MULTILATERALISM v UNILATERALISM

Multilateralism v Unilateralism: Policy Choices in a Global Society

Edited by

J.B. ATTANASIO and J.J. NORTON

A Paul C. Carrington Lecture Series Project

BIICL
British Institute of
International and
Comparative Law
and
The SMU Dedman School of Law

Published and Distributed by
The British Institute of International and Comparative Law
Charles Clore House, 17 Russell Square, London WC1B 5JP

British Library Cataloguing in Publication Data

ISBN 0–903067–44–7

Typeset by Cambrian Typesetters
Frimley, Surrey
Printed in Great Britain by Biddles Ltd
King's Lynn

TABLE OF CONTENTS

IN MEMORIAM: ARTHUR C. HELTON ix

ACKNOWLEDGEMENTS xi

EDITORS' NOTE xi

PART ONE—THE CONFERENCE PAPERS

FOREWORD—PART ONE
Professor Vaughan Lowe 3

Chapter One
INTRODUCTION: MULTILATERALISM, UNILATERALISM, AND LEADERSHIP 11
Dean John B. Attanasio

Chapter Two
UNILATERAL ACTION IN AN IMPERFECT WORLD ORDER 25
Professor W. Michael Reisman & Scott Shuchart

Chapter Three
A MULTILATERALISM VS. UNILATERALISM: PRINCIPLE OR POLICY?
Ambassador Christopher Ashby 41
B CHINA'S WTO ACCESSION AND THE PROSPECT OF ASIA'S ECONOMY 49
Professor Gao Shangquan
C MULTILATERALISM AND AMERICAN POLICY: A DIPLOMAT'S VIEW 57
Ambassador Robert W. Jordan

Chapter Four
UNILATERALISM AND CURRENT TRANSATLANTIC RELATIONS 61
Professor Rudolf Dolzer

Chapter Five
GLOBAL ECONOMY—GLOBAL LAW? 83
Professor Werner F. Ebke

Chapter Six
THE INTERNATIONAL CRIMINAL COURT: AMERICA'S RETURN
TO UNILATERALISM 99
Professor Whitney R. Harris

Chapter Seven
REACTION AND INATTENTION WITHIN THE U.S. GOVERNMENT 115
A. Helton

Chapter Eight
MULTILATERALISM VERSUS U.S. UNILATERALISM: THE ROLE OF THE UN SECURITY COUNCIL AS THE AUTHORIZING BODY FOR THE UNITED STATE'S USE OF FORCE 145
Ambassador Yutaka Kawashima

Chapter Nine
THE LEGITIMACY OF EXTERNAL RESPONSE TO PROTECT THE RIGHT TO DEMOCRATIC GOVERNANCE AND FREE CHOICE 161
Professor Ndiva Kofele-Kale

Chapter Ten
MULTILATERALISM AND UNILATERALISM IN A NEW SECURITY ENVIRONMENT 197
Professor Alexander Konovalov

PART TWO—THE SUPPLEMENTAL PAPERS

FOREWORD—PART TWO
International Financial and Trade Law in the Age of Unilateralism. 227
Dr. Mads Andenas

Chapter Eleven
A FURTHER CONTOUR TO 'LIMITED MULTILATERALISM': THE INTERVENTION OF PRIVATE SECTOR INVOLVEMENT TO GLOBAL FINANCIAL STABILITY AND THE PRUDENTIAL CONTROL OF LARGE COMPLEX GLOBAL BANKING ORGANIZATIONS 231
Professor Joseph J. Norton

Chapter Twelve
UNILATERALISM, MULTILATERALISM AND INTERNATIONAL SECURITIES OFFERINGS 255
Dr. Douglas W. Arner

Chapter Thirteen
A DECADE OF OPEN REGIONALISM IN LATIN AMERICA: THE NEED FOR EFFECTIVE AND EFFICIENT ARTICULATION, COORDINATION, COOPERATION AND CONVERGENCE 297
Mauricio Baquero-Herrera

Chapter Fourteen
EXPANDING TRADE REMEDIES UNILATERALLY: THE *BYRD AMENDMENT* CASE AND THE UNITED STATES AGAINST THE WORLD 345
Professor Raj Bhala

Chapter Fifteen
THE MULTILATERALISM OF BRETTON WOODS REVISITED: THE CRUCIAL ROLE OF THE WTO IN THE INTEGRATION OF TRANSITION ECONOMIES 365
Dr. J.H. Hoogmartens

Chapter Sixteen
MULTILATERALISM VERSUS UNILATERALISM IN THE SOVEREIGN DEBT RESTRUCTURING CONTEXT: WILL EITHER APPROACH PREVENT DEFAULT? 393
Kristin McFetridge

Chapter Seventeen
LEGAL DEVELOPMENT COOPERATION: CONDITIONS, PRINCIPLES AND METHODS 423
Professor Claes Sandgren

Chapter Eighteen
'CLUB MULTILATERALISM' AND GLOBAL SUPRANATIONALISM: THE CASE OF FATF 459
Dr. Heba M. Shams

Chapter Nineteen
INTERNATIONAL FINANCIAL STABILITY – THE NEED FOR A MULTILATERAL RESPONSE. 483
Dr. George A. Walker

In Memoriam

ARTHUR C. HELTON
(1949–2003)

The international community suffered an enormous loss on August 19, 2003. On that day, we heard about the horrible bombing of the United Nations headquarters in Baghdad and learned that among the dead was our friend and colleague, Arthur C. Helton. As so many know, Arthur was an ardent champion of human rights, particularly for refugees displaced by war, and so it was no surprise that he went to Baghdad at a very difficult time to assist the U.N. in its humanitarian efforts to relieve the suffering of the Iraqi people. It is believed that Arthur was meeting with Sergio Vieira de Mello, the U.N.'s chief envoy to Iraq who was also killed in the bombing.

In a world marked by conflict and tragedy, it is rare to meet an individual who has the courage, intellect, and passion to do what most of us would find impossible. Despite formidable barriers, Arthur succeeded in convincing others that refugees, regardless of their country of origin, were worthwhile and deserving of humane treatment. His remarkable compassion for people inspired hope among those who became the invisible and powerless remnants of unresolved hostilities. As former director of the Refugee Project at the Lawyers Committee for Human Rights and as founder and former director of the Forced Migration Projects at the Open Society Institute, Arthur was instrumental in fighting the legal and political battles necessary to secure basic rights for Haitian detainees held in U.S. custody and to expand opportunities for thousands of refugees from war torn countries to seek asylum in this country. More recently, his position as Director of Peace and Conflict Studies and Senior Fellow for Refugee Studies and Preventive Action at the Council on Foreign Relations allowed Arthur to continue what he did best—helping others who were affected most cruelly by the ravages of war.

Arthur's contributions as a tenacious human rights lawyer, prolific scholar, and consummate teacher and mentor will long be remembered throughout the international community. I am personally grateful to him for his contribution to this book and join those who honor his memory.

John B. Attanasio
May 2004

ACKNOWLEDGEMENTS

Special Acknowledgement is extended with deepest appreciation to the following:

Paul C. Carrington Lecture Series, which provided the support for the Spring 2002 SMU Conference upon which this volume is derived.

Staff of the SMU International Law Review Association for their excellent and responsive editorial support.

EDITORS' NOTE

Various of the Chapters in this volume were finalized before the U.S. invasion of Iraq in March 2003.

Part One—Conference Papers

FOREWORD	*Vaughan Lowe*	3
CHAPTER ONE	Introduction: Multilateralism, Unilateralism, and Leadership *Dean John B. Attanasio*	11
CHAPTER TWO	Unilateral Action in an Imperfect World Order *Professor W. Michael Reisman & Scott Shuchart*	25
CHAPTER THREE		
A	Multilateralism vs. Unilateralism: Principle or Policy? *Ambassador Christopher Ashby*	41
B	China's WTO Accession and the Prospect of Asia's Economy *Professor Gao Shangquan*	49
C	Multilateralism and American Policy: A Diplomat's View *Ambassador Robert W. Jordan*	57
CHAPTER FOUR	Unilateralism and Current Transatlantic Relations *Professor Rudolf Dolzer*	61
CHAPTER FIVE	Global Economy—Global Law? *Professor Werner F. Ebke*	83
CHAPTER SIX	The International Criminal Court: America's Return to Unilateralism *Professor Whitney R. Harris*	99
CHAPTER SEVEN	Reaction and Inattention Within the U.S. Government *A. Helton*	115
CHAPTER EIGHT	Multilateralism versus U.S. Unilateralism: The Role of the UN Security Council as the Authorizing Body for the United State's Use of Force *Ambassador Yutaka Kawashima*	145
CHAPTER NINE	The Legitimacy of External Response to Protect the Right to Democratic Governance and Free Choice *Professor Ndiva Kofele-Kale*	161
CHAPTER TEN	Multilateralism and Unilateralism in a New Security Environment *Professor Alexander Konovalov*	197

Foreword—Part One

*By Vaughan Lowe**

The meeting that preceded the 2002 Carrington Lecture at the SMU Dedman School of Law was convened to discuss the nature and implications of the fact that the major threats currently facing the world can be addressed in either of two broad ways, which may loosely be called unilateral mechanisms and multilateral mechanisms. Again speaking in broad terms, there is undeniably a perception in many parts of the world that powerful States, and in particular the USA, are content to use multilateral mechanisms such as the United Nations for as long as those mechanisms secure or advance their national interests, but that these States quickly abandon multilateral mechanisms in favour of unilateral approaches when those approaches serve their interests better. It appears, on this view, that after a century of experimenting with inter-State co-operation and international organizations the world is reverting to a condition where might is right and the law is no more than one of the instruments used by the rich and powerful to keep the poor and weak in their place. While the foregoing account may caricature the argument, it is a serviceable caricature, adequate as a starting point for analysis.

The discussions that took place in the summer of 2002 under the auspices of the SMU Dedman School of Law in Dallas, Texas, focussed upon three key areas of international activity: security, trade and the environment. No-one doubted that international co-operation is in principle useful and desirable even if, as Arthur Helton's paper shows, it is sometimes difficult to arrange national administrations in such a way as to facilitate co-operation. The need for co-operation is a matter of plain observation and common sense, well captured by one former European foreign minister, writing in 1997:

> . . . nation states are incompetent. Not one of them, not even the United States as the single remaining super-power, can adequately provide for the needs that its citizens now articulate. The extent of that incompetence has become sharply clearer during this century. The inadequacy of national governments to provide security, prosperity or a decent environment has brought into being a huge array of international rules, conferences and institutions; the only answer to the puzzle of the immortal but incompetent nation state is effective co-operation between those states for all the purposes that lie beyond the reach of any one of them.[1]

* Chichele Professor of International Law, Faculty of Law University of Oxford.

[1] Douglas Hurd, *The Search for Peace* (London, 1997), p. 6.

That quotation elides two concepts: co-operation, and multilateral action. They are by no means the same. Much international trade is carried out within the multilateral framework and procedure of which the institutional incarnation is the World Trade Organization. That is a complex, permanent international organization which operates continuously to oil the wheels of international trade and keep it on the tracks agreed by States at the great multilateral trade conferences of the latter half of the twentieth century. The organs of the European Union, whose powers are so extensive as to give the Union many of the characteristics of a sovereign State, are an even more striking example of multilateralism in action. Even a form of informal, multilateralism is evolving in the setting of international financial standards. The papers by Gao Shangquan on the WTO, Joseph Norton on international financial standards and by Whitney Harris on international criminal tribunals record some of the notable developments in co-operation of this kind. Yutaka Kawashima examines a variant of this kind of action, in which the organization does not act itself but authorizes specific States to act for it and for its members. Kawashima takes the example of the Security Council as the authorizing body for uses of force by States. But co-operation does not need any permanent international institutions, let alone complex and powerful bodies. It does not even need any developed system of internationally agreed rules. One State may seek and obtain the extradition of a wanted person from another State, or two States may negotiate a rescheduling of public debts, without the interposition of any international body and without being constrained by any specific international rules. Co-operation may be informal, *ad hoc*, and ephemeral; and it may be bilateral or multilateral. Examples of such co-operation feature in two papers in this volume. Alexander Konovalov writes about the need for co-operation to address the emerging threat of international terrorism in his paper on multilateralism and unilateralism in the new security environment; and Werner Ebke writes in his paper on the global economy of the ways in which States co-operate through harmonizing their unilateral actions.

Where States are unable to proceed jointly to deal with problems that they face, it is inevitable that some States will attempt to deal with the issues unilaterally, as best they can. Indeed, the very act of setting the agenda for international discussions may bear the imprint of unilateralism, as a powerful State insists that a particular matter is included in or excluded from discussions. Differences may arise when there are discussions over the best policy for addressing an international problem. The United States, for example, is sometimes criticised for a retreat into isolationism and unilateralism because of its 'failure' to participate in initiatives such as the establishment of the International Criminal Court and the Kyoto Protocol. But in neither case was the United States under any obligation to participate in those initiatives; and if a State considers a particular approach to a problem to be misconceived, it is difficult to see why it should be expected to subscribe to that approach—at least, if it has a coherent and practical alternative to offer. The position is, however, very different if the State has already committed itself to a particular multilateral procedure for addressing the problem. In such cases the other participants will have expectations that the agreed procedures will be followed. Indeed, they may have made their own commitments to follow those procedures on the basis of an understanding that all participants renounce their right to take unilateral measures and accept the discipline of the multilateral procedure—whether that be in the field of trade, security, human rights, disarmament or any other matter of international concern. Departure from the agreed multilateral procedures is a much more troublesome matter in these circumstances.

There was much discussion during the conference of what, precisely, multilateralism means. The question is visited from two rather different perspectives in the papers by Rudolf Dolzer and by Michael Reisman and Scott Shuchart. Dolzer points out that multilateralism is more a matter of the general disposition or attitude of a State than of any particular conduct or measure. It is an attitude that generally, though not necessarily invariably, accords priority to agreed procedures involving collaboration with other States in decision making. The contrast is not with a crude unilateralism that abandons agreed procedures whenever the national interest appears to demand it. Though criticism of the United States and other powerful States may sometimes seem to suggest that they practice this brand of unilateralism, that suggestion is misconceived. Modern States rarely, if ever, justify their actions on the basis that they are entitled to pursue their own interests unconstrained by rules and principles of international conduct. Rather, the claim tends to be that the State is entitled to the preservation of certain interests, or that other States are obliged to behave in a certain manner, and that if existing international mechanisms are inadequate to secure compliance with those rights and obligations the State may act itself in order to secure that end. This is not an entire repudiation of international law: it is an approach to international law that attaches a greater importance to substantive obligations than to procedural obligations. It is an argument that the end that is sought, the upholding of the substantive right or duty, justifies a departure from the procedural means that are prescribed for achieving that end. While one may, of course, find individual cases where States act in a manner that is inconsistent not only with procedural obligations but also with substantive obligations under international law—and the 'Coalition' action against Iraq that began in March 2003 is a prime candidate for that miserable distinction—less dramatic withdrawals or departures from multilateral procedures with the declared aim of upholding substantive rules may have equally significant consequences.

Many of the consequences are, given a moment's thought, obvious. If a State asserts that it is free to depart from agreed procedures, such as the need to obtain Security Council authorisation for the use of force against another State, other States will ask if that State can be relied upon to keep any other commitments that it has entered into or may enter into in the future. They will ask why they, too, should not feel free to abandon commitments if they consider themselves to be unduly constrained by them. They will ask whether, when another State violates international law, they should necessarily align themselves against the law-breaker or should feel free to take their position according to political or economic considerations, largely disregarding questions of legality. The logic of this situation points to a development towards a condition where even the most solemn undertakings of States, given as formal and explicit commitments to be bound by the express terms of international treaties, cannot be relied upon. Every commitment is liable to be reviewed in order to determine if it is 'useful' to adhere to it. If the world were ever to reach that condition, diplomacy would become extremely difficult. The transaction costs of making even simple international arrangements would rise dramatically. But even short of that position, the efficiency and effectiveness of the international legal system in providing a vehicle for international co-operation may be steadily and seriously eroded by repudiations of procedural obligations.

One of the main criticisms of unilateral action is that it compromises efforts to secure international justice. If justice demands that like cases be treated alike, the usurpation of key functions in the international legal system (such as the enforcement of the law) by powerful States entails a risk that cases will be treated according to their significance for those States, rather on some more 'objective' basis. The risk is greatest when an individual State or group of States regards itself as uniquely qualified to understand and protect 'international' values and institutions. Aspects of this problem are addressed in the paper by Ndiva Kofele-Kale on the legitimacy of external responses to human rights abuses within other States. Of course, the process of characterising situations and identifying characteristics that mark out situations as 'alike' or 'not alike' can never be truly objective; but locating that process of characterization in an international organization at least increases the chance of it proceeding on the basis of shared values and understandings.

On the other hand, if international procedures fail, what is to be done? Should violations of rights and breaches of obligations be ignored? If, for example, the Security Council fails to discharge what the UN Charter refers to as its 'primary responsibility for the maintenance of international peace and security,' acting on behalf of the Members of the United Nations, can no-one else act in its stead? That example illustrates the need for care in pinning down the exact questions in issue. One must determine whose view of what is necessary for international peace and security is to prevail. It can scarcely be argued that every State has the right to insist that its own view of the necessities be accepted and acted upon by the Council. One must determine whose view of 'failure' is to prevail. There are many different configurations of the matter. The Council may decide to act, but may do more or less than a particular State thinks is necessary and desirable. The Council may decide not to act at all; or it may expressly postpone a decision; or it may simply not take a decision. One must also consider the nature of any action that is to be taken without the Security Council's authority. There is a world of difference between pursuing, for instance, the path of the Uniting for Peace resolution and seeking action through the UN General Assembly and, on the other hand, abandoning the UN entirely in favour of purely unilateral action. Again, there is a difference between taking inherently lawful measures of retorsion against another State, such as breaking off diplomatic relations, and imposing sanctions that involve what are *prima facie* violations of the target State's rights and which would have to be justified as lawful counter-measures. Measures involving the use of force take the unilateral action into another distinct realm again. There are many kinds of unilateralism, which give rise to quite different issues; and those that are considered by the international community to be appropriate or acceptable are likely to differ from field to field—trade, environment, security, and so on.

The conference repeatedly came back to questions of power, responsibility, authority and leadership. Those attributes do not necessarily go together, but they are certainly interlinked. The military might of the United States is peerless. Military might is not, however, the same as military power. Power is the product of military might coupled with the effects of whatever moral, political, economic and logistical constraints exist upon its unbridled deployment. Massive might and technologically unrivalled weaponry may exist; but a determination to avoid civilian deaths and unnecessary suffering, and the costs of rebuilding a community, and an unwillingness to accept massive deaths among the State's own forces, may result in only of a fraction of that potential power being brought to bear. Even then, military resources designed for a classical inter-State, cross-border war may be of little use against terrorist or guerilla attacks.

The fact that the United States, NATO States, regional powers, and indeed any State with a minimal military capacity, is capable of assuming a policing role may, as Reisman and Shuchart suggest, be thought to entail a responsibility so to act. The difficulty lies in finding procedures that enable such States to act in the role of policemen rather than vigilantes. The Rule of Law is no less important internationally than it is domestically. Vigilante action lacks legitimacy, and it undermines the authority and leadership of those who take it. The same principle applies to applications of economic power; but here the factual situation is different. There is no single economic superpower. The economy of European Union is outstripping that of the United States; and patterns of trade establish particular local and global dependencies upon suppliers of particular resources and give States an economic power that is not proportionate to their military power—the power of the oil States is a clear example. Because economic power is more evenly spread and because, unlike the episodic deployments of military power, economic interests are continuously in play, the interdependence of States is more clearly recognised and international co-operation is much more highly developed. Perhaps, too, intellectual factors assist this development. The economic advantages of multilateral trade regimes in contrast to bilateral arrangements are demonstrable using the techniques of quantitative economics which have, at least in recent decades, been regarded in the west as paths to an understanding of basic truths.

Authority and leadership are more elusive characteristics; and they cannot be bought or imposed by force. Leadership is plainly an attribute of a particular State or person; authority is a quality of a particular policy or course of conduct that is being urged upon others. Authority only exists when all can see the justice and the benefits that flow, at least in the long term, from the policies in question; and that is a perception which is closely tied to questions of legitimacy and of the willingness to accept that those rules of international conduct that have the status of rules of law do indeed operate as constraints upon the freedom of action of States and may not simply be ignored. Unilateral action in breach of rules of law undermines claims to authority, unless there is an overwhelmingly clear moral case for such action. Even unilateral action that involves no violation of the law may undermine claims to authority unless it can be seen that the unilateral conduct is an application of a sound general principle and not merely a matter of the pursuit of self-interest. A State may have authority but decline to take the role of a leader. Some may think that France acted in much this way in opposing the authorisation by the Security Council of the use of force against Iraq but without leading the Council towards the adoption of some other clear and viable strategy. A State may act as a leader but lack authority. It may coerce or cajole other States into following a policy that they regard as illegitimate or ill-advised. One of the central problems addressed at the conference is that there are clear signs that many in the world think that power is becoming detached from authority, that leadership is imposed rather than freely given, and that only the acceptance of a responsibility to act in accordance not only with the agreed substantive principles of international conduct but also with agreed multilateral procedures can reverse this worrying trend.

These issues are canvassed in the papers that follow in Part One, submitted after the 2002 conference and before the U.S. Iraqi invasion. John

Attanasio's introduction surveys the topic and sets the context for the more specialised papers. Those other papers offer expert reflections upon the failures and successes of international co-operation in key areas. It is hoped that the collection (including the series of supplemental papers contained in Part Two of this volume) offers some insights into the strengths and weaknesses of unilateralism and multilateralism and in some small way advances the debate on these vitally important issues.

CHAPTER ONE

Introduction: Multilateralism, Unilateralism, and Leadership

*by John B. Attanasio**

CHAPTER OUTLINE

I. The Post-Cold War World
II. Consent
III. Leadership
IV. The New World Order
V. The Conference

I. THE POST-COLD WAR WORLD

1989: The wall that divided the city of Berlin suddenly fell; the Second World War and the Cold War ended even more abruptly than they had begun; and the mantle of leadership fell on the United States—the driving force behind victory, particularly in the Cold War. It was unclear whether the United States desired this mantle of leadership. After all, our first President, George Washington, warned of 'foreign entanglements' in his famous Farewell Address; isolationism has influenced our foreign policy ever since.[1]

In the immediate aftermath of the fall of the Soviet Union, the United States was mostly stunned and suspicious of the completeness of victory. We had been at war—hot or cold—for so long during the 20th century that we anxiously awaited the inevitable bad news that some mistake had occurred somewhere. It all seemed too good to be true.

* Dean and William Hawley Atwell Professor of Constitutional Law, Dedman School of Law at Southern Methodist University. I want to thank Heather Stobaugh and Kathleen Spartana for their excellent work on this essay. I also want to thank Tina Brosseau for her assistance in typing this manuscript. *Editors' note*: This chapter was finalized before the U.S. invasion of Iraq.

1 George Washington, Farewell Address (Sept. 19, 1796), reprinted *in* Matthew Spalding & Patrick J. Garity, *A Sacred Union of Citizens: George Washington's Farewell Address and the American Character* (1996) [hereinafter, Farewell Address].

In a way it actually was. But unlike some feared, Russia did not come back as our enemy with a renewal of the Cold War. In fact, Russia not only desired to make peace but also wanted to be our friend. But a different phenomenon took the place of the Cold War.

As the Report of Chancellor Willy Brandt asserted nearly 20 years before, north-south conflict began to replace east-west conflict.[2] Today these words seem prescient. The Brandt Report was not alone in making such assertions. When I was in college some years ago, a number of distinguished international relations scholars were asserting that northsouth conflict would replace eastwest conflict in the not-so-distant future. These scholars used the term 'northsouth' in a figurative sense to describe the wealthy nations of the first world—which for these scholars definitely included Russia—with the poor nations of the third world. Ironically, the neoMarxian struggle of the Cold War would be replaced by another of the haves warring with the havenots. One of the contributors of this symposium has put the situation this way: one billion people in the world currently live well, while five billion live on less than $3 a day.[3] In 25 years, the population of the world will increase to eight billion people;[4] still, one billion will live well and seven billion will live on less than $3 a day. Such disparities do not lead to stability.

Whether intentional or not, the mantle of leadership has remained upon the United States after the Cold War. The strong leadership we displayed in the Cold War helped to ensure an encore performance.

II. CONSENT

If leadership is the issue, one question is who does the leading power lead? But before we get to that inquiry, we must describe what leadership is. What does leadership mean? No one would dispute that the United States is the greatest military power on earth, whose muscle relative to other countries is discontinuous even by historical standards. But does that military might translate into leadership? Was Rome the leader of the ancient world? To be a leader, one must have followers. It would also seem that those followers must be voluntary, that is, an element of volition comprises a necessary condition to being a follower.

Consequently, someone who asserts himself purely by coercion is not a leader. But just as surely, following does not have to be on a purely voluntary basis. For example, a prime minister in a democratic polity securing the

[2] Brandt Commission, North–South: A Program for Survival (1980).

[3] Rudolf Dolzer, *Unilateral and Current Transatlantic Relations* (2003).

[4] U.S. Census Bureau, International Data Base 10-2002, *at:* http/www/img/worldpop.gif (last visited Jan. 31, 2003).

support of another political leader may not be purely voluntary in the strict sense of the term. A collision of wills occurs, and each individual decides what she will do under the circumstances. For example, if a member of the British Parliament opposes a particular piece of legislation, the Prime Minister may try to obtain it by asserting party discipline. Does securing support by means of party discipline eradicate consent? Surely not, as in a democracy, consent is often secured in this fashion. Indeed, in the United States 'consent' is often won by the threat of political retaliation at the polls for lack of support on a major issue. Granted different cultures may have different notions of consent, but many cultures with which I am familiar would embrace the hypothetical outlined above.

One can claim that the above scenarios do not entail real consent at all. Under an extreme version of the circumstances posited above, the Member of Parliament might even oppose the legislation at issue in principle, but vote for it because he feels that he has no other choice, that is, if he wishes to have a political future. Has the person who consents under those circumstances really consented at all? Is it an act of free will or has his will been supervened? Again, withdrawing political support for lack of consent is widely regarded as legitimate under many circumstances.

Suppose, however, we shift the adverse consequence from political defeat to escaping starvation, that is, instead of withholding political support, suppose one withholds all food if another refuses to engage in a particular act? Suppose the refused act is murder? Could anyone seriously claim true consent under these circumstances? But how far does one have to go? Is withholding food a valid means to secure consent—what about if there is a danger of starvation? One readily sees how relevant this example is in a world in which one billion people have all the cookies. Moreover, in a highly interdependent world, economic sanctions often inflict severe deprivation on people. Suppose instead one country refuses to give free energy to another country whose climate is very cold? Suppose the country cannot pay for the energy? Suppose its poverty stems from having a ludicrous political and economic system? Suppose that it seeks to 'pay,' or secure consent, for the free energy by refraining from building weapons of mass destruction? So the means used to effectuate consent might affect its legitimacy.

Does the nature of the act that one is seeking to persuade another to perform make any difference? For example, in the above hypothetical, murder is the act for which consent is being sought. This presents an easy case because the act is assumed to be illegitimate. Suppose instead the act was legitimate killing—say in self-defense. Who delineates the moral difference between murder and legitimate killing? Who defines legitimacy?

Suppose the activity is war rather than individual killing. Who is consenting to what? After all, consent in the international arena is virtually always derivative; that is, government consents on behalf of the governed.

At times, consent truly reflects the popular will, but often it does not. Even in a democracy—which in most instances is actually a republican or representative form of government—consent is supposed to, and frequently does, reflect the will of the governed. Unfortunately, in the mix of issues for which people vote, international matters are often unimportant. For those international issues which do matter at the polls, voters commonly defer to politicians until they grow disillusioned. And even after disillusionment occurs, it can take a long time to extricate a nationstate from a 'foreign entanglement.'[5] Take, for example, the experiences of France and then the United States in Vietnam.

Shifting even more distinctly to the international arena, consent surely must mark a key difference between unilateral and multilateral action. Essentially, unilateral action comprises conduct by a single nation-state. As sketched above, however, even what forms consent by a single nation-state is a complex question. To avoid these messy issues, the international system determines consent merely by looking at consent by the government; it simply assumes that a government that exerts effective power over the population of a nationstate can consent on behalf of the governed on virtually any issue. Niceties about consent of the governed are ignored altogether.

But in certain areas—notably the emergent power of humanitarian intervention—the intervening government, governments, or international entities by definition lack the consent of the government whose will they would supervene.[6] In fact, the *raison d'etre* for humanitarian intervention is government persecution. Because sovereignty has traditionally been the bedrock of the international legal system,[7] outside intervention is always a risky business. At bottom, the argument behind humanitarian intervention asserts that an outside government better perceives the interests of a country's people and is more likely to carry out those interests than is the domestic government. Of course, the doctrine of humanitarian intervention is not new. Hitler used something resembling it in the Sudatenland to save the German minority from persecution by the Czechs.[8] The Soviet Union used it frequently—everywhere from Ukraine to Afghanistan.[9] Thus, history

[5] *See* Farewell Address, *supra* note 1.

[6] *See, e.g.*, President & Fellows of Harvard College, *Recent Development: Restoring Hope: U.N. Security Council Resolutions for Samalia and an Expanded Doctrine of Humanitarian Intervention,* 34 HARV. L.J. 624 n.2 (1993) (discussing the various definitions of humanitarian intervention).

[7] *See generally,* John B. Attanasio, 'Rapporteur's Conclusions,' *in International Law Decisions in National Courts* 373-95 (Transnational Pub., Inc. 1996); 28 N.Y.U. INT'L L. & POL. 1-33 (1996).

[8] *See* Jack L. Goldsmith & Eric A. Posner, *Moral and Legal Rhetoric in International Relations: A Rational Choice Perspective,* 31 J. LEGAL STUD. S115 (2002).

[9] *See* W. Michael Reisman & James Silk, *Which Law Applies to the Afghan Conflict?*, 82 A.J.I.L. 459 (1988).

teaches us to regard unilateral intervention—for humanitarian or any other reasons—with deep suspicion. Multilateral agreement on humanitarian intervention helps to ensure that altruism, rather than pretextual self-interest, is at least an important motivator driving the intervention.

Under the current state of international law, perhaps the best basis for external intervention remains a resolution of the U.N. Security Council. Curiously, at the public part of the conference, none of the 11 participants even mentioned the United Nations in their presentations. Indeed, President Clinton ignored the United Nations in his action against Serbia, preferring to remain in the more friendly confines of NATO.[10] President Bush openly challenged the United Nations to show its continuing relevance in the situation in Iraq.[11]

This inattention contrasts sharply with the postwar vision of the United Nations as the centerpiece for keeping peace. Despite its many problems, the world has not descended into world war since the creation of the United Nations. Whether the United Nations is primarily responsible for this era of relative peace is impossible to know; the ominous threat of nuclear war may also have played some role.

The framework provided by the United Nations—imperfect though it might be—also provides a way of dealing with the first conundrum described earlier. The United Nations, or some other type of multilateral agreement at least among a number of major powers—and hopefully including some interested countries, for example, other countries in the region in question—helps to validate coercive means to obtain the consent of a hostile power.

Perhaps certain kinds of coercive means eradicate any true consent. However, in autonomy theory, the sanctioned nationstate is being coerced for a reason, generally that its behavior impairs or threatens to impair the autonomy of other nationstates. As typically defined, autonomy does not include the ability to harm others.[12] At that point surely the person or entity being harmed has some right of self-defense to protect its own autonomy. This points to the interdependencies inherent in achieving true autonomy when a number of free actors inhabit the same planet. The tough questions become: What harms to freedom of action may sufficiently justify invoking the doctrine of self-defense? What sorts of responses comprise reasonable selfdefense? What kinds of actions engage a right to collective self-defense as provided in the U.N. Charter? And under what circumstances (short of the right of collective selfdefense) might a state have the power under some sort of agency authority to help another state that has been wronged? What

[10] 'Rhetoric Doesn't Make War Any Nicer,' *Newsday* (June 9, 2000), at A50.

[11] 'War Averted for Now?' *The Business Times Singapore* (Sept. 18, 2002).

[12] *See generally,* John Stuart Mill, *On Liberty* (David Spitz, ed., W.W. Norton & Co. 1975) (1859); I. Berlin, 'Two Concepts of Liberty' *in Four Essays on Liberty* (1969).

sorts of wrongs attract such a response? Must they only be against other nation-states? Can they be against populations within nation states? What types of wrongs count in each case? Do they differ depending on whether the victim is a state, people within a state, or perhaps even an international organization?

Assuming an international wrong sufficient to justify some remedy of intervention, what sorts of calls for help attract such a response? What sorts of responses are appropriate under what circumstances? When are public censures, economic sanctions, and military sanctions legitimate? How do these types of respective sanctions differ? For example, do food sanctions differ from raising tariffs? Suppose the food cut off comprises .01% of a nation's food supply whereas the tariff reduces the exports of a poor nation by 75% and its per capita income by 50%? Do whatever sanctions pertain incorporate some notion of proportionality? Must a number of nations endorse the response in question? Are the answers to all of these dilemmas made merely by reference to *realpolitik*, or do some of these questions have ethical content? Even if none have ethical content, or if decision-makers should ignore ethical systems to maximize the 'neutrality' in their approaches, can human beings blithely shed whatever ethical moorings they may have? If some of these questions have ethical implications, which ones are they? What ethical systems should help in formulating responses? What consideration should be afforded the dramatic cultural differences among ethical systems? Should religious beliefs be taken into consideration? For believers, can they be totally ignored? How should differing interpretations among adherents of a particular ethical system be treated?

Needless to say, the responses to these and countless other quandaries are not obvious, and I certainly will not attempt them here. Suffice it to say that most of the answers become easier in a multilateral context when several nations consent to the response—whatever it may be. Obviously, when many nations agree, the questions become easier because the likelihood of arbitrary treatment driven by pretextual self-interest, or even misunderstanding, declines. Moreover, broad-based consent, particularly by ethically diverse powers, may indicate that the behavior and its accompanying remedy or sanction is so universally condemned that they engage ethical considerations which are fundamental to the human condition.

Assuming some consensus can be achieved, how widespread must it be to count? Do all nations count the same? Should the opinions of nations with greater power count more? What about the opinions of nations with greater wealth? What about those with larger populations? Should any weight be afforded to differences of opinion within a nationstate? Suppose the overwhelming majority of the population differs with the opinion of its government? Who should make this determination—a Gallup poll? Do the opinions of international organizations other than the U.N. Security

Council matter? What about the U.N. General Assembly, the International Red Cross, Amnesty International, or Conintern when the Soviet Union still existed?

Obviously, the five permanent members still dominate the Security Council. The consent of this group and perhaps some key members of the G8 major economic powers will almost always do the trick. Of course, this comprises a tiny minority of all nationstates. When one takes population into consideration, the consent of these major powers becomes more formidable, but still not a majority of the world's population—not even close if one removes China from the mix.

Indeed, securing multilateral agreement on issues of armed intervention—humanitarian or otherwise—is easier said than done. When the conference which catalyzed this book took place, the United States was having great difficulty securing support for enforcing UN weapon inspections in Iraq. Several months later, the United States and Great Britain had secured a unanimous resolution of the Security Council demanding that Iraq comply with its disarmament obligations.[13] The resolution was the product of much conversation and negotiation. Demonstrating the fragility of multilateral action, some nations have stated that they would not support the use of force if Iraq is found in further material breach.[14] Thus, consent is not always one discontinuous event. Consent for military action is commonly a process that must be nurtured over time rather than a oneshot conclusive event.

As previously noted, sovereignty remains the defining characteristic of the international system.[15] Sovereigns can consent to a wide range of international actions, but sovereigns also have an easier time withdrawing consent than most of the rest of us. After all, enforcement mechanisms must be used against fellow sovereigns, particularly relatively powerful fellow sovereigns, and consent only marginally changes the underlying power relations that preceded the agreement. Military or economic action must proceed against some relatively strong interdependent nation.

World War I resulted in part from perceived enforcement powers exercised by relatively powerful sovereigns. The enforcement was on behalf of surrogates and was highly pretextual. Still, it illustrates the inefficacy of military action in solving problems of world public order outside some level of multilateral cooperation among at least the major powers. The importance of consent to military action by smaller powers should not be ignored, however. Look at how important having bases in Uzbekistan was to the Afghan conflict.

[13] 'Threats and Responses: The Rationale for the U.N. Resolution on Iraq, in the Diplomats' Own Words,' *The New York Times* (Nov. 9, 2002), at A10.

[14] *See* Dolzer, *supra* note 3.

[15] *See generally*, Attanasio, *supra* note 7.

Understandably, multilateralism also carries distinct advantages with regard to economic sanctions. First, in a globalized, interdependent world[16] even lesser economic actors can inflict significant harm on much larger economies—for example, if they possess an important commodity like oil or uranium. Other nations may inflict damage by possessing less attractive commodities like pollution. September 11 vividly demonstrated the military and economic dangers posed by even socalled failed states like Afghanistan.

The number and complexity of the above questions also paradoxically demonstrates the limits of multilateralism. After all, complete consent from everyone represents a sure recipe for inaction in a world where interests among nationstates differ systematically and tremendously. The myriad questions posed above may or may not be discerning, but they certainly can cause policy paralysis. In fact the more difficult they are, the more paralysis they may cause.

III. LEADERSHIP

The tension between consent and paralysis calls to mind the age-old problem of leadership. One of the most insightful discussions of that dilemma occurs in the preface to John F. Kennedy's Pulitzer Prize winning book *Profiles in Courage*.[17] Focusing on tension in a democracy between representing one's constituency and standing alone to do what is right, Kennedy examines the age-old dilemma of leadership. In a republican-democracy, consent legitimates the exercises of power inherit to leadership. Of course, leaders must have vision. By definition, 'vision' entails seeing things. In the context of leadership, Americans have come to use the word vision to signify seeing things that others do not. Speaking in the context of an elected public official in American democracy, Kennedy thought that the leader must normally represent the will of his constituents, but occasionally, the leader must stand against the will of his constituents for compelling moral reasons.[18]

Kennedy's analysis has limited applicability to the international arena. After all, according to traditional thinking about international relations, the United States is not obliged to represent anyone except its naked self-interest; and as the pure unilateralist argument goes, can exert the full measure of its might to assert those interests. The United States can, of course, do this. But the irony is that this selfish, overbearing approach is not in the long-term interests of the United States or anyone else. Rapacious unilateralism is the antithesis of leadership. Measured unilateralism is occasionally

[16] *See* John B. Attanasio, *Foreword: The Globalization of the American Law School*, 46 J. Legal Educ. 311 (1996).
[17] John F. Kennedy, *Profiles in Courage* (Harper, 1961) (c.1956).
[18] *Id.*

required to lead. Constant formulation, communication, and deliberative persuasion of visionary ideas for world order also comprise a necessary condition for leadership.

Historically, Americans generally side with underdogs. We have detested and often fought against bullies.[19] We certainly do not want to behave like bullies ourselves. A bully does not inspire followers; instead, a bully only attracts resentment and competition. In a highly interdependent world, other nations can make life more difficult and costly for us. In some ways, the mantle of leadership has certainly burdened the United States, but it has benefited us much more. In the wake of the global financial crisis, our stock market soared largely because the dollar is regarded as the safest currency on earth and because we are regarded as the safest place on earth.[20] But the benefits of being the leader of the world can be whittled away if we grow unpopular from excessive unilateral action.

Analogizing to *Profiles in Courage*, we must choose carefully those moral imperatives which dictate unilateral action on our part.[21] In the best traditions of the United States, we must lead by persuasion rather than by coercion, or dictation. Such leadership breeds trust which, in the long run, gives a leader far greater freedom of action. And trust begets more trust.

To maximize world public order, the trick is to try to act with maximum cooperation while minimizing inaction or ineffectual action. Besides posing short-term dangers, either lack of cooperation or ineffectual action can lay the foundation for inaction in the future.

IV. THE NEW WORLD ORDER

A dangerous idea that arose in the United States during the mid1990s was that the existence of a single superpower obviates the need for multilateral action. Instead, a single superpower can act very effectively on a unilateral basis. Contrary to popular opinion in the United States and around the world, this idea did not arise during the current administration. It clearly arose during the previous administration. At times even our Secretary of State called us the essential, sole superpower.[22] Unfortunately, this was not a rhetorical flourish, but mirrored policy realities.

[19] *See generally,* Ernest Hemingway, *For Whom the Bell Tolls* (Charles Scribner's Sons ed., 1968) (1940).

[20] *See generally,* John B. Attanasio, *Symposium: Law-Based Nature of the New International Financial Infrastructure: Foreword: The Asian Financial Contagion–A Global Epidemic*, 33 INT'L LAW. 847 (1999).

[21] *See* Kennedy, *supra* note 17.

[22] Madeleine Albright, *Newsmaker: Secretary of State Albright*, interview with Jim Lehrer (Oct. 28, 1997) *available at:* http://www.pbs.org/newshour/bb/asia/July-dec97/albright_10-28.html (last visited Jan. 31, 2003).

After a magnificent demonstration of multilateralism in the Iraq conflict, the United States proceeded in a very different way in the Kosovo conflict. The United States never obtained United Nations' approval for the war in Kosovo.[23] One or two of its five permanent members would almost certainly have vetoed the resolution.[24] In fact, we did not even secure Congressional approval; rather than the Security Council or our own Congress, the administration relied on NATO approval as a kind of substitute.[25] Much of the war was conducted by the United States with some help from Great Britain. Incidentally, the Yugoslavian crisis was not an isolated example of unilateralism by the Clinton administration. At the beginning of the administration, it forged a strategy of using 301 sanctions to get its way in economics and trade that eventually culminated in the global financial crisis[26] and later hurled cruise missiles at what turned out to be a drug factory in Sudan a day before an impeachment vote. Incidentally, just to show that the democrats have no lock on unilateral behavior, section 301 was a republican brainchild.

This repeated unilateralism of the Clinton administration contrasts sharply with that of the first Bush administration in which President Bush forged a magnificent seamless coalition which included the Security Council, the major economic powers, our Congress and even the Arab nations. This coalition, and the patient process by which it was forged, was put forth as a model for a post-Cold War world, a model of leadership based on a kind of noblesse oblige. Almost like Camelot, the remaining superpower would lead not by 'might but by right.' Other nations would be carefully consulted and their approval won in a process a bit like the round table. The President would lead in forging the peace in a New World Order. Unfortunately, this emergent paradigm, which was only born in the last two years of the Bush administration, wilted in the political winds of electoral defeat.

Granted, the New World Order was formed at a propitious time. Saddam Hussein's occupation of Kuwait made a multilateral coalition much easier to build. After all, Yugoslavia at some level was an internal intervention or at least an intervention when a state was in the process of dismembering. Moreover, the current Iraqi crisis does not involve occupation of another power. Iraq's history of extreme aggression against neighboring powers and its own people, together with its pursuit of weapons of mass destruction in violation of the U.N. Resolution,[27] have been advanced as reasons for pursuing war with Iraq.

23 Inocencio Arias, *Essay: Shumanitarian Intervention: Could the Security Council Kill the United Nations*, 23 FORDHAM INT'L L. REV. 1005, 1024 (2000).

24 *Id.* at 1024-25.

25 *Id.* at 1024.

26 *See* Attanasio, *supra* note 20, at 847.

27 S.C. Res. 687, U.N. SCOR, 46th Sess., 2881st mtg. PC 8, U.N. Doc. S/RES/687 (1991).

The jury is still very much out on whether the current Bush administration will embrace the paradigm resembling the New World Order or a more unilateralist approach. Before the United Nations and Congressional vote on Iraq, this administration was beginning to look considerably unilateralist. Its actions at Kyoto, steel quotas, and the War Crimes Tribunal only buttressed this characterization.

Except for steel, these initiatives began during the previous administration. This point is not made to criticize the previous administration, but rather to state that after a propitious beginning, the 1990s witnessed considerable American unilateralism. The fact that the second Bush administration showed distinct signs of unilateral behavior indicated that this behavior might be emerging as a bipartisan model for the conduct of American foreign policy. The emergence of unilateralism as a potential bedrock of American foreign policy prompted this conference.

One of the ways we designed the conference was to show how the spillover effects of unilateral action in one area affect international relations in other areas, notably economics and the environment. For example, it may be that the United States is the sole superpower in military terms; however, it is certainly not the sole super power in economic terms. Our total foreign debt reaches the trillions. Moreover, the GDP of the European Union has been gaining force in recent years.[28] We are even less disparate when it comes to environmental issues. While certain types of environmental degradation are localized, such as, pollution in a lake that does not produce fish for export, other environmental degradation affects all of us, notably the hole in the ozone. In any case, the range of unilateral action available to the United States militarily is greater than its economic or environmental range. Even in the military realm, our range of unilateral action has distinct limits. Without considerable cooperation from countries like Great Britain, Russia, and Uzbekistan, our operations in Afghanistan would certainly have been more costly in terms of life and limb, time, money, and success.

V. THE CONFERENCE

These papers emanate from a conference on unilateralism versus multilateral responses to global threats. The conference was organized by the Dedman School of Law at Southern Methodist University under the auspices of the Carrington Lecture Series. It sought to bring together a distinguished group of policymakers and academics to discuss these

[28] Martin Wolf, 'Europe Risks Destruction to Widen Peace and Prosperity,' *The Financial Times (London)* (Dec. 11, 2002), at 23.

momentous issues. To encourage a frank exchange of views, part of the conference was held in private with the intention that these views would inform this publication. The distinguished list of participants in the conference is as follows:

CHRISTOPHER ASHBY, former U.S. Ambassador to Uruguay

JOHN ATTANASIO, Dean and William Hawley Atwell Professor of Constitutional Law at SMU

AL CASEY, former CEO of American Airlines and former U.S. Postmaster General

RUDOLPH DOLZER, former Director General of the Federal Chancellery of Germany and Professor of Law at the University of Bonn (Germany)

WERNER EBKE, International Business Law and Taxation Chair at the University of Konstanz School of Law (Germany) and Global Professor of Law at NYU School of Law

WHITNEY HARRIS, former Nuremberg Prosecutor and former Professor of Law, SMU

ARTHUR HELTON, Director, Peace and Conflict Studies; Senior Fellow for Refugee Studies and Preventive Action, Council on Foreign Relations; and former Vice President of the Soros Foundation

RAY HUNT, CEO—Hunt Oil Company

ROBERT JORDAN, U.S. Ambassador to Saudi Arabia

YUTAKA KAWASHIMA, former Vice Minister of Foreign Affairs in Japan and Japanese Ambassador to Israel, former Distinguished Visiting Fellow at the Center for Northeast Asian Policy Studies at Harvard University and former Fellow of the Brookings Institute

NDIVA KOFELE-KALE, Professor of Law at SMU

ALEXANDER KONOVALOV, President of the Russian Institute for Strategic Analysis, Political Consultant of the First Channel for Russian TV and Professor of Moscow State Institute of International Relations

VAUGHAN LOWE, Chichele Professor of Public International Law & Fellow—All Souls College

LT. GENERAL JAMES T. SCOTT (RET.), Former Director of National Security Program, Harvard University; Former Special Operations Force Officer

W. MICHAEL REISMAN, Myres S. McDougal Professor of Law, Yale University

GAO SHANGQUAN, Senior Research Fellow, Professor and Former Vice-Minister of the State Commission for Restructuring the Economic Systems, and President of the China Research Society for economic reform and development in China

SHEILA SISULU, South African Ambassador to the United States

Most sadly, two of the conference's distinguished participants have passed away: Arthur Helton (see *In Memoriam* above) and Al Casey (after a most distinguished career in the public and private sectors) at the ripe age of 84.

This conference was inspired by a July 1, 2001, article in *The New York Times* on American unilateralism.[29] Michael Reisman and I discussed the article and thought that these issues merited discussion. Vaughan Lowe at Oxford agreed, and our own distinguished alumnus Lee Schepps rounded out the team. While *The New York Times* article prompted our interest in the idea of the conference, we quickly determined that the focus of that article was too narrow and that the focus of the conference should expand to unilateralism by nations around the world. It was also designed to show the interaction in unilateral behavior in the context of the military, economics, the environment, and international organizations. When the tragedy of September 11 occurred, the conference was already well into the planning stage. We changed the focus of the conference not so much to be a critique of unilateralism, but a comparison of unilateral versus multilateral behavior in the above four areas.

The results far exceeded our expectations. We hope that this volume will help to enrich the discussion of these important issues. The flavor of the conference is well captured by the introduction of one of its planners, Professor Vaughan Lowe.

[29] William Safire, 'The Way We Live Now: On Language; Quick, Henry, the emoillient!' *The New York Times* (July 1, 2001), at 26, sec. 6, col. 3.

CHAPTER TWO

Unilateral Action in an Imperfect World Order

*by W. Michael Reisman & Scott Shuchart**

CHAPTER OUTLINE

I. Introduction
II. The Parameters
III. The Role of the Dominant Actor Generally
IV. The United States and Unilateral Action
V. Conclusion

I. INTRODUCTION

Recent events have cast substantial doubt in the minds of many international elites on the commitment of the United States, easily the world's most influential state, to act within multilateral structures. NATO bombing in Kosovo, American repudiation of the Rome Statute of the International Criminal Court,[1] and the Bush administration's schizoid alternation between courting and rejecting United Nations involvement in its invasion and occupation of Iraq have made clear—to some, uncomfortably clear—the extent to which multilateral organs and a multilateralist ideology are seen by powerful states as instruments to be used in the pursuit of national interests rather than as a substitute for national organs and national interest. By the same token, the failure of multilateral entities to act to secure their pronounced aims at critical junctures has made overt what some would prefer politely to deny: namely, the immaturity and impotence of

* W. Michael Reisman, Myres S. McDougal Professor of International Law, Yale Law School; Scott Shuchart, Clerk to Judge Marsha S. Berzon, U.S. Court of Appeals for the Ninth Circuit; J.D., Yale Law School, 2003.

[1] *See* Letter from John R. Bolton, Under Secretary of State for Arms Control and International Security, to Secretary General Kofi Annan (May 6, 2002), *available at* http://www.state.gov/r/pa/prs/ps/2002/9968.htm (last visited Nov. 16, 2003) ('[I]n connection with the Rome Statute . . . the United States does not intend to become a party to the treaty. Accordingly, the United States has no legal obligations arising from its signature. . . .').

multilateral structures when they cannot harness the political, economic, or military energies of actors for whom multilateral action is not the only conceivable vector for obtaining international policy outcomes.

Angst about the success, failure, bolstering, or undermining of a regime for multilateral action by unilateral actors presupposes both a potentially effective multilateral decision-making regime and an operative consensus about the duties of especially powerful states within such a regime. Both presumptions merit examination, for unilateral action is hardly extraordinary: Since 1990, unilateral foreign interventions in internal military conflicts have numbered as many as United Nations-authorized foreign interventions.[2]

II. THE PARAMETERS

A 'unilateral action' is an act by a formally unauthorized actor that effectively pre-empts any official decision by an entity legally designated to act. The unilateral actor claims that its action is, nonetheless, lawful on the grounds that (1) the relevant legal regime allows such an action in particular circumstances, provided substantive criteria for lawfulness are satisfied; (2) circumstances surrounding the unilateral act satisfy the relevant criteria; and (3) notwithstanding procedural irregularities, the act is claimed to satisfy those substantive criteria. Hence a 'unilateral action' necessarily amounts to an effective displacement of decision-making by what would be the appropriate decision-maker were the legally recognized procedure followed. Actions that merely prompt a logy official decision-maker into action are then not unilateral, as they do not preclude an effective action through procedures sanctioned by relevant norms of recognition. A unilateral action is claimed by its author to be substantively *lawful*—in conformity with the ultimate goals of the relevant system, and productive of legitimate effects[3]—even if not procedurally *legal*.

As unilateral action necessarily displaces other action, a given action's propriety depends crucially on the likely decision or range of action it obviates. Hence, the appraisal of any unilateral action depends on an understanding of the international decision-making apparatus outside of which the action is taken. Arguments against unilateralism are weakest when the displaced decision-maker is incapacitated or otherwise unresponsive. Unilateral action is most plainly unacceptable when an officially designated actor could have solved the problem were it not pre-empted. The lawfulness of a unilateral action that sidelines a multilateral decision-maker will

[2] *See* PATRICK M. REGAN, CIVIL WARS AND FOREIGN POWERS 102 (2000).
[3] *See* VLADIMIR D. DEGAN, SOURCES OF INTERNATIONAL LAW 272 (1997).

depend in large part on the efficacy of the constitutive structure through which the multilateral decision might be taken.

The international decision-making system, no less than any other system governed by quasi-legal concepts, includes a constitutive process that establishes and maintains decision-making procedures. This structural process is distinct from the decisions the apparatus so constituted produces, but it is not insulated from it. The first test of the lawfulness of a unilateral action is whether the constitutive process allows the unilateralist to displace the competence of formally designated decision-makers. The relevant constitutive process will, at a level of great abstraction, be one of four types:

An unorganized or non-hierarchical constitutive structure. In these systems, unilateral action is the primary means of decision-making; unilaterality therefore cannot be per se an indicator of the unlawfulness of the action. Though some participants and observers may note and bemoan the lack of effective multilateral processes, in their continued absence, unilateral action remains the norm and so not, *eo ipso*, unlawful.

An ineffective constitutive structure. These all-too-common systems tend to have purely semantic structures, processes that purport to abide by elaborate law-governed processes but which in fact operate on an entirely different value calculus and through channels distinct from those superficially recognized. An 'operational code,'[4] not a public constitution, regulates decision. Where the relevant decisionmaker cannot reach a decision through official methods, frequent unilateral action can be expected. Nonetheless, the cognitive dissonance generated by such systems can make effective operation within them quite difficult, as the presence even of empty legal symbols can make those undertaking action in derogation of the symbols seem unlawful and corrupting. Agents who move between effective domestic structures and ineffective international ones are liable to underestimate the emptiness of legalisms in these defective structures.

A partially effective constitutive structure. Limited effectiveness of a constitutive process may result from a lack of political power, authority, or coordination, but it may also arise as a conscious, or at least a useful, technique for mediating among the incompatible values, interests, and aspirations of a varied constituency. On areas of normative dissensus, partially effective structures will recognize claims as 'valid' while providing no means to enforce them. Such generally effective systems may retain contingent *exceptios* for unilateral action where the decision maker has, at least at times, insufficient power to make effective the clear standards and procedures to which it subscribes. The 'right of self-defense' in article 51 of the U.N. Charter is a prime example. Rather than some atavistic remnant of the

[4] *See* W. MICHAEL REISMAN, FOLDED LIES: BRIBERY, CRUSADES, AND REFORMS 1 (1979).

pre-Charter right of each state to wage war, article 51 carves out devolution to unilateral action from the general monopoly on force delegated to the Security Council.

An effective constitutive structure. It is in the presence of an effective institution capable of responding to the justified demands of its participants that unilateral action becomes generally unjustified, and so presumptively delictual. Though some unilateral action might be tolerated—if, in particular, it is not simply self-serving—an effective structure can be expected to condemn and to sanction any such action, lest the constitutive process be undermined and devolve into a structure of merely limited effectiveness.

There simply is not, at present, sufficient consensus on which of these forms describes the instant world public order to provide a clear, categorical assessment of unilateral action. The United Nations may have been meant to be a fully effective institution, but the Cold War quickly relegated it to the third, limited sort, as the Security Council became effectively paralyzed in virtually all the situations in which the drafters of the Charter anticipated it would operate. A tide of unilateral actions filled the vacuum, often by expanding the conception of 'self-defense.'

The tide has not waned significantly since the end of the Cold War, which accounts for the genuinely uncertain legal status, and indeed wisdom, of actions taken outside of world constitutive structures. To imagine that the Security Council retains a full and effective monopoly on economic, political, or military sanction is to conjure away all the occasions on which it has failed to act as it is supposed to in an effective constitutive structure. Yet to suggest that the Council acts with only the simulacra of effectiveness is perhaps equally unfair. It is no surprise, then, that the world—and its jurists—are in a quandary about the role of unilateral action in the system.

Arguments for the desirability of a fully effective multilateral order are too easily mistaken for reasons to treat the extant order as though it were fully effective. Quite often, current multilateral mechanisms are unable to induce steps supported by the values of most participating states. The comparatively easily-achieved consensus authorizing a response to Iraq's 1990 invasion of Kuwait[5] responded to a manifest violation of a state's security in its borders and contrasts with reaction since then to internal human rights abuses, over which the Security Council has remained essentially sessile. Indeed, the mismatch between the process of international law-making by which human rights norms are enunciated and the Security Council's processes for enforcement of those norms has in recent years

[5] *See, e.g.*, S.C. Res. 678, U.N. SCOR, 45th Sess., 2963d mtg. at 27, UN Doc. S/RES/678 (1990) (implicitly authorizing use of force against Iraq).

provided the primary justification for unilateral actions thought to preempt matters within the Council's remit. Because some veto-holders on the Security Council reject what others consider to be the consensus norms on human rights values and standards, the broader human rights constituency has tried to work through the larger constitutive process—in which the United Nations is embedded—to implement those norms. For these matters, the Security Council is at best only a partially effective institution, hobbled by its internal legal arrangements from giving effect to values it is pledged to support.

In many circumstances, the judgment of ineffectiveness of the official decision-making system that might justify unilateral action will depend on whose ox is being gored. In a system whose effectiveness varies with respect to different domains and to the issues at stake there, participants may profoundly disagree as to whether the officially designed decisionmaker *is* effective with regard to a class of events. These disagreements may rest on differing factual assessments, but they may just as often turn on value conflict, with the result that proponents of a unilateral action may believe the official decisionmaker incapable of effective action while opponents take official inaction to be an effective, and so preclusive, decision. The current action in Iraq serves as a prime example. When less powerful states stand up for territorial integrity safeguarded by absolute sovereignty and against unilateral military interventions for humanitarian purposes, they do so in part because their own ability to remain vital participants in international affairs depends on the conceit that an official decisionmaker committed to humanitarian values might choose to refrain from intervention. For states unthreatened by the erosion of a non-intervention norm, official inaction in a humanitarian crisis is a defect, whereas for the smaller states, enforced inaction seems the apotheosis of multilateral decision-making, displacing the ability of powerful players to act by their own lights.

The coexistence of domains in which members of the Security Council and other official decisionmakers can fairly claim to be effective and those in which these claims are mere palaver creates genuine uncertainty as to the nature of public order and the duty of individual actors to hew to the formal prohibitions of international law. In times of crisis, actors capable of acting outside the official structure may be inclined to do so—not because they reject the authority of the official decisionmaker, but because they cannot for whatever reason abide the long process of ascertaining whether the decisionmaker will prove effective. The continued existence of genuine exigencies, and the continued failure of official decisionmakers to respond in a reliably timely or efficacious manner, makes a sweeping anti-unilateralist position untenable.

III. THE ROLE OF THE DOMINANT ACTOR GENERALLY

Regardless of the degree of effectiveness manifested in the official international decisionmaker, there is reason to suppose that some states might competently and justly bear distinct responsibilities, especially for security functions. Even under a capable multilateral decisionmaker, asymmetries among national resources, technologies, and competencies are conducive to a recurrent apportionment of decision-implementing functions among participating states. Only a minority of states have the logistical technologies to mount a major humanitarian relief operation; some states are better able to bear the political costs of long-term peacekeeping deployments than are others. While many states maintain substantial military forces as a share of population, they may not be large in the international sense or trained for foreign deployments. Support of states capable of such deployments is thus a prerequisite for any international security undertaking. These asymmetries are, perhaps, even more pronounced in the current climate, where differential competence leads some actors to take the lead in implementing norms on which the official decisionmaker fails to act. By and large, these are the 'major powers'—states with the demographic and economic wherewithal to project force across the globe in the service of political activities. The truly difficult question is, then, whether in the absence of a fully effective regime possessed of its own capable international military instrument, these major-power states might justly bear special responsibility, especially for international security. Finding an answer to that broad question is beyond the scope of this chapter, but there do appear to be domains in which differential responsibility has been recognized as justifying displacement of the official decisionmaker by some forms of unilateral action.

In the case of nuclear security especially, the fact that the 1970 Nuclear Non-Proliferation Treaty (NPT)[6] imposes different responsibilities on non-nuclear and 'grandfathered' nuclear states indicates a system of asymmetric duties. The basic obligation imposed by the NPT, after all, is that the allowed powers not transfer nuclear weapons or assistance in producing such weapons to the non-nuclear state parties.[7] This 'seemingly unequal treaty . . . reflected the reality of the international relations in the 1970s and 1980s'[8] and in effect endeavored to freeze the extant balance of power. With that balance now shifted, under the regime established in the 1995

[6] Treaty for the Non-Proliferation of Nuclear Weapons, July 1, 1968, 21 U.S.T. 483, 729 U.N.T.S. 161.

[7] *See id.* art. II.

[8] Legality of the Threat or Use of Nuclear Weapons, 1996 I.C.J. 226, 330 (July 8) (dissenting opinion of Judge Oda); *see also* W. Michael Reisman, *The Political Consequences of the General Assembly Advisory Opinion*, *in* INTERNATIONAL LAW, THE INTERNATIONAL COURT OF JUSTICE, AND NUCLEAR WEAPONS 473 (Laurence Boisson de Chazournes & Philippe Sands eds., 1999).

treaty extension, the five Permanent Members of the Security Council covenanted not to use nuclear weapons against any non-nuclear state party to the NPT.[9] The regime then essentially turns on assurances given by the nuclear powers to the other states to limit the spread and use of the weapons. This system, approved by the Security Council,[10] amounts to a regime of differential responsibility for the maintenance of security through the management of nuclear weapons. The nuclear powers are barred from using their weapons against non-nuclear NPT signatories and are expected to come to the assistance of any non-nuclear state threatened or attacked with nuclear weapons.[11]

Economic and development issues are inseparable from security, and the major powers dominate these institutions as well. The *Grundnorm* of multilateral economic agencies holds that power be distributed on the basis of the size of contributions. Where dominant economic power may be used to further partial economic interest rather than that of the world economy, the major economic powers may have special duties to constrain their ability to manipulate the constitutive world economic institutions to their own ends. Moreover, whatever asymmetric duties the major powers hold for physical security surely entail duties to contribute adequately to economic development projects, the inadequacy of which often forms the predicate for military instability. Alas, the major powers often make economic decisions of international import with an eye toward their own national economic interest, largely for domestic political reasons.

Differential responsibility is also encoded in the U. N. Charter through the special status accorded to the five Permanent Members of the Security Council, notably the veto power.[12] Just as possession of nuclear weapons has been taken by the NPT regime as a basis for imposing special security obligations, so too might the major powers be under some obligation to utilize the veto in a way that furthers world order. Use of the veto in a way that advances only the holder's interest is antinomian and, under the Charter, inappropriate. It would be plainly inappropriate, for example, for a state to take unilateral action after its veto (or threatened veto) kept the Security Council from taking an effective decision to create a multilateral solution. The possibility of a General Assembly 'Uniting for Peace' resolution[13] provides some check on abuse of the veto, but special obligations for the Permanent Members remain.

[9] *See* U.N. Doc. S/1995/261, 262, 263, 264, & 265.

[10] *See* S.C. Res. 984, U.N. SCOR, 50th Sess., 3514th mtg., U.N. Doc. S/RES/984 (1995).

[11] *See id.* at 2 (providing that, in the event a non-nuclear state is threatened or attacked by nuclear weapons, 'the nuclear-weapon State Permanent members of the Security council will . . . seek Council action to provide . . . the necessary assistance to the State victim').

[12] U.N. CHARTER art. 2, para. 3.

[13] *See* G.A. Res. 377, U.N. GAOR, 5th Sess., Supp. No. 20, at 10, U.N. Doc. A/1775 (1950).

The factual dominance of one Permanent Member in particular makes differential responsibility inevitable. Given its extraordinary economic, military, and political centrality to a variety of constitutive regimes, both internal and international political pressures make it extremely difficult for the United States to forego unilateral action in support of consensus norms to which it subscribes.[14] The existence of such a preeminent actor may itself tend to reduce a fully effective constitutive procedure to one of only limited effectiveness; this occurs through both that actor's ability to act and to stand apart from official decisionmakers, and through a crowding-out effect whereby the official decisionmaker foregoes political costs that the preeminent actor is willing to bear itself. And, it should not be forgotten that arguments for differential responsibility resonate with the decision-making elites within powerful states, who appreciate the political benefits that come from projecting unilateral strength.

So long as one actor plays such a dominant role, acknowledgement of special duties on its part may be the only vector for achieving a variety of policy outcomes. By the same token, a public order largely dependent on the presumed altruism of the most powerful actors is dangerously prone to moral hazard. Given the frequent ineffectiveness of multilateral decision-making and the fact of broad inequalities of military and economic means among states, some realistic theory of asymmetric obligations to mediate these perils would be helpful.

IV. THE UNITED STATES AND UNILATERAL ACTION

In light of the frequent ineffectiveness of the multilateral constitutive decision-making structure and the substantial arguments favoring special responsibility for some states, unilateral action is apt to coexist for some time with multilateral policies adopted by partially effective international decisionmakers. Yet some contemporary defenses of unilateral action often overstate the ineffectiveness of multilateral bodies and minimize the political values participation in such bodies serves.

The international myth system depends crucially on the principle of sovereign equality set forth in the United Nations Charter.[15] Yet it is quite evident that members of the United Nations have unequal rights and obligations, with respect to budget and security matters especially. U.N. practice has been to speak the language of equality but to act on the maxim 'each

[14] *See generally* Ruth Wedgwood, *Unilateral Action in a Multilateral World*, *in* MULTILATERALISM & U.S. FOREIGN POLICY: AMBIVALENT ENGAGEMENT 167, 169 (Stewart Patrick & Shepard Forman eds., 2002) (describing ways in which asymmetries of power tend to bolster American claims to legitimacy of unilateral action).

[15] U.N. CHARTER, art. 2, para. 1.

according to his ability, each according to his needs.'[16] For states with little ability, multilateral institutions have begun to become the principal avenues for diplomacy. Whereas for the United States the formal institutions of international law are often little more than means to an end determined by domestic elites,[17] these smaller states find substantial value in process itself. Their votes in multilateral bodies are their chief power-base in international relations, far greater than any leverage they might hope to exercise on a bilateral basis outside, perhaps, of their geographic region. Though the major powers cannot, of course, afford to ignore multilateral structures, they simply do not depend on them in the same way.

The United States is not the only state to see the United Nations largely as a means to obtaining bilateral outcomes. The other permanent members, even while they use the Security Council as a device to counterbalance U.S. dominance, have bilateral tools at their disposal that the majority of states almost entirely lack. U.S. impatience with the cumbersome procedures of multilateral diplomacy may spring from the national tendency to 'can-do-ism' and sometimes from a genuine desire to obtain legitimate policy outcomes, but dispensing with those procedures oftentimes looks, to all the world, like impatience with the deliberative involvement of any state that dares not fall immediately in line behind American preferences. Respect for international deliberation is not the same as deference to international diplomats, but expressions of such respect are oftentimes the prerequisites to political acquiescence by other states. When America is seen not even to care whether other nations acquiesce in its actions, it raises legitimate questions regarding its apparent indifference to the lawfulness of its undertakings.

While the United States in one sense uses multilateral instruments more than any other state to project its values,[18] these uses are distinctive and, from the standpoint of states more dependent on formal international institutions, often manipulative. By and large, these U.S. practices reflect a political culture and the foreign policy of an actor that is, in many respects, distinctively altruistic, by its own lights. Nonetheless, the manifestations of distinctive U.S. views at times threaten to undermine the viability of the international myth system that allows less powerful states to engage in multilateral structures under a claim of equality of status.

The United States engages with and engineers international institutions in a variety of modalities. First, as reformer, the United States often

[16] *See* KARL MARX, *Critique of the Gotha Programme: Marginal Notes on the Programme of the German Workers Party*, *in* Marx: Later Political Writings 208, 215 (Terrell Carber ed., 1996) (1891).

[17] *See* John C. Ikenberry, *Multilateralism and U.S. Grand Strategy*, *in* MULTILATERALISM & U.S. FOREIGN POLICY, *supra* note , at 121.

[18] *See id.* at 122.

attempts international 'social engineering' in the expectation that new institutions and procedures could transform international politics. In this modality, law and legalism are central—as central as Americans believe law to be to their own politics. Second, as a factor within a wide range of international organizations, the United States is surprisingly restrained, generally deferring to and defending established constitutive procedures despite its ability to manipulate them to its favor. Because of the reformist role, however, the United States is generally held to a higher standard, and expressions of its own partial interests are often subject to special scrutiny. Some of these expressions may be America defending itself within approved bureaucratic procedures, procedures designed to function best when states vigorously advocate for themselves. However, other aspects may be manifestations of the fact that, in a regime of only intermittently effective legal procedures, many key institutions remain conduits for expressions of power, and the United States, like any other player, acts to preserve the power it has acquired. These roles can prove quite complex, as when America has supported expansion of the General Assembly's power, at the expense of the Security Council's, to circumvent veto roadblocks in the latter.[19]

Third, and uniquely, is the U.S. role as custodian of international values and institutions. At times, the inherent defects of multilateral decisionmakers render them incapable of action; multilateral success in forming an institution to implement certain norms does not always translate into successful execution. These institutions function in a regime of international politics largely dominated by actors representing their national perspectives, a fact far less transient than the Cold War. Rather, despite a homogenizing global culture (especially among elites, and particularly with regard to certain humanitarian values), states do act with different aims, different expectations, and divergent interests. When these conflicting aims threaten to undermine a multilateral entity, unilateral action that displaces official action may save the institution from itself. The United States, for all its devotion to legalism, is more willing and more capable than many actors of taking sole action in part to safeguard the future viability of a paralyzed institution. While states threatened by the potential for U.S. hegemonism may confuse these custodial actions with aggressive unilateralism, calls for America to fill this role often originate in *other* supporters of the crippled institution. A state's unchecked aggression threatens to undermine the United Nations' ultimate value as guarantor of international security; yet defects in its procedures or international politics may prevent it from authorizing a collective defense. Here it may be the U.S. interest in future U.N. competence that leads it to take unauthorized action to secure tranquility—

[19] *e.g.*, the 'Uniting for Peace' Resolution, *supra* note and accompanying text.

not because the aggression in question threatens any particular U.S. interest, but because international stability is a goal for which America will act even without multilateral sanction. Such action may be reformist, too—a forceful implementation of the anti-aggression norm. The irony that, sometimes, a multilateral institution must be set aside in order ultimately to be saved is not lost on American decisionmakers, but neither should it always inhibit them from acting on reformist and custodial impulses.

Fourth, the United States role is heavily conditioned, more so than the diplomatic postures of many states, by internal political considerations, both electoral and intra-governmental. Values of state and local officials, whose activities are increasingly the subject of multilateral treaties, have substantial influence on federal diplomacy. The legislature, especially when the Senate is controlled by a political party other than the one holding the presidency, may have a large role in foreign policymaking; and, legislators influence and are influenced by their constituents' international concerns. These varied interests can put stress on the ability of federal diplomacy to speak in the single voice sometimes required for effective international politicking. They may also create especially great pressure for foreign-policymakers to see that the interests of the domestic constituency be honored even though doing so will involve extraordinary or unilateral action. Individual interest groups will almost invariably be willing to deplete the political capital available for other causes in the service of their own, meaning that an opportunity for unilateral involvement on a given issue will be quite appealing to some, usually vocal, constituent in the domestic decisionmaking apparatus.

None of these institutional functions is aided, of course, by overt attempts to marginalize multilateral decisionmakers or to undermine the myth system that allows less powerful states to draw political benefits from their active participation in those institutions. Some in the U.S. foreign policy establishment would appear to underestimate both the instrumental and rhetorical value of multilateralism. As a result, they have fostered an erroneous sense in some corners that the United States has retreated from its custodial role, altering its intra-institutional posture to favor its own interests and backing off from its reformist vision of a world order composed of legalized institutions.[20] The manipulative signature and retrenchment[21] on the Rome Statute for the International Criminal Court,[22] the abandonment of U.S. commitment to the Kyoto Protocol on climate

[20] *See* Stewart Patrick, *Multilateralism & Its Discontents*, *in* MULTILATERALISM & U.S. FOREIGN POLICY, *supra* note , at 1, 10 (noting value of multilateral institutions to breadth and success of U.S. diplomatic initiatives).

[21] *See also* Letter from Bolton to Annan, *supra* note (claiming that, with no intention of ratification, U.S. signature of treaty had no legal effect).

[22] U.N. Doc. A/Conf.183/9 (1998).

change,[23] and the country's failure to ratify the Comprehensive Nuclear Test Ban Treaty,[24] the Convention on the Elimination of All Forms of Discrimination Against Women,[25] the Land Mines Convention,[26] and the Convention on the Rights of the Child[27] have seemed to many an abdication of America's reformist role. Its disinclination to involve official decisionmakers in its policy towards non-state terrorist actors and rogue authoritarian states has, similarly, appeared to be a retreat from the custodial vision and a move towards a hegemonic, imperial sense of America not as ultimate underwriter of security, but as primary and exclusive guarantor.

These steps, combined with an apparent failure of many in the policy elite to recognize the abiding value—even if only instrumental—of international legal arrangements, have unnecessarily undermined the United States' ability to execute its reformist and custodial roles and have left even its well-intentioned attempts to serve those goals tinged with an unhealthy air of self-interestedness. The new robust unilateralism also evidences an almost willful blindness to the seemingly obvious point that internationalist fetters on unilateral U.S. action are liable to be fully offset by the benefits of corresponding strictures on the unilateral actions of other states.[28]

Domestic political concerns in part explain, but scarcely excuse, the frequent hostility to multilateral undertakings, institutions, and ideology expressed by and through policymaking and diplomatic elites. Especially since the end of the Cold War, consensus among elected officials on foreign policy matters has substantially collapsed, with the major political parties taking up adversarial views on the merits of international involvements. This new political culture has latched on to the tense relationship between the United States and United Nations that accompanied the growth of the non-aligned movement during the 1970s and its control of the General Assembly.[29] The right-wing lunatic fringe now worries not about the Communist International, but about the U.N.'s black helicopters seeking to subjugate America to world government. The Republicans' electoral success

[23] Kyoto Protocol to the United Nations Framework Convention on Climate Change, Conference of the Parties, 3rd Sess., Agenda Item 5, U.N. Doc. FCCC/CP/1997/L.7/Add.1 (1997).

[24] Comprehensive Nuclear-Test-Ban Treaty, U.N. Doc. A/50/1027, 35 I.L.M. 1439, opened for signature Sept. 24, 1996.

[25] 1249 U.N.T.S. 13, 19 I.L.M. 33 (1980) (opened for signature March 1, 1980).

[26] Convention on the Prohibition of the Use, Stockpiling, Production and Transfer of Anti-Personnel Mines and on Their Destruction, 36 I.L.M. 1507 (1997) (opened for signature Dec. 3, 1997).

[27] Nov. 20, 1989, 1577 U.N.T.S. 3, 28 I.L.M. 1448 (1989).

[28] *See also* MICHAEL J. GLENNON, LIMITS OF LAW, PREROGATIVES OF POWER: INTERVENTIONISM AFTER KOSOVO 198 (2001) (arguing that multinational support for a policy is a good indication that the active states are acting on overt, not ulterior, motives).

[29] See Margaret P. Karns and Karen A. Mingst, *The United States as 'Deadbeat'? U.S. Policy and the UN Financial Crisis*, *in* MULTILATERALISM & U.S. FOREIGN POLICY, *supra* note , at 267, 269.

in 1994 hinged on their 'Contract with America' platform, one plank of which called for legislation to ensure that 'No U.S. troops [operate] under U.N. command. . . .'[30] The decade-long refusal of the United States to pay its full mandatory dues to the United Nations emerged from the same sort of politics, joined with legitimate custodial concerns about fiscal and administrative management in the organization.[31] American presidential politics, long the electorate's focus for foreign-policy concerns, have of late directed attention to the values implicated by a commitment to multilateralism.[32]

Whatever the merits of unilateral undertakings, there is no value at all in the world's most powerful state issuing gratuitous insults to multilateral fora. Yet some in the United States persist in doing just this, through policy behavior and the anti-internationalist rhetoric of distinguished commentators. For example, Charles Krauthammer has written that the United General Assembly is 'a playground for the most powerless nations on earth to rant and vent their rage at the powerful.'[33] One knowledgeable observer captured the needless hostility American tactics engender:

> The United States is, by its actions, setting a devastating example. The wealthiest nation in the world has chosen not to honor its dues to the organization that it helped create, and of which it is the most important member. . . . The leader of the free world went over a year without appointing an ambassador to the body entrusted with the task of securing and upholding international peace. . . . The United States does not even sign or ratify treaties whose propriety is acknowledged unanimously by the international community. . . . All these actions harm the United Nations beyond description, not only because the United States is one of the world's foremost democratic states, but also because of the U.S. standing as the sole superpower. The immediate effect thereof is both contagious and harmful.[34]

This indignation at times deprives the United States of participation in selective decision-making panels, as when the U.S. delegates were for a time voted off the U.N. Advisory Committee on Administrative and Budgetary Questions or the U.N. Human Rights Commission.[35]

[30] Republican Contract with America, *available at* http://www.house.gov/house/Contract/CONTRACT.html (last visited Nov. 18, 2003).

[31] *See generally* Karns & Mingst, *supra* note .

[32] *See* J.M. Spectar, *Elephants, Donkeys, or Other Creatures? Presidential Election Cycles & International Law of the Global Commons*, 15 AM. U. INT'L L. REV. 975 (2000).

[33] Charles Krauthammer, *A World Imagined: The Flawed Premises of Liberal Foreign Policy*, NEW REPUBLIC, March 15, 1999, at 23 (quoted in Edward C. Luck, *The United States, International Organizations, and the Quest for Legitimacy*, *in* MULTILATERALISM & U.S. FOREIGN POLICY, *supra* note , at 47, 61).

[34] Inocencio Arias, *Humanitarian Intervention: Could the Security Council Kill the United Nations?*, 23 FORDHAM INT'L L.J. 1005 (2000). The author was the Spanish Ambassador to the United Nations.

[35] *See* Patrick, *supra* note , at 25; *Election of the United States to the UN Human Rights Commission*, 96 AM. J. INT'L L. 718 (2002).

There is a good reason debate and process are valuable to states lacking the wherewithal to act outside of sanctioned institutions, and even officials animated by *Realpolitik* and committed to preserving unilateral options should by word and deed allow multilateral institutions to fill whatever space they may competently and effectively occupy. American victory in the Cold War destabilized the balance that had earlier provided many smaller states with some measure of security, if only the thin assurance of predictable antagonisms. When that balance was lost, those states turned even more urgently to the international order just as some in the United States felt liberated to conduct policy without substantial multilateral consultation.[36] Lingering distaste for the General Assembly among U.S. policy elites appears at times to emerge as a concern that even engagement with the Security Council might subordinate American action to dominance of the poorer, southern nations in the membership as a whole. This is a serious mistake; both the General Assembly and Security Council can serve or impair U.S. interests, but they do so in profoundly different ways, and the general ineffectiveness of the General Assembly—which was, in a sense, designed to be ineffective—reflects little on the potential effectiveness of the Security Council when sitting in its role as guarantor of security.

V. CONCLUSION

Cognitive dissonance regarding the nature of the international order can produce destructive reverberations throughout international politics. As some states become comparatively incapable of executing major diplomatic enterprises outside of multilateral bodies, their own resentments at this fact may surface in the form of excessive faith in the competence of the body to succeed in whatever it undertakes.[37] Failures by the multilateral organ will then only reinforce a dominant actor's tendency to see the organ as an unnecessary, even silly, sideline to the real business of international politics, further alienating the two. Neither strategy is stable, for all the same reasons that the present world constitutive institutions were built following the Second World War: Without a means for dissipating political costs throughout the states favoring a costly undertaking, norms will be under-

[36] *See* Raymond F. Hopkins, *Anomie, System Reform, and Challenges to the U.N. System, in* INTERNATIONAL ORGANIZATIONS AND ETHNIC CONFLICT 72 (Milton J. Esman & Shibley Telhami eds., 1995).

[37] Hence the prematurity of the view of many international legal scholars that humanitarian intervention is lawful only when vetted by the authorized decisionmaker. *See, e.g.*, Edmundo Vargas Carreño, *Humanitarian Intervention, in* INTERNATIONAL LAW ON THE EVE OF THE TWENTY-FIRST CENTURY: VIEWS FROM THE INTERNATIONAL LAW COMMISSION 339 (1997); PETER MALANCZUK, HUMANITARIAN INTERVENTION AND THE LEGITIMACY OF THE USE OF FORCE (1993).

enforced and miscreants allowed to thrive. Without a reliable way to involve the wealthiest states in the affairs of the poorer, the former will grow inattentive and the latter unstable.

Just as unilateralists may now overlook these instrumental values, so too have multilateralists come to adopt an excessively Kantian view of unilateral pursuits, supposing that the admixture of a single nation's interest irrevocably taints an otherwise worthwhile undertaking. But, nation-states are not mere atavisms, national interest is not synonymous with hegemony, and political elites cannot be expected to move about the international plane with disregard for the demands of or possible benefits to domestic constituencies. At the same time, though marginal states may hope to expand their own political resources through the legitimacy of multilateral regimes, opposition to the affairs of a dominant actor is hardly the *reason* such states find international procedures so attractive. The interdependency of the multilateral and the unilateral, the decision-making powers of the group and the executive efficiency of the strong, are likely more than transient phenomena. Scarce political capital ought not be wasted disparaging a worthwhile arrangement.

CHAPTER THREE A

Multilateralism vs. Unilateralism: Principle or Policy?

*by Christopher Ashby**

CHAPTER OUTLINE

I. How Do We Define Unilateralism and Multilateralism?
II. For an Approach to be Multilateral, Do the Various Parties involved have to Agree on the Eventual Policy Decision?
III. Are Discussions and Consultations That do not Reach Consensus Considered to be Unilateral?
IV. And of Course the Logical Extension is, if Multilateral Consultations are Undertaken but No Consensus or Agreement is Found, Does That Make Any Policy or Action Taken by any of the Involved Parties Illegal?
V. What Level of Multilateralism Must be Reached for Such Action to be Deemed in Accordance with the Rule of Law?
VI. What Roles do the Various International Tribunals Play?
VII. Clearly the Great Multilateral Body is the United Nations. Does the Discussion of the Rule of Law Imply That Actions which the UN Endorse are Legal, and Those That They do not Illegal?
VIII. Is Unilateralism vs. Multilateralism a Quest for Policy or Principle?

At the concluding event of the seminar, each participant made a short presentation and then the panel took questions from the audience. One of the questioners stated something akin to the following: 'I was surprised to hear in this discussion very little about the rule of law. I was especially surprised that Ambassador Ashby would state that multilateralism versus unilateralism was a question of policy, not principle.' In this statement is embedded a number of questions worth examining.

* President, Houston World Affairs Council; Former U.S. Ambassador to Uruguay.

I. HOW DO WE DEFINE UNILATERALISM AND MULTILATERALISM?

I suppose technically speaking, unilateralism involves one state or party, bilateralism involves two, and multilateralism involves three or more. As with most technical definitions, this is inadequate. The definitions of multilateralism and unilateralism in the literature and in common usage in the United States are, by design, ambiguous. Taken to its logical conclusion, submission to multilateralism involves the voluntary surrender of sovereignty. Although purists would argue that there is no such thing as 'some sovereignty,' in actual application there are clearly degrees of sovereignty. There are also temporal surrenders, for a fixed period or until the state changes its mind. With the change of administration, the United States reclaimed its willingness, and right, to act unilaterally in abrogating the ABM treaty and 'unsigning' the Kyoto accords. Unilateralism, or the ability to act in one's own interest, as defined by the nation, is part of the historical definition of sovereignty. Therefore, to the extent that multilateralism implies requirement, it impinges sovereignty. If an international organization or agreement prevents or requires some action, it is clearly reducing the ability of a nation to act as it sees fit.

In general practice, the definition of multilateralism implies an effort to agree among more than two. I emphasize 'effort.' For multilateralism to be anything approaching requirements or prevention, it is a restriction on sovereignty. If the dilution of sovereignty is voluntary, then multilateralism can imply agreement. To the extent that it is enforced, then multilateralism becomes coercive.

There are further differentiations of multilateralism, which are those implying an establishment of a non-state entity to manage the multilateralism. The United Nations (UN) is a multilateral organization established to enforce the rules of multilateralism. NAFTA is a multilateral agreement, without a non-state entity for enforcement. To the extent that a non-state agent enforces multilateralism, it implies a dilution of sovereignty. To the extent that it is a voluntary participation that can be ended, such as NAFTA, then it is not.

Therefore, a critical element in the definition of multilateralism, insofar as it is involved with the rule of law, is the level of voluntary versus involuntary restriction implied. By definition, multilateralism that is involuntary is more likely to be governed by the rule of law than multilateralism that is voluntary and restrictive only by mutual agreement. It is difficult to state that abrogating a treaty is illegal, if there were provisions for abrogation in the treaty itself.

It would appear that multilateralism and unilateralism do not have agreed upon definitions. It is a matter of context and the argument being put forward. What is important to note is that there is no legal definition of multilateralism or unilateralism, which would tend to indicate that these terms are not legal topic.

II. FOR AN APPROACH TO BE MULTILATERAL, DO THE VARIOUS PARTIES INVOLVED HAVE TO AGREE ON THE EVENTUAL POLICY DECISION?

If multilateralism is voluntary, it is an approach to a situation or problem with the consent of the participants. It is therefore non-binding unless previously agreed to. The U.S. participation in the Land Mines negotiations was clearly multilateral. We were a prime mover in the effort, and we were intimately involved with the process over time. However, we did not participate as a signatory to the Ottawa Convention. Although our approach was clearly multilateral, we did not give up our right to disagree with the final outcome. Our eventual role as a non-signatory party group was not a question of legality or the rule of law.

III. ARE DISCUSSIONS AND CONSULTATIONS THAT DO NOT REACH CONSENSUS CONSIDERED TO BE UNILATERAL?

Discussion and consultation with more than one other party is multilateral. The approach to finding a solution is multilateral. If a solution is found, then the voluntary restriction that the agreement might imply is a multilateral solution. However, a multilateral approach to finding a solution does not imply a priori accession to the majority will of the group. To do so would clearly be beyond the requirements of a sovereign nation. Therefore, the lack of agreement or consensus as a result of a multilateral approach is not in any way a contravention of the rule of law.

IV. AND OF COURSE THE LOGICAL EXTENSION IS, IF MULTILATERAL CONSULTATIONS ARE UNDERTAKEN BUT NO CONSENSUS OR AGREEMENT IS FOUND, DOES THAT MAKE ANY POLICY OR ACTION TAKEN BY ANY OF THE INVOLVED PARTIES ILLEGAL?

The current situation involving the U.S. effort to generate a resolution from the UN on Iraq is very illustrative. The United States is clearly trying to take a multilateral approach to the problem of chemical and biological weapons that Iraq maintains. UN Security Council Resolution 1441, passed last year, demanded that President Saddam Hussein allow unfettered access to inspectors searching for weapons of mass destruction. The White House has been careful not to commit itself to having to seek a second UN resolution before starting military action. If there is a breach of Resolution 1441, the UN is expected to honor the undertakings that are given to uphold the will of the UN. It is quite possible that no additional resolution that authorizes the use of force will be passed. If that is the case and the United States takes military action in Iraq without the international consensus that a UN resolution conveys in order to find and destroy those weapons, is that illegal?

This is one area in which the rule of law might come into play. By voluntarily signing the UN charter, the United States accepted a considerable reduction of sovereignty. For one thing, the rules of war, such as the Geneva Convention, are honored by the Security Council of the UN. However, because the UN has unfortunately been frequently ineffective, due to the power of one permanent member to veto resolutions, it was often bypassed during the Cold War, with the notable exception of the Korean Conflict. When the military forces of the Democratic People's Republic of Korea moved southward across the 38th Parallel in June 1950, the United Nations supported the efforts of the Republic of Korea to halt the Communist invasion. The United States bore the brunt of the burden, as the United Nations first contained, then drove back the North Koreans in defeat. Only the entry of the Chinese Communists into the war in November prevented the UN from attaining a clear-cut military victory as well as a potential political triumph in the unification of Korea. Now, it is generally felt that the consent of the UN through the Security Council is politically important, perhaps crucial, especially when the conflict ends short of a clear-cut victory, as was the case in Korea in the early 1950s. But it is not generally maintained that the United States would violate the rule of law to unilaterally move to dispose of those weapons, because it would be upholding UN Security Council Resolution 1441, which calls upon Iraq to disclose its weapons of mass destruction. The Resolution says that any 'omissions or false statements' in the arms statement Iraq presents would constitute elements of a serious breach. However, military action is not the only method available to uphold Resolution 1441, and several nations disagree on military action coming before containment by weapons inspectors has at least been given a chance.

V. WHAT LEVEL OF MULTILATERALISM MUST BE REACHED FOR SUCH ACTION TO BE DEEMED IN ACCORDANCE WITH THE RULE OF LAW?

Again, the current situation is an interesting example of this conundrum. Is a 'coalition of like-minded countries' multilateral? Is it multilateral enough to be viewed as legitimate? Who decides? I think the answer to this is going to be very important to the United States if we choose to take action without the blessing of the UN. Then the question becomes, is multilateralism policy or principle? Is it a smart, effective, and politically intelligent way to proceed, or is it also legal while unilateralism is not? Each country, especially the United States, is multilateral when it wants to be, unilateral when it must be. Certainly, a transnational legal and economic world order implies an ideal of cooperation, as organized around the UN, the International Criminal Court, the World Trade Organization, and other international human rights and environmental institutions. The United States has signed on to the parts of the international legal order that served its interests (the World Trade Organization, for example), while ignoring other parts (the Kyoto Protocol or the International Criminal Court) that do not.

VI. WHAT ROLES DO THE VARIOUS INTERNATIONAL TRIBUNALS PLAY?

It may have been assumed that a multilateral order would essentially level the playing field and constrain American power projection, where the rule of law applied. That was before such international agreements, as the case of the International Criminal Court. The United States was instrumental in establishing the ICC and was very involved in the negotiations that led up to its creation. But as with land mines, the United States did not agree to the final document, and opted out of the consensus. So the question is, does the US position *vis-à-vis* the International Criminal Court constitute a unilateral act or a legitimate act of a sovereign nation? I think the answer is both. The creation of the court was a multilateral act, in which the United States was a major participant. Our final decision not to participate in the jurisdiction of the court was a unilateral act. However, there is no argument that it was an illegal act. It was a decision taken by a sovereign power not to participate in an international agreement. Now that the court is formed, our unwillingness to abide by its authority, or to allow our service men to be subject to its decisions, is causing considerable agitation among our allies and adversaries. However, our position has been labeled arbitrary, arrogant, and unilateral, but not illegal.

VII. CLEARLY THE GREAT MULTILATERAL BODY IS THE UNITED NATIONS. DOES THE DISCUSSION OF THE RULE OF LAW IMPLY THAT ACTIONS WHICH THE UN ENDORSE ARE LEGAL, AND THOSE THAT THEY DO NOT ILLEGAL?

The use of the UN by the United States since 1990 has been one of the most dramatic consequences of the end of the Cold War. When President Bush went to the United Nations to get agreement for the invasion of Iraq (but not Panama), and President Clinton for the U.S. military action against

Haiti, we showed that we believed the support of the UN was preferable in those circumstances. However, we had never stated that such support was necessary for the action to be legal. In fact, during the Cold War, we rarely approached the UN for such support. Were such actions legal without UN support during the Cold War but illegal afterward? No such assertion was ever made. In fact, the action in Kosovo was a NATO military undertaking without the support of the UN because of the opposition of Russia. So in fact we are saying that support of the UN has nothing to do with legality or the rule of law. It is politically preferable, perhaps even required for a conclusive peace, maintained by UN peacekeepers. The extent that the United States is going to get Security Council support for disarming Iraq is an impressive demonstration of the political necessity of UN support for such actions. The fact that President Bush has repeatedly stated that the United States will act without UN support if he cannot get it clearly means that he does not feel that UN support affects the legality of the action. He feels that it is good policy.

VIII. IS UNILATERALISM VS. MULTILATERALISM A QUEST FOR POLICY OR PRINCIPLE?

The choice between multilateral and unilateral approach to problem solving and action alternatives is a very important, and at times, critical decision. It can affect international support and the reaction by the adversary. However, it is a matter of policy, not principle. It is almost never a question of the rule of law.

The one possible exception to this might be the use of force, which is clearly regulated by the UN Charter. Although this stipulation has been obviated many times in the history of the UN, it is clearly covered by the charter. However, there are of course times when the stipulations of the charter might conflict with the principle of a nation's right of self defense, which has seldom been challenged in the international arena. Even when Israel launched a preemptive attack on its neighbors in 1967, there was little international denial that it was doing so in self-defense and therefore had that right, regardless of the provisions of the UN charter, and regardless of the unilateral nature of its actions.

Because of cold war relations between the United States and the Soviet Union prior to 1992, the UN was virtually never the arena for armed conflict resolution. Only the Korean 'police' action of 1950 went to the Security Council. And even after the fall of the Soviet Union and a more moderate Russia took the Security Council seat, the United States used the Organization of American States as the deliberative body to approve military action in Panama, and NATO to approve the attack on Kosovo.

But the political efficacy of multilateral approaches has been demonstrated many times, such as Presidents Bush and Clinton seeking UN approval about pending military action in Somalia and Haiti. However, the realization of the need for multilateral action has never been more dramatic than the current confrontation with Iraq. The United States has consistently maintained that it did not need UN approval to take military action against Iraq, and has just as consistently sought that approval.

But in all the discussion about Iraq, few have used the term 'rule of law.' The basis of discussion has been on the existence of sufficient provocation in the form of weapons of mass destruction, and the ability and means to prove their existence.

Security Council Resolution 1441, passed last November, stipulated that Saddam Hussein allow UN inspectors unimpeded access to search for weapons of mass destruction. According to the Resolution, Iraq has been and remains in material breach of its obligations under relevant resolution, in particular through Iraq's failure to cooperate with UN inspectors and the IAEA (International Atomic Energy Agency). And in paragraph 13 in the Resolution, 'the Council has repeatedly warned Iraq that it will face serious consequences as a result of its continued violations of its obligations.'

Note that according to the Resolution itself, it is the Security Council that decides (1) non-compliance, and (2) defines what will be the 'serious consequences.' There are two schools of regarding non-compliance: the Bush Administration maintains that it is up to Iraq to prove that it has no weapons of mass destruction. The administration's case is resting so far on two elements: (A) Iraq's failure to list weapons that the inspectors already found before they were ejected in 1998 is already, according to the Bush Administration, sufficient evidence to indicate that Iraq has not given a full account of its weapons. (B) Any weapons the inspectors now find that were not listed in the declaration it gave to the Security Council last month is a violation of Baghdad's international obligations. The other school of thought is that it is completely up to the UN inspectors to declare serious violations. Already there is a problem of timing in the delivery of the UN inspection team's reports. The head of the UN inspection team, Hans Blix, recently stated that a March meeting is required in order to give a new report on Iraqi disarmament. In Blix's view, the March meeting is required under the 1999 UN Resolution (1284) that created the inspection agency, the United Nations Monitoring, Verification and Inspection Commission (UNMOVIC). The Bush Administration, however, holds that the tough new November UN Resolution, superceded all elements of the earlier Resolution.

In any case, is it a material breach of the November Resolution, because Iraq only passively complied and did not give a full accounting? Or is it a material breach of the November Resolution if and when the UN inspector team declares it? The latter determination has two advantages: that Iraq is officially declared by the international body of the UN to be violating a Resolution, and secondly that the Resolution itself has embedded in it the phrase 'serious consequences.' The 'serious consequences' phrase could lead to a second UN resolution authorizing the use of force.

The Bush Administration has been careful not to commit itself to seeking a second UN resolution before commencing military action. President Bush said on January 16: 'In the name of peace, if he does not disarm, I will lead a coalition of the willing to disarm Saddam Hussein.' That means that the United States may not wait for the second UN resolution, but will interpret the Iraqi's lack of accountability as a reason to go to war with a more limited 'coalition of the willing.'

The choice to decide on 'breach' independent of the UN inspectors' report is a policy decision, as would be a war plan with a coalition of the willing, rather than a UN force. Opinions about the legality of both of these actions would likely be long debated. It is clear, however, that international opinion supports UN determination of breach as well as specific UN authorization of the use of force. Policy decisions normally take into account legality as well as the probable outcome in the international arena. UN authorization of force has the advantage of UN peacekeepers in the period of rebuilding.

CHAPTER THREE B

China's WTO Accession and the Prospect of Asia's Economy

*by Gao Shangquan**

CHAPTER OUTLINE

I. The Impacts of September 11 on the Asian Economy
II. China's Accession into WTO
III. The Relationship of Trade and Investment between China and Other Asian Countries
   A. Development of China's Economy and Trade between China and Asian Economies
   B. Foreign Investment from Asia
IV. Implications of China's WTO Accession on Asian Economics
   A. The Enhanced Market Opportunity made Available to Asian Economies
   B. Competition on Labor-intensive Manufacturing Products
   C. Competition Between China and other Asian Economies for Third Party Markets
   D. Impact on Capital Flow
V. Strengthening Regional Economic Cooperation to Promote the Development in Asia

I. THE IMPACTS OF SEPTEMBER 11 ON THE ASIAN ECONOMY

The slowdown of the world economy caused by the September 11 tragedy added to the difficulties Asian countries already faced. From luxury hotels to computer manufacturers to shipping agents, Asian companies are suffering from a much deeper-than-expected economic downturn. Unlike the Asian tempest of the late 1990s, which was largely rooted in home-grown excesses, people here feel swept by events out of their control.

* The author is a former Vice-Minister of State Commission for Restructuring the Economic System. Now he is president of China Society for Research On Economic System Reform, Professor and Doctorate Advisor at Peking University.

The current drop in Asian exports is due more to the slump in electronics demand, causing China's Taiwan, Korea, Singapore and Malaysia all to record a 20–30% decrease in year-on-year exports. Exports of electronics will drop even further not only because of continued reduction in demand but also from supply disruption resulting from the disturbance in air transport.

The imminent recession in the United States and its extension in Asia are likely to encourage corporations to cut back their investments even further and continue to implement layoffs. This will undoubtedly adversely affect consumer sentiment. In some countries, like Thailand, Indonesia, the Philippines and Korea, growth in domestic consumption becomes a major support to otherwise relatively depressed economics.

Tourism will also be affected. In Malaysia, visitor arrivals rose by 43.3% in the first seven months of 2001. Thailand, China's mainland, Hong Kong and Taiwan China also saw reasonably decent growth in visitor arrivals. These statistics will almost certainly be hard hit by the fear air travel following September 11.

What is more important is next year's growth forecast. Due to the impacts of the September 11 tragedy, it is likely that about one to three percentage point cuts on top of the real GDP growth forecast in many Asian countries in 2002. Though China probably is an exception where domestic demand remains strong, its exports will likely see more a pronounced contraction and the growth rate of foreign tourists might drop somewhat.

In the foreign exchange rate front, it is unlikely that Asian currencies will enjoy any major appreciation against the U.S. dollar in the short term, as their central banks will take this opportunity to further ease monetary policy, rather than letting their currencies rise. Consistent capital outflow to the United States in the past few years has been putting pressure on many Asian currencies. This currency pressure has been restraining some central banks' ability to ease monetary policy. The increase in the United States could slow the capital flow from Asia to the U.S., providing more support to local currencies.

In sum, Asian countries will almost certainly be adversely affected by the September 11 tragedy through their close link to the U.S. commodities and financial markets. However, aggressive public policies, including strong fiscal stimulus, a further increase in banking liquidity, and a drop in real interest rates, could provide a good foundation for the recovery of Asian economies.

II. CHINA'S ACCESSION INTO WTO

Mike Moore, The WTO Director-General, once said, 'With China's membership, the WTO will take a major step towards becoming a truly world organization. The near-universal acceptance of its rules–based system will serve a pivotal role in underpinning global economic cooperation.'

The major points of China's commitments are as follows:

- China will provide non-discriminatory treatment to all WTRO members as well as eliminate dual pricing practices and differences in treatment accorded to goods produced for sale in China in comparison to those for export.
- The WTO Agreement will be implemented by China in an effective and uniform manner by revising its existing domestic laws and enacting new legislation in full compliance with the WTO Agreement.
- Within three years of accession, all enterprises will have the right to import and export all goods and trade them throughout the customs territory with limited exceptions.
- China will not maintain or introduce any export subsidies on agricultural products.
- China will gradually reduce trade barriers and expand market access to foreign goods. China has bound all tariffs for imported goods. After implementing all the commitments, China's average tariffs level will decrease to 15 percent for agricultural products and 8.9 percent for industrial goods.
- China will join the WTO Agreement on Basic Telecommunication. The transitional period for abolishing the location restrictions on various categories of services shall be two years for paging and value-added services, five years for mobile communications service, and six years for domestic cable service. However, restrictions will remain on foreign equity share, and management control rights and the entrance and exit of international communications will continue to be subject to state restrictions.
- China will join the WTO Agreement on Financial Service and has committed to gradually lift the customer and location restrictions on foreign banks' transactions in foreign exchanges and the local currency RMB within five years.
- Within three years after its WTO accession, China will phase out its restrictions on the scope and location of foreign insurance companies. However, foreign equity share of life insurance companies shall not be allowed to exceed 50 percent.
- Foreign investors will be allowed to hold shares of securities fund management companies, but the controlling shareholder must be on the Chinese side. There will be virtually no restrictions on the business scope after three years.
- Distribution includes trade, wholesale, retail, repairs, transportation,

storage and other auxiliary services. Except for a few commodities, China will phase out its restrictions on the equity share, product varieties, quantities and location of foreign invested enterprises. Except for salt and tobacco, foreign investors will be allowed to engage in the distribution of virtually all kinds of industrial products after five years.

III. THE RELATIONSHIP OF TRADE AND INVESTMENT BETWEEN CHINA AND OTHER ASIAN COUNTRIES

A. Development of China's Economy and Trade between China and Asian Economies

Due to deepened economic reform and political stability, China's economy has maintained rapid growth since 1978, making it one of the fastest growing economies in the world during the last two decades. By 2001, China's GDP had exceeded $1000 billion in U.S. dollars. Economic growth has been driven by more efficient allocation of resources in most sectors of the economy as central planning has been replaced by a more market-oriented approach, in which international trade and investment have been significant. China's share of world exports had risen from less than 1 percent in the late 1978 to 3.9 percent in the last year.

China's merchandise exports to Asia have reached $132.3 billion in U.S. dollars, accounting for 53 percent of its total exports. Moreover, China's imports from Asia have amounted to $141.3 billion U.S. dollars, accounting for 62.8 percent of its total imports. China's most important trade partners in Asia are Japan, Hong Kong, Korea, ASEAN, and Chinese Taipei. China's exports and imports with these countries and regions account for about 90 percent of its total exports and 86 percent of its total exports imports.

Among China's major trade partners in Asia, it is a common tendency that their shares of intra-regional imports have expanded during the last decade. As to the destinations of exports, NIEs have changed their export market from North America and West Europe to Asian economies, along with the intra-regional industries transfer and the expansion of processing trade in the coastal area. As China has emerged as 'a global manufacturing base' of labor intensive that Japan and the NIEs have lost competitiveness.

B. Foreign Investment from Asia

FDI flow to China has been steadily increasing since the early 1990s. Ten Asian economies have served as major sources of FDI absorbed by China. By the end of 2000, China had accumulatively absorbed a paid-in foreign investment of $231.4 billion in U.S. dollars, of which 75 percent came from these 20 Asian economies. In addition to large investors, thousands of small and medium-sized enterprises, particularly involving overseas Chinese, have made a major contribution to output, employment, and export growth in China over the last decade.

IV. IMPLICATIONS OF CHINA'S WTO ACCESSION ON ASIAN ECONOMICS

The potential impact on Asian economics of China's WTO accession is essentially on our important decisions.

A. The Enhanced Market Opportunity made Available to Asian Economies

First, China's WTO entry is expected to provide a strong stimulus to China's economy. As long as the Chinese economy continues to maintain a 7 percent annual growth rate in the next 10 years, its economic aggregate would be doubled, exceeding $2 trillion in U.S. dollars, and its economic structure would shift towards industrialization. Accordingly, China's domestic demand for capital goods, energy, raw material, and component inputs will increase to feed the expansion and upgrading of its industrial sectors.

Second, the reduction of tariffs in large margin and abolition of quantitative restrictions within 5 years will benefit imports from Asian economies with revealed comparative advantage. As there continues to be expansion of production and exports of China's labor-intensive products and raw materials, almost all of related exports sectors in Japan, NIE and other Asian developing countries will benefit.

B. Competition on Labor-intensive Manufacturing Products

After WTO accession, all the prohibitions, quantitative restrictions, or other measures maintained against imports from China that are inconsistent with WTO agreements would be phased out by its trade partners. Since China enjoys comparative advantages in labor- intensive products, such as textiles and clothing, and miscellaneous products and electronics, improvement of the export environment will probably intensify competition with other developing countries based on market rules.

C. Competition Between China and other Asian Economies for Third Party Markets

It is quite common for China and other developing Asian economies to be dependent on the same large market. Furthermore, there is a significant overlap in their export products. For example, in the U.S. market, ASEAN and China are major exporters of clothing and electronics; in the Japanese and EU markets, ASEAN and China are major exporters of electronics. However, more than half of China's exports take the form of processing trade and conducted by foreign invested enterprises. The competition between China and other Asian developing countries could be eased with diversification of production and markets operated by multinationals.

D. Impact on Capital Flow

Great concern has been raised about the impact of FDI flow to China on other developing countries. This concern is supported by facts that FDI inflow into China rose by 20 percent during the first half of 2001, Southeast Asia's share of total FDI in Asian developing countries continue to shrink and FDI inflow into South Asia were still below the 1997 peak. However, it is recognized that the decision to invest in a country is a complex one, and that the contraction of FDI inflow to Asian developing economies in recent years is obviously resulted from the 1997 financial and economic crisis.

Another concern about FDI booming in China is that FDI outflow will cause de-industrialization and unemployment in home countries of investments. As economies are getting more and more integrated, it is almost impossible for the government to prevent enterprises from moving out of the country. For example, the emerging horizontal division of labor between China and Japan mostly exists in capital-intensive and technology-intensive industries, which has led to the increase of China's exports of machinery and electronic products to Japan. Since processing trade are mainly conducted by Japan-invested companies and parent companies generally control the import sources of components and the export channels of the final products, such kind of trade between China and Japan is actually the intra-company trade.

V. STRENGTHENING REGIONAL ECONOMIC COOPERATION TO PROMOTE THE DEVELOPMENT IN ASIA

In order to ensure long-term steady economic growth for Asia, the enlargement of the intra-regional trade and the expansion of regional markets are important measures for regional economic cooperation. The different stages of economic development of Asian countries and regions provide great potential for trade and investment based on a high degree of complementarily. Along with economic restructuring and industrial transfer, there is a bright future for intra-industry and intra-company trade. Faced with the challenge of regionalism, it is the common desire of enterprises in Asia to strengthen institutional cooperation as well as trade and investment liberalization. While controversies over the relationship between regionalism and multilateralism exist, it is well-known that regional trade agreements (RTAs) usually contain a higher level of obligation for liberalization than multilateral trade agreements. Thus, they can pursue a more relevant liberalization scheme with a smaller group of nations. As a member of WTO, China can actively participate in bilateral or plurilateral negotiations on RTA. For example, under the '10 + 3' framework, a joint research team on forging closer China-ASEAN economic relations has been established by China and ASEAN to probe into the possibility of forming the China-ASEAN Free Trade Area within 10 years. With China's entry into the WTO, penetrating more aggressively into the Chinese market may become one of the important motives for countries to negotiate with China or its neighboring countries on RTA.

Trade facilitation can also be a priority of the institutional cooperation among Asian countries, as simplification of trade procedures can result in considerable savings in time, money and human resources. At the same time, a comprehensive technical assistance program in trade facilitation will be needed to encourage ongoing work in this area in Asian developing countries.

CHAPTER THREE C

Multilateralism and American Policy: A Diplomat's View

*By Robert W. Jordan**

I would like to offer a brief commentary from the perspective of a 'practitioner' of foreign policy working in the field. My arena, Saudi Arabia, is a long-standing ally of the United States, a country of great strategic importance, but without the ties of culture, history, and common outlook that bolster our relationships with other major allies.

The debate over 'unilateralism versus multilateralism' has always had heavy transatlantic overtones. As a global power, America often prefers to remain unfettered in the exercise of its power. An ambitious European Union or an insecure Russia are apt to see multilateralism as a means of leveling the playing field. These are natural inclinations and perhaps we should not worry too much as long as the effect of such rivalry is limited to spheres such as finance, the environment, intellectual property, trade, or even arms control.

It is obviously a caricature of the truth to suggest that this or any previous U.S. Administration is concerned only with U.S. interests and rejects any constraint on its freedom to act in the international sphere. President Bush is a strong supporter of the World Trade Organization, the North Atlantic Treaty Organization, and the North Atlantic Free Trade Association. In fact, the percentage of international treaties that President Bush has said he wants to review is tiny. The United States consistently has taken the lead in developing international institutions to grapple with international problems that are difficult for a single government to resolve, or that no single country has an interest in solving alone. As the president has stated in The National Security Strategy of the United States of America, 'No nation can build a safer, better world alone. Alliance and multilateral institutions can multiply the strength of freedom-loving nations.'

The threat to global security highlighted by the terrorist attacks of September 11 put the issue of multilateralism into a different context. The theoretical aspects of the debate over multilateralism quite properly were

* U.S. Ambassador to the Kingdom of Saudi Arabia.

put aside for a time. The role of the United States as world leader came into focus. The global community was confronted with an immediate and very real threat, and only the United States had the means to muster a global response.

On one hand, the United States has responded by calling for a war against terrorism in all its dimensions. On the other hand, U.S. leaders have reminded us that this will be an unprecedented kind of war. It will not be over quickly, it will require patience, and we will not be able to fight it alone.

It is readily apparent to me from my vantage point in Saudi Arabia why we cannot expect to prevail in this effort with a strictly unilateral policy. The struggle will have to be waged in many countries, including our own, where small cells of terrorists may reside. There is an obvious military dimension to the struggle, but it may not be the most important part of what we do. Military force may neutralize bin Ladin and the al-Qaeda network, but without a more comprehensive strategy, the broader phenomenon of terrorism will not necessarily be fundamentally weakened. There will be a need for careful police and intelligence work to undermine the networks of terrorists. We will have to trace the flows of money, arms, training, and motives that can lead to the carrying out of terrorist attacks.

We need allies at times like this, including many in the Arab and Islamic worlds. There simply is no debate here between multilateralism and unilateralism. Borders, political systems, language, culture and all the other trappings of the modern nation state have no relevance to the fanatic. And when small cells of radical extremists have the means and the will to wreak destruction on a scale that would be possible with the acquisition of weapons of mass destruction, that is a global threat unlike any other we have had to confront before.

As Ambassador to Saudi Arabia, I have been deeply troubled by the degree of alienation from the United States that I have encountered at a popular level. Such sentiments will make it harder for us to conduct the kind of multilateral campaign that will eventually reduce the risk of terror. There is no single answer to the question of why there is so much anti-American sentiment in the Arab and Islamic world, but it is clear to me that as a government we urgently need to be thinking of ways to encourage moderate voices in the Middle East. We cannot casually dismiss the resentments directed at the United States when our interests are so closely tied to developing cooperation with governments like that of Saudi Arabia.

As our National Security Strategy makes clear, regional crises such as the Israeli-Palestinian conflict can strain our alliances, and we must build international relationships that can help manage these crises. We also must support global and regional initiatives, such as free trade, economic and educational reform, and exchanges of students and teachers.

Finally, we must enhance our efforts to improve international understanding of America. While the war on terrorism is not a clash of civilizations, we are engaged in a struggle of ideas. If we do not involve all the major countries in the region in a cooperative effort to fight against global terrorism, the war will never be won.

CHAPTER FOUR

Unilateralism and Current Transatlantic Relations

*by Rudolf Dolzer**

CHAPTER OUTLINE

I. Unilateralism and Multilateralism: Evasive Usages and Values
II. Unilateralism and the Preservation of Global Order
III. Unilateralism and Multilateralism: Different Conditions and Experiences
IV. Unilateralism and Multilateralism in Areas of Global Concern
V. Unilateralism and Multilateralism: Reflections on Strength and Weakness
VI. Limitations of U.S. Unilateralism
VII. Unilateralism and Long-term Transatlantic Relations

I. UNILATERALISM AND MULTILATERALISM: EVASIVE USAGES AND VALUES

The notion of unilateralism in international relations is not subject to a clear-cut definition. In its core, the term refers more to a general disposition of a particular state or government in its conduct of foreign relations than to a particular act or measure. Where a state takes a position different from the majority of the international community only in one setting or in rare circumstances, it will be more appropriate to speak of this as an instance of substantive disagreement. A precise point in the spectrum between occasional disagreements and a mode of unilateralism can hardly be pointed out in the abstract. In general, we may speak of unilateralism in a setting in which a state or government decides to act within a broader pattern of conduct towards the international community that is characterised by an attitude of separateness and of disregard for processes of international coordination and agreements.

The crux of the concept so understood is that, at least prima facie, it is

* Director, Institute of International Law, and Professor of Law, University of Bonn.

not related to any particular set of substantive values. It relates to procedure and to orientations in decision-making. The basic, albeit disputed, question today is whether or not a unilateralist mode of deciding will necessarily be seen as negative and disruptive for the fabric of international relations and the substantive outcome as judged in a normative context; in other words, the issue is whether, under the specific contemporary conditions of a globalised world based on nearly two-hundred nation states, multilateralism will be seen as the appropriate disposition for all states, small or large, weak or powerful. Must we consider multilateralism as a value in itself? Is consensus, or at least the orientation toward the majority, to be granted a higher priority under current conditions than the substantive outcome of an international decision inasmuch as unilateralism is inconsistent with the current fabric and by itself unduly threatens values rightly embedded in the international community?

A simple answer dictated by considerations of substantive value would initially point to the formal dimensions both of the concepts of unilateralism and multilateralism and would argue that the contribution of a policy or measure could only be assessed in the light of its suitability to promote the well-being of the international community. If considered, however, in a national context, such an argument would directly collide with the concept of constitutionalism. A basic value in itself, constitutionalism is characterised by an emphasis on the architecture of procedures for decision-making. Does the same principle apply for international decision-making, for instance in the context of the United Nations? Or does a national constitution set forth procedural rules only because of the existence of a consensus on substantive values whereas on the international level such a consensus cannot be a presumed, with the consequence that a procedural emphasis comparable to the domestic constitutional setting would be devoid of substantive orientation and therefore find no justification? To what extent is the United Nations built on sovereign equality and diversity? To what extent should it be assumed on the international level that the requirements of diversity, of multilateralism and pre-agreed rules of procedure converge? Are they comparable to a domestic constitutional setting in which different constituencies are designed to express different experiences, perspectives, and interests on decisions which affect different groups?

Considerations of these concerns are general and abstract in nature. In today's world, unilateralism is discussed mainly in relation to the foreign policy of one state—the United States. The issue here is obviously not so much the singularity of any particular policy, but the ability of the United States to impose its point of view on other states and, sometimes, on the international community. Myanmar's or North Korea's peculiar views of the world and their positions on foreign policy matters are hardly discussed under the heading of unilateralism. Thus, a major dimension behind the debate on unilateralism relates to the current, dominant international political position of the United States that derives from its military and economic power. Obviously, those states and commentators who do not share the substantive positions of the United States may be inclined to phrase their criticism by way of referring to the concept of multilateralism as an inherently appropriate tenor of foreign policy and to the concept of unilateralism as an approach which in itself invokes associations of national egoism in disregard of the real exigencies of the international community. A third variation of the current use of the term 'unilateralism,' linked but not identical with the second, will be observed when it is applied as a synonym for Anti-Americanism; in today's world, the blame for unilateralism has more political appeal than the polemical expression of an outright Anti-American attitude. While this usage exists, it will be ignored at this point and only the first two variants of unilateralism will be addressed.

II. Unilateralism and the Preservation of Global Order

The starting point for the following observations lies in the assumption that special benefits or insights can be gained only to a limited extent from an abstract vantage point in the discussion of the drawbacks or virtues of unilateralism. In systemic terms, to what extent the exercise of unilateral power will be compatible with the functioning and the stability of the current architecture of international relations may be asked. This perspective will form the subject of our initial remarks which consider whether and to what extent a position of unilateralism is compatible with the foundations of the current international order as reflected in the principles and rules of international law. This discourse assumes that international legal rules reflect, in principle, the collective wisdom of the international community based upon past experience. Beyond this aspect of the preservation of the existing structure of the international system, the value of unilateralism will need to be discussed in terms of issues as they exist in reality, in terms of the suitability to address them in practice through unilateral or multilateral process and in terms of the priorities and values which need to be fostered on the international level. Subjective attitudes and preferences will necessarily play a role in such an effort inasmuch as no internationally agreed criteria for values and priorities exist.

Compliance with international law forms one of the most meaningful yardsticks to measure and to assess unilateralism in terms of the burden on the international community and the future viability of an orderly and stable system of relations. Customary international law, based on the practice of states and their legal opinion, reflects the collective experience of the international community. Disregard of these rules prima facie will be considered to have a disruptive effect on the fabric of international relations and will necessarily raise questions regarding the willingness of the offending state to act as a reliable partner in the framework of a 'level playing field'. A second vantage point by which unilateralism may be measured within the coordinates of international law concerns a state's record in complying with international treaties that it has accepted and by which it is bound. Third, connected with these two previous aspects, in Europe, a state's general willingness to accept the judgments of international tribunals will also be seen as an expression of its respect for the international legal system. On a fourth level, in Europe, the acceptance of a state to actively participate in constructive discussions about new arrangements and treaties which respond to evolving international concerns will often be seen as a reflection of the degree to which a state is willing to keep the international system viable and to protect transnational interests, taking into account both the national interest and the interests of other members of the international community.

From a legal point of view, a strict necessity exists to differentiate in the identification and weighing of these four international levels of concern. In contrast to the first two concerns, the third and the fourth do not involve issues of regards for positive existing obligations. As to the third aspect, no state is under an obligation to settle a dispute by way of submitting it to an international tribunal unless it has specifically consented to it in the past. Of course, questions will arise in case a state consistently refuses to accept the jurisdiction of neutral courts set up on the basis of internationally agreed rules and instead seeks to reach a settlement by way of power-based negotiations.

Complex as the issues related to this last aspect may be, the most frequent and wide ranging accusations of unilateralism against the United States were heard in Europe concerning Washington's willingness to participate in international negotiations and conferences entrusted with setting new rules, especially when accompanied by agreements on judicial or arbitral settlement of disputes. The negotiation of the Kyoto Protocol, the efforts to set up rules for land mines issues, the adoption of the regime on biological weapons, and most visibly, the international effort driven mainly by Europe to set up the International Criminal Court illustrate the dimensions of the problem. In all these areas, some governments in Europe consider that Washington has blocked the evolution of appropriate new rules which are considered necessary to protect legitimate transnational interests. But, contrary to direct issues of compliance with existing law in the first two aspects and the enforcement of existing law by international tribunals, this fourth area has an entirely different character inasmuch as it concerns the direction and substance of the future international legal order, in other words an essentially political rather than a legal matter. Of course, legal policy and political will are intricately linked, but they do not relate to existing law, or to existing commitments and their enforcement. As to shaping of future law and policy, international law does not prevent a state relying upon his influence and power; the principle of sovereign equality relates only to the subordination under existing law.

A detailed discussion of the performance of the United States within these four categories relating to the international legal process would require a broad empirical study. Presumably, the outcome of such a study would be that the record of the United States in terms of compliance with existing international law, is by and large comparable to that of other industrialized countries. Possibly, the single coherent area with a distinct U.S. course of conduct concerns the extension of national jurisdiction to transnational factual settings without a clear nexus to U.S. interests.[1] The most remarkable illustrative field concerns human rights. The United States has hesitated to accept relatively weak international machinery of monitoring while at the same time it aggressively pursues, through its national courts, world-wide violations without a demonstrable nexus to U.S. interests on the basis of the opaque Alien Tort Claims Act of 1798.[2] The U.S. Government would likely sharply protest against comparable assertions of jurisdiction by third countries when directed toward its nationals and officials.[3] Sovereign equality, however, requires that jurisdictional rules apply to all states in the same way. In a globalised world with increasing contacts of firms and citizens all over the world, the traditional function of international law to allocate and to limit rules of national jurisdiction so as to avoid constant friction has acquired a new urgency. Unilateralism in this field would present a major systematic challenge which would eventually call for a response of the international community.

As to the third level of legal cooperation noted above, the United States has been, in principle, on the retreat since withdrawing its consent to the jurisdiction of the International Court of Justice following the Nicaragua proceedings in 1985.[4] Of course, the United States has agreed to the establishment of a system of dispute settlement under the WTO and has actively relied on these procedures. Concerning the United States as a defendant, the

[1] *See* Rudolf Dolzer, *Extraterritoriale Anwendung von nationalem Recht aus der Sicht des Völkerrechts*, BITBURGER GESPRÄCHE JAHRBUCH 2003, 71.

[2] *See* ANTHONY D'AMATO & RALPH G. STEINHARDT, THE ALIEN TORT CLAIMS ACT: AN ANALYTICAL ANTHOLOGY (1999).

[3] *See* Belgium's Amendment to the Law of June 15, 1993 (as amended by the Law of February 10, 1999) Concerning the Punishment of Grave Breaches of Humanitarian Law, 42 ILM 749 (2003) and the report on contemporary practice of the United States Relating to International Law *U.S. Reaction to Belgian Universal Jurisdiction Law*, 97 AJIL 984 (2003).

[4] *See* U.S. Withdrawal from the Proceedings Initiated by Nicaragua in the ICJ, Jan. 18, 1985, DEPT. ST. BULL., Mar. 1985, at 64.

original scepticism of the U.S. Congress (see the Dole Amendment[5]) seems to have vanished to some extent. Nevertheless, frictions have appeared, sometimes with sharp edges. In one case, for instance, in spring 2000, the United States was found to be in violation on both levels of the dispute settlement system, but the U.S. Congress has failed to take the necessary remedial action without any discernible reason.[6] Other cases of a less spectacular degree of obviousness have presented similar issues. In the field of foreign investment, the NAFTA multilateral dispute settlement system has been actively used in the past years by U.S. foreign investors as plaintiffs while proceedings of foreign investors against the United States have not only led to protest by U.S. environmental groups but also by political groups which consider these proceedings to amount to an undue interference with the domestic U.S. legal systems.[7] Of course, the sharpest clash between the U.S. and European governments over the role and the acceptance of international tribunals has occurred in past years in the negotiations on the jurisdiction of the International Criminal Court. While the United States has not objected to the establishment of the Court as such, Washington has vigorously objected to every way in which the Court might exercise jurisdiction over U.S. nationals.[8]

Quite obviously, differences exist in the trust and confidence of European governments and of the U.S. government concerning the neutrality and objectivity, as well as the usefulness in general, of international tribunals. While European foreign offices are inclined to support such tribunals as a way to strengthen the rule of law and the legal process on the international level, the United States constantly expresses concern over a possible lack of objectivity and a bias against the United States. For the European observer, it is not always easy to distinguish between such genuine concerns and hesitation on the part of the United States to accept third party settlement instead of retaining the power to settle disputes in direct negotiations.

The fourth and last category of concerns in Europe over U.S. legal unilateralism relates to treaty-making and the willingness of the United States to

[5] Proposal to create a 'WTO Dispute Settlement Review Commission', *see, e.g.* Homer E. Moyer, *How Will The Uruguay Round Change the Practice of Trade Law in the United States?* 30/3 JOURNAL OF WORLD TRADE 63, 76–80 (1996).

[6] *See* Panel report on *US—Anti-Dumping Act of 1916*, WT/DS136/R, 14 Feb. 2000; *see* Appellate Body report on *US—Anti-Dumping Act of 1916*, WT/DS136/AB/R adopted on 26 Sept. 2000.

[7] *See, e.g.* Charles H. Brower, II, *Structure, Legitimacy, and NAFTA's Investment Chapter*, 36 VANDERBILT JOURNAL OF TRANSNATIONAL LAW 37 (2003); Howard Mann, *NAFTA's Investment Chapter: Dynamic Laboratory, Failed Experiments, and Lessons for the FTAA*, ASIL Proceedings of the 97th Annual Meeting, 2003, 247.

[8] *See* report on contemporary practice of the United States Relating to International Law on the American Servicemembers' Protection Act: *U.S. Efforts to Secure Immunity from ICC for U.S. Nationals*, 97 AJIL 710 (2003).

constructively engage in multilateral negotiating fora addressing areas of international reform. The view from Europe in the past decade has been that Senator Helms' statement that he has sworn an oath to the Constitution of the United States and not to the Charter of the United Nations has echoed the sentiments of a large part of the U.S. Congress making it difficult for the U.S. Administration to submit any treaty project to the advise and consent of the Senate and thus to approval by the United States. Occasionally, doubts have been voiced whether the U.S. Administration is at times hiding behind the threat of blocking by the Senate, but on the whole, this suspicion does not seem to reflect reality.

Whatever the details may be, European complaints about unilateralism of the United States in international negotiating fora often merely paper over the fact that the United States defends a substantive position which is not shared in European capitals. Substantive disagreement however must, in principle, not be identified with support for multilateralism or a preference for unilateralism. International law does not require that a state supports an existing majority in the international arena. The clearest example is found in the voting procedure of the Security Council, more precisely in the veto power of its permanent members. Indeed, this system forms one of the pillars of the current international order. Occasionally questioned as a matter of principle, occasionally the subject of proposals for modification, and recently modified at least in practice in the area of humanitarian intervention,[9] it is safe, nevertheless, to assume that the principle will not be changed in the foreseeable future.

Thus, we do not find the principle of majority voting at the power centre of the current system, but a version of unilateralism: the right of each of the five states to say no to any international military action in response to a breach of the peace, with the consequence of preventing all others from acting with military means. Unilateralism is an accepted mechanism in the most central area of international legal relations. Of course, everyone may question the relevant rules of the United Nations Charter, but no alternative has so far been acceptable to the international community. Along the same lines, no rule of international law prevents one state from assuming a role of dominance in international relations, be it on a military, the political or economic level, or to use this power without threatening the use of force. In the postcolonial world, especially after the down fall of the Soviet Union, the principle of sovereign equality has become even more of a fiction than it was before.

[9] *See, e.g.* Antonio Cassese, Ex iniuria ius oritur: *Are We Moving towards International Legitimation of Forcible Humanitarian Countermeasures in the World Community?* 10 EUROPEAN JOURNAL OF INTERNATIONAL LAW 23 (1999); Daniel Thürer, *Der Kosovo-Konflikt im Lichte des Völkerrechts: Von drei—echten und scheinbaren—Dilemmata*, 38 ARCHIV DES VÖLKERRECHTS 1 (2000).

III. UNILATERALISM AND MULTILATERALISM: DIFFERENT CONDITIONS AND EXPERIENCES

In the following part, we shall turn to the preconditions and the effects of U.S. unilateralism in the current setting of transatlantic relations. These relations have evolved historically, and while they never have been entirely stable, the close partnership between the United States and Europe has, since 1945, not only dominated foreign policy on both sides of the Atlantic, but has also formed a central factor in the agenda and the shaping of global political relations. Any major change in the transatlantic relations would necessarily imply a tectonic shift for the foreign policy coordinates in Washington and in European capitals, as well as in global political structures.

In principle, two fundamental questions are raised by a trend toward unilateralism in Washington. The first concerns the general issue as to how much U.S. unilateralism is compatible with the existence and the foundations of transatlantic relations as they have been characteristic for the second part of the 20th century. A much broader question concerns the continued value of these relations for the United States in its role as the dominant global superpower; the more this value should vanish, the less the United States leaders will need to reflect on the parameters of a policy combining a continuing close relationship with Europe and the current position of global leadership of Washington.

The United States has acquired its current status of a dominant power entirely with its own resources and means, and every other state or region is free to challenge this status. Today, the U.S. GNP is more than twice as large as that of Japan, the second power. The U.S. military budget is fifteen times larger than that of the UK as the second power. Europe, for whatever reasons, has lagged behind the United States in these respects. The disparity has become glaringly obvious in the 1990's when the European governments were not able to deal with the Balkan crisis, a short distance away from the borders of the European Union. The United States was called in and had to send their troops and their airplanes, and Richard Holbrooke had to put an end to the chaos and the murdering. The United States did not do so for domestic reasons or to strengthen their national interests, but as a surrogate power making up for the failure of the European powers to act decisively. This was a key experience for many politicians in Washington and many European intellectuals, who, occupied with the power of diplomacy, the need for peace, and a disdain for military power, remained silent for a period because their coordinates did not allow criticism of the use of force by the United States or an expression of relief at the end of the cruel bloodshed.

The Balkan war of the 1990's highlighted fundamental political attitudes in European capitals and in Washington. European powers today believe in diplomacy based on the rule of law, in multilateral fora, in the power of reason and persuasion.[10] The emphasis on the nation state, on national action and on the use of force which was so dominant before 1914 has receded and negative or ambivalent connotations are attached to these forms of organization and politics. 'Nationalism, this is war' ('Le nationalisme, c'est la guerre') was a motto often used by French President Mitterand and German Chancellor Kohl. And, in the European context, this was indeed the only lesson which reason allowed to draw after 1918 and after 1945. The complex merging and modification of national sovereignty in favor of a supranational European authority has become the dominant theme of European politics since the founding of the Economic Union in 1956, with an unprecedented era of peace, solidarity and prosperity, albeit under an umbrella of protection granted by the United States as a leader of the West. Many Europeans fundamentally mistrust the use of force by the United States, not just in the Balkans, but also in Afghanistan and in other places of murder and terror, but have accepted the necessity to resort to military power, so to speak, with regret.

The historical connotations of political elites and public opinion in the United States attached to the nation state, the military and the use of force has been radically different, Vietnam notwithstanding. The necessity to defend freedom in times of crises, if need be with military power, constantly formed an accepted part of the canon of political life in Washington. Where Europeans are inclined to explain, or to explain away, the peculiarities of the situation of each country in historical, political and cultural terms and believe in peaceful ('critical') dialogue, the U.S. Government has been much more willing to draw lines, to distinguish between good and evil, and to stop evil governments and terrorists. Religious beliefs are not without significance in this context. In a sense, Europeans deprived themselves to make such choices when they set their budgets and allocated smaller and smaller sums to the departments of defence, presumably always aware of the existence of the military strength of the United States and its power to project that strength around the globe within a few months or shorter if need be.

When the United States pushed for NATO expansion in the 1990's, the same European voices warned against a Russian backlash, which in 2002 celebrated the victory of freedom when the Baltic countries joined the Alliance. In the past decade, even major segments of the European peace movements have accepted the traditional philosophy embodied in the UN Charter that under certain conditions the use of force becomes a necessary

[10] *See* European Security Strategy, 'A Secure Europe in a Better World' adopted 12.12.2003.

ingredient to protect basic values of humanity and to restore peace. The existence of forces of destruction in a modern globalised world has in the past decade become more difficult to ignore or to deny.

Against this background of a radically different historical experience with the nation state, with the military, with the use of force on the two sides of the Atlantic, combined with the ability and willingness to defend western values in times of crisis by the United States, and by the United States only, many accusations in Europe directed against U.S. unilateralism or the U.S. emphasis on military responses to international crisis situations are bound to sound hollow and essentially irrelevant to Washington. A system of multilateralism which does not allow enforcement of the distinction between good and evil, between inhumane conduct and civility, between oppression and freedom, will not, and should not, appear to be a viable choice in Washington. Of course, this position does not, in itself, speak to the question of a possible overreliance on the use of force as an alternative to peaceful negotiations. No one will deny the temptation for a nation in a unique position of global power to resort to military power instead of messy negotiations with difficult compromises forced by third parties. But, no one will deny that the checks and balances in the U.S. system of government have historically acted as powerful barriers against arbitrary and unjustified use of force.

Mainly France and Germany have raised their voices since President George W. Bush moved into the White House. From the point of view of the British Government, the 'special relationship' which has evolved since 1941 has remained vital enough, certain differences notwithstanding, to allow and to require separate analysis and assessment. On the European continent, current Italian and Spanish foreign policy are in many respects more closely aligned with Washington than are the governments in Paris and in Berlin. France and Germany have by no means taken a coordinated, common position against actions which are considered as unilateral in Bonn and/or in Paris. However, in both capitals, the theme of United States unilateralism has been prominent in the analysis of U.S. foreign policy and in reflections on appropriate responses. Occasionally, these critical voices are blended with traditional elements of Anti-Americanism. In France, Jean Jacques Schreibers classic challenge of U.S. politics exposed in his 'Le Défi Americain' in 1967 is cited and discussed these days much more often than a decade or two ago. In Germany, open governmental criticism of U.S. foreign policy after 1945 has never been as loud as in 2002, especially during the election campaign period.

Beyond those spokesmen who are convinced of the general necessity to preserve and protect European cultural values, environmentalists in particular deplore U.S. unilateralism when they address the U.S. position on the Kyoto protocol. Legal departments in foreign offices complain bitterly about the diplomatic unilateral fight of the United States against the new International Criminal Court. In the area of disarmament and arms control, it is mainly NGO's who have raised their voices against U.S. unilateralism in abandoning the ABM Treaty, against Washington resistance to ban landmines and against U.S. indifference to the international process of reviewing and renegotiating the existing agreements aimed at protecting people against biological weapons. In Germany, in particular, the determination of the U.S. Administration and Congress to use military force, if need be, against Iraq to remove the threat emanating from Saddam Hussein's regime have contributed to a growing feeling in public opinion and in the highest governmental levels that a divide has opened between the political cultures in Washington and in Europe that may be more serious than the nearly continuous series of problems and issues which have occupied the United States and Europe during the more quiet decades of partnership after 1945. Occasionally, it is argued that the current problems are merely temporary expressions of the distinct political style of President Bush and his aides; this view does not pay sufficient attention to earlier signs of tensions during the Clinton Administration and, especially, the mood in the U.S. Congress and its emphasis on U.S. national interests in the past years. Indeed, lack of information and outright ignorance of the motifs of the other side in Europe and in the United States have not seldom contributed to public opinion. In the media, commenting on and speculating about unilateralism and transatlantic relations has become a kind of pastime, or required exercise, albeit not always with emphasis on rigorous analysis. The definition of unilateralism, the reasons for unilateralism and its evaluation in an ideal world and in the real world, are indeed less frequently explored than is blame for unilateral attitudes and measures.

In a certain perspective, the signs of increasing stress in the transatlantic relationship are not coming as a surprise. With the downfall of communism, the fall of the Berlin Wall and the new relationship of the United States and of Europe with Russia deprived of its previous military conventional strength, the communality of transatlantic interests has thinned out, with tough economic competition on global markets between U.S. and European firms increasing at the same time[11]. The war against terrorism has in fact not contributed to a fundamental reorientation of the transatlantic relationship so far, official declarations in the months after September 2001 notwithstanding. On both sides of the Atlantic, official speechwriters

[11] In general, transatlantic economic relations have remained stable and have intensified in the past years, and it has shown that during a period of political crisis a firm economic pillar will help to stabilize the situation. Indeed, the contribution of the transatlantic business community to support the political fabric might be supported with more resources and imagination in the future. It will not be overlooked that, in the long run, economic relations will suffer from a deterioration on the political side.

and politicians keep correctly citing, at least on special events, the joint roots, the common values and the common interests of Europe and the United States. On the level of daily operational politics, these expressions of historic cooperation still inform the transatlantic relations, but it would be incorrect to argue that the relations have not been weakened in part or downgraded in the past years.

A prognosis for the future course of these relations, as based on current trends and their projections into the coming years, points to more rivalry, less trust, and a slow drifting apart rather than a growth of commonality. A second related trend concerns the current preference in the United States to focus more attention than before on the Pacific region and the strengthening of the European inclination to build a stronger relationship to its Eastern European neighbors. A third parallel trend points to an expansion and corresponding gradual strengthening of the European Union as an economic and, possibly, political actor on the global level in the coming decade, while focusing on a new sense of mission of diplomacy, rules and the sharing of sovereignty accompanied by weak conventional military forces.

IV. UNILATERALISM AND MULTILATERALISM IN AREAS OF GLOBAL CONCERN

A few short remarks on three global issues as seen from the different perspectives of multilateralism and unilateralism will question the thesis that multilateralism necessarily offers an optimal systemic approach to effectively address problems that are inherently global in nature. In varying degrees, this is illustrated in policies on non-proliferation, of the combat against poverty and on environmental matters.

Reservations about strict multilateralism, as it is often advocated in Europe, come from special considerations of issues emanating from the proliferation of weapons of mass destruction. Given current conditions, this central problem of international relations will not be resolved by emphasis on diplomatic negotiations in the United Nations or other international fora alone. What is needed in this area is multilateralism combined with active and effective leadership. My personal experience indicates that the United States has been much more able and willing than any other country to insist and pursue matters of global concern in this area. Other states have expressed the same objectives, but in practice they have not shown the resolve or the resources to act decisively. Not all major states of today or tomorrow have demonstrated a sense of global responsibility when it comes to the spreading of technology necessary to produce weapons of mass destruction. European states and other regional powers have attempted to contribute in their own ways to relevant international efforts but without the same conviction and strength as the United States, often hindered by considerations of national priorities in other areas on international politics.

In short, United States unilateralism in this crucial area of international politics must be welcome. Indeed, the hope for more global responsibility in the future largely rests on the hope for more U.S. unilateralism. These remarks are not meant to imply that the non-proliferation efforts by the U.S. Government have always been free of influence by narrower considerations of national interest, and the complexities of global nuclear disarmament are also beyond the scope of this article. The fact remains that global order and the concept of multilaterlism depend in major respects on the willingness of the United States to exercise leadership with a healthy dose of U.S. unilateralism.

One area in which the definition of the national interest and the distinction from a global interest raise difficult issues of judgment and directly bring up the limits of national U.S. resources concerns the need to combat poverty on the global level. Today four out of six billion people live in poverty, and in the coming decades, an additional two billion young people may live on the planet in the current areas of poverty. Not only in sub-Saharan Africa most young people lack access to basic opportunities and have little reason for hope and new perspectives. One response to this situation lies in relying on each country and government to care for its citizens. The establishment of the IMF and the World Bank after 1945 and their operations have pointed in a different direction. In the shrinking world of CNN and modern means of communication, the politics of isolation of areas of absolute poverty may not be a long-term option under all circumstances. Moreover, issues of migration, of health management, of environmental degradation and of terrorism breeding in areas of gross poverty may acquire dimensions which will directly affect the national interest of a superpower, not just the organisations of charity.

Of course, the balance sheet of development politics for the past decades is mixed at best, and the results are hardly encouraging in times when no global rival exists and the taxpayer is sceptical about new foreign expenditure. At the same time, it is recognized that the methods of development politics have shifted. The emphasis on individual projects and macroeconomic politics have been complemented and in part replaced by efforts for institution building and a focus on education and training ('human resources'). Generally, the awareness of cost-benefit calculations and the willingness to set benchmarks for aid programmes has increased, and questions such as corruption and good governance have received much more attention than it was the case a decade ago. The opportunity of private-public partnership will require additional attention in the future.

As for aid granted by the United States, European governments have frowned upon the low figures as measured by GNP, often conveniently ignoring that Europe rather than the United States has been blocking agricultural reform within the WTO, thus depriving developing countries of benefits much greater than the difference in aid contributions from the United States. Since September 2001, the commitment of the United States to development matters has significantly increased, at least in financial terms, without significant echo in Europe. A deficit remains, sometimes glaring, in the allocation of aid programs concerning coordination among donors to ensure optimal use of scarce resources. In this area of assistance for the poor, a stronger sense of global responsibility, as opposed to unilateral emphasis on national priorities, has often been promised but seldom followed in the past; more multilateralism, essentially based on policies of the World Bank and other international financial instructions, is needed.

In many European circles, the most deplorable dimension of U.S. unilateralism is its refusal to participate in international efforts to provide global solutions to problems concerning the global environmental agenda. Climate change, biodiversity and the protection of waters and forests remain key areas of perceived U.S. indifference to what are considered high priority values in Europe and sometimes in other regions.

To some extent, national conditions, lifestyles and experiences may explain differences in attitude and outlook. It will, however, also be noted that two decades ago, European states attempted to block the efforts of the strong leadership of the United States to protect the stratospheric ozone layer and acquiesced to these efforts only in a late stage of the negotiations.[12] Another demonstration of U.S. pro-environmentalist unilateralism in the recent past concerns the protection of dolphins and sea turtles in the oceans. Contrary to widely accepted rules of the WTO, the United States was prepared to take measures, at times fiercely resisted, to prevent unnecessary destruction of dolphins and sea turtles in the process of fishing.[13] Thus, the record is more complicated than black and white statements in Europe may suggest. So far, in the area of biodiversity, the U.S. Government has tended to give priority to pharmaceutical interests to the detriment of environmental concerns.

In climate change, issues of lifestyle, issues of energy efficiency, and the impact of energy prices on the U.S. economy have led Washington to resist what it considers to be the 'quick fixes' of environmental activists without sound economic basis, thus reinforcing views of European governments that consider the United States willing to sacrifice its role of protector of global values to short-term economic interests. The United States has found it difficult to state precisely whether or not it accepts the scientific finding

[12] *See* RICHARD E. BENEDICK, OZONE DIPLOMACY, 1998.

[13] *See* the Tuna-Dolphin Cases and Shrimp-Turtle Cases reported in: INTERNATIONAL ENVIRONMENTAL LAW REPORTS, Vol. 2 (2001).

that anthropogenic greenhouse gas emissions threaten the stability of the global climate in the past decades. Some observers may be reminded by the Bush Administration's current position of the reversal of the U.S. strategy in 1981 during the negotiations for a Law of the Sea Convention, when President Reagan announced that the U.S. Government would no longer participate in a conference which had steered a course inimical to the forces of the free market.[14] Initially, U.S. policy change was met with stiff resistance, but the U.S. reversal ultimately laid the foundation for a modified Convention in which concepts like the forced transfer of technology, upper limits for production of natural resources or the sharing of production fields were eliminated.[15] Today, most European governments probably consider this practical outcome of the stark exercise of U.S. unilateralism twenty years ago preferable to the version rejected by the United States.

V. UNILATERALISM AND MULTILATERALISM: REFLECTIONS ON STRENGTH AND WEAKNESS

Generally speaking, the current debate on multilateralism and unilateralism echoes the old rule that the rule of law protects the weaker segments of a community while the more powerful actors often consider the law to prevent them from exercising their power. With the disparities of power between the United States and Europe growing, it is not surprising that European complaints about the United States 'going it alone' have become louder. Perhaps a politically more appropriate response from a European point of view would be to turn the light on the weakness of Europe as a global power, its causes and possible strategies for change. As long as the United States retains its strength and Europe speaks with many voices backed up by weak economic and military power, European complaints about U.S. unilateralism essentially amount to lamenting about the sheer existing of national strength and weakness in global policies.

In the United States, the joint military efforts in the former Yugoslavia in the mid 90's have led military leaders and others to believe that efforts in joint preparation, coordination, targeting and implementation may rise to a degree of operational complexity which, in effect, highlight the virtues of unilateralism or quasi-unilateralism. Along similar lines, certain phases of Middle East politics in recent years have raised similar questions in Washington, reminiscent of Henry Kissinger's famous questions of a telephone number of a spokesman for Europe. At times, Javier Solana, as the

[14] *See* U.S. Policy and the Law of the Sea, Jan. 29, 1982, DEPT. ST. BULL., Mar. 1982, at 54. *See also* Rüdiger Wolfrum, *Die amerikanische Seerechtspolitik*, EUROPA ARCHIV 1984, 317.

[15] *See* Agreement relating to the implementation of Part XI of the United Nations Convention on the Law of the Sea of 10 December 1982, 33 ILM 1309 (1994).

High Representative for the European Union, issued certain statements while the presidency of the European Council, represented by an inexperienced prime minister, voiced its opinion; the President of the Commission gave his own point of view and both Prime Minister Blair and Chancellor Schröder expressed their positions while on the telephone with the U.S. president. Of course, such diversity and heterogeneity will lead to questions in Washington about the costs and benefits of pursuing a 'European' effort.

By and large, Europe has in recent years not managed to organize itself as a unified and reliable partner in foreign relations, and the United States has correspondingly dealt with its European allies on a case-by-case basis. Whether or not the United States has felt this to be advantageous or cumbersome for the formulation and conduct of its foreign relations is essentially an academic question which can hardly be answered in general terms for all situations. What is clear, however, is that European complaints against the occasional heavy weight of U.S. unilateral foreign policy in essence amounts to little more than a reflection of the lack of the European policy, often sounding like the echo of antecedent failure to manage the internal European process. If Berlin or Paris cannot persuade their European partners to adopt a certain position, there will hardly be a basis to complain subsequently if Washington adopts and follows its own position. In other words, more influence of Europe on the conduct of global foreign policy does not primarily call for 'less Washington,' but for 'more Europe.'[16]

The point is illustrated in the trade field where Europe speaks with one voice in accordance with its rules and procedures, exerting a stronger European influence. Indeed, the trade sector, more than any other sector, today represents the kind of multilateralism generally favored by Europe: a rule-based regime founded on a broad consensus with a standing dispute settlement mechanism. The creation of this order was prompted by multidimensional factors and influences with the existence of a single European voice as a key component.

On the financial side, the Euro has established itself in past years as a leading currency without so far coming close to the dominating role of the U.S. dollar. With regard to the use for transaction purposes and, more importantly, as an investment currency, the Euro has not reached strength equal to the dollar, despite that in regard to short-term financing and the trend on bond-markets, no major difference in strength exists between the two currencies. The remaining discrepancy is not surprising given prospective growth rates, the lack of practical integration of the still-dominant

[16] *See, e.g.* for a study on the Balkans: Jan Wouters & Frederik Naert, *How Effective is the European Security Architecture? Lessons from Bosnia and Kosovo*, 50 International and Comparative Law Quarterly 540 (2001).

national European financial markets, and remaining legal obstacles for a common European financial space. Most experts seem to assume that the Euro's international role will grow over the next five years with the expansion of the European Union and the widening and deepening of European financial integration. Against this background, room for U.S. unilateralism in global currency matters may be reduced in coming years unless issues such as growth or fiscal discipline weaken the Euro.

VI. LIMITATIONS OF U.S. UNILATERALISM

No one will doubt that significant limitations for the exercise of unilateral measures and policies exist even for a state with the current powers of the United States. In practice, several important elements relevant to the present context were recognized and played out in the preparation and execution of the international response to destroy the Taliban regime in Afghanistan in 2001–2002. The crucial military dimension of this effort was, in essence, organized, driven, and implemented by the United States. But even on the military front, the United States, for good reasons, preferred a strategy which relied on some involvement and assistance by foreign forces, with the Northern Afghan forces playing a key role in the initial part of the battle and a number of other countries assisting in the second part of the military effort.

Beyond the military campaign, the United States has successfully devised a strategy that has placed a major part of responsibility both for humanitarian matters, during and after the military campaign, and for post-conflict security organization into the hands of allies. In the exaggerated words of a senior UN diplomat, 'The United States fights, Europe funds and the UN feeds.'

Practical limitations of funding global policies connected with concepts of global leadership in the military and the civilian area are not easy to quantify. With an economy running on ten trillion dollars per year, the United States has the power of conducting expensive and long-lasting operations if need be, and the people of the United States have no doubt that in times of peril they are prepared to sacrifice some of their wealth to restore and to preserve national and international security. Nonetheless, attention to the taxpayer's concerns and the need for a degree of fiscal balance will necessarily occupy Congressional and administrative decision-makers. Thus, financial burden-sharing has remained and will remain an essential theme on the international agenda of the United States; especially if situations calling for long-stretched operations, simultaneous or consecutive, would arise. At the request of the United States, the division of burdens has been, for understandable reasons, a constant theme of the past decades within NATO.

These considerations do not imply that the option of unilateralism does not exist under certain circumstances as a viable financial alternative. But, it is fairly clear that unilateralism as an option for international politics on a broad basis will hardly be seen by Washington as a practical way to conduct foreign policy and military politics. Within the spectrum between extreme versions of unilateralism and modest versions of multilaterlism, a point exists in practice beyond which unilateralism becomes a financial burden which even the United States will not be prepared to carry.

Of course, one option is to separate military and political decision-making from the funding side, in the sense that the United States elects to rely on unilateralism on the military and political side and opts for multilateralism on the financial side. However, such a strategy is based on the power of persuasion by the United States, and it will be difficult or impossible for Washington to push with success for a general strategy that would call for financial contributions of the European allies without corresponding political dialogue or participation.

A further limitation of unilateralism, which is impossible to quantify but is nevertheless real, concerns the standing of the United States in foreign public opinion. This aspect is much more acute at this moment in the Arab world where antagonism towards the United States is growing and the repercussions of the public sentiment may reach a level at which it needs to be considered as a significant issue in itself. The number of militant religions is growing and, especially in Asian regions, more and more young people join these groups. This troubling trend might raise broader questions regarding the stability of governments, states and borders. So far, it has been widely assumed that the states founded during the process of decolonization would ultimately be met with popular acceptance despite religious and ethnic divisions which run counter to historical units of organization.

Obviously, it is much easier to point to this situation than to come up with an appropriate remedy. But, it is equally clear that the United States will have to devote more resources, energy and imagination to this front in order to avoid new issues further down the road. The power of persuasion has always been complex to build and more cumbersome to employ than military machinery. But, the challenge of the coming years may well stem from the need for more recognition in Europe that a free world without military strength would face unacceptable challenges and sacrifices, as well as for parallel awareness in the United States that the power of the word, the idea, and global compassion forms the basis for long-term international stability.

As to Europe, public opinion is far from hostile toward the United States, and major social segments support most U.S. policies. The trend, however, in the past years has not been positive. The issue here concerns not the short-term, but the long-term perspective.

VII. UNILATERALISM AND LONG-TERM TRANSATLANTIC RELATIONS

One of the most difficult and important issues in measuring the values of multilateralism and unilateralism concerns the differentiation between the impact for the short-term and the long-term perspective. Goodwill and confidence emanate from mutuality and trust; they cannot be produced or negotiated over a few weeks or months. The side effect, albeit not intended, of unilateralism will, in principle, always consist of a sense of separateness and dominance. In such an atmosphere, fostered or tolerated for a longer period, it will be difficult, or in any event costly, to establish a new sense of commonality and joint mission for a coalition against new enemies and threats in the short run. This view does not fully coincide with the often quoted principle that states have no friends but only interests. In reality, the latter maxim appears to be a semi-truth inasmuch as the pursuit of national interests itself requires a degree of cooperation and confidence among allies and neighbors.

These observations do not imply that coalition building will be impossible from the high plateau of unilateralism, but it will be more difficult, more costly, and perhaps less effective. And it would be unrealistic to assume that in a globalising world the causes and occasions for coalition forming could disappear or become less frequent. The past decade, although freed from the cold war, illustrates the point.

The parameters of European-U.S. relations have not been fundamentally altered in the past decade, but they have been evolving in light of changing circumstances. The common roots of the enlightenment and the Judeo-Christian civilization still are reflected in shared values which underlie and shape the identity of the peoples on both sides of the Atlantic. So far, changing demographic structures, particularly in the West and South of the United States, are not strong and deep enough to alter these common foundations. However, in the past decade some centrifugal forces were at work which have led to a certain weakening of relations. Of course, communism as a joint vital challenge has disappeared. In the words of a prominent U.S. Congressman, this change has led to a feeling that 'the job in Europe has been done.' The perspective underlying such a statement seems to assume that the United States post-war interest in Europe has consisted of building democratic and peaceful structures and protecting them from the Communist threat. If so, then the historic task has been achieved with success. It is a different matter whether it is politically necessary or desirable to build a relationship with Europe beyond the post-war challenges that will allow common interests in matters of joint concern to be successfully pursued, in particular in the evolving context of global challenges.

The differentiation between long-term considerations vis-à-vis short-term issues in the pursuit of unilateralism may bring to the fore a most important aspect in transatlantic relations that might deserve further reflection in Washington.

Economists may debate the vulnerabilities of the United States and the European economies, but it is likely that the pending expansion of the European Union with a single market of about 500 million people will contribute to stability and growth in Europe, thus promoting the global role of Europe and reducing the political space for U.S. unilateralism. Even today, the division of power specifically in trade negotiations between the United States and Europe does not allow for a general approach of unilateralism of the United States, the reason being that, in this arena, the national power of European Member States has been transferred to the European level and has ensured a European position. While no one can predict the course of progress in European integration, the United States should take the scenario of a stronger Europe into account and avoid the demonstration of undue unilateral strength in order to avoid a climate of antagonism and escalation that might haunt Washington in subsequent years, keeping in mind the consequences of instabilities in trade and foreign investment.

Empirical knowledge indicates that long-term predictions of international relations based on past trends will more often than not turn out to be incorrect due to unforeseeable events and factors. If taken to an extreme and reinforced by thinking in the time span of legislative periods, a school of thinking relying on this maxim supports the choice for the short-term benefits of the unilateral exercise of power. Under current transatlantic circumstances, a strategy based on these considerations would clearly risk a gradual and continuous atmosphere of deterioration that presumably would lead, not to any rupture or breakdown of relations, but to a business-like attitude on both sides that would no longer take any mutual support or favors for granted and would eventually make progress easier in the future for those groups on both sides who would not in principle regret loosening of the relations.

Washington will have to consider the relevant choices about the desirability of the future course of transatlantic relations in general, and, more specifically, the alternatives of increasing unilateralism at the price of weakening bonds vis-à-vis a Europe with an economically and politically growing potential on the one hand or a stronger dialogue with less demonstrations of unilateral strength and the preservation in principle of a transatlantic relationship of confidence and mutuality on the other. The third alternative of increasing unilateralism and a long-term strengthening of transatlantic relations does not seem practical. Business-as-usual will likely favor increased unilateralism. Thus, any reorientation towards additional emphasis on transatlantic relations will come only from increased awareness of the long-term implications and deliberate choices in decision-making that speak to and express the need to foster transatlantic relations.

In the current transatlantic context, the values of procedure and of multilateralism lie in expressing awareness of the willingness to preserve the foundations of the relationship as it evolved in the post-war period in the wake of unprecedented magnanimity and long-term strategic thinking on the part of the United States, followed by a half century of peace and prosperity. Most people living in Europe today were born after the Marshall Plan was conceived and brought food and hope into an age of destruction and gloom, and the attitude toward the United States is no longer generally characterized by this unique historical experience. Never before was it so true that gratitude cannot be considered a long-term category of political thinking.

The Western alliance under the military umbrella of NATO turned out to be the most successful concept of peacemaking in modern history. Politically, this alliance was formed as a partnership. The United States acted as a leader who, in principle, accepted the status of equality and independence of its European partners; the European States, in principle, accepted the strength and the values characteristic of the United States. The inherent fragility of such an alliance has made it dependent on intangibles and imponderables such as mutual familiarity, the willingness to consult and to listen, the acceptance of strength and weakness and, when appropriate, the sacrifice of short-term interest in exchange for long-term stability given the vagaries of foreign policy making in democratic societies and the increasing linkage of foreign relations with domestic constituencies and interests.

In hindsight it may appear surprising that an alliance dependent on such soft characteristics has lasted so long. The justification for its price lies in its success in the preservation of peace and in its creation of wealth and prosperity. So far, its many dimensions of sensitivity notwithstanding, the alliance has always successfully coped, and sometimes benefited, from the occasional selective resort to unilateralism. Under current circumstances and the unique strength of the United States, the relative dominant weight of Washington will continue to test the foundations of the transatlantic relations by calling for the willingness of the United States not to exercise all national power available in relation to Europe and for the willingness of Europe to accept more than before the factual power of the United States. Leadership along these lines will not always contribute to popularity and will only come forth with a renewed sense of joint values and purpose. A lengthy period of sustained unilateralism would gradually erode the common fabric of understanding and mutual confidence weaved and nurtured in the past decades. A new dialogue will be required if the short-term convenience and the benefits of unilateralism shall not be allowed to overshadow the more subtle and indirect values of the historical alliance. At this moment, this dialogue remains to be initiated, and the auspices for a new partnership in a post-communist world with increasing opportunities and challenges of globalisation remain vague.

CHAPTER FIVE

Global Economy—Global Law?

*by Werner F. Ebke**

CHAPTER OUTLINE

I. Introduction
II. Territoriality
  A. Conflicts
  B. Competition of Institutions
  C. Limits of Competition
III. Private Ordering
IV. Power of the Markets
  A. Antitrust Law
  B. Securities Regulation
  C. Financial Accounting
V. The Search for Institutional Solutions
VI. Conclusion

I. INTRODUCTION

'Globalization' has become an emotive subject.[1] Increasingly, anti-globalization protests at the scene of major international events turn into violent clashes between demonstrators and security forces. Seattle, Prague, Nice, Davos, Naples, and Genoa are just some examples of this controversy in 2000–2001. Such incidents may forewarn organizers of future international economic summits of the potential problems that they may face. The anti-

* Professor of Law, Chair of Business Law and Taxation, University of Konstanz School of Law, Konstanz, Germany; Global Professor of Law, New York University School of Law, New York, New York; Distinguished Visiting Professor of Law, Southern Methodist University Dedman School of Law, Dallas, Texas (Spring 2001 and Spring 2004). Referendar (J.D.), University of Muenster School of Law, Muenster, Germany, 1977; LL.M., University of California at Berkeley School of Law (Boalt Hall), 1978: Dr. jur. (J.S.D.), 1981, and Habilitation (post-doctoral degree), 1987, University of Muenster School of Law; Member, New York Bar.

[1] *See, e.g.*, Werner Ebke, *Globalisierung: Wirtschaft und Recht*, in HANDBUCH INTERNATIONALISIERUNG: GLOBALISIERUNG—EINE HERAUSFORDERUNG FÜR DIE UNTERNEHMENSFÜHRUNG 125–37 (Ulrich Krystek & Eberhard Zur eds., 2nd ed. 2002).

globalization movement has mobilized itself. Calls for a return to the 'Local' are becoming increasingly forceful.[2] Globalization of almost all areas of the economy, however, is not only associated with apprehension, but also hope. An increasing number of companies realize that the globalization of businesses and transactions is an opportunity for all those involved including investors, employees, consumers, markets and policymakers as well as the environmental, research and development, technology and cultural sectors. At the same time, one should not underestimate the difficulty of overcoming the barriers of distance, time, and culture in an economy of global markets.[3]

The process of globalization has affected almost all aspects of the private exchange of goods and services, capital transactions, current international payments, and, last but not least, the employment market and public goods. The search of nation-states for possible policy responses to their international market position was at the forefront of academic study into the consequences of globalization.[4] For states that cooperate in larger economic or political unions (e.g., European Union, NAFTA), the research also focused on the interaction between and among the member states themselves as well as the union vis-à-vis non-member states.[5] Recently, the interdependence of globalization and legal systems has become a focal point of academic interest.[6] Therefore, international economic law (e.g., GATT, GATS, WTO and IMF) plays an ever increasing role in overcoming the deficiencies of national legal systems.[7] In terms of creating an international economic-political regulatory system to police the globalization of the economy, the path towards globalization of the law is still in its embryonic

[2] JERRY MANDER & EDWARD GOLDSMITH, THE CASE AGAINST THE GLOBAL ECONOMY AND FOR A TURN TOWARD THE LOCAL (1996). *See also* HAROLD JAMES, THE END OF GLOBALIZATION: LESSONS FROM THE GREAT DEPRESSION (2001).

[3] Bernhard Grossfeld, *Loss of Distance: Global Corporate Actors and Global Corporate Governance—Internet v. Geography*, 34 INT'L. LAW. 963 (2000).

[4] GLOBALISIERUNG, SYSTEMWETTBEWERB UND NATIONALSTAATLICHE POLITIK (Karl-Ernst Schenk, Dieter Schmidtchen, Manfred Streit & Viktor Vanberg eds., 1998).

[5] EUROPÄISCHE INTEGRATION UND GLOBALER WETTBEWERB (Martin Henssler, Thomas Kolbeck, Hans-Werner Moritz & Hannes Rehm eds., 1993).

[6] GLOBALISIERUNG UND RECHTSORDNUNG (Karl-Ernst Schenk, Dieter Schmidtchen, Manfred Streit & Viktor Vanberg eds., 1999); INSTITUTIONAL ARRANGEMENTS FOR GLOBAL ECONOMIC INTEGRATION (Hans-Jürgen Vosgerau ed., 2000); CARSTEN T. EBENROTH & ERNST STIEFEL, INSTITUTIONELLER WETTBEWERB ALS HERAUSFORDERUNG FÜR DIE GLOBALISIERUNG DER WIRTSCHAFT (1995); RÜDIGER VOIGT, GLOBALISIERUNG DES RECHTS (2000).

[7] CHRISTOPH STADLER, DIE LIBERALISIERUNG DES DIENSTLEISTUNGSHANDELS AM BEISPIEL DER VERSICHERUNGEN. KERNELEMENTE BILATERALER UND MULTILATERALER ORDNUNGSRAHMEN EINSCHLIESSLICH DES GATS (1992); MATTHIAS KOEHLER, DAS ALLGEMEINE ÜBEREINKOMMEN ÜBER DEN HANDEL MIT DIENSTLEISTUNGEN (GATS) (1999); BETTINA STEINHAUER, DIE AUSLEGUNG, KONTROLLE UND DURCHSETZUNG MITGLIEDSTAATLICHER PFLICHTEN IM RECHT DES INTERNATIONALEN WÄHRUNGSFONDS UND DER EUROPÄISCHEN GEMEINSCHAFT (1997).

stages.[8] Furthermore, the gap between the ideas of the developed countries and the less industrialized regions of the world concerning the institutional formation of a global allocation system for private and public goods remains too wide. The creation of a world economic allocation system is further complicated by the lack of a consensus on the role and the function of markets, as well as the deeply differing views of the states on the meaning and importance of the 'rule of law' and the relationship between freedom and equality in law and economy.

'Globalization' as a field of research includes not only the relationships between states, but also the international role and impact of non-governmental entities. In addition to trans-national enterprises, internationally active trade unions belong to this group.[9] The area of economic activity of transnational enterprises is more extensive than that of the territorially restricted sovereign states or the territories of supranational unions of states that have developed since World War II as 'alliances of reason'.[10] The operating areas of multinational enterprises are regional, multiregional, and in many cases even global.[11] For example, except for exceptional cases, internet companies almost always appeal to international markets.[12] The same is true for the leading companies in the automotive, aviation, and telecommunications industries as well as other global players. For many years, worldwide industry and trade have relied on cooperative means through the use of a high division of labor, which maintains developed production and marketing techniques that do not recognize national borders.[13] This trend is accompanied by large-scale changes in contractual regulatory frameworks such as in the area of licensing agreements that regulate the usage of intangible property (e.g., patents, trademarks, copyrights, design and know-how) through continuous involvement of third parties.[14] Similarly, globalization has affected employment contracts.[15]

[8] *See generally* GLOBALISIERUNG UND WELTWIRTSCHAFT (Karl-Ernst Schenk, Dieter Schmidtchen, Manfred Streit & Viktor Vanberg eds., 2000).

[9] *See generally* BERNHARD GROSSFELD, INTERNATIONALES UND EUROPÄISCHES UNTERNEHMUNGSRECHT. DAS ORGANISATIONSRECHT TRANSNATIONALER UNTERNEHMEN (2nd ed. 1995).

[10] Werner Ebke, *Die Zukunft der Rechtsetzung in multijurisdiktionalen Rechtsordnungen. Wettbewerb der Rechtsordnungen oder zentrale Regelvorgabe am Beispiel des Gesellschafts- und Unternehmensrechts*, 1999 ZEITSCHRIFT FÜR SCHWEIZERISCHES RECHT [ZSR] 106, 112.

[11] HANS-JÖRG SCHMIDT-TRENZ, AUSSENHANDEL UND TERRITORIALITÄT DES RECHTS. GRUNDLEGUNG EINER NEUEN INSTITUTIONENÖKONOMIK DES AUSSENHANDELS (1990).

[12] KLAUS GREWLICH, GOVERNANCE IN CYBERSPACE. EUROPA- UND WIRTSCHAFTSVÖLKERRECHTLICHE REGULIERUNG (2001).

[13] For a more detailed exposition, *see* KNUT LANGE, DAS RECHT DER NETZWERKE (1998).

[14] *See, e.g.*, RETO HILTY, LIZENZVERTRAGSRECHT (2001); HERBERT STUMPF & MICHAEL GROSS, DER LIZENZVERTRAG (7th ed. 1998).

[15] For a thorough analysis, *see, e.g.*, MARTINA LÜHKER, NEUE ARBEITS- UND PRODUKTIONSKONZEPTE UND NOTWENDIGKEIT DER VERÄNDERUNGEN DES ARBEITSRECHTLICHEN REGELUNGSRAHMENS. EINE BETRACHTUNG UNTER EINBEZIEHUNG ZUNEHMENDER

The impact of the globalization of the economy can also be felt in the service industry. The 'Big Four' international accounting firms are probably the single most important example of this impact. Their predecessors were globally active as early as the Nineteenth Century. In the 1980s, the big international accounting firms each founded an international association or 'world-firm' to offer their clients competitive prices for auditing and consulting services on a large scale, implemented under unified global standards by highly qualified specialized staff, and all within temporal and spatial proximity.[16] Other examples include the insurance and re-insurance industries as well as financial services companies.[17]

The focus of the present article is private law and its nationally and internationally important framework and regulatory function.[18] Considering the complexity of the topic and the means at one's disposal, no definitive institutional solutions can be given here. Rather, the article depicts historical events and developments, addresses some fundamental questions, and analyzes possible starting points for strategic solutions and further suggestions. The specific legal perspective from which the present article has been written is not intended to exclude economic, political, or social aspects. On the contrary, institutional solutions to cope with the challenges of the law resulting from the globalization of the economy can only be developed inter-disciplinarily and without the widespread belief of some scholars that several academic disciplines are in a better position than others to solve the problems of globalization.

II. TERRITORIALITY

Economic activities and business transactions between economic entities are based on legal institutions. An economic system is functional only if an operational legal framework exists. This observation is true for both domestic economic processes and cross-border transactions. The changing of economic conditions for businesses calls for changes to the legal system

DEZENTRALISIERUNGS-, GLOBALISIERUNGS- UND VERNETZUNGSTENDENZEN IN DER ARBEITSWELT (1999); Christian Meier-Schatz, *Über die Internationalisierung des Arbeitsrechts*, *in* RECHT UND INTERNATIONALISIERUNG: FESTGABE DER JURISTISCHEN ABTEILUNG DER UNIVERSITÄT ST. GALLEN ZUM JURISTENTAG 2000 253 (Christian Meier-Schatz & Rainer Schweizer eds., 2000).

[16] Werner Ebke, *Internationaler Dienstleistungshandel, Unternehmenskooperation und das Problem des 'Holding-out'*, *in* FESTSCHRIFT FÜR ERNST-JOACHIM MESTMÄCKER 863 (Ulrich Immenga, Wernhard Möschel & Dieter Reuter eds., 1996); FRANK IMMENGA, INTERNATIONALE KOOPERATION UND HAFTUNG VON DIENSTLEISTUNGSUNTERNEHMEN (1998).

[17] *See, e.g.*, HERMANN GEIGER, THE COMPARATIVE LAW AND ECONOMICS OF REINSURANCE (2000).

[18] For a thoughtful analysis of the role and function of private law, *see* BERNHARD GROSSFELD, ZIVILRECHT ALS GESTALTUNGSAUFGABE (1977).

on both national and international levels. Legal rules are traditionally produced by the national legislature or the judiciary. As a general rule, therefore, law is territorially limited. This is especially applicable to public law ('revenue rule'), but is also true for private law.[19]

A. *Conflicts*

Conflicts of laws resulting from the claims of several legal orders to have their substantive law applied in a given case involving more than one state have traditionally been solved with the help of national conflict-of-laws principles. The principles, however, regulating the conflict of laws in transnational economic matters could hardly be more diverse.[20] Legal restrictions on national principles for the conflict of laws may come from public international law or even from supranational law (e.g., the law of the European Union). The highly controversial issue of reconciling the 'real seat' doctrine (*Sitztheorie*) with the EU Treaty's provisions on the free movement of companies is a classic example in support of this proposition.[21] The rules on conflict of laws set the nation state's private law free from its territorial bonds and present the law with the opportunity to gain universal consideration and validity. The rules on conflict of laws are therefore a cornerstone of the law's grasp of the globalization of markets.[22] Efforts to harmonize the law of international judicial jurisdiction and the recognition and enforcement of judicial decisions in civil and commercial matters complement the conflict-of-laws rules.[23] Such efforts are designed

[19] For details, *see, e.g.*, Werner Ebke, *Das Internationale Devisenrecht im Spannungsfeld völkerrechtlicher Vorgaben, nationaler Interessen und parteiautonomer Gestaltungsfreiheit*, 100 ZEITSCHRIFT FÜR VERGLEICHENDE RECHTSWISSENSCHAFT [ZVGLRWISS] 365, 373 (2001). *See also* NICOLA NEUMANN, INTERNATIONALE HANDELSEMBARGOS UND PRIVATRECHTLICHE VERTRÄGE (2001).

[20] *See, e.g.*, STEFAN HABERMEIER, NEUE WEGE ZUM WIRTSCHAFTSKOLLISIONSRECHT. EINE BESTANDSAUFNAHME PRÄVALENTER WIRTSCHAFTSKOLLISIONSRECHTLICHER METHODOLOGIE UNTER DEM BLICKWINKEL DES KRITISCHEN RATIONALISMUS (1997); ANTON SCHNYDER, WIRTSCHAFTSKOLLISIONSRECHT (1990).

[21] Werner Ebke, *The 'Real Seat' Doctrine in the Conflict of Corporate Laws*, 36 INT'L. LAW 1015 (2002); Werner Ebke, *Centros—Some Realities and Some Mysteries*, 48 AM. J. COMP. L. 623 (2000). The issue of whether the 'real seat' doctrine complies with the free-movement-of-companies provisions of the EC Treaty was recently solved by the European Court of Justice in Case C-208/00, Überseering BV v. Nordic Construction Company Baumanagement GmbH *(NCC)*, 2002 ECRI-079/9.

[22] Peter Behrens, *Die Bedeutung des Kollisionsrechts für die 'Globalisierung' der Wirtschaft*, *in* AUFBRUCH NACH EUROPA: 75 JAHRE MAX-PLANCK-INSTITUT FÜR PRIVATRECHT 381 (Jürgen Basedow, Reinhard Ellger, Klaus Hopt, Hein Kötz, Rainer Kulms & Ernst-Joachim Mestmäcker eds., 2001).

[23] *See generally* JAN KROPHOLLER, EUROPÄISCHES ZIVILPROZESSRECHT: KOMMENTAR ZUM EUGVÜ UND LUGANO-ÜBEREINKOMMEN (6th ed. 1998); HANS MICKLITZ & PETER ROTT, VERGEMEINSCHAFTUNG DES EUGVÜ IN DER VERORDNUNG (EG) NO. 44/2001, 12 EUROPÄISCHE ZEITSCHRIFT FÜR WIRTSCHAFTSRECHT [EUZW] 325 (2001); Fritz-René Grabau & Jürgen

to prevent conflicts over judicial jurisdiction and to safeguard the enforcement of the rights of private parties in an increasingly cross-border economy.

Since the middle of the last century, it has become recognized that some transnational conflict-of-laws rules are needed or at least are desirable to promote the development of international economic cooperation between private parties. The European Convention of June 19, 1980, on the Law Applicable to Contractual Obligations is probably the single most prominent example of such a transnational set of effective conflict-of-laws principles.[24] The Treaty of Amsterdam of October 10, 1997, also recognizes the need for the harmonization of the EU member states' rules on conflicts of laws.[25] There is even a truly global rule on conflicts of laws to be found in Article VIII, Section 2(b) of the IMF Agreement of December 27, 1945, which specifies whether and to what extent the courts of IMF member states are to give effect to a member state's restrictions on current international payments or cross-border capital transfers.[26] Internationally harmonized principles of conflict of laws are intended to harmonize a court's decision of the applicable law regardless of which nation's courts are called upon to decide the issue in a given case.

B. Competition of Institutions

Within the harmonization of rules for the conflict of laws there is certainly recognition and perhaps even an acceptance of the differences between and the variety of the substantive laws that regulate the activities of economic entities and cross-border business transactions. Within the EU,[27] but also at

Hennecka, *Entwicklung des weltweiten Zuständigkeits- und Anerkennungsübereinkommens—Aktueller Überblick*, 47 RECHT DER INTERNATIONALEN WIRTSCHAFT [RIW] 569 (2001).

[24] Werner Ebke, *Erste Erfahrungen mit dem EG-Schuldvertragsübereinkommen*, *in* EUROPÄISCHES GEMEINSCHAFTSRECHT UND INTERNATIONALES PRIVATRECHT 77 (Christian von Bar ed ., 1991).

[25] *See* Treaty of Amsterdam, Oct. 10,1997, arts. 61(c), 65(b).

[26] Articles of Agreement of the Int'l Monetary Fund, *open for signature until* Dec. 31, 1945, art. VIII, §2(b). For details of Article VIII, Section 2(b) of the IMF Agreement, *see, e.g.*, WERNER EBKE, INTERNATIONALES DEVISENRECHT 158–311 (1990); RICHARD EDWARDS, INTERNATIONAL MONETARY COLLABORATION 389–490 (1985); JOSEPH GOLD, THE FUND AGREEMENT IN THE COURTS: VOLUME IV: SOME PROBLEMS OF THE UNIFORM INTERPRETATION OF MULTILATERAL TREATIES (1989); JOSEPH GOLD, THE FUND AGREEMENT IN THE COURTS: VOLUME III: FURTHER STUDIES IN JURISPRUDENCE INVOLVING THE ARTICLES OF AGREEMENT OF THE INTERNATIONAL MONETARY FUND (1986); F.A. MANN, THE LEGAL ASPECT OF MONEY 364–96 (5th ed. 1992). For the latest developments, *see* Werner Ebke, *Commentaries: Anhang zu Art. 34 EGBGB*, *in* JULIUS VON STAUDINGER, KOMMENTAR ZUM BGB 634–76 (13th ed. 2002).

[27] *See generally* WOLFGANG KILIAN, EUROPÄISCHES WIRTSCHAFTSRECHT (1996); HANDBUCH DES EU-WIRTSCHAFTSRECHTS (Manfred A. Dauses ed., 2000).

international level,[28] there is not a lack of effort to achieve standardization or at least harmonization of the substantive law relating to commercial and business transactions. Broad areas of commercial and business law, however, are still regulated primarily by national law. In itself, this observation is not a negative one. On the contrary, differences in the substantive law can lead to institutional competition (provided that the parties involved in cross-border transactions are free to choose the applicable law) whereby, at least theoretically, the best solution will prevail. Doubts, however, immediately arise.

For example, may we leave the governance of the internal and external affairs of corporations exclusively to the 'trial-by-error' market in the hope that some day the 'best solution' (from whose point of view: management, shareholders, employees, creditors, the public?) will prevail in the 'market for corporate laws'?[29] This question is particularly important in the case of large publicly-held corporations in which the principal-agent problem is quite evident. Additionally, the interests of third parties such as employees, creditors, and other stakeholders are at issue, not to mention the overall balance of social and political power that may be affected by the activities of large, internationally operating public companies.

C. Limits of Competition

Law as a 'product' of competition between and among legislatures is necessarily spontaneous and unsystematic. In the long run, such competition does not necessarily bring about sensible and efficient solutions at a lower cost.[30] A regulatory system based solely on the principle of competition would run the risk of failing to deal satisfactorily with the complexities of institutional realities, political decision-making processes, and market mechanisms as well as the behavior of market participants. Particularly, it is unrealistic to assume that nation states will always pursue interests for the collective benefit of the community of states rather than at the expense of other states. Seemingly, national egotism is a fact of life. It is similarly unrealistic to assume that national regulations do not tend to protect the

[28] *See* Jan Kropholler, Internationales Einheitsrecht (1975); Wolfgang Witz et. al., International Einheitliches Kaufrecht (2000); Joachim Frick, *Die UNIDROIT-Prinzipien für internationale Handelsverträge*, 47 RIW 416 (2001); Hansjürgen Sonnenberger, *Der Entwurf eines Europäischen Vertragsgesetzbuches der Akademie Europäischer Privatrechtswissenschaftler—ein Meilenstein*, 47 RIW 409 (2001).

[29] For a more detailed analysis of this question, *see* Werner Ebke, *Unternehmenskontrolle durch Gesellschafter und Markt*, *in* Internationale Unternehmenskontrolle und Unternehmenskultur 7 (Otto Sandrock & Wilhelm Jäger eds., 1994).

[30] For details, *see* Werner Ebke, *Unternehmensrecht und Binnenmarkt—E pluribus unum?*, *in* 62 Rabels Zeitschrift für ausländisches und internationales Privatrecht [RabelsZ] 195 (1998).

local economic entity against foreign economic entities or that courts are not inclined to use these regulations to achieve that end. One only needs to recall the international debt crisis and the numerous cases of international loan agreements in the 1980s in which foreign sovereign states, as debtors of private domestic banks, found themselves in financial difficulties.[31] The key question for both lenders and borrowers at that point in time was '2(b) or not 2(b).'[32]

Additionally, the positive effects of competition are limited by the fact that national legislatures frequently only react to changes in the market as opposed to using the legislative process proactively as an organizing tool to safeguard economic freedom, raise trans-boundary factor-mobility, ensure access to markets, reduce transaction costs, and fortify the private law as the central organizational means of the global economy. As a result, legal lacunae arise that are free from state regulation, and therefore, binding regulations need to be created for the first time. Further legal vacuums arise because national and even supranational lawmakers are no longer in the contemporary position to adapt the legal framework to the needs of changing economic conditions because of the decreasing ability of many legislatures of developed and increasingly diverse nations to reach consensus on the creation and passing of rules.[33]

III. PRIVATE ORDERING

The vacuum of regulation that is formed as a result of the above is increasingly filled by private arrangements. Although privately set standards can function alongside the non-mandatory national regulations, they can also replace them. The relevance of private ordering for internationally operating economic entities is somewhat reflected by the increasing importance of the *lex mercatoria* as well as the growing significance of private international commercial arbitration.[34] The parties thereby rely more frequently on non-

[31] *See, e.g.*, Werner Ebke, *Internationale Kreditverträge und das Internationale Devisenrecht*, 46 JURISTENZEITUNG [JZ] 335 (1991); Werner Ebke, *Sir Joseph Gold and the International Law of Exchange Controls*, 35 INT'L. LAW. 1475 (2001); CARSTEN T. EBENROTH & LOUISE E. TEITZ, BANKING ON THE ACT OF STATE. INTERNATIONAL LENDING AND THE ACT OF STATE DOCTRINE (1985); Carsten T. Ebenroth, *The Changing Legal Framework for Resolving the Debt Crisis: A European's Perspective*, *in* FESTSCHRIFT IN HONOR OF SIR JOSEPH GOLD 39 (Werner Ebke & Joseph Norton eds., 1990).

[32] *See* Werner Ebke, *Artikel VIII Abschnitt 2(b) des Übereinkommens über den Internationalen Währungsfonds und die Schweiz: '2(b) or Not 2(b)'*, *in* BANKEN UND BANKRECHT IM WANDEL: FESTSCHRIFT FÜR BEAT KLEINER 303 (Bruno Gehrig & Ivo Schwander eds., 1993).

[33] Werner Ebke, *Renaissance-Juristinnen und -Juristen für das 21. Jahrhundert*, 51 JZ 995, 996 (1996).

[34] *See, e.g.*, ALAN REDFERN & MARTIN HUNTER, LAW AND PRACTICE OF INTERNATIONAL

governmental regulations, proceedings, sanctions, and legal enforcement. Increasing private ordering, however, affects not only transactions of economic entities and the enforcement of their rights, but also the entities themselves. The large entities and the capital market's very important sector of financial accounting provide a ready example of this outcome.

The standards of consolidated financial accounting of internationally operating companies, which were traditionally the domain of national regulation and since the middle of the 1980s the object of harmonization at EU level, are today mainly defined by the Financial Accounting Standard Board (FASB) in the United States and the International Accounting Standards Committee (IASC) based in London.[35] The significance of the impact of the International Accounting Standards (IAS) of the IASC in Germany[36] is sufficiently demonstrated by the German Accounting Standards (DRS) that are developed by the German Accounting Standards Committee (DRSC) and published by the Federal Ministry of Justice.[37] The effects of the privately set IAS can also be felt in the EU. On July 19, 2002, the EU adopted the so-called IAS Regulation that requires listed companies incorporated under the laws of any of the fifteen EU member states to prepare their consolidated financial statements in accordance with International Accounting Standards (IAS).[38] It is only a matter of time before we will witness the application of the IAS to the financial statements of independent unaffiliated companies.[39]

COMMERCIAL ARBITRATION (3rd ed. 1999); STEPHEN SCHWEBEL, INTERNATIONAL ARBITRATION: THREE SALIENT PROBLEMS (1987); ROLF SCHÜTZE, SCHIEDSGERICHT UND SCHIEDSVERFAHREN (3rd ed. 1999).

[35] For a more detailed exposition of this view, *see* Werner Ebke, *Accounting, Auditing and Global Capital Markets*, *in* CORPORATIONS, CAPITAL MARKETS AND THE LAW: LIBER AMICORUM RICHARD M. BUXBAUM 112 (Theodor Baums, Klaus Hopt & Norbert Horn eds., 2000). *See also* DIE ZUKUNFT DES DEUTSCHEN BILANZRECHTS IM ZEICHEN INTERNATIONALER RECHNUNGSLEGUNG UND PRIVATER STANDARDSETZUNG (Detlef Kleindiek & Wolfgang Oehler eds., 2000); SEBASTIAN DAUB, RÜCKSTELLUNGEN NACH HGB, US GAAP UND IAS (2000). For the effects on tax accounting, *see, e.g.*, FRANK BROER, MASSGEBLICHKEITSPRINZIP UND HARMONISIERUNG DER RECHNUNGSLEGUNG (2001); Andreas Oestreicher & Christoph Spengel, *Anwendung von IAS in der EU—Zukunft des Massgeblichkeitsprinzips und Steuerbelastung*, 47 RIW 889 (2001).

[36] INTERNATIONAL ACCOUNTING STANDARDS (International Accounting Standards Board ed., 2002).

[37] For details, *see, e.g.*, Werner Ebke, *Der Deutsche Standardisierungsrat und das Deutsche Rechnungslegungs Standards Committee: Aussichten für eine professionelle Entwicklung von Rechnungslegungsstandards*, 20 ZEITSCHRIFT FÜR WIRTSCHAFTSRECHT [ZIP] 1193 (1999). *See also* BORIS PAAL, RECHNUNGSLEGUNG UND DRSC (2001).

[38] O.J.EU L 243 at 1 (Sept. 11, 2002). For details of the IAS Regulation, *see* Arbeitskreis Bilanzrecht der Hochschullehrer Rechtswissenschaft, *Zur Fortentwicklung des deutschen Bilanzrechts*, 57 BETRIEBS-BERATER [BB] 2372 (2002).

[39] *See* Hans-Joachim Böcking, *IAS für Konzern- und Einzelabschluss?*, 54 DIE WIRTSCHAFTSPRÜFUNG [WPG] 1433 (2001); Rudolf Niehus, '*Auch für Einzelabschlüsse gelten grundsätzlich die IAS?'—Ein Beitrag zu den (möglichen) Grenzen einer 'Internationalisierung' der Rechnungslegung im Einzelabschluss*, 54 WPG 737 (2001).

As a result of changes in the markets or prevailing economic conditions, the work of the IASC shows that private regulation is able to react faster to challenges facing the regulatory framework than the legislature or large supranational bureaucracies. On the other hand, international regulation by private standard setters is exposed to intense institutional competition. Whether the IAS are capable of becoming established as internationally accepted accounting standards as opposed to the US Generally Accepted Accounting Principles (US GAAP) will neither be determined by the IASC in London nor by the EU Commission in Brussels, but rather by the most important capital markets, their 'guardians' (e.g., the Securities Exchange Commission—SEC), and the investors who will decide whether or not they wish to invest in a company whose financial statements are prepared in accordance with IAS.

IV. POWER OF THE MARKETS

Additionally, it is important to note that in our global economy markets make law irrespective of whether national legislatures approve.[40]

A. Antitrust Law

This concept was demonstrated shortly after the end of World War II in antitrust law when the 'effects doctrine' had its heyday in the famous decision of the United States Court of Appeals for the Second Circuit in *United States v. Aluminum Co. of America*.[41] The 'effects doctrine' allows the politically and economically strong market to impose its own standards of conduct on foreign businesses.[42] Of course, conflicts with other states are inevitable. Expectedly, the opposition outside the United States was especially strong when the link of facts to the United States was comparatively weak or if the application of American law seemed to offend the principle of reasonableness. The opposition had little effect despite the 'blocking statutes' that have remained few in number and rather insignificant in practice. Economically important states, however, reacted to the 'effects doctrine', which they considered a form of 'legal imperialism', by adopting similar doctrines. Thus, for example, the 'effects doctrine' is laid down in Section 130(2) of Germany's Antitrust Law just as forcefully as it is in the

[40] For details, *see* Werner Ebke, *Märkte machen Recht—auch Gesellschafts- und Unternehmensrecht!*, *in* FESTSCHRIFT FÜR MARKUS LUTTER 17 (Uwe Schneider, Peter Hommelhoff, Karsten Schmidt, Barbara Grunewald & Tim Drygala eds., 2000).

[41] United States v. Aluminum Co. of America, 148 F.2d 416 (2d Cir. 1945).

[42] *See* BERNHARD GROSSFELD, *supra note* 9, at 31.

EU's antitrust laws.[43] As applied on both sides of the Atlantic, the 'effects doctrine' is becoming a 'political trump card.' German commentators have pointed out as a precaution that the 'effects' of anti-competitive behavior should not only be judged on real facts, but also from a 'normative' standpoint.[44] While this statement is legally accurate, the 'normative' perspective should not hide the fact that the realization and use of the 'effects doctrine' depends on the relative power of a state to make its views and standards prevail over those of foreign countries.

B. Securities Regulation

Similar developments can be observed in the area of securities regulation. The desire of economically and politically influential markets to apply their own regulations to foreign business entities and persons is especially pronounced where sanctions punishing securities fraud are concerned.[45] On the other hand, the markets are much more reluctant if the extraterritorial application of registration or reporting requirements is at issue. How far courts in the United States are willing to go in cases of securities fraud is illustrated by the decision of the United States Court of Appeals for the Second Circuit in *Itoba Ltd v. LEP Group Plc*[46] and the Ninth Circuit Court's decision in *Butte Mining Plc v. Smith*.[47] *Butte Mining* vividly demonstrates that a far-reaching extraterritorial application of securities regulations, 'blocking statutes' to block such application, 'anti-suit injunctions,' and subsequent 'anti-anti-suit injunctions' are detrimental to a harmonious and prosperous coexistence of securities regulations in different markets.[48] The decision also illustrates that unilateral measures to ensure a balanced extraterritorial application of securities regulation (such as the 'balancing test' pursuant to §403 of the Restatement [Third] of the Foreign Relations Law of the United States or the 'shared values approach') at best achieve something if they are observed by the courts in the interpretation and application of the relevant

[43] For details, *see* Knut Lange, *Einführung*, *in* HANDBUCH ZUM DEUTSCHEN UND EUROPÄISCHEN KARTELLRECHT 46 (Knut Lange ed., 2001); VOLKER EMMERICH, KARTELLRECHT 21–3 (9th ed. 2001).

[44] *See* MARTIN HEIDENHAIN ET. AL., GERMAN ANTITRUST LAW 97 (1999).

[45] *See, e.g.*, Werner Ebke, *Die Haftung des gesetzlichen Abschlussprüfers im Internationalen Privatrecht*, *in* FESTSCHRIFT FÜR OTTO SANDROCK 243, 261 (Klaus Berger, Werner Ebke, Siegfried Elsing, Bernhard Grossfeld & Gunther Kühne eds., 2000).

[46] Itoba Ltd. v. LEP Group PLC, 54 F.3d 118 (2d Cir. 1995), *cert denied*, 116 S.Ct. 702 (1996).

[47] Butte Mining Plc v. Smith, 76 F.3d 287 (9th Cir. 1996), *aff'g* 876 F.Supp. 1153 (D. Mont. 1995).

[48] Werner Ebke, *supra* note 40, at 20.

law.[49] In the case of the United States, however, such an approach does not seem to be assured at the moment.[50]

C. Financial Accounting

In the financial accounting sector, too, the market has illustrated its ability to enforce its own standards vis-à-vis foreign enterprises. The differences in the financial accounting and reporting principles and the consequential lack of comparability of (consolidated) financial statements have induced countries with important securities and capital markets (particularly the United States) to require foreign capital-seeking businesses to speak the 'local' accounting language if they want to gain access to those stock exchanges. As a result, the applicable rules of the game are determined by the market rather than by national principles of conflict of laws that as a general rule lead to the application of the financial accounting principles of the enterprise's state of incorporation.[51] Because the observance of such market-set accounting principles is a prerequisite to entry into the market, the relationship between the market and the market participant is effectually governed by a 'contract of adhesion' that is not necessarily based on the 'better' principles of financial accounting, but rather on local principles that the market has the power to impose on foreign issuers.

For capital-seeking enterprises this development means that they need to prepare their (consolidated) financial statements either according to the rules set by the market in question, by internationally accepted financial accounting principles (possibly in addition to the accounting principles required by the law of their state of incorporation if there is no exemption in that law), or with the help of a so-called 'reconciliation' in order to meet the preconditions and expectations of the target market. The capital-seeking companies' only other option is to stay away from foreign capital markets (with all the economic and political consequences that such a decision will have!) or operate exclusively in the less heavily regulated and typically less attractive OTC market, which normally is not an attractive option.[52] In the 1990s, the German legislature and the legislatures of several other EU Member States responded to this development by abolishing the obligation of companies listed on their stock exchanges to produce

[49] *Id.* at 21.

[50] *See* Paul Rogers, *A Comment on the Extraterritorial Application of American Law in the 1990's*, *in* FESTSCHRIFT FÜR BERNHARD GROSSFELD 901, 913 (Ulrich Hübner & Werner Ebke eds., 1999).

[51] *See, e.g.*, Bernhard Grossfeld, *Internationales Bilanzrecht als Internationales Unternehmensrecht*, 36 WIRTSCHAFTSPRÜFERKAMMER-MITTEILUNGEN [WPK-MITT.] 25 (spec. issue June 1997).

[52] *See generally* Werner Ebke, *Rechnungslegung und Abschlussprüfung im Umbruch*, 36 WPK-MITT. 12 (spec. issue June 1997).

consolidated financial statements according to domestic accounting principles.[53] These concessions opened the way for the application of US GAAP and IAS.[54] The Member States' unilateral measures are now superseded by the EU's IAS Regulation of July 19, 2002, which gives effect to the IAS for consolidated financial statements of listed companies incorporated in any of the fifteen Member States.[55]

V. THE SEARCH FOR INSTITUTIONAL SOLUTIONS

Our discussion reveals which strategies legislatures may pursue in their search for institutional responses to the globalization of the economy. Legislatures may:

(1) attempt to hold on to their national rules by defending them against the onset of foreign rules (which would not exclude a material improvement of a national rule in light of a foreign rule) and apply those rules through their conflict-of-laws principles to foreign business enterprises;
(2) release all or some of their own business enterprises with cross-border economic activities from the obligation to abide by national rules and permit them to apply relevant foreign rules (such a change could be unconditional or be subject to certain conditions, such as functional equivalence of such foreign rules);
(3) to arrange for the mutual recognition of national rules through entering into international agreements with other states (such agreements could be bilateral or multilateral);
(4) agree supranationally on a harmonization of relevant rules, whereby the harmonization could be effectuated by governmental agencies, quasi-governmental institutions or private entities;
(5) reach an international agreement on the standardization of relevant rules, which could again be effectuated by international agencies, quasi-governmental institutions or private entities;
(6) create a global market regulatory system with the other states that, among other things, could protect rights and lay down the institutional foundations for cross-border activities.

[53] *See, e.g.*, § 292(a) HGB.

[54] For the possible effects of the internationalization of financial accounting principles on the financial statements of unaffiliated companies, *see supra* note 39.

[55] For the background of the IAS Regulation, *see* Christoph Ernst, *Bilanzrecht: quo vadis?—Die kommende Reform des europäischen Bilanzrechts und mögliche Auswirkungen auf die deutsche Rechnungslegung*, 54 WPG 1440 (2001); Michael Niehus, *EU-Rechnungslegungsstrategie und Gläubigerschutz*, 54 WPG 1209 (2001).

Although each option has different costs, consequences, and temporal perspectives, all aim to overcome the territorial limitations of the law. Each sees the universal opening of the law as an institution in an increasingly global economy as the ultimate objective. The choice between the above options will be influenced by a number of factors in each different area of law. The choice cannot and need not be analyzed here. In any event, it is not a question of one or the other (for example competing regulatory systems versus a centralized system) nor is it an 'all or nothing' situation. From case to case in the broad spectrum of circumstances to the local institutional infrastructure and its interaction with the international structure, there is a long road ahead to developing internationally acceptable solutions with the aim of creating an enabling legal framework for a free world economy. The need to create as many trading opportunities as possible for enterprises and individuals and to widen the scope of private autonomous trade as far as possible is a common goal.[56] Therefore, it is necessary to balance the pros and cons of a competition of systems against a globally unified market law. How difficult the choice between the various approaches can be in an individual case is demonstrated by the controversial debate over the creation of an International Antitrust Code.[57] In this context, one must not overlook the fact, however, that there is a path dependency that in many cases cannot be overcome without cost and hardship and in some cases may actually be insurmountable.

VI. CONCLUSION

The process of globalization has created numerous problems for the economy and the law. Nothing demonstrates this point better than the internet whose unprecedented directness, flexibility, and interaction renders the traditional legal principles like territoriality and legislative, executive, and judicial jurisdiction stretched to their limits. There are no easy answers to the globalization of the economy. Legislatures have, however, several options available to them to create sensible and innovative solutions. The aim should be the creation of a liberal world economy that offers enter-

[56] HORST SIEBERT, WELTWIRTSCHAFT (1997).

[57] For details of the debate, *see, e.g.*, WOLFGANG FIKENTSCHER & ULRICH IMMENGA, DRAFT INTERNATIONAL ANTITRUST CODE. KOMMENTIERTER ENTWURF EINES INTERNATIONALEN WETTBEWERBSRECHTS MIT ERGÄNZENDEN BEITRÄGEN (1995); Karl Meessen, *Das Für und Wider eines Weltkartellrechts*, *in* GLOBALISIERUNG UND WELTWIRTSCHAFT, *supra* note 8, at 336–55; Andreas Fuchs, *Ziele, Formen und Grenzen einer internationalen Vereinheitlichung des Kartellrechts*, *in* GLOBALISIERUNG UND WELTWIRTSCHAFT, *supra* note 8, at 356–72; TOWARDS WTO COMPETITION RULES—KEY ISSUES AND COMMENTS ON THE WTO REPORT (1998) ON TRADE AND COMPETITION (Roger Zäch ed., 1999); Klaus Grewlich, *Wettbewerbsordnung als Bestandteil völkerrechtlicher Konstitutionalisierung*, 47 RIW 641 (2001).

prises and individuals the most trading opportunities and that widens the scope of private autonomous trade as far as possible. The law's answer to the demands put upon it by the globalization of the economy cannot be static, but rather must be part of a dynamic process. Not only enterprises and their managers, but also shareholders, employees, consumers, policymakers, and, last but not least, lawyers themselves need to adapt continuously to the new challenges.

CHAPTER SIX

The International Criminal Court: America's Return to Unilateralism

*by Whitney R. Harris**

CHAPTER OUTLINE

I. War Crimes Trials at the End of World War I
II. War Crimes Trials at the End of World War II
III. Proposals for an International Criminal Court
IV. The Rome Conference for an International Criminal Court
V. Crimes Within the Jurisdiction of the ICC
VI. Principles and Procedures of the ICC
VII. Ratification of the Rome Statute
VIII. The ICC and Terrorism

A state is a self-governing political community occupying its own territory. The treaties of Westphalia, signed on October 24, 1648, which marked the end of the Thirty Years' War in Europe, established the principle, since recognized and observed in international law, that the basic political unit in international relations is the state which may act alone or, pursuant to agreements, covenants, or treaties, with other states.

In the Twentieth Century, in which violence among coalitions of states reached an historical apogee, the single most significant act of treachery may have been the assassination of the Archduke Francis Ferdinand, heir to the Hapsburg throne, and his wife, in Sarajevo, then the seat of Bosnia-Herzegovina, on June 28, 1914.

At that time the uneasy peace of Europe hinged on the balance of power of the triple alliance—Germany, Austria-Hungary, and Italy—and the triple entente—Great Britain, France, and Russia. When Austria-Hungary declared war on Serbia to avenge the Sarajevo murders, Russia came to the aid of Serbia, and the skein of treaties upon which the peace of Europe depended, unraveled. Germany sided with Austria-Hungary, France supported Russia, and Great Britain aligned herself with France. Thus

* Prosecutor at the Trial of the Major German War Criminals, Nuremberg, 1945–46, and author of *Tyranny on Trial*, and Professor of Law, SMU School of Law.

began the first of the two world wars of the Twentieth Century. Facing defeat on the battlefield, Germany's KaiserWilhelm II fled to Holland on November 10, 1918 and on the following day an armistice was signed at Compeigne.

I. WAR CRIMES TRIALS AT THE END OF WORLD WAR I

At the end of World War I a commission of inquiry recommended that an *ad hoc* International tribunal should be established to try persons charged with the commission of war crimes and crimes against humanity during the war. The Treaty of Versailles of June 28, 1919, called for the prosecution of Wilhelm II, under Article 227, and of German war criminals, under Articles 228 and 229. This was the first attempt, after a major war, to bring war criminals to justice by multilateral legal process. The proposed trials did not materialize. The Netherlands refused to surrender Wilhelm for trial and the Allies ultimately acceded to a German proposal to conduct its own war crimes trials in Leipzig. These were less than a success. Of the 896 persons accused of the commission of war crimes by the Allies, only twelve were brought to trial. Six were convicted and given small sentences. The Treaty of Peace between the Allied Powers and Turkey of August 10, 1920, called for the prosecution of Turkish officials responsible for the Armenian massacre of 1915. This, too, failed, and a general amnesty was granted on adoption of the Treaty of Lausanne on July 24, 1923.

World War II, essentially a revengeful and expansionist continuation by Nazi Germany under Adolf Hitler of the earlier struggle, began on September 3, 1939 with Germany's assault on Poland. It ended with the unconditional surrender of Germany on May 8, 1945. Of primary concern was the punishment of the leaders of Germany who had inflicted incomparable harm upon the world in the intervening years.

II. WAR CRIMES TRIALS AT THE END OF WORLD WAR II

The genesis of the trial of the major German war criminals at the end of World War II was the Moscow Conference of October, 1943 at the conclusion of which a statement was signed by President Roosevelt, Prime Minister Churchill, and Premier Stalin declaring the determination of the three powers to hold Germans individually responsible for the crimes committed by them in the course of the war.

The statement did not declare whether such offenders would be punished by executive action or pursuant to the judicial process. In Britain, Lord Chancellor Simon and Prime Minister Churchill were of the view that major war criminals should be disposed of by executive action- a view echoed in the United States by Secretary of the Treasury Henry Morgenthau, who proposed to President Roosevelt that German arch criminals be shot upon capture and identification.

Secretary Morgenthau was opposed in the Cabinet by Secretary of War Henry L. Stimson, who believed that leading Nazis should be brought to trial before an international military tribunal. Stimson's views ultimately prevailed, and a memorandum recommending a trial was prepared for the use of President Roosevelt at the three-power Yalta conference in February, 1945. The memorandum stated that condemnation of German war criminals after a trial would command maximum public support and receive the respect of history, and it noted that use of the judicial method would make an authentic historic record of Nazi crimes.

Supreme Court Justice Robert H. Jackson was appointed by President Truman on May 8, 1945 as the United States Chief of Counsel, charged with obtaining the agreement of the Allies to a trial of the major German war criminals before an international military tribunal, and he entered upon this daunting task with unswerving determination. He succeeded in persuading the British to accept the proposal to punish German war criminals after trial by an international military tribunal established for that purpose.

Representatives of the United States, Great Britain, France and the Soviet Union met in London on June 26, 1945 for the purpose of drafting an agreement to establish an international military tribunal for the trial of major war criminals, a charter for the tribunal, and an indictment of the principal leaders of Nazi Germany.

The London Agreement was adopted on August 8, 1945. The Charter created the International Military Tribunal 'for the just and prompt trial and punishment of the major war criminals of the European Axis.'

The Charter set forth three basic crimes charged to the defendants: the crime of initiating and waging aggressive war, war crimes, and crimes against humanity committed in the course of the war. In addition, under the American prosecution theory, the defendants were charged with engaging in a common plan or conspiracy to commit all of these crimes. All persons who willingly joined with Hitler necessarily supported these criminal objectives and were liable for the crimes committed in furtherance of the conspiracy.

Each prosecuting power appointed a judge and alternate judge. Similar appointments were made of chief prosecutors, who were directed to act as a committee to select the persons to be tried, and to draft the indictment and lodge it with the Tribunal.

It was provided that each accused person should be served with a copy of the indictment in a language understood by him, that preliminary examinations should be conducted in such language, that defendants should have the right to conduct their own defense or to have the assistance of counsel, selected by them, and that they should have the right to present evidence in their own behalf and to cross-examine any witness called by the prosecution.

The Tribunal was given the powers essential for the proper conduct of the trial and was directed to apply to the greatest possible extent expeditious and non-technical procedures and to admit any evidence which it deemed to have probative value. Berlin was named the permanent seat of the Tribunal and Nuremberg as the place of trial. All official documents were to be produced, and all court proceedings conducted, in the English, French, and Russian languages, and in the language of the defendant.

The trial opened on November 20, 1945. The President of the Tribunal, Lord Justice Lawrence of Great Britain, set the tone for the proceedings of that day, and all the days to follow, when he said:

> The Trial which is now about to begin is unique in the history of the jurisprudence of the world and it is of supreme importance to millions of people all over the globe. For these reasons, there is laid upon everybody who takes part in this Trial a solemn responsibility to discharge their duties without fear or favor, in accordance with the sacred principles of law and justice. The four Signatories having invoked the judicial process, it is the duty of all concerned to see that the Trial in no way departs from these principles and traditions which alone give justice its authority and the place it ought to occupy in the affairs of all civilized states.[1]

The indictment was read at length into the record after which the defendants were called upon to enter their pleas. Ley was dead by his own hand, and the Tribunal had postponed proceedings against Krupp von Bohlen because of his physical incapacity. Bormann was absent and a not guilty plea was entered for him. Kaltenbrunner was hospitalized and later made his personal plea of not guilty. All other defendants were present in court and entered 'not guilty' pleas. In his opening statement, which has become a jurisprudential classic, Justice Jackson began:

> The privilege of opening the first trial of history for crimes against the peace of the world imposes a grave responsibility. The wrongs which we seek to condemn and punish have been so calculated, so malignant, and so devastating, that civilization cannot tolerate their being ignored because it cannot survive their being repeated. That four great nations, flushed with victory and stung with injury, stay the hands of vengeance and voluntarily submit their captive enemies to the judgment of the law is one of the most significant tributes that Power has ever paid to Reason.[2]

During the next several months evidence was introduced against the

[1] Harris. *Tyranny on Trial*, 3rd ed,. P. 34. [2] *id.*

twenty-two individual and five organizational defendants. The evidence consisted primarily of captured German documents supplemented by the testimony of witnesses.

The defendants were given the benefit of both the common law and civil law systems of jurisprudence. As in the common law, they were permitted to testify under oath in their own defense, and all, save Rudolf Hess, did so. At the conclusion of the trial each of the defendants including Hess, was allowed to make an unsworn statement to the Tribunal in his on defense, permitted under the civil law. Convictions were required to be supported by evidence of guilt beyond a reasonable doubt.

No significant difficulty was experienced in the conduct of the trial, despite its multi-national composition. It was conducted by professional judges and attorneys, respectful of the law and knowledgeable of rules of procedure and standards of evidence common to all advanced legal systems. And it was conducted in the spirit of truth-seeking and not of revenge. Convictions were based upon evidence, and evidence was required to be relevant and preponderant. The trial established, irrefutably, that justice could be effectively dispensed by a multi-national tribunal.

On the afternoon of October 1, 1946 the International Military Tribunal convened in final session. Every chair in the courtroom was occupied except the twenty-one chairs in the prisoners' dock. The four judges and their alternates sat on the bench. Defense counsel faced them across the room. To the left were the four tables of the prosecuting staffs. Behind them, members of the press and guests packed the visitors gallery. The defendants were to be brought into the courtroom, one at a time, to hear the sentences pronounced against them.

At ten minutes to three, the paneled door in the back of the prisoners' dock slid silently open. The defendant Hermann Goering stepped out of the elevator which had brought him from the ground floor where the defendants waited. Goering was emotionless when the residing judge, Lord Lawrence, announced the verdict in a steady voice: 'Defendant Hermann Wilhelm Goering, on the counts of the indictment on which you have been convicted, the International Military Tribunal sentences you to death by hanging.'

The number two Nazi turned on his heel and passed through the paneled door into the waiting elevator. The door closed, and there was a hum of whispered voices in the courtroom as those present awaited the arrival of the next defendant, Rudolf Hess. Hess, who had flown his Messerschmitt to England in a futile effort to persuade the British to abandon the fight with Germany, was sentenced to imprisonment for life.

The other defendants appeared in turn and received their sentences. Twelve, including Martin Bormann, who had been tried *in absentia* were given death sentences; three, Hans Fritzsche, Hjalmar Schacht, and Franz von Papen, were acquitted; and the remaining seven received varying terms of imprisonment. After delivering the sentences, the International Military Tribunal adjourned *sine die*.

An International Military Tribunal for the Far East was convened under the authority of General Douglas MacArthur as the Supreme Commander of Allied Forces in the Far East. MacArthur appointed judges from eleven nations, and the Far East Tribual thus acquired, like the Nuremberg Tribunal, a multi-national character. The Tokyo War Crimes Trial followed closely the Nuremberg precedent. Twenty-seven Japanese political and military leaders indicted. The trial lasted from April 29, 1946 until April 16, 1948. Judgment was handed down on November 4–12, 1948. It was the second multi-national tribunal to function successfully at the end of World War II.

While many war crimes trials were held after World War II by national military and other tribunals, a precedent was set by the Nuremberg and Tokyo proceedings for bringing military aggressors, in a multi-national war, to trial before multi-national tribunals. It was clearly established that the problems of conducting trials in several languages, and in accommodating diverse legal systems, could be overcome in such proceedings and that multi-national criminal tribunals could have a positive role in international affairs.

III. PROPOSALS FOR AN INTERNATIONAL CRIMINAL COURT

Shortly after the Nuremberg judgment was handed down an international Conference was convened in Paris under sponsorship of the *Mouvement National Judicaire Francais*. The Congress, which consisted of lawyers from twenty-two countries, including all of the prosecuting powers before the International Military Tribunal, called for the establishment of an international criminal court. Judge Henri Donnedieu de Vabres, the French judge on the International Military Tribunal, proposed the following year that a criminal chamber of the International Court of Justice should be established to hear certain cases and that, in addition, a permanent criminal court should be established.

The General Assembly considered the proposal for an international criminal court when drafting the Convention on the Prevention and Punishment of the Crime of Genocide, but failed to approve it. On the day it adopted the Genocide Convention, December 18, 1948, however, the General Assembly requested the International Law Commission to undertake a study of permanent international criminal court. This was in addition to a directive of the General Assembly of November 21, 1947, requesting the International Law Commission to formulate the principles of international law which it considered to have been promulgated by the Charter of the International Military Tribunal as constructed by the tribunal.

In August, 1951, a Committee on International Criminal Jurisdiction, composed of representatives of seventeen member states, submitted a draft statute to the General Assembly calling for the formation of a court to try persons accused of crimes under international law. Thus began a long period of international negotiations culminating in a General Assembly resolution of December 17, 1996 calling for a diplomatic conference of plenipotentiaries to meet in 1998.

IV. THE ROME CONFERENCE FOR AN INTERNATIONAL CRIMINAL COURT

The Conference convened in Rome on June 15, 1998 under the chairmanship of Phillip Kirsch of Canada.[3] In opening the conference United Nations Secretary General Kofi Annan declared:

After the defeat of Nazism and Fascism in 1945, the United Nations was set up in an effort to ensure that world war could never happen again. The victorious powers also set up international tribunals at Nuremberg and Tokyo, to judge the leaders who had ordered and carried out the worst atrocities. And they decided to prosecute the Nazi leaders not only for 'war-crimes'—waging war and massacring people in occupied territories- but also for 'crimes against humanity' which included the slaughter of their own fellow citizens and others in the tragedy we now know as the Holocaust.

Was it enough to make an example of a few arch-criminals in states that had waged aggressive war, and leave it at that? The General Assembly of the United Nations did not think so. In 1948 it adopted the Convention on the Prevention and Punishment of the Crime of Genocide. And it requested the International Law Commission to study the possibility of establishing a permanent international criminal court. In this area, as in so many, the Cold War prevented further progress at that time.

Events in the former Yugoslavia and in Rwanda overtook the slow processes by which the world was considering the creation of a permanent international criminal court. Ad hoc tribunals had to be set up for these two countries. These tribunals are showing, however imperfectly, that there is such a thing as international criminal justice, that it can have teeth. But ad hoc tribunals are not enough. People all over the world want to know that humanity can strike back- that whatever and whenever genocide, war crimes, or other such violations are committed, there is a court before which the criminal can be held to account . . .[4]

[3] The author was an NGO delegate, representing the Committee of Former Nuremberg Prosecutors for a Permanent International Criminal Court, of which he was founder and coordinator.

[4] *United Nations Press Release, Dept. Pub. Info. L/ROM?6/Rev.1, June 14, 1998.*

On June 17, the United States Ambassador to the United Nations, Bill Richardson, addressed the conference. After pointing to United States support of the establishment of the *ad hoc* tribunals for the former Yugoslavia and Rwanda, he introduced a note of caution into the coming deliberations. He endorsed the inclusion of serious violations of international humanitarian law—genocide, large-scale war crimes and crimes against humanity—but declared it premature 'to attempt to define a crime of aggression for purposes of individual criminal responsibility.' He opposed the concept of self-initiating prosecutor and called for a dominant role by the Security Council in referring cases to the court. Within such limitations he advocated bringing to justice individuals 'responsible for genocide, crimes against humanity, and war crimes' and preventing 'the recurrence of such unspeakable acts in the future.[5]'

The Conference deliberated on the proposed Statute for an International Criminal Court over a period of five weeks. The Statute was adopted by consensus on July 17, 1998. United States Ambassador David Scheffer, the head of the U.S. delegation, held fast to the limitations suggested by Ambassador Richardson and opposed adoption of the Statute at the end of the conference. The United States called for a roll call and the unrecorded vote showed 120 in favor to 7 against, with 21 abstentions. Voting against the statute were Iraq, Libya, Qatar, Yemen, China, Israel, and the United States. The Arab countries opposed the statute primarily because it omitted the death penalty. China was concerned with the possibility of charges of offenses against human rights. Israel believed that the shifting of population into occupied territory should not have been included as a war crime. And the United States feared that its role as a primary peace-keeper with American military forces deployed around the world might be adversely affected by spurious charges of war crimes. The United States championed, while India deprecated, while India deprecated, the significant role of the Security Council in the initiating of cases before the Court. But the overwhelming majority of the nations represented at the Rome Conference approved the statute as the principal international document of peace and justice of the latter half of the twentieth century. Chairman Kirsch declared: 'This is an extraordinary moment, a historical moment. I am not sure to what extent those present here know how important this is for the future of mankind.[6]'

The mayor of Rome, the host of the ceremony, observed that representatives of the United Nations had gathered at the end of the century to give to the world a crucial instrument to fight against crime, violence, and genocide and to establish law, justice and peace in the 'spirit of Rome.' Professor

[5] *United Nations Press Release, Dept. Pub. Info. L/ROM/8, June 17, 1998.*

[6] *Terraviva, No. 26, Rome, July 18, 1998, p.1.*

Gerhard Hafner, speaking on behalf of the European Union, declared that delegates to the Conference could justifiably say: *Roma Iocuta, causa finita*—when Rome has spoken, the task is finished.

V. CRIMES WITHIN THE JURISDICTION OF THE ICC

The Preamble of the Rome Statute recalls the millions of children, women and men who were victims of the 'unimaginable atrocities' of the twentieth century, observing that 'such grave crimes threaten the peace, security and well-being of the world.' It declares that these crimes of concern to the international community must not go unpunished. It reaffirms that all States must refrain from the threat or use of force against the territorial integrity or political independence of any State. And it calls for the establishment of an independent permanent International Criminal Court, complementary to national criminal jurisdictions and in relationship with the United Nations system, to take jurisdiction over the most serious crimes of concern to the international community. The seat of the Court is at the Hague in the Netherlands.

The Court is given the right to exercise its functions and powers on the territory of States Parties and by special agreement on the territory of other States. Its jurisdiction is limited to the most serious crimes which are of concern to the international community as a whole, namely, (a) genocide, (b) crimes against humanity, (c) war crimes, and (d) aggressive war (when defined).

In a stunning reversal of legal concepts, the United States opposed the inclusion of the crime of aggression in the category of crimes within the jurisdiction of the Court. In the London negotiations leading to the inclusion of aggressive war as a principal crime within the jurisdiction of the Tribunal, Justice Jackson had said: '. . . launching a war of aggression is a crime and no political or economic situation can justify it. . . the great crime of crimes of our century was the launching of a needless war in Europe.[7]' And in its final judgment the Tribunal said: 'War is essentially an evil thing. It consequences are not confined to the belligerent states alone, but affect the whole world. To initiate a war of aggression, therefore, is not only an international crime, it is the supreme international crime differing only from other war crimes in that it contains within itself the accumulated evil of the whole.[8]' Moreover, on December 14, 1974, the General Assembly of

[7] *Report of Robert H. Jackson, United States Representative to the International Conference on Military Trials, London, 1945, Washington, D.C. Department of State Publication 3080 (Government Printing Office , 1949).*

[8] *Trial of the Major War Criminals (Nuremberg: International Military Tribunal, 1947–49, p.186).*

the United Nations by Resolution 3314 (XXIX) adopted a consensus definition of aggression as 'the use of armed force by a State against the sovereignty, territorial integrity or political independence of another State, or in any other manner inconsistent with the Charter of the United Nations.'

Crimes against humanity are cognizable by the Court whether or not committed during an external or internal conflict. The International Military Tribunal was restricted to finding that crimes against humanity were cognizable only when committed in connection with aggressive war or war crimes. In defining crimes against humanity as crimes in and of themselves, without reference to war or war crimes, the Statute confirms the right of humanity to freedom from inhuman crimes.

VI. PRINCIPLES AND PROCEDURES OF THE ICC

The Court may exercise jurisdiction only with respect to crimes committed after the Statute came into effect on July 1, 2002. If a State becomes a party to the Statute after that date the Court may take jurisdiction for that State only over crimes committed after it becomes a party. The Court may take jurisdiction only if the State on the territory of which the alleged crime occurred, or the State of which the accused is a national, is a party to the Statute or has accepted its jurisdiction.

The Court may assume jurisdiction if a State Party has referred the case to the prosecutor, the Security Council has referred the case to the prosecutor under Chapter VII of the UN Charter, or the prosecutor has initiated an investigation *proprio motu.* The prosecutor may proceed *proprio motu* only upon authorization of the Pre-Trial Chamber. No investigation or prosecution may be undertaken for a period of twelve months after the Security Council has requested abeyance under Chapter VII. The Court shall declare a case to be inadmissible where it is being investigated or prosecuted in good faith by a State which has jurisdiction over it. No person shall be prosecuted for a crime of which that person has been convicted or acquitted in a prior judicial proceeding.

The Statute sets forth other fundamental principles of criminal law, including the doctrines of *nullem crimen sine lege, nulla poena sine lege,* and *mens rea.* Persons who commit or order the commission of crimes are held individually responsible and are not exempt because of official capacity. Military commanders are responsible for crimes committed by forces under their command as a result of failure to exercise proper control over such forces. The statute sets out normal grounds for excluding criminal responsibility such as mental incapacity, duress, and self-defense. Acting pursuant to superior orders will not relieve a person from liability if the accused knew that the order was unlawful, as in the case of orders to commit genocide or crimes against humanity, but can be considered in mitigation of punishment.

A State Party may, by written notice to the Secretary-General of the United Nations, withdraw from the Statute one year after the date such notification has been received. Seven years after the entry into force of the Statute the Secretary-General of the United Nations is required to convene a Review Conference to consider any amendments to the Statute. With respect to a State Party which does not accept an amendment, the Court may not exercise jurisdiction regarding a crime covered by the amendment when committed by that State's nationals or on it territory.

VII. RATIFICATION OF THE ROME STATUTE

With virtually unprecedented speed, reflecting the desire of nations and their citizens to find a substitute for war in resolving international disputes and to punish assaults upon humanity, the Statute for a Permanent International Criminal Court gained and surpassed the sixty ratifications necessary for entry into force, less than four years after the Rome Conference of 1988. At a special ratification ceremony held on April 11, 2002 at the United Nations headquarters in New York City ten countries simultaneously deposited their instruments of ratification. The tribunal came into being on July 1, 2002, an historic landmark in the enforcement of the rule of law in international relations.

The Rome Treaty is the vision and product of the western world- the world which gave America its life, its beliefs, and its conscience. Canada, its neighbor to the north, of like heritage, traditions and principles, ratified the treaty on July 7, 2000. The United Kingdom from which our legal system largely derives, ratified the treaty on October 4, 2001. And Germany, whose leaders stood trial at Nuremberg in the great trial which gave meaning to crimes of aggressive war, genocide, war crimes and crimes against humanity in international law, ratified the treaty on December 11, 2000 upon the *unanimous vote* of the Bundestag.

Why has America, in this issue of law versus force, abandoned its traditional friends and allies and chosen the company of nations it has mistrusted in the past, such as Iraq, Russia and China? Certainly is it not because it prefers the policies of the latter states. It is rather that, as the world's remaining superpower, the United States feels that it may serve its interest more effectively through a unilateral approach to conflict resolution in international affairs.

The International Tribunals for the former Yugoslavia and Rwanda were established by the Security Council in furtherance of its peace-keeping functions. It is not to be expected that there will be need for new *ad hoc* judicial bodies after July 1, 2002. The availability and utilization of the permanent tribunal will avoid the *ex post facto* objection to the *ad hoc* courts. The ICC is international judicial body with published jurisdiction and procedures. No tyrant may complain that he was without knowledge of the law and his possible indictment, trial, and punishment thereunder, when he committed his tyrannical acts.

The ready availability of the *permanent* court will avoid the delays in organizing and staffing *ad hoc* tribunals. In the several months required to establish and convene special courts evidence is frequently lost and witnesses disappear. Sir Richard Goldstone, the first prosecutor for the Yugoslavian and Rwandan tribunals, has noted this defect in the *ad hoc* approach to international criminal procedure.

The existence and functioning of the ICC, recognizing and utilizing the most advanced legal procedures and principles available to international legal systems will demonstrate to unsophisticated societies the benefits in applying to their own societies such principles and procedures. The courtroom will displace the machete. Primitive societies will endeavor to emulate the ICC. Criminal law and procedures around the world may be expected to improve through the example of the ICC in conducting criminal trials and dispensing justice.

The Security Council will continue to play a vital role in the use of the judicial process in the maintenance of world peace and order. The permanent court will eliminate the need for *ad hoc* tribunals which have been set up by the Security Council in the past. But the Security Council will supervise the ICC in important respects. It may refer cases to the Prosecutor under Chapter VII of the UN Charter, and it may order that no investigation or prosecution be commenced or undertaken for a period of twelve months after a request to that effect, subject to right of renewal, has been made by the Security Council. The Security Council represents a form of multilateralism, although each of its five permanent members, including the United States, may exercise the veto power.

The first nation to ratify the Rome Treaty was Senegal, on February 2, 1999. It is a country on the west coast of Africa with a population of approximately 10,000,000 and a military of approximately 20,000. Because of its small size and limited military strength it cannot be a significant factor in the maintenance of world peace, although, to be sure, its leaders might be subject to trial for the commission of war crimes or crimes against humanity in any military action in which Senegal might become involved.

But the risks and responsibilities are much greater for the United States. Its military leaders and personnel may be engaged in military actions across the world. Was the bombing of Afghanistan wedding party an excusable error of judgment or such an act of recklessness as to warrant a war crimes charge against responsible military personnel? Was the legal response of the United States to the bombing adequate to meet the good faith standards of the Rome Statute? The possibility of charges of this kind being brought before the ICC by its prosecutor, even with the approval of the Pre-Trial Chamber, has been a significant factor in the reluctance of the United States to join its most trusted allies in ratifying the Rome Statute.

As one of his final acts of office President Bill Clinton directed Ambassador David Scheffer, or chief negotiator at the Rome Conference, to sight the Treaty on behalf of the United States. By signing the Treaty the United States would be entitled to participate in meetings of the Preparatory Commission here rules of procedure and other ancillary matters are reviewed. President Bush rescinded the signature of the United States to the treaty in May, 2002. This had the effect of excluding the United States from any further contact with the proponents of the Statute. It was an act of self-exclusion from one of the most significant instruments for international justice ever approved by the world community. The United States is no longer entitled, as would a signatory which has not yet ratified the Treaty, to participate in negotiations for improvements of the Statute in the review conference of 2009. It was an act of futile defiance, intended to show the world, friend and foe alike, that the United States intends to stand against the Rome Statute for a permanent International Criminal Court- a position of extreme unilateralism.

A signed treaty need not be submitted by the President to the Senate for ratification. The treaty declaring and defining the crime of genocide was not approved by the Senate for over forty years after its enactment. It is now accepted international law. The United States, reluctant to ratify the Rome Statute, fails in its mission to serve world peace by aligning itself with other non-signers such as Iraq, China and Cuba. In doing so it divorces itself from its historical friends and allies for whom multilateralism is the key to peace.

VIII. THE ICC AND TERRORISM

Terrorism, like aggressive war, is a crime which is difficult to define but easily recognizable when it occurs. The International Military Tribunal had no difficulty in finding Nuremberg defendants guilty of the crime of waging aggressive war. Every element of unlawful aggression was present in Hitler's attack upon Poland on September 3, 1939. In national trials of individuals involved in the September 11, 2001attacks on the World Trade Center there is little doubt that the accused will be found guilty of acts of terrorism where justiciable under national statutes.

No generally accepted definition of terrorism could be agreed to by the negotiators of the Rome Statute.[9] Like aggressive war, it is not an international crime, which, at this time, lies within the jurisdiction of the ICC. Under certain factual conditions, however, terrorist acts may qualify as crimes against humanity.

Crimes against humanity include murder and inhuman acts, widespread or systematic, committed against a civilian population. They are not required to be committed in connection with aggressive war or war crimes.[10] The September 11 assaults were clearly in violation of laws of the United States against murder, willful destruction of property, and other criminal statutes. But September 11 as not merely an offense against the World Trade Center and its occupants, it was, and was intended to be, an assault against the United States. If the terrorist acts of September 11 had been committed by another nation they would have constituted an act of war. Committed by civilians, in furtherance of a private conspiracy, they were a crime against humanity, clearly outlawed by the Rome Statute.[11]

If these terrorist assault had occurred on September 11, 2002, rather than the year before, and the United States had by then ratified the Rome Treaty, the International Criminal Court could have taken jurisdiction over the terrorists. Co-conspirators of those who had killed themselves in the c\action could have been held for trial before this international criminal court. The process would have gained the support of other nations whose citizens were killed in the World Trade Center assaults. The effect would have been to elevate the criminal conduct from an act of inhumanity against the United States of to an act of terrorism against the civilized world.

The September 11, 2001 terrorist attack was directed primarily against the most powerful nation in the world, capable of mounting a swift and powerful counter-attack. What if the attack had been made against a lesser power, Great Britain, perhaps, or the Netherlands, less able to pursue the criminal suspects across the globe? Would it not be preferable for an indictment ot have been lodged in the ICC against such criminals, calling for a world response to this crime of world dimensions?

The three great crimes in the international law which demand universal response are those defined and enforced at the trial of the major German war criminals at Nuremberg half a century ago- aggressive war (where one state attacks without legal provocation another state with force of arms), war crimes (crimes against the laws of war committed against military personnel in time of war), and crimes against humanity (murder, torture or

[9] Rome, Statute, Resolution F.

[10] The Charter of the International Military Tribunal did not require that crimes against humanity be systematic, but they had to be committed in connection with other crimes within the jurisdiction of the tribunal namely, aggressive war or war crimes.

[11] Ramer and Adams, *Accountability for Human Rights Atrocities in International Law: Beyond the Nuremberg Legacy* (1997), 140–41.

inhumane acts forming part of a widespread or systematic attack upon civilians). War crimes and crimes against humanity, as defined in the Rome Statute, are now subject to the jurisdiction of the ICC in cases arising after July 1, 2002.

These crimes better suited to the jurisdiction of an international criminal court, specializing in such cases, and handling them routinely, than in national courts of general jurisdiction on sporadic occasions.[12] Te ICC will have a significant place in the lexicon of courts. Its role will not be to replace, but rather to support, national judicial systems in the struggle against tyrants and terrorists. It will serve as a multinational legal instrumentality in furtherance of a system of justice intended and designed to subject tyrants and terrorists to the law and to establish and maintain a world of peace under the law.

[12] Even so, the ICC will not take jurisdiction in cases where courts of the State of which the accused person is a citizen undertake to prosecute the case against him in good faith.

CHAPTER SEVEN

Reaction and Inattention Within the U.S. Government

*by A. Helton**

CHAPTER OUTLINE

I. Organizing Humanitarian Policy
II. Executive Branch
III. The Bureaucratic Architecture of U.S. Responses
IV. The January 2000 Executive Branch Humanitarian Review
V. The Politics of Bureaucratic Reform
VI. A Proposal for a New U.S. Agency for Humanitarian Action (AHA)
VII. A First Task: Contributing to Rule of Law Initiatives in Post-Crisis Settings
VIII. Congress

It was an uncharacteristically cold day in Washington, DC, in December 2000. The renaissance-style facade of the Old Executive Office Building was projected against the breaking dawn as I arrived for my breakfast meeting with Eric Schwartz, then Special Assistant to the President for National Security Affairs and Senior Director for Multilateral and Humanitarian Affairs at the National Security Council (NSC). Schwartz, whom I have known for many years, had worked on humanitarian issues at the NSC since 1993. He was already at his office computer when I arrived at 7:10 a.m. for our breakfast meeting. I sat in the waiting area outside his office, having made my way through the building that reflected an odd mix of grandeur and standardized office furnishings.

Schwartz's tenure at the NSC had coincided with a series of profound humanitarian challenges to the Administration of President Bill Clinton in the 1990s. Humanitarian emergencies in places such as Bosnia, Herzegovina, Cambodia, East Timor, Haiti, Iraq, Kosovo, Rwanda, Sierra

* Mr. Helton was the Director of Peace and Conflict Studies and Senior Fellow for Refugee Studies and Preventative Action at the Council on Foreign Relations at the time of his untimely death in the August 19, 2003 bombing of the U.N. Headquarters in Baghdad.

Leone, and Somalia had shaken the U.S. government bureaucracy. The office Schwartz directed had a staff of seven persons. In the prior President George H. W. Bush Administration, only one person at a lower level in the NSC had the brief on humanitarian and multilateral issues.

Schwartz explained that his office had become 'an outpost of concern on human rights and humanitarian issues' during the Clinton Administration. But his responsibilities had grown to involve traditional political and security issues relating to United Nations (UN) matters, which he believed made him much more influential in the policy arena. 'I go to so many more high level meetings with this brief,' he noted. An exclusive focus on human rights and humanitarian issues risks marginalization in the foreign affairs bureaucracy, a dynamic reflected, for example, by the difficulties in influencing policy experienced by the State Department's human rights bureau over the past several years.

Schwartz found the idea of a humanitarian response 'toolbox' to be an extremely important notion. Political will is often informed—indeed, on occasion fundamentally—by the responses that are available. Frequently, objections in senior-level government meetings on crisis responses are not stated in terms of high policy. The objectors do not say: 'Don't alleviate the horrible suffering of people.' Rather, they claim that such action is 'too hard to do.' Debates within government often swirl around issues of capacity and feasibility, and it can be crucial at Cabinet-level meetings to rebut the assertion that something is too hard to try. Of course, making the case can mean that you get the job as well. Making a showing that there are skilled professionals, money, and accepted procedures in place and ready to undertake an initiative can make all the difference.

Crises arise in specific situations demanding a survey of feasibilities, in effect a rummage through the policy toolbox. Schwartz noted that it potentially could be a waste of time to agonize in advance over the general guidelines for humanitarian intervention, that is, the proportionate use of military force for humanitarian reasons. The 1999 Kosovo conflict has given rise to several wide-ranging reviews of the legitimacy of such endeavors. But attempting to formulate broad policy is of limited value where the key issues are almost invariably operational: how to get from here to there in a particular crisis. 'I tell my staff they are not op-ed writers. We have a responsibility to make specific suggestions,' said Schwartz.

Schwartz drew a distinction between those crises that are unanticipated and not of highest geopolitical concern, those that are thus 'low on the radar screen' of decision-makers, and those of long-standing duration. Prolonged crises such as the humanitarian emergencies in Bosnia, and Herzegovina, and Kosovo over the past decade are more amenable to a deliberate planning process. But even in these circumstances there can be important conceptual and institutional gaps. The oft-cited failure to integrate humanitarian considerations into military and political planning in relation to Kosovo is illustrative.

A toolbox notion could be particularly valuable in addressing unanticipated crises that are catapulted onto the agendas of decision-makers. Political will in such instances can be informed significantly by having in hand operational options, such as the capacity to deploy troops or international police or to respond to requests for help by the training of indigenous forces in Africa or elsewhere. Also, transitional administration capacities in the UN system can clearly encourage decision-makers to undertake such daunting initiatives.

Schwartz, however, was skeptical given the obstacles facing the UN in this area. Turf squabbles are endemic. The UN Development Programme (UNDP) is reluctant to cede authority in this area to the Department of Peacekeeping Operations. But it is far from clear whether UNDP will be able to meet the challenges of becoming more operational and integrated into immediate post-conflict peace-building operations. The issue of UN reform and humanitarian action is increasingly bogged down in bureaucratic turf wars and in a long-standing debate between developed and developing countries on questions of intervention and national sovereignty. Nevertheless, Schwartz saw investing greater capabilities in international organizations as a key tool for the United States for addressing future humanitarian catastrophes around the world in a multilateral context.

Not only does the United States not need to act alone in formulating such responses, but also it normally should not act alone. International institutions can be indispensable mechanisms for mounting effective humanitarian action. In addition, while the United States will often have to play a key role, it need not play a dominant role: witness the intervention response to the East Timor crisis in 1999. U.S. support was helpful in terms of military logistics, but the United States was relieved when Australia took the lead on the mission.

Within the U.S. government, moreover, policy coordination can proceed along informal as well as formal lines. The Clinton Administration used Presidential Decision Directives (PDDs) to promulgate presidential decisions about national security, and Schwartz discussed PPD 56, which dealt with managing complex contingency operations. He noted that the planning procedures of PDD 56 had not been formally invoked in every complex humanitarian crisis, but the processes embodied in that document operated nevertheless. According to Schwartz, formally invoking a planning process could, in some circumstances, impose elements of bureaucratic paperwork and distract from effectiveness. Also, bureaucratic dynamics can become disruptive. PDD 56 suggests that planning should be under the aegis of a functional office, and the regional offices within the U.S. Department of State and the NSC can be jealous and seek to guard their prerogatives. Planning can also pose diplomatic or security concerns if plans are leaked. Conversely, one can imagine a situation in which public revelation of a plan could also be useful in achieving a foreign policy objective.

The dynamics of crisis response described by Schwartz were echoed by Princeton Lyman, who has held leadership positions at the State Department in bureaus that are functional—refugees and international organizations—as well as regional (Africa). In his view, governmental humanitarian responses had been 'remarkably ad hoc' and often the product of bureaucratic rivalries. 'Very few decision-makers have all of the options,' he asserted. Lyman gave, as an example, his chairing of an informal inter-agency working group that sought to address a severe drought in Ethiopia in 1984 and 1985. In order to overcome reluctance by the NSC to aid the Mengistu regime, the working group organized a cross-border assistance effort from Sudan into Ethiopia to aid drought victims under the control of forces fighting the regime. While NGOs had used such an approach before, this was an innovation for the UN, which has since become a well-established humanitarian option. In the mid-1980s, agency turf battles could be avoided through such creative methods. But this flexibility seems 'less possible today; it's more bureaucratic now,' according to Lyman.

Of course, a propensity for ad hoc approaches runs the risk of failing to appreciate what has worked in the past and what might work in the future. On the lack of institutional memory, Lyman cited the way policymakers apparently failed to embrace the safe-enclave option when Kosovar Albanians sought to enter Macedonia in 1999. A safe haven, such as the one established in northern Iraq in 1991, could have changed the situation on the ground. If declared, conceivably Serbian forces would have held back, and the potentially devastating influx into Macedonia could have been averted through an arrangement to protect and assist the Albanians in Kosovo proper. But humanitarians have been wary of safe enclaves ever since the Bosnian city of Srebrenica was overrun in 1995. Faced with the influx, Macedonia closed its border to asylum seekers, and an extraordinary refugee relocation program was undertaken by North Atlantic Treaty Organization (NATO) countries. Similar experiences of relocating asylum seekers from Haiti and Indo-China could have helped guide policymakers to understand the political implications of this extraordinary resettlement effort. The controversial proposal, quickly withdrawn, to keep Kosovars at the Guantanamo Bay U.S. naval base in Cuba was another product of the failure to appreciate fully prior political ramifications relating to refugee policy responses. The prospect of images of Kosovars in a U.S. military compound behind barbed wire repulsed humanitarians within the Clinton Administration.

Knowing what has worked and what could be refined and used to respond to a future crisis could be quite valuable, in the estimation of Lyman, who also underscored the importance of seeing international organizations as important adjuncts in humanitarian action. He advocated an annotated policy toolbox, which would be useful for the next U.S. presidential administration.

The new political leadership in the United States is supported by permanent staff that functions effectively as an institutional memory, particularly in the refugee bureau of the State Department, according to Julia Taft, a self-described operational person, who headed that bureau during the second Clinton Administration. But this will not necessarily be true in the regional bureaus, she noted, nor at the Agency for International Development (AID). Taft reports only one person remains at AID's Office of Foreign Disaster Assistance—which Taft characterized as a 'revolving door'—since she headed it from1986–89. AID's Office of Transition Initiatives is entirely new and did not even exist when she was there. A toolbox that surveyed the international machinery, including non-governmental organizations (NGOs) and international organizations, as well as their respective capacities would be 'a great reminder' as policymakers confront humanitarian crises in the future.

For example, in Taft's view, the experience in northern Iraq indicated that safe havens, while rare, should be promoted under appropriate circumstances. In addition, refugee camp insecurity has bedeviled arrangements from Goma to West Timor over the past decade and the efforts to respond to this persistent problem should be cataloged. 'We need a principles guide for donors,' she said, urging the creation of a reference guide setting out the best ways to deal with such crises. Such a guide would promote coordination and be an invaluable resource for new policymakers coming onto the scene. Taft felt certain that the new Bush Administration would retain a significant function at the NSC on humanitarian issues. She noted that her colleagues in the regional bureaus covering the Balkans and East Timor are grateful to this day for her bureau's efforts. The reason is basic: in her view, the end of the cold war had fundamentally changed perspectives and expectations. Humanitarian action is deeply political and now firmly part of the new national agenda. There is no choice: 'It will have to exist. And this is some of the hardest stuff in the world to do.'

My conversation with Schwartz in December 2000 turned, as one might have predicted at the end of a presidential Administration, to prospects and possibilities. The White House mess, where we had breakfast that day, was crowded and there was a buzz of conversation. Occasionally, I could overhear a reference to the U.S. Supreme Court argument, scheduled later that morning, concerning the legality of a recount ordered by the Florida Supreme Court in the disputed presidential election between George W.

Bush and Al Gore. But our world seemed strangely insulated from this political controversy, and more enduring.

We hurriedly finished our breakfast in time for Schwartz to return to his office and participate in an 8:30 a.m. conference call on UN arrears owed by the United States for peacekeeping operations. I departed, leaving him to conduct his business at the end of the Clinton Administration on that cold and dreary December morning, wondering who would be the workers in the next administration who would reach for a refugee policy toolbox.

As of May 2001, after the first 100 days of the Administration of George W. Bush, the question remained unanswered. The size of the NSC contingent working on multilateral and humanitarian issues had been reduced to an Acting Senior Director and four professionals, all career personnel. The reduction in size of the office is reflective of a general reduction in NSC staff and an approach designed to decentralize operational decision making. The NSC's role is to broker inter-agency disputes and fill the gaps in governmental structures in this Executive Branch. Political appointments have been made at the NSC and are on the horizon at the State Department.

Following the issuance of National Security Presidential Directive 1, two directly relevant policy coordinating committees were set up at the Under-Secretary/Assistant Secretary level. One committee, Democracy, Human Rights, and International Operations, is to be chaired by the NSC and will be responsible for rapid-onset humanitarian emergencies. The other, International Development and Humanitarian Assistance, is to be chaired by the State Department and will be responsible for longer-term development and humanitarian relief issues. This structure could be seen as seeking to formalize the type of inter-agency coordination that occurred during the 1999 Kosovo crisis. The regional policy coordinating committees are also likely to play important roles, as is the case with the humanitarian crisis in Afghanistan, given the customary regional emphasis in the foreign policy bureaucracy. While the new bureaucratic structure is largely untested, the humanitarian crisis in Afghanistan in late 2001 has presented an early challenge.

I. ORGANIZING HUMANITARIAN POLICY

If asked to design from ground zero an institutional structure for delivery of our civilian humanitarian assistance, few would come up with our current structure. From a January 2000 Executive Branch review of humanitarian assistance programs, the past decade has presented a series of new challenges to U.S. decision-makers as they have tried to organize responses to global refugee emergencies, denominated as complex contingency operations in the bureaucratic language of the Executive Branch. These challenges resulted in a series of dilemmas which were addressed in the Clinton Administration by three Presidential Decision Directives, issued to provide guidance to U.S. government agencies and departments involved in such operations. Such directives are customarily reviewed by an incoming administration, which may or may not decide to retain them as guidance.

No single inter-agency forum in the U.S. government formulates international humanitarian policy. By default, the White House—NSC—plays a coordination role; indeed, in the words of a senior NSC official in the Clinton Administration, at times 'too great of a coordination role.' A presidential directive was considered but not issued on international migration policy. According to this same NSC official, the lack of attention to this substantive issue is simply another example of urgent matters precluding attention to important matters. Nevertheless, the considerations that animated the issuance of three Presidential Decision Directives on humanitarian operations over the past decade are enduring, and they thus merit discussion here.

II. EXECUTIVE BRANCH

The proliferation of peacekeeping deployments at the end of the Cold War, coupled with the misadventure in Somalia, prompted an inter-agency review in 1993 by the Clinton Administration of US peacekeeping policies and programs. This review resulted in a 1994 Presidential Decision Directive—PDD 25—which sought to improve the way the U.S. government manages and coordinates such operations in a multilateral context. A public White Paper summarizes the rationale for PDD 25. [1]

During the Cold War, the UN could resort to multilateral peace operations only in the few cases when the interests of the Soviet Union and the West did not conflict. In the new strategic environment such operations can serve more often as a cost-effective tool to advance American as well as collective interests in maintaining peace in key regions and create global burden-sharing for peace.

Territorial disputes, armed ethnic conflicts, civil wars (many of which can spill across international borders), and the collapse of governmental authority in some states are among the current threats to peace. While many of these conflicts may not directly threaten American interests, their cumulative effect is significant.

The White Paper specifically identifies what value is added by working

[1] White House White Paper: Reforming Multilateral Peace Operations, *The Clinton Administration's Policy on Reforming Multilateral Peace Operations*, (May 1994), *available at* http://library.whitehouse.gov/WH/EOP/NSC/html/documents/NSCDoc1.html.

collectively in such operations: UN and other multilateral peace operations will at times offer the best way to prevent, contain, or resolve conflicts that could otherwise be more costly and deadly. In such cases, the U.S. benefits from having to bear only a portion of the burden. We also benefit by being able to invoke the voice of the community of nations on behalf of a cause we support. Thus, the establishment of a capability to conduct multilateral peace operations is part of our National Security Strategy and National Military Strategy.

Building on the intervening experiences of military and civilian deployments in Haiti and the former Yugoslavia, a further Presidential Decision Directive—PDD 56—concerning the management of such 'complex contingency operations' was issued in May 1997.[2] Its rationale is detailed in another public White Paper:[3]

> In the wake of the Cold War, attention has focused on a rising number of territorial disputes, armed ethnic conflicts, and civil wars that pose threats to regional and international peace and may be accompanied by natural or manmade disasters which precipitate massive human suffering. We have learned that effective responses to the situations may require multidimensional operations composed of such components as political/ diplomatic, humanitarian, intelligence, economic development, and security: hence the term complex contingency operations.[4]

PDD 56 also requires that a political-military implementation plan be developed for each operation. The plan is to include a comprehensive situation assessment, mission statement, agency objectives, and the desired end state. An after action review involving those who participated in or monitored the operation is to be prepared at the conclusion of each mission.

Following the experience of the deployment of NATO forces in Kosovo, another Presidential Decision Directive—PDD 71—was issued in February 2000 to strengthen criminal justice systems in support of complex peace operations. While rule of law issues have been implicated in humanitarian operations throughout the decade, from Cambodia onwards, the stark situation of impunity in Kosovo in late 1999 gave impetus to this new policy review. PDD 71 surveys an array of existing U.S. government initiatives, focusing on rule of law issues, and seeks to deal with issues of international civilian police, development facilitate inter-agency cooperation of indigenous police forces, and the establishment of justice systems in transitional settings.

[2] White House, White Paper: Managing Complex Contingency Operations, *The Clinton Administration's Policy on Managing Complex Contingency Operations*, (May 1997). *available at* http://library.whitehouse.gov/WH/EOP/NSC/html/documents/ NSCDoc2.html.

[3] *Id.* at *1.

[4] *Id.* at *12.

III. THE BUREAUCRATIC ARCHITECTURE OF U.S. RESPONSES

Below the presidential realm in the U.S. government, there is a complicated administrative framework that deals with forced migration emergencies. There are two broad categories of agency actors. One set of activities deals with refugee protection, resettlement, and asylum, principally undertaken by the State Department and the Justice Department's Immigration and Naturalization Service. The other broad category of agency actors—namely, USAID's Bureau for Humanitarian Response and Office of Foreign Disaster Assistance—deals with humanitarian assistance. The NSC provides the mechanism at the presidential level to bring both sets of actors together for coordination in complex humanitarian emergencies, including to identify the contribution that the military may be uniquely situated to provide, for example by airlifting large quantities of relief supplies. Together, the combined budgets of these U.S. government offices total upwards of two billion dollars annually.

The main offices in the State Department that deal with migration-related humanitarian operations are the Bureau of Population, Refugees and Migration (PRM), established originally in 1980, which offers assistance to refugees and conflict victims primarily by providing funding through multilateral international organizations like the United Nations High Commissioner for Refugees (UNHCR) or the International Committee of the Red Cross (ICRC), and the Bureau for Democracy, Human Rights and Labor (DRL), which publishes annual country reports on human rights conditions that can address refugee issues.

At the AID, the Bureau for Humanitarian Response serves as a focal point for the development of humanitarian policy. USAID's Office of U.S. Foreign Disaster Assistance (OFDA) provides urgent humanitarian assistance as well as undertakes prevention, mitigation, and preparedness activities in cases of natural or human-made disasters abroad. OFDA's usually provides assistance in the form of grants to NGOs or international organizations and addresses population displacements in the context of disasters. USAID's Office of Food for Peace (FFP) provides food assistance in crises through the World Food Programme and other agencies; its Office of Transition Initiatives (OTI) focuses on assisting the return to normal governance and development of capacities in countries that have been driven by crisis.

The legislative framework for complex humanitarian operations has evolved over the past forty years. In particular, the Migration and Refugee 236 *Reaction and Inattention* Assistance Act of 1962 (MRA) provides the basic authority for U.S. government assistance for refugees and migrants. The current annual budget for programs managed by PRM is approximately

$700 million.[5] Of this total, 70 percent goes to Overseas Assistance programs for refugees and migrants, channeled primarily through international agencies such as the UNHCR and ICRC.

The Foreign Assistance Act of 1961, which authorizes OFDA's activities, provides a general statutory framework for assisting displaced persons, with specific authority to assist disaster victims. Significant assistance may also be provided to displaced persons under Title II of the Agricultural Trade Development and Assistance Act of 1954, commonly referred to as P.L. 480 or the Food for Peace Act. Title II programs provide agricultural commodities to foreign countries to address famine, malnutrition, and the alleviation of hunger.

The culture of a bureaucracy clearly affects the quality of its work product. In terms of perceptions, humanitarian officers are often viewed by senior policymakers as technical implementers, and not as experts who should be present and heard when foreign policy is discussed and formulated. Humanitarian programs are seldom seen as policy instruments that require prior strategic analysis, contingency planning, and policy advocacy. Instead, emphasis is placed on the management of relations with operational partners, including NGOs. As a consequence, both within the State Department and USAID, humanitarians have relatively weak influence as compared with those in regional and even other functional bureaus.

This dynamic is not a new. Within the State Department and the NSC, regional perspectives predominate. In the words of a former senior NSC official involved in humanitarian affairs: 'Policy will always be regionally focused.' Functional offices such as PRM or the humanitarian directorate at the NSC normally react to regional initiatives and seek to ensure a measure of consistency in response. Internal tensions between functional and regional offices are often present in decision making in the foreign affairs bureaucracy.

While perhaps obvious, another important factor is the quality and stature of leadership. Competent and credible leadership adds weight to the advocacy of a policy option. Considerations are heard and listened to that might not otherwise have emerged from the debate. This awareness is a crucial matter that can make virtually all the difference in crafting humanitarian policy.

Bureaucratic biases are often intertwined with substantive considerations in Executive Branch decision-making on the issues. The political process often requires responses with short-term perspectives and an emphasis on

[5] Press Release, U.S. Committee for Refugees, Congress Approves $700 Million Budget for Refugee Aid,(Oct. 26, 2000), *available at* http://www.refugees.org/news/press_releases/2000/102600.htm. *See also* U.S. Department of State, *The Budget for Fiscal Year 2002*, 731–32, *available at* http://www.whitehouse.gov/omb/budget/fy2002/sta.pdf.

immediate responses. In the words of one seasoned bureaucrat, 'it is a luxury to ask the question: What is the best way to solve the problem?' Nevertheless, that is precisely the question that was posed in an interagency review of humanitarian activities completed at the end of the Clinton Administration in late 1999.

IV. THE JANUARY 2000 EXECUTIVE BRANCH HUMANITARIAN REVIEW

The Kosovo crisis in 1999 frightened U.S. officials. They had stared into an abyss and felt fortunate that a victory had been snatched from the jaws of a potential quagmire. Among the lessons they learned from the emergency was the importance of considering humanitarian dimensions in military and political planning. When the crisis had ended and the vast majority of Kosovars had returned, the Clinton Administration initiated an Interagency Review of U.S. Government Civilian Humanitarian and Transition Programs.[6]

The basic objective was to encourage a more coherent policy and unified leadership in such situations. A wide range of options was considered, and three broad approaches emerged in the review. But no decision on the options was taken during Clinton's tenure and, while the report has no status in the new Bush Administration, the issues are endemic. For that reason, the substance of the report remains highly relevant.

The Interagency Review report, which was initiated by Morton H. Halperin, then Director of Policy Planning at the State Department, characterizes the current administrative architecture as '[a] less than logical structure, with unclear lines of accountability.'[7] 'Overlapping bureaucratic mandates' and 'duplication of effort' are particularly noted in the report.[8] In extraordinary circumstances, such as the humanitarian crises relating to Hurricane Mitch or Kosovo, high-level political appointees become involved in decision-making. Otherwise, such crises are normally handled by officials below sub-cabinet rank who interact without assignment of lead responsibility or formal coordination procedures. The review made recommendations on humanitarian and transition assistance policy and identified organizational options for making this assistance most effective.

The rationale for the review is articulated as follows: Since the end of the Cold War, the foreign policy stakes of U.S. civilian humanitarian programs have risen significantly, driven by profound changes in the complex crises

[6] U.S. Department of State, *Interagency Review of U.S. Government Civilian Humanitarian & Transition Programs* (January 2000), *available at* http://www.gwu.edu/~nsarchiv/NSAEBB/NSAEBB30.

[7] *Id.* at 10.

[8] *Id.* at 4.

themselves and the prominent place these now occupy in our overall foreign policy. The humanitarian factor has become central to senior policymakers' deliberations over U.S. foreign policy priorities and possible diplomatic, economic, or military interventions to ease crises and facilitate humanitarian relief.

As our global humanitarian interests have become more complex and vital to our national policy, the need has grown for the USG [United States Government] to have unified, coherent humanitarian leadership. This need does not imply that humanitarian considerations will or should dictate foreign policy outcomes. Rather, USG leadership is needed to guarantee that humanitarian considerations are present and an active force within the foreign policy-making process. As we have witnessed in Rwanda, Bosnia, Kosovo, Timor, Sudan, and elsewhere, major foreign policy challenges typically feature, at their very center, complex humanitarian emergencies that demand coherence in our policy responses.[9]

The review report noted significant gaps in program capacity to deal with issues such as internal exiles, and framed the problem in the following terms:

Our humanitarian achievements notwithstanding, we can and should do better to empower the humanitarian agenda and overcome the fragmentation of USG humanitarian affairs. Internal conflict victims now figure as a major and growing humanitarian challenge, yet they have traditionally been a secondary or indirect priority for both State and USAID. Neither agency has a clearheaded responsibility for addressing this humanitarian problem, even though it now exceeds that posed by refugees . . . Increasingly, complex emergencies generate a complex mixture of refugees and internally displaced. However, neither [USAID's Bureau for Humanitarian Response] natural disaster competencies and primarily bilateral response nor PRM's multilateral emphasis and refugee response provide the basis for a comprehensive approach. . .[10]

Overall, the current split between State and USAID's civilian emergency programs has impeded coherent leadership on humanitarian issues, domestically and abroad, and complicated the coordination of civilian and military humanitarian efforts. The humanitarian voice in Senior USG policy-making has often been absent at critical moments, such that the humanitarian implications of political-military choices in crisis situations do not receive adequate consideration. Overlapping bureaucratic mandates

[9] *Id.* at 3.

[10] The absence of overall policy and of a lead office on issues of internal displacement was again recognized in August 2001 in a report of the U.S. General Accounting Office. There are six offices within the State Department and USAID that directly assist internally dis-placed persons, plus several other agencies and offices involved in related functions. *See* U.S. General Accounting Office, *Internally Displaced Persons Lack Effective Protection*, GAO-01-803 (Aug. 2001), at 30.

and duplication of effort hinder both the operational efficiency of our humanitarian programs, especially with respect to internally displaced persons, and the inter-linkage of programs.

> . . . [T]he central aim of creating unified leadership is to strengthen consideration of the humanitarian implications of political-military choices in crisis situations, including the mandate and role of external military interventions. This essential step will not, it must be said, necessarily guarantee there is always adequate high-level political will to take the appropriate political-military decisions necessary to advance USG humanitarian interests. Ultimate decision responsibility rests with political authorities above the officials who manage our humanitarian programs. This reality notwithstanding, our top political authorities will be far better equipped to reach decisions that must advance US humanitarian interests when they are served by unified humanitarian leadership.[11]

The review concluded that: 'The current structure results in less than coherent leadership on complex humanitarian issues in our foreign policy making process.'[12]

We do achieve effective operational coordination, but only through significant effort in a context of continued mandate overlap and some duplication of effort. We do not optimally leverage our humanitarian influence abroad, in proportion to the level of effort and resources expended and the general prestige attached to our programs.

There is inadequate interlinkage among emergency, transitional, and development programs. The report is succinct in its ultimate assessment: Given these conclusions, the present status quo is not an optimal basis for promoting U.S. humanitarian interests. We can and should do better.[13]

The report identifies three approaches to enhance U.S. leadership in humanitarian action. The review report's first option, called by one State Department official the 'can't we all live together better?' variant, calls for closer consultation, communication, and cooperation. Formally denominated as discrete measures, this option would call for the creation of a senior humanitarian policy seat at NSC meetings and a joint State–USAID Policy and Planning Task Force. Collaboration in training and evaluation activities is advocated, as is outreach to Congress and the media. These efforts would be undertaken within the existing structures. One legacy of the U.S. response to the Kosovo crisis is that this collaboration may already be happening to some extent. However, the Interagency Review sounds a note of caution:

Since this approach works within the current division of responsibility between State and USAID, it does not answer the question of each respon-

[11] U.S. Department of State, *supra* note 6, at 3.
[12] *Id.* at 4.
[13] *Id.* at 3–5.

sibility or eliminate overlapping mandates and duplication of effort and may even increase duplication.[14]

The second approach, called by the same State Department official the 'who is in charge?' option, is a designated lead agency model. In each emergency situation, a particular agency would be designated to manage and coordinate the response. The method of designation is the subject of an additional array of choices. One variation is based on the current system, in which the USAID Administrator, who is also the President's Special Coordinator for International Disaster Assistance, would make the decision. While this is the current arrangement, it has not been implemented in practice.

This choice, therefore, would be to strengthen the role of the USAID Administrator in order to make this approach real.

Another proposal is for the designation to be made on a case-by-case basis with the National Security Council serving as the mechanism, subject to the Secretary of State's ultimate direction, for choosing the lead agency depending upon the character of the emergency and the relative advantages of the agency in question.

A further option would be to promulgate in advance a rule for decision making, with PRM taking the lead in complex humanitarian emergencies, and USAID's Bureau for Humanitarian Response addressing natural disasters such as famines or floods, unless the Secretary of State decides that a higher leadership level is warranted in a particular case. Of course, an overall coordinator for the U.S. government humanitarian response could be named by the president in exceptional cases. Consultation with Congress would be required, but no modification of statutory authorities would be necessary. Each of these choices would be accompanied by the creation of a senior humanitarian advisory council.

In comparing the last two options—case-by-case or by-rule designations of the lead agency—a case-by-case approach might act as a disincentive for U.S. government agencies to develop their own specialized comparative advantage because they would never be sure on what basis they would be chosen to act as the lead. A rule-based approach in advance, on the other hand, might encourage pre-designated agencies to enhance planning capacities.

A third variant identified in the Interagency Review is the administrative consolidation of U.S. government humanitarian activities. This outcome would clearly require legislation. One institution and one senior official would be accountable. The function could be located in one of three places: within the State Department, within the Agency for International Development, or in a separate foreign affairs agency reporting to the Secretary of State. As the review explains:

[14] *Id.* at 13.

Central to deciding among the three possibilities is what priority is attached to competing policy goals: to integrate humanitarian affairs into foreign policy; to create an empowered single-focus humanitarian entity; and to integrate relief, transition and development assistance.[15]

Situating the function in the State Department would promote humanitarian and foreign policy integration. Refugee situations are caused by political situations and are often linked to political solutions. If USAID were the location, this would encourage the integration of relief and development perspectives. This integration could address the customary gap between emergency response and longer-term development. A separate office would enhance the focus—as well as, perhaps, promote the marginalization—of humanitarian policy formulation. No consensus was reached in the review on which option to recommend to the Secretary of State. In any event, the humanitarian review came too late in the Clinton Administration to result in reform. The problem of bureaucratic fragmentation thus remains to be unearthed again in future crises.

V. THE POLITICS OF BUREAUCRATIC REFORM

The State Department's Bureau of Population, Refugees, and Migration can be seen as a guardian of humanitarian sensibilities that can foresee problems coming in the formulation of foreign policy initiatives within the State Department. As a senior humanitarian official at the State Department who served in the Clinton Administration explained, 'AID is never involved in these questions. As a different agency, they never find out soon enough.' Some would also question whether there would be a loss of leverage in multilateral relations by removing the $700 million budget from the State 242 *Reaction and Inattention* Department, arguing this would likely serve to dissociate the funding from foreign policy goals.

'AID does not take direction from State,' said Julia Taft, who characterized the provision of humanitarian assistance as 'the human face of foreign policy.' To buttress this point, she cited several conversations with foreign ministers of donor countries who longed for a budget, which was situated in the development bureaucracy of their country, to implement humanitarian policy. Moreover, she noted, somewhat ruefully, that 'NGOs do not want to be stuck with just one interlocutor.' They like to shop among different policy and funding entities, whether it is AID, NSC, or the State Department.

A contrary position has been taken by J. Brian Atwood, former Administrator of USAID during the Clinton Administration, who recommended in connection with the 1999 humanitarian review that relief

[15] *Id.* at 14.

assistance be consolidated and located at AID in order to encourage consideration of development impacts and perspectives. Atwood sees such an outcome as a step toward the organization of a cabinet-level agency on development and humanitarian responses, which he proposed after leaving government in 2000.

During much of the Clinton Administration, USAID was fending off a proposed merger of the State Department and USAID advocated by U.S. Senator Jesse Helms.[16] For USAID, therefore, the issue is one of institutional survival, in the words of a former AID staff member. The reform question is necessarily very political as it involves an agency that is in a struggle for its life.

For instance, the establishment of the OTI could be seen as an effort to become more relevant in an era of diminished resources for development and in the course of the tussle with Congress over the fate of the agency. USAID, recognizing the attraction of an integrated approach to economic, political, and social rehabilitation in post-conflict situations, established OTI as a response to working in countries emerging from conflict. Located in the Bureau for Humanitarian Response, OTI has been featured in U.S. government responses in many post-conflict situations, such as Angola, Bosnia, Guatemala, Haiti, Liberia, Rwanda, Sierra Leone, and more recently in Colombia and Nigeria.

A former AID official noted the 'politicization of humanitarian assistance,' with increasing involvement by the White House—that is, the National Security Council—during the Clinton Administration in directing the day-to-day management of relief activities. She attributed this development in part to a post-cold war lack of conceptual clarity. Humanitarian assistance can be a relatively easy tool to employ in response to the political imperative to 'do something.'

The new administrator of USAID, Andrew Natsios, has a reputation for dynamism and candor. He testified at an April 2001 Senate hearing that the agency's 'career officers are demoralized and frustrated' and that efforts to reform AID have been 'too slow, and neither innovative nor sweeping enough to get the job done.'[17] He made a pledge: 'things are going to change.'[18] Natsios, who worked at AID from 1989 to 1993, is familiar with military and civilian humanitarian issues, and he sees the return of refugees and displaced persons as an essential objective of the agency's work in post-conflict situations. But whether his energetic expressions of intention will translate into broader bureaucratic reform remains to be seen.

[16] Republican, North Carolina.

[17] Andrew S. Natsios, *Statement before the U.S. Senate Committee on Foreign Relations* (Apr. 25, 2001). *at* http://www.usaid.gov/press/spe_test/testimony/2001/an_conf_stmt.html.

[18] *Id.*

For Mort Halperin, the initiator of the 1999 review, it is less important which institutional arrangement is chosen. Indeed, he suggested that a single official could wear dual agency hats and be housed in one of the agencies. The most important point is that just one person is responsible. When humanitarian crises emerge, 'no one knows who is in charge,' he concluded. Nevertheless, Halperin leans toward consolidation within AID in order to retain the speed of bureaucratic responses to crisis and to avoid the cumbersome clearance processes that operate within the State Department. Halperin noted that, ironically, AID's assistance is often more closely linked to foreign policy objectives as it is deployed through NGOs at the behest of U.S. ambassadors in embassies abroad, while PRM's funding is mostly given through multilateral channels that are somewhat more insulated from U.S. political direction.

VI. A PROPOSAL FOR A NEW U.S. AGENCY FOR HUMANITARIAN ACTION (AHA)

Recent experiences, particularly the Kosovo crisis, have pushed the humanitarian components in the U.S. government to work together more closely, including through information exchange and a greater degree of joint engagement in the planning, implementation, and evaluation of programs. But much more needs to be done to improve the coherence of U.S. government responses to humanitarian and refugee emergencies. This effort would include such matters as designing protection strategies for internal exiles or improving the capacity to deploy rule-of-law expertise in post-crisis situations. A place is needed to forge and collect the new conceptual tools to deal with new forms of humanitarian action. These activities are not handled adequately in the current structure.

The 1999 inter-agency humanitarian review pointed to three ways to organize U.S. responses more effectively, but no consensus was achieved in the deliberations in terms of the direction of bureaucratic reform, leaving the location of the function: (1) within the State Department in order to relate humanitarian considerations to foreign policy objectives; (2) within USAID to relate the considerations to longer-term development strategies; or (3) in a separate agency reporting to the Secretary of State.

Given the continued fragmentation in the governmental structures for humanitarian responses, fundamental reform is warranted. In particular, a new separate civilian agency reporting to the Secretary of State, here called the Agency for Humanitarian Action (AHA), should be created to discharge U.S. government functions in this field. This proposed agency, foreshadowed in the 1999 humanitarian review discussed earlier, could retain appropriate linkages to foreign policy objectives by virtue of oversight by the Secretary of State. As it stands now, the policy preferences of regional bureaus at the State Department can smother the perspectives of a functional bureau like PRM, even with its substantial budget. Also, appropriate linkages between humanitarian action and development work could be retained as well through the Secretary's oversight of USAID. The arrangement would also preserve the comparative speed of crisis response that characterizes AID's work.

But the primary point is that just one entity and person would be in charge.[19] Location in an agency such as AHA could help profile the humanitarian voice in Executive Branch deliberations. The principal critique of the separate agency outcome—that distancing humanitarian issues from foreign policy and development imperatives might marginalize the humanitarian voice—could be remedied by ensuring that the person appointed to administer the new agency has political stature and relates closely to the Secretary of State and the President of the United States. The increasing importance of this area of governmental action in fashioning international humanitarian responses would justify the appointment of just such a person of stature. This person should also have deep expertise on the issues in order to relate humanitarian policy appropriately to diplomatic and developmental perspectives. The executive office of AHA should be physically located at the State Department to ensure a presence at key high-level meetings, as proximity is often half the battle in bureaucratic deliberations.

A further justification for the establishment of a new civilian agency is one that the 2000 humanitarian review simply did not address: the creation of an appropriate mechanism for civilian-military planning to respond to complex humanitarian emergencies. The U.S. military is a key player in foreign humanitarian and refugee operations. In 1999, the U.S. Department of Defense estimated that it expended 864,239 staff days on such operations.[20]

The overarching lesson from Kosovo was the recognition that humanitarian considerations have to be better integrated into military and political planning. But little has been done to realize this received wisdom, and there is a growing recognition that there will be more of these kinds of operations over the next years. More capacity is needed within the U.S. government to plan to undertake them. This realization has recently prompted the new Bush Administration to consider organizing separate military forces and specialized headquarters units to handle humanitarian missions, such as refugee emergencies. The military would swiftly hand over operations to civilians and NGOs thirty days after being deployed. This would seek to

[19] The absence of budgetary and program authority was a fatal institutional weakness of the U.S. Coordinator for Refugee Affairs, a position that was created within the State Department in 1979 and abolished in 1993.

[20] U.S. General Accounting Office, Military Personnel: Full Extent of Support to Civil Authorities Unknown but Unlikely to Adversely Impact Retention (January 2001), at 7.

remedy a customary disjunction between the time when the military deploys in complex operations, the establishment of the basic security (often accompanied—if not preceded—by civilian humanitarian agencies providing immediate relief), and the time when activities are undertaken to provide policing, basic human security and the rudiments of law and order.

Experience teaches that more needs to be done, however, to strengthen headquarters structures in the U.S. military to relate to civilian humanitarians. The most ambitious outcome would be a dedicated headquarters structure for humanitarian and peace operations, including appropriate liaison relationships with NGOs. However, a new structure would have to overcome the current political and bureaucratic reluctance to see military capacities develop in this direction, including force structure and funding constraints, as well as congressional skepticism on the issue. But if a dedicated structure were created, it would become a bureaucratic advocate, seeking to maximize available budgetary resources. The development of the special operations and space commands are examples of such arrangements within the U.S. military.

A less dramatic, but perhaps somewhat more realistic, outcome would be to identify personnel in the planning and operations components of headquarters structures responsible for being the liaisons and points of contact for humanitarian operations. These personnel would be expected to remain knowledgeable about international organizational and NGO activities before, during, and after deployments in such situations. This is what retired U.S. Marine Corps General Anthony C. Zinni, who oversaw military force deployments in northern Iraq and Somalia, calls a virtual organization in headquarters, meaning one that exists on paper and that can be activated to deal with an emergency situation. One weakness in such an approach is that this function could be crowded out by the perceptions and realities of other priorities.

Any integrated civilian and military mechanism to plan and implement programs of reconstruction and rehabilitation in post-crisis settings could involve international institutions, such as the United Nations at the universal level, or the European Union (EU), NATO, or OSCE at the regional level. But as U.S. Army retired General George Joulwan has noted, the U.S. government needs an internal capacity as well to plan such transitional responses. 'There must be a better way of doing these things,' he said. Joulwan, who commanded U.S. military deployments in Bosnia and Rwanda, has seen many instances of lack of coordination and cooperation between the civilian and military sectors. As a result, he urges that a joint military and civilian mechanism be created to plan for crisis responses involving the United States, which is a possible function for the new AHA that could provide an authority to interrelate military and humanitarian perspectives.

The military is familiar with operational coordinating mechanisms such as Civil Military Operation Centers. But this broader humanitarian coordination function should not be situated within the military. Many NGOs will be understandably wary of close involvements with the military, and vice versa. AHA would thus be an appropriate integrated civilian umbrella to associate those NGOs that are willing, or could be persuaded, to engage with the military in crisis management planning.

The Administration of George W. Bush will inevitably confront the need to mount responses to refugee emergencies, and the new cadre of officials would be well advised in advance to address the question of the optimal agency architecture to provide adequate humanitarian responses. To fail to address the issue will simply condemn the bureaucracy to repeat the mistakes and inefficiencies of the past. And such an outcome would have profound human costs. Bureaucratic delay in this area translates into loss of life and terrible hardships.

Ultimately, the value of such anticipatory planning efforts will have to be demonstrated in the real world. But lack of preparedness is not a defensible *Reaction and Inattention* 247 option. Rather, it is itself a decision to disfavor involvement. As General John Abizaid of the U.S. Army warned when I met with him in Germany in 2000, 'muddling through is not good enough.' The ultimate truth is simple: the U.S. government needs more capacity to plan comprehensively for effective humanitarian action.

VII. A FIRST TASK: CONTRIBUTING TO RULE OF LAW INITIATIVES IN POST-CRISIS SETTINGS

An obvious place for AHA to start its work is to assemble the currently fragmented efforts within the U.S. government to deal with threshold issues of human security and refugee return in post-conflict settings. These problems are at the international level, discussed later in this book, but they also pose a policy coordination challenge within the U.S. government.

The February 2000 White Paper relating to Presidential Decision Directive 71 recounts relevant recent experiences: In Somalia, for example, the police simply left their posts in 1991 when a new government failed to emerge after the Siad Barre government was deposed. In Haiti and Bosnia, the police were involved in the conflict and consequently were viewed as biased combatants rather than public servants by large segments of the population. Even before the conflict arose, the public safety forces in Haiti, as in many areas where peace operations are conducted, were the primary instrument for state sponsored repression of the citizens.[21]

[21] Presidential Decision Directive 71, Strengthening Criminal Justice Systems in Support of

PDD 71 was premised on the notion that indigenous law enforcement and criminal justice frameworks are a prerequisite to achieving a sustainable peace in post-crisis situations. Among the U.S. national interests in the establishment of a workable rudimentary justice system are the successful completion of peace operations and the deterrence of criminal activities. As the White Paper notes, '. . . such wrongdoers often include organizers of terrorism, illicit drug and arms trafficking, and international criminal syndicates.' Finding a workable methodology for disengagement is viewed by many in the Executive Branch as a prerequisite to undertaking such military humanitarian deployments in the future. The new focus on addressing a bundle of these basic rule-of-law issues early in a post-conflict setting may provide such a methodology.

The political and military plan developed in each operation is to address public safety and the restoration of the criminal justice system. The process currently used to recruit, train, and deploy civilian police officers in such operations is not adequate, and there is a need to improve the speed of deployment as well as to enhance the discipline and accountability of those deployed.

The Office of International Narcotics and Law Enforcement (INL) in the State Department is to take the lead on these issues. As the White Paper explains:

> This office shall be responsible for policy development, all aspects of provision and oversight of US CIVPOL [civilian police] to field operations, development and implementation of training and technical assistance plans and programs for foreign police forces, and priority setting and coordination among other US activities relating to the criminal justice system, among other tasks.[22]

INL has a budget of ten million dollars for Fiscal Year 2001 to organize a 2000-person standing roster of civilian police[23] and is hiring staff to develop training for police candidates and reach out to local police authorities to facilitate recruiting. As of August 2001, no political decision had been made on how to establish the US CIVPOL program on a permanent basis, and discussions are ongoing between the State Department and the Department of Justice on these issues. USAID's Center for Democracy and Governance focuses on the justice system issues, which a State Department official characterized as much more complex.

Apart from the capacity to train and develop foreign police forces, arrangements are needed as well to develop assistance in judicial and penal matters. In the words of the White Paper:

Peace Operations 1 (February 2000),, *at* http://www.fas.org/irp/offdocs/pdd/pdd-71-4.htm [hereinafter White Paper on the Clinton Administration's Policy].

[22] *Id.* at 3.

[23] In 2001, approximately one million dollars a week was being spent on the U.S. CIVPOL contingent in Kosovo.

When such systems break down or are destroyed, the damage is felt in a variety of ways, ranging from economic interests, to humanitarian concerns, to the physical safety of American citizens. We must therefore continue to expand and improve cooperation and development activities with other countries, especially those emerging from periods of instability where havens of criminal impunity might otherwise develop.[24]

The White Paper specifically recognizes the value of a multilateral approach to build such capacities:

. . . U.S. government capabilities should not become the international community's instrument of first resort whenever CIVPOL-related requirements arise. Many other countries and organizations have similar interests and responsibilities and should share the burden of these activities. Therefore, the US government shall seek to enhance the capacities of non-US entities including those of other countries, international organizations, and non-governmental organizations.[25]

The PDD 71 White Paper refers specifically to constabulary forces and paramilitary forces present in other countries to conduct crowd control and basic law and order functions and to the expertise of the United Nations as well as the OSCE in Europe in the deployment of international police. The White Paper emphasizes that, in general, civilian police are not to exercise executive authority except in exceptional circumstances such as Kosovo and East Timor where the international community is responsible for the administration of a territory.[26]

PDD 71 is in effect the product of a survey of current U.S. government local capacity building efforts that are highly relevant to the management of forced migration emergencies. It seeks to address the public security gap by enhancing U.S. capabilities to recruit, train, and deploy police officers and to provide the necessary criminal justice resources. The directive reflects the notion that a discrete set of measures designed to enhance the rule of law can promote normality and refugee repatriation preliminary and can facilitate the much more ambitious objectives of reviving economies, rehabilitating societies, or building Western-style democracies. These justice system issues are a discrete package of human security elements in the context of a much more complex and long-term endeavor that would ultimately require greater indigenous support and participation to succeed in fostering the rule of law.

A more coherent structure within the U.S. government, such as AHA, to address such problems in the future would facilitate the development of doctrine and mechanisms at the national level. This structure could be the first step toward contributing most usefully to a model rule of law service

[24] White Paper on the Clinton Administration's Policy, *supra* note 21, at 5.
[25] *Id.* at 6.
[26] *Id.* at 10.

package to be assembled under a framework of international standards for deployment in post-crisis situations.

A cautionary note, however, is in order. Having been involved in efforts to build the capacity of legal systems in Bosnia, Haiti, and Rwanda, Ian Martin (who oversaw UN efforts in these places), expresses concern about the poor performance of bilateral donors in building criminal justice institutions. They are, in his words, 'badly coordinated.' Donors concoct projects with no real idea about the justice system in the country in question. 'No one does it well,' he said ruefully. Oftentimes, the bilateral donors are influenced mainly by their own judicial systems. There simply is no forum for international policy coordination—a possible role for the intergovernmental mechanism for Strategic Humanitarian Action and Research (SHARE) described in this book.

VIII. CONGRESS

The complexities of the U.S. legislative process have produced reams of scholarship and commentary, although relatively little has been written in terms of Congress and the formulation and implementation of U.S. government humanitarian responses. How the process is organized, however, may not be the most salient factor. Senior congressional staffers on both the Democrat and Republican sides emphasized that perhaps the most significant considerations are the 'politics and personalities involved.' Notably, just how few staff persons, a mere handful, addressed refugee issues in Congress. Nor is there any single member who has made generic humanitarian action his or her top issue currently. Thus, refugees in general do not have what can serve as a powerful engine for action: a congressional champion. Nevertheless, certain dynamics and trends are discernible.

The manner in which the U.S. government responds to international refugee emergencies is shaped at least to some extent by how Congress is organized in relation to the Executive Branch. This relationship concerns funding and policy oversight. 'We are concerned with the bottom line, not the details of policy,' explained one senior Democratic staffer. The committee structures of Congress in some ways mirror the work of the foreign policy bureaucracy in the Executive Branch. In other respects, the interface is less obvious.

Like many policy areas, several congressional committees deal with refugee issues. In terms of substantive policy oversight, where the admission of refugees to the United States from abroad is concerned, the House Committee on the Judiciary, particularly the Subcommittee on Immigration and Claims, has jurisdiction. On the Senate side, the Subcommittee on Immigration of the Committee on the Judiciary has responsibility. These involvements flow from the fact that those committees oversee the Immigration and Naturalization Service, a sub-agency within the Department of Justice, which implements refugee admissions programs under U.S. immigration law. International refugee protection policy, however, implicates other sets of legislative actors.

Where the international response involves humanitarian relief, on either a multilateral or a bilateral basis, the congressional committees overseeing foreign policy and international development have jurisdiction. In the House of Representatives, this is the Committee on International Relations, notably the Subcommittee on International Operations and Human Rights. On the Senate side, it is the Committee on Foreign Relations, particularly the Subcommittee on International Operations. These committees relate directly to the work of the State Department and the USAID. However, as in the Executive Branch, since the staff of the International Operations subcommittees are oriented more around regions than functions, thematic issues such as refugees can receive relatively low priority.

Sometimes international financial institutions seek to address funding issues in post-conflict reconstruction and rehabilitation efforts. In these instances, the House Committee on Banking and Financial Services and the Senate Committee on Banking, Housing and Urban Affairs are interested.

When a military deployment is an aspect of a U.S. government response to a humanitarian crisis, then the House Armed Services Committee and the Senate Armed Services Committee have substantive policy oversight. Recent experience suggests that the Armed Services committees have little interest in refugee issues, and they have exhibited a bias against the military's preparation for and participation in refugee-related missions. This participation has been referred to somewhat derisively as nation building since the 1993 withdrawal of US forces from Somalia. This hostility stems from a variety of causes, including the drain on defense resources, which is a persistent complaint voiced by some military leaders and their supporters in Congress. In recent times, the committees' deliberations have reflected the reluctance of the Pentagon to have the U.S. military become engaged in nontraditional humanitarian activities, such as peacekeeping or peace-building operations, for which the record has been mixed.

Aside from policy oversight, congressional committees also are deeply involved in funding the responses to international refugee emergencies. Indeed, as one senior Republican staffer noted, funding appropriators are often more important to legislative outcomes than the policy authorizers in Congress, except perhaps when substantive committees with considerable political influence are involved, such as the Armed Services. As a foreign policy committee staffer bemoaned in relation to the dynamics of Executive Branch and congressional Appropriations Committee negotiations, "They try to pretty much ignore us.'

Refugee issues are often considered somewhat obscure and they frequently arise episodically, thus falling between the cracks even for policy authorizers. This obscurity is compounded by the fact that refugee issues in broad terms have not had congressional advocates in recent times. More often, particular ethnic groups have been championed, according to one senior Democratic staffer involved in appropriations. His explanation was pointed, 'There is no real political pay off at home.' As a result, there is no incentive to develop expertise on refugee issues and provide a counterweight to the Executive Branch. Nevertheless, in general terms, refugee programs have done 'better than most,' said this staffer, noting both Democrats and Republicans like humanitarian aid more than long-term development aid.

Refugee-related issues frequently end up being raised as reactions to administration initiatives. Also, because there was not much consensus over the substance of foreign policy during the Clinton Administration, Congress focused its energy on considering the annual budget, which is primarily the domain of the funding appropriators. To the extent that refugee issues are embodied in budget considerations, the members and staff who are appropriators became the key actors.

In the House and Senate Committees on Appropriations, for example, a powerful Senator or Representative, or even a strong staffer on the Subcommittees on Commerce, Justice, State, and Judiciary or the Foreign Operations Subcommittees, can do more to shape a policy outcome than the committee responsible for substantive policy. The substantive authorizing committee has to take the initiative to prevail; as one Republican staffer puts it, 'we have to legislate.'

The dynamics of interactions between Congress and the Executive Branch in this policy area are illustrated by recent congressional efforts to grant U.S. resettlement to Vietnamese refugees. One of the signature modern events of refugee exodus concerned Indo-China after the end of the Vietnam War. The first refugees from Laos reached the Thai border in early 1975, followed shortly thereafter by Cambodians after Phnom Penh collapsed. The end of the Vietnam War in 1975 marked the beginning of a refugee emergency, which was characterized by a flotilla of boat people, brutal high-seas attacks by pirates, and summary rejection of asylum seekers as well as their harsh treatment in nearby countries in south-east Asia. The peak period for arrivals was between 1979 and 1981, when some 640,000 arrivals from Vietnam, Laos, and Cambodia were registered for asylum in countries in the region.[27]

An international conference in Geneva in 1979 sought to guarantee

[27] Minot, Michael, *Refugees from Cambodia, Laos and Vietnam, 1975–1993*, *in* THE CAMBRIDGE SURVEY OF WORLD MIGRATION 452 (Robin Coven ed., 1995).

reception for these arrivals in return for a promise of resettlement in the West, mainly in Australia, Canada, France, and United States. The United States then led one of the most generous resettlement programs of all time to rescue allies who had assisted the war effort. Over the next twenty years, more than 1.4 million Vietnamese were admitted to the United States; 900,000 gained entry into other countries.[28] An extraordinary pact was struck: countries of resettlement, notably the United States, would accept refugees in return for a guarantee that they would be permitted to land and stay in countries of asylum.

As the years passed, the need for the resettlement commitments by the United States and other countries was increasingly questioned. Some policy administrators were concerned that the admissions scheme had become a magnet for economic migrants instead of refugees with a fear of persecution. Forced return was introduced in 1989 under the aegis of an internationally-agreed Comprehensive Plan of Action (CPA) in order to discourage Vietnamese and others in the region from undertaking unauthorized, risky journeys. Refugees were to be screened in nearby countries of asylum. Those who were found to have a well-founded fear of persecution if returned were to be resettled abroad. Those who failed to qualify were to be sent back to Vietnam. This proved to be a prolonged exercise. The last Vietnamese asylum seekers under the CPA were released and expelled from a detention camp in Hong Kong only in 2000.[29]

Concerns over the accuracy of the screening process established under the CPA prompted action by House Republicans in 1995, led by Congressman Christopher Smith,[30] then the chair of the Subcommittee on International Operations and Human Rights of the House Committee on International Operations. Representative Smith introduced a bill that would have mandated a second case examination for Vietnamese who had been rejected under the CPA procedures. This approach was strongly opposed by the U.S. State Department and UNHCR, among others, on the grounds that it would undermine the deterrent effect of the CPA. While this re-screening provision was part of a broader foreign aid bill that ultimately was vetoed for a variety of reasons by President Clinton, it was clear that the provision was likely to emerge again in subsequent legislative efforts.

The legislative incentive coincided with a debate within the Executive Branch about the proper course of action. 'This was an NGO proposal that

[28] Press Release, U.S. Dep't of State, Bureau of Population, Refugees, and Migration, East Asian Refugee Admissions Program, (Jan. 18, 2000). *See generally* United Nations High Commissioner for Refugees, *Flight from Indochina, in* The State of the World's Refugees: Fifty Years of Humanitarian Action 79–103 (2000).

[29] Vietnamese Migrants, Enforcement and Liaison Branch, Hong Kong Special Administrative Region, Government Information Center. *at*: http:/www.info.gov.hk/immd/a_report/right4.htm (last visited Jan. 25, 2003).

[30] Republican, New Jersey.

we argued, that we agreed with,' explained a senior humanitarian official at the NSC during Clinton's tenure. The official acknowledged that there were 'significant screening errors' under CPA procedures that rendered the outcomes of cases uncertain. 'We wanted to make peace with Congress and avoid a diplomatic train wreck, since our ASEAN [Association of South East Asian Nations] partners would not have accepted a re-screening requirement.' An initiative to provide additional opportunities for resettlement to Vietnamese previously rejected under CPA procedures was thus imposed by the NSC on an acquiescing State Department.

The result of the negotiations was an administrative program, called Resettlement Opportunities for Vietnamese Refugees (ROVR), for those refugees deemed of special interest to the United States who returned to Vietnam under the terms of the CPA. The new interviews were to occur in Vietnam as part of an in-country refugee program that had existed for many years. Despite some delays in implementation by the Vietnamese authorities, after 1996 approximately 20,000 Vietnamese were admitted to the United States as refugees under the ROVR program, which ended only in 2000.[31]

The saga of the ROVR program is a lesson in power politics between the leaders of a Republican Congress and a Democratic Administration. The Administration's position was negotiated by a handful of foreign policy officials. The legislative effort was led by a highly committed individual member who garnered leadership support. The outcome was an Executive Branch reaction to a congressional initiative, although an NSC official cautioned that 'if we had decided to oppose instead of co-opting the initiative, we may well have succeeded.' Instead, the result was a last spasm of generosity for a discrete group of Vietnamese refugees.

There are many other forms of policy leverage in the legislative process. Appropriations generally and, on the Senate side, nominations and confirmations can provide a passive form of pressure. There are numerous examples. An initiative in 2000 by U.S. Senator Judd Gregg,[32] who chaired the Appropriations Committee's Subcommittee on Commerce, Justice, State, and the Judiciary, is illustrative. Senator Gregg unblocked funding for UN peacekeeping to Sierra Leone in return for an agreement by the Administration to exclude the leader of a rebel group from a power-sharing arrangement negotiated in a peace agreement signed by the combatants in July 1999 and to assist in reconstituting a more effective peacekeeping force. Upon the accommodation with the Administration, Senator Gregg

[31] Congressional Record, 146, 3 146 CONG. REC. H2421 (May 23, 2000), *available at* http://www.access.gpo.gov/su_docs/aces/aces150.html (relating to continuing human rights violations and political oppression in Socialist Republic of Vietnam).

[32] Republican, New Hampshire.

agreed to release fifty million dollars to fund the United States' share of peacekeeping expenditures in Sierra Leone.[33]

The impact of the system of congressional committees on the legislative agenda can be summarized as follows. The involvements of the appropriations committees and strong substantive committees, such as Armed Services, can be determinative. Ironically, the substantive foreign policy oversight committees have in recent years largely been talk shops and not very consequential in the legislative mix.

This pecking order is illustrated well by the lack of even informal consultation concerning the 1999 review of humanitarian assistance undertaken by the Executive Branch. Some of the options set forth in the review, particularly those regarding the consolidation of functions at the State Department and USAID, would require legislation. But as a key senior staffer, involved in international operations noted in May 2000 in relation to the review, said, 'I did not even know about it.' His ignorance of the exercise illustrates graphically a lack of consensus and communication on humanitarian issues between important policy overseers in the Republican Congress and Democratic Executive Branch.

Of course, certain unique dynamics are at play in a situation where one political party holds the White House and the other the Congress. Ordinarily, in such a circumstance, a great deal of legislative business gets done at the end of the year in omnibus spending bills, in which the authorizers may have only a limited role. A veteran Republican staffer repeatedly noted in 2000 the reactive posture of Congress, with a Democratic Administration undertaking policy initiative that it negotiates with the Republican leaders. 'In the end it very much depends on what the Republican leadership thinks,' observed this staffer, who cited the military deployment in Kosovo as an example. 'The Administration usually gets what it wants.'

It remains to be seen whether this disjunction will be repaired in a situation where one party has captured both Congress and the Executive Branch, particularly with a Congress so finely divided that a change in party affiliation by one Senator propelled the Democrats into the majority in the Senate in June 2001.[34] But a senior NSC staff person in the new Bush Administration noted in May 2001 that old bad habits in Congressional and Executive Branch relations are hard to break. He was referring to a vote in the House of Representatives that day, over the Administration's

[33] Press Release, Amnesty International—USA, Amnesty International USA Applauds Senator Gregg's Release of Sierra Leone Funds, (Jun. 7, 2000), *available at* http://www.amnestyusa.org/news/2000/sierra_leone06072000.html.

[34] Helen Dewier, Jeffords Staged a 'Coup of One,' Angry Lott Says, WASH. POST, May 31, 2001, at A8.

opposition, to block part of the payment of UN dues in reaction to the United States not being re-elected to the UN Human Rights Commission. Whether new political leadership will change these dynamics remains to be seen.

CHAPTER EIGHT

Multilateralism versus U.S. Unilateralism: The Role of the UN Security Council as the Authorizing Body for the United States' Use of Force

*by Yutaka Kawashima**

CHAPTER OUTLINE

I. Introduction
II. Appraisal of the Past Mechanism of Collective Security
III. The Gulf War and the Formation of Multinational Force
IV. Evolution throughout the '90s
  A. Somalia
  B. Genocide in Rwanda
  C. Haiti
  D. Bosnia after Dayton Accords
  E. East Zaire and Great Lakes Region
  F. Albania
  G. Kosovo
  H. East Timor
  I. Afghanistan
V. Some Lessons and Future Challenges
  A. Multinational force was formed to fight war against the aggressor
  B. Multinational force was formed to enforce the order
  C. Multinational force was formed to grapple with humanitarian disaster
VI. Conclusion

I. INTRODUCTION

Contrary to the Charter of the United Nations' original assumption that the UN itself would be equipped with the military capability to suppress whatever threat to international peace and security, it became evident that in the

* Senior Fellow, John F. Kennedy School of Government, Harvard University.

foreseeable future the formation of the UN force was unlikely because a number of major member states were reluctant to place their respective military under the command of the UN. It became imperative, therefore, to find a kind of second-best formula in which the international community could collectively carry out the task of grappling with threats to international peace and security. This is the reason why since the end of the cold war we have witnessed the evolutionary practice of forming multinational force pursuant to resolution by the Security Council with the participation of the major world powers, notably the United States.

The Gulf War was the first case in which multinational force under the U.S. command effectively expelled invading Iraqis from Kuwait and restored peace in the region. Since then, multinational forces were formed on number of occasions, such as in the aftermath of the wars in Balkan, to stop appalling bloodshed and to restore peace and security in affected countries and areas. Under these circumstances, the new function of the Security Council has become giving the green light to major countries to take whatever military measures necessary to accomplish the stipulated objectives in the relevant resolution by the Security Council. Today, the U.S. administration is consulting with other permanent members of the Security Council for the adoption of the Council's resolution that would authorize military action against Iraq. Twelve years after the Iraqi invasion of Kuwait, the role of the Security Council has once again become crucial in deciding the legality of the use of force by member states, in this case by the United States.

This paper seeks to review the evolutionary change concerning the practice of forming multinational force and to reflect upon the future prospect of this practice in the context of possible war against Iraq.

II. APPRAISAL OF THE PAST MECHANISM OF COLLECTIVE SECURITY

Long before the concept of multilateralism was introduced, after the end of the WWI, the approach of collective security in the global context was attempted for the first time by creating the League of Nations pursuant to the initiative by President Wilson. The League failed, however, to function effectively for the maintenance of the international security and could not prevent the tragedy of the WWII, partly because many key players, namely the United States, the newly emerging Soviet Union, and defeated Germany, were not effective participants in this system. Still, article 15 of the League's Charter provided for the imposition of economic sanction by member states on the country that was starting war in contravention of the Charter. As such, this Article embodied the first multilateral attempt ever to grapple with international security challenges.

In preparing the Charter of the UN, the allied powers were fully aware of the lesson that the League had failed to prevent the outbreak of the WWII and therefore attempted to strengthen the competence of the UN in such a way that, unlike the case of the League, the UN itself should be equipped with its own military capability to overwhelm those who tried to disrupt international peace by starting military adventure against other countries. The basic assumption was that the combined military strength of the major allied powers, most notably the United States and the Soviet Union, would suffice in the foreseeable future to effectively suppress threat posed by any country, possibly the remilitarized former axis powers who might be tempted to a return match. The step-by-step procedure, including the formation of a UN force, is stipulated in chapter 7 of the UN Charter, which the Security Council was supposed to follow in taking military measures to counter threats to international peace and security. The logical structure is as follows:

First, the use of force by states is deemed illegal except to exercise the right of self-defense. Second, in the event that some country launched military invasion into another country, the Security Council determines that such invasion constitutes threat to international peace and security and tries non-military measures, such as economic sanction, first. Third, if it becomes evident that non-military measures would not lead to resolution of the crisis, the Council decides to take military measures and for that purpose, takes steps to form UN force to be engaged in military campaign against the invading state. Meanwhile the use of force by the invaded side for the exercise of right of self-defense is legally permitted as provided for in the article 51 of chapter 7. Such was the way by which any threat to peace and security was supposedly addressed in the UN's collective security system.

However, as military confrontation soon developed between the key allied powers, namely the United States and the Soviet, this assumption was quickly shattered. As the advent of the cold war in the immediate aftermath of the WWII seemed inevitable in hindsight, it would not make much sense to question whether the UN could have functioned effectively pursuant to the chapter 7 of the Charter, had the Soviet continued to work with the United States and, in essence, remained a well-behaved player in international politics. During the cold war, the function of the UN had been substantially curtailed, simply because the Security Council—whose decision-making is subject to veto by five permanent members—could not make a decision on any issue that could have an impact, one way or another, on the ongoing zero-sum game of the cold war confrontation. One exception took place, in the very early phase when the Security Council adopted the resolution to send UN troops to the Korean War, as the Soviets boycotted the deliberation of the issue in the Council. The UN force, which was sent to the Korean Peninsula and fought against the North Korean force and eventually against Chinese voluntary force, was the de-facto alliance force of the free world to be commanded by the United States. In that sense, it was different from what the chapter 7 had originally assumed.

The only area that the UN was able to carry out the commendable task pertaining to peace and security during the cold war was the peacekeeping operations ('PKO') activities that were meant to keep peace by sending infantry with blue helmets for various missions, such as the observance of cease-fire, once cession of hostilities was agreed upon among belligerents. Obviously, the PKO as such was not envisaged by the original drafters of the Charter. Thus, the PKO was aptly described as measures of chapter 6.5, meaning that it did not belong to those measures stipulated in chapter 7. In spite of the basic zero-sum nature of the cold war confrontation, the Soviet side had occasionally shared strategic interest with the West in containing regional crisis that could otherwise disrupt the delicate balance between the two camps. As a result, the Soviet side often acquiesced in the dispatch of various PKO by the UN.

In those days, as far as international security was concerned, the juxtaposition of multilateralism and unilateralism was irrelevant since the fundamental issue of war and peace was decided not in the multilateral system of the UN, but in the context of the cold war confrontation where the key parameter for the maintenance of peace was mutually assured destruction between the United States and the Soviet Union. Simply put, the international community could not take effective collective measures to counter any threat to peace and security when the international community was split into two fiercely contending blocs. Multilateralism versus unilateralism became the difficult issue in the cold war context in the case of imposition of sanctions by the West on the Soviet side. When other allies in the West were reluctant to follow such imposition initiated by the United States, the United States often went ahead with unilateral imposition and occasionally attempted to press other allies to follow in its footsteps. In this case, whether the approach was unilateral or multilateral was primarily related to the test of solidarity within the Western alliance.

III. THE GULF WAR AND THE FORMATION OF MULTINATIONAL FORCE

It was only after the end of the cold war that the multilateral approach could have a better chance of success in grappling with the security challenges in the international community. It became increasingly clear, however, that the possibility of creating UN force pursuant to the chapter 7 of the UN Charter was extremely remote. The basic difficulty concerning the notion of UN force is that it is quite unlikely that every major player with credible military capability shares the same judgment about the worthiness to shed the blood of their soldiers in dealing with the concrete crisis, since the stakes for each player are bound to vary according to their respective national interests. They are, therefore, reluctant to delegate the decision-making of engaging their respective military to the UN, which could lead to automatic engagement. After all, decision about when and under what circumstance the military should be engaged belongs to the hard core of sovereign decision-making. Given this difficulty, it became a new challenge to find some formula in which the UN's system of multilateral approach was compatible with the member states' sovereign decision about the engagement of respective military.

The first challenge was the Iraqi invasion of Kuwait in the summer of 1990. At first, the imposition of economic sanction was attempted pursuant to article 41 in order to force Iraq's withdrawal from Kuwait. It became increasingly evident, however, that military measures would be needed to resolve the crisis, since Iraq did not show any sign of succumbing to the economic sanctions. Iraq's invasion was perhaps the classical case of threat to international peace and security that the original drafters of the UN Charter had in mind; in that sense, had UN force been created, it could have been the typical case of engaging such UN force to fight against the Iraqis. But since UN force was non-existent, the second-best option of forming multilateral force had to be pursued.

Resolution 678 was adopted by the Security Council in November, the gist of which was: The Security Council authorizes member states to use all necessary means (i.e., military measures) to uphold and implement Resolution 660 and subsequent relevant resolutions and to restore international peace and security in the area (i.e., to expel Iraqis from Kuwait). Thus, extremely important precedent was established in that the Security Council assumed the new function of deciding when and under what circumstance the use of force by individual member states could be authorized, so that such use of force would be deemed perfectly legal in addressing threats to international peace and security. In essence, the Security Council decided to entrust member states to carry out multilateral endeavors in place of non-existent UN force to fight against perpetrator of aggression.

As far as member states were concerned, it was up to each member state to judge whether it would be in its own interest to participate in such multilateral endeavors. Although broad objectives of the authorized use of force are stipulated in relevant resolutions, such as Resolution 660 in the case of the Gulf War, concrete modality of carrying out the use of force for the purpose of achieving these objectives is not subject to the judgment of the

Security Council but rather subject to the judgment of member states who send their troops to join multinational force. Obviously, for the new formula to be successful, the pre-requisite would be the existence of a state or a group of states prepared to and capable of resorting to the use of force authorized by the Security Council to grapple with pending crisis. Since the Gulf War, we have witnessed a number of cases in which the formation of multilateral force was crucial in resolving the crisis, and in almost all of these cases NATO force led by the United States constituted the core of such forces.

IV. EVOLUTION THROUGHOUT THE '90S

After the victory of multilateral force in the Gulf War and the end of the cold war, the beginning of the '90s was marked with high hopes for the effectiveness of multilateral approach in the realm of peace and security. The report by the Secretary General ('SG') of the UN in 1992, entitled 'An Agenda for Peace, Preventive Diplomacy, Peace Making and Peace-Keeping,' introduced the notion of creating a peace-enforcing unit within the UN that would be made available by member states on an on-call basis and be placed under the command of the SG.[1] In essence, it was proposed that the UN should play a much more proactive role, including the use of force by the UN itself, for enforcing peace as envisaged in the chapter 7 of the UN Charter.

Meanwhile, in the field, the combination of the PKO under the command of the UN and multinational force organized by authorizing resolution was attempted to deal with a number of crises.[2] In retrospect, classical international crisis involving military clash between states, such as the Gulf War, was not repeated throughout the decade. We have mostly witnessed a total breakdown of internal peace and order within a state where appalling atrocity was perpetrated in the course of internal warfare. The impression was that all sorts of ethnic hatred and xenophobia that had been frozen during the cold war became suddenly defrosted as the cold war had ended. As Kofi Annan, SG of the UN, recounted in looking back at the

[1] Report of Secretary General, *An Agenda for Peace Preventive Diplomacy, Peace-Making, and Peace-Keeping*, U.N. Doc. A/47/277-S/24111 (1992), *available at* http://www.un.org/Docs/SG/agpeace.html (in paragraph forty-three, it is suggested that the Security Council should initiate a negotiation with Member States to form UN force pursuant to article 43 of the UN Charter).

[2] Report of Secretary General on the Work of the Organization, *Supplement to an Agenda for Peace: Position Paper of the Secretary-General on the Occasion of the Fiftieth Anniversary of the United Nations*, U.N. Doc. A/50/60-S/1995/1 (1995), *available at* http://www.un.org/Docs/SG/agsupp.htm (the SG, while acknowledging the practice of forming a multinational force, argued that there were positive and negative sides to this practice).

'90s, the proportion of civilian casualties in the total war dead in the decade was estimated to be somewhere in the region of 75 percent. In the WWI, the civilian death accounted 10 percent of the total war dead, and in the WWII, the civilian death including holocaust victims was 50 percent of the total war dead. This horrifying increase in the proportion of civilian casualty testifies the nature of crisis that the international community had to grapple with in that decade.[3] All cases other than the Gulf War in which multinational force was formed pursuant to the Security Council resolution are briefly described below:

A. Somalia

Today, Somalia is remembered in terms of TV coverage in 1993 of Somali people joyfully dragging bodies of dead American soldiers. This coverage had a profound impact on the national psyche of the United Stated regarding the wisdom of sending U.S. forces to an area where the United States did not have any strategic interest. Throughout the autumn of 1992, the humanitarian situation was rapidly deteriorating in Somalia because of the total breakdown of internal order with intensified armed struggles among clans. Alarmed by the prospect of humanitarian disaster, President Bush, who had lost the presidential election in the previous month, decided to send U.S. troops to Somalia to facilitate the distribution of humanitarian assistance. Thus, the Security Council adopted Resolution 794 in December 1992, authorizing member states to form multinational force to carry out humanitarian missions. This multinational force was different in structure from the Gulf War multinational force in that it was deployed in tandem with the PKO sent by the UN, with which coordinated operation had to be undertaken. Since the SG was in commanding position of the PKO, much interaction between the SG and multinational force was inevitable, unlike the case of Gulf War. In any event, the operation by the U.S. forces of facilitating humanitarian relief activities was initially well-received by Somalis. However, eventually the nature of the operation changed, as the SG tried to restore internal order by subduing leading clans, notably the one led by Aidid. The end result was that, in October 1993, eighteen American soldiers were killed while they were engaged in an attempt to capture Aidid and his people. The U.S. government swiftly withdrew troops, and the notion of enforcing peace by deploying UN PKO and multinational force suffered a serious setback.[4]

[3] Kofi Annan, *Human Rights and Humanitarian Intervention in the Twenty-First Century*, *in* REALIZING HUMAN RIGHTS: MOVING FROM INSPIRATION TO IMPACT 312 (Samantha Power & Graham Allison eds., 2000).

[4] Takahisa Kawakami, Safety of Personal Serving on Peace Operations, in The Rule of Law on Peace Operations, ch. 3 (Jessica Howard & Bruce Oswald eds., 2002), available at http://www.apcml.org/Ruleoflawbookfinal.pdf.

B. Genocide in Rwanda

The expectation that the international community could effectively deal with international crisis involving immense humanitarian tragedy was further shattered in Rwanda. Although a small PKO was deployed in Rwanda in the earlier phase of the crisis, its physical capacity and mandate were totally inadequate to halt the deterioration of the situation. The sign was abundant in the spring of 1994 that following the collapse of the order and outbreak of tribal strife, the massive killing of Tutsis tribe people was about to be perpetrated by Hutus tribe. The UN could not take effective action to prevent the debacle, however, and no country expressed its readiness to engage its military to avert the crisis. It is estimated that by the time the massacre was over in the summer of 1994, some eight hundred thousand Tutsis had been killed. It was only after the cruelest part of the tribal war was over that France and some African countries expressed their readiness to send their troops to Rwanda to alleviate the humanitarian disaster. As a result, the Security Council managed to pass Resolution 929, authorizing member states to conduct the operation for the protection of displaced persons, refugees, and civilians in Rwanda. The fact that no country dared to risk lives of their soldiers in the possible intervention in the bloody tribal war, while massive atrocity was being committed, illustrated the fundamental difficulty for the international community in addressing this type of challenge to peace and humanity. In that instance, it was argued that because the atrocity was committed in Africa, the emotional upheaval among populace in the developed part of the world was not as heated as it would have been if the atrocity had been committed in other region, such as Balkan.[5]

C. Haiti

The situation in Haiti was an example of international effort to restore order in a country where because of the nature of the regime, internal order had totally disintegrated, and therefore, the creation of a whole system of governance was urgently needed. In 1991, the junta headed by Cedras took over power by ousting President Aristide, who was elected through free-election held a year before. In 1993, the junta accepted what was called the Governors Island Agreement, which would pave the way for the transfer of power to Aristide. The junta eventually backed away from the implementation of the Agreement, however, and the systematic violation of civil liberties by the junta started to escalate. In the summer of 1993, as the United States expressed its readiness to engage its troops in Haiti, the Security

[5] David Halberstram, War in a Time of Peace 273–278 (Simon & Schuster 2001).

Council adopted Resolution 940 authorizing member states 'to form a multinational force under unified command and control and, in this framework, to use all necessary means to facilitate the departure from Haiti of the military leadership, consistent with Governors Island Agreement, the prompt return of the legitimately elected President.'

In any event, the use of force as authorized by the resolution did not materialize, as last minute negotiations between the United States team led by former President Carter and the junta managed to produce a deal in which the junta finally agreed to step down and transfer power to Aristede. Since the negotiation was conducted when military operation by the United States was about to be launched, it can be concluded that the threat of impending use of force was quite effective in forcing the junta to give up. The PKO, called UNMIH, assumed the function of looking after the restoration of internal order, including professionalizing the Haitian armed force and creating civilian police. Thus, in this case, the working relation between multinational force and the PKO was not in tandem but consecutive. This pattern of deployment of multinational force followed by the PKO activities was repeated in a number of cases throughout the '90s.

The Haitian case was also notable for the non-use of the force by multinational force. Perhaps the simple lesson is that when the multinational force is overwhelmingly strong, and in addition, if a local leader, be it clan leader or junta leader turns out to be a relatively effective player with whom negotiated settlement is feasible, deployment of multinational force at the initial phase can be quite effective. However, the ensuing task of constructing the effective structure of civilized governance can be a difficult and awfully time-consuming endeavor for which physical strength of multinational force cannot be an answer.

D. Bosnia after Dayton Accords

In Bosnia, the UN tried to expand the role of the PKO with a dismal result. The basic assumption of the traditional PKO was that parties to the conflict would consent to accept the PKO's efforts. For example, in the case of a typical state-to-state armed conflict, both belligerents would agree in the cease-fire accord that the PKO would be deployed along a certain zone of disengagement. It was a totally different matter to try to carry out the PKO in the area where parties to the conflict were not prepared to give full-fledged consent to the activities of the PKO by the UN, and that was precisely what the UN tried in Bosnia.

As the internal war intensified in the early '90s, the UN decided to send the PKO, called UNPROFOR, into Bosnia. UNPROFOR's mission was to protect, by the use of force if necessary, various humanitarian activities, such as the distribution of foodstuff to civilians. UNPROFOR was not adequately equipped with the capability of carrying out protection of civilians as such. Besides, it was feared that if UNPROFOR was engaged in military operation against one of the belligerents, namely Bosnian Serbs, the impartiality of the UN in the conflict could be violated. Especially tragic was that when Srebrenica fell in the summer of 1995 after three years of siege, the small contingent of UNPROFOR deployed in the city could not prevent the massacre of civilians perpetrated by Bosnian Serbs.[6] This was another case in which the injection of robust military strength would have been the only answer to prevent such atrocity. But then the question was whether major military powers, notably the United States and perhaps other NATO countries, were prepared to shed the blood of their soldiers for the purpose of preventing atrocities. Balkan was well known for difficult terrain in terms of war fighting, and casualties of dispatched troops were estimated to be quite high. The basic question then was whether nations should be ready to shed the blood of their soldiers for humanitarian purposes even though a strategic interest was not at stake. In any event, due to the commendable efforts of the United States, in the fall of 1995, Dayton Accords was reached among belligerents in Bosnia. In accordance with the Accords, a multinational peace implementation force called IFOR was formed by Security Council Resolution 1031. The United States sent to IFOR twenty thousand men, who functioned as the central pillar of the whole operation. Thirty four countries, including all NATO members (except Iceland, Egypt, Russia, Malaysia, the three Baltic countries, Poland, Hungary, Austria, and Pakistan) participated in IFOR. The total number of personnel in IFOR was roughly 60,000. A year later, Resolution 1088 was adopted in which the mission of multinational force was extended for another eighteen months, but with a new title of 'multinational stabilization force (SFOR).' The number of personnel in SFOR was roughly 35,000.

In the case of most past peace agreements between various belligerents, it was often safe to assume that parties to the peace agreement would abide by the terms and conditions stipulated in the peace agreement and would consent to PKO deployment for observation purposes. In the case of Bosnia, however, it was obvious that deployment of strong military force was essential in enforcing the peace agreement on local belligerents. Since IFOR and SFOR were equipped with robust capability far superior to local belligerents, military provocation by local belligerents was effectively deterred. It was judged from the outset that deployment of PKO was out of the question, as they were likely to be ignored by the belligerents, and the hostilities could easily be rekindled. Thus, the new formula of forming multinational force for the purpose of enforcing the peace agreement was created.

[6] Numerous authors took up the tragedy of Srebrenica. See *id.*; PHILIP BOBBIT, THE SHIELD OF ACHILLES 411–67 (Knopf 2002).

E. East Zaire and Great Lakes Region[7]

The internal strife between the Zairian army and the rebels led by Kabila, who later became the president of Zaire by successfully dismantling the regime of President Mobutu in 1996, triggered a massive inflow into Eastern Zaire of Rwandan Hutus refugees, who were trying to flee from the possible revengeful attacks from Tutsis. In the autumn of that year, the Security Council adopted a resolution authorizing the establishment of a temporary multinational force to facilitate the voluntary repatriation of refugees back to Rwanda and the immediate return of humanitarian organizations to the area, so these organizations could resume humanitarian relief activities. It was initially planned that developed countries, such as Canada, the United States, the United Kingdom, France and Netherlands, as well as underdeveloped, African countries, such as South Africa, Senegal, and Cameroon, would send their troops. By the time the temporary force was to be deployed, however, it was discovered that the majority of refugees had already returned to Rwanda, that the remaining numbers had been dispersed over large areas of Eastern Zaire, and that international humanitarian agencies had had growing access to displaced persons. As a result, in December 1996, the Security Council terminated the mandate of the temporary multinational force.[8]

F. Albania

Following the collapse of the pyramid investment schemes, the total meltdown of law and order in Albania took place in 1997. Hundreds of thousands of people broke into armories and looted weapons for 'self-defense,' and many of them engaged in violent criminal activities. A massive wave of destruction of public, private, and institutional property ensued. A large number of refugees started to arrive at ports in Italy, who was compelled to proclaim a State of Emergency. The Albanian Government requested that the Security Council authorize the formation of multinational force to provide security for the delivery of humanitarian aid throughout Albania and to help create a durable, safe environment for the provision of international assistance. In response to this request, the Security Council adopted Resolution 1101, in March 1997, authorizing the formation of multinational protection force with 7,000 personnel from Italy, France, Turkey, Greece, Romania, Austria, Spain, and Denmark. This was unprecedented in that the collapse of economic policy triggered a total breakdown of order that required the dispatch of multinational force.

[7] G.A. Res. 1078, U.N. SCOR, 3710th Mtg., U.N. Doc. S/RES/1078 (1996), *available at* http://daces-ods.un.org/TMP/778706.1.html.

[8] Letter from the Canadian Permanent Representative to the UN to the SG (Dec. 23, 1996), *available at* http://www.africanaction.org/docs97/un9702.afr.htm.

G. *Kosovo*

The unique feature of the Kosovo case was that the multinational force, which was called 'international security presence,' was deployed only after the use of force in the form of a bombing campaign to force the Federal Republic of Yugoslavia to stop atrocity in Kosovo was completed by NATO without the authorization of the Security Council. As a result of heavy bombing by NATO, the Federal Republic of Yugoslavia accepted a set of principles, including an immediate and verifiable end of violence and repression in Kosovo and verifiable withdrawal from Kosovo of all military, police, and paramilitary forces. The legal implication of Kosovo has already been amply debated. Essentially, the question is whether the use of force against a sovereign state can be legally tolerated even though the Security Council does not give authorization, as long as extreme atrocity is perpetrated against the nationals of that state by the state authority. Certainly, the precedent established in Kosovo about possible use of force against any state that perpetrates atrocity against its own nationals because of ethnic hatred or other wrongful motivation would reduce the possibility of the recurrence of such atrocity, as leaders of any state would have second thoughts before proceeding with such atrocities. And if that is the case, perhaps we will be living in a somewhat more civilized world.

In any event, in the case of Kosovo, multinational force was deployed only after the event was settled by NATO bombing. Still, because of its superior military capability, multinational force functioned as an effective deterrent to the recurrence of violence.

H. *East Timor*

In 1974, Portugal withdrew from East Timor, and Indonesia intervened and later declared East Timor its twenty-seventh province. Since then, alleged human rights abuses in East Timor by the Indonesian authority has been a thorny issue between Indonesia and many developed counties, notably EU member countries. It was the departure of President Suharto and the coming into power of Habibi as a successor of Suharto in 1998 that made possible the political resolution of the issue. In May 1999, an agreement was reached between Indonesia and Portugal to the effect that the UN Mission in East Timor (UNAMET) would be in charge of conducting the popular consultation (i.e., referendum among local people) of the East Timorese through a direct ballot. Pursuant to this agreement, the direct ballot was conducted on August 30 where 78.5 percent opted for secession and independence, and 21.5 percent opted for integration with Indonesia. Following the announcement of the result, pro-integration militia started a campaign of violence, which resulted in the deaths or displacement of many East Timorese.

On September 15, the Security Council adopted a resolution that authorized the establishment of multinational force, called INTERFET, pursuant to the request of the Indonesian Government. INTERFET had the task of (a) restoring peace and security in East Timor, (b) protecting and supporting the UNAMET in carrying out its task, and (c) within force capabilities, facilitating humanitarian assistance operations. Twenty three countries participated in INTERFET with the strength of 10,000 personnel under the Australian command. In response to the expressed preference of the Indonesian Government that a majority of the force would consist of personnel from Asian countries, many ASEAN countries, such as Thailand, the Philippines, Malaysia, and Singapore, participated in INTERFET. As order was eventually restored, and the Indonesian Consultative Assembly formally recognized the result of the ballot of August 30, the Security Council adopted a resolution in October establishing the UN Transitional Administration in East Timor (UNTAET) which was entrusted with the task of looking after practically all aspects of the administration in East Timor, including the implementation of elections during the transitional phase until the new independent state was formally established. The command of military operation was handed over from INTERFET to UNTAET in February 2000. This was an instance in which, at the initial phase, the readiness to use force by multinational force was needed to restore order, and once the order was successfully restored, the UN operation could be launched to prepare the region for the eventual independence.[9]

I. Afghanistan

This was the memorable case in the aftermath of September 11. The United States started the military campaign in Afghanistan in the autumn of 2001 with the objectives of hunting down Al Qaeda terrorists and dismantling the Taliban regime that had provided sanctuary and assistance for these terrorists. This campaign was deemed the classical case of the exercise of the right of self-defense, as provided for in the article 51 of the UN Charter, and therefore, authorization by the Security Council was not required. As the U.S. campaign successfully liberated Kabul and dismantled the Taliban, the urgent task was the creation of an effective structure of governance by Afghans that could restore order and normalcy within the whole country.

In December, agreement was reached in Bonn among Afghans regarding provisional arrangements, including the deployment of international security

[9] Press Release, Security Council, *Security Council Hears Detail of Free and Fair Elections in East Timor*, G.A. Res. 7139, U.N. SCOR, 4367th Mtg., U.N. Doc. S/7139 (2001), *available at* http://www.un.org/News/Press/docs/2001/SC7139.doc.htm.

forces pending the reestablishment of permanent government institutions. In support of this Bonn Agreement, the Security Council adopted Resolution 1386 authorizing the establishment of an International Security Assistance Force to assist the Afghan Interim Authority in the maintenance of security in Kabul and surrounding areas. At the time of this writing, there remains much to be achieved in order to stabilize the country because of the deadly feud among various tribes, as well as the threat from the remnant of Al Qaeda forces. Thus, there exists a dual structure in which U.S. forces are still engaged in the campaign against terrorists and the International Security Assistance Force commanded by the UK is engaged in the maintenance of the security.

V. SOME LESSONS AND FUTURE CHALLENGES

It may be useful to divide these cases into a few groups:

A. *Multinational force was formed to fight war against the aggressor*

The Gulf War falls into this category. Assuming that some resolution will be adopted by the Security Council, whether the Gulf War II is going to be characterized as the war against aggressor, or the war against the state that poses the gravest security threat, is debatable.

B. *Multinational force was formed to enforce the order*

In the case of Kosovo and Afghanistan, the use of force was carried out without the Security Council's authorization. In the case of Kosovo, it was NATO's aerial bombing campaign, and in the Afghan case, it was the U.S. military campaign to fight terrorists. The deployment of multilateral force took place after military campaign was effectively over to enforce the restoration of order. Robert Kagan referred to this division of labor in his essay, 'As some Europeans put it, the real division of labor consisted of the U.S. making dinner and the Europeans doing the dishes.'[10]

A peace agreement or some other agreement was reached among belligerents or other related parties, and multinational force was formed to enforce that agreement (e.g., IFOR, SFOR and East Timor).

[10] Robert Kagan, *Power and Weakness*, POLICY REVIEW (June 2002), *available at* http://www.newamericancentury.org/kagan-052002.htm.

C. Multinational force was formed to grapple with humanitarian disaster

Atrocities were committed in the context of ethnic strife (e.g., Rwanda and East Zaire). It should be noted that the option of forming multinational force to alleviate humanitarian disaster during the internal war in Bosnia could not be pursued by the international community because of the possible high casualties that would be sustained due to the notoriously difficult terrain.

Cases of failed states where the total breakdown of order resulted in humanitarian disaster requiring the engagement of multinational force to enforce order and to facilitate humanitarian relief activities (e.g., Haiti, Somalia, and Albania).

VI. CONCLUSION

Now, after having witnessed all sorts of internal strife, many of which were the product of ethnic hatred, and cases of failed states, which was the characteristic symptom of the decade since the end of the cold war, at the time of this writing the impression is that we have drifted back to square one, namely the Gulf War of 1990. As noted above, the Gulf War set the precedent in the formation of multinational force to grapple with various threats to international peace and security. That is the reason why all the Security Council's resolutions authorizing the formation of multinational force invoked the chapter 7 of the UN Charter. Since the Gulf War, the only instance in which the use of force could not be explained by the traditional international law was NATO's campaign in Kosovo. Otherwise, the legality of the use of force was assured by the authorizing resolution of the Security Council or the invocation of the right of self-defense in case of the U.S. campaign in Afghanistan. And that is what the multilateral approach to the use of force is all about.

If some formulation is agreed upon among the five permanent members of the Security Council about the adoption of resolution that would authorize the use of force against Iraq once again, then multilateralism pertaining the use of force can be maintained. Moreover, if the United States starts the Gulf War II without such resolution, perhaps the legal justification, if any, might be the extension of the right of self-defense. It may be argued that state A can be justified in taking unilateral military action against state B which, because of the possession of the weapons of mass destruction, constitutes imminent and immeasurable danger to state A.

As the United States has proclaimed the new doctrine of preemptive strike against terrorist and rogue states with weapons of mass destruction, the task of reconciling this posture with multilateral approach is extremely important but difficult. Because of the very nature of preemptive action, it is difficult to envisage that prior to preemptive military action by the United States the Security Council would adopt, in a timely manner, a resolution authorizing such action. Therefore, we have to assume that U.S. preemptive action may be taken without the authorization of the Security Council. It might be argued that it would actually serve the security interest of allies and many other countries, if the threats accruing from the possession of weapons of mass destruction by Al Qaeda-type terrorist groups or by the rogue states could be effectively eliminated as a result of such unilateral action by the United States. After all, in view of the role that the United States has thus far played, as what Joe Nye described, as the provider of public good in terms of international security, it is hopefully assumed that unlike some of the past dominant states, such as France under Louis XIV that utilized their strength for aggrandizing their interest, the United States would not exploit one's dominant military strength with possible unilateral strikes for their own advantage at the expense of other normal and civilized states.

The obvious problem, however, is the possible emulation of unilateral preemptive doctrine by other states that may be tempted to proclaim that they are also entitled to resort to the unilateral preemptive use of force. It would be extremely difficult to argue legally that unilateral preemptive action by the United States could somehow be acceptable and might be beneficial for the security of other states, while similar actions by other states would utterly destabilize existing international order. To avoid this possible dilemma of the seemingly double standard, it seems all the more desirable that some compromise be reached among the five permanent members of the Security Council, so that authorization resolution can be adopted.

CHAPTER NINE

The Legitimacy of External Response to Protect the Right to Democratic Governance and Free Choice

*by Ndiva Kofele-Kale**

CHAPTER OUTLINE

I. Introduction
II. The Legal Framework for Global Community Involvement
III. Contrasting Responses to Human Rights Violations
IV. Failure of World Community to Protect the Right to Democratic Governance
V. Concluding Statement

I. INTRODUCTION

The universality of human rights[1] and the elevation of a select few to the level of *jus cogens*[2] have imposed on the community of nations an obligation

* Professor of Law, Southern Methodist University Dedman School of Law. The research assistance of Catherine Bamugemereire, LL.B. (Makerere), LL.M. candidate (SMU Dedman School of Law) and the research support from a 2002 Summer Research Grant are gratefully acknowledged.

[1] The Universal Declaration of Human Rights which was adopted by the United Nations General Assembly in 1948 [by an affirmative vote of 49 states, with no state voting against and 8 states abstaining] proclaims in its preamble that this Declaration is intended to serve as the 'common standard of achievement for all peoples and all nations' and exhorts 'every individual and every organ of society . . . to strive by teaching and education to promote respect for [the rights and freedoms contained in the Declaration] and by progressive measures, national and international, to secure their *universal and effective recognition and observance*, both among the Member States themselves and among the peoples of territories under their jurisdiction.' *See* UNIVERSAL DECLARATION OF HUMAN RIGHTS. Adopted by the UN General Assembly, Dec. 10, 1948, G.A. Res. 217A, UN GAOR, 3rd Sess., Pt. I, Resolutions, at 71, UN Doc. A/810.

[2] Article 53 of the Vienna Convention on the Law of Treaties defines *jus cogens* as 'a peremptory norm of general international law . . . accepted and recognized by the international community of States as a whole as a norm from which no derogation is permitted and which can be modified only by a subsequent norm of general international law as having the same

erga omnes[3] to respond affirmatively to violations of these rights wherever and whenever they occur.[4] However, the haphazard manner in which the global community has reacted to human rights abuses around the world and Africa in particular has led to well-earned criticism that the community of nations employs an *Orwellian* double standard in the enforcement of *universal* human rights law.[5] It is argued that the major actors on the global stage (United States, France, Germany, United Kingdom, Japan) have opted for an à *la carte* approach when it comes to faulting States that are not in compliance with the international human rights regime.[6] As a result, the passion, intensity and persistence of their condemnation of human rights abuses are calibrated on the basis of their strategic *national interests* and the region of the world where these abuses are occurring.[7] Thus, on the basis of this parochial *state-centric* national interests template, the killing fields

character.' *See* VIENNA CONVENTION ON THE LAW OF TREATIES. Concluded at Vienna, May 23, 1969. Entered into force, Jan. 27, 1980. 1155 U.N.T.S. 331. Reprinted in 8 I.L.M. 679. Signed (Apr. 24, 1970) but not ratified by the United States. [Hereinafter 'Vienna Convention']. Examples of *jus cogens* norms would include: genocide, torture, crimes against humanity, war crimes, the doctrine of *pacta sunt servanda,* and the right to self-determination.

[3] The concept of obligations *erga omnes* was framed by the International Court of Justice by way of an *obiter dictum* in its judgment in the *Barcelona Traction Case*. The Court wrote that 'an essential distinction should be drawn between the obligations of a State towards the international community as a whole, and those arising vis-à-vis another State in the field of diplomatic protection. By their very nature the former are the concern of all States. In view of the importance of the rights involved, *all States can be held to have a legal interest in their protection; they are obligations erga omnes.' See* International Court of Justice, *Barcelona Traction, Light and Power Company, Limited, Second Phase.* 1980 I.C.J. Rep. 3 , 32 (Judgment of Feb. 5) (Emphasis added). The Court then went on to cite several examples of obligations of an *erga omnes* character: '[s]uch obligations derive, for example, in contemporary international law, from the outlawing of acts of aggression, and of genocide, as also from the principles and rules concerning the basic rights of the human person, including protection from slavery and racial discrimination.' *Id.*

[4] This *erga omnes* duty to respond in the internal affairs of states has been exercised in the following instances: India's intervention in East Pakistan now Bangladesh in 1971; Tanzania's intervention in Uganda in 1978–1979; the United States intervention in Grenada in 1983, Nicaragua in the mid-1980's, in the Panama in 1989, in Iraq in 1991, and in Haiti in 1994.

[5] *See* Marc M. Boutin, Somalia: The Legality of U.N. Forcible Humanitarian Intervention, 17 SUFFOLK TRANSNAT'L L. REV. 138 (1994) [Hereinafter cited as 'Forcible Humanitarian Intervention'].

[6] Tired of being picked on by the United States State Department for its less than sterling human rights record, China finally issued its own report on America's own human rights situation. *See* Information Office of the State Council of the People's Republic of China, HUMAN RIGHTS RECORD OF THE UNITED STATES IN 2000 (February 26, 2001; HUMAN RIGHTS RECORD OF THE UNITED STATES IN 2001 (March 11, 2002).

[7] *See e.g.*, David M. Kresock, 'Ethnic Cleansing' in the Balkans: The Legal Foundations of Foreign Intervention, 27 CORNELL INTL'L.L.J. 203, 226 (1994) (NATO intervention was inevitable since its European members found it unacceptable to have this kind of instability in their own backyard, so to speak)[Hereinafter cited as 'Ethnic Cleansing']; Douglas Eisner, Humanitarian Intervention in the Post-Cold War Era, 11 B.U.INT'L.L.J. 195, 214 (1994) (The West could not sit still and allow Saddam Hussein to seize the rich oil fields of Kuwait on which the West depended for its energy needs thus intervention imperative to oust Saddam Hussein)[Hereinafter cited as 'Postwar Humanitarian Intervention'].

of Rwanda[8] and Cambodia, littered with *black* and *brown* bodies, went virtually unnoticed by the family of nations[9] while the *white* victims of equally horrific crimes against humanity in Bosnia-Herzegovina would arrest the attention of no less a 'policeman' than the entire membership of the North Atlantic Treaty Organization (NATO)![10] Electoral mal-practices are condemned in some countries but ignored in others.

A. A Framework for Analysis

The propriety of external involvement in the domestic affairs of States in

[8] The world 'stood around with its hands in its pockets,' is how General Kagame, commander of the Tutsi-dominated Rwanda Patriotic Front, and subsequently Vice-President and Minister of Defense in the reconstituted Rwanda, described it. *See* Philip Gouvrevitch, WE WISH TO INFORM YOU THAT TOMORROW WE WILL BE KILLED WITH OUR FAMILIES 163 (1998) [Hereinafter cited as 'We Wish to Inform']. The General was referring to the roughly *800,000 thousand and a million Rwandans who were killed in a hundred days.* As the genocide reached its peak in the early summer of 1994, French President Francois Mitterrand would callously dismiss this unimaginable human tragedy with the observation that 'In such countries, genocide is not too important.' *Id. at* 325. Clearly, from their collective inaction one can safely conclude that the other major powers shared this view! Mitterrand's successor as President of France, Jacques Chirac, would continue this policy of turning a blind eye to the atrocities that took place in Rwanda. In 1995 Chirac refused to invite Rwanda's new President, Pasteur Bizimungu, to the annual Francophonie conference holding in Biarritz. To add insult to injury, at the opening ceremony President Chirac presided over a moment of silence to honor the memory of President Habyarimana—the man most responsible for the extermination of fellow Tutsi citizens—and *NOT* the hundreds of thousands of victims of the genocide committed in Habyarimana's name. *Id.* at 292.

[9] The official French government position while the genocidal killings were occurring in Rwanda was that the massacres of Tutsis by the Hutus were the result of mass popular outrage following President Juvenal Habyarimana's assassination; that the population had risen as a single man to defend itself; that the Hutu-led government and army wanted only to restore order; in short, that Rwandans were simply killing each other as they were wont to do, for primordial ethnic reasons, since time immemorial. *Id.* at 154. *See also* Samantha Power, NEVER AGAIN: THE WORLD'S MOST UNFULFILLED PROMISE (1998) [Hereinafter cited as 'Never Again'] (The major genocides of the post-war era—Cambodia, northern Iraq, Bosnia and Rwanda—have yielded virtually no American action and few stern words; the U.S. has not merely refrained from sending American troops to combat genocide, when it came to atrocities in Cambodia, Iraq and Rwanda, the U.S. also refrained from condemning the crimes or imposing economic sanctions, and again in Rwanda, the U.S. refused to authorize the deployment of a multinational U.N. force, and also squabbled over who would foot the bill for American transport vehicles). President Clinton would later apologize for America's failure to respond quickly and decisively to the mass killings in Rwanda. *See* 'Clinton in Africa; Clinton's Painful Words of Sorrow and Chagrin,' *New York Times*, 26 March 1998, Late Edition, sec. A; p. 12; col. 5.

[10] *See* Ethnic Cleansing, *supra* note 7, at 226; Postwar Humanitarian Intervention, *supra* note 7, at 214. According to Major-General Romeo Dellaire, the Canadian commander of the UN peace keeping force, United Nations Assistance Mission in Rwanda, (UNAMIR) sent to Rwanda in late 1993, 'more people were killed, injured, and displaced in three and half months in Rwanda than in the whole of the Yugoslavian campaign in which [the international community] poured sixty thousand troops and the whole of the Western world was there, and [they are still] pouring billions in there, still trying to solve the problem.' *See* We Wish to Inform, *supra* note 8, at 169.

defense of the people's right to freely choose who they want to govern them is the focus of this essay. The disparate global community response to systematic and persistent abuses of this fundamental right is a sub-theme. Thus, the interest in human rights in this essay is specifically limited to the enjoyment of the right to democratic governance and the obligation of the international community to vindicate or secure this legal right.[11] The locus is sub-Saharan Africa where '[a] decade of democratization has resulted in disappointing results and unfulfilled expectations, frustrating the democratic promise of peace and development. . .'[12] It will be argued that the right to vote out a government that is unresponsive, and/or to vote in one that is responsive, to the people's democratic aspirations is a fundamental right entitled to global community protection. Some have argued that the right to pro-democratic intervention has not yet attained the status of *lex lata*[13] while others submit that it at least qualifies as *de lege feranda.*[14] Some believe that this duty to promote democratic governance, to the extent that it exists at all, should be advanced through collective action bearing the

[11] *See* Christina M. Cerna, Universal Democracy: An International Legal Right or the Pipe Dream of the West? 27 N.Y.U.J.INT'L L. & POL. 289, 299 (1995) (arguing that the right to live under a democratic form of government has become an international legal right).

[12] *See* Augustin Loada & Carlos Santiso, Landmark Elections in Burkina Faso: Towards Democratic Maturity, 1,2 International IDEA's Burkina Faso Project: [Hereinafter cited as 'Landmark Elections']. Available at http://www.idea.Burkina.

[13] Tom J. Farer, An Inquiry into the Legitimacy of Humanitarian Intervention, in LAW AND FORCE IN THE NEW INTERNATIONAL ORDER 185 (Lori Fisler Damrosch & David J. Scheffer eds. 1991) [Hereinafter cited as 'Legitimacy of Intervention']. *See also* Oscar Schachter, The Legality of Pro-Democratic Invasion, 78 AM. J. INT'L L. 645, 649–50 (1984) (who argues that pro-democratic invasions must be weighed against the dangerous consequences of legitimizing armed attacks against peaceful governments).

[14] *See e.g.,* Thomas M. Franck, Intervention Against Illegitimate Regimes, in LAW AND FORCE IN THE NEW INTERNATIONAL ORDER 159, 164 (Lori Fisler Damrosch & David J. Scheffer eds. 1991) [Hereinafter cited 'Illegitimate Regimes'] (Argues that intervention against gross 'domestic' human rights abuses already has become relatively normative in the system. What is new is the idea that the system would include among those gross abuses triggering international concern those instances where governments deny their own populations the right to participate democratically in the process of governance). *See also* Thomas M. Franck, The Emerging Right to Democratic Governance, 86 AM. J. INT'L L. 46 (1992) (submits that representative democracy is gradually evolving from moral prescription to an international legal obligation based in part on customary law and in part on the collective interpretation of treaties); Ibrahim J. Gassama, Safeguarding the Democratic Entitlement: A Proposal for United Nations Involvement in National Politics, 30 CORNELL INT'L L.J. 287 (1997) [Hereinafter cited as 'Safeguarding Democratic Entitlement']; Lois E. Fielding, Taking the Next Step in the Development of New Human Rights: The Emerging Right of Humanitarian Assistance to Restore Democracy, 5 DUKE J. COMP. & INT'L L. 329 (1995) (arguing that the overthrow of a democratic government can constitute a threat to peace and security under Article 39 of the U.N. Charter and that support for this emerging right of humanitarian assistance to restore democracy is found in various U.N. documents, declarations and resolutions) [Hereinafter cited as 'Restore Democracy']; Gregory H. Fox, The Right to Political Participation in International Law, 17 YALE J. INT'L L. 539, 540–41 (1992) [Hereinafter cited as 'Political Participation'].

imprimatur of the United Nations Security Council.[15] We say that it does not really matter what vehicle moves this right forward: unilateral, bilateral or multilateral, because a) not each case of abuse of the democratic entitlement will invite the same type of external response and b) the effectiveness and legitimacy of these responses may depend on who is doing what and where. For instance, a unilateral intervention by France in an English-speaking West African State may be resented while a similar intervention from the Nordic countries may provoke the opposite reaction. It is therefore important that the discourse on the relative merits of unilateralism and multilateralism should focus more on which of the two approaches, in a given context, can successfully advance this fundamental entitlement to democracy. If in a given situation of domestic violation of the right to free choice, a resolution which favors the right holders is obtained but only through the unilateral involvement of a neighboring State or of a powerful distant one, then for that situation unilateralism is clearly the appropriate response. Other cases of such violations may merit a collective response involving a coalition of nations or initiated by such powerful and influential global financial agencies like the Bretton Woods institutions. In the latter instance, the effective multilateral response could well be lending conditions imposed by the International Monetary Fund or the World Bank on the offending State. External response as used here is not limited only to situations involving the use of force but encompasses a wide range of responses on a continuum of varying degrees of intrusion[16], such as the withdrawal of aid, the suspension of diplomatic relations, economic sanctions, and so on. An external response that is backed by force of the threat of it becomes an option only in the most extreme cases.

It has been insisted and with some justification that any form of external involvement should be aimed at arresting a situation that threatens international peace and security in conformity with U.N. Charter prescriptions. Since the Charter's provisions regulating external intervention in the domestic affairs of states represent the 'common will' of the founding members of the United Nations, so this argument goes, then this will must be given full effect. In response, we submit that when in 1945 the founding members spoke of threats to the peace and security they had as their point of reference their long experience with *inter-state* conflicts that culminated in two major world wars in the space of twenty-five years—the First and Second World Wars.[17] The conflicts of our time are in the main *intra-state* in nature

[15] Safeguarding Democratic Entitlement, *supra* note 14. Lois Fielding takes the contrary view arguing that the right of humanitarian assistance to restore democracy supports a unilateral right of humanitarian intervention when the U.N. is not in a position to act. *See* Restore Democracy, *supra* note 14, at 330.

[16] *Id.* at 330.

[17] In the Preamble to the Charter, the peoples of the United Nations unequivocally reaf-

though with the potential for grave trans-boundary effects.[18] This new genre of disputes occurs with remarkable frequency in regions of the world that were not fully represented nor whose interests were articulated during the drafting of the Charter. Now that they have become *bona fide* members of the U.N., it seems only fair and just that in construing the 'common will' of the parties to the Charter, account should be taken of their realities along with those of the 50 or so mostly Euro-American States that met in San Francisco to form the United Nations Organization. To do so would require a dynamic and functional interpretation of the 'threat to peace and security' provisions of the Charter.[19] Only through such an approach will it be possible to address domestic human rights abuses that can and *do* pose a threat to world public order. An uncompromising reliance on the 'common will' of U.N. members as expressed over a half century ago, in a world that has radically and dramatically changed since that time, works against the progressive development of the law of nations in general and human rights law in particular.

1. *Questions Put*

To the extent that the widespread *perception* of a tendentious enforcement of universal human rights law by the family of nations reflects global realities[20] then it raises a number of questions which this essay intends to confront. The questions to which I shall address myself are these: First, whether the 'threats to *international* peace and security' that invite some kind of external response should be limited to the more dramatic security threats that tend to dominate the front pages of the major newspapers (like the U.S. military campaign in Afghanistan against *al-Qaeda* terrorism provoked by the World Trade Center attacks of 11th September 2001) and which tend to focus attention, fairly or unfairly, on whether the United

firmed their determination 'to save succeeding generations from the *scourge of war, which twice in [their] lifetime has brought untold sorrow to mankind. . . .*' (emphasis added)

[18] David Wippman acknowledges that almost any case of significant internal disorder creates trans-boundary effects 'to permit the Security Council to find a plausible threat to the peace if it wishes to authorize intervention.' However, it does not follow, he argues, 'that the Council will utilize its power to authorize intervention with any frequency.' *See* David Wippman, Defense of Democracy and Non-Intervention: Remarks, 19 HOUS. J. INT'L L. 659, 673 (1997) [Hereinafter cited as 'Defense of Democracy'].

[19] *See* W. Michael Reisman, Comment, The Constitutional Crisis in the United Nations, 87 AM. J. INT'L L. 83, 93 (1993) (finds the Security Council's application of the term 'threat to the peace' to be 'quite elastic').

[20] *See e.g.*, Information Office of the State Council of the People's Republic of China, HUMAN RIGHTS RECORD OF THE UNITED STATES IN 2001 (March 11, 2002) (The report accuses the United States of assuming the role of the 'world judge of human rights' and of turning a blind eye to its own human rights-related problems while distorting human rights conditions in many countries and regions of the world, including China).

States, as the lone superpower, will respond unilaterally or as part of a multilateral coalition? This focus overlooks other global threats not necessarily linked to issues of military security such as the ravaging effects of the HIV/AIDS pandemic, the almost Sisyphean struggle to eradicate river blindness, smallpox, and other infectious diseases that continue to ravage Third World populations and for which the external response, whether unilateral or multilateral, may not be as critical as the resolution itself.

Second, whether external response to human rights abuses is defined by the type of abuses? Differently put, whether certain categories of human rights abuses deserve an international response while others do not? And if so, which ones and who decides? The concern here is whether the community of nations should be required to focus its attention only on those human rights violations that touch on a people's right to *self-determination* or those connected to *flawed elections* which deny a people their fundamental right to elect leaders of their choosing or those in which *human dignity/the human condition*[21] is under threat? Or should the imperative to act be limited only to those instances where the *national interests* (strategic or otherwise) of a major power (United States, Russia, France, Germany, Great Britain) are implicated or in response to threats to the '*world order*' (whatever that means)?

Thirdly, to what extent should the desire to intervene in the 'domestic' affairs of States, ostensibly to stop governments from systematically depriving citizens of their fundamental human rights, be tempered with some respect for the bedrock principle of state sovereignty. How and where should international law strike that delicate balance between state sovereign rights and the international obligation to intervene in domestic crises situations to protect citizens from their own repressive governments? Finally, to what degree should regional perceptions and expectations, on when and how the international community should react to human rights violations, be factored into the unilateral versus multilateral discourse? This question is on interest because of the possibility that this Manichaen split could be an artificial one to the degree that in some parts of the globe choosing one over the other is no choice after all. For instance, in francophone Africa, the 'gendarme of record' has always been France *not* the United States and it is from France that outside help to resolve domestic problems in this region is traditionally expected.[22] This *franco-dependence* or perhaps *francophilia*

[21] One scholar has defined human dignity as 'the particular cultural understanding of the inner moral worth of the human person and his or her proper political relations with society.' *See* Rhoda E. Howard, Dignity, Community, and Human Rights, in HUMAN RIGHTS IN CROSS-CULTURAL PERSPECTIVE 81, 81–91 (A. AN-NA'IM ed., 1992).

[22] We Wish to Inform, *supra* note 8, at 154 ('France has rarely hesitated in the past to conduct unilateral, partisan military invasions to prop up its African clients.'); *see also* Never Again, *supra* note 8.

while problematic to post-colonial nationalists is understandable nonetheless since it is the unfortunate by-product of a long colonial history, cemented by a shared language and culture and a dense and extensive network of commercial, financial and defense arrangements.

II. THE LEGAL FRAMEWORK FOR GLOBAL COMMUNITY INVOLVEMENT

A useful starting point for any legal analysis of the right to intervene in the domestic affairs of another state in defense of fundamental human rights is the Charter of the United Nations, the Constitution of the world and the highest instrument in the international hierarchy of international and domestic documents on human rights. In the wake of the most massive and systematic violations of human rights in modern history the United Nations Organization was born. The Preamble to the Charter reaffirms 'faith in fundamental human rights, in the dignity and worth of the human person, in the equal rights of men and women.' It goes on to declare the determination of the peoples of the United Nations 'to promote social progress and better standards of life in larger freedoms.' Article 1 which speaks to the purposes and principles of the United Nations includes in its paragraph 3 international cooperation 'in promoting and encouraging respect for human rights and for fundamental freedoms for all without distinction as to race, sex, language or religion.' This principle comes up again in Article 55, paragraph (c). In article 13, paragraph 1, subparagraph (b), human rights are listed among the responsibilities for study and recommendation of the General Assembly and the Economic and Social Council. Article 68 authorizes the Economic and Social Council to set up commissions on human rights while Chapters XI and XII dealing with non-self-governing territories and the international trusteeship system also include numerous human rights provisions. Finally in article 56, Members pledge themselves to cooperate with the United Nations organization for the achievement of its human rights goals.Clearly article 56 intended for the enforcement of human rights to be a cooperative effort with Members working in concert with the United Nations and *not* unilaterally.

The drafters may have unwittingly set up a clash between the responsibility of the international community to promote and protect human rights and the principle of non-intervention in the internal affairs of member states. Where Article 1 of the Charter acknowledges that a fundamental purpose of the United Nations is the promotion and respect for human rights and fundamental freedoms, Article 2, paragraphs 4 and 7 make clear that U.N. Members must 'refrain in their international relations from the threat or use of force against the territorial integrity or political independence of any state, or in any manner inconsistent with the Purposes of the United Nations,'[23] and

> Nothing contained in the present Charter shall authorize the United Nations to intervene in matters which are essentially within the domestic jurisdiction of any state or shall require the Members to submit such matters to settlement under the present Charter; but this principle shall not prejudice the application of enforcement measures under Chapter VII.[24]

Article 2, paragraphs 4 and 7 reflect the priority given to the principle of state sovereignty by the drafters of the Charter.[25] However, the prohibition against external intervention in matters that are domestic in nature does not entirely foreclose such action. Chapter VII of the Charter outlines the limited circumstances under which the United Nations may take action, forcible or non-forcible, against a sovereign nation. The juxtaposition of Articles 1.3 and 2.4 gave rise to two inter-related questions. First, when does the doctrine of non-intervention yield to the international responsibility to promote and encourage respect for human rights? Secondly, at what point do domestic human rights abuses pose a threat to international peace to justify a response from the community of nations?

A. The Doctrine of Non-Intervention

The doctrine of non-intervention is to international law what the Hippocratic Oath is to medicine—first do no harm.[26] Any discussion on external response to domestic human rights abuses must commence with the principle of non-intervention—the norm from which any departure has to be justified. It took a multinational effort that spanned five continents to bring an end to the barbarous Nazi regime, so it was not that much of a surprise that the drafters of the United Nations Charter showed a strong preference for multilateral over unilateral action in defense of the rights enshrined in the Charter.

The authority for collective intervention is granted by Articles 39, 41, and 42 of Chapter VII. Article 39 gives the Security Council the general authority to take action when there is a threat to the peace:

> The Security Council shall determine the existence of any threat to the peace, breach of the peace, or act of aggression and shall make recommendations, or decide what

[23] U.N. Charter, art. 2, para 4.

[24] *Id.* art. 2, para 7.

[25] 24 Forcible Humanitarian Intervention, *supra* 5, at 141.

[26] International Commission on Intervention and State Sovereignty, THE RESPONSIBILITY TO RESPOND: REPORT OF THE INTERNATIONAL COMMISSION ON INTERVENTION AND STATE SOVEREIGNTY 33, para. 4.12 (December 2001) [Hereinafter 'ICISS Report']; *see also* DECLARATION ON THE INADMISSIBILITY OF INTEVENTION IN THE DOMESTIC AFFAIRS OF STATES AND THE PROTECTION OF THEIR INDEPENDENCE AND SOVEREIGNTY

measures shall be taken in accordance with Articles 41 and 42, to maintain or restore international peace and security.[27]

Article 41 of Chapter VII governs the use of non-forcible collective measures to ensure compliance with Security Council decisions:

> The Security Council may decide what measures not involving the use of armed force are to be employed to give effect to its decisions, and it may call upon Members of the United Nations to apply such measures. These may include complete or partial interruption of economic relations and of rail, sea, air, postal, telegraphic, radio, and other means of communication, and the severance of diplomatic relations.[28]

Finally, the authority to employ military force is granted in limited circumstances by Chapter VII, Article 42:

> Should the Security Council consider that measures provided for in Article 41 would be inadequate or have proved to be inadequate, it may take such action by air, sea, or land forces as may be necessary to maintain or restore international peace and security. Such action may include demonstrations, blockade, and other operations by air, sea, or land forces of Members of the United Nations.[29]

Article 42 is invoked only in response to crisis situations that threaten 'international peace and security.' This language has been used to justify United Nations collective actions in defense of human rights.[30]

1. *The Problem with the Language of Intervention*

Strong reservations continue to be registered over the use of the term 'humanitarian intervention' in human rights abuse situations. After an exhaustive study of external reactions to domestic human rights violations, the International Commission on Intervention and State Sovereignty[31] came to the conclusion that the expression 'humanitarian intervention' is not particularly helpful in carrying forward the debate for or against the 'right

[27] U.N. Charter, *supra* note 23, art. 39.

[28] *Id.* art. 41.

[29] *Id.* art. 42.

[30] Ravi Mahalingam, The Compatibility of the Principle of Nonintervention With the Right of Humanitarian Intervention, 1 UCLA J. INT'L L. & FOREIGN AFF. 221, 245 (1996).

[31] This cross-national independent body was set up in September 2000 by the Canadian Government in response to a statement made by the United Nations Secretary-General challenging the international community to try to build to build consensus around the basic questions of principle and process with respect to the so-called 'right to humanitarian intervention.' The Commission's mandate was 'to promote a comprehensive global debate on the relationship between intervention and state sovereignty.' After twelve months of intensive research, worldwide consultations and deliberation, the Commission issued its report: The Responsibility to Protect.

to intervene' and proposed in its stead the term 'responsibility to protect.'[32] The Commission justifies this change in nomenclature because it re-focuses 'attention where it should be most concentrated, on the human needs of those seeking protection or assistance.'[33] In a similar vein, in this essay the term 'responsibility to respond' is preferred over the term the 'right to intervene' because the former properly focuses attention where it should be—on those who are on the receiving end of human rights abuses. They are the ones best placed to assess the effectiveness of external responses to their plight. As Jean-Jacques Rousseau is reputed to have observed, the view of the tree from the branches is quite different from that as seen from its roots. So too the effectiveness of international response to human rights abuses are likely to elicit different reactions from the victims and their rescuers. While the latter might get bogged down over the legality of their right to intervene, the victims for their part worry about the nature and effectiveness of international responses.

The discussion will treat external responses on a continuum of responses of varying degrees of involvement with military intervention at one extreme and mere condemnation at the other.[34] United Nations Secretary-General, Kofi Annan, has underscored the importance of defining external responses to domestic violations of human rights 'as broadly as possible, to include actions along a wide continuum from the most pacific to the most coercive.'[35] Responses would include, in ascending order of gravity, diplomatic isolation, denial of visa privileges to high-ranking State officials and their relatives, withdrawing air landing rights, denying it loans, denying MFN status, removing the country from the General System of Preferences, cutting off foreign aid and freezing assets, imposing trade embargo (exempting humanitarian supplies), and military intervention.[36]

[32] The traditional language's preoccupation with 'the of humanitarian intervention' or the 'right to intervene' was found unhelpful for three reasons: 'First, it necessarily focuses attention on the claims, rights and prerogatives of the potentially intervening states much more so than on the urgent needs of the potential beneficiaries of the action. Secondly, by focusing narrowly on the act of intervention, the traditional language does not adequately take into account the need for either prior reventive effort or subsequent follow-up assistance, both of which have been too often neglected in practice. And thirdly, although this point should not be overstated, the familiar language does effectively operate to trump sovereignty with intervention at the outset of the debate: it loads the dice in favour of intervention before the argument has even begun, by tending to label and delegitimize dissent as anti-humanitarian.' *See* ICISS Report, *supra* note 25, at 17, para 2.4, 21, para. 2.28.

[33] *Id.* at p. 20, para. 2.22

[34] *See* John C. Pierce, Note, The Haitian Crisis and the Future of Collective Enforcement of Democratic Governance, 27 LAW & POL'Y INT'L BUS 477, 482 (1996) [Hereinafter 'Haitian Crisis'].

[35] 35 Secretary General Presents His Annual Report to General Assembly, Press Release SG/SM/7136 GA/9596, 20 Sept. 1999. [Hereinafter '1999 Annual Report']

[36] *See also* Harold Hongju Koh, Democracy and Human Rights in the United States Foreign Policy?: Lessons from the Haitian Crisis, 48 S.M.U. L. REV. 189, 196–197 (1994).

2. The Reach and Scope of 'Threat to the Peace' and 'Breach of the Peace'

Before a decision to respond, unilaterally or collectively, in the internal affairs of another State is taken, the Security Council must first determine, under Article 39 of the Charter, whether there exists 'any threat to the peace, breach of the peace or act of aggression.' What types of domestic human rights situations meet this standard in order to justify derogation from the principle of non-intervention. The answer to this question depends heavily on whether the terms 'threat to the peace' or 'breach of the peace' are given a narrow and restrictive interpretation or are read broadly.

a) *The Narrow Interpretation.* The terms 'any threat to the peace,' and 'breach of the peace,' have been interpreted somewhat restrictively to include 'gross and systematic violations . . . with grave human consequences,'[37] or 'massive violations of humanitarian law and crimes against humanity,'[38] or 'overwhelming humanitarian catastrophes,'[39] or situations of 'extreme humanitarian distress on a large scale requiring urgent relief'[40] or violations which genuinely 'shock the conscience of mankind'[41] or which present such a 'clear and present danger to international security'[42] or serious breaches 'on a widespread scale and a consistent pattern of serious violations.'[43] One proponent of this restrictive interpretation contends that nothing in the *travaux* of the United Nations Charter suggests that the parties envisioned a government's treatment of its own nationals as likely to catalyze a threat or breach of peace within the meaning of Article 39 and related articles.[44] The problem with this view is that the historical conditions in which this language was drafted have changed radically leaving us to ask how the founding fathers of the U.N. would have wanted these words construed in today's world. We submit that they would have shied away from a narrow interpretation because it makes a mockery of the human rights instruments that followed on the heels of the Charter. More importantly, this restrictive interpretation has the effect of ruling out most cases of human rights abuses because of the frightfully high threshold it sets for determining the kinds of human rights violations that pose a threat to international peace. It is true that the United Nations was formed while memories of the holocaust were still fresh on the minds of its founding

[37] 1999 Annual Report, *supra* note 35.

[38] *See* Robin Cook, Guiding Humanitarian Intervention, Speech by the Foreign Secretary, Robin Cook, American Bar Association Lunch, QEII Conference Centre, London, Wednesday 19 July 2000.

[39] *Id.*

[40] *Id.*

[41] ICISS Report, *supra* note 26, at 33–34, para. 4.13.

[42] *Id.*

[43] Louis Henkin, Human Rights and 'Domestic Jurisdiction,' in HUMAN RIGHTS INTERNATIONAL LAW AND THE HELSINKI ACCORDS, 22, 33 (Thomas Buergenthal ed. 1977).

[44] *See* Legitimacy of Intervention, *supra* note 13, at 190.

[45] *See* Restore Democracy, *supra* note 14, at 330.

members who were determined to avoid a repetition of the unspeakable assaults on human dignity that characterized the Nazi regime. But they could not have intended that the horrors of the holocaust—one of the worst crimes against humanity in all of history— would serve as the yardstick against which to measure human rights violations that pose a threat to international peace.

The focus on the *exceptional or extraordinary* human rights situations is misplaced because it leaves out a whole range of domestic human rights abuses whose potential for threatening international peace and security is equally as potent as the traditional types. The international commitment to the universality of human rights is absolute and cannot afford to be relativized. In order to avoid falling into this relativist trap, it would be necessary to give the 'threat to peace' clause of Article 39 a broader reading. Such an expansive interpretation would expand the kinds of domestic situations that pose a threat to international peace and would likely include such arguably internal matters as the denial of democratic governance.

b) *The Need for an Expansive Interpretation of the Democratic Entitlement.* Increasingly the right to democratic governance is gaining recognition as a fundamental human right—what Professor Thomas Franck calls the 'democratic entitlement.' A violation of this right to democracy necessarily gives rise to an international responsibility to assist democratic restoration. Unfortunately contemporary discussion of the right to live under a democratic form of government has been preoccupied with situations where there has been a 'usurpation of the sovereign prerogative of a population to be governed by those it has democratically elected.'[45] As a result, calls for democratic restoration, i.e., international response to violations of the right to democracy, have been limited to measures designed to restore democratically elected governments that fall victims to military coups.[46] On the other hand, efforts directed at the removal of repressive and authoritarian governments have been few and far in between.

W. Michael Reisman has rightly observed that '[m]ilitary coups are terrible violations of the political rights of all the members of the collectivity and

[46] Examples would include the United States intervention in Haiti under United Nations authorization or the ECOWAS (Economic Community for West Africa) interventions in Liberia and Sierra Leone. *See* e.g., W. Michael Reisman, Humanitarian Intervention and Fledgling Democracies, 18 FORDHAM INT'L L.J. 794, 795 (1995) [Hereinafter 'Humanitarian Intervention'] (support for democratic governments that find themselves imperiled by violent domestic anti-democratic forces). President Tejan Kabbah of Sierra Leone was overthrown in a coup on 25 May 1997, forcing him into exile in neighboring Guinea. Kabbah was eventually helped by the United States, Britain, and the Organization of African States to get his presidency back. But while in Guinea the U.S. and the U.K. paid the expenses of Kabbah's government in exile. *See* Baffour Ankomah, 'Chuck your bloody constitution in the dustbin,' Jacques Chirac to Pascal Lissouba, NewAfrican, May 1998.

they invariably bring in their wake the violation of all the other rights.'[47] One could not agree more. The very idea of military participation in civil politics, leaving aside for the moment how this involvement comes about, offends the spirit of participatory democracy. When this involvement is secured through the violent overthrow of a popularly elected government then it undermines the participatory rights that constitute the democratic prerogative. But there are other equally insidious means for violating popular sovereignty that do not carry the high drama of a *coup d'Jtat* nor, for that matter, arrest for long the attention of the global community. How else can one describe the deliberate and systematic violation of the agreed rules of the game for electing a democratic government? The democratic entitlement implies the right of the people to be able to remove repressive and authoritarian governments through constitutional means. Free and fair elections are inextricably linked to this human right to democratic governance.[48] A flawed electoral process ineluctably contributes to the obstruction of legitimate democracy in much the same way as a violent overthrow of a popularly elected government. Should the two not be treated similarly?

3.The Right to Democratic Governance in International Law

The right of a people to elect a government of their choice is a fundamental right recognized in numerous international and regional instruments. The Universal Declaration of Human Rights, the fountain of all subsequent human rights instruments, provides:

> The will of the people shall be the basis of the authority of government, this will shall be expressed in periodic and genuine elections which shall be universal and equal suffrage and shall be held by secret vote or by equivalent free voting procedures.[49]

Article 25 of the International Covenant on Civil and Political Rights also recognizes the importance of elections as the means for building a democratic government:

> Every citizen shall have the right and the opportunity . . .To take part in the conduct of public affairs, directly or through freely chosen representatives; To vote and to be elected at genuine periodic elections which shall be universal and equal suffrage and shall be held by secret ballot, guaranteeing the free expression of the will of the electors.[50]

[47] *Id.*
[48] *See* United Nations General Assembly Resolution 46/137, UNGA Res. 46/137, U.N. GAOR, 46th Sess., Agenda Item 98, addendum pt. 1, at 2, U.N. Doc. A/46/721/Add. 1 (1991).
[49] Universal Declaration of Human Rights, *supra* note 1.
[50] INTERNATIONAL COVENANT ON CIVIL AND POLITICAL RIGHTS. Concluded at New York, 16

With the exception of the European Convention on Human Rights, virtually all the extant regional human rights instruments provide for the right to free and fair elections as the sine qua non of participatory democracy. Article XX of the American Declaration of the Rights and Duties of Man states:

> Every person having legal capacity is entitled to participate in the government of his country, directly or through his representatives, and to take part in popular elections, which shall be by secret ballot, and shall be honest, periodic and free.[51]

Similar language is contained in the 1969 American Convention on Human Rights which provides in its Article 23:

> Every citizen shall enjoy the . . . [right] . . . [t]o vote and be elected in genuine elections, which shall be by universal and equal suffrage and by secret ballot that guarantees the free expression of the will of the voter. . . .[52]

And the more recent African Charter on Human and Peoples Rights recognizes the right of every citizen 'to participate freely in the government of his country, either directly or through freely chosen representatives in accordance with the provisions of the law.'[53]

International commitment to democratic governance has also been exprcssed in General Assembly Resolution 45/50 which strongly affirms the conviction of U.N. members:

> That periodic and genuine elections are a necessary and indispensable element of sustained efforts to protect the rights and interests of the governed and that, as a matter of practical experience, the right of everyone to take part in the government of his or her country is a crucial factor in the effective enjoyment by all of a wide range of other human rights and fundamental freedoms, embracing political, economic, social, and cultural rights.[54]

In addition to the articulation of principles there is also wide agreement on the criteria that define a free and fair election. These have been summarized by Gregory Fox as: (1) periodic elections at reasonable intervals; (2) a secret ballot; (3) honesty in vote tabulation; (4) universal suffrage, with

Dec, 1966. Entered into force, 23 March 1976. 993 U.N.T.S. 171, 1966 U.N.J.Y.B. 193; 1977 U.K.T.S. 6, Cmnd. 6702; reprinted in 6 I.L.M. 368 (1967).

[51] AMERICAN DECLARATION OF THE RIGHTS AND DUTIES OF MAN. Adopted at Bogota by the Ninth International Conference of American States, 30 March–2 May 1948. O.A.S. Res. XXX, O.A.S. Off. Rec. OEA/Ser. L/V/1.4 Rev. (1965).

[52] AMERICAN CONVENTION ON HUMAN RIGHTS. Concluded at San Jose, 22 November 1969. Entered into force, 18 July 1978. 1114 U.N.T.S. 123; O.A.S.T.S. No. 36, O.A.S. Off. Rec. O.E.A./Ser. L/V/II.23 doc. 21 rev. 6 (1979); reprinted in 9 I.L.M. 673 (1970).

[53] AFRICAN CHARTER ON HUMAN AND PEOPLE'S RIGHTS. Concluded at Banjul, 26 June 1981. Entered into force, 21 October 1986. O.A.U. Doc. CAB/LEG/67/3 Rev. 5; reprinted in 21 I.L.M. 59 (1982).

[54] UNGA Res. 45/150 (Feb. 21, 1991).

minor exceptions permitted minors, prisoners, the mentally ill, and the like; (5) an absence of discrimination against voters and candidates; (6) freedom to organize and join political parties, which must be given equal access to the ballot, and an equal opportunity to campaign; (7) to the extent the government controls the media, the right of all parties to present their views through the major media outlets; and (8) supervision of the election by an independent council or commission not tied to any party, faction, or individual, whose impartiality is insured in both law and practice.[55]

It is evident from the foregoing discussion that treaty law recognizes free, fair and transparent elections with universal suffrage and secret balloting as the means by which a people can express its will and on which the legitimacy of a government is based. It is imperative therefore that means be made available to the people through which they can vindicate this legal right if it is to mean anything—*ubi jus ibi remedium.* This rule was framed in the context of fundamental rights in *Marbury v. Madision:*

> The very essence of civil liberty certainly consists in the right of every individual to claim the protection of the laws, whenever he receives an injury. . . . It is a general and indisputable rule, that where there is a legal right, there is also a legal remedy by suit or action at law whenever that right is invaded. . . .[56]

It goes without saying that international human rights instruments must furnish a remedy for the violation of human rights norms. The primary responsibility for enforcing these internationally accepted human rights norms falls on the community of nations.[57] It means therefore that this community cannot routinely ignore widespread and repeated violations of the people's right to elect leaders of their choice in non-coerced elections without running the risk of diluting this treaty-protected right and transforming it into a legal right without a legal remedy.

III. CONTRASTING RESPONSES TO HUMAN RIGHTS VIOLATIONS

In the section that follows we present three examples of human rights violations in Sub-Saharan Africa which elicited conflicting external responses. The first case-study does not quite fall in the category of the right to a democratic government but it raises questions about the disposition of the world community to extend its policing reach in the internal affairs of a

[55] *See* Political Participation, *supra* note 14, at 251.

[56] *See* Marbury v. Madison, 5 U.S. 137, 163 (1803)(citing Blackstone Commentaries 23).

[57] The Members of the United Nations have pledged themselves to jointly and severally take action to promote the 'universal respect for, and observance of, human rights and fundamental freedoms for all without distinction as to race, sex, language, or religion.' *See* U.N. Charter, articles 55 (C) and 56.

Sub-Saharan African State especially when the violations of human rights clearly shock the conscience of human kind. The other two examples speak directly to violations of the right to free choice, a core element of the democratic entitlement. The Zimbabwean and Cameroonian electoral cases lend context and perspective to this discourse on the trade-offs and pay-offs from unilateralism and multilateralism as appropriate responses to threats to international peace and security.

A. Genocide in Rwanda as the World 'Stood Around With Its Hands in Its Pockets!'

In his 1999 Annual Report to the General Assembly, U.N. Secretary-General Kofi Annan sadly noted that 'the genocide in Rwanda will define for our generation the consequences of inaction in the face of mass murder. . . .'[58] The indifference of the international community to the horrors of Rwanda[59] raises serious doubts about its commitment to the rule of law. This blight neglect has been described in these graphic terms by Alain Destexhe, Secretary General of *Médecins Sans Frontières*:[60]

> The international community barely realized that it was confronted with a repeat of a singular crime unknown since the Second World War. Haunted by the ghost of the recent conflict in Somalia, the United States and the Security Council abandoned the

[58] *See* 1999 Annual Report, *supra* note 35.

[59] In the weeks following April 16th1994, between 500,000 and one million Rwandans were killed. The majority of the killers were members of the Hutu ethnic group who constituted approximately 85% of the population while the victims, in the main, were Tutsis who comprised about 14% of the Rwandan population as well as a small number of moderate Hutus. The Belgians who colonized Rwanda ruled through a privileged class of Tutsis and by the time that Rwanda gained independence in 1961the persecution of the Tutsis had begun. As a result, a large number of Tutsis were forced to flee to neighboring Uganda. In the following decade the Hutu-dominated government prevented these refugees from returning to Rwanda. Thirty years later, on October 1, 1990, the Rwandan Patriotic Front (RPF), comprising largely of Tutsis began a military campaign invading Rwanda from Uganda. There followed a period of fighting and negotiations which resulted in the signing of the Arusha Peace Accord on August 4, 1993 between the Government of Rwanda and the RPF. The Accord provided for power sharing between the two groups, but the Hutu hardliners in the government took steps to obstruct its implementation. *See* We Wish to Inform, *supra* note 8; Alain Destexhe, RWANDA AND GENOCIDE IN THE TWENTIETH CENTURY (1995) [Hereinafter '20th Century Genocide]; Human Rights Watch, LEAVE NONE TO TELL THE STORY: GENOCIDE IN RWANDA (1999) [Hereinafter 'Genocide in Rwanda'].

[60] Winner of the 1999 Nobel Peace Prize, Médecins Sans Frontières (MSF) is an independent humanitarian medical aid agency committed to providing emergency medical assistance to populations in danger in more than 80 countries. It first got involved in Rwanda in 1991. MSF organized a highly successful public campaign in France in May and June 1994, denouncing the French government's complicity in the Rwanda genocide through its support of the Habyarimana regime. In 1998, MSF together with other NGOs and prominent academics called for the creation of a French parliamentary commission of inquiry into the role of the French government in the organization and execution of the Rwandan genocide between 1990 and 1994.

Tutsi. And when they finally did decide to take action, it was under the ambiguous banner of humanitarianism that pushed the genocide into the background as universal shock, horror and compassion moved the refugees in the cholera-stricken camps to centre stage.

When the massacres began in Kigali, the western world appeared concerned only for the fate of its own nationals. Within a few days, French and Belgian troops had evacuated almost every *white* person from Rwanda. . . . Throughout the world people watched film of armed soldiers helping to save their compatriots. *Those same soldiers were ordered to turn their backs on women and children being slaughtered by adolescents armed only with machetes and sticks. Rarely has then been an episode in history when differences in status and destiny of groups of human beings has been so obvious.*[61]

Since no international action can be taken without the leading role of the United States, the widely acknowledged global superpower, America's indifference to the Rwanda genocide was particularly telling. To begin with, the U.S. government was not even prepared to admit that what was occurring in Rwanda satisfied the definition of genocide under the 1948 Genocide Convention,[62] preferring instead to engage in semantic double-speak and 'shameless evasions.'[63] Understandably, smarting from its humiliation in Somalia, the U.S. not only chose to remain on the sidelines during the Rwanda crisis but appeared to have gone out of its way to block the United Nations from acting. In Destexhe's own words, the U.S. refused:

any new deployment of UN Blue Helmets unless all the necessary conditions (logistical, financial, troop deployments, etc.) were fulfilled—yet they could never be fulfilled *without* the active support of the superpower. . . . This Catch 22 situation was further complicated by the added condition that if America was too involved in any such operations they must have a direct bearing on US national interests.. . . As a result, the United States blocked the adoption of any firm resolution for action by the UN and refused to agree to resolution 719 of 17 May 1994, authorizing the

[61] *See* 20th Century Genocide, *supra note 59,* at 48 (emphasis added).

[62] *See* CONVENTION ON THE PREVENTION AND PUNISHMENT OF THE CRIME OF GENOCIDE. Done at New York, Dec. 9, 1948. Entered into force, Jan. 12, 1951; for the United States, Feb. 23, 1989 (defines genocide as the systematic destruction, in whole or in part, of a national, ethnical, racial or religious).

[63] For example, the following colloquy between Christine Shelley, a State Department spokeswoman and the press corps during a routine briefing captures this effort at obfuscation: 'Q: So you say genocide happens when certain acts happen, and you say that those acts have happened in Rwanda. So why can't you say that genocide has happened? Ms. SHELLEY: Because, Alan, there is a reason for the selection of words that we have made, and I have—perhaps I have—I'm not a lawyer. I don't approach this from the international legal and scholarly point of view. We try, best as we can, to accurately reflect a description in particularly addressing that issue. It's—the issue is out there. People have obviously been looking at it.' *See* We Wish to Inform, *supra* note 8, at 153 (emphasis added).

deployment of a maximum of 5500 men, until it had ensured that there was no risk of any real American commitment.[64]

Under U.S. prodding, the U.N. Security Council slashed the UNAMIR force by ninety percent, barely a week after its commanding officer, Major General Dellaire, had publicly declared, on April 21, 1994, that with just a force of 5,000 well-equipped soldiers and a free hand to fight the Hutu, he could bring the genocide to a rapid halt.[65] Three weeks later, May 13, 1994, as the Council, now confronted with mounting evidence of genocide in Rwanda, prepared to vote on restoring UNAMIR's strength, Ambassador Madeleine Albright, the permanent representative of the United States at the United Nations, succeeded in getting that vote postponed for four days.[66] Now fed-up with the foot-dragging at the U.N., a group of eight African countries expressed their willingness to dispatch an intervention force to Rwanda, provided the United States would provide 50 armored personnel carriers. Instead of lending the transport vehicles to the Africans, the U.S. 'decided *lease* [them] to the UN—where Washington was billions in arrears on membership dues—for a price of *fifteen million dollars*, transportation and spare parts included.'[67]

B. Protecting the Right to Vote and to Elect a Democratic Government

As the preceding discussion has tried to demonstrate, there is now a growing realization that the holding of free and fair elections is central to democratization. The understanding following the 1990 Copenhagen Meeting of the Conference of Security and Co-operation in Europe highlights this aspect of the democratic entitlement by linking governmental legitimacy to respect for the popular will.[68] The will of the people, freely and fairly expressed, through periodic and genuine elections is now seen as the basis of the authority and legitimacy of all governments. The much earlier International Covenant on Civil and Political Rights which now binds over two-thirds of the world community including the major powers, entrenches the free expression of the will of the electors in the second clause of Article 25 which prescribes the right 'to vote and to be elected at genuine, periodic

[64] *See* 20th Century Genocide, *supra* note 59, at 50; *see also* We Wish to Inform, *supra* note 8, at 150–154.

[65] *Id.* 150.

[66] *Id.* at 151.

[67] *Id.* [Emphasis added]; *see also* Genocide in Rwanda, *supra* note 59, at 646. The United Kingdom, for its part, contributed a grand total of 50 trucks. *Id.*

[68] *See* DOCUMENT OF THE COPENHAGEN MEETING OF THE CONFERENCE ON THE HUMAN DIMENSION OF THE CONFERENCE ON SECURITY AND CO-OPERATION IN EUROPE. Adopted by the Conference on Security and Co-operation in Europe at Copenhagen, 29 June 1990. *Reprinted in* 29 I.L.M. 1305 (1990) [Hereinafter 'Copenhagen Meeting'].

elections, which shall be universal and equal suffrage, and shall be held by secret ballot.' It would appear from the *travaux prJparatoires* that in the drafting of the Civil and Political Rights Convention, greater stress was placed on the election clause rather than the 'take part in the conduct of public affairs' clause in Article 25.[69]

1. *Zimbabwe's 2002 Controversial Presidential Election*

Zimbabwe's recent controversial presidential election that returned Robert Mugabe to power was watched with great interest in capitals around the world.[70] On the eve of the election, the *Sunday Times* of London carried a headline: 'Shadow over Africa.' What shadow, some asked?[71] At the close of the polls, the Observer Team dispatched by the Commonwealth of Nations declared the election flawed and called on Mugabe to conduct fresh elections consistent with the Harare Principles. When Mugabe declined their invitation, Zimbabwe was promptly suspended for one year from this venerable organization grouping together 54 States under the leadership of the United Kingdom. It did not take long thereafter before veteran observers of elections in sub-Saharan Africa began to question the speed with which the Commonwealth reacted to the Zimbabwean elections.[72] They pointed out that this was not the first election in this region to have been declared coerced, unfair and totally undemocratic by the Commonwealth—Cameroon's flawed 1997 and 2002 legislative elections, discussed below, come readily to mind. Nor was Zimbabwe's presidential election the first such poll in the continent that was accompanied by gross violations of human rights including targeted killings of opposition supporters. All things considered, the March 2002 presidential election in Zimbabwe was hardly a world-shaking event as one critic noted.[73]

If that is all it was then how does one begin to explain this harsh multilateral response to an event that has become fairly routine in sub-Saharan Africa? Some have speculated that were it not for the few thousand white

[69] *See* Henry Steiner, Political Participation as Human Right, 1 HARV. HUMAN RIGHTS Y.B. 77, 87–88, 90, 93 (1988). *See also*Ved Nanda, Commentary on International Intervention to Promote the Legitimacy of Regimes, in LAW AND FORCE IN THE NEW INTERNATIONAL ORDER, 181, 182 (Lori Fisler Damrosch & David J. Scheffer eds. 1991) (Argues that the focus on non-coerced and fair elections is not enough to determine governmental legitimacy. Rather, what matters is the genuineness of these elections, as measured in terms of the quality of electoral participation, degree of equality of access of different classes and ethnic groups in the political processes, the relative freedom of the media, and on.).

[70] *See* Desmond Davies, 'Letter from the Editor: Commonwealth Acts at the Right Time,' West Africa, 25th–31st 2002, p. 7.

[71] *See* Yolande Agble, 'What Shadow over Africa?' West Africa, 25th–31st March 2002, p. 8; col. 1 ('The Zimbabwean presidential elections were not really a world-shaking event and were it not for the few thousand white farmers whose future depended on which way the poll went, it would have excited little interest in the world at large.')

[72] *Id.*

[73] *Id.*

farmers whose fate hung precariously on the outcome and where a Mugabe win spelt disaster,[74] Zimbabwe's March 2002 presidential election would have excited little interest in many Western capitals. In other words, the outcome of this flawed election would have elicited the same spineless response from the Commonwealth as has been the case in many other flawed elections witnessed by high-powered Commonwealth Observer Missions.

2. *Cameroon's Flawed Parliamentary Elections—1997*

Cameroon's return to multiparty politics dates back to 1990. Since that time the Government has organized six elections. Of these, only two, the 1992 legislative and 1996 municipal elections, were considered relatively free, fair and transparent. But the parliamentary and presidential elections that were held in May and October, 1997, respectively, and the 2002 local government and legislative elections, were *universally* dismissed as falling below minimum international standards for democratic elections. Fortunately for those interested in exploring methods used by despicable governments to subvert the peoples' right to free choice, the 1997 elections were monitored by external observers whose reports provide firsthand eye witness account of how badly the polls were conducted. The focus of this brief case history is on the 1997 legislative elections, for two reasons. First, because these polls proved to be a dress rehearsal for future elections as the flaws that were observed would be reproduced on a greater scale five years later. Secondly, because this case demonstrates that a government bent on maintaining its monopoly on power becomes emboldened in pursuing this goal when it is fairly certain that the international community will not sanction it for gross electoral malpractices.

Months in advance of the polls (the same is true of the June 2002 twin legislative/municipal polls) spokesmen for the ruling party were already announcing the number of seats each of the contesting party would win. This turned out to be a self-fulfilling prophecy as the ruling Cameroon Peoples' Democratic Movement (CPDM) won the exact number of seats the

[74] Wafula Okumu who readily confesses to having once, but no more, 'hero-worshipped 'Comrade Bob', as Mugabe was and is still fondly referred to by millions of his admirers in Africa,' points to Mugabe's radical land reform program which promises to re-distribute land to landless Zimbabweans as the root of his problems with the West. About 4,400 white commercial farmers, including some members of the British House of Lords and other individuals connected to the British establishment, own 12.2 million hectares of Zimbabwe's prime farming land. While a few whites, including a number of absentee landlords, have alienated large tracts of land, 1.2 million black communal households are crammed into 15.4 million hectares of land, much of it not arable. *See* Wafula Okumu, Is it Democracy or Democrazy for Africa? (Reflections on Elections: Zimbabwe, Congo and Madagascar), THE PERSPECTIVE, March 19, 2002, at 3 [Hereinafter cited as ['Democrazy']. Available in http://www.theperspective.org/democrazy.html.

Minister of Communications had predicted it would win; enough seats to assure it an absolute majority in the National Assembly.[75] The quest to secure a dominant position for the CPDM in the National Assembly was accomplished at TWO LEVELS, at the level of electoral processes and procedures and at the level of structures; and in THREE STAGES: before and after the elections and on polling day itself.

Drawing on the reports prepared by two observer mission– the Commonwealth Observer Group and the U.S.-based International Foundation for Election Systems (IFES)— who were in Cameroon at the invitation of the Government, how the May 17, 1997—we show how this electoral exercise failed to meet the most elementary standards of fairness and transparency.[76]

(a) *ELECTORAL PROCESS/PROCEDURES* were manipulated in several ways with the result that the playing field was tilted to the advantage of the ruling party and at the expense of the opposition parties.

(1) Demarcation of *constituency boundaries* was done haphazardly since the objective was gerrymandering in order to create a disproportionate number of seats in constituencies where the President of the Republic and leader of the ruling party enjoys strong ethnic support. Special constituencies were also carved out in under-populated rural areas where traditional rulers beholden to the Government were able to intimidate their subjects to vote for the CPDM. The Observer Team 'noticed very wide discrepancies between the sizes of population represented by constituency seats' and called for a formula for boundary demarcation that would 'give effect to the cardinal principle of equal representation by population while taking into account peculiar local circumstances.'[77]

(2) *Inadequacy of Programs for Voter Education and Training of Polling Officials*: An internationally-funded program to train some 2000 or more domestic polling observers was inexplicably canceled by the Ministry of Territorial Administration.[78] As the Observer Group noted: 'This meant

[75] In 1997 the CPDM won 116 of the 180 seats in the National Assembly; five years later in the June 2002 elections this number was increased to 150 seats. The leading opposition party, the Social Democratic Front (SDF) managed 43 seats in 1997 only to see this number reduced to 22 in 2002.

[76] *See* Cameroon's Recent Parliamentary Elections: Observations and Recommendations, Submission by Professor Ndiva Kofele Kale to Honorable Edward R. Royce, Chairman, Subcommittee on Africa, U.S. House of Representatives, Washington, D.C., Friday, 26 September, 1997.

[77] *See* Commonwealth of Nations, Commonwealth Observer Group Report 1 (1997) [Hereinafter cited as 'Commonwealth Observer Report']; *see also* International Foundation for Electoral Systems, Report 1, 20–23, 55 #6 (1997) [Hereinafter cited as 'IFES Report'].

[78] In the 2002 legislative/municipal elections, Cameroon's churches had organized training in election monitoring for more than 3,000 local observers but the Ministry of Territorial; only accredited 50! *See* Cameroon's Opposition wants elections annulled. Available at http://www.afrol.com/News2002/cam011.

that the number of independent local observers was greatly reduced' which accounts for the 'few local monitors on polling day.'[79] The stuffing of ballot boxes, multiple voting, underage voting and other such fraudulent practices were evident in polling stations where there were no independent observers.[80]

(b) The process was undermined through a process of deliberate and *SELECTIVE DISENFRANCHISEMENT* of eligible voters before the polls and on election day. This began with the registration process which, as the Observer Group found out, was seriously flawed.[81]

(1) *Before the polls*. The Observer Group observed in its report that: (a) 'very many' eligible voters 'who wished to register . . . were prevented from doing so,' (b) the unavailability of voter registration cards for registered voters prior to the polls and even at polling stations on polling day 'contrary to assurances given by the authorities; (c) the distribution of voters' cards by unauthorized persons such as quarter heads, traditional rulers, etc., a process which was open to abuse; (d) the failure by the Ministry of Territorial Administration to publish or otherwise make available voters' registers to citizens in advance of polling day.[82]

The manipulation of the registration process largely accounts for the significant drop in the number of eligible voters on the register by 'some 300,000 from the number of voters who were on the register used for the municipal election in January 1996.'[83] Out of a population of roughly 14 million, only 3,719,774 eligible voters were on the register and as the Observer Group noted: '. . . one would have expected the number of voters to have been substantially higher,'[84] to which IFES adds 'particularly given the 2.9% annual increase in the population.' IFES puts the blame on low registration on the registration process itself: 'It is unlikely,' their Report notes, 'that this drop in registration is completely based on voter apathy as some have suggested. Widespread shortcomings in the registration process were mostly to blame for the low registration figures for the 1997 elections.'[85] 'Voter registration and preparation of the voters' register are fundamental to the conduct of a credible election' so observed the Commonwealth Group. This view is shared by IFES.[86] When a process so fundamental to the conduct of an election is tampered with then the outcome predictably cannot be a true and honest representation of political realities on the ground. The process of disenfranchising voters continued right up to the day of election.

[79] *See* Commonwealth Observer Group Report, *supra* note 77; *See also* IFES Report, *supra* note 77, at 39, 42–43.

[80] *Id.* at 39, 42–43.

[81] *Id.* at 38.

[82] *Id. at* 28.

[83] *See* Commonwealth Group Report, *supra* note 77.

[84] *Id.*

[85] *See* IFES Report, *supra* note 77, at 27.

[86] *Id.* at 26–28.

(2) *On Polling Day*: (a) 'many potential voters with evidence of registration' were not allowed to vote 'because their names were not on the register' even though they could establish their identity through their national identity cards. (b) the late publication of the list of polling stations which 'resulted in many voters being unable to locate their designated station.' (c) the lack of election materials including ballots; (d) inappropriate presence of security officials, intimidation and harassment by party supporters.[87]

(c) *The Lengthy Period for Processing Electoral Returns*: 'The present system under which electoral returns are processed over an extended period of time before official results can be announced [20 days after the polls]' detracts 'from the transparency of the elections, and is detrimental to public confidence.' Over 140 petitions were submitted to the Constitutional Council detailing how senior representatives of the Administration, notably Senior Divisional Officers (SDO's) and Divisional Officers (DO's) took advantage of this time lag to engage in massive falsification of the results sheets.

ELECTORAL STRUCTURES: The entire election machinery was compromised. The structural checks-and-balances built into the electoral code to guarantee fairness and transparency were simply swept aside by SDOs and DOs who were hell bent on securing a victory for the ruling party.

1. *The Partisan Role of the Ministry of Territorial Administration*: '[I]t is our view that the administration of the election apparatus by a government department under the leadership of a Minister of Government undermined confidence in the process,' was one of the conclusions reached by the Commonwealth Observer Group.[88]

2. *The Partisan Role of Auxiliary Agents*: The use of traditional rulers and quarter heads who were members of the ruling party in the registration of voters and distribution of voters' cards and the use of their residences as polling stations was in violation of the electoral laws. The Observer Group found 'the practice of locating polling stations in or adjacent to [the] private residences [of these auxiliary agents] to be detrimental to the progress that has been made towards the establishment of a neutral and transparent electoral system. . .' and made it clear that.' any participation by the chiefs [in the electoral process] should be clearly defined by law in order that the neutrality of the election machinery is not compromised.'[89]

3. *The Creation and Composition of Key Electoral Institutions*: Their creation was delayed until the last minute and they were usually packed with members beholden to the Administration. In the case of (a) the National Commission for Final Counting of Votes , the Observer Group complained about its composition: '[W]e . . . do not consider that the composition of the National Commission for the Final Counting of Votes,

[87] *Id.* at 39–40. [88] *Id.* at.18. [89] *Id.* at 40.

with its large number of government officials provided sufficient assurances of transparency. . . . We urge that the constitution of such an important body, as well as of all the various other commissions involved in the electoral process, should take place early in the electoral time frame ;' (b) the Constitutional Council: 'Some of the processes and institutions envisaged by the Constitution which would have increased the consensual climate were either not enacted or created. The most important of these is the Constitutional Council. . . . [whose] intended responsibilities were given to the Supreme Court, all of whose members are appointed by the Head of State.'

4. *The Subversion of State Institutions:* Because no effort has been made to separate the state apparatus from that of the ruling party, resources from the former were blithely appropriated by the latter. Weeks before the elections, Yaounde was emptied of its offices as Ministers and other ranking officials were sent out to their provinces of origin to campaign for the CPDM. Government vehicles and those belonging to state corporations were very much in evidence during the campaigns; money, T-shirts, food and drinks were used unabashedly by Government Ministers and their agents to buy votes. The CPDM's unlimited access to the resources of the state gave 'the ruling party a marked residual advantage' as the Observer Group found out.

5. *The Aftermath of the Elections:* The handling of election petitions by the Constitutional Council confirmed public cynicism about Cameroon's republican institutions; that no institution whose members are appointees of the Head of State can summon the courage to 'do the right thing.' The Constitutional Council heard 145 petitions in 14 hours![90] This pace was so furious that it raised serious questions about the quality of judicial review. In the end, the Constitutional Council let stand the results that were fixed at the level of the divisional offices. Cameroonians were not surprised nor fooled. And the international observers who came to monitor these elections also took note.

At the close of the 1997 polls, the independent foreign monitors were unanimous in their observation that the flaws which contributed immensely in undermining voter credibility and confidence in the electoral system stemmed from one source, the Ministry of Territorial Administration. Its partisan role in the conduct and organization of elections made it possible for the government-cum-ruling party to be both player and referee in every election organized and to be in a position to dictate the number of seats it desired. In six elections between 1992 and 2002, the Ministry has demonstrated its inability or unwillingness to serve the Cameroonian people in an impartial way.[91] In order to create a level playing field, the entire electoral

[90] *Id.* at 47ff. [91] *Id.* Appendix III, p. 3.

process must be entrusted to a neutral body free of the control and influence of the executive branch. The Commonwealth Observer Group went on record with its:

> [F]irm view that to hold a viable poll in Cameroon the creation of an impartial and autonomous institution, such as an independent electoral commission, with the necessary legal and financial authority, is a given requirement. The creation of such a body will accomplish two things (1) enhance the credibility of the outcome of the poll and (2) divorce the administration and conduct of the election from the structures and institutions of the executive arm of government and the ruling party.[92]

This and other recommendations made by the international observers were intended to contribute toward improving the electoral system in and strengthening Cameroon's grip on the democratization process. These recommendations were ignored;[93] not surprisingly when the next round of multiparty elections were held in June 2002, the same flaws observed five years earlier were everywhere evident. Yet the thoughtful recommendations of 1997 which represented the minimum response a community of nations committed to democratic governance could have offered to help consolidate democracy in Cameroon were never implemented. Electoral reforms of the kind contained in the Commonwealth Observer Group Report have been credited for the immense success of the May 2002 Burkinabe parliamentary elections:

> Although broader factors contributed to the dismay of the ruling party in the context of a protracted crisis of governance since 1998, several technical electoral reforms have played a critical role. These include in particular the reform of the electoral system, the introduction of the single ballot and *THE STRENGTHENING OF THE INDEPENDENCE OF THE ELECTORAL COMMISSION*.[94] (Emphasis added).

Not only have these reforms contributed to legitimizing elections as 'a genuine mechanism of democratic change' but they came about through generous international assistance.[95]

IV. FAILURE OF WORLD COMMUNITY TO PROTECT THE RIGHT TO DEMOCRATIC GOVERNANCE

Against a background of such overwhelming evidence of treaty law and state practice in support of the right of political participation and democ-

[92] *See* Commonwealth Observer Group Report, *supra* note 77.

[93] To the recommendation to create an independent elections commission, the government responded with a defanged National Elections Observatory which saw nothing, heard nothing and therefore did nothing to correct gross and ubiquitous electoral mal-practices.

[94] *See* Landmark Elections, *supra* note 12.

[95] *Id.*

ratic governance as a fundamental human right, what explains the tepid response of the international community to case after case of gross electoral fraud in sub-Saharan Africa. Justifying the international response to restore a popularly elected government in Haiti, America's onetime Permanent Representative to the United Nations, Jeanne Kirkpatrick, observed that 'if political democracy is viewed as 'a human right' shared by all persons, and if the 'world community' has an obligation to use force to protect those rights, then of course it is appropriate to use force to depose Haiti's military government—or any other military that achieves power by force and violates its citizens' rights.'[96] If Ambassador Kirkpatrick is right in asserting that democracy is a universal entitlement then the world community has a responsibility to protect and defend it wherever and whenever it is threatened. It is generally acknowledged that the core of the institutional architecture of democratic governance is the electoral system.[97] This system generates credibility, reliability and legitimacy when elections it organizes are free, fair and transparent. The reality on the ground in much of sub-Saharan Africa is that this key tenet of the democratic entitlement is repeatedly violated by autocratic leaders bent on perpetuating their stay in power with hardly an eyebrow raised by the world community. There are no extant cases where the world community took collective action to remove a repressive leader who has systematically abused the electoral process. The reasons for the lackluster international response, unilateral or multilateral, to this type of human rights abuses, i.e., electoral fraud, are fourfold.

A. *Interpretational Problems Associated With the 'Threat to the Peace' Language*

Part of the reason for the relative lack of attention world leaders accord electoral violations can be attributed to a perception that human rights abuses of this sort do not have trans-boundary effects. On the strength of this belief the 'threat to the peace' clause of Article 39 has been interpreted to exclude from its scope the after-effects of a flawed election. This interpretation does not conform to realities on the ground where abuses of the electoral system have been known to have spill-over effects. It is therefore necessary to broadening of the scope of Article 39's 'threat to the peace' to make room for violations of the rights to political liberty found in almost every human rights instrument in force today.

[96] See Jeanne Kirkpatrick, Is Democracy an Entitlement?, Wash. Post, Sept. 12, 1994, at op. ed.

[97] *See* Landmark Elections, *supra* note 12.

1. Vienna Convention Rules of Treaty Interpretation

Following the rules of treaty interpretation set forth in Section 3 of the Vienna Convention on the Law of Treaties, the general rule requires an interpretation that accords 'with the ordinary meaning to be given to the terms of the treaty in their context and in the light of its object and purpose.'[98] This is what is generally referred to as the textual method since it lays stress on the text of a treaty as the best expression of the common will of its parties. Article 1 of the U.N. Charter which enumerates the object and purpose of the United Nations lists as one of the Organization's main purposes the maintenance of '*international* peace and security, and to that end: to take effective *collective measures for the prevention and removal of threats to the peace, and for the suppression of acts of aggression or other breaches of the peace, and to bring about by peaceful means, and in conformity with the principles of justice and international law, adjustment or settlement of international disputes or situations which might lead to a breach of the peace.*' The operative word here is '*international,*' it is the adjective that modifies the word '*peace.*'[99] Given its ordinary meaning within the context of the avowed goals of the Charter, the words 'threat to the peace' when they appear in the charge to the Security Council in Article 39 would clearly be referring to situations that threaten *international* peace. The plain and ordinary meaning of the word 'international' is worldwide. Its use in Articles 1 and 39 is in reference to a threat that is global or worldwide in nature. A textual interpretation must take this as expressing the original will of the parties that adopted the Charter back in 1945. But what should one make of threats to the peace that have transnational though not worldwide effects. Should these be ruled out of the reach of Articles 1 and 39? It is submitted that to do so would unduly restrict the reach and scope of the United Nations Charter.

The Vienna Convention's treaty interpretation rules also provide that when the 'ordinary meaning', according to Article 31 (1), is 'ambiguous or obscure' or is likely to lead to a result that is 'manifestly absurd or unjust' then recourse to supplementary means of interpretation are permitted.[100] This subjective method as a supplementary method of interpretation allows for the examination of preparatory works or recourse to the circumstances surrounding the adoption of the Charter as adequate means of getting to the 'common intention of all the parties.'[101] Following the subjective method of interpretation, words used in a treaty have no meaning unless

[98] *See* Vienna Convention on the Law of Treaties, art. 31 (1).

[99] Art. 1, para. 1, U.N. Charter.

[100] Vienna Convention, *supra* note 98, Article 32.

[101] *See* V. D. Vegan, SOURCES OF INTERNATIONAL LAW 493 (1997) [Hereinafter 'Sources of Law'].

they express the common intention of its parties at the time of its conclusion. The paternity of this rule of treaty interpretation is usually traced to Grotius who rendered it in Latin as '*In fide quid senseris, non quid dixeris cogitandum*' (In matter of promises more important is the intention than the words used.).[102] Even though our preference is for the teleological method, it is submitted that reliance on the subjective method articulated in Article 32 of the Vienna Convention produces results that are manifestly absurd and unjust. Such would be the case for ignoring the fact that systematic and deliberate efforts to prevent a democratic government from coming into being have frequently produced effects that transcend national boundaries.

(a) The need for a dynamic approach in interpreting 'threat to the peace.'

The subjective method has been found of limited utility especially where treaties constituting international organizations, like the U.N. Charter, are concerned:[103]

> the object and purpose of these treaties at *the time of their interpretation* can sometimes prevail over the original wills of the parties. For this reason a functional or teleological interpretation of these treaties can in these circumstances be more justified to recourse to the subjective method.[104]

It is not only the subjective method of Article 32 of the Vienna Convention that is equally wanting, both are. Relying only on them is a sure way of arresting the progressive development of international human rights law by freezing it in time, the 1940's that is. At the time the Charter was drafted in 1945 the threats to peace and security that its framers feared the most were *inter-state* conflicts that potentially could expand to engulf much of the globe. Now the focus has shifted to *intrastate* conflicts many of which have trans-boundary effects. It has been argued that the drafters of the Charter did not envision a government's treatment of its own nationals (including denying them the right to exercise the franchise) as likely to pose a threat to the peace, breach of the peace, or an act of aggression.[105] It is conceivable that at the time the Charter was drafted consolidating and strengthening the democratic entitlement around the world may not have been a priority and for good reason.

In 1945 over one half of the peoples of the world were under European colonial domination and the major international concern then was how and when to free them from this colonial yoke. Not surprising therefore the

102 *See* Hugonis Grotii, DE JURE BELLI AC PACIS, libri tres, Janae 1680, Liber II, Caput XVI, '1/1 in V.D. Vegan, SOURCES OF INTERNATIONAL LAW 493 (1997).

103 *Id.*

104 *See* Sources, *supra* note 101, at 495.

105 *See* Legitimacy of Intervention, *supra* note 13, at 190.

founding fathers recognized the right of colonized peoples to self-determination and made provision for it in the Charter.[106] The many conflicts including wars of liberation that were waged to enjoy this right were seen as threats to international peace and subject to external intervention—Congo, Palestine, are a few examples. Self-determination has now moved into the domestic context as the right to democratic governance. This fundamental right of a people to determine how they will be governed is the functional equivalent of internal self-determination. Where the right to self-determination in its 1945 formulation envisioned a struggle between the colonized peoples and their colonizers, its internal manifestation transforms this struggle into one which pits the governed and their governors. The drafters of the Charter may not have anticipated this struggle nor considered its likely consequences as among the kinds of conflicts that represent a threat to international peace.

A more dynamic definition of the term 'threat to peace' is called for, one which recognizes the changed historical conditions in which the United Nations Charter must now operate; and second, that the Charter is a flexible document to be interpreted broadly especially when fundamental human rights are concerned. In this respect the teleological or functional method is much more useful than the objective or subjective approaches in the Vienna Convention in interpreting the 'threat to the peace' clause found *inter alia* in Articles 1 and 39 of the U.N. Charter. This functional approach allows for the recognition that at this historical juncture the threats to peace and security are no longer those originally thought of when the U.N. Charter was drafted over a half a century ago. Internal conflicts including those provoked by assaults on the right to democratic governance, broadly construed, have now become potent threats to world peace. While these may fall short of a threat that has *worldwide* reach, the fact that they transcend the frontiers of a single State and more often than not involve a number of neighboring States, makes them *inter-national.*

(b) The problem of global fatigue

A second reason for the noticeably lack of interest in domestic violations of the right to free choice may have to do with the problem of 'global' fatigue. Flawed elections in sub-Saharan Africa like official corruption have become almost a way of life in this part of the world so much that the community of nations may simply have become jaded by the frequency of their occurrence.[107] With some qualified exceptions, few elections in Africa in the last

[106] Among the purposes of the United Nations included in Article 1 of the Charter is respect for the principle of equal rights and self-determination of peoples.

[107] There are notable exceptions to this catalog of flawed elections in country after country in sub-Saharan Africa. The recent May 2002 parliamentary elections in Burkina Faso have been described as a 'breakthrough for democracy.' These elections marked the end of an era,

ten years have come anywhere close to meeting the minimal international standards set for free and fair elections.

c) Democracy is not for the Africans

Related to the sense of *déjà vu* discussed above is the patronizing view of democracy in Africa current in certain Western circles. This notion that Africans are congenitally unsuited for democratic governance and, if at all, only a 'tropicalized' version of democracy is good for them was confirmed by French President Jacques Chirac during a four-nation swing through francophone Africa in the summer of 1999. During a stop in Conakry, Guinea, Chirac appealed to the West to respect 'the African rhythm' of democratization; an implicit support for the slow pace of democratic reforms marked by persistent electoral frauds. Many Africans found Chirac's remarks an affront to the continent[108] but they may very well explain France's reluctance to intervene to put right flawed elections or its willingness to certify them to be otherwise. The remarks also confirm a view that the international community merely pays lip service to basic principles of democratic governance in so far as this relates to the Third World.[109]

d) External Involvement only when strategic interests are threatened

An African scholar has rightly observed that: '[t]rue democracy is not only about 'free and fair elections' that are certified to be so by the international election observers. Care should be exercised for elections not to be used to certify bad leadership or promote the interests of foreigners.'[110] The truth is that elections in Africa have routinely been used to validate repressive and autocratic governments because it fits in with the *realpolitik* interest of certain members of the international community. This much can be seen in the response to the Haitian crisis in the mid-1990's which offers a textbook

as they ended the dominance of the ruling Congress for Democracy and Progress ('CDP') which has monopolized political power since the return to multiparty democracy in that country in 1991. The May 2002 elections saw the ruling CDP losing its crushing majority in the 111-seat National Assembly. CDP's saw its share of seats shrink from 101 to 57 while the opposition increased its share from 7 to 54. The May 2002 presidential elections in Mali also saw the defeat of the candidate of the long-standing ruling ADEMA party and the election of an opposition candidate Amadou Toumani Toure to the presidency. *See* Landmark Elections, *supra* note 12, at 2.

108 *See* TIME.com, Aftermath of Empire, Aug. 16, 1999. Available in http://www.time.com/time/magazine/intl/article.

109 For an exposition of this thesis, *see* David Wippman, Defense of Democracy and Non-Intervention: Remarks, 19 HOUS. J. INT'L L. 659, 665 (1997) (Dismisses those who claim that international law recognizes a right to democracy justifying external intervention in its defense. Argues that there is as yet no broad right of democratic intervention and rhetoric over its existence has outpaced reality).

110 *See* Democrazy, *supra* note 74, at 3. Available in http://www.theperspective.org/democrazy.html.

example of an external involvement driven by the intervening state's own agenda. The United States' involvement was as much for altruistic humanitarian reasons as it was in pursuit of self interest. First, the U.S. government harbored genuine fears about the potential for an enormous influx of refugees to American shores.[111] These fears were understandable as hundreds of Haitian 'boat people' had been streaming to the U.S. long before the military overthrow of the Aristide government. It is also likely that U.S. support for the Haitian intervention had much to do with American economic interests. This was evident in the deliberate weakening of the 1992 Organization of American States' trade embargo against Haiti by allowing a series of exemptions for U.S. companies in the Haitian assembly sector was done ostensibly on humanitarian grounds to relieve the suffering of some 40,000 Haitian workers. Many observers saw through this gesture as a 'hollow cover for a blatant concession to U.S. business at the expense of an effective sanctions regime.'[112] For Lori Damrosch, by the action, the U.S. government was pursuing its 'self interest in flows of profits rather than of refugees.'[113] Of course, it would be naïve to expect that when States respond to defend domestic violations of human rights, it is always for altruistic reasons, after all, 'good international citizenship is a matter of national interest.'[114] Canada's International Commission on Intervention and State Sovereignty which explored this issue at length offers this sobering conclusion on what motivates States to respond to domestic human rights violations.

> The budgetary cost and risk to personnel involved in any military action may make it politically imperative for the intervening state to be able to claim some degree of self-interest in the intervention, however altruistic its primary motive might actually be. Apart for economic or strategic interests, that self-interest could, for example, take the understandable form of concern to avoid refugee flows, or a haven for drug producers or terrorists, developing in one's neighborhood.[115]

2. *Denial of the Right to Free Choice Represents a Real Threat to World Peace*

World community indifference to electoral mal-practices in sub-Saharan overlooks the potential threat these pose to international peace and security. Examples from sub-Saharan Africa where elections results have been

[111] *See* Julie Ann Waterman, Note, The U.S. Involvement in Haiti's Tragedy and the Resolve to Restore Democracy, 15 N.Y.L. SCH. J. INT'L & Comp. L. 187, 213 (1994).
[112] *See* Haitian Crisis, *supra* note 34, at 498.
[113] *See* Lori Fisler Damrosch, The Civilian Impact on Economic Sanctions, in ENFORCING RESTRAINT COLLECTIVE INTERVENTION IN INTERNAL CONFLICTS 274, 306 (Lori Fisler Damrosch ed., 1993).
[114] *See* ICISS, *supra* note 26, at 38, para. 4.36.
[115] *Id.* at 39, para. 4.35.

contested by public opinion, opposition parties and civil society underscore how the failure to preempt and prevent mal-practices could easily lead to a messy conflict with spill-over effects. Several consequences flow from popular contestation of the legitimacy of the polls and could include withdrawal of mass confidence and support in the electoral system and ultimately the central government itself. This can express in peaceful non-violent ways, for instance, when people simply refuse to take part in elections which are dismissed as State organized charades. It could also express itself in overt and violent confrontations with central authority.[116] The recent crisis in the Ivory Coast is a case in point where persistent and widespread complaints about the fairness and transparency of past elections went ignored until they reached a boiling point. First, it was the presidential election of October 2001 where a serious contender, Alassane Ouattara, a former Prime Minister of the Ivory Coast, was stripped of his Ivorian citizenship which disqualified him from being a candidate in that election. This was followed by elections to the National Assembly in July 2002 in which supporters of Ouattara's party, drawn mainly from the Muslim north, were systematically denied voting cards on account of their ethnicity and presumed sympathy for Ouattara. These deliberate and systematic attempts to subvert the electoral system immensely contributed to a full-blown civil war pitting a largely Muslim North against a predominantly Christian south from whence the current President Laurent Gbagbo hails.

The specter of a once stable Ivory Coast cleaved into two antagonistic parts caught in a savage fratricidal war with the potential of endangering the stability of the region has not been lost on African statesmen like President Olusegun Obasanjo of Nigeria who recently acknowledged that '[a] threat to Ivory Coast is a threat to all of us.'[117] With refugees streaming from both sides of the north/south divide into the six countries that share boundaries with the Ivory Coast—Mali, Ghana, Guinea, Sierra Leone, Liberia and Burkina Faso—[118] will most certainly add to an earlier

[116] Contested elections in the Congo Republic ended up in a destructed rebellion which split the country into war zones controlled by warlords, the Ninjas under the command of the former mayor of Brazzaville, Kolelas, and the Cobras led by Sassou-Nguesso, current president. In Cameroon, repeated electoral mal-practices have contributed to a home-grown secessionist movement, the Southern Cameroons National Council, which seeks to take the English-speaking section out of the present union. The troubles in Congo were not localized but had trans-boundary consequences; the secessionist impulse in Cameroon will likely spill into neighboring Nigeria where groups like the Ogoni and the Efiks are also asserting their right to self-determination.

[117] *See* Briony Hale, Ivorian Unrest Threatens West Africa Economy, Available athttp://www.news.bbc.co.uk/2/hi/business/2288938.stm .

[118] The United Nations food agency, the World Ford Program (WFP), has already warned of a humanitarian crisis in Ivory Coast on a scale comparable to the crisis in the Great Lakes region where millions have died in conflicts in Rwanda, the Democratic Republic of Congo and Burundi. According to the WFP 'all the ingredients are present for a large-scale humani-

massive displacement of hundreds of thousands of people fleeing from the civil wars in Liberia and Sierra Leone. The Ivorian crisis which has its roots in a democratization process gone awry could have been avoided—and this point bears emphasizing—but for the lack of international will.

Doing nothing in the Ivory Coast may have contributed to the present crisis. The Commission on Intervention and State Sovereignty takes the position that the *international* responsibility to protect also implies a concomitant *responsibility to prevent*, noting that 'the failure of prevention can have wide international consequences and costs.'[119] The collapse of the Ivorian state will entail unimaginable consequences and costs. To begin with, the disintegration or balkanization of the Ivory Coast represents a threat to regional stability that could ultimately endanger international peace and security. As long as the civil war rages on it will undoubtedly trigger an arms race in this corner of the globe as the combatants will aggressively enter the international arms market in search of weapons to destroy each other. The government has in fact admitted to spending over $1 billion to purchase arms from private companies in Angola. President Gbagbo conceded this much in response to rebel accusation that foreign soldiers had been imported from Angola to reinforce government troops: 'We bought weapons and ammunition in Angola at the beginning of the crisis, we paid for them, and they are now arriving,' he said.[120] In addition to involving Angola through arms purchases, the Gbagbo government has also imported mercenaries from South Africa to help contain rebel forces holding most of the country's north.[121] As if that is not enough, a 2,000 strong West African force is preparing to move into the Ivory Coast to begin peace-keeping duties. They will be relieving the more than 1,000 French troops who were flown in the early days of the conflict to ensure the security of French and other Western nationals. Here then is a crisis that began life as a purely localized affair now snowballing into an international conflict as it slowly but surely sucks in other countries into its dragnet.

tarian crisis through a massive displacement of people in the country and possible outflow of immigrant workers into neighbouring countries.' About 200,000 people have already been displaced. *See* BBC NEWS, Ivory Coast Defence Minister Axed, Available at http://www.bbc.co.uk/2/hi/world/africa/2323577/stm.

[119] *Id.* at 23, para. 3.3. The international efforts to comply with this responsibility to prevent are not unidirectional: they can take the form of inducements in some cases or tough measures including punitive measures. *Id. See also* Yogesh K. Tyagi, The Concept of Humanitarian Intervention Revisited, 16 MICH. J. INTL L. 883 (1995) (Where the author argues that once a humanitarian crisis breaks out, it is difficult to control, so instead of providing relief to refugees it is better to arrest situations that create refugees).

[120] *See* BBC NEWS, Ivorian Rebels Meet Mediators, Available at http://www.news.bbc.co.uk/2/hi/world/africa/2335745.stm.

[121] *See* Reuters, Pro-Government Mercenaries Reported in Ivory Coast, Available in BBC News, Ivorians Confirm Mercenary Presence, Available in http://story.news.yahoo.com/news; BBC News, Ivorians Confirm Mercenary Presence, Available in http://news.bbc.co.uk/1/hi/world/africa2449049.stm

Secondly, it would have been economically for the global community to have funded the organization of free and transparent elections. The funds that will now be used to rebuild a collapsing or collapsed Ivorian state are likely to outstrip what it would have taken to repair the flawed electoral system in the first place. Reforms that would have helped in inspiring confidence among a cross-section of the Ivorian population, Christian as well as Muslim, that is now on each others throats. Ivory Coast is the world's largest cocoa producer attracting a large number of migrant workers on the cocoa and tropical fruits plantations. With a $10 billion economy, four times the size of its neighbors of Mali and Burkina Faso, a sizeable services industry and a regional hub for banking, insurance and advertising, Ivory Coast was able to provide an environment where an estimated five million non-Ivorian Africans could find gainful employment.[122] If this economy is destroyed as a result of the current crisis, it will not be all that easy to rebuild it. More important, the scarce resources that would be earmarked for economic reconstruction would most likely be diverted from resources that should be directed at resolving Africa's perennial problems, those scourges that continue to plague this region: poverty, HIV/AIDS, malaria, river blindness, environmental degradation, and so on.

V. CONCLUDING STATEMENT

With due apologies to the relativists, this essay takes as a given that the human rights contained in the International Bill of Rights were meant to be *universally* enjoyed. Among the fundamental rights people in Sub-Saharan Africa are yearning to enjoy is the right to live under a democratic form of government. A key component of this democratic entitlement is the right to political participation. Agreement is fairly widespread that the means to give expression to this right is through periodic and genuine elections. The centrality of the right to participation in legitimizing governance imposes an affirmative duty on the community of nations to safeguard and deepen this right in regions where its observance is more in the breach. around the world. In sub-Saharan Africa, popular expectations that elections to democratically choose a government will be free and fair have not been borne out in practice. The reality has been one of *widespread, persistent and systematic* violations of this fundamental right. This then raises the question on whether the best approach to restoring this right is through external unilateral or multilateral action. The position taken here is that the form of external response is not as critical as the effort made to treat *comparable* cases

[122] *See* Briony Hale, Ivorian Unrest Threatens West Africa Economy, available at http://www.news.bbc.co.uk/2/hi/business/2288938.stm.

of violations of this right in like manner. That is, *consistency and equality of treatment* should be the hallmark of any form of external response, whether unilateral or bilateral or multilateral, to human rights abuses wherever these have occurred. Such a response should be seen as balanced and even-handedness in order for it to be well-received by the victims of those abuses. An external response should not be driven *primarily* and *exclusively* by the external actor's own narrow national and strategic geo-political interests but must be fully committed to democratic restoration as the ultimate goal. It is such commitment that guarantees a sustainable response without which success in the restorative quest becomes questionable.

CHAPTER TEN

Multilateralism and Unilateralism in a New Security Environment

*by Alexander Konovalov**

CHAPTER OUTLINE

I. Introduction
II. What is New in a 'New Security Environment'?
III. From 'Black September' 2001 in America to 'Black October' 2002 in Moscow: Strategy and Goals of the World Terrorism
  A. The events of September11, 2001 in America
  B. Attack on the French Supertanker
  C. The Explosion in Bali Island, Indonesia
  D. Terrorist Act in Moscow 23-26 October 2002
IV. Fighting International Terrorism: What are the Primary Targets
  A. Problem of Terrorists' Space
  B. Terrorism and its Sources of Finance
  C. Liquidation of Secret Terrorist Network and Combat Groups
  D. Islam and Islamic Extremists
V. Multilateralism Versus Unilateralism in Dealing With Contemporary Security Problems: Which Way to Go?

'In relations between nations, the progress of civilization may be seen as movement from force to diplomacy, from diplomacy to law.'
Louis Henkin. How Nations Behave. (1979)

* Professor at Moscow State Institute of International Relations; President of the Institute for Strategic Assessments; Lecturer at Columbia University, Princeton University, Brown University, University of Illinois, Naval War College, University of California at Los Angeles, Rand Corporation, University of Bundesvehr (Germany). From 1990 through 1999, Dr. Konovalov taught regularly at NATO Defense College (Rome). From 1995 through the year 2000, Dr. Konovalov was a Professor at the George C. Marshall European Center for Security Studies, Garmisch-Partenkirchen, Germany.

I. INTRODUCTION

The question—how the states should behave to insure national security and international stability in a changed security environment that appeared after the terrorist acts of September 11, 2001—remains open. The dilemma, a collective and multilateral response based on international law and institutions, versus individual unilateral actions based on common moral principles and undertaken possibly under dramatic time pressure, possesses numerous pros and cons for each choice. The September 11 terrorist attacks on the United States radically changed the global security environment and traditional stereotypes of threat assessments. Of course, the events of September 11 resulted from new trends in the world's economic, political, and security situation that began much earlier but were, for different reasons, not seen or at least dramatically underestimated by political leaders. September 11 brought the curtain down and it became clear that the non-state actors on the world political scene, including international terrorist networks and the like, that were threatening international security and stability were not part of a Hollywood thriller, but a political reality. The world after September 11 is seen in a substantially different way than the virtual stereotypes that prevailed in the minds of many analysts and political leaders before that day.

II. WHAT IS NEW IN A 'NEW SECURITY ENVIRONMENT'?

Even preliminary analyses of the events of September 11 allowed the formulation of some fundamental characteristics of the new political situation:

First, the United States stopped serving as the world's guarantor in the field of security. Of course America remains the only superpower, the militarily and economically most advanced, strongest, and most powerful state. But at the same time it became evident that in the face of new security threats, the United States alone would be unable to guarantee security not only to its European allies, but also to its own home territory. After September 11, America had to comprehend that it was no longer a self-sufficient country and could hardly be one in the foreseeable future.

Second, the events of September 11 clearly demonstrated the vulnerability of modern societies that contain numerous built-in mechanisms able to cause damage or even to destroy a state or shake its financial and economic systems when used by terrorists. The attacks on New York and Washington, D.C. were undertaken by essentially unarmed (not counting box cutters) combatants. The real and deadly weapons were the products of technological developments: a wide-body civilian jet—consisting of 200 tons of metal containing 80 tons of fuel—accelerated to a velocity of several hundred kilometers per hour.

Third, the September 11 terrorist attacks put American traditions and values to the test. As a result of the attacks, it became clear that liberal democratic states are not the most efficient for dealing with problems of terrorism. Nevertheless, it was surprising to see how easily the majority of Americans agreed to sacrifice, at least temporarily, some of their basic personal freedoms in exchange for the *FEELING OF* greater personal safety. (Absolutely the same tendency was clearly seen in Russia after the October 2002 terrorist act in Moscow. Needless to say, democratic traditions were much weaker in Russia than in the United States. In practically all public polls taken after the October tragedy in Moscow, an absolute majority of Russian respondents were ready to sacrifice at least part of their individual rights and freedoms in exchange for guarantees of personal safety).

Fourth, a wide spectrum of modern technology, combined with the consequences of globalization, has resulted in the appearance of a new factor in world policy: non-state actors. They operate outside the field of international law, are not clearly linked to any one state, and are able to inflict damage to a state comparable or even exceeding that of the aggression of a hostile nation. Modern terrorists act globally and attack non-conventionally.

Fifth, in the light of the new risks and challenges in international security, it became clear that practically all existing institutions, national (armed forces, police, secret services) and international (UN, OSCE, NATO, and the like), established to guarantee the security of individual states and the international community failed to perform their missions. New threats demand new instruments to deal with them.

After the terrorist attack on America, it became apparent that not even a state as strong and rich as the United States would be able to successfully fight the new terrorist threat alone. It needed allies and partners, and Russia, given its geo-strategic position, its relatively recent combat experience in Afghanistan, and its long engagement in fighting terrorism in Chechnya, had much to offer. For the first time since the end of the Second World War, Russia and the West appeared to have a common threat to face, a threat that was durable and global in nature. No less important was the fact that the strategic interests of the two sides were united, *NOT ONLY* by the fight against terrorism and the need to bring members of the same criminal group to justice, chief among them Osama bin Laden, but also by the comprehension that they both belong to the same civilization.

Russia's choice to side with the United States was not a religious one in favor of Christianity and against Islam. To do so would be a grave mistake for Russia, which is a multi-religious state. It was driven by sober strategic considerations based on choosing in favor of international law, human rights, and democratic values.

President Putin was the first foreign state leader to express his strong support for the United States and to identify Russia as a U.S. partner, if not ally, in the war against terrorism. This statement and further practical actions undertaken by Russia were not an easy decision for the Russian president. For the first time during his presidency, he put his high political rating at stake and took a position that was likely to be opposed by influential political circles in Russia.

The key problem related to Putin's political choice was put into words by Nikolai Zlobin, Director of Russian and Asian programs at the Center for Defense Information: 'the political elites of both countries are not yet ready to follow decisively the course taken by the Presidents.'[1] It is clear now that the American political class dramatically underestimated Russia and its possible role on the international scene. In all fairness, the Russian political elite deserves no less criticism than its American counterpart because many of its representatives continue to see the United States in the stereotypes of the Cold War period. They refrain from openly opposing President Putin's course on close relations and cooperation with the United States, but continue to see America as the main potential threat to Russian security and genetically are unable to believe that new relations between the two states are not a zigzag in Russian foreign policy, but rather a durable trend based on new realities and a new understanding of Russian vital national interests.

Public polls taken in October 2001 in Russia revealed a wide gap between presidential policy and its prevailing understanding in society. For instance 57 percent of respondents in Moscow (where the most politically advanced part of the Russian society is concentrated) did not support the military operation in Afghanistan, and only 37 percent of them considered it a well thought-out military operation. Sixty-three percent of respondents considered the military operation in Afghanistan nothing more than a 'demonstration of American military power,' and another 72 percent of respondents would not support such military actions against other countries placed on the American list of rogue states—Iraq, Iran, Libya, and others.[2]

Thus, the fact that we are in a new type of global war with world terrorism was not yet understood in Russia. Unfortunately, the same conclusion could characterize the situation in all the leading capitals around the world. As it was mentioned earlier, new actors started to dominate in defining the situation in the world political scene. They were not formalized as traditional subjects of international relations—sovereign and internationally

[1] Nikolai Zlobin, *Russia is Facing a Painful Collapse of Political Stereotypes*, IZVESTYA, May 27, 2002, at 4.

[2] G. Iljichev, *Russian Society is Not Ready to Support the Presidential Foreign Policy*, IZVESTYA, Oct. 15, 2001, at 4.

recognized states. These new actors were not subordinated to any legal government. It looked difficult, if not impossible, to attribute them to the territory of any single state. They act globally through and beyond national borders. Of course, they use territories of sovereign states, but never ask for permission from these state governments. These structures exert more and more impact on the development of the world situation in security, political, and economic fields, but neither state can ratify a treaty with them or exchange diplomatic missions. All traditional economic measures that the world community could use to apply pressure to any state, like sanctions or a trade embargo, are meaningless and inapplicable to the terrorist networks. Even the use of military power in its traditional form does not appear efficient. Those states that expressed a firm readiness to fight terrorism face similar problems. They fail in searching defensive lines to be attacked, armies to be defeated, territory to be occupied, or capitals to be captured. The war is waged without front lines or rear areas, and without precise knowledge of where the next target for a terrorist attack will be located.

In sum, the whole system of international relations, basic principles of military strategy, key approaches towards international security, and stability look irrelevant or completely inadequate in the face of the contemporary situation. To discuss an optimal correlation in using unilateral or multilateral approaches to meet these new threats and challenges demands more precise description of the enemy, its nature, its means, and its goals.

III. FROM 'BLACK SEPTEMBER' 2001 IN AMERICA TO 'BLACK OCTOBER' 2002 IN MOSCOW: STRATEGY AND GOALS OF THE WORLD TERRORISM

To begin, it would be useful to note that the new character of threats to security resulted in the necessity to deeply reconsider the definitions of such basic terms as war, military victory, and military power. Military operations conducted by terrorists are aimed primarily, not at armed forces or military installations, but at the civil population and the most vulnerable elements of modern postindustrial society's infrastructure. The main goals of such attacks are not classical military victory, but spreading panic, threatening civil population, shaking and destroying the economic and financial system, and changing the government or its policy. Analyses of the terrorists' activities for the period from September 11, 2001 in America until October 23–26, 2002 in Moscow allow us to identify a definite logic in their behavior.

A. The events of September11, 2001 in America

The selection of targets for terrorist attacks in Washington, D.C. and New

York looks very illustrative. Terrorists who planned the attack on the Pentagon, the heart of the world's strongest military machine, hardly expected to defeat the American army or even to cause substantial damage to the U.S. armed forces. A much more important goal was to create feelings of personal un-safety and insecurity among typical American citizens and to demonstrate the inefficiency of military means, and the lack of protection against new threats. The Twin Towers of the World Trade Center were chosen very deliberately. The terrorists calculated that the destruction of these buildings, symbolizing the most prosperous global economic system and directly linked to the world's most important trade and financial centers, would inflict enormous damage on the American economy and financial system as well as on global economic and financial stability. One has to accept that this was a correct calculation.

According to American sources, by the end of 2001, direct losses in the American economy resulting from the September terrorist acts were valued at $639 billion and two million jobs.[3]

B. Attack on the French Supertanker

Terrorists attacked the French supertanker Limburg on October 6, 2002 near the Yemen shores. The explosion was caused by a collision of this huge vessel with a terrorist boat loaded with explosives. The methodology was tested previously more than once, for example, the same type of attack was launched against the American destroyer, the U.S.S. Cole, at Yemen's harbor, Aden, on October 12, 2000. A small boat, driven by two terrorists and loaded with 300 kilos of explosives, collided with an American combat ship resulting in serious damage. Seventeen American seamen were killed and more than forty were seriously injured as a result of the explosion.[4] Terrorist activities at sea could be the theme of a special study exceeding the limits of this paper. It would be useful to stress here that the world's oceans are no longer safe, and terrorist attacks can happen with almost equal probability on the land, at sea, or in the air.

Returning to the incident with the French tanker, one should take into consideration that this terrorist act had a highly precise aim, oil markets. The tanker itself survived the attack and did not sink. It was a huge modern ship with a reliable system of passive protection. The ship transported 400,000 barrels of crude oil from Saudi Arabia to eastern Asia. The terrorists knew well that oil markets are extremely sensitive and that reliability of the oil supply is vitally important for economic stability in nearly all devel-

[3] Vladimir Kusmin & Andrey Mirochnichenko, *The Third World War is Continuing*, NEZAVISIMAYA GAZETA, Oct. 25, 2002, at 4.

[4] Mark Shteinberg, *Shachids Attack from at Sea*, NEZAVISIMAYA GAZETA, June 28, 2002, at 9.

oped countries. Demonstrating the vulnerability of these supply lines had an immediate effect. The day after this explosion, oil prices went up and exceeded the level of $30 per barrel. This effect was not durable, but very visible.

It is important to note that oil tankers are an extremely important element of the world's oil supply network. For instance, three-fifths of Russian oil exports are shipped by oil tankers (mainly Greek and Liberian). Tankers are the key means of oil supply for the economies of Asian and European countries. This key supply source is why the situation in the oil markets depends not only on the correlation between the total amount of produced oil and the consumer's demand at the moment, but also on freight price. Freight price includes a risk factor as one of its main components. A week after the French tanker was attacked, the freight price for big tankers (250-300 thousand tons deadweight) jumped twice; the freight price for smaller ships (70-150 thousand tons deadweight) increased by 20–25 percent. At the beginning of October, the shipment price for a barrel of oil delivered from the Russian harbor of Novorossisk to the harbor of Augusta in Italy was $0.54, but a week later it rose to $0.64. During the same week, the oil shipment price from the Baltic harbor of Venspils to the German harbor of Vilgelmshaffen increased from $0.65 to $0.84 per barrel.[5]

C. The Explosion in Bali Island, Indonesia

The explosion in Bali, one of the most popular Asian resorts at high season, took the lives of almost 200 people, primarily tourists from Australia and many other nations. The incident shook stock exchanges worldwide, and seriously undermined tourism, the main branch of the Indonesian economy, on which the country crucially depends. The tourism business represents 12 percent of the Indonesian economy. Foreign tourists annually brought a hard currency income equal to 10 percent of the country's total export. The tourism business provides work to 5.75 million people, or to 6.1 percent of the country's total labor force. Last but not least, Bali was the main gate through which foreign tourists visited the country. Roughly one quarter of all foreign tourists arriving in Indonesia landed in Bali.

There was a visible growth of foreign tourists visiting Bali annually. At the end of 2001, the average number of foreign tourists visiting Bali was 85,000 people per month. Half a year later, by mid 2002, the number had grown to 150,000 people per month. Now this trend is over. Evidently, the big flight companies were among the first victims of this change. Shares of Air France dropped by 4.76 percent, Lufthansa by 0.45 percent, and British

[5] N. Babasijan & M. Ignatova, *If Tanker War Starts Tomorrow*, IZVESTYA, Oct. 17, 2002, at 1, 10.

Airways by 2.16 percent. Shares of the French company, Accor, which owns hotels in Bali, fell by 2.62 percent. The Bali explosion shook the economy of the whole region of Southeast Asia.[6]

A few days after the terrorist act, the business activity index of the Jakarta stock exchange dropped 10 percent, to the lowest level in four years. The national currency lost a substantial share of its value and continues to decline. During one weekend, all savings and other Indonesian assets became 10 percent cheaper. Analysts from JP Morgan considered that by the end of 2002, the exchange rate between the Indonesian rupee and the U.S. dollar would reach 10,000:1 instead of 8700:1 as forecasted some days before the terrorist act.[7] According to the local paper, the *Jakarta Post*, 'Foreigners are leaving and local investors are saying that the existing level of insecurity practically blocks any new investments.'

In sum, the terrorist act in Bali resulted in a negative change in the investment climate in the Asian region. According to the Overseas-Chinese Banking Corp.'s assessment, 'Now investors will consider South East Asia a more risky place for business. This in turn will impact negatively on share prices, currency exchange rates, and obligations income and will threaten potential investors.'[8]

It would be important to mention here that the second biggest victim of the Bali terrorist act in Indonesia was the local oil industry. Indonesia is a member of OPEC and the oil industry is the second biggest pillar of the country's economy. The 'tanker war' discussed above is linked directly to the economic stability of Indonesia and the region as a whole. One quarter of the annual world oil trade passes through Southeast Asia. The diminishing reliability of these supply lines could shock the economies of several important regions. For instance, an attack on an oil tanker in the Malacca Straits would have been a direct strike on the economies of northeast Asia (Japan, China, and Korea).

Indonesian authorities place responsibility for the Bali terrorist act on the radical Islamic organization Jemaah Islamiyah, which is linked closely to Al Qaeda. Special military operations could be undertaken to fight terrorism in the region. The United States has experience in fighting Islamic terrorist groups in the Philippines and keep a substantial military contingent in the area. But even possible success in military attacks on local Islamic extremists would be an inefficient means for changing the economic situation in the short or medium term. Regions of military instability and insecurity where combat actions are going on can hardly be seen as an attractive zone for foreign or local investors. As previously mentioned, the terrorists' main

[6] Aleksey Efimov & Abdret Terekchov, *Bali—A Lost Paradise*, NEZAVISIMAYA GAZETA, Oct. 16, 2002, at 3.

[7] *Id.*

[8] *Id.*

goals are to spread panic, to threaten people, and to paralyze business activities. As we see, they chose the targets for attack to reach these goals in the shortest and most efficient way.

D. Terrorist Act in Moscow 23–26 October 2002

It is beyond the scope of this paper to analyze in detail how the group of fifty armed terrorists seized the Theater Center located five kilometers outside the Kremlin walls, took almost 1000 hostages, and put their lives at deadly risk by installing mines and putting on 'shachid belts' containing a total of approximately 120 kilos of highly efficient explosives. My task is less ambitious: to identify the goals these terrorists planned to reach. In public declarations, the terrorists stated that their aims were to stop war in Chechnya and to force the Federal Government to withdraw Russian armed forces from the area. But from the very beginning of this terrorist act, it was absolutely clear that its organizers had absolutely different results in mind. First of all, it was evident, even to the terrorists themselves, that to finish the war and to withdraw a military contingent of more than 80,000 soldiers and officers is a time-consuming process. To demand this as a condition for the hostages' release was deliberately unrealistic as it was not a realizable goal.

In reality, the terrorist act was aimed at reaching goals opposite to those being loudly pronounced. The first and perhaps most important aim was to destroy any prospect of a political settlement of the deadlocked situation in Chechnya. During the previous months, several hopeful signs appeared that reinforced federal authorities' efforts to establish contacts with more or less adequate representatives of Chechen separatists leaders who could participate in talks with Moscow. It was very well known that several months before the events in Moscow, Akhmet Zakaev, who served as Aslan Maskhadov's international emissary, met with Viktor Kazantsev, Russian Presidential Representative to the South Federal District, at the neutral zone of the Sheremetjevo International Airport in Moscow. The political process in Chechnya started to develop, very slowly overcoming huge obstacles.

But the moment terrorists seized the building where the Nord Ost musical was playing, took around 1000 hostages, and killed some of them, the political situation changed radically. This was particularly true after evidence emerged proving that Shamil Basaev was among the key organizers of this raid, and Aslan Maskhadov together with Akhmet Zkaev were most likely informed about its preparation. The window of opportunity for any contacts with these people was closed hopelessly. The attack served as an intentional strike against those who tried to find a political way out of the war in Chechnya. This made the situation much more difficult politically for President Putin. After this event, he faced a dramatic problem: to find figures who could capably represent the Chechen interests in future talks.

It seems important to note that the participants of the raid on the Moscow Theater Center, with whom Russian authorities had to deal, represented a new generation of terrorists. They were all around twenty years old. Consequently, they were roughly ten when the war in Chechnya began, and their last ten years had been spent in mountain forests sleeping with machine guns. They spent their time studying the Koran, installing mines and shooting tanks and helicopters. They knew very little if anything about the United States or Europe, but they knew for sure that their holy mission was to kill Russians and other non-Muslims and to spread the most radical version of Islam around the world. They lacked the ability to participate in political talks, to search for compromise, and to make mutually acceptable concessions.

By the way, the same characteristic easily could be attributed to all extremist Muslim organizations today. We are witnessing growing ideological fanaticism and a tendency toward global expansionism and world domination of radical Islam. This should hardly be seen as a clash of civilizations. Most likely we are witnessing a dangerous trend: Islam as a great religion and Islamic culture are becoming more and more a hostage of radicals and terrorists who are espousing Islamic dogmas and using Islam as a flag to camouflage pretense for their goal to dominate the world.

Of course, the other traditional terrorist goals were present in the October attack in Moscow: to spread panic, to threaten people, and to demonstrate that the city of Moscow is not a much safer or more secure place than the city of Grozny, the Chechen capital. The organizers of that terrorist act did not wish to stop war in Chechnya, but instead to bring it to the heart of Russia to threaten its internal political stability. The war in Chechnya began as a conflict between the separatist movement and the federal center trying to save the territorial integrity of the Russian state. It was presented to the world as a legitimate struggle for the national liberation and human rights of the Chechen people, but soon after, international terrorists took this territory and the separatists' combat activities under their control. Under this leadership, the separatist movement was quickly transformed into an integral part of world terrorism's global strategy.

The same can be said about separatist and ethnic movements in other countries like Indonesia or Israel. It was not an accident that in an audiotape broadcast by the Al Jazeera channel on November 12, 2002, terrorist guru Osama bin Laden welcomed all terrorist acts described above, including the attack on the Moscow Theater Center, as links in one chain. 'Combatants from Al Qaeda are acting in the Russian territory,' stated President Bush in an interview given to the Russian paper *Izvestya*. 'Russia has to fight them to bring them to justice. When Osama bin Laden praised the terrorist act undertaken by Chechens in Moscow he proved clearly that he has his own interests in Chechnya.'[9]

The appearance of international terrorism as one of the key players in the world's political scene has dramatically changed the security environment. Immediately after the terrorist attack on September 11, it became evident that neither states, alliances, nor international institutions were prepared to meet this challenge efficiently. As Army General K. Nauman, former Chairman of NATO's Military Committee, stated recently:

> We already can't see how people are killed. In our historical development we passed the stages when murder legal or not was a part of normalcy. But today we have to accept that never ever will we feel completely safe and secure whatever technical innovations are invented and new protection means are used. We can defend the military but are incapable of completely insuring the security of the civilian population. But 'they' will behave asymmetrically. The stronger and more invincible we are in the military field, the more precisely they will target their strikes on innocent civilians.[10]

All of these events have raised the level of urgency in working out new approaches and strategies, unilateral and multilateral, to accept this challenge and to win the war imposed on us by the 'destroyers of civilization.' New threats demand new assets.

IV. FIGHTING INTERNATIONAL TERRORISM: WHAT ARE THE PRIMARY TARGETS

International terrorism on a global scale is a new phenomenon. Of course, terror as a political instrument has been used in different historical circumstances for centuries. In the September 1792 Convent, a legislative council of revolutionary France discussed the problem: 'About inclusion the terror as an actual means in today's agenda.' One of the Great French Revolution's leaders, Marat, wrote at that time in *The Peoples' Friend* newspaper:

> It does not matter if hundreds of people die for the bright future of millions. If necessary we will liquidate thousands. We will shoot them down without court verdicts or judicial inquiry. We are ready to liquidate tens of thousands. Nothing could stop us on the way to the great civil society. Terror and more terror will lead us to the bright future.[11]

Deepest social inequality, the inability to find personal identity in a quickly

[9] President Bush interview to Izvestya Paper, IZVESTYA, Nov. 20, 2002, at 1.

[10] Klaus Naumann, Interview to Novaya Gazeta, NOVAYA GAZETA, Feb. 14–17, 2002, at N 11, p.5.

[11] Alexander Asmolov, *Settling the Agenda of Terror*, NOVAYA GAZETA, Nov. 24, 2002, N 86, at 5.

changing environment, lost social status, and marginalizing substantial parts of society resulted in 'red terror' in Russia after 1917 and 'brown terror' in Germany after 1933.

Now the world has to deal with a more difficult problem. The face of modern international terrorism is vague and even its precise definition presents a serious problem. It would be enough to say that specialists think that more than 120 different definitions of international terrorism presently exist. Professor Zbigniev Brzezinski, who does not need special introduction, expressed some concern in this respect. 'Terrorism is transforming,' says Brzezinski, 'in some abstract phenomenon. It looks like heartless terrorists act under the guidance of evil will, without any reasons and motivations.'[12] However, we are speaking not about terrorism in general, but about the most serious contemporary threat that follows from global expansion of Islamic radicals using terror as a principal means for reaching the goal of global domination. At the beginning of the 20th century, the Muslim population on the planet was about 150–170 million people. Now 1.1–1.3 billion Muslims constitute one fifth of the world's total population. Approximately half of them are below the age of twenty.[13] The demographic explosion in the Muslim world has made the youth the most numerous strata of their society, but the impossibility of socio-economic self-realization has predefined their aggressiveness.

Oil sales provided the ruling elites of Arab and other Muslim countries with enormous financial resources. Arab countries earn $120–150 billion annually from oil exports. At the same time, these enormous natural resources have not helped modern economies to grow there. According to James Woolsy, former Director of the CIA, 'The whole Muslim East exported in mid 90s (not counting oil) less than Finland alone. 260 million people produced and sold less than 5 million Finns.'[14] It is no surprise that these factors created a favorable climate for spreading extremist ideology masked with religious dogmas and slogans about a 'just' reorganization of the world order. To some extent, this was a reincarnation of a distorted primitive version of Marxist ideology for failed states or speaking globally for failed areas. Of course, in fighting international terrorism, one should not forget that the struggle against global poverty and social inequality constitutes one of the factors that creates the productive soil for growth of terrorism seeds. However, the two tasks, struggling with poverty and fighting international terrorism, must be clearly distinguished. Poverty is not the main force guiding international terrorist actions and definitely cannot be used as an excuse to approve it. Unfortunately the actions of Islamic

[12] Zbignev Brzezinski, *How to Curb an Anti-Americanism?* MOSKOVSKIE NOVOSTY, Nov. 10, 2002, N 35, at 5.

[13] V. Rudakov et. Al., *Generation Next*, PROFILE, Oct. 2002, N 41, at 17–21.

[14] James Woolsy, Interview to Novaya Gazeta, NOVAYA GAZETA, Sept. 26, 2002, at 6, 7.

extremists are more likely based on ideological roots than on material reasons.

Specialists identify several forms of radical Islamic territorial expansion. First, there is an infiltration of extremist radical mullahs to work with their colleagues, forcing them to shift from traditional non-militant forms of Islam toward a belligerent version. A second type of activity involves circulating propaganda containing the extremist version of Islam among regular believers, who practice traditional non-belligerent forms of the religion. Last but not least, creation of religious-political organizations of an extremist nature is an important part of this expansion. The main task of such organizations is to form a political opposition to secular governments in their own countries and abroad. These organizations struggle not only to spread extreme forms of Islam abroad, but also to forcefully transform secular Muslim states into radical religious ones like Afghanistan when it was governed by the Taliban.

The Islamic extremists do not accept secular forms of state organization. That is why extremists view other Muslims, who practice non-radical forms of Islam, in the same light as their non-Muslim enemies. In this respect, Islamic radicals represent a deadly threat to Islam as a religion and to Islamic culture as a whole. The threat is similar to those that Hitler and the Nazis represented to the German state and culture. According to a prominent Russian specialist on Islam, Alexander Ignatenko, not less than 200 organizations of that character now exist in different countries on practically all continents.[15]

Thus, the lack of a single universal definition of international terrorism should not disarm us in a situation of urgent necessity to fight this phenomenon. Prominent Russian social psychologist Alexander Asmolov considers that the phenomenon of international terrorism should not be seen as less than a threat of civilization regress. According to his assessment, three factors combine to define the regress of civilization: terror technology, extremist Islamic ideology, and fanaticism psychology.[16]

The threat of civilization regression is not only linked to the direct and indirect damage terrorist acts cause modern civilization. The bigger danger is linked to the fact that fighting terrorism should be seen as an 'interactive process.' The state engaged in a struggle against international terrorism is under serious pressure. It is very easy to respond to the international terrorist conspiracy with retaliatory terror actions. However, it is very difficult to avoid the incentives for 'temporary' limits on basic democratic rights and freedoms to create optimal conditions for fighting terrorism. To follow this path would signal the terrorists' success, at least partially, and would be a step back in the development of civilization.

[15] Rudakov et al., *supra* note 13.

[16] Asmolov, *supra* note 11.

Having said that, it is possible to identify some primary targets the world community should concentrate on when endeavoring to meet the new challenge. Four areas of primary importance should be emphasized. With some reservations they could be called shrinking and liquidation of terrorists' space, cutting the terrorists' financial resources to bankrupt them, infiltrating terrorists' secret network cells and working toward their liquidation, and breaking the links between Islam and Islamic extremists.

A. Problem of Terrorists' Space

As has been discussed already, modern terrorists prefer not to be identified with any one single country. Terrorists act through and beyond national borders. Nevertheless, they need bases for training their combatants, and for planning and preparing for terrorist offenses. They need territory for recovery and reinforcement and for shelters to escape to after terrorist attacks. They find this space in the territories of sovereign states. Conditions that allow terrorism to grow in the territory of the nation state appear in two cases. The first occurs when the national government directly or indirectly supports international terrorism by hosting terrorists as 'guests of honor' and granting them space and material support. The most prominent example of this is Al Qaeda's bases hosted by the Taliban on Afghan soil. This situation is comparatively easy to deal with, at least in the legal sense. If a national government hosts and supports terrorists, it bears full responsibility for all actions undertaken by terrorists from its territory. In this case, a retaliatory strike, unilateral or multilateral, on terrorists' bases is nothing but the realization of a legitimate right of a nation to defend itself, and would be in full compliance with international law.

The other case is much less evident and judicially much more difficult to deal with. There are more and more states whose governments are weak and incapable of efficiently controlling the whole of their national territory. Such a situation can be characterized as limited or invalid sovereignty. A government's inability to realize full sovereignty over national territory results in the appearance of enclaves quickly saturated by all sorts of criminals and international terrorists. Examples of such areas include south Lebanon, parts of the Philippines, the northern part of Sumatra Island (Indonesia), and enclaves in Sudan, Algeria, Nigeria, and Somalia. Serious tensions between Russia and Georgia in 2002 were only about the situation in the Pankissi Gorge, the Georgian territory bordering Chechnya and populated by ethnic Chechens. According to Russian officials, Chechen criminals and international terrorists, including Al Qaeda members, extensively used this territory as a bridgehead for organizing terrorist raids against Russian territory and as a shelter to which they could easily escape following terrorist attacks.

The growing number of such enclaves worldwide puts before us a new problem of international law: how should we treat these governments and what should we do with such terrorist nests? With respect to Pankissi Gorge, Russian President V. Putin and Russian Defense Minister S. Ivanov stated numerous times that 'Russia reserves the right to retaliatory strike by all available means, terrorists, their bases, their financial sponsors, and their ideological centers, wherever they were located.'[17] Contrary to Ivanov's statement, former Georgian President Ed. Shevardnadze insisted that any Russian attack against terrorists in Pankissi Gorge would be a direct violation of Georgian sovereignty and territorial integrity. Officially, President Shevardnadze did not support Chechen terrorists' activities in Georgia's territory and would have preferred not to have the extra political headache related to this problem. However, at the same time he had neither the political will nor the power and necessary instruments to stop terrorist activities in the Pankassi Gorge region of his own country.

Thus, it is necessary for the international community to develop norms of international law that would allow fighting, and liquidating, terrorist enclaves while fully respecting the sovereignty of an independent nation-state. The 'invalid sovereignty' of weak states should not become an insurmountable obstacle in fighting international terrorism. The battle against terrorist threats will succeed only when terrorists fail to find one square foot of this planet's soil where they feel comfortable, safe, and secure.

B. Terrorism and its sources of finance

After September 11, American authorities froze thirty-nine bank accounts belonging to organizations and individuals who are suspected of links with terrorists.[18] The U.S. government undertook titanic efforts to destroy the terrorists' financial bases and bankrupt them. But the more intense this struggle against the international criminal empire became, the more evident was the fact that Osama bin Laden was not its only emperor. In particular, it appeared that a network of organizations of honey suppliers were among the key financial sponsors of Al Quaeda, and their product, honey, played an important role in financing terrorist activities. The struggle against terrorist sponsors and their financial network is an even more complicated problem than fighting the terrorists themselves. This is because terrorism sponsors and the terrorists they support live in the same countries and use the fruits of the same civilization, including the global financial network.

Only a few of the bank accounts frozen by American authorities were

[17] *See* Sergei Ivanov, *We Love the Georgian People*, KOMMERSANT VLAST, Sept. 2002, at 46.

[18] G. Bovt, '*It is Impossible to Defeat Terrorists Without Reorganization of the Modern World Order*,' IZVESTYA, Oct. 15, 2001, at 1, 4.

based in Persian Gulf countries. Their official business was the supply of honey and sweets. Three of these firms were based in Yemen—Al Hamati Sweets Bakeries, Al Nur Honey Press Shops, and Al Shifa Honey Press. These 'honey suppliers' were connected to partners in sixty-six countries worldwide. Further, the American Department of the Treasury identified three huge 'charity' organizations linked to Osama bin Laden. Among them was the Moowafac Foundation, whose headquarters were based in Saudi Arabia. This 'charitable' organization transferred millions of dollars to this 'number one' terrorist. Its head—Yasin al Quady—is living in Jedda. Financial links from the Moowafac foundation went to Tunisia and Germany. After American authorities imposed financial sanctions on the Moowarac foundation, its head expressed astonishment saying that the foundation was closed six years ago. But according to British intelligence sources, the foundation was not closed but merely changed its legal status and became a semi-underground organization.

The second center, the Institute of Islamic Culture, was based in Milan (Italy). Americans believe that this Institute was 'the main center of Al Qaeda in Europe.' The main function of this Institute was to provide money and weapons to Islamic terrorists worldwide. The third organization, Human Concern International, was based in Canada and linked to bin Laden through Afghanistan.[19] The bin Laden family itself is a very rich and diversified clan. Publicly they stated that they cut all links with their prominent relative, but that seems highly unlikely. One of the reasons to doubt the sincerity of this statement is the fact that nobody can discern Middle Eastern capitalists working in the economies of the United States and Europe from those supporting the terrorist activities of Islamic extremists. According to American sources, terrorists organized an efficient world-wide network to transfer huge sums of money in cash. Its accounting offices were located around the globe and combined illegal terrorists' supply operations with legal transactions. This means that focused efforts aimed at cutting out and removing the sources of financing for international terrorism would hardly be possible without affecting the world financial system.

A separate question is how many foundations, 'charitable organizations,' and 'cultural centers' in Europe and the United States were nothing more than fundraisers for international terrorists in Chechnya. Shortly before the September 11 terrorist acts in America, a three-month campaign was organized to raise money for Chechen extremists. More than $5 million was donated and transferred into the accounts of the Islamic Charity Society. No one could definitively prove that all of these sums were spent in Chechnya and not used at least partially for those who were busy preparing the attack on the World Trade Center and the Pentagon. Other so-called

[19] *Id.*

'pro-Chechen' foundations existed in Germany, and similar organizations have also acted in Sweden, Denmark, Czech Republic, Poland, and the like.

The U.S. Congress was preparing a package of bills aimed at making nearly all financial transactions transparent. High-ranking Saudi officials made several statements about changes in their banking and financial control systems that would exclude the possibility of any illegal money transfers to support terrorist activities. It is evident, however, that the task of depriving international terrorism of its financial resources and bankrupting it represents an enormous challenge to the world financial system. 'Good' and 'bad' money and the channels they are traveling through are so close, so interlaced and interconnected, that a very exacting methodology must be used to distinguish, using President Bush's terminology, 'those who are with us' from 'those who are against us.'

It is clear now that the world financial system, which is the product and the achievement of the modern post-industrial, information society and the result of the globalization processes, can become a deadly weapon when used by terrorists. As previously mentioned, today's terrorists tend to use the developments of modern civilization as weapons. This conclusion could be fully applicable to the financial sphere. One has to accept that the modern global financial system allowed terrorists to quickly, secretly, and efficiently collect and transfer huge amounts of money using legal and semi-legal channels. Therefore, international terrorism, to a large extent, did not face financial problems. Such a situation cannot be allowed to continue. It is not absolutely clear yet what sort of changes to the world financial system will be necessary to ensure success in the anti-terrorist war, but it is evident that these changes will need to be on a massive scale.

C. Liquidation of Secret Terrorist Network and Combat Groups

Analyses of international terrorist activities from September 11, 2001 until October 23–26, 2002 and beyond (for example, the attempt to shoot down the Israeli civil jet and the bombing of the hotel in Kenya) proved our initial conclusion: all institutions (national and international) existing to ensure security and stability need serious reorganization to efficiently meet the new threats and challenges of international terrorism. As already mentioned, no state, whatever its reach and power, is able to defeat world terrorism alone. To deal with this global threat, a global coalition is needed. Formally speaking, such a coalition appeared just after September 11, 2001. However, the question which remains is how durable and reliable it will be.

This coalition requires its members to dramatically reconsider traditional approaches to very sensitive issues related to national security. For instance, the exchange of intelligence information received by national technical means and by agents who infiltrate terrorist organizations must increase.

The sharing of intelligence information has not been the norm even among the closest allies. Now, however, such intelligence sharing is a necessity and must even occur between nations who were recently political and military opponents. Such an exchange should be comprehensive, systematic, and regularly occurring. However, one should bear in mind the level of specificity and delicacy that cooperation of this sort requires, especially when dealing in such a sensitive area. For instance, information received from an infiltrated agent is expensive, both directly and indirectly. Providing information gathered by such a source to a coalition partner can disclose the source and put the agent's life at risk. Therefore, it is prudent for nations seeking to share intelligence to jointly plan and organize an agent's work.

Human intelligence comes from several sources: satellite imagery, signal intelligence, and electronic intelligence. But the tragedy of September 11 clearly demonstrated that it is not enough to rely solely on technical means, no matter how sophisticated such means are. To fight terrorism efficiently, we need to place substantially more attention on espionage (the infiltration of agents into terrorist networks and cells). As General K. Naumann stated in the previously mentioned interview, 'According to my personal view, the role of the agent's intelligence grows again. We need "good old" espionage. It cannot be substituted for any technical innovations.'[20]

All of these arguments bring us to the conclusion that Russia and other leading anti-terrorist coalition partners should organize special information banks with channels for quick information exchange and coordination of activities. Success in this area should be seen not only as the ability to respond to terrorist attacks quickly and flexibly, but primarily to prevent them from happening at all. To sum up, dealing with the new threats of global terrorism requires groups of well-trained, well-equipped, and highly motivated individuals who can infiltrate and destroy terrorist networks.

With regard to military cooperation between Russia, the United States, the nations of the North Atlantic Treaty Organization (NATO), the European Union, and others, it is important to mention that both Russia and the West need special forces to deal with the terrorist threat; forces which are currently not available to either side in large quantities. The most famous of western Special Operation Forces (SOF) are Great Britain's Special Air Service (SAS), an organization that was established after 1941. Most SOF units—Australia's Special Air Service Regiment; Holland's Bijzondere Bijstands Eenheid (BBE); France's new joint Commandment des Operation Speciale (COS) units; Germany's Grenzschutsgruppe (GSG)-9; Israel's Sayeret Matkal/Unit 269; and U.S. Army 1st Special Forces Operational Detachment, Delta Force, and Naval Special Warfare

[20] K. Naumann, *We Need an 'Old Good Spy' Again*, NOVAYA GAZETA, Feb. 14–17, 2002, N 11, at 5.

Development Group—were established in the 1970s as a direct response to terrorist incidents. According to prominent Dutch expert Rob de Wijk, 'Western militaries have extremely limited true SOF capabilities, probably no more than 3,000–5,000 for all of NATO.'[21] In addition, Western governments have forces trained to perform specific covert missions. The United States has approximately 45,000 such troops and its NATO allies have 20,000–30,000. The US Army Rangers battalions specialize in seizing airfields; the 82nd Airborne Division is the world's largest parachute force. The main task of these specialized units is to seize key targets and to prepare the area for the general-purpose forces that follows them.

Counter-terrorist operations demand the creation of SOF's that are capable of dispersing after deployment, covering large areas, and using a wide spectrum of modern communication means, such as satellites, to guide different types of manned and remote-controlled combat platforms for the purpose of hitting high value targets.

The evident gap between demand and the availability of these types of forces creates an opportunity for cooperation among anti-terrorist coalition partners. Such cooperation could take the form of practical experience exchange, unification, if not standardization, of training programs for SOF, and the working out of joint tactics for such forces and joint training for acquiring interoperability between Russian and Western SOF units. General K. Nauman believed that we were on the eve of a breakthrough in training and equipping future infantrymen:

> As I perceive we will see shortly new infantry special operation forces able to land deeply inside the enemy's rear, operate and survive there for a long time. They should be equipped with special instruments to search out targets and to guide to them precision weapons from platforms deployed hundreds of kilometers outside the area.[22]

The 'high-tech' SOF infantryman of tomorrow could become a very powerful and capable combat unit.

Efficiently fighting global terrorism will require the reconsideration of force structure, training, equipment, as well some fundamental contemporary military concepts. However, many of them may have little value as applied to the counter-terrorist war. Terrorists fight unconventionally, and we are therefore faced with a problem: how should we deal with the basic rules of conventional war? According to Rob de Wijk's assessment, the list of strategic concepts that need to be rethought should include the following items:

[21] Rob de Wijk, *The Limits of Military Power*, THE WASHINGTON QUARTERLY, Winter 2002, at 75–92.

[22] *See* Naumann, *supra* note 20.

Proportionality of response. Terrorists act with the goal of inflicting a maximum amount of losses on the civilian population. For instance, the terrorist attack on the Twin Towers of the World Trade Center could be compared in material and human losses to an explosion of two tactical nuclear weapons. Taking the proportionality-of-response concept literally, one should see the retaliatory use of a few low-yield nuclear weapons as a justifiable response to the September 11 terrorist act. But a literal understanding of 'proportionality' in fighting international terrorism is hardly rational and applicable at all.

Extremely low collateral damage among the civil population. It seems very difficult, if not impossible, to draw a clear distinction between combatants and civil populations in counter-terrorist operations, especially in cases where a majority of the local population supports the combatants. The combat units engaged in the counter-terrorist war face a dramatic choice: either insure the efficiency of the counter-terrorist operation and accept the inevitability of substantial or high collateral damage, or minimize human loses among civil population by sacrificing at least part of the operation's military goals.

Extremely low human losses in forces engaged in antiterrorist operations. It is well known that developed democracies are extremely sensitive to losses of their own troops. Politicians, whose positions depend on the electorate, can allow themselves (without the risk of political failure) only short, victorious wars with practically no soldiers killed in action. Usually, such results can be achieved by using overwhelming air superiority, precision guided weapons, information processing complexes, and so forth. This allows their armies to avoid large-scale ground operations and saves the lives of their servicemen. However, the same tactics are hardly applicable to the war on terrorism. In such a war, ground operations occur in very difficult terrain against an enemy who has absolutely no incentive to surrender and is ready to sacrifice his life. This predefines the inevitability of substantial human losses and the moral preparedness that is necessary to accept them. In other words, a price must be paid for success in the counter-terrorist struggle.

The meaning of the deterrence concept. First, we must accept that the states where the deterrence concept still works do not need to deter each other. But deterrence does not completely work against individual fanatics or their groups, and does not work at with regard to failed states. This leads us to the necessity of discussions on whether low-yield nuclear weapons can be seen not only as a deterrent, but as a battlefield weapon in fighting the counter-terrorist war. According to media information, the U.S. government has already allocated significant sums of money to develop deeply penetrating, low-yield nuclear warheads to be used for hitting hardened mountain shelters and the command centers of the terrorist network. Of course, this path looks extremely dangerous. The nuclear threshold would be significantly lowered in military and political mindsets, and might result in grave consequences. To avoid this, new means and concepts should be designed to substitute for traditional deterrence ideas, ideas which have become almost completely useless in the global antiterrorist war.

D. Islam and Islamic Extremists

A significant component of any war is the campaign to win the popular support of those previously on the side of one's military opponent. In the case of the global anti-terrorist war, this means waging a battle for the hearts and minds of the people in the Islamic world. This battle will not be an easy one, but is achievable and is absolutely necessary. This propaganda war should be waged in several directions. First, a clear message should be delivered to Muslims all over the world: the war against terrorism is not a war against Islam. When organizing this campaign, one should bear in mind that international terror is not the desperate actions of wretched people or the historical revenge of colonial populations on its former 'sahibs.'

Relatively well-educated individuals from middle class families have perpetuated the largest terrorist acts. Needless to say, those who really organized terrorists' attacks had billion dollar bank accounts at their disposal. In authoritarian Third World countries, including Muslim ones, the 'poor' social strata of society are not engaged in policy-making. At best they can take part in fighting between one local clan and another. The Islamic religion does not demand its believers to take weapons and to kill representatives of other religions. The problem is that masses of Muslims can be mobilized under the green banner of Islam if they are convinced that somebody is trying to attack their religion, cultural identity, values, traditions, or their principles of societal organization.

One has to accept that the people of the Middle East Islamic states feel growing fears with respect to the possibility of losing their cultural and civil identity. They will never agree to be absorbed by the globalization process and brought under a single universal standard symbolized by the American way of life. Any attempts to impose democratic values or to spread the liberal democratic model all over the globe would hardly be seen as a wise policy. Any American attempt to unilaterally use force in international relations that bypass international institutions and neglects international law and norms would trigger new terrorist activities. In September 2001, Italian prime minister Silvio Berlusconi characterized Western civilization as superior to that of the Islamic world. He called on Europe 'to reconstitute itself on the basis of its Christian roots.' He also talked about the 'superiority of our civilization, which consists of a value system that has given people widespread prosperity in those countries that embrace it. . .'[23] Such actions and such statements like President Bush's declaration about a 'crusade against international terrorism' only help bin Laden and his lieutenants to recruit new 'kamikaze' to realize their evil plans.

For the propaganda campaign in the Muslim world to be successful, it is extremely important to understand why extremist Islamic organizations are getting more and more popular among the 'men in the street' in Muslim countries. One should bear in mind that in many Muslim countries radical Islamic organizations substitute for governments by building up the social and cultural infrastructure that provide health care, education, and welfare to those who needed it most—the poor. It is not a surprise that in these states, Koran study centers have become the recruiting firms supplying extremist organizations with new members from the youth. Emissaries of these organizations are extremely active in recruiting wherever Muslim enclaves exist. For example, the President of the World Islamic League recently visited the small town of Pervouralsk located deep in the Russian heartland. He found the time and will to teach the Koran to boys from local Muslim families and selected the most talented among them for further free education in Saudi Arabia.

Struggling for the hearts and minds of the populations of Islamic states can bring positive results only in cases where several important factors are taken into consideration. Muslim society has its own values and cultural identity. It would be a grave mistake to propagate Western values, standards, and principles of societal organization in Muslim areas, or try to impose them by force. The main goal of an antiterrorist campaign should not be the reorganization of Muslim societies and political systems in the style of a Western democracy, but rather should provide the people in Islamic countries with positive alternatives to the self-destructive ideas of radical Islamic world expansion. To oppose these extremist ideas, numerous respected spiritual leaders are needed, including Mullahs and Imams who are capable of breaking the links between Islam and the terrorists who use Islamic phraseology to conceal their criminal intentions. Respected Russian specialist on Middle East issues Professor Ge. Mirski wrote,

> All civilizations are compatible enough for coexistence but not necessarily for friendship and mutual love. Civilization differences like poverty and misery are only a fertilizer but not a legitimate and non-removable bases [sic] for international terrorism, which is driven in reality by the evil will of a not so numerous group of people. They simply use sincere and bordering with the fanaticism belief of the youth to channel it in a false way.[24]

[23] *Berlusconi Vaunts West's Superiority*, INTERNATIONAL HERALD TRIBUNE, Sept. 27, 2001.

[24] G. Mirski, *Terrorist Act in Manhattan: is it a Clash of Civilizations?*, NEZAVISIMAYA GAZETA, Sept. 20, 2001, at 11.

V. MULTILATERALISM VERSUS UNILATERALISM IN DEALING WITH CONTEMPORARY SECURITY PROBLEMS: WHICH WAY TO GO?

The security environment in the 21st century has become more dangerous and less predictable than ever before. Therefore, answering the question formulated above is neither a trivial nor evident task. On the one hand, the threat of international terrorism as well as the threat of proliferation of weapons of mass destruction and missile technologies is global in nature and demands world-scale cooperation to oppose these new challenges efficiently. On the other hand, unilateralims proponents actively use the inefficiency of existing international institutions, the lack of commonly accepted international rules and regulations useful in a new security situation, and the dramatic pressure of decision-making within short time spans that is caused by the novel character of terrorist threats.

According to Rob de Wijk

> . . . the year 1998 seems to be a turning point in recent history. Events that took place in 1998 and 1999 indicated that the U.S. approach had once and for all shifted to a narrow and more selective foreign and national security policy of unilateralism and preservation of the nation's dominant position in the world.[25]

The most illustrative example that proves the inefficiency of old institutions in dealing with new security challenges is the situation within the NATO alliance after the terrorist acts of September 2001.

For NATO, the military operation in Afghanistan could be seen as an 'irony of history.' The NATO alliance was created first and foremost to provide U.S. security guarantees to Europe and to protect it against Soviet communist expansion. Article V of the Washington Treaty, which speaks about collective defense, was implemented the first and only time in just the opposite case—when America was attacked by an aggressor in the heart of its home territory and needed help from the outside. No less important, the proposed NATO military assistance was practically rejected by America. The U.S. did not need NATO to meet the new threat to its security, but crucially needed Russia. This was due to several factors: the Russian geostrategic position, the Russian influence in the post-Soviet region of Central Asia, the rich Russian combat experience in Afghanistan, Russian relations with the only then existing Afghan opposition force, the Northern Alliance, and last but not least, the Russian experiences in fighting international terrorism in Chechnya.

The situation did not change radically after the NATO Prague summit and the admission to the alliance of seven new member states in 2002. Of course, high-ranking officials spoke all the necessary words about the

[25] Wijk, *supra* note 21, at 87.

bright future of the organization, but it was absolutely clear that NATO had lost both its mission and its enemy—the worst thing that could happen to a military-political alliance of collective defense. Now NATO is planning a dramatic reorganization with the goal of acquiring the abilities to fight international terrorism, to oppose the proliferation of nuclear and other weapons of mass destruction, and to perform peacekeeping missions. In practice, some of these plans seem very difficult to realize, some seem completely unrealistic. This explains why Russia stopped opposing, and then became practically indifferent to, NATO's enlargement.

The Prague Summit has indicated several other important changes in the American attitude towards the NATO alliance. First, analysts mentioned that 'quality admission criteria' for newcomers were at their lowest level compared to any previous cases of enlargement. This is especially visible when compared to the admission of Poland, Hungary, and the Czech Republic. Practically all experts determined that the armed forces of Bulgaria, Rumania, and the Baltic states were substantially below the minimal quality requirements for alliance newcomers. If NATO is seriously discussing further enlargement and the admission to the alliance of Croatia, Macedonia, and Albania in the foreseeable future, one can forget about qualitative military standards at all. It does not appear accidental that NATO Secretary General Ge. Robertson recently mentioned that now, 'NATO puts much more attention not on armed forces abilities of the candidate state but on its adherence to democratic values, human rights, and a market economy.'

The main element of the NATO reorganization plan proposed in the Prague summit is the decision to form a NATO Rapid Reaction force consisting of 21,000 troops designed to support possible U.S. military antiterrorist operations worldwide. For an alliance of twenty-seven member states whose armies number roughly 3.5 million, such a task looks less than modest.

All these changes lead us to inevitable conclusions. First, the United States does not plan to launch a serious military operation together with all or even a majority of NATO state armies in the foreseeable future. Second, the traditional task of collective defense of Europe by all member-states armies has departed from American military planning and is absolutely irrelevant under the new political and military circumstances. In the Fiscal Year 2002, the U.S. defense budget has grown by roughly $48 billion. This sum is substantially higher than the total defense budget of any NATO state. Even the most advanced members of NATO are gradually losing interoperability with the United States and do not perform some of the high-tech missions the American army does. This gap supports the unilateralist tendencies in American foreign and national security policy.

The unpredictability of the international security situation and the new character of risks and challenges explains to a very large extent the dualism present in the last version of the U.S. national security strategy. The strategy tries to combine two approaches—multilateralism and unilateralism. On the one hand, a recent U.S. national security document states, 'We are also guided by the conviction that no nation can build a safer, better world alone. Alliances and multilateral institutions can multiply the strength of freedom-loving nations.'[26] But later on it reads,

> For centuries, international law recognized that nations need not suffer an attack before they can lawfully take action to defend themselves against forces that present an imminent danger of attack. Legal scholars and international jurists often conditioned the legitimacy of preemption on the existence of an imminent threat—most often a visible mobilization of armies, navies, and air forces preparing to attack. We must adapt the concept of imminent threat to the capabilities and objectives of today's adversaries . . . The United States has long maintained the option of preventive actions to counter a sufficient threat to our national security. The greater the threat, the greater is a risk of inaction—and the more compelling the case for taking anticipatory action to defend ourselves, even if uncertainty remains as to the time and place of the enemy's attack. To forestall or prevent such hostile acts by our adversaries, the United States will, if necessary, act preemptively. [27]

It is interesting to note that the American concept of a 'right to preemptive strike' was taken with enthusiasm by the Russian leadership with respect to the situation in the Pankissi Gorge in Georgia where, according to Russian intelligence sources, there were international terrorist bases. On September 11, 2002, President V. Putin sent a very strong message to the Georgian leadership. He accused Georgia of allowing its territory to be used for terrorist activities and ordered the Russian General Staff 'to prepare plans for strikes on terrorists' bases on Georgian territory.'[28] In October 2002, shortly after the terrorist act in Moscow, Russian President V. Putin made several very important and tough statements. In particular, he said,

> International terrorism has the insolence to threaten us with the use of means comparable to weapons of mass destruction. If somebody even tried to use such means against our country Russia would retaliate by means adequate to the threat, attacking all places where terrorists, their leaders, financial sponsors and ideological inspirers escape.[29]

Besides that, President Putin met with the power Ministers and ordered them to prepare a new version of Russia's National Security Strategy to reflect the fundamental changes in the international security environment

[26] THE WHITE HOUSE, A NATIONAL SECURITY STRATEGY (2002)

[27] *Id.* at 15.

[28] President V. Putin, *Statement on September 11, 2002*, VLAST WEEKLY MAGAZINE, Sept. 16–22, 2002, at 48.

[29] A.Gamov, *Putin Starts a Frontal Offense on Terrorism*, KOMSOMOLSKAYA PRAVDA, Oct. 30, 2002, at 8.

that have occurred after January 2000, the date the previous version was issued.

Of course, the adoption of a preemptive strike concept is a dangerous development. First, there are no criteria that would allow a nation to lawfully identify whether a preemptive strike is a means of self-defense or an instrument of military-political blackmail. At the same time, one has to accept the fact that if air strikes against Al Qaeda training camps in Afghanistan were undertaken preemptively, when these bases were saturated with terrorists, the tragedy of September 11 would possibly have been avoided. Fortunately, we have not yet dealt with nuclear terrorism, where the price of preemptive strike inaction could be much higher. As prominent Russian nuclear expert Major General V. Dvorkin wrote, 'It's time to say openly: we can't defend ourselves by defensive means only against weapons of mass destruction used by totalitarian rogue state confessing radical Islam or by transnational terrorism.

> 'Preemptive measures should be agreed. They should allow to forcefully disarm terrorists or terrorist regimes and launch exterritorial attacks on terrorists' bases but not to respond on irreparable consequences of terrorist acts.'[30]

It is useful to repeat once more that the new threats of the 21st century, and international terrorism in particular, are of a global nature, and no state can efficiently oppose them alone. It seems likely that we are shifting from big military alliances of the past towards 'flexible ad hoc coalitions' like those used in Afghanistan. The situation makes multilateralism an imperative for the war on counter-terrorism. Worldwide cooperative efforts can successfully fulfill the gaps of the exchange of intelligence information, the creation of Special Operation Forces with the proper level of interoperability, the organization of a global support infrastructure to act quickly and globally when necessary, the waging of a counter propaganda campaign in the Islamic world, and many other vitally important tasks.

Two tasks seem especially important: working out legal bases for acting in the new environment that do not neglect international law, and reorganizing international institutions to make them relevant to the new situation. The international community should develop and adopt a code of commonly accepted rules and regulations. We must know how to use force against terrorist enclaves in countries with weak governments and 'invalid sovereignty.' We need international laws and instruments to forcefully disarm the regimes that neglect common rules and represent a direct threat to the world's security and stability. The first priority should be the strengthening and modernization of the United Nations (UN) structures.

[30] V. Dvorkin, *Prophylactic Instead of Retribution*, RUSSIA IN GLOBAL AFFAIRS, Nov.–Dec., 2002, at 33.

Recently, the UN was on the eve of complete collapse and a repetition of the destiny of the League of Nations. The American decision to launch a military operation against Iraq without UN Security Council mandate could have devalued the role of this organization to near zero.

The contemporary situation in Iraq is far from a final solution, but it gives some ground for expectations to be gradually returned to the legal field. There is hope that the world's community will manage to keep it there, and finally find a way to stabilize a domestic situation in Iraq. It is evident that international law needs further development to cover situations that could have been foreseen several decades ago. However, a lack of commonly accepted norms for dealing with new situations should not be used as a pretext for neglecting international law or as a right to use force in the international arena simply because such military force is available.

The war in which we are now engaged is not a Huntington's clash of civilizations. This is more likely a war between barbarity and civilization in all its plurality of cultures and religions. Barbarians do not accept any laws, rules, or moral norms. But to follow the same path in neglecting international law, destroying international institutions, and the like, would be a very serious sign of civilization regression and concessions to barbarity. It is not coincidental that after the terrorist act of September 2001 more and more studies appear that seriously discuss the perspective of the 'World Government.' Russian diplomat and former Deputy Foreign Minister of Russia A. Adamishin titled his article 'On the Way to the World Government.' In this article he says, 'What should be the answer to systemic crises? Deeply thought build up of the new world order.' In the same article he quotes Henry Kissinger who said, 'The war against terrorism is not hunting terrorists only. First of all this should be a protection granting us a unique opportunity to reorganize the international system. It sounds paradoxical but international terrorism brought to life a feeling of the world's unity.'[31]

[31] A.Adamishin, *On the Way to the World Government*, RUSSIA IN GLOBAL AFFAIRS, Nov.–Dec., 2002, at16.

Part Two—The Supplemental Papers

FOREWORD	International Financial and Trade Law in the Age of Unilateralism *Dr. Mads Andenas*	227
CHAPTER ELEVEN	A Further Contour to 'Limited Multilateralism': The Intervention of Private Sector Involvement to Global Financial Stability and the Prudential Control of Large Complex Global Banking Organizations *Professor Joseph J. Norton*	231
CHAPTER TWELVE	Unilateralism, Multilateralism and International Securities Offerings *Dr. Douglas W. Arner*	255
CHAPTER THIRTEEN	A Decade of Open Regionalism In Latin America: The Need for Effective and Efficient Articulation, Coordination, Cooperation and Convergence *Mauricio Baquero-Herrera*	297
CHAPTER FOURTEEN	Expanding Trade Remedies Unilaterally: The *Byrd Amendment* Case and the United States against the World *Professor Raj Bhala*	345
CHAPTER FIFTEEN	The Multilateralism of Bretton Woods Revisited: The Crucial Role of the WTO in the Integration of Transition Economies *Dr. J.H. Hoogmartens*	365
CHAPTER SIXTEEN	Multilateralism versus Unilateralism in the Sovereign Debt Restructuring Context: Will Either Approach Prevent Default? *Kristin McFetridge*	393
CHAPTER SEVENTEEN	Legal Development Cooperation: Conditions, Principles and Methods *Professor Claes Sandgren*	423
CHAPTER EIGHTEEN	'Club Multilateralism' And Global Supranationalism: The Case of FATF *Dr. Heba M. Shams*	459

CHAPTER NINETEEN International Financial Stability—The Need for a Multilateral Response. 483
Dr. George A. Walker

Foreword—Part Two

International Financial and Trade Law in the Age of Unilateralism

*By Mads Andenas**

It is a great pleasure for me to contribute with a Foreword to *Multilateralism v Unilateralism: Policy Choices in a Global Society.* John Attanasio and Joe Norton are to be congratulated on this very distinguished collection of essays in this book. The issues of the book are the foundations of international law, including if there is a role for the rule of law. Vaughan Lowe has in his Foreword to Part I set out the background for the book and the discussions that took place at the SMU Dedman School of Law in Dallas Texas in the Summer of 2002. He adds a hope that this book, including the essays in Part II, will offer 'insights into the strengths and weaknesses of unilateralism and multilateralism and in some small way advance the debate on these vitally important issues'.[1] The book has most certainly succeeded in advancing the debate, and in more than 'some small way'. The supplemental essays in Part II, not presented at the conference in 2002, complement the main part in a rather important way. It deals with the different forms of modern international cooperation, in particular in the financial and banking sectors.

The new and informal ways of international cooperation have an increasingly important function. In Anne-Marie Slaughter has developed an interesting perspective on global governance.[2] In today's world, government officials exchange information and coordinate activities at a horizontal level. They establish informal networks and deal directly with one another. The traditional treaty mechanism, with involvement of the ministries of foreign affairs and their diplomats, making use of the international conference or organization, is side-stepped. Anne-Marie Slaughter makes use of different forms of government cooperation, with or without

* PhD (Cambridge) MA DPhil (Oxford). Director, British Institute of International and Comparative Law, London, Senior Fellow, Institute of European and Comparative Law, University of Oxford. Visiting Professor of Law, Queen Mary, University of London..

[1] V Lowe 'Foreword for Part One', above, 2, 6

[2] A M Slaughter *A New World Order* (Princeton University Press Princeton and Oxford 2003) and in several articles.

a base in international organizations, to develop her perspective. She makes particular use of the cooperation in the financial and banking sectors.

In the financial and banking sectors, the development of international standards and the cooperation between supervisors in enforcing them, have now created a radically new situation where not only the traditional diplomatic negotiation model but also the domestic legislative model is subordinated. Both create new issues of international legitimacy and domestic democratic control. They demonstrate the limitations on the traditional concepts of national sovereignty. Standard-setting and enforcement have changed character: it is no longer primarily a domestic enterprise. The international process or transaction is no longer of some extra-ordinary character: it has become the ordinary or usual mode of operation.

In international banking regulation, the standards of banking regulation is developed by a committee of banking supervisors meeting in a committee under the auspices of the Bank of International Settlements. Their work is not presented to national legislatures before (and only if) national legislation is required to transpose the new standards. The countries that take part form a small group of ten or so nations, which are the financially most developed in the world.

One starting point is that this form of cooperation works. The countries involved have managed to agree on the standards. The rest of the world more or less passively also accept the standards. The discussion has a highly professionalized level where concepts of banking regulation dominate. Conflicts with other polices, for instance those of international development, are not acknowledged. So if state loans to developing states are considered to involve higher risks than lending to the richest states, such loans are given a rating involving higher costs to the lending banks. Which will be passed on to the borrowers in the form of higher interest rates. Seen in a development perspective, developing states will in this way pay for the solidity of the banks in the rich states. If bank solidity and banking prudence is regarded in isolation, and this may be natural for a group of banking supervisors, the development perspective is irrelevant. It would not be irrelevant for a legislature or general assembly of an international organization.

The cooperation works but one can ask at what price. Before one replies to that, one should remember that traditional forms of international cooperation never managed to get results in most of the field where the new informal forms of cooperation are developing. A return to the previously restricted forms of international cooperation is not a viable proposition.

The study of international financial and trade law in the age of unilateralism is an interesting one. The processes and instruments are developing in different directions, and their relationship to traditional international law and domestic law is complex. The achievements in practical cooperation are considerable, even if there are many problems of legitimacy and transparency that remain. There is no new international legal order based on informal international cooperation that can resolve the problems of self-defence, humanitarian intervention or humanitarian law of war. But informal international cooperation has increased in these times of unilateralism. It must be understood also on this background.

The issues of informal international cooperation require more attention than international lawyers have yet devoted to it. International lawyers willingly recognize this, and much helpful scholarship will no doubt emerge, and change our concepts of the international legal order and the tasks of international law. The essays in Part 2 form a contribution to this scholarship which can only be based on a solid understanding of the ways in which the new and informal cooperation actually works in different sectors.

CHAPTER ELEVEN

A Further Contour to 'Limited Multilateralism': The Intervention of Private Sector Involvement to Global Financial Stability and the Prudential Control of Large Complex Global Banking Organizations

*By Joseph J. Norton**

CHAPTER OUTLINE

I. Introduction: Globalization and its Discontents
II. The Subject-Matter of Risk-Focused Bank Regulation/Supervision: The Backdrop
III. The 'Public-Private Partnership' Notion
A. In General
IV. Public-Private Partnership Dynamics
V. Elite Bank Risk-Focused Supervision and Qualified Self-Regulation
VI. Concluding Observations

I. INTRODUCTION: GLOBALIZATION AND ITS DISCONTENTS

In his Chapter Eighteen, Dr Walker paints a curious picture of a qualified 'multilateralism' in the area of global financial stability and the prudential

* S.J.D., D.Phil, LLD (h.c.). James L. Walsh Distinguished Faculty Fellow and Professor in Financial Institutions Law, SMU Dedman School of Law, Dallas, Texas and Sir John Lubbock Professor of Banking Law, CCLS, Queen Mary, University of London. The author would like to express his appreciation for the substantial input and comments provided by his colleagues, Dr. H. M. Shams, and Mr. C. D. Olive. This article is derived from a 1997 research study conducted by the author and Mr. Olive (*see* note 3 *infra*), and a recent 2002 paper presented with Dr. Shams (*see* note 10 *infra*) for an Oxford University Symposium on 'Law and Privatization' (2002). A version of this Chapter has appeared in the Spring 2003 issue of the *International Lawyer* published by SMU Dedman Law School, in conjunction with the ABA Section of International Law and Practice.

'safety and soundness' of international banking institution through the workings, collateral extensions, collaborative efforts and 'soft law' of the core international financial/economic institutions making up the Financial Stability Forum (FSF), which includes among other institutions the industriualized countries' Basel Committee on Banking Supervision (Basel Committee). Prof. Arner, in his Chapter Twelve depicts a companion, but rather more 'democratic' multilateral process in the area of international securities transactions and institutions though the International Organization of Securities Commissioners (IOSCO)—albeit another 'soft law' which now also comes under the FSF 'umbrella'-based process and one that in recent years has become closely linked to the Basel Committee process. Dr Shams in her Chapter Seventeen critically examines what she sees as 'club' form of limited multilateralism, using the example of the Financial Action Task Force (FATF) (which also is now under the FSF), whereby the strongest core members come to dominate the process and to transform their agenda onto a broader multilateral stage.

This Chapter considers an area of concern to the Basel, IOSCO and FATF processes, as well as to domestic and regional authorities: that is, the subject of large and complex international banking institutions and their sophisticated area of non-traditional banking activities. In considering this subject-matter, this Chapter will focus on a further variant of *limited multilateralism* in the area of global financial stability, by demonstrating that both the involved multilateral and domestic institutions require linkage with and active participation by the private financial industry sector to achieve the desired governmental/intergovernmental goals.

A perceived trend in the context of international economic activities is the shift towards forms of *private governance* or at least greater reliance by the public sector on private sector involvement.[1] This Chapter observes this trend in the area of international banking regulation and supervision.[2] It is concerned with what the author perceives to be an evolving 'public-private partnership' among governments, banking authorities, and large and complex banking organizations (LCBO), referred to below as 'elite banks,' with respect to fundamental dimensions of modern international financial regulation.[3] Because of time and space constraints, this Chapter will focus

[1] For background of this trend as embedded in the ongoing modern 'globalization processes,' see Heba Shams, *Law in the Context of 'Globalization': A Framework of Analysis*, 35 INT'L LAW. 1589 (2001). As to financial markets, see Douglas W. Arner, *Globalisation of Financial Markets: An International Passport for Securities Offerings?* 35 INT'L LAW. 1543 (2001).

[2] *See generally* JOSEPH JUDE NORTON, DEVISING INTERNATIONAL BANK SUPERVISORY STANDARDS (1995).

[3] Joseph J. Norton & Christopher D. Olive, *The Ongoing Process of International Bank Regulatory and Supervisory Convergence: A New Regulatory-Market 'Partnership'*, 116 ANN.

solely on this trend in the context of the international regulation and supervision of the modern genre of financial institution risks.[4] However, the author's informed intuition suggests that this trend can be detected and analyzed in other areas of international financial regulation including international capital markets, corporate governance, economical/financial criminality, and anti-terrorism issues.[5]

The rise of LCBOs through consolidation and diversification into new activities and risks has been swift and defining over the past decade.[6] This consolidation trend of LCBOs will most likely continue, as new legislation recently enacted by the United States and other major financial jurisdictions (e.g., Japan and Korea) paves the road to even more powerful and diverse financial institutions in the form of 'financial holding companies.'[7]

In this sense, these LCBOs and financial conglomerates (sometimes referred to as LCFIs, 'large complex financial institutions')[8] will be the major 'actors' in international financial transactions and markets.[9] In specific terms, as to these 'actors,' financial transactions and markets, this article explores the notion of a 'risk-focused' supervisory regime coupled with a 'self-regulatory' regime (i.e., 'qualified self-regulation') as a modern manifestation of and a trend towards 'a quasi or partial privatization' of what traditionally would have been the exclusive domain of government.[10]

REV. BANKING L. 67 (1997) [an abbreviated, but revised and update version also appeared in 1 J. INT'L FIN. REG. 16 (2000)].

4 *See* Symposium, *Law-Based Nature of the New International Financial Infrastructure*, 33 INT'L LAW. 847 (1999); J. B. ATTANASIO & J. J. NORTON (eds.), A NEW INTERNATIONAL FINANCIAL ARCHITECTURE: A VIABLE APPROACH? (2001).

5 *See, e.g.*, Symposium, *Terrorism's Burdens on Globalization*, 36 INT'L LAW. 1 (2002).

6 *See* Joseph J. Norton & Christopher D. Olive, *A By-Product of the Globalization Process: The Rise of Cross-Border Bank Mergers and Acquisitions—The U.S. Regulatory Framework*, 56 BUS. LAW. 591 (2001). *See also* Andrew Crockett (Chairman of the Financial Stability Forum), Statement at International Monetary and Financial Committee Meeting (Apr. 29, 2001); Lawrence H. Meyer, Remarks before a National Bureau of Economic Research Conference: Supervising LCBOs: Adapting to Change (Jan. 14, 2000).

7 *See, e.g.*, Gramm-Leach-Bliley Financial Modernization Act, Pub. Law. 106–102 (codified at 12 U.S.C (1999) on bank modernization and creating regulated FHC possibilities, previously in U.S. there were only regulated bank holding companies). Also in 2002, Korea legislated such possibilities. *See* BYUNG-TAE KIM, KOREA'S BANKING LAW REFORM: POST ASIAN CRISIS (2002).

8 LCBOs are, in effect, a type of 'financial conglomerate' with the bank as the center-piece. The LCFIs would be financial conglomerates that might be dominated by another type of financial institution, such as a specialties firm or insurance company.

9 On financial conglomerates, see generally George A. Walker, *The Law of Financial Conglomerates: The Next Generation*, 30 INT'L LAW. 57 (1996); and LUTGART VAN DEN BERGHE (ed.), FINANCIAL CONGLOMERATES: NEW RULES FOR NEW PLAYERS? (1995).

10 *See* Joseph J. Norton & Heba M. Shams, Privatisation in Modern Bank Regulation, presented in Oxford University Symposium on Privatisation and the Law (Wolfson College, Dr. M. Litkosky, Coordinator) (June 2002).

II. THE SUBJECT-MATTER OF RISK-FOCUSED BANK REGULATION/SUPERVISION: THE BACKDROP

The evolution of bank activities and the development of bank regulatory and supervisory frameworks on domestic, regional, or international bases have been underscored by frequently occurring periods of distress and crises throughout recent history.[11] The recent Asian, Russian, Turkish, Argentine, and Brazilian financial crises and their globally contagious impact are but several contemporary examples.[12] Even developed countries and regions have not been immune. In particular, banking authorities in the United States and Japan have encountered systemic periods of distress and crisis while attempting to maintain the 'safety and soundness' of their respective banking and financial systems and specific banking institutions. The U.S. thrift and banking crisis of the 1980s and early 1990s, as well as temporary crises generated during the financial market turbulence of 1998, graphically illustrate this point.[13]

Yet, within and through these recurring periods of crisis, banking activities have continued, over the past several decades, to evolve from traditional deposit-taking and lending activities into a diverse range of non-traditional counterparty activities that transverse the entire sphere of financial products and services. The 'traditional' bank lending and depository activities are becoming less significant, relegated more or less to 'relationship banking,' as global competition leaves banking institutions with diminishing opportunities to profit from traditional business lines.[14] In particular, the U.S. banking industry and especially LCBOs have experienced extraordinary growth and diversity over the past two decades into new activities through rapid advancements in information technology,

[11] *See generally* CARL-JOHAN LINDGREN ET AL., BANK SOUNDNESS AND MACROECONOMIC POLICY (1996). *Cf*, recent efforts to address these problems through the creation of a 'new international financial architecture.' On this, see J. B. ATTANASIO & J. J. NORTON (eds.), THE NEW INTERNATIONAL FINANCIAL ARCHITECTURE (Sir Joseph Gold Memorial Series 2001); Symposium, *Law-Based Nature of the New International Financial Infrastructure*, 33 INT'L LAW. 847 (1999).

[12] *See* DOUGLAS ARNER ET AL., FINANCIAL CRISES IN THE 1990S (2002). *See also* Joseph J. Norton, *The Modern Genre of Infrastructural Law Reform: The Legal and Practical Realities—The Case of Banking Reform in Thailand*, 55 SMU L. REV. 235 (2002).

[13] *See e.g.*, G. N. OLSON, BANKS IN DISTRESS: LESSONS FROM THE AMERICAN EXPERIENCE OF THE 1980S (2000); Symposium, *The S&L Crisis: Death and Transfiguration, Annual Survey Issue on Financial Institutions and Regulations*, 59 FORDHAM L. REV. S1 (1991); L. WILLIAM SEIDMAN, FULL FAITH AND CREDIT: THE GREAT S&L DEBACLE AND OTHER WASHINGTON SAGAS (1993) (former FDIC Chairman memoirs of the U.S. S&L and banking crises).

[14] Marc R. Saidenberg & Philip E. Strahan, *Are Banks Still Important for Financing Large Businesses?*, *in* Federal Reserve Bank of New York, CURRENT ISSUES IN ECONOMICS AND FINANCE, vol. 5, no. 12 (Aug. 1999).

telecommunications, and financial innovation, as well as through deregulatory initiatives from the respective U.S. banking authorities.[15]

The U.S. banking industry's expansion into new and increasingly complex activities has significantly increased competition both within the banking industry (LCBOs in particular) and between the banking industry and other financial service industries, particularly securities and insurance.[16] This enhanced competition, in turn, has facilitated systemic consolidation within the banking and financial services industries.[17] The result of this consolidation is the relatively recent formation of a distinct class of LCBOs undertaking complex risks in conducting sophisticated financial activities, services, and products across increasingly volatile financial markets.[18] The expansion of LCBOs into non-traditional and diverse activities and cross-border structures has established even more diverse and complex risks and linkages within and among banking systems and financial markets in developed and developing nations alike.[19]

These risks and linkages have expanded also the nature and scope of banking-customer relationships particularly over the past decade. LCBO underwriting, dealing, issuing, and proprietary trading activities in capital markets, structured finance markets, and over-the-counter (OTC) derivatives markets has become the new 'engine' of the modern global banking business.[20] Thus, advances in technology and financial innovation, as well as deregulatory initiatives of the U.S. banking authorities, which eventually set the stage for the enactment of dramatic financial modernization legislation in 1999, have consistently expanded the range of activities and risks conducted by large banks and LCBOs. These activities and risks, particularly activities involving, and risks arising in connection with, OTC derivatives and structured financial products, have increasingly refined LCBO and supervisory methodologies for measuring and managing risk.

The evolution of LCBOs as a cognizable class has occurred often through opaque maneuvering by the Basel Committee on Banking Supervision (the 'Basel Committee'), the key Central Bank Supervisors [e.g.,

[15] *See* Laurence H. Meyer, Board of Governors of the Federal Reserve System, *Market Discipline as a Complement to Bank Supervision and Regulation*, Statement at the Conference on Reforming Bank Capital Standards (June 14, 1999).

[16] Joseph Norton & Christopher Olive, *Regulation of the Securities Activities of Banks: A Comparison of U.S. Deregulation and Japanese Liberalization*, *in* INVESTMENT BANKING: THEORY AND PRACTICE (EDWARD P. M. GARDENER & PHILIP MOLYNEUX eds. 2d ed., 1996).

[17] Susan M. Phillips & Alan N. Rechtschaffen, *International Banking Activities: The Role of the Federal Reserve in Domestic Capital Markets*, 21 FORDHAM INT'L L.J. 1754, 1760 (1998).

[18] Comptroller of the Currency, Advisory Letter No. 99-4, *Leveraged Lending* (May 3, 1999) (reviewing breakdowns in lending discipline).

[19] *See generally* ROBERT C. EFFROS (ed.), CURRENT LEGAL ISSUES AFFECTING CENTRAL BANKS, vol. 5 (1998).

[20] Phillips & Rechtschaffen, *supra* note 17, at 1765–66.

the U.S. Board of Governors of the Federal Reserve System (FRB), and the U.S. Comptroller of the Currency (OCC, a bureau of the U.S. Treasury Department)] in support of continued global banking industry consolidation.[21] In the global bank supervisory context, the evolution of LCBOs has been explicitly addressed and implicitly supported through consistent efforts of the Basel Committee on several fronts. First, the Basel Committee has recognized certain LCBOs as 'financial conglomerates,' and has worked jointly since 1995 with the International Organization of Securities Commissions (IOSCO) and other authorities through the 'Joint Forum' platform to develop regulatory and supervisory guidance on handling these institutions. Second, the Basel Committee has increasingly issued guidance that focuses on global bank risk management and internal control systems, as well as public and regulatory disclosure of complex activities and risks arising from such activities. Third, the Basel Committee has increasingly vested discretion in LCBOs to identify and to measure risk, subject to generally objective criteria using 'internal models,' such as through the Market Risk Amendment to the Capital Accord and in the more recently proposed modifications to the credit risk-based provisions of the Capital Accord. Fourth, the Basel Committee has recently proposed major revisions to the Capital Accord in an attempt to refocus emphasis with respect to global banks.[22]

In effect, the Basel Committee and key national bank regulators attempt to meet the challenges presented by the global banking consolidation trend and new complex activities and risks by developing and implementing distinct 'risk-based supervision' frameworks.[23] By this, they redirect examination techniques to emphasize risk management and internal control systems, as opposed to determining through transaction testing and other static means whether a bank or LCBO is operating in a safe and sound manner at a given time. This evolution to risk-focused supervision is a direct response to dramatic changes in the banking industry and the rapidly

[21] *See generally* Lisa M. DeFerrari and David E. Palmer (members of the FRB's Division of Banking Supervision and Regulation), *Supervision of Large Complex Banking Organizations*, Fed. Res. Bull. 87 (Feb. 2001).

[22] The Basel Committee maintains a comprehensive Web site, through the Bank for International Settlement, which contains a 'compendium' of documents provided by the Basel Committee on Banking Supervision, along with a full collection of Basel Committee 'publications' (Nos. 1–93 from March 1982 through October 2002), joint publications, newsletters, and Working Papers. *See* http://www.bis.org/publ.htm.

[23] Federal Reserve Board, SR 97-24, Risk-Focused Framework for Supervision of Large Complex Institutions (Oct. 27, 1997) and related SR 99-15 and 99-18 (1999); and Joint Forum on Financial Conglomerates, Supervision of Financial Conglomerates, Basel Committee Publications No. 47 (Feb. 1999) (consultation documents on 'financial conglomerates' released by the Basel Committee), *available at* http://www.bis.org/publ/bcbs34.htm. *See also* Professor Howell E. Jackson & Cameron Half, *Background Paper on Evolving Trends in the Supervision of Financial Conglomerates* (Harvard Law School, June 2002) (draft) (copy on file with author).

declining time in which risk profiles can change significantly. The risk-focused supervision approach is intended to be more 'forward looking' than the 'transaction testing' approach, and to focus on bank risk management practices and internal control systems to manage current and prospective risks. The risk-focused approach facilitates the development of supervisory plans that are tailored for each individual bank or LCBO risk profile and organizational structure.

III. THE 'PUBLIC-PRIVATE PARTNERSHIP' NOTION

A. In General

The expansion and diversification of large banks and LCBOs into complex activities and cross-border structures through consolidation has generally separated certain global banks and LCBOs into a fairly small class of global banking organizations (i.e., 'elite banks' referred to above). The majority of global bank resources are undoubtedly concentrated in certain of the elite banks. The elite banks are engaged in intense global competition in all activities, have complex cross-border organizational structures, and undertake increasingly greater and more complex risks to enhance revenues and profits.[24] The elite banks are the primary vehicles for the transmission of government monetary, credit, and exchange rate policies, and hold significant assets and counterparty linkages throughout global banking and financial markets.

Therefore, home and host nation authorities are either directly or indirectly subjected to a 'public-private partnership' to some extent with the elite banking industry. The elite banks are the institutional fabric that connects domestic and international banking and financial markets through their credit, intermediary, and proprietary functions. As such, the vestiges of this public-private partnership define the parameters of elite bank regulation and supervision. This 'partnership' may not necessarily exist between governments and other financial institutions, although this point is certainly debatable with several of the largest and most complex securities and insurance conglomerates at this time.

[24] *See* Laurence H. Meyer, *Moving Forward into the 21st Century*, Remarks at the Conference of State Bank Supervisors (June 3, 1999) (stating that the FRB began 'sharpening its focus' on twenty U.S. banks and ten international banks last year in response to their increasing size and complexity), *available at* http://www.bog.frb.fed.us/boarddocs/speeches/1999/19990603.htm.

1. The 'Special Relationship'

The distinguishing implementation of elite bank regulation and supervision in the form of a public-private partnership is premised in part on the uniquely complex risk profiles, and global capital and organizational structures, of elite banks as compared to other non-bank financial institutions.[25] For example, elite banks maintain a complex funding profile that consists, to a significant extent, of customer and interbank deposits withdrawable on demand, short-term debt relationships derived from capital markets, and significant counterparty linkages developed through securitization and OTC derivatives markets. Further, elite banks generally maintain substantial degrees of leverage relative to capital. In addition, bank loan and other credit assets, which represent a significant percentage of total assets, are generally more illiquid than securities and other financial instruments held by securities firms or other financial institutions.[26]

The elite banks are also generally either implicitly or explicitly, supported by some form of explicit or implicit government 'guaranty' to prevent or mitigate the systemic effects of bank insolvency, such as a deposit insurance scheme or other guaranty of deposit/lending obligations. Deposit insurance or government guarantees to elite banks exist in order to contain the real (or perceived) threat of contagion and potentially enormous macroeconomic costs of liquidity problems in times of market stress.[27] The uncertainty and inconsistency over primary and secondary market credit valuations of elite banks and their respective assets, liabilities and hedging transactions, however, necessarily leads to more difficulty and less transparency in determining the financial condition of an elite bank at any given time.[28] Nonetheless, the range of elite bank activities involving other non-traditional, complex financial services and products clearly extends the scope of explicit or implicit safety nets.[29]

The elite banks should, therefore, be viewed as 'special' institutions; and these factors, along with the credit, intermediary, and proprietary functions

[25] *See, e.g.*, Edward W. Kelley, Jr., Board of Governors of the Federal Reserve System, *Are Banks Still Special?*, presented at the Seminar on Banking Soundness and Monetary Policy in a World of Global Capital Markets, International Monetary Fund, Washington, D.C. (Jan. 29, 1997) (on file with author). The genesis of the author's interest in this theme of 'public-private partnership' is Norton & Olive, *supra* note 3.

[26] *See, e.g.*, Thomas Glaessner & Ignacio Mas, *Incentives and the Resolution of 3f Bank Distress*, 10 WORLD BANK RESEARCH OBSERVER No. 1 53–73 (1995).

[27] *See, e.g.*, George G. Kaufman, *Bank Failures, Systemic Risk, and Bank Regulation*, FEDERAL RESERVE BANK OF CHICAGO WORKING PAPER SERIES IN FINANCIAL REGULATION (Working Paper No. 96–1, 1996).

[28] *See generally* Group of Thirty, *International Insolvencies in the Financial Sector; A Study Group Discussion Draft* (1996).

[29] *See generally* James R. Smoot, *Striking Camp and Moving to Higher Ground: The Hazardous Subtleties of 'Subtle Hazards' in Bank Regulation*, 4 GEO. MASON L. REV. 21 (1995).

necessitate that governments and elite banks are bound by certain flexible constraints inherent to the partnership.

The parameters of their partnership are worth exploring; and, although the theoretical and practical examination of these parameters is currently in its infancy, several observations may be noted. First, the partnership is both formal (established through banking laws, regulations, and other supervisory guidance) and informal (established through certain supervisory and market practices and understandings not necessarily reduced to writing). Second, there are various responsibilities of the partnership to be fulfilled by governments and/or banking authorities. Third, there are various responsibilities to be fulfilled by the elite banking institutions in this configuration.

2. *The Governments and/or Banking Authorities*

Banking authorities have the incentive to avoid undertaking regulatory or supervisory actions that unnecessarily hinder opportunities for their constituent elite banks to remain competitive and profitable on a domestic or international basis. Instead, the banking authorities maintain the incentive to support and to enhance elite bank opportunities to diversify into new activitics and otherwise to earn greater profits so long as the risks arising from such activities are not *per se* disproportionately excessive or beyond the scope of supervisory oversight. For example, the U.S. banking authorities have engaged, consistently and actively, in deregulation to ensure that large banks and LCBOs remain able to increasingly engage in nonbank activities. The U.S. banking authorities also strive to achieve a balance in regulating and supervising foreign banking organizations operating in the United States to promote 'level playing fields' and to ensure that U.S. banking organizations receive equal access to foreign markets. These U.S. regulatory incentives are supplemented by prudential 'safety and soundness' considerations through appropriate administration of risk-based to capital requirements.

Banking authorities arguably maintain certain interesting incentives as part of this partnership. For instance, banking authorities have the incentive to ensure that monetary policy objectives do not unnecessarily create undue conflicts between their constituent LCBO industry and bank regulatory and supervisory objectives. The banking authorities would necessarily desire to avoid implementing policy objectives that would submit the banking system to unnecessary macroeconomic volatility, asset-liability or foreign exchange mismatches, or inflationary expectations that would fuel asset price bubbles and speculative lending or derivatives such that the policy objectives disadvantage or threaten the banking system.[30]

[30] A most difficult concept to address is how developing nations should adjust their macro-

Banking authorities also generally lack the expertise or resources available to elite banks and, therefore, have the incentive to seek out the counsel and advice of constituent elite banks on issues pertaining to monetary, supervisory, and regulatory policies prior to or during their implementation. Banking authorities further have the incentive to alert and to protect their constituent elite banks from risks or conditions that may not be entirely within their ability to control, such as political risk of untimely or inappropriate government action. Banking authorities also have the incentive to create, promote, and enhance 'market discipline' mechanisms for elite banks to engage in 'self' and 'collective' regulation and supervision of risks that are generally within their ability to control.

Finally, banking authorities have the incentive to punish or to eliminate the demonstrably reckless partners of the partnership or to facilitate their consolidation into other stronger banking institutions so that the partnership may continue to evolve. Effectively, banking authorities have every incentive to address the most problematic or systemic issues that arise with their constituent banking organizations largely out of the public domain where they can be handled 'appropriately' with as much discretion as possible and without the onset of destabilizing or politically motivated intervention.

3. The Elite Banks

The elite banks have the incentive to work with the banking authorities, directly or indirectly, to ensure that monetary, supervisory, and regulatory policies are effectively balanced, developed, and implemented. The elite banks also have the incentive, implicitly or explicitly, to engage in political action or inaction to protect and to support their respective banking authorities when they come under political scrutiny for risks undertaken by the banks. The elite banks allow banking authorities to view the 'secrets of the temple,' including sensitive proprietary information such as risk management and internal control systems, in order to protect against risks within their control and anticipate risks beyond their control. Finally, and perhaps most importantly, the elite banks have the incentive to assist banking authorities in preserving the safety and soundness of the domestic and international banking system through non-transparent but quasi-orderly workouts of large distressed borrowers and other counterparties (such as OTC derivatives counterparties). The elite banks and their respective banking authorities, in turn, work with governments and international financial

economic and exchange rate policies to address volatile private capital flows. *See, e.g., Hearing on Proposals for a New International Financial Architecture*, Committee on Banking and Financial Services, U.S. House of Representatives (May 20, 1999) (testimony from various experts).

institutions (IFIs) to ensure ultimately that large borrowers or counterparties in distress are dealt with 'appropriately.'

4. A Symbiotic Framework?

The 'public-private partnership' evidences particular understandings between elite banks and their banking authorities that represent a form of a symbiotic framework of 'safe passage' among and between them. The partnership parameters are defined through the bank regulatory and supervisory frameworks as well as the implicit balances of power that necessarily exist between elite banks and banking authorities. As the elite banks represent crucial policy vehicles to their respective governments, the government authorities conducting monetary policy and the banking authorities conducting bank regulation and supervision (to the extent that such agencies are separate) have every incentive to ensure that their constituent elite banks remain sound, competitive, and robust. The elite banks presumably prefer to have discrete self-regulatory frameworks, but may also desire supervisory oversight relationships as additional checks and balances against complex risks overtaking their risk management and internal control systems.

The elite banks are already subject to an extensive global regulatory and supervisory framework. The current global bank regulatory and supervisory framework is nonetheless arguably tilted in favor of elite banking interests versus the interests other bank classes. In other words, banking authorities naturally seek to implement and to enforce regulatory and supervisory policies so as to enable the elite banks to:

- engage in bank and nonbank activities that present maximum opportunities for profit;
- diversify within and among different lines of business to maintain competitiveness;
- remain relatively free of unnecessary government restraints, burdens and costs that work against these objectives;
- maintain access to necessary funding and certain protections in times of crisis (such as government liquidity or intervention guarantees or deposit insurance); and
- simultaneously develop, implement, and enforce effective risk management and internal control systems and preserve capital to cushion losses from those activities.

The larger and more influential elite banks, the interests of which are more readily acknowledged and addressed by the political and regulatory processes (but nonetheless are aligned in most respects to the partnership) presumably enjoy a stronger and more mutually beneficial relationship with their respective banking authorities. The banking authorities are often faced with external market shocks and monetary, supervisory, and regulatory policy decisions where a given policy decision would likely affect different banks and economic sectors or regions differently, or otherwise might diminish the profit opportunities of the elite bank class as a whole. If conflicting policy decisions become self-evident, then banking authorities presumably would tend to adopt policies that favor the interests of the larger and more influential elite banks, perhaps to the detriment of the smaller and less influential banks, economic sectors, and safety and soundness concerns. The larger and more influential elite banks have global interests spread across the international financial markets. The safety and soundness of elite banks is enormously important to the banking authorities; once again, perhaps to the detriment of other banking institutions and economic interests. The reality is that more influential elite banks, in all likelihood, exert greater influence upon banking authorities than the authorities exert upon them. Accordingly, to the extent that elite banks and banking authorities diverge on issues affecting the partnership, the elite banks would presumably exert far greater influence on the banking authorities to set agendas and priorities as such.

These basic deductions are supplemented by the realization that the larger and more influential elite banks have considerably greater financial and intellectual resources at their disposal than the government agencies in terms of expertise in dealing with increasingly complex and global risk exposures. The subtle conclusion here is that, notwithstanding regulatory influence upon elite bank risk management infra-structures and upon associated risk-focused supervision, banking authorities arguably may have little choice in the medium- to long-run but to defer to 'market discipline' to have a greater impact on elite bank 'business judgment' in such matters than risk-focused supervision (or to form a primary element of risk-focused supervision). The reliance on 'market discipline' as an element of risk-focused supervision for elite banks may render bank regulatory frameworks as mere parameters for the partnership to address problems after they arise, as supplemented by close supervisory oversight of and implication of public disclosure requirements on elite banks to ensure that potentially significant problems are anticipated and pre-empted by market forces before they arise. The concepts of close supervisory oversight, enhanced regulatory enforcement of risk management and internal control systems, and, most importantly, the use of 'market discipline' through elite bank public disclosures of certain risks or structural characteristics, should be used to rebalance the partnership parameters.[31]

[31] *See generally* DeFerrari & Palmer, *supra* note 21, which discusses all key, related FRB supervision and regulation (SR) letters from 1999 through 2000.

IV. PUBLIC-PRIVATE PARTNERSHIP DYNAMICS

The parameters of this public-private partnership become especially dynamic, such as in the United States, where different classes of banking interests exist and similar banking and financial conglomerates are subjected to different strains of regulatory and supervisory oversight by different and/or multiple government financial authorities. In recent history, the U.S. financial authorities lacked uniformity in how they work with, supervise, or regulate their respective financial organizations, both within and beyond the United States. Thus, 'supervisory and regulatory arbitrage' opportunities existed in legion on domestic and international bases.[32]

The elite banks have had every incentive to (and generally do) exploit such arbitrage opportunities through financial and legal innovations. In fact, the financial authorities often encouraged such behavior with respect to authorizing their respective institutions to diversify into new activities, and to devise new financial structures at different times and in different ways. The regulatory and supervisory arbitrage opportunities place the financial authorities in the situation where they have had to compete with each other, from a 'regulatory jurisdiction' perspective, in order to preserve the rationale for their existence.[33]

As partnership parameters, such as described above, become more dynamic, however, special interests involved in the banking and financial service industries become increasingly vested in the legislative and regulatory processes. The elite banking interests become more entrenched, and fight to prevent losses of market share or explicit or implicit regulatory subsidies that previously sustained them. The elite banks continuously search the world over for business opportunities abroad that they might be limited or prohibited from conducting within their home nations, and they press their interests forward with foreign governments to establish and protect their opportunities and interests. This is particularly evident as one realizes the enormous opportunities for regulatory arbitrage and regulatory jurisdictional ambiguities existing at the international level, particularly between and among developing nations with far less transparent and less meaningful regulatory and supervisory frameworks.[34] The consistent

[32] *See generally* James R. Barth et al., *Commercial Banking Structure, Regulation, and Performance: An International Comparison*, OFFICE OF THE COMPTROLLER OF THE CURRENCY WORKING PAPER 97–6 (1997).

[33] *See, e.g.*, Joseph J. Norton, *The Glass-Steagall Act and Related Legislative Reform in the United States: Non-Legislative Bank Deregulation and Modernization—The Recent Comptroller of the Currency 'Op-Sub' Regulation* , 14 BANK & FIN. L. REV. 1 (1998); Bevis Longstreth & Ivan E. Mattei, *Organizational Freedom for Banks: The Case in Support*, 97 COLUM. L. REV. 1895 (1997); Phillips & Rechtschaffen, *supra* note 17, at 1759–60.

[34] *See, e.g.*, Morris Goldstein & Philip Turner, *Banking Crises in Emerging Economies:*

exploitation of regulatory arbitrage opportunities by elite banks effectively forces developing nations to take measures to protect their domestic banking and financial service industries from foreign influence and control, which cuts against any incentives for establishing meaningful international 'free trade' in banking and financial services.

The modern public-private partnership also consistently provides elite banks with incentives consistently to 'push the envelope' of complex risk-taking in their activities. The development and implementation of legitimate risk management and internal control systems becomes most critical as elite banks and national banking and financial systems consistently encounter periods of systemic risk, distress, crisis, and failure. Banking and financial system crises generally have multiple and diverse causes and any given crisis generally cannot be explained by a single cause. The causes of any such crises usually arise from basic ambiguities, gaps, omissions, or outright failures to perform under the public-private partnership by elite banks or banking authorities. The basic ambiguities, gaps, or failures to perform under the partnership generally results in 'boom-bust' periods underscored by elite bank credit, market, operational, or other risk exposures in excess of what they can or will adequately manage and, therefore, tend to cause the banking authorities to react or to intervene only on an 'after the fact' basis.[35]

The banking authorities' reaction to 'boom-bust' periods and to excessive risk-taking may be to intervene directly or indirectly in an untimely and/or inappropriate manner through monetary, supervisory, or regulatory policy. The intervention methods themselves may incorporate 'lessons learned' from risk management and internal control failures in the short run, but likely will reinforce 'moral hazard' incentives in the longer run to inadvertently encourage elite banks to continue to engage in excessive risk-taking without meaningful risk management and enforcement of internal control.

The basic decision of a banking authority to intervene comes down to another 'business judgment'; should the authority intervene directly or indirectly and meaningfully address the situation, or otherwise should it engage in *forbearance* and trust that the elite bank or banks will address the perceived inequities? The nature and extent of the business judgment is related necessarily to the following conceptual questions. First, how and on the basis of what information should elite bank risk management and internal control systems be continuously supervised and evaluated by banking

Origins and Policy Options, BANK FOR INTERNATIONAL SETTLEMENTS ECONOMIC PAPER NO. 46, *available at* http://www.bis.org/publ/econ46.pdf (1996).

[35] *See generally Banking Soundness and Monetary Policy: Issues and Experiences in the Global Economy Papers Presented at the Seventh Seminar on Central Banking* (Charles Enoch & John H. Green eds.,1997).

authorities over time? Second, how can the credit, market, and operational risks undertaken by an elite bank be measured and its capital adequacy evaluated in *real time*? Third, how can elite bank senior management be held accountable for meaningful deficiencies in risk management and internal control systems and for capital inadequacy? Fourth, how should such accountability be defined and determined (in terms of regulatory enforcement or public disclosure or both), and what is the objective of holding persons or institutions accountable? Fifth, what should be the standard for holding such senior management accountable for risk management and internal control failures that result in substantial losses to the banks and/or jeopardize the national on global banking and financial systems? These questions should be cautiously explored in developing future reforms to large bank supervision and capital adequacy frameworks.

The path of least resistance for banking authorities faced with such challenges and business judgments will be to take no direct enforcement actions against elite banks for such failures in this regard, but to pursue forbearance policies in the name of 'market discipline.' The concept of 'market discipline' as an emerging regulatory paradigm provides that the market participants will allocate accountability for excessive elite bank risk-taking that actually or potentially results in substantial risk management and internal control failures and losses under an increasingly 'self-regulatory' regime. The pursuit of forbearance policies by banking authorities, however, may lead to political intervention, loss of banking authority credibility, and increased costs for resolution of ensuing bailouts.

However, effective market discipline will occur only if meaningful information regarding elite bank risk management and internal control failures are disclosed to the public and/or other government authorities. If significant elite bank risk management or internal control failures occur, then the issues of accountability and compensation in terms of who will be held accountable for the condition of the organization, and who will or will not be compensated in times of crisis become even more significant? The resolution of these issues generally should be developed by consensus between the elite banks and banking authorities under the public-private partnership framework. But, if the balance of power in the public-private partnership generally lies with the elite banks, then banking and financial interests will generally govern the solution, and that solution will generally facilitate non-transparent relations between elite banks and banking authorities.

V. ELITE BANK RISK-FOCUSED SUPERVISION AND QUALIFIED SELF-REGULATION

The U.S. banking authorities' and the Basel Committee's approach as to elite banks has generally resulted in the development of a regulatory and supervisory framework for elite banks comprised of risk-focused supervisory oversight coupled with qualified 'self-regulation.' There is little question that elite banks generally possess far greater expertise and resources to identify, measure, monitor, and manage complex risk exposures, using sophisticated risk measurement and aggregation methodologies, than is available to most (if not all) domestic banking authorities. The 'risk-focused supervision' concept essentially redirects responsibility and accountability for the design, development and implementation of risk management and internal control systems to the elite banks themselves, subject to general and objective (and, at times, subjective) standards for such systems established by the banking authorities, and to supervisory oversight of such systems.

This approach admittedly leaves significant discretion to the elite banking community (in terms of development and implementation of such systems, and the provision of timely and meaningful information generated by such systems disclosures to the banking authorities) and the banking authorities (in terms of relative degree of supervisory oversight and enforcement of those systems and access or diligence in obtaining such information). The nonbank activities of elite banks, carried on through financial holding companies, bank holding companies, bank subsidiaries, and nonbank affiliates, may be subject to both supervisory oversight by the banking authorities and functional regulation by other respective financial authorities, depending on the jurisdiction (particularly in the United States). The elite banks operationally are increasingly managing their activities and systems along business lines on a more centralized basis, as opposed to distinguishing approaches based on legal entities.

The risk-focused supervision framework essentially provides elite banks with substantial discretion to develop, implement, and enforce risk management and internal control systems, subject to the development and application of objective and subjective supervisory standards and narrowly focused supervisory oversight on material risks arising from elite bank activities. The risk-focused supervision framework is also being used to refine appropriate risk-based capital requirements for elite banks. Finally, the banking authorities maintain substantial discretion on how to conduct supervisory oversight of large banks and LCBOs under this guidance.

The movement towards risk-focused supervision and qualified 'self-regulation' became primarily evident through the Basel Committee's introduction of the Market Risk Amendment to the Capital Accord in January 1996, as implemented by the U.S. banking authorities and other authorities at the domestic level.[36] There is little question that elite banks were the 'primary drivers' behind the Basel Committee's adoption of the Market

[36] *See* Basel Committee on Banking Supervision, *Amendment to the Capital Accord to Incorporate Market Risks* (1996).

Risk Amendment in its current form and its most significant aspect, the 'internal models' approach for determining market risk capital requirements as a basis for capital adequacy regulation for elite banks with significant trading activities. The 'internal models' approach authorizes certain qualifying elite banks to develop and to utilize their own risk management (particularly, risk measurement) systems to measure capital requirements using models tailored from the collection of 'value-at-risk' (VaR) methodologies, subject only to certain quantitative and qualitative parameters established by the Basel Committee.[37] The 'internal models' approach essentially provides elite banks with significant discretion to determine their own market risk capital requirements using individually tailored VaR methodologies.

The Market Risk Amendment represented a paradigm shift in global bank supervision, but the activities covered are a fairly small part of global risks assumed by the elite banks. The far more significant impact of the Market Risk Amendment was the clear signal that such an 'internal models' approach could eventually be introduced for credit risk, in the form of revised credit risk-based capital requirements under a new Basel Capital Accord. The Basel Committee moved decisively closer to this state of affairs by proposing an entirely new capital adequacy framework to replace the currently existing Basel Capital Accord in June 1999, and then re-proposing this new framework in January 2000, updating it in June 2000, revising it in December 2001, and elaborating further on it in July 2002 (Basel II).[38] The new Basel II capital adequacy framework proposes a three-pillar approach towards addressing credit risk: (i) 'minimum capital requirements,' (ii) 'supervisory review of capital adequacy,' and (iii) 'market discipline.' A review of the restated framework and subsequent statements by leading bank authorities indicates a clear intent to shift responsibility for the design and implementation of credit risk capital requirements more to the banks themselves under such an 'internal models' approach.[39]

[37] *See, e.g.*, Darryll Hendricks & Beverly Hirtle, *Bank Capital Requirements for Market Risk: The Internal Models Approach*, *in* Federal Reserve Bank of New York, ECONOMIC POLICY REVIEW, at 1 (Dec. 1997).

[38] *See* Basel Committee on Banking Supervision, *A New Capital Adequacy Framework* (June 1999), as repurposed and revised. *See* Basel Committee on Banking Supervision, *The New Basel Capital Accord* (July 2002). For history of the new Basel Capital Accord, see www.bis.org/publ/bcbsca.htm (last visited Feb. 21, 2003). The Basel Committee provided extensive further elaboration on Basel II on July 10, 2002.

[39] *See* Federal Reserve Bank of New York, *Consultative Paper on a New Capital Adequacy Framework*, *available at* http://www.ny.frb.org/pihome/news/speeches/mcd990603.html (June 3, 1999). Also for a critique, see Christopher Olive, *Market Risk Capital and the Basel Internal Models Approach: Some Preliminary Reflections on the Public-Private Model*, *in* INTERNATIONAL MONETARY AND FINANCIAL LAW IN THE NEW MILLENNIUM ch. 25 (J. Norton & M. Andenas eds., 2002). The Basel Committee received more than 250 comments on its January 2001 Basel II proposal.

The clear trend towards risk-focused supervision and qualified 'self-regulation' is also demonstrated by banking authorities' reluctance to regulate OTC derivatives markets directly. The U.S. and other banking authorities have conducted various studies of the OTC derivatives market since 1993, and have weathered periods of significant market stress dominated by events involving OTC derivative activities. These events, including recent Russian financial crises in 1998 and the financial LTCM debacle, arguably demonstrated that enhanced prudential standards and supervisory oversight of these activities may be desirable.[40] Nonetheless, elite banks and their respective banking authorities jointly engaged in considerable efforts over the past several years to pre-empt any momentum towards adopting any distinct 'regulatory framework' for OTC derivative activities, and even meaningful public disclosures of these activities.[41] Notwithstanding progress made in disclosure of such activities to banking authorities themselves as evidenced by Basel Committee annual surveys of elite bank OTC derivative activities conducted over the past several years. These positions have been established and maintained notwithstanding available information that suggests that OTC derivatives, and the handful of global elite banks acting as primary dealers and counterparties in these instruments, collectively assert a dominant yet volatile influence over spot and exchange-traded interest rate, foreign exchange and even equity and commodity markets, and facilitate excessive leverage and illiquidity in such markets, which (in turn) facilitate or exacerbate periods of market stress.[42] These trends are readily acknowledged in several important reports issued by the U.S. President's Working Group on Financial Markets, consisting of the U.S. banking authorities, Treasury Department, SEC, and CFTC, but

[40] *See, e.g.*, Basel Committee on Banking Supervision & Technical Committee of the International Organization of Securities Commissions (IOSCO), *Framework for Supervisory Information about Derivatives and Trading Activities* (1998); Bank for International Settlements, *Report on OTC Derivatives: Settlement Procedures and Counterparty Risk Management* (1999); U.S. General Accounting Office, *Commodity Exchange Act: Issues Related to the Commodity Futures Trading Commission's Reauthorization*, GAO/GGD 99–74 (2000).

[41] This has occurred most visibly through the battle over adopting and implementing accounting standards for OTC derivatives, and in various regulatory authorities collaborating to stifle the CFTC's attempt to raise and address various unresolved issues pertaining to OTC derivatives in its May 1998 Concept Release.

[42] *See, e.g.*, Bank for International Settlements, *Central Bank Survey of Foreign Exchange and Derivatives Market Activity*, 30 Sec. Reg. & L. Rep. (BNA) 24, at 908, (1998) (reviewing preliminary opposition of U.S. regulatory authorities to the *CFTC Concept Release on OTC Derivatives*, 63 Fed. Reg. 26,114 (1998)). *See also* Basel Committee on Banking Supervision & Technical Committee of the International Organization of Securities Commissions (IOSCO), *Recommendations for Public Disclosure of Trading and Derivatives Activities of Banks and Securities Firms* (1999) (joint consultative paper). *See, e.g.*, Bank for International Settlements, *Central Bank Survey of Foreign Exchange and Derivatives Market Activity*, UP, FENCED IN OR TAMED?, AMEX BANK REVIEW (1995) (on file with author). For latest BIS analysis of the global OTC derivatives market activities, see its Press Release of Nov. 8, 2002.

nonetheless significantly influenced by the banking authorities, and in various post-1998 Basel Committee papers.[43]

The risk-based capital amendments and proposals for the Basel Capital Accord and regulatory postures adopted for OTC derivatives markets are facilitated by a recent plethora of 'best practices' guidance for risk management and internal control systems. This guidance was developed and issued primarily through the Basel Committee in close consultation with the elite banking industry and other international regulatory forums (e.g., IOSCO, Joint Forum, and Financial Stability Forum).[44] The industry groups consulted in this regard included the Counterparty Risk Management Policy Group, International Swaps and Derivatives Association (ISDA), the Group of Thirty, and the Institute of International Finance (IIF).[45] These reports focus primarily on the development and implementation of 'best practices' with respect to identifying, measuring, monitoring and managing credit risk, market risk, operational risk and liquidity risk management, and managing relationships with and risk exposures to highly leveraged institutions such as hedge funds.

The driving force behind the guidance issued to address these complex areas is the dangerously consistent occurrence of episodes of market stress, suggesting (if not demonstrating) that elite banks may not consistently implement and enforce risk management and internal control systems. A careful review of these public-private efforts to develop guidance, and the market stress events and risk management and internal control failures on

[43] *See* Report of the President's Working Group on Financial Markets, *Hedge Funds, Leverage, and the Lessons of Long-Term Capital Management* (1999); Report of the President's Working Group on Financial Markets, *Over-the-Counter Derivatives Markets and the Commodity Exchange Act* (1999). On Basel Committee papers, see, *inter alia*, Publications No. 64 (1999).

[44] *See generally* Basel Committee on Banking Supervision, *Internal Audit in Banks and the Supervisor's Relationship with Auditors: A Survey* (2002); Basel Committee on Banking Supervision, *Sound Practices for the Management and Supervision of Operational Risks* (2002); Basel Committee on Banking Supervision, *Operational Risk Management* (1998); Basel Committee on Banking Supervision, *Framework for Internal Control Systems in Banking Organisations* (1998); Basel Committee on Banking Supervision, *Framework for the Evaluation of Internal Control Systems* (1998). *See also* Technical Committee of the International Organization of Securities Commissions (IOSCO), *Risk Management and Control Guidance for Securities Firms and their Supervisors* (1998); *Joint Forum, Intra-Group Transactions and Exposures and Risk Concentrations Principles* (1999) (consultation papers). The work of the Basel Committee, IOSCO, and the Joint Forum (formerly known as the Joint Forum on Financial Conglomerates, established in 1996 and consisting of members of the Basel Committee, IOSCO, and the International Association of Insurance Supervisors (IAIS)), are generally well known in the international financial law community. The Financial Stability Forum was developed following the G-7 Finance Ministers' meeting in Bonn, Germany, in February 1999. The group consists of finance officials from both developing and developed nations, regulatory authorities, central bankers, and members of international financial institutions. *See* http://www.fsforum.org.

[45] *See, e.g.*, Counterparty Risk Management Policy Group, *Improving Counterparty Risk Management Practices* (1999).

which they are premised, also suggests that the recommended 'best practices' are well-articulated and user-friendly principles addressing complex matters (but not inherently complex in themselves nor are they entirely new ideas to the elite banking community). The guidance instead represents a series of ambitious restatements of fairly elementary risk management and internal control principles already inherent in law, regulation, accounting and common sense that elite banks, with their expertise and resources, already have integrated into their global banking and trading operations.

Nonetheless, elite banks and their banking authorities have repeatedly been caught in significant risk management and internal control failures in recent times. The specific institutional and regulatory failures include, among others, the well-known Barings Bank plc, Daiwa Bank (New York) and Sumitomo Bank 'rogue trader' episodes of 1995–1996, the NatWest derivatives pricing/internal control debacle and similar failures in 1997, and the money laundering scandals involving the Bank of New York and other major U.S. and European global banks of August 1999-present.[46] The more significant 'industry' failures certainly include the OTC derivatives and counterparty credit episodes underscoring the Asian and Russian financial crises over 1997-1998, and most importantly the LTCM episode of 1998, and the current Argentine and Brazilian financial crises respectively.[47]

These above referenced examples cumulatively suggest that the risk management and internal control standards established through Basel Committee and U.S. banking authority guidance may not, from time to time, be successfully implemented or meaningfully self-enforced by the elite banks. The intellectual frameworks for risk management and internal control systems have undoubtedly been organized and articulated to the elite banking industry through the Basel Committee and U.S. regulatory channels. The collective motivation and incentives for elite banks to successfully implement and meaningfully enforce these standards appear to be absent or compromised by profitability concerns. An important question in this regard is whether the appropriate ingredients for 'market discipline' are lacking because of complexities underlying the implementation and enforcement of these systems in complex global financial markets, or

[46] *See, e.g.*, Joseph Norton & Christopher Olive, *Globalization of Financial Risks and International Supervision of Banks and Securities Firms: Lessons from the Barings Debacle*, 30 INT'L LAW. 2, at 301 (1996); R.T.I. Moonen, *The LTCM Crisis and its Consequences for Banks and Banking Supervision*, FINANCIAL MARKET TRENDS, No. 73, at 97 (June 1999) (reviewing facts and circumstances behind LTCM 'hedge fund' debacle and bailout); Sharon Walsh & Kathleen Day, *Money Laundering Suspected: Russian Mob Said to Send Billions Through N.Y. Bank*, WASH. POST, Aug. 20, 1999, at E01 (reviewing facts and circumstances behind inquiry involving Bank of New York and laundering of Russian mafia funds, possibly including commingled IMF funds previously distributed to the Russian Government).

[47] *See, e.g.*, Basel Committee on Banking Supervision, *Supervisory Lessons to be drawn from the Asian Crisis* (1999); Basel Committee on Banking Supervision, *Sound Practices for Banks' Interactions with Highly Leveraged Institutions* (1999).

because of voluntary, knowing, or subliminal decisions rendered at the middle or highest levels of elite bank senior management to avoid full enforcement of systems given perceived effects of such enforcement on elite bank profits.

The Basel Committee (and U.S. banking authorities) may have presupposed too much at the outset by assuming that 'market discipline' incentives implicitly would guide the elite banks to implement and meaningfully to enforce their own comprehensive risk management and internal control systems. The recent financial market events, particularly with respect to the LTCM episode and FRB-induced private-sector bailout, exhibited clear elite bank breakdowns or outright failures to enforce risk management and internal control systems at the highest levels of these institutions. The relative absence of banking authority enforcement actions or consent orders against elite banks addressing such failures as 'unsafe and unsound' banking practices in the U.S. or addressing the periodically excessive risk exposure incurred by elite banks in OTC derivative activities, arguably demonstrates that U.S. banking authorities may be unable or unwilling to hold elite banks directly and fully accountable for their actions or omissions in this regard. How all this 'sounds' for the viability of the newly evolving public-private partnership in banking supervision remains, at minimum, highly problematic.

VI. CONCLUDING OBSERVATIONS

The genesis of systemic capital impairment is traceable to basic conflicts in the role of government intervention in banking systems and international financial markets. The role of government in this sense is necessarily defined by the parameters of the public-private partnership, however. The imposition of more stringent and detailed risk-based bank capital requirements, without more, cannot unilaterally resolve this issue without changes in the public-private partnership dynamics regarding supervisory oversight and enforcement of risk management and internal control systems. The major issues relating to bank capital adequacy now focus on the changing nature and transparency of risk measurement techniques, including valuation and revaluation of complex OTC derivatives, and other financial instruments and structured transactions, and portfolios thereof, in the context of domestic and international, legal and economic events. The application of the aforementioned objectives to address elite bank capital impairment should be conducted with a clear understanding of the various significant interests, relationships and linkages which establish the boundaries and pressure points of the public-private partnership. The framework for risk management and internal control systems needs to establish a careful and transparent rebalancing of power such that elite banking interests do not unduly influence or overcome the 'safety and soundness' interests of banking authorities.

In general, a breakdown in the public-private partnership will usually precede the manifestation of elite bank or banking system crises such that it becomes difficult or impossible to isolate the independent effects of an ensuing crisis. The success of rebalancing the public-private partnership may well be inherent in the continued evaluation application and analysis of the risk-focused supervision and examination schemes for elite banks by the banking authorities. The effectiveness of elite bank risk-focused supervision and examination techniques will depend on many things, but primarily on the ability of examiners to identify and measure the risks presented by a given large bank or LCBO. The success of this approach will also depend on bank examiner expertise, independence, and access to proprietary information and to senior management and internal audit functions and understanding of present or emerging risks to the banking industry in its entirety through the examination process.

The most important challenges in this regard, however, include the following. First, ensuring that elite banks actually implement their risk management and internal control systems and use them as they are intended, and that examiners are actually able to identify and measure complex anomalies generated by these systems or otherwise or significant changes in elite bank risk profiles in a timely manner. Second, ensuring that the supervisory issues noted from bank risk management and internal control systems and/or during examinations or ongoing monitoring are actually raised directly to the appropriate bank senior management and addressed or resolved in a timely manner. The bottom line is that if examiners do not correctly identify and measure critical risks in particular business lines, they may go unaddressed until events overtake the respective institutions.

The LTCM debacle presents an excellent example of this because, quite clearly, bank examiners were not aware of the material risks incurred by elite banks in their lending and OTC derivatives counterparty activities with the hedge fund could cause to respective large banks and LCBOs through OTC derivatives counterparty activities and other credit-related activities with the hedge fund. The large banks and LCBOs involved in this episode clearly did not implement or enforce their own credit risk or market risk management and internal control systems with respect to LTCM (and presumably other hedge funds and highly leveraged clients). Additionally, bank examinations are generally not designed to reveal operational risks such as insider fraud. Finally, bank examiners are enormously challenged by the complexity and diversity of bank risk management systems that utilize differing 'internal models' to measure and account for risk on a real-time basis.

Large banks and LCBOs each undoubtedly design and apply 'internal models' to measure market risk and credit risk that reflect their individual risk profiles. As such 'internal models' are designed to be applied to specific risk profiles; elite bank internal risk models will likely differ even if intended to cover similar risk profiles. This ultimate 'model subjectivity' renders it quite difficult for bank examiners, who are trained to rely on more objective bank models and measurements, to assess similar risks in a consistent manner. Of course, the accuracy of the output of these 'internal models' depends on the nature of the input data used, and much of this input data is derived from internal and proprietary valuations of financial instruments such as OTC derivatives. There is little question that the 'internal models' approach to risk-focused supervision of elite banks is in its infancy, and the banking authorities will need to take every step to ensure that their supervisory process does not get marginalized.

To summarize, banking authorities in developed nations in seeking to create the desired conditions for stability, predictability, and safety and soundness in their increasingly global financial markets have tended towards 'risk-focused supervision' coupled with a qualified form of 'self-regulation' vis-à-vis the major international banking institutions. This undoubtedly ties the potential for success to a proactive, constructive and transparent 'public-private partnership.' However, the ultimate question remains whether the international regulator/supervisors and international banks are up to the task of their new-founded 'partnership' and whether the creation of an elite group of international banking institutions will prove a wholesome event in the evolvement of a 'global financial system.'[48] The duties of these new functions are expanding continuously, and this leaves open, serious fundamental questions of due process and compatibility with the core functions of financial institutions.

[48] The reliance on financial institutions as agents of governance did not remain confined to the area of self-regulating their own 'safety and soundness.' Instead, for example, through a set of anti-money laundering regulatory requirements, financial institutions, in a very broad sense, are increasingly required to police the illegal activities of other private actors acting individually or in organized criminal groups. As most recently emphasized by the U.S. Treasury Department's General Counsel, financial institutions and their related professionals 'have become the ears and eyes of the government. . . and, whether [they] like or not, [they] all have been deputized. . . It is a default mechanism because we [i.e., governmental authorities] do not have perfect intelligence, so we have to do something else, and that something else is watchfulness.' *See* reported remarks of U.S. Treasury Department General Counsel David Aufhauser made on October 23, 2002 concerning the USA PATRIOT Act in 79 BNA Banking Rep. No 16, at 682–683 (2002). For further discussion, see Joseph J. Norton & Heba Shams, *Money Laundering Law and Terrorist Financing: Post-September 11 Responses—Let Us Step Back and Take a Deep Breath?* 35 INT'L LAW. 103 (2002); and Norton & Shams, *supra* note 10.

CHAPTER TWELVE

Unilateralism, Multilateralism and International Securities Offerings

*by Douglas W. Arner**

CHAPTER OUTLINE

I. Introduction
II. Development of International Securities Markets
   A. The Euromarkets
   B. Unilateralism Internationalisation: Domestic Efforts to Encourage International Listings
III. Internationalisation of Standards for Securities Offerings: Bilateral, Regional and Multilateral Initiatives
   A. The United States and Canada: The Multi-jurisdictional Disclosure System
   B. European Securities Markets
IV. Multilateral Development of International Disclosure Standards for Securities Offering and Listings
   A. Objectives and Principles of Securities Regulation
   B. International Disclosure Standards for Cross-border Offerings and Initial Listings by Foreign Issuers
   C. Multilateral Harmonisation of Accounting Standards
V. Implementation of International Standards for Offerings and Listings of Securities
   A. Domestic Implementation of International Disclosure Standards
   B. Accounting and Auditing Standards
VI. Conclusion: A Future for Multilateral Efforts to Support Globalisation of Securities Offerings?

* B.A. (Drury), J.D. (SMU), LL.M (London). Associate Professor; Deputy Director, Asian Institute of International Financial Law; and Director, LL.M (Corporate & Financial Law) Programme, Faculty of Law, The University of Hong Kong; and Visiting Fellow, Centre for Commercial Law Studies, University of London. The author would like to thank the following for their comments and assistance: Prof. Joseph J. Norton, Southern Methodist University and University of London; Christopher D. Olive, Jones Day Reavis & Pogue (Dallas); Matthew S. Morgan, Allen & Overy (London); Chantal Hébert, Baker & McKenzie (Hong Kong); and Dr. Iain MacNeil, University of Glasgow. Any errors of course lie with the author. In addition, the author would like to thank the University of Hong Kong's Research Initiation Grant program for financial support.

I. INTRODUCTION

Securities regulation has been and is likely to remain ultimately a matter of domestic law (with the increasing exception of the on-going efforts of the European Union (EU)). Historically, the jurisdiction with the largest and best developed capital markets (i.e. the United States (US)) and its domestic regulator (the Securities and Exchange Commission (SEC)) have tended to try to dominate international securities regulatory developments. Though this attitude shifted from a primary focus on unilateral export of US standards after the world-wide market collapse of 1987 towards a more multilateral approach in the late 1980s and 1990s, with major financial scandals at the beginning of the twenty-first century, the US attitude has once again shifted towards a more unilateral approach. At the same time, in the 1980s, the EU began to look to the successes of securities markets in the US and the United Kingdom (UK) and from 1985 began serious regional multilateral efforts through a series of Directives (European laws required to be implemented by individual EU Member States) aimed at developing a true integrated 'European' capital market.

As the US, EU and other countries around the world (especially developing and transitioning) became more interested in securities market development and financial market 'internationalisation' (as highlighted by the 1987 market collapse) and 'globalisation' (highlighted by the series of financial crises in the 1990s),[1] efforts became centralized in the multilateral securities forum: the International Organisation of Securities Commissions (IOSCO). During the 1990s, IOSCO became in many ways the centre of a dynamic global process of domestic, regional and international endeavours. However, with financial scandals in the US and EU, the focus has once again shifted towards a more unilateral focus, centred on the SEC (and to some extent, the Attorney General of New York) and the European Commission (the quasi-civil service of the EU).

International sales and trading of securities are nothing new. In fact, studies suggest that international securities activities existed at least from the initial formation of stock exchanges in Europe at the end of the seventeenth century. Over the last twenty years, there has been an increasing interest in international securities, their issuance, trading, and regulation.[2] This trend slowed somewhat with the spate of financial crises in emerging markets around the world in the late 1990s and the collapse of the telecoms and technology share prices, but has been increasing again from the end of

[1] *See* Douglas Arner, Mamiko Yokoi-Arai and Zhongfei Zhou (eds.), Financial Crises in the 1990s: A Global Perspective (2001).

[2] HAROLD JAMES, INTERNATIONAL MONETARY COOPERATION SINCE BRETTON WOODS 12 (1996).

2002. As equity markets stalled in 2001, with the collapse of the Internet bubble and terrorist attacks in the United States, new issues activity in international securities markets became quiet, but not silent, with global issues shifting towards debt rather than equity and discussion of related issues continuing. With the collapse of Enron and WorldCom in the US and Parmalat in Europe, attention has shifted somewhat to corporate governance and accounting issues; however, the results (Sarbanes-Oxley in the US and proposed Directives in the EU) are already having a major impact on international securities activities.

While securities markets have always encompassed international participants and sales, prior to the First World War, such activities were essentially unregulated. During the period from the First World War to the 1960s, international capital movements were tightly regulated and restricted through legislative efforts of individual countries under the Bretton Woods system. In fact, one purpose of the Bretton Woods system was to prevent financial instability of the sort seen in the first half of the twentieth century—often blamed on free movement of capital.

Beginning in the 1960s, restrictions on capital movements began to be relaxed, with a resulting growth of international financial activities, culminating in the collapse of the Bretton Woods fixed exchange rate system in 1973. Following the collapse of Bretton Woods, the remainder of the 1970s was characterised by petrodollar recycling, culminating in the emerging market debt crisis of the 1980s.

As the move towards state dominance of individual economies began to reach its limits, the worldwide trend towards privatisation of state-owned companies and assets beginning in the 1980s, in the United Kingdom under Margaret Thatcher, led to interest and the need for offerings of equity securities in multiple capital markets throughout the world,[3] creating the first 'global offerings,' and highlighted the 'internationalisation' of financial markets. Nonetheless, most of these activities have taken place in the context of individual domestic markets, with foreign participants (whether issuers, purchasers, or intermediaries) forced to meet the individual national requirements of any given jurisdiction of interest, a situation not dissimilar to that originally envisioned under Bretton Woods, but now in a far different context.

As a result of the pressures of internationalisation of financial markets, beginning with a number of regional experiments, steps have been taken toward the acceptance of foreign credentials for offerings and listings of securities on an equal basis with those of domestic participants, of which

[3] For development of this thesis, see DANIEL YERGIN & JOSEPH STANISLAW, THE COMMANDING HEIGHTS: THE BATTLE BETWEEN GOVERNMENT AND THE MARKETPLACE THAT IS REMAKING THE MODERN WORLD 370–71 (1998).

the European efforts to develop a single market for capital in the context first of the European Communities and now the EU are the most advanced. For a variety of reasons, most of these efforts have not been entirely successful, often due to lack of synchronisation of domestic legal systems, with the increasingly open and internationalised character of international financial markets. As a result of increasing 'globalisation' of financial markets in the 1990s, efforts focused on the development of international standards applicable to securities markets, with the aim to harmonise minimum standards and eventually to support mutual recognition based upon common standards, including offerings and listings of securities.

After describing the trends noted above in general terms, this chapter analyses the issue of whether, for the first time, international efforts may lead to the development of a standard format for the content of an international offering/listing document acceptable in jurisdictions around the world, i.e., a 'global prospectus' or 'international passport prospectus', or whether we will instead see a return to unilateral regulation. Recent cross-border corporate mergers and acquisitions, proposed mergers and alliances between stock exchanges around the world, and the development of 'global shares,' traded on multiple markets underscore the growing importance and usefulness of such a mechanism.

Section II of this article briefly discusses the historical development of international securities markets. The most significant developments in this respect are the development of the Euromarkets and initiatives seeking to encourage international listings through relaxation of domestic standards for foreign issuers. These initiatives, however, do not truly foreshadow the development of a single global offering document, but rather reflect the needs and requirements of internationalisation of competition between markets for business opportunities represented by cross-border offerings and listings.

Section III discusses the development of two significant regional initiatives supporting mutual recognition of securities offerings: the multi-jurisdictional disclosure system (MJDS), a bilateral structure involving the United States and Canada; and the securities Directives of the European Union (EU), a regional multilateral process. These initiatives are the precursors to recent multilateral efforts to promote the creation of a single offering document for offering and listing securities around the world, involving the efforts of IOSCO and the International Accounting Standards Board (IASB—formerly the International Accounting Standards Committee (IASC). Section IV discusses the content of the international standards as devised at the multilateral level, both non-financial international listing requirements and financial and accounting harmonisation and standards. Section V discusses the implementation process in the United States, EU, and elsewhere. Finally, section VI concludes with a short discussion of the implications of the development of a global prospectus for further globalisation of financial markets.

This author concludes that these changes are driven by a search for high standards of regulation (necessary to encourage investor participation), and by the move toward creation of a single capital market in Europe to rival that in the United States. These trends will focus consolidation in other smaller markets (e.g., the various countries of east Asia), along with a move towards higher international standards in markets, in such jurisdictions around the world, if they are to maintain the interest of international investors. Nonetheless, even with an international passport for securities offerings and listings, domestic requirements will continue to address issues of enforcement and corporate governance. As we have seen in the past several years, these issues may in fact signal a return towards a more unilateral approach, focusing on the competing standards of the US and the EU. However, there is hope for bilateral cooperation between the two jurisdictions, which in time may yield the basis for a truly multilateral set of standards acceptable around the world.

II. DEVELOPMENT OF INTERNATIONAL SECURITIES MARKETS

In the seventeenth and eighteenth centuries, the international capital markets of Europe were dominated by Amsterdam, with some competition from Geneva and Genoa. Dutch investments centred on (in consecutive periods) its Empire and the Continent, on Britain until the Anglo-Dutch Wars, then on France and the United States, until the occupation of Amsterdam during the Napoleonic Wars.[4] Throughout this period, activities took place through a variety of instruments, such as loans, bonds, annuities, and equity securities, and involved sophisticated techniques, such as short selling, puts, calls, and futures.[5] While loan contracts were in use, company law, including law governing equity securities, was quite undeveloped. The essential absence of any sort of regulation of securities markets or offering requirements in all likelihood exacerbated the frequency and severity of periodic panics and crashes.

In the nineteenth century, London became the leading centre for international financial activities, although Paris provided strong competition. By the beginning of the First World War, the London financial markets were involved in wide and varied international financial transactions, rivalling the sophistication and extent of those today.[6] In fact, measurements of the

[4] *See* CHARLES KINDLEBERGER, A FINANCIAL HISTORY OF WESTERN EUROPE 208–14 (2d ed. 1993).

[5] *Id.* at 210.

[6] *See id.* at 214–20.

degree of financial integration in the world economy indicate that at the beginning of the twentieth century, the world was more interconnected than at any subsequent time, at least up to the 1990s and possibly today.[7] Such developments were not limited to London, Paris, and Amsterdam; records indicate that foreign issues and listings of both foreign bonds and other tradable securities were relatively common in Frankfurt in the nineteenth century.[8]

While the link has not been made explicitly, it is probable that the development of standardised company law (including basic requirements for financial reporting) in Britain and the United States encouraged the development of the markets.[9] Nonetheless, regulation of market activities and abuses remained largely governed by the common law in both England and the US, making redress often difficult.[10]

While World War I significantly reduced international securities activities, the Crash of 1929 and the Great Depression drastically reduced securities activities outside of Europe and the United States until the 1960s (centred during this period in New York, reflecting the United States' position as the world's banker). These reductions were not only the result of market decisions but also of a wide variety of unilateral (and multilateral following World War II) restrictions imposed to severely limit movements. This drastic reduction in international financial activity reflected a conviction that the fundamental destabilisation of the previous decades had 'stemmed from volatile and irresponsible flows of capital ('hot money')' and that the international financial system could only function effectively if such flows were curtailed.[11]

In the US, congressional studies in the 1930s led to the conclusion that one of the causes of the market crash and the depression that followed was excessive speculative activities in the financial markets and market abuses that both encouraged such activities and prejudiced the proper operation of the markets.[12] As a result, the US enacted the first comprehensive legal regime for the regulation of securities activities, including issues, issuers,

[7] JAMES, *supra* note 2, at 12.

[8] *See* KINDLEBERGER, *supra* note 4, at 223–24.

[9] *See* Bernard S. Black, *The Legal and Institutional Preconditions for Strong Securities Markets*, 48 UCLA L. REV. 781 (2001); Brian R. Cheffins, *Does Law Matter? The Separation of Ownership and Control in the United Kingdom*, 30 J. LEGAL STUD. 459 (2001); Lucian Ayre Bebchuk & Mark J. Roe, *A Theory of Path Dependence in Corporate Ownership and Governance*, 52 STAN. L. REV. 127 (1999); John C. Coffee, Jr., *The Future as History: The Prospects for Global Convergence in Corporate Governance and its Implications*, 93 NW. U. L. REV. 641 (1999).

[10] *See generally id.* In the United States, 'blue sky' laws began to develop early in the twentieth century. *See* Jonathan R. Macey & Geoffrey P. Miller, *Origin of the Blue Sky Laws*, 70 TEX. L. REV. 347 (1991).

[11] JAMES, *supra* note 2, at 32. *See id.* at 87–92, 125.

[12] *See* S. REP. NO. 73–47 (1933).

financial intermediaries and market participants, all based on the premise of full and fair disclosure of all material information.[13] (It is worth noting that these laws were not restricted to the US domestic market, but on their face apply to all securities market activities, wherever occurring.)

This marked the beginning of a period of increasing regulation of financial institutions and markets in the developed world, primarily as a response to varied crises—largely of a unilateral nature. Outside of the US, securities activities continued to be regulated through company law and individual exchange rules, although in many cases they continued to remain unregulated outside of traditional sources of remedies in the domestic legal system. As will be discussed in the following section, this trend towards increased regulation, especially in the US, combined with largely closed national financial markets, had an unintended consequence: the development of an international and unregulated capital market based in London (largely the result of unilateral decisions taken by the Bank of England to allow such activities, the US financial authorities' attempts to limit capital flows in and out of the US, and omissions to restrict such activities in other (mainly European) jurisdictions).

A. The Euromarkets

A post-war market in US dollar deposits and lending began in the late 1940s, when the new Chinese communist government began to place its dollar earnings with a Soviet bank in Paris (the Banque Commerciale pour l'Europe du Nord).[14] In 1957–58, European banks, primarily in London and Switzerland, began to deal more extensively in dollars.[15] The markets that developed, first in syndicated lending, then in bonds (Eurobonds) in the 1960s, became known as the 'Eurodollar' markets. Rapidly, however, these markets expanded beyond US dollars and beyond Europe, although they are still known as the Eurocurrency markets or the Euromarkets.[16] The Euromarkets developed as a truly international market, structured to avoid domestic regulatory restrictions, and their success has stimulated internationalisation of domestic markets and (increasingly) globalisation of financial markets. While the Euromarkets, with their emphasis on syndicated loans and bond offerings, fall somewhat outside the scope of the analysis of this chapter, given its focus on the development of a single set of issuing and

13 *See* JOEL SELIGMAN, THE TRANSFORMATION OF WALL STREET: A HISTORY OF THE SECURITIES AND EXCHANGE COMMISSION AND MODERN CORPORATE FINANCE (1982).

14 JAMES, *supra* note 2, at 179.

15 KINDLEBERGER, *supra* note 4, at 439.

16 According to Kindleberger, a 'eurocurrency' is any currency borrowed and lent (whether through term loans, syndications or bonds) outside the country that uses the currency. *Id.* at 440. The market in fact travels around the world daily, shifting from market to market as the time zone advances, although London remains the hub.

trading requirements for international equity offerings, they are nonetheless important as an illustration of the possibilities available in the development of global capital markets.

As noted, the Euromarkets sought to avoid domestic regulation, and in fact grew partly as the result of such restrictions in the US. The development of the Eurobond market was partly stimulated by the registration requirements of US securities regulation, and partly by the Interest Equalization Tax (IET) imposed in the United States in 1963, to reduce the borrowings of European countries in the United States.[17] With the repeal of the IET and all other restrictions on capital movements out of the United States in 1973, bonds began to be issued simultaneously in New York (through allowances by the SEC) and European financial centres, and eventually in financial centres around the world, such as Hong Kong, Singapore, and Tokyo; thus marking the beginning of the first multi-jurisdictional offerings of securities, albeit debt securities.

The development of the Eurocurrency markets was stimulated further by the Oil Price Shocks of 1973 and 1979, leading to recycling of increased earnings of oil states, earned in US dollars and deposited mainly in London and Switzerland (so-called 'petrodollars'), by international banks.[18] While this process of recycling was successful following the first shock in 1973, it was less successful after the second shock in 1979, when combined with a global surplus of liquidity.[19] Until the Debt Crisis of the 1980s (which began with Mexico's default in 1982),[20] lending dominated the Euromarkets in the form of both bilateral term loans and multi-lender syndications. These sorts of transactions were and are typically documented through a loan and syndication agreement, both of which have assumed a relatively standardised form, changed only slightly to reflect the experiences of each new crisis.[21]

During the resolution of the Debt Crisis throughout the 1980s, bonds began to take precedence as banks securitised rescheduled debt and sought to decrease their risk exposure and increase their margins through a preference for bonds.[22] Syndicated lending nonetheless remained significant.[23]

[17] *Id.* at 441; JAMES, *supra* note 2, at 179.

[18] *See* JAMES, *supra* note 2, at 309–46.

[19] *See id.* at 347–408.

[20] *See* YERGIN & STANISLAW, *supra* note 3, at 130–33.

[21] *See* Joseph J. Norton, *International Syndicated Lending: The Legal Context for Economic Development in Latin America*, 21 NAFTA L. REV. 21 (1996); ROSS CRANSTON, PRINCIPLES OF BANKING LAW ch. 11 (1997); PHILIP R. WOOD, INTERNATIONAL LOANS, BONDS AND SECURITIES REGULATION chs. 1–7 (1995).

[22] *See* Ross P. Buckley, *A Tale of Two Crises: The Search for Enduring Reforms of the International Financial System*, 6 UCLA J. INT'L L. & FOREIGN AFF. 2 (2001). *See also* WILLIAM R. CLINE, INTERNATIONAL DEBT REEXAMINED (1995).

[23] *See* Norton, *supra* note 21.

Like loans, Eurobonds have developed standardised forms, such as trust indenture agreements and offering documents.[24] As well, Eurobonds remain essentially unregulated (though this is set to change to some extent with recent changes in European law), and as with the Euromarkets generally, their structures were developed to avoid regulation in domestic legal systems. Unlike loan agreements, which remain essentially contractual undertakings, bonds are traditional securities and therefore typically subject to domestic regulatory concern and therefore scrutiny. As a result, Eurobonds have traditionally not been listed in the United States, and instead have focused on exchanges such as London and Luxembourg with simple rules governing offer, sale, and listing of international bonds. Further, over time, the Eurobond market has been specifically exempted from most regulation in Europe, primarily in order to protect the position of London's financial markets and as a reflection of the institutional nature of the market and the consequent view that such players do not require the same level of protection as small investors. In order to encourage international offerings in the United States (and to curtail the facial extraterritorial application of the U.S. securities laws), the U.S. SEC has made special efforts to support access to the U.S. market through the promulgation of Regulation S and, more specifically, Rule 144A, and their predecessors.[25]

As highlighted above, unlike domestic capital markets, the Euromarkets are essentially unregulated and unsupervised (although the financial standing of participants is carefully monitored, both by government agencies (in the case of financial institutions) and private ratings agencies such as Standard & Poor's and Moody's). Participants (almost exclusively financial institutions, major international corporations, and sovereigns and their agencies) operate outside the traditional requirements of domestic securities markets, primarily because these sorts of participants are deemed capable of guarding their own interests and because the main operating arenas for the Euromarkets fear loss of business and stature. Therefore, arrangements are made through contracts (loan agreements, syndication and participation arrangements, and trust indenture agreements). Thus, while these markets are global in nature and the legal arrangements involved are quite standardised, they are also organic by nature, having grown up between and around domestic legal requirements.

[24] *See generally* Roy C. Smith & Ingo Walter, Global Banking ch. 9 (1997); Wood, *supra* note 21, chs. 8–10 (discussing the standard content of trust indentures and bond offerings).

[25] For a discussion, see generally Mark Steinberg, International Securities Law: A Contemporary and Comparative Analysis ch. 4 (1999).

B. Unilateralism and Internationalisation: Domestic Efforts to Encourage International Listings

As a result of the increasing awareness of firms, securities exchanges, and governments of the advantages of securities markets for accessing capital (reflected at least partially in the successes of the Euromarkets), individual countries and securities exchanges have undertaken generally unilateral initiatives to encourage foreign listings on domestic exchanges and in domestic markets.[26] While some advances have been made in encouraging such activities, the remaining expense and complexity have largely remained prohibitive as each individual jurisdiction developed its own requirements.[27] Recent international consolidation of securities exchanges (discussed in the final section, *infra*) is the most recent example of these efforts.

During the 1980s, privatisation of state-owned assets, including such companies as British Steel and British Telecommunications, required access to investors in markets outside of the home jurisdiction, essentially due to the massive amounts of securities required to be offered and sold. In such circumstances, the cost of compliance with the domestic offering requirements of multiple jurisdictions could be absorbed by the large value of the offering itself. With the success of multi-jurisdictional offerings in such circumstances, financial institutions and their legal advisors realised the possibilities for truly 'global offerings' by private companies, as well as the future of privatisation throughout the world. Likewise, states saw the advantages that could be gained for their own markets and firms by encouraging market access by foreign firms through the possibility of enhanced liquidity. Finally, developments in investment theory (especially portfolio theory) and relaxations of restrictions on institutional investors encouraged such investors to diversify their portfolios through investments in foreign securities.

The result was the development of different mechanisms to allow foreign issuers to list and/or sell their securities to domestic investors, most importantly through the development of 'depository receipts,' whereby securities listed on a foreign exchange could be traded on a domestic exchange, if certain requirements were met.[28] In addition to depository receipts, securities regulators and stock exchanges began to allow certain derivations from

[26] *See id.* ch. 1.

[27] *See* Howell E. Jackson & Eric J. Pan, *Regulatory Competition in International Securities Markets: Evidence from Europe in 1999—Part I*, 56 BUS. LAW. 653 (2001).

[28] *See* Jorge Gonzalez, Jr. & Christopher D. Olive, *Foreign Issuer Disclosure and Accounting Compliance in U.S. Public Offerings and Securities Listings*, 1 NAFTA L. & BUS. REV. AMS. 39 (1995).

domestic requirements for foreign issuers.[29] The most important of these has been the minimal deviation allowed by U.S. SEC from traditional home country requirements, in the area of accounting standards, shelf-registration, and short form registration statements.[30]

The dangers of the increasing internationalisation of financial markets, however, were graphically shown during the worldwide collapse of stock market values in October 1987. Following drastic falls and halts in trading on numerous exchanges (including the New York Stock Exchange (NYSE) and the Stock Exchange of Hong Kong), domestic regulators began to analyse the new risks, as well as the new opportunities, presented by internationalisation. The result was not only a unilateral strengthening of domestic standards and systems in many cases, but also increased international dialogue, not only among securities regulators, but also among central bankers and treasury officials, especially from the major industrialised countries.

III. INTERNATIONALISATION OF STANDARDS FOR SECURITIES OFFERINGS: BILATERAL, REGIONAL AND MULTILATERAL INITIATIVES

Because of the difficulties of international financial cooperation and agreement on standards, regional efforts have been undertaken with increasing frequency since the late 1950s in an attempt to arrive at pragmatic solutions to the problems and needs of international financial markets.[31] Until the period following the worldwide market collapse of 1987, however, securities regulation was typically not considered significant enough to merit much multilateral attention. On a regional basis, the most significant efforts to date are those involving the United States and Canada (bilateral) and the countries of Europe (multilateral), respectively.

A. The United States and Canada: The Multi-jurisdictional Disclosure System

The MJDS originally began life as a proposal of the U.S. SEC to create a system for the facilitation of multinational securities offerings in the United

[29] *See* STEINBERG, *supra* note 25, chs. 1, 4 (discussing domestic initiatives to encourage foreign listings and issues).

[30] *See* Gonzalez & Olive, *supra* note 28. Regulation S also falls under this categorisation to some extent, in that it relaxes extraterritorial application of U.S. securities laws (but not of antifraud provisions). In reality, this only reflects a realisation that the rest of the world is in fact unlikely to adopt standards identical to those in the United States and that actual application of such a principle of universal extraterritoriality was impracticable and politically disadvantageous in discussions with other sovereign states.

[31] *See* JAMES, *supra* note 2, at 467–89; KINDLEBERGER, *supra* note 4, at 436–50.

States, the United Kingdom, and Canada.[32] According to the SEC, 'to provide a context for public comment on internationalisation,' it presented 'two conceptual approaches' to 'facilitate multinational offerings': (1) 'the reciprocal approach' and (2) 'the common prospectus approach,' and requested comment on a series of questions dealing with these approaches.[33] Under the reciprocal approach, each country would agree to accept a prospectus, which was accepted in the issuer's domicile and met certain minimum requirements.[34]

Under the common prospectus approach, a common prospectus would be developed, which would then be filed simultaneously with each country's respective securities regulatory authority.[35] Following comment on the original release, the SEC, the Ontario Securities Commission, and the Commission des valeurs mobilieres du Quebec proposed the MJDS between the United States and Canada in 1989, reflecting a 'hybrid' between the reciprocal and the common prospectus approaches.[36] The United Kingdom was not included for a number of reasons,[37] including differences in registration, accounting and auditing requirements,[38] and potential illegality interposed with the United Kingdom's acceptance of the Single European Act in 1986.[39]

As adopted, the MJDS is not an international legal agreement, but rather parallel sets of domestic administrative rules. In the United States, the SEC promulgated one set of rules governing securities transactions covered by U.S. federal securities laws,[40] which, if necessary under state law, could be adopted by the various state securities regulatory agencies in order to apply to offerings within each respective state. In Canada, the Canadian Securities Administration, a non-governmental association of provincial regulatory authorities,[41] agreed and published a 'national policy,'[42] which was then

[32] Facilitation of Multinational Securities Offerings, Exchange Act Release No. 33-6568, 1985 SEC LEXIS 2074 (Feb. 28, 1985).

[33] *Id.* at *1.

[34] *Id.* at *3.

[35] *Id.*

[36] *See* Multijurisdictional Disclosure, Exchange Act Release Nos. 33-6841, 34-27055, 39-2217, 1989 SEC LEXIS 1377, at *4 (July 24, 1989).

[37] *See* DAVID JOHNSTON & KATHLEEN DOYLE ROCKWELL, CANADIAN SECURITIES REGULATION 319–20 n.99, 102 (2d ed. 1998).

[38] *See* Cally Jordan, *The Thrills and Spills of Free Riding: International Issues before the Ontario Securities Commission*, 23 CAN. BUS. L. J. 379, 381 (1994).

[39] *See generally* J. Lipsius, *The 1996 Intergovernmental Conference*, 20 EUR. L. REV. 235, 237 (1995); J. Kingston, *External Relations of the European Community—External Capacity Versus Internal Competence*, 44 INT'L COMP. L. Q. 659 (1995).

[40] Multijurisdictional Disclosure and Modifications to the Current Registration and Reporting System for Canadian Issuers, Exchange Act Release Nos. 33-6902, 34-29354, 39-2267, 1991 SEC LEXIS 1217 (June 21, 1991) [hereinafter Multijurisdictional Disclosure].

[41] A non-statutory self-regulatory organisation.

[42] CANADIAN SECURITIES ADMINISTRATION, MULTIJURISDICTIONAL DISCLOSURE SYSTEM, NI 71-101 (1991).

implemented in each province through provincial legislation, or statutorily delegated agency rule-making powers.

In practice, the MJDS has not fulfilled its potential. While it was intended to be a first step towards international harmonisation (albeit largely on the basis of the U.S system),[43] in reality it has resulted only in increased harmonisation of U.S. and Canadian regulation, with the various Canadian authorities making most of the compromises.[44] It has, however, increased Canadian access to U.S. markets and stimulated some interest on the part of U.S. issuers in Canadian markets.[45]

B. European Securities Markets

While both the oldest stock exchange[46] and the world's most significant international financial centre[47] are located in Europe, widespread individual ownership of securities was not common outside of the United Kingdom during the twentieth century prior to the 1990s.[48] The development of securities markets in Europe, however, has become an objective of national policy in most member States of the EU, beginning in the 1980s.

A study of capital markets by the European Economic Community (EEC) in 1966 addressed impediments to the effective functioning of national markets and their availability to foreign borrowers. The Segré Report[49] (so-called after the chairman of the group of experts and the principal author, Claudio Segré) found that national markets in Europe discriminated in favour of domestic borrowers, especially national governments, as against foreign, primarily through regulations governing the investment of funds of savings banks and insurance companies. In addition, few European securities were listed on stock exchanges outside the domicile of the issuing company. As a result of practical governmental needs (combined with the forces of harmonisation, access deregulation, and prudential re-regulation inherent in the process of opening developed the 'Maastricht' objective of free movement of capital), national securities regulation in western Europe has developed significantly in recent years.[50] Prior to the 1990s, however, securities regulation in western Europe was virtually non-existent outside of

43 *See id.* at 6.

44 JOHNSTON & ROCKWELL, *supra* note 37, at 319–20. *See* Jordan, *supra* note 38, at 381.

45 JOHNSTON & ROCKWELL, *supra* note 37, at 320.

46 Amsterdam Stock Exchange.

47 London.

48 *See* BENN STEIL ET AL., THE EUROPEAN EQUITY MARKETS: THE STATE OF THE UNION AND AN AGENDA FOR THE MILLENNIUM (1996).

49 EEC, THE DEVELOPMENT OF A EUROPEAN CAPITAL MARKET (1966) [hereinafter SEGRÉ REPORT]. *See* KINDLEBERGER, *supra* note 4, at 438–39.

50 *See* Manning Gilbert Warren, *Global Harmonization of Securities Laws: The Achievements of the European Communities*, 31 Harv. Int'l L.J. 185, 194 (1990).

the United Kingdom.[51] Although company law was well-developed across western Europe, European stock exchanges have been historically self-regulating, with little or no direct oversight by national governments.[52] Moreover, European states historically did not mandate full disclosure systems for the distribution or trading of securities, nor did they prohibit insider trading or other market manipulative practices long prohibited by the United States.[53]

Most of the EU Member States only started to develop broad-based equity markets in the late 1980s. Further, the EU financial services market is still absent any comprehensive and consistent regulation and enforcement as in the United States (despite increasing efforts to achieve this goal). While the current EU system is complex, it is still not so complex as that of the U.S. system, though the EU system is striving to be a comprehensive and coherent regulatory system.

The EU framework for investment services provides minimum standards for accounting and auditing standards, listings and stock exchange regulation, company law, market conduct regulation, and regulation of institutional investors. It should be borne in mind, however, that this framework is not complete. Since its purpose is to ensure the harmonisation of the laws of the Member States, insofar as this is necessary for the achievement of a single market, and to fill gaps relating to cross-border activities, it builds on the existing national systems of company and securities laws, rather than trying to replace them with a complete new system. The purpose of this chapter is not to evaluate the specific provisions of the EU framework; however, a general appreciation of the key elements of the EU framework is necessary to understand the development of the European passport prospectus.

1. The Creation of a Common Market in Investment Services

The EU legislative framework for financial markets seems to be grounded in a concept that can be thought of as a search for equivalence among disparate regulatory and legal systems, while taking into account the continuing reality of separate and distinct national legal and regulatory regimes as the basis of any overall EU initiatives.[54] Initially, efforts focused

[51] *Id.*

[52] *Id.*

[53] When the Public Offers Prospectus Directive was proposed in 1981, only five members of the EU required prospectus disclosure to investors in public offerings of securities, namely: Belgium, France, Ireland, Luxembourg, and the United Kingdom. 1980–1981 EUR. PARL. DOC. (COM. 893) (1980); 1981 O.J. (355) 39. As of 1990, West Germany still imposed no prospectus upon issuers in connection with public offers of securities not listed on an exchange. Warren, *supra* note 50, at 195 n.54.

[54] *See* STEIL, *supra* note 48, at 113.

on harmonisation of rules across Member States, however, this proved impossible in many areas and in the 1980s, efforts moved to the development of mutual recognition based upon common minimum standards. The key principles were outlined in the European Commission White Paper[55] and enshrined in the 1986 Single European Act,[56] implementing the common internal market on the basis of 'mutual recognition,' based on common minimum standards applicable in all Member States through European Directives and implemented through domestic legislation.[57] According to this methodology, all Member States agree to recognise the validity of one another's laws, regulations, and standards, thereby facilitating free trade in goods and services without the need for prior harmonisation,[58] while limiting the scope for competition among rules by mandating Member State conformity with a 'floor' of essential minimum European requirements.[59] As such, investment services regulation in the EU seeks to avoid the problem of competitive deregulation and regulatory arbitrage that may undermine the letigimacy and efficiency of financial markets.[60]

As a general matter, the EU system of securities regulation rests on the EU company law and corporate governance directives and financial reporting directives. In turn, the basic framework for the EU securities regulatory regime is founded upon a series of directives known as the stock exchange Directives[61] (enacted prior to the 1986 Single European Act, but subsequently amended to provide for mutual recognition) and now consolidated into a single directive, as well as directives dealing with collective investment schemes (e.g., mutual funds), unlisted prospectuses, and insider dealing.

The second level of EU investment services regulation deals with the establishment of a single market in financial services, based on the common minimum framework provided by the basic company law and corporate governance, financial reporting and securities directives. This level centres around the Investment Services Directive (ISD) and the Capital Adequacy Directive (CAD). To put this in a broader perspective, the single market is rooted in basic tenets of the Treaty of Rome respecting the free movement of capital, establishment and services, and is manifested in the various

[55] EUR. COM, COMPLETING THE INTERNAL MARKET: WHITE PAPER FROM THE COMMISSION TO THE EUROPEAN COUNCIL, COM (85)310 FINAL (1985).

[56] SINGLE EUROPEAN ACT, 1987 O.J. (L 169) 1 (1987) (effective July 1, 1987).

[57] *Id.*

[58] *See* STEIL, *supra* note 48. This principle underlies the Second Banking Directive (2BCD) as well as the ISD. *Id.*

[59] *Id.* at 114. According to commentators, the Commission has recently followed the mutual recognition principle to a much greater extent than the harmonisation principle. *Id.* at 115; *see also* Warren, *supra* note 50.

[60] *See* Warren, *supra* note 50.

[61] The Stock Exchange Listing Directives include: the Admission Directive, the Listing Particulars Directive, the Interim Reports Directive and the Major Holding Directive.

single 'passport' directives.[62] Under the concept of the 'single' passport, an EU firm authorised in one Member State (its 'home state') and wishing to operate in other Member States ('host states') will generally be able to choose to supply services through branches or to supply services on a cross-border basis without having a permanent physical presence in the host state.[63] The intended benefit of the passport is that it should increase competition by opening markets to a wider range of participants and by allowing firms to choose the most cost-effective means of supplying services to a particular market.[64] Combined with the basic framework established in the company law and securities directives and the capital standards of the CAD, the ISD was meant to establish the framework for a comprehensive European system of securities regulation. At present, it is the subject of a proposals for change to address the current needs of the markets.

2. *The Underlying Legal and Financial Infrastructure: Company Law and Corporate Governance*

Many areas traditionally considered in the United States as matters of securities law, rather than corporate law, are covered under the company law framework in Europe and elsewhere. EU company law is based on the prohibition of discrimination within the EU, and is based on the nationality of an entity organised within a Member State under Article 7 of the Treaty of Rome.[65] Companies organised under the laws of one Member State have the right to establish branches in other Member States.[66] Further, regulation for the protection of shareholders, employees, and creditors must be equivalent throughout the EU.[67] As a result of the political impossibility of achieving strict harmonisation in this very diverse area,[68] the EU began to propose directives that prescribed only basic, essential principles, with a requirement of mutual recognition among the Member States.[69]

Companies are organisations which are created and administered according to legal requirements, and involve different categories of

[62] The passport directives in the financial services area include: (1) the First and Second Banking Coordination Directives (1BCD and 2BCD) (banking); (2) the Investment Services Directive (ISD) (investment firms and securities markets); (3) the UCITS Directive (collective investment schemes); (4) the First, Second and Third Life Assurance Directives (life assurance); (5) the First, Second and Third Non-Life Insurance Directives (non-life insurance); and (6) the proposed First Pension Funds Directive (pension funds).

[63] *See The EU Single Market in Financial Services*, BANK OF ENG. Q. BULL., Feb. 1993, at 92.

[64] *Id.*

[65] Treaty Establishing the European Economic Community, Mar. 25, 1957, art. 7, 298 U.N.T.S. 11 [hereinafter Treaty of Rome].

[66] *Id.* art. 58.

[67] *Id.* art. 54(3)(g).

[68] *See* Warren, *supra* note 50, at 197-98 (discussing development of EU company law).

[69] *Id.*

persons—shareholders, employees, creditors, and third parties—who are all concerned in some way with the activity of the undertaking.[70] The first objective of the approximation or harmonisation of company law in the EU is to ensure an equivalent degree of protection for the interests of these various constituencies.[71]

Most significant are the First Company Law Directive,[72] and the Second Company Law Directive.[73] Other significant company law and corporate governance directives include: the Third Company Law Directive,[74] introducing a common procedure for mergers; the Eleventh Company Law Directive,[75] providing for consolidated reporting; the Twelfth Company Law Directive,[76] dealing with single-member limited liability companies; and the Regulation on the Statute for a European Company (SE) and the Regulation on the European Economic Interest Grouping (EEIG),[77] creating a Community level instrument permitting cooperation of undertakings from different Member State jurisdictions.

[70] EUR. COMM., White Paper on the Preparation of the Associated Countries of Central and Eastern Europe for Integration into the Internal Market of the Union, COM(95) 163 final 2, Annex, at 308 [hereinafter White Paper].

[71] *Id.* The basic legal approach to harmonisation of company law has a two-fold aim: (1) to remove obstacles to companies' freedom of establishment in order to expand and improve market competitiveness; and (2) to establish an equivalent degree of protection throughout the Community for the various constituencies. *Id.* at 309. *See* Treaty of Rome, *supra* note 65, art. 54. The second approach is to allow enterprises to create new or combine existing cross-border operations on the basis of EU rather than national laws. White Paper, *supra* note 70, at 309. *See* Treaty of Rome, *supra* note 65, arts. 235, 100A

[72] First Council Directive 68/151/EEC of 9 March 1968 on Co-Ordination of Safeguards Which, for the Protection of the Interests of Members and Others, are Required by Member States Companies Within the Meaning of the Second Paragraph of Article 58 of the Treaty, With a View to Making Such Safeguards Equivalent Throughout the Community, 1968 O.J. (L 65), as amended by Directive 2003/58/EC of 15 July 2003 amending Council Directive 68/151/EEC, as regards disclosure requirements in respect of certain types of companies, 2003 O.J. (L 221).

[73] Second Council Directive 77/91/EEC of 13 December 1976 on Co-Ordination of Safeguards Which, for the Protection of the Interests of Members and Others, are Required by Member States of Companies Within the Meaning of the Second Paragraph of Article 58 of the Treaty, in Respect of the Formation of Public Limited Liability Companies and the Maintenance and Alteration of Their Capital, With a View to Making Such Safeguards Equivalent, 1997 O.J. (L 26), as amended by Council Directive 92/101/EEC, 1992 O.J. (L 347).

[74] Third Council Directive 78/885/EEC of 9 October 1978 Based on Article 54(3)(g) of the Treaty Concerning Mergers of Public Limited Liability Companies, 1978 O.J. (L 295).

[75] Eleventh Council Directive 89/666/EEC of 21 December 1989 Concerning Disclosure Requirements in Respect of Branches Opened in a Member State by Certain Types of Companies Governed by the Law of Another Member State, 1989 O.J. (L 395).

[76] Twelfth Council Directive 89/667/EEC of 21 December 1989 Concerning Single Member Private Limited Companies, 1989 O.J. (L 395).

[77] Regulation (EC) 2001/2157 of 8 October 2003 on the Statute for a European Company (SE), 2001 O.J. (L 294); Council Regulation 2137/85/EEC on the European Economic Interest Grouping (EEIG), 1985 O.J. (L 199) 1, 2.

3. The Stock Exchange Directives

The overall objective of these directives is to provide a set of minimum standards capable of operating on a uniform basis throughout the EU, and in a way which removes some of the barriers which would otherwise result from the existence of conflicting requirements in a number of different markets. The result permits greater flexibility of access to the EU capital markets than might otherwise have been the case.

In July 2000, the European Commission proposed a simplification of the legislative framework governing stock exchange listings into a single Directive.[78] The four major Directives covered are:

- The Directive on the conditions for the admission of securities to official stock exchange listing (79/279) (Admission Directive);[79]
- The Directive on the listing particulars to be published for the admission of securities to official stock exchange listing (80/390) (Listing Particulars Directive);[80]
- The Directive on information to be published on a regular basis by companies, the shares of which have been admitted to official stock-exchange listing (82/121) (Interim Reports Directive);[81] and
- The Directive on the information to be published when a major holding in a listed company is acquired or disposed of (88/627) (Major Holdings Directive).[82]

Directives not included are those not directly linked to the listing of or limited to listed securities, namely:

- The Directive on undertakings for collective investment in transferable securities (85/611/EEC) (UCITS Directive);[83]

[78] Securities: Commission proposes simplification of legislative framework, July 24. 2000; Proposal for a Directive of the European Parliament and of the Council on the Admission of Securities to Official Stock Exchange Listing and on Information to be Published on Those Securities (codified version), 2000 O.J. (0174) 2.

[79] Council Directive 79/279/EEC of 5 March 1979, Coordinating the Conditions for the Admission of Securities to Official Stock Exchange Listing, 1979 O.J. (L 66) 1, 2.

[80] Council Directive 80/390/EEC of 17 March 1980 Coordinating the Requirements for the Drawing up, Scrutiny and Distribution of the Listing Particulars to be Published for the Admission of Securities to Official Stock Exchange Listing, 1980 O.J. (L 100) 2.

[81] Council Directive 82/121/EEC of 15 February 1982 on Information to be Published on a Regular Basis by Companies the Shares of Which Have Been Admitted to Official Stock Exchange Listing, 1982 O.J. (L 48) 2.

[82] Council Directive 88/627/EEC of 12 December 1988 on the Information to be Published When a Major Holding in a Listed Company is Acquired or Disposed of, 1988 O.J. (L 348) 2.

[83] Council Directive 85/611/EEC of 20 December 1985 on the Coordination of Laws, Regulations and Administrative Provisions Relating to Undertakings for Collective Investment in Transferable Securities (UCITS), 1985 O.J. (L 375) 2, 3.

- The Investment Services Directive (93/22/EEC) (ISD);[84]
- The Directive on investor-compensation schemes (97/9/EC) (Investor Compensation Schemes Directive);
- The Directive on prospectuses in the case of a public offer (89/298/EEC) (Public Offer Prospectus Directive);[85] and
- The Directive on insider dealing (89/592/EEC) (Insider Dealing Directive).[86]

The finalised consolidated listing Directive was adopted on May 28, 2001, in a substantially identical format to the initial proposal and repealing the underlying directives.[87] Specifically, the consolidated listing directive details requirements for five major areas respecting listed securities, namely: official listing of securities[88] and information to be included,[89] conditions relating to official listing of securities,[90] ongoing obligations relating to securities admitted to official listing,[91] publication and communication of information,[92] and competent authorities and cooperation between Member States.[93]

4. *Public Offer Prospectus Directive*

The Public Offer Prospectus Directive[94] adopted in 1989 after ten years of negotiation,[95] sought to harmonise the disclosure standards of the Member States for public offerings of securities regardless of their listed or unlisted status. Like the consolidated listing directive, its underlying policy is to protect investors by providing information necessary to assess the risks of investment in securities; to reinforce confidence in securities markets; to contribute to the correct functioning and development of securities markets; and to establish an equivalent level of securities disclosure among the

[84] Council Directive 93/22/EEC of 10 May 1993 on Investment Services in the Securities Field, 1993 O.J. (L 141) 4.

[85] Council Directive 89/298/EEC of 17 April 1989 Coordinating the Requirements for the Drawing-Up, Scrutiny and Distribution of the Prospectus to be Published When Transferable Securities are Offered to the Public, 1989 O.J. (L 124) 2.

[86] Council Directive 89/592/EEC of 13 November 1989 Coordinating Regulations on Insider Dealing, 1989 O.J. (L 334) 3.

[87] Directive 2001/34/EC of the European Parliament and of the Council of 28 May 2001 on the Admission of Securities to Official Stock Exchange Listing and on Information to be Published on Those Securities, 2001 O.J. (L 184) (the 'consolidated stock exchange Directive').

[88] *Id.* tit. II. [89] *Id.* ann. I. [90] *Id.* tit. III.

[91] *Id.* tit. IV. [92] *Id.* tit. V. [93] *Id.*, tit. VI, arts. 105–107.

[94] Council Directive 89/298/EEC of 17 April 1989 Coordinating the Requirements for the Drawing-up, Scrutiny and Distribution of the Prospectus to be Published When Transferable Securities are Offered to the Public, 1989 O.J. (L 124). *See* Manning G. Warren III, *Regulatory Harmony in the European Communities: The Common Market Prospectus*, 16 BROOK. J. INT'L L. 19 (1990).

[95] Warren, *supra* note 50, at 215.

Member States.[96] The Directive, however, has largely been ineffective and not used in practice.[97]

5. *The Investment Services Directive*

The most relevant of the passport directives (for present purposes) is the ISD,[98] adopted in 1993. The ISD is intended to provide a 'single passport' for EU securities firms to conduct cross-border operations anywhere in the EU, based on a license issued by their respective home states.[99] As originally proposed, the ISD was designed to achieve the goal of breaking down the various EU Member States' protectionist, non-tariff barriers to domestic market entry.

6. *European Economic and Monetary Union and the Creation of a Single European Capital Market*

On January 1, 1999, the individual currencies of the eleven EU Member States that met the relevant criteria and accepted the relevant obligations of the Maastricht Treaty (Austria, Belgium, Denmark, France, Germany, Ireland, Italy, Luxembourg, the Netherlands, Portugal, and Spain) became permanently fixed in exchange rate and ceased to exist, thereby creating a single European currency, the 'euro', and European Economic and Monetary Union (EMU). From January 1, 2001, the twelve (Greece has since been added) different sets of notes and coins were quickly replaced by a single physical currency. While significant differences still exist in European capital markets, with the introduction of the euro, financial statements and offering documents have begun to become comparable. This shift is beginning to produce, when combined with the painfully developed securities regulatory framework discussed in the previous sections, the development of a unified European capital market for the first time.

Prior to the signing of the Maastricht Treaty in 1992, there existed little impetus for Member States to actively implement the securities and company law directives. However, with the coming into force of the Treaty in 1994, and its requirements for adoption and implementation of the framework supporting freedom of capital movements necessary to underpin EMU, Continental Member States have adopted and implemented legislation quite foreign to the securities markets of their domestic systems. The

[96] Council Directive 89/298/EEC, 1989 O.J. (L 124), *supra* note 85, at 8.

[97] *See* Jackson & Pan, *supra* note 27, at 680–83.

[98] Council Directive 93/22/EEC on Investment Services in the Securities Field, 1993 O.J. (L 141).

[99] Manning Gilbert Warren III, *The European Union's Investment Services Directive*, 15 U. PA. J. INT'L BUS. L. 181 (1994).

result has been an increased awareness of the use of capital markets and the realisation that the legislative changes, when combined with the advent of the single currency, will change (and have already changed) the nature of finance throughout the EU, but most especially in the Euro-12 members.

While the ultimate result is yet to be seen, significant movements have already taken place with the significant and continuing development of domestic capital markets in the EU. Further, new initiatives are coming rapidly, seeking to take advantage of new opportunities and to place competitors at an advantage in the European markets that are, in all likelihood, to arrive in short order. Although numerous impediments to such developments remain (most notably in the area of taxation), activity is set to continue increasing at a rapid pace, putting pressure on the barriers that remain. One example of the recognition of continuing impediments and the pressure to remove them is the establishment of a triumverate of 'wise men' to review the EU capital markets and to develop proposals to remove remaining barriers to the creation of a single European capital market.

It is this 'real world' experience of the countries of the EU and their moves to develop a single regional capital market with an agreed and mutually acceptable issuing and trading framework that indicates the real advantages of the path of multilateral that may lie ahead in the globablisation of capital markets. The development of European capital markets, and other countries' nervousness respecting the same, has provided the impetus to international organisations, such as IOSCO and the IASB (and their previously recalcitrant members, such as the United States), to consider the multilateral development of an internationally acceptable offering document.

IV. MULTILATERAL DEVELOPMENT OF INTERNATIONAL DISCLOSURE STANDARDS FOR SECURITIES OFFERING AND LISTINGS

Originally formed in 1973 as an initiative of the U.S. SEC to facilitate cooperation among securities regulators of the Americas (largely to support export of U.S. standards), IOSCO encompasses over 100 members, representing securities regulatory authorities from developed and developing countries around the world, as well as over fifty affiliate members, representing self-regulatory organisations (SROs) and stock and futures exchanges.[100] Today, IOSCO is the leading multilateral international financial organisation coordinating cooperation, standardisation and establishment of minimum internationally agreed standards in the area of securities regulation.

100 *See* IOSCO, 1999 Annual Report (2000), *available at* http://www.iosco.org.

Following the meetings of its Executive and Technical Committees in Paris in May 1998, IOSCO announced the release of two significant documents for securities regulators and market participants:[101] (1) *Objectives and Principles of Securities Regulation*;[102] and (2) *International Disclosure Standards for Cross–Border Offerings and Initial Listings by Foreign Issuers*.[103] These two documents, taken together, establish the underlying standards for securities regulation and the form and content of an internationally acceptable offering document. The combination, accepted at IOSCO's Annual Meeting in September 1998 in Nairobi, Kenya, is in turn to be implemented by the membership through domestic legislation and regulation with the intention to create a truly global set of standards for issuing and trading securities.

A. *Objectives and Principles of Securities Regulation*

Following an initiative of the Group of Seven (G-7) at their Lyon Summit in 1995, the Group of Ten (G-10) and representatives of sixteen emerging market economies published a framework for promoting financial stability in domestic economies around the world.[104] As part of this initiative, international financial organisations, such as IOSCO, were instructed to develop internationally acceptable principles and standards for their respective disciplines. IOSCO's *Objectives and Principles* are the key standard in the area of securities regulation and reflect its membership's agreement that there are certain principles that form the basis for an effective system of regulation of securities and derivatives markets.

B. *International Disclosure Standards for Cross-border Offerings and Initial Listings by Foreign Issuers*

In order to build upon the general principles respecting offering and listings standards in the *Objectives and Principles*, IOSCO has developed a framework for the minimum content of public offer prospectuses. This latter document is intended to set a basic framework for international offering documents acceptable to regulators and stock exchanges around the world. Such a framework could serve as an internationally acceptable basis for the

[101] IOSCO, Press Communique (1998), *available at* http://www.iosco.org/news/pdf/IOSCONEWS46.pdf.

[102] IOSCO, Objectives and Principles of Securities Regulation: A Report of the International Organisation of Securities Commissions (1998) [hereinafter Objectives and Principles]. The IOSCO Objectives and Principles were updated and re-released in October 2003: IOSCO, Objectives and Principles of Securities Regulation (2003).

[103] IOSCO, Report of the Technical Committee, International Disclosure Standards for Cross–Border Offerings and Initial Listings by Foreign Issuers (1998) [hereinafter IDS].

[104] Group of Ten, Financial Stability in Emerging Market Economies (1997).

further development of stock exchange listing requirements and prospectus regulations throughout the world. According to IOSCO, 'this report presents a set of non–financial statement disclosure standards (financial statements standards are the subject of another project) that will apply to foreign companies seeking to enter a host–country market, facilitating cross–border offerings and initial listings.'[105] The intention is that these standards will allow issuers to prepare a single disclosure document that will serve as an 'international passport' to capital raising and listing in more than one jurisdiction at a time. If successful, the implementation of these standards will represent an important step forward in reducing the costs of raising capital for companies, enabling them to issue or list shares in multiple jurisdictions without concern for the burdens of complying with a multiplicity of non-financial statement disclosure requirements. Following the receipt of comments from the IOSCO Emerging Markets Committee, and from the international financial community, the standards were approved by the membership of the entire organisation, including the U.S. SEC.

1. *Scope of the Standards*

Part I sets out *International Disclosure Standards (IDS)* for use by companies in connection with cross-border public offerings and listings of equity securities. The Standards are to apply to listings, public offers, sales of equity securities for cash, and unless otherwise indicated, the Standards are intended to be used for prospectuses, offering and initial listing documents and registration statements.[106] The Standards relate to non-financial statement disclosure requirements and do not address a number of issues, including:[107] (1) 'which bodies of accounting or auditing principles may be followed by the issuer in preparation of its financial statements;' (2) 'disclosure requirements that may apply in some countries in connection with other types of transactions, such as business combinations, tender offers, exchange offers, 'going private' transactions or interested party transactions;' (3) 'collective investment schemes or 'start up' companies with no history of operations;' (4) 'continuous reporting disclosure mandates which may arise, for example, out of insider trading laws, requirements to disclose material developments or antifraud prohibitions;' and (5) 'suitability criteria that may be imposed by stock exchanges in connection with listings of equity securities, such as the company's operating history, asset size, profitability, market float, share price, etc.'[108]

[105] Press Communique, *supra* note 101.

[106] IDS, *supra* note 103, at 3.

[107] *Id.* at 3–4.

[108] *Id.* at 4.

In addition, '[c]ompanies engaged in specialised industries (i.e., banking, insurance, mining and oil and gas companies) may be required to provide additional information in certain countries, and the sources of these requirements are set forth in Part II,' which addresses disclosure issues outside of the Standards and includes 'information of a general nature and other disclosure requirements that may apply in certain countries.'[109] The disclosure requirements for certificates representing shares, such as depository receipts, voting trust certificates, or similar forms of ownership representation, are also referenced in Part II.

The Standards are intended to apply to cross-border offering and listings. Under the IDS, an offering or listing of securities is considered to be 'cross-border' 'when it is directed to one or more countries other than the company's home country (whether or not the offering or listing also is being made concurrently in the company's home country).'[110] As a general matter, according to IOSCO, all foreign companies, subject to certain exceptions, can apply the IDS to offerings or listings in a particular host country.[111]

2. *Additional Requirements*

The IDS were issued 'with a recommendation that IOSCO members accept in their respective home jurisdictions a disclosure document containing the information set forth in the Standards.'[112] According to IOSCO, additional actions, however, 'may be needed in some jurisdictions to implement the Standards, and issuers are encouraged to verify that the Standards are in effect in the host country jurisdiction prior to their use.'[113] While the IDS are not necessarily intended to substitute for or to replace disclosure requirements applicable to any jurisdiction's domestic issuers, they are intended to provide alternative standards for the preparation of a single disclosure document by foreign issuers.[114]

In addition to the specific disclosures required in the Standards, according to IOSCO, 'most countries rely on an overriding principle that in connection with a registration or listing of securities or a public offering of securities, a company should disclose all information that would be material to an investor's investment decision and that is necessary for full and fair disclosure.'[115] Accordingly, information called for by specific requirements contained in the Standards may need to be expanded under this general principle of disclosure of material information, where supplemental information is deemed to be material to investors and necessary to keep the

[109] *Id.* at 3.
[110] *Id.* at 4.
[111] IDS, *supra* note 103, at 4.
[112] *Id.* at 3.
[113] *Id.*
[114] *See id.* at 3.
[115] *Id.* at 5.

mandated disclosure provided pursuant to specific requirements from being misleading.[116]

The Standards also address omission of information and supplementary information.[117] Specifically, '[i]f a disclosure requirement is inapplicable to an issuer's sphere of activity or legal form, no information need be provided in response to that requirement, although equivalent information should be given, if possible.'[118] Further, '[a]ny significant change or any inaccuracy in the contents of the document which may materially affect the company or its securities, that occurs between the date of publication of the document and the date of sale or listing also must be adequately disclosed and made public.'[119]

3. *The Standards*

Following an introduction (summarised in the previous section) and a glossary of terms, the Standards, in Part I, outline the contents of an acceptable document. Part II provides country specific information on areas not covered within the standards, necessary to validate the document in a given jurisdiction, which should be incorporated as a 'wrapper' to the IDS prospectus. In outline form, the cross-border prospectus is to comprise the following ten information categories: (1) identity of directors, senior management and advisers; (2) offer statistics and expected timetable; (3) key information; (4) information on the company; (5) operating and financial review and prospects; (6) directors and employees; (7) major shareholders and related party transactions; (8) financial information; (9) the offer and listing; and (10) additional information.

C. Multilateral Harmonisation of Accounting Standards

Accounting standards provide the essential means of communication for valuation of companies regarded as necessary to any sort of investor choice in equities, and therefore necessarily underlie any efforts to harmonise and/or standardise international offering requirements. At present, accounting standards are nationally determined, so preparers and users of financial statements from different countries essentially speak different languages.[120] The collapses of Enron, WorldCom and Parmalat have underlined the significance of national differences and also perhaps may serve as a spur to further multilateral action along the lines discussed below; at the least, these

[116] *Id.* [117] *Id.* [118] *Id.* [119] *Id.*

[120] *See* Glenn Alan Cheney, *Western Accounting Arrives in Eastern Europe*, 170 J. ACCT. 40, 43 (Sept. 1990) (describing accounting as the 'language of production and transaction' and discussing difficulties in integrating Eastern Europe and Western countries due to differences in accounting).

events have spurred unilateral efforts by the United States and the EU to attempt to address existing deficiencies. Specifically, major initiatives are underway to establish multilaterally internationally agreed accounting standards, with the most significant achievements to date involving, respectively, the (1) EU and (2) IOSCO and the IASB.

The Office of the Chief Accountant of the U.S. SEC surveyed international accounting and auditing standards in 1987 and found significant disparities in a number of respects.[121] In general terms, systems of accounting rules in different countries at the time could be grouped into two categories:[122] (1) countries 'where business finance is provided more by loans than by equity capital, where accounting rules are dominated by taxation considerations and where legal systems customarily incorporate codes with detailed rules for matters such as accounting;'[123] and (2) countries 'in which equity sources of finance are more important, accounting measurements are not dominated by taxation considerations because tax breaks can be enjoyed independently of [the mechanism of reporting], and common law systems prevail.'[124] Overall, however, at the time of the SEC's study, no one system seemed to have such clear merits as to deserve adoption by the entire world.

The task of harmonisation is especially important in the area of securities regulation because of the critical link between information and stability in the world's securities markets.[125] The disharmony in accounting standards that exists today creates difficulties for both users and preparers of financial statements,[126] and presents obstacles to the process of international capital formation.[127] Overall, the usefulness of financial statements

[121] SEC, INTERNATIONALIZATION OF THE SECURITIES MARKETS (1987). At least as a partial result of this study, the SEC insists, in connection with financial statements used by foreign issuers, that assurances be provided that the auditing standards followed are the equivalent to U.S. generally accepted accounting standards (GAAS). *Id.* at IV-34. *See also* Gonzalez & Olive, *supra* note 28.

[122] Bryan Carsberg, *Harmonising Accounts Worldwide*, FIN. TIMES, Jan. 12, 1996, at XII.

[123] *Id.* Reporting under these systems often leads to a 'lack of full transparency' for investors due to their basis on the tax systems. Major countries in this category include France, Germany, and Japan. *Id.*

[124] 'These countries generally have some private sector system for setting accounting standards, often within a general statutory framework,' and 'capital market pressures (lead to the increased) quality of available information to investors. Major countries in this category include the United States, the United Kingdom, Australia, and the Netherlands. *Id.*

[125] UNITED NATIONS, U.N. CENTRE ON TRANSNATIONAL CORPORATIONS, INTERNATIONAL ACCOUNTING AND REPORTING ISSUES: 1989 REVIEW III (1990). *See also* Barbara S. Thomas, *International Accounting and Reporting—Developments Leading to the Harmonization of Standards*, 15 N.Y.U. J. INT'L L. & POL. 517 (1983).

[126] THOMAS G. EVANS ET AL., INTERNATIONAL ACCOUNTING AND REPORTING 85–86 (2d ed. 1994).

[127] *See* SEC, INTERNATIONALIZATION OF THE SECURITIES MARKETS, *supra* note 121, at IV-8. A study of international accounting problems has confirmed that the lack of international accounting standards greatly diminishes the utility of financial statements in world markets.

prepared on the basis of varying accounting standards is limited because it is difficult and time consuming to understand what the information means.[128] Further, from the standpoint of preparers of financial statements and the companies involved, disharmony of accounting standards is an impediment to both international securities offerings and cross-border mergers and acquisitions.[129]

Globalisation of stock markets and other trading markets is driving the movement toward international harmonisation of accounting standards. Further, businesses and capital markets desire both uniformity and higher quality, thereby stemming fears of regulatory arbitrage and a race for the 'lowest common denominator.'[130] Interestingly, the debate surrounding the collapses of Enron, WorldCom and Parmalat also appears to be focusing on certain philosophical questions such as rules-based systems (e.g., U.S. standards) versus more judgment-based systems (e.g., U.K. standards or IAS).

1. *Multilateral Harmonisation of Accounting Standards in the EU*

The EU has undertaken a number of initiatives to improve financial reporting among its Member States from both a qualitative and a quantitative standpoint. Accounting harmonisation is part of the company law harmonisation program aimed at furthering freedom of establishment. As such, it is aimed not only toward the equivalent protection of all investors, but of all third parties dealing with Member States' companies.[131]

EU legislative harmonisation in the accounting field presupposes the existence of a national accounting system.[132] EU accounting directives include the First Company Law Directive; the Fourth Company Law

See also GEORGE M. SCOTT, EIGHTY-EIGHT INTERNATIONAL ACCOUNTING PROBLEMS IN RANK ORDER OF IMPORTANCE: A DELPHI EVALUATION (American Accounting Assoc. ed., 1980).

128 The case of Daimler-Benz is illustrative in this context: 'in 1994, its reported profit under German accounting rules was DM 895 million, whereas its profit under U.S. accounting rules was DM 1,052 million. In 1983, however, accounting under German rules showed a profit of DM 615 million, but U.S. (rules) led to . . . a loss of DM 1,839 million.' Carsberg, *supra* note 122, at XII. *See also* Gonzales & Olive, *supra* note 28.

129 A survey of multinational corporations indicated that 'the greatest potential benefit' of harmonisation would be the acceptance by stock exchanges around the world of 'one set of accounts' complying with international accounting standards, instead of requiring different financial information prepared in 'accordance with local accounting standards.' *Support for International Standards*, 169 J. ACCT. 15, 16 (1990).

130 FINANCIAL ACCOUNTING STANDARDS BOARD, INTERNATIONAL ACCOUNTING STANDARDS 540 (*quoting* Dennis Beresford, chairman of the U.K. Financial Accounting Standards Board (FASB)).

131 See Marc I. Steinberg, Christopher D. Olive & Douglas Arner, 'The Development of Internationally Acceptable Accounting Standards: A Universal Language for Finance in the 21st Century?' 27 SECS. REG. L.J. 324 (1999).

132 *Id.*

Directive;[133] the Eighth Company Law Directive;[134] the Insurance Accounting Directive;[135] the Seventh Company Law Directive;[136] and the Bank Accounting Directive.[137]

In 1995, the Commission presented the outline for a 'new accounting strategy,'[138] which was subsequently endorsed by the Council of Ministers in June 1996. Key objectives of the strategy are 'easier access for European companies to international capital markets and improved comparability of consolidated accounts prepared by those companies which are important players in the Single Market.'[139] Under this 'new strategy,' the Commission has determined to associate its work with that of the IASB and IOSCO in pursuit of international accounting standards, rather than establishing a European Accounting Standards Board or a new layer of EU accounting standards. In addition, the Commission's work in the area of accounting standards has been significantly spurred by the needs of EMU, which formally began on January 1, 1999.

According to Mario Monti, 'the accountancy sector has a fundamental role to play in an efficient Single Market. The preparation, publication and widespread circulation of financial information relating to companies allow economic actors to make appropriate choices and constitute the necessary basis for management to take the right decisions.'[140] As part of its 'new accounting strategy,' the Commission adopted an Interpretative Communication[141] in January 1998, covering three main issues: consolidated accounts; the relationship between the Accounting Directives and IAS; and environmental issues in financial reporting. The Communication's conclusions regarding compatibility with IAS are based on the comparison

[133] Fourth Council Directive 78/660/EEC of 25 July 1978 Based on Article 54(3)(g) of the Treaty on the Annual Accounts of Certain Types of Companies, 1978 O.J. (L 222), as amended by Directive 84/569/EEC, 1984 O.J. (L 314), Directive 90/604/EEC, 1990 O.J. (L 317), Directive 90/605/EEC, 1990 O.J. (L 317), and Directive 94/8/EU, 1994 O.J. (L 82).

[134] Eighth Council Directive 84/253/EEC of 10 April 1984 Based on Article 54(3)(g) of the Treaty on the Approval of Persons Responsible for Carrying out the Statutory Audits of Accounting Documents, 1984 O.J. (L 126).

[135] Council Directive 91/674/EEC of 19 December 1991 on the Annual Accounts and Consolidated Accounts of Insurance Undertakings, 1991 O.J. (L 374).

[136] Seventh Council Directive 83/349/EEC of 13 June 1983 Based on Article 54(3)(g) of the Treaty on Consolidated Accounts, 1993 O.J. (L 193).

[137] Council Directive 86/635/EEC of 8 December 1986 on the Annual Accounts and Consolidated Accounts of Banks and Other Financial Institutions, 1986 O.J. (L 372).

[138] Accounting Harmonisation: A New Strategy vis-à-vis International Harmonisation, Communication from the Commission, Eur. Comm. (COM 508) 95. *See* Eur. Comm., Commission Proposes a New Strategy for the Improvement of the Financial Reporting Framework for Companies in Europe, Press Release IP/95/1234 (1995).

[139] *Id.*

[140] Mario Monti, Speech at the Conference on the Role, the Position and the Liability of the Statutory Auditor in the E.U., Dec. 6, 1996 (on file with author).

[141] Commission Proposal for an Interpretative Communication Concerning Certain Articles of the Fourth and Seventh Council Directives on Accounting, XV/7009/97.

undertaken between the EU Accounting Directives and IAS by a special Task Force of the Contact Committee on the Accounting Directives.[142] In addition, the Commission's work in the area of accounting standards has been significantly spurred by the needs of EMU. In this regard, the Commission has produced two sets of guidelines to assist companies in dealing with the practical financial implications of the advent of the euro.[143] Overall, despite significant general progress in establishing minimum accounting standards, the multilateral efforts in the EU have not reached the level of a coherent and comprehensive system and recognition of this fact has led to the decision to adopt IAS.

2. *International Accounting Standards Board (IASB)*

Formed initially in 1973 by agreement among the accounting bodies of ten industrialised countries,[144] by 1989, the International Accounting Standards Committee (IASC) had grown to include approximately 100 accountancy bodies from eighty countries.[145] Renamed the International Accounting Standards Board (IASB) in 2001, it is engaged in an effort to harmonise and improve accounting principles 'for the benefit of the public.'[146] This task is especially difficult for two reasons: first, the IASB seeks harmonisation on a worldwide basis,[147] and second, since the IASB has no official status, its standards are essentially recommendations.[148] Further, the IASB standards are generally broad and allow alternative practices; hence, they achieve no real uniformity.[149]

The IASB's overall objectives are to formulate and publish accounting standards to be observed in the presentation of financial statements and to promote their worldwide acceptance, and to work generally for the improvement and harmonisation of regulations, accounting standards, and

[142] Commission Proposal for an Examination of the Conformity Between the International Accounting Standards and the European Accounting Directives (1996).

[143] *Id.*

[144] The founding members were Australia, Canada, France, Germany, Japan, Mexico, the Netherlands, the United Kingdom, Ireland, and the United States. International Accounting Standards Committee, Objectives and Procedures § 9000.24 [hereinafter Objectives and Procedures].

[145] Stephen H. Collins, *The Move to Globalization*, J. ACCT. 83 (1989). Note that the membership of the IASB consists of accountancy bodies rather than nations. Evans, *supra* note 126, at 89.

[146] Objectives and Procedures, *supra* note 144, § 9000.33.

[147] *See IASC Moves to United Worldwide Standards*, 165 J. ACCT. 22, 26 (1988).

[148] *See* LeRoy J. Herbert, *Developments in the Harmonisation of Accounting Standards*, 3 J. COMP. CORP. L. & SEC. REG. 175, 177 (1981).

[149] Note, however, that the IASB in recent years has been making efforts to eliminate alternatives, thereby increasing the possibility of real harmonisation. *See* Carsberg, *supra* note 122, at XII.

procedures relating to the presentation of financial statements.[150] By agreement, members of the IASB are bound to persuade governments and other standard setting bodies that financial statements should comply with the international accounting standards (IAS) promulgated by the IASC.[151] (IAS issued since 2001 have been named International Financial Reporting Standards (IFRS); however, IAS is the term generally used in the markets). These standards are not binding on nations or the IASB members themselves, and the IASB has no enforcement authority.[152]

The reaction of nations to IASB IAS has been divided into three categories: (1) for some countries that do not have a developed national system of accounting, IAS have been given essentially the same status given domestic standards;[153] (2) a number of countries have accounting systems that are for the most part compatible with IAS;[154] and (3) some countries have well-developed accounting standards that in large part are incompatible with IAS.[155] Given the general reception and the overall necessity of harmonisation, increasing use of IAS appears likely.[156]

3. *International Federation of Accountants (IFAC)*

The IFAC, organised in 1977, which includes the International Auditing Practices Committee (IAPC), is charged with the responsibility of developing and issuing guidelines on generally accepted auditing practices and the content of audit reports.[157] Overall, the problems facing the IAPC are quite similar to those facing IASB; however, the focus of the IAPC is on auditing rather than on accounting standards.

4. *Cooperation between IOSCO and the IASB*

In the area of international accounting standards for financial reporting connected with stock exchange listings, the barriers created by the lack of a single financial language are especially significant to the process of international capital formation. IOSCO, however, had always withheld any endorsement of the various IAS, feeling that a core set of standards that

[150] Objectives and Procedures, *supra* note 144, §9000.58.

[151] *Id.* §9000.60.

[152] *Id.*

[153] EVANS, *supra* note 126, at 94. *Cf.* Cheney, *supra* note 120.

[154] EVANS, *supra* note 126, at 95 (e.g., United States, Canada, and the United Kingdom).

[155] *Id.* (e.g., Japan, although this may be changing somewhat).

[156] Note that the London Stock Exchange began accepting IAS soon after the foundation of the IASC. *See* Carsberg, *supra* note 122, at XII. The U.S., Canada, and Japan, however, still refuse to permit the use of IAS for stock exchange purposes. *Id.*

[157] *See* INTERNATIONAL FEDERATION OF ACCOUNTANTS, PREFACE TO INTERNATIONAL AUDITING GUIDELINES OF THE INTERNATIONAL FEDERATION OF ACCOUNTANTS, AICPA PROFESSIONAL STANDARDS, 8000.01-02 (1979).

dealt comprehensively with all the main financial reporting issues should be completed first.[158] In 1993, IOSCO agreed on 'the necessary components of a reasonably complete set of accounting standards (core standards) that would comprise a comprehensive body of principles for enterprises undertaking crossborder offerings and listings.'[159] IOSCO's list identified forty core standards.

The IASB (then IASC), however, was unwilling to undertake such a process, until July 1995, at which time the IASB and IOSCO published a joint agreement agreeing to complete a comprehensive set of core standards agreed between the two organisations by 1999.[160] Under the agreement, IASB and IOSCO agreed to collaborate to produce a comprehensive set of core standards for the global listing of securities, which then would be submitted to IOSCO for endorsement by its membership.[161] The IASB proposal has now been submitted and approved by the membership of IOSCO[162] and has also been reviewed both by domestic authorities and other international institutions and organisations, such as the Basel Committee on Banking Supervision.[163] The standards were subsequently approved by the full membership of IOSCO (including the U.S. SEC), with a recommendation for implementation in member jurisdictions.[164] As a result, there exists the clear possibility for the eventual employment of core standards developed by the IASB and approved by IOSCO being thereafter acceptable by the SEC for acceptance in the U.S. capital markets.

V. IMPLEMENTATION OF INTERNATIONAL STANDARDS FOR OFFERINGS AND LISTINGS OF SECURITIES

International standards developed on a multilateral basis may be interesting from an academic standpoint, but real impact on financial markets only comes with domestic implementation in the world's most significant capital markets, namely the U.S. and the EU

Recognising the importance of implementation, in May 2000, IOSCO

158 Carsberg, *supra* note 122, at XII.

159 Paul Pacter, *International Accounting Standards: The World's Standards by* 2002, CPA J. ONLINE (1998).

160 *See* Steve Burkholder, *International Accounting Standards Panel Accelerates Release of Rules*, 28 SEC. REG. & L. REP. 540 (1996)

161 *Id.* at 540.

162 IOSCO Technical Committee, IASC Standards—Assessment Report (May 2000; see IOSCO, Final Communique of the 25th Annual Conference of the International Organization of Securities Commissions (2000).

165 Basel Committee on Banking Supervision, Report to G7 Finance Ministers and Central Bank Governors on International Accounting Standards (2000).

164 IOSCO, Resolution and List of IASC 2000 Standards (May 2000).

produced a *Report on Implementation of IDS*.[165] The Report surveyed the progress of implementation of IDS among the seventeen members of the Working Party.[166] Sixteen indicated either that they:

(1) currently accept documents prepared in accordance with the IDS from foreign companies, or
(2) have taken steps to be in a position to do so at some point in 2000.

According to information supplied by those surveyed, progress in implementation fell into five categories: (1) those that had implemented IDS through changes in laws or rules by May 2000 (four jurisdictions: Spain, the United Kingdom, Mexico, and Italy); (2) those that were in the process of implementing IDS through changes in laws or rules by end-2000 (two jurisdictions: France and the United States); (3) those that permitted use of IDS without any need for rule changes, through discretionary authority or other means (eight jurisdictions: Australia, Belgium, Germany, Hong Kong, Japan, Luxembourg, the Netherlands, and Switzerland); (4) those that planned to undertake rule changes to implement IDS, but in the interim would permit use through discretionary authority (two jurisdictions: Ontario and Quebec); and (5) those that would not allow use of IDS (one jurisdiction: Sweden).

Another survey (an informal one) of the implementation of IDS conducted by Samuel Wolff of Akin, Gump, Strauss, Hauer & Feld was published in February 2001.[167] Of the respondents to the informal survey, Wolff found four in which IDS had been implemented through rule and/or legislative changes applicable to foreign and domestic issuers[168]: two (Italy and Mexico) required use of IDS for both foreign and domestic issuers; one (Argentina) required IDS for foreign issuers and intended to apply the same requirements to domestic issuers by sometime in 2002; and one (Singapore) required IDS with modifications for both foreign and domestic issuers.

Of the respondents, Wolff found five jurisdictions which had implemented IDS for foreign issuers only by rule and/or legislative change[169]: in two (the United States and Switzerland), IDS were optional for foreign issuers, but different standards applied to domestic issuers, although foreign issuers could also comply with the domestic requirements; in one (France), changes were in progress during 2001 to allow use of IDS by

[165] IOSCO, Report on Implementation of International Disclosure Standards (May 2000).
[166] The seventeen Working Party members surveyed were: Australia, Belgium, France, Germany, Hong Kong, Italy, Japan, Luxembourg, Mexico, the Netherlands, Ontario, Quebec, Spain, Sweden, Switzerland, the United Kingdom, and the United States.
[167] Samuel Wolff, *Implementation of International Disclosure Standards*, 22 U. PA. J. INT'L ECON. L. 91 (2001). Wolff surveyed twenty IOSCO member organisations. *Id.* at 94.
[168] *See id.* at 95–104.
[169] *See id.*

foreign issuers; one (Spain) required use of IDS for foreign issuers; and the listing rules of one (United Kingdom) exempted foreign issuers complying with IDS from certain provisions, but would nonetheless be required to furnish listing particulars in accordance with the remaining provisions of the listing rules.[170] Wolff found that seven of the respondents anticipated no legislative and/or rules changes were necessary, but IDS were acceptable for issuers: in four (Luxembourg, Hong Kong, the Netherlands and Belgium), IDS would be accepted under discretionary authority; in one (Germany), IDS were deemed to meet listing requirements; in one (Japan), IDS would be accepted on a discretionary basis, but only if in Japanese proper format; and in one (Australia), Wolff was not able to confirm the response to the IOSCO survey indicating that IDS would be accepted under discretionary authority. In one jurisdiction (South Africa), it was unclear whether IDS would be accepted, and IDS were not acceptable in four jurisdictions (Israel, Canada, India, and Taiwan).

From these surveys, use of IDS by different jurisdictions appears to be falling into four categories: (1) required for all companies, foreign and domestic; (2) optional for all companies, foreign and domestic; (3) inapplicable to domestic companies, but required for foreign companies; and (4) inapplicable to domestic companies and optional for foreign companies. Wolff concludes:

> the record so far, two and one-half years after promulgation of the IOSCO Standards, is mixed at best . . . While some progress has been made toward the implementation of International Disclosure Standards, the more toward implementation has probably been slower than IOSCO contemplated. There is still a hodgepodge of prospectus and listing rules which foreign issuers have to sort through as before on a country-by-country basis to determine applicable disclosure standards. More often than not, there is no reference at all to the IOSCO Standards.[171]

While Wolff's conclusion does not appear optimistic, closer analysis of implementation of IDS and IAS in the two most significant capital markets (the United States and the EU) actually suggests that significant progress is in fact being made.

A. Domestic Implementation of International Disclosure Standards

1. United States

The primary securities legislation in the United States remains the Securities Act of 1933 (1933 Act) and the Securities Exchange Act of 1934 (1934

170 Public offerings without listing are governed by POS Regulations (based upon EU POP Directive), to which no change had been made in respect to IDS.

171 Wolff, *supra* note 167, at 105.

Act), the former regulating the initial public offering of securities and the latter secondary dealings in them. Although much amended by subsequent Congresses, and added to by SEC rules and regulations, the original purpose of the legislation remains unchanged, namely to protect investors by requiring the provision of accurate and timely information.[172] Specifically, in relation to disclosure in securities offerings, providing shareholders with better tools with which to scrutinise companies issuing securities (especially public/listed corporations) was one of the U.S. Congress's central purposes in adopting the 1933 and 1934 Acts.[173]

The key obligation imposed by the 1933 Act is the requirement for registration of any offering of securities, absent a specific exemption.[174] Initial disclosure obligations are supported by a liability framework, including criminal and civil (private and administrative) actions, as well as requirements for on-going disclosure of public companies, under the 1934 Act. General disclosure requirements are contained in Regulation S-K. In order to increase the attractiveness of U.S. capital markets for non-U.S. issuers, the SEC has made a number of accommodations over the years, including respecting disclosure standards.[175]

On September 28, 1999, the U.S. SEC adopted a complete revision of Form F-20,[176] which contains the basic disclosure requirements applicable to foreign private issuers under the U.S. Securities Acts, largely along the lines proposed previously in February 1999.[177] Under the SEC Final Rule and Form F-20 there under, the IOSCO IDS are substantially implemented into U.S. securities regulation, although the F-20 requirements remain more detailed and stringent than those of IDS. According to Allan Beller of Cleary, Gottlieb, Steen & Hamilton:

[172] Alistair Alcock, *Rise and Fall of Private Actions under Rule 10b-5*, J. BUS. L., May 1998, at 230–49.

[173] H.R. REP. NO. 85, 73d Cong., 1st Sess. (1933).

[174] *Id.* § 5.

[175] Accommodations include:

- Interim reporting on the basis of home country and stock exchange practice rather than quarterly;
- Exemption from proxy rules and the insider reporting and short swing profit recovery provi sion;
- Aggregate executive compensation disclosure rather than individual disclosure, if permitted in issuer's home country;
- Acceptance of 3 IAS: cash flow statements (7), business combinations (22) and operations in hyperinflationary economies (21);
- Offering document financial statements updated principally on a semi-annual rather than a quarterly basis; and
- Exemption from 1934 Act registration under Section 12(g) for foreign private issuers that have not engaged in a US public offering or whose securities are not traded on a national exchange or NASDAQ.

[176] Exchange Act Release No. 33-7745 (Sept. 28, 1999).

[177] Exchange Act Release No. 33-7637 (Feb. 2, 1999).

foreign issuers that register with the Commission for the first time will not find the new disclosure regime any more hospitable than the old . . . Unless the IOSCO Standards are adopted for home-country disclosure, most issuers will probably continue to prepare substantially different offering documents and annual reports to satisfy home-country requirements and to satisfy U.S. requirements.[178]

Most significantly, the F-20 revision does not address issues respecting financial information, with reconciliation to U.S. GAAP continuing to be required. Nonetheless, IDS have been implemented in the United States.

2. *European States*

As a result of EMU, EU Member States and the European Commission have re-examined the Single Market project and sought to take steps to remedy structural problems not addressed in the earlier Single European Act and Maastricht processes.

The European Council endorsed the European Commission's Single Market Action Plan on June 16–17, 1997 in Amsterdam. The Action Plan establishes four 'Strategic Targets' for implementation under a three phase timetable: making rules more effective, addressing key market distortions, removing obstacles to integration, and delivering a 'Single Market' for the benefit of all citizens of EU Member States.[179] As one aspect of the Single Market Action Plan, the Commission developed a Framework for Action for creating a single market in financial services in 1998.[180] A Financial Services Policy Group (FSPG) was established in January 1999 to develop specific recommendations. Following meetings of the FSPG, the Commission produced its Financial Services Action Plan for the establishment of a single market in financial services by 2005.[181]

Included within the FSAP were decisions to focus on, inter alia, developing a single prospectus for securities offerings and a single set of financial statements for listed companies. The Commission, the FSPG and a variety of specially created groups of market experts have since moved forward with proposals in a wide variety of areas, including the development of a single prospectus and single set of financial statements.[182] Most significantly, the Commission established a so-called 'Committee of Wise Men' or

178 A. Beller, *SEC Adopts New Disclosure Requirements for Non-U.S. Issuers*, *in* 32D Annual Institute on Securities Regulation, Practising Law Institute, Corp. L. & Prac. Course Handbook Series, 1213 PLI/Corp 183, 186 (2000).

179 *Id.*

180 Financial Services: Building a Framework for Action, COM(625) (Oct. 1998)

181 Financial Services: Implementing the Framework for Financial Markets: Action Plan, COM(232) (May 1999).

182 *See generally* Financial Services Priorities and Progress: Third Report, COM(692/2) final (Nov. 2000); Progress on Financial Services: Second Report, COM(336) (May 2000); Financial Services Action Plan: Progress Report (Nov. 1999).

the Lamfalussy Committee, chaired by Alexandre Lamfalussy.[183] The European Council endorsed the recommendations (including for a controversial new legislative process for EU securities legislation) of the Lamfalussy Committee by in Stockholm in March 2001.[184] Key recommendations of the Lamfalussy Committee include adoption by the end of 2003 of a single prospectus for issuers and modernisation of requirements respecting admission to listing. Other key recommendations include home country control for all wholesale members, definition of the meaning of professional investor (important for many exemptions from securities regulation), modernisation of investment rules for UCITS, adoption of IAS, and the creation of a single passport for recognised stock markets. Recommendations so far have resulted in the creation of the Committee of European Securities Regulators (CESR)[185] and the European Securities Committee (ESC),[186] both of which have been active.

As noted above, as one aspect of the creation of a single prospectus, the Commission has codified the four basic listing directives.[187] As a very significant follow-on development, the Commission, following the Lamfalussy recommendations, proposed a single prospectus, valid EU-wide, covering all listing and public offers of securities. According to the Commission, the key features are:[188]

(1) Definition of clear conditions for offering securities to the public and for admission to trading;
(2) Harmonisation of the essential definitions in order to avoid loopholes and different approaches, thus ensuring a level playing field throughout the EU;
(3) Introduction of enhanced disclosure standards in line with international standards (IOSCO) for public offer of securities and admission to trading;

[183] Committee of Wise Men, Final Report of the Committee of Wise Men on the Regulation of European Securities Markets (Feb. 2001); Initial Report of the Committee of Wise Men on the Regulation of European Securities Markets (Nov. 2000).

[184] Results of the Council of Economics and Finance Ministers, 22 March 2001, Stockholm—Securities legislation' (Mar. 23, 2001).

[185] Commission Decision 2001/527/EC of 6 June 2001 Establishing the Committee of European Securities Regulators, 2001 O.J. (L 191).

[186] Commission Decision 2001/528/EC of 6 June 2001 Establishing the European Securities Committee, 2001 O.J. (L 191).

[187] Directive 2001/34/EC of the European Parliament and of the Council of 28 May 2001 on the Admission of Securities to Official Stock Exchange Listing and on Information to be Published on Those Securities, 2001 O.J. (L 184).

[188] Financial services: Commission Proposes Single Prospectus Valid EU-Wide (May 30, 2001); Proposal for a Directive of the European Parliament and of the Council on the Prospectus to be Published When Securities are Offered to the Public or Admitted to Trading, COM(280) final (May 2001). An amended version of the proposal was adopted at the end of 2003: Directive 2003/71/EC of the European Parliament and of the Council of 4 November 2003 on the prospectus to be published when securities are offered to the public or admitted to trading and amending Directive 2001/34/EC, 2003 O.J. (L 345).

(4) Introduction of the registration document system for issuers whose securities are admitted to trading on regulated markets in order to ensure a yearly update of the key information concerning the issuer;
(5) Concentration of the responsibilities in the Home State's administrative competent authority; and
(6) The 'single passport' enabling the possibility to offer or admit securities to trading on the basis of a simple notification of the prospectus approved by the home competent authority.

Significantly, the requirements for information included in the prospectus are identical to those of the IOSCO IDS, albeit with much less detail present in the Commission proposal.[189] As adopted, the Directive is set to have a major impact on European (and Euromarket) securities transactions once it comes into force in 2005. Implementing regulations are currently being worked out.[190] In addition to proposals on accounting standards and prospectuses, the Commission has also initiated consultation on on-going disclosure obligations of listed companies.[191]

B. Accounting and Auditing Standards

As noted, the IASB core programme has been approved by IOSCO, reviewed and largely recommended by the Basel Committee, and included as one of the key standards for sound financial systems by the Financial Stability Forum.[192] In addition, they have been accepted for international offerings and listings by a wide range of stock exchanges around the world.[193] Among the largest capital markets in the world, the EU has determined to use IAS as the basis for reporting by all EU listed companies by 2005, while the United States is currently discussing future usage of IAS in its markets. Significantly, with the on-going debate over Enron, WorldCom,

[189] *Id.*, Annex I (prospectus), Annex II (registration document), Annex III (securities note) & Annex IV (summary note).

[190] *See* http://www.europa.eu.int/comm/internal_market/en/finances/mobil/prospectus_en.htm for current status.

[191] Proposal for a Directive of the European Parliament and of the Council on the harmonisation of transparency requirements with regard to information about issuers whose securities are admitted to trading on a regulated market and amending Directive 2001/34/EC, COM(2003) 138(01); Internal Market Directorate General, Towards an EU Regime on Transparency Obligations of Issuers whose Securities are Admitted to Trading on a Regulated Market, MARKT/11.07.2001 (July 2001).

[192] Financial Stability Forum, International Standards and Codes to Strengthen Financial Systems (2001). *See also* Financial Stability Forum, Compendium of Standards, *available at* www.fsforum.org/standards/repiscsfs.html. The FSF is the key coordinating organisation for international financial standards, now a key aspect of the so-called 'new international financial architecture (NIFA)'. *See, e.g.*, M. Giovanoli, *A New Architecture for the Global Financial Market: Legal Aspects of International Financial Standard Setting*, *in* INTERNATIONAL MONETARY LAW: ISSUES FOR THE NEW MILLENNIUM (2000).

[193] For a current summary, see the IASB website at http://www.iasb.org.

Parmalat and others (such as Shell), pressure for adoption of a set of accounting standards agree between the US and the EU around the world may increase. At the moment, though, both jurisdictions are focusing on their internal markets (including standards applicable to foreign issuers) and are unprepared to agree to any deviation from their respective positions.

1. European Union

In the EU, the Accounting Directives have provided a base level of minimum standards for accounting; however, as noted above, they never reached the level of a complete, coherent, integrated system of accounting, with the result being that the accounting standards and practices varied significantly across Member States.

As a result of this realisation and of the increasing emphasis on the importance of developing a single capital market in the Euro Area and the EU as a whole, the Commission investigated whether to develop a complete system of European accounting standards—an European GAAP, perhaps through an European Accounting Standards Board or similar organisation—or whether to instead rely on the work of the IASB. In the event, the decision taken was to work with the IASB process and to adopt IAS as the EU standard. As the most concrete step to date, the Commission determined in 2001 to adopt the use of IAS as a requirement applying to all companies listed on any securities exchange within the EU by the end of 2005[194]—a requirement that will fundamentally effect the financial reporting of approximately 7,000 listed companies listed in the EU, including many foreign companies. As a result of the Commission's determination to work directly with the international standards-setting process and to require all EU listed companies to report according to IAS by 2005, recent and developing international efforts in this area are of considerable interest and importance.

2. United States

In the United States, the SEC has responsibility for setting accounting standards for securities issuers under the securities laws, which it delegates to the Financial Accounting Standards Board (FASB). The FASB in turn establishes U.S. GAAP, which govern accounting practices in the United States. The Public Company Accounting Oversight Board (created by the

[194] Regulation (EC) No 1606/2002 of the European Parliament and of the Council of 19 July 2002 on the application of international accounting standards, 2002 O.J. (L 243); Proposal for a Regulation of the European Parliament and of the Council on the Application of International Accounting Standards, COM(80) final (Feb. 13, 2001).

Sarbanes-Oxley Act of 2002) is responsible for overseeing auditors of public companies, under the supervision of the SEC.

Historically, by far the greatest barrier to foreign issuer access to the U.S. capital markets has been the requirement for use of U.S. GAAP for required financial information and reporting.[195] In order to partially address these concerns, the SEC has allowed foreign issuers to use either GAAP or home country (or IAS) reconciled to GAAP. Reconciliation, however, is an expensive and time-consuming process and can still be regarded as the major barrier to foreign issuer access to U.S. markets.

Notwithstanding IOSCO endorsement of IAS (and participation of the U.S. SEC in that process), the U.S. SEC is considering the IAS package independently with no underlying legal obligation to follow IOSCO endorsement. Congressional testimony of SEC officials indicates that in order for IAS to be adopted, the standards must (1) constitute a comprehensive basis of accounting; (2) be of high quality and result in comparability and transparency and provide for full disclosure; and (3) be rigorously interpreted and applied.[196] The SEC has repeatedly stated that its decision to adopt IAS would be premised upon an evaluation of the impact of IAS upon capital formation, cost of capital for domestic registrants, and investor protection.[197] The SEC concluded that the IASB's efforts have already contributed greatly to raising the level of accounting standards worldwide and reducing the number of differences between international standards and accounting principles used in the United States. These and other efforts at the international level are encouraging development of accounting principles that have the needs of investors and capital markets as their primary focus.[198]

The SEC at present has a request for public comment respecting adoption of IAS pending.[199] In respect to the IAS proposal, the United States is looking at four options: (1) retain the current reconciliation system; (2) remove some reconciliation requirements for selected IAS; (3) allow IAS for recognition and measurement, with GAAP and SEC supplemental footnote disclosure; or (4) allow IAS without reconciliation. The first (no change)

[195] *See* Gonzales & Olive, *supra* note 28.

[196] *See, e.g.*, Remarks by Jane B. Adams, Deputy Chief Accountant, Office of the Chief Accountant, U.S. Securities and Exchange Commission, at the 17th Annual SEC and Financial Reporting Institute Conference, Leventhal School of Accounting, University of Southern California, Los Angeles (May 14, 1998). These factors have been repeated on numerous occasions in SEC testimony and speeches since April 1996, when the SEC released a statement in support of the efforts of IOSCO and the IASB. *See* SEC News Digest, SEC Statement Regarding International Accounting Standards, Issue 96-67, *reprinted in* 1996 SEC LEXIS 873 (Apr. 11, 1996).

[197] *See, e.g.*, Remarks by Mary B. Tokar, Senior Associate Chief Accountant, Office of the Chief Accountant, U.S. Securities and Exchange Commission, at the 2nd Annual International Accounting Standards Conference, Belgium (Mar. 10, 1998).

[198] *See* SEC INTERNATIONALIZATION OF THE SECURITIES MARKET, *supra* note 127, at 23.

[199] *See* Tokar, *supra* note 197, at 5.

and last (adopt IAS for foreign issuers) are both unlikely. At present, the discussion is largely on hold following Enron and Sarbanes-Oxley. However, active discussions of possible convergence are taking place between the European Commission, the SEC, IASB and FASB.

In relation to the specific proposals, in respect to the first, the SEC (through IOSCO) has endorsed the use of IAS for foreign issuers. As a result of this, combined with congressional pressure, it would seem as if the SEC would have to make some allowances in respect to IAS. In respect to the last, given the comments of both the SEC and domestic constituents, it appears unlikely (even in the context of the Enron debate) that IAS will be adopted wholesale, at least at this point in time. It therefore seems probable that the SEC will allow use of IAS to some extent by foreign issuers at some point. The SEC may decide to endorse certain IASB core standards but not endorse other standards. Notably, the SEC has previously endorsed three IASB standards for partial use by foreign issuers without requiring reconciliation to U.S. GAAP.[200] The SEC could decide to endorse IAS for use by foreign issuers coupled with a requirement that issuers explore U.S. GAAP on particular issues not addressed or inadequately addressed in the opinion of the SEC. The SEC could also exclude one or more of the core standards adopted by IOSCO from domestic endorsement.

VI. CONCLUSION: A FUTURE FOR MULTILATERAL EFFORTS TO SUPPORT GLOBALISATION OF SECURITIES OFFERINGS?

As noted at the outset, the key issue is globalisation of financial markets, specifically truly global securities offerings and listings, at present largely impossible due to disparities between domestic legal and regulatory standards. Essential to true 'globalisation' of securities offerings and listings is the issue of whether, for the first time, multilateral efforts may lead to the development of an agreed format for the content of an international offering/listing document acceptable in jurisdictions around the world, i.e., a 'global prospectus' or 'international passport prospectus.'[201]

In summary, the area of regulation of international securities offerings has several and differing dynamics involving the domestic, regional and international levels. Certainly the SEC is a driving domestic force, both unilaterally, bilaterally and multilaterally: we have the US-Canada situation—back-to-back unilateral mutual recognition; and we have US participation in IOSCO, as well as the current focus on domestic accounting

[200] *See A Window of Opportunity*, CORP. ACCOUNTING INT'L 10 (1996).

[201] For a discussion of other issues, see Douglas W. Arner, Globalisation of Financial Markets: An International Passport for Securities Offerings?, 35 Int'l Law.1543, 1583-1587 (2002).

standards. Second, we have also seen the relative success of regional multilateral efforts of the EU. Third, there has been some success of multilateral efforts through IOSCO and the IASB. At present, though, domestic concerns with financial scandals in the US and the EU have created a conflict between the two major players. It remains to be seen whether the US and EU can come to a common position, which in turn could serve as the basis for further multilateral efforts through IOSCO and/or the IASB.

Based upon the analysis above, this author suggests the following as a possible pragmatic approach to the development of mechanisms to support true global offerings, while at the same time maintaining high standards of disclosure and adequate investor protection across jurisdictions.

Countries should continue to implement the IOSCO IDS, along with improving IAS to an acceptable level within a short period, thus continuing domestic implementation of areas of multilateral agreement. Companies (whether domestic or foreign) seeking to sell securities to the public (either through a stock exchange listing or through a public offering) should be required to use IDS in conjunction with IAS or have the option to use domestic standards (if such exist). Companies would have to comply with the distribution rules of each jurisdiction in which it is desired to list or make an offering to the public (as is presently the case). IOSCO (and where relevant, regional organisation such as the EU) would seek to develop harmonised distribution standards, a process that in all likelihood will be facilitated and encouraged by consolidation and international expansion on the part of securities exchanges. In the interim, companies and their legal advisors are well equipped to deal with divergent systems. By accessing the public markets of a given jurisdiction, companies would become subject to the domestic enforcement standards applicable. The risks would be limited by registration requirements of exchanges and securities regulators. For institutional investors (the major constituency of the Euromarkets), exemptions/relaxations should be in place to reduce the more stringent disclosure requirements appropriate for the public (and used in all listings). This however will necessitate convergence in respect to definitions of public offers.

Clearly, companies are in a better position than individual investors to monitor their potential legal and regulatory risks. Companies would also be subject to the legal regime of their jurisdiction of incorporation and/or domicile. As stock exchange linkages develop, standards of enforcement will move upwards, as individual exchanges seek partners with exchanges from countries with higher regulatory standards or choose such standards for market reasons. Institutional investors pursuant to exemptions from the stringent requirements of public offerings in turn would rely on the standards of the home jurisdiction, as well as listing jurisdictions, as appropriate in the given case. The end result is a placing of the burden on companies in the context of listings and public offerings and allowing the public in a given jurisdiction to use the rules available in their own jurisdiction for enforcement. Institutional investors operating outside of the standards appropriate for the investing public should be able to enforce on the basis of the home jurisdiction of the issuer, as well as on the basis of the rules of any jurisdiction on which the issuer is listed.

The United States should continue to emphasise high minimum standards for disclosure and enforcement, but should be flexible in their actual form and work through IOSCO to achieve harmonisation of standards. Mutual recognition will in all likelihood increase as minimum international standards are established, implemented, and enforced, reflecting the experiences of the EU in its ongoing project to create a single European capital market.

CHAPTER THIRTEEN

A Decade of Open Regionalism in Latin America: The Need for Effective and Efficient Articulation, Coordination, Cooperation and Convergence

*By Mauricio Baquero-Herrera**

CHAPTER OUTLINE

I. Open Regionalism and the Main Features of the Regional Integration Processes in Latin America
II. Differential Treatment and Preferences
   A. Complexity: The Damaging Effect of The Latin American Area of Economic Preferences
   B. Mechanisms Used To Grant Differential Treatment and Preferences Among The Laia Members
III. Highly Institutionalised Structures and Forums
   A. Institutional Structures
   B. Institutions Created or Acting With the Aim of Promoting Articulation, Coordination, Cooperation and Convergence Within the Region
   C. Association of Caribbean States (ACS)
   D. Rio Group
IV. Antithetic Policies and Positions Towards External Markets
   A. From Import-substitution Policies to Neo-liberal Policies and Still Fragile
   B. Are the Economies in the Region Really Open?
V. Concluding Remarks

* The author is a Colombian Lawyer specialising in Colombian Financial Law, LLM in Banking and International Financial Law (London), and a member of the Economic Law Department of the Universidad Externado de Colombia. Part of the research work was conducted while a Research Fellow at the Centre for Commercial Law Studies (CCLS), Queen Mary, University of London. The author is Latin American Head of the Secretariat of the London Forum for International Economic Law and Development.

Regional Integration in Latin America comprises four important features, which can be described as the granting of differential treatment and preferences, politically led processes, highly institutionalised structures and forums, and antithetic positions towards external markets. These qualities have played a key role in the successes and failures of the diverse schemes established within the region. Differential treatment is considered not only a peculiarity but also a principle of economic integration in the region. However, it may create complexities and bring about weakness and legal uncertainty. Political direction could become political intrusion. Institutions, structures and forums may turn dysfunctional and external relations could be based on policies which leave the region vulnerable to external shocks. These core aspects of South-South Latin American integration are embodied within the definition of open regionalism, a policy upon which countries have relied since the mid 1990s. After a decade of being implemented its purpose is far from reached. There is a need to articulate the various regional, sub-regional trilateral and bilateral treaties in order to direct open regionalism towards more effective multilateralism. The evolution and dynamism of the process have produced a complex network of bodies, institutions and organs, which have lost their influence in procuring the required convergence, coordination and cooperation. By reexamining the Latin American and the Caribbean integration framework and correcting the weaknesses present in the features to be considered, the region as a bloc will find a balanced immersion in the global economy. In order to discuss these issues, the Chapter is divided into five sections. The first four identify, describe and evaluate each one of the qualities present in the South-South Regional Integration processes in Latin America considering their interdependence with the concept of open regionalism. Section five summarises and provides some concluding remarks.

I. OPEN REGIONALISM AND THE MAIN FEATURES OF THE REGIONAL INTEGRATION PROCESSES IN LATIN AMERICA

Regional integration is not a novel concept in Latin America. Prominent citizens and statesmen had already discussed the prospect of integrating the nations of the South of the Continent during the first decades of the XIX Century.[1] Latin American Integration was the unfinished political dream of 'El Libertador' Simon Bolivar after emancipating Andean countries from the Spanish rule by 1817–1820. Bolivar, without succeeding, acted towards

[1] Juan Mario Vacchino & Telasco Pulgar, *Integration Agreements and the Latin American Community of Nations*, 53 CAPITULOS DEL SELA 113, 113 (1998) (discussing the early stages of regional integration).

the accomplishment of this aim by inviting neighbouring Heads of States to meet in Panama to consider the creation of a Confederation of States.[2]

The first intention of establishing a free trade area among the countries in South America was proposed in 1889 at the First International Conference of the American States[3]. Diverse approaches have been applied in order to obtain the desired goal of sustained development through economic integration. After more than three decades of regional, sub-regional and bilateral efforts, differential treatment, politically led processes, highly institutionalised structures and forums, and antithetic positions towards external markets are regarded as the main features of regional integration in Latin America.

In addition, Open Regionalism is the principle upon which different models of regional integration in developing countries, such us APEC[4] and the six arrangements actually in place in Latin America and the Caribbean[5], have carried out economic integration. Different attempts to define it have been made. Some conceive open regionalism as the reduction in barriers on imports from non-member countries as a consequence of the liberalisation of trade among members.[6] Others go beyond trade liberalisation and relate open regionalism with social access.[7]

Bergsten[8] proposes five possible definitions as follows: 1. Open

[2] *See* Article 2 of the unsigned Treaty for perpetual unity, league and confederation of the Latin American Countries or the Amphictyonic Congress of Panama, 1824 quoted in SELA, GUIDE TO LATIN AMERICAN AND CARIBBEAN INTEGRATION 2001, 4 (Permanent Secretariat of SELA 2001). Document available at http://lanic.utexas.edu/~sela/AA2K1/ENG/docs/Integra/SPDi5-01/SPDi5-01-2.htm, last visited September 09, 2003 [hereinafter *Guide*].

[3] *Id.* at 5. *See also* Rubens Antonio Barbosa GCVO, *The Evolution of the Integration Process in South America. Introduction* to MARTA HAINES FERRARI, THE MERCOSUR CODES, at xi (BIICL 2000).

[4] APEC is the Asia-Pacific Economic Cooperation established in 1989. APEC's 21 Member Economies are Australia; Brunei Darussalam; Canada; Chile; People's Republic of China; Hong Kong, China; Indonesia; Japan; Republic of Korea; Malaysia; Mexico; New Zealand; Papua New Guinea; Peru; The Republic of the Philippines; The Russian Federation; Singapore; Chinese Taipei; Thailand; United States of America and Viet Nam.

[5] They are the Latin American Integration Association, LAIA (regional); the Central American Integration System, SICA (sub-regional); the Central American Common Market, MCCA (sub-regional); the Caribbean Community and Common Market, CARICOM (sub-regional); the ANDEAN COMMUNITY (sub-regional, countries located in the North Cone of South America); and the Common Market of the South, MERCOSUR (sub-regional, countries located in the North Cone of South America).

[6] Defined as external liberalization by trade blocs. *See* Wei Shang-Jin & Jeffry A. Frankel, OPEN REGIONALISM IN A WORLD OF CONTINENTAL TRADE BLOCS 440-453 (IMF Staff Papers 45, no. 3 1998), http://www.imf.org/external/Pubs/FT/staffp/1998/09-98/pdf/wei.pdf, last visited March 17, 2004.

[7] *See* Clark W. Reynolds, OPEN REGIONALISM LESSONS FROM LATIN AMERICA FOR EAST ASIA (Working Paper #241 1997), http://www.nd.edu/~kellogg/WPS/241.pdf, last visited March 17, 2004.

[8] C. Fred Bergsten, OPEN REGIONALISM (Institute for International Economics, Working Paper 97-3 1997), http://www.iie.com/publications/WP/1997/97-3.htm, last visited March 18, 2004.

Membership in the regional arrangement. 2. Unconditional most-favoured-nation (MFN) treatment by which trade liberalisation would be extended unconditionally to all of the members' trading partners. No new preferences or discrimination would be created. 3. Conditional MFN. A group would offer to generalise its reductions of barriers to all non-members that agreed to take similar steps. 4. Global liberalisation, meaning continuous reduction of barriers on a global basis while pursuing each group's regional goals. 5. Trade facilitation through non-tariff and non-border reforms.

This Chapter in turn considers 'Open regionalism' from the perspective introduced by ECLAC[9] in the mid 1990s. It was a response to the changes towards regional integration in the early 1990s. Although the policy of import substitution, which it advocated in the 1960s was left aside, ECLAC continued providing guidance to the process of economic integration within the context of openness in which all economies of the region were involved.

As stated by ECLAC, it is 'a process of growing economic interdependence at the regional level, promoted both by preferential integration agreements and by other policies in a context of liberalization and deregulation, geared towards enhancing the competitiveness of the countries of the region and, in so far as possible, constituting the building blocks for a more open and transparent international economy'.[10]

Open regionalism contains two antithetical propositions.[11] On the one hand, it advocates regional integration as opposite to multilateral or global integration. Regionalism implies certain preferences among the members and a degree of protection against non-members. On the other, it proposes openness to other countries, blocs and economies through different means, among them, multilateralism.

This two-folded definition implies an enormous degree of multiple inter-

[9] ECLAC is the United Nations Economic Commission for Latin America and the Caribbean. Its Spanish acronym is CEPAL. ECLAC has developed its own school of thought being extremely influential within the region during the 1950s and 1960s. Its 'Historical structuralism' was based on the ideas and work of Raul Prebisch, Celso Furtado and Jorge Ahumada, among others. *See* http://www.eclac.cl/acerca/default-i.asp, last visited July 28, 2003. *See also* Bela Balassa, *Regional Integration and trade liberalisation in Latin America*, X No. 1, JOURNAL OF COMMON MARKET STUDIES 58, 59-60 (1971).

[10] ECLAC, OPEN REGIONALISM IN LATIN AMERICA AND THE CARIBBEAN. ECONOMIC INTEGRATION AS A CONTRIBUTION TO CHANGING PRODUCTION PATTERS WITH SOCIAL EQUITY. (1994), http://www.eclac.cl/cgi-bin/getProd.asp?xml=/publicaciones/xml/7/4747/ P4747. xml&xsl=/tpl-i/p9f.xsl&base=/tpl-i/top-bottom.xsl, last visited September 26, 2003 [hereinafter *open regionalism]*. *See also* Gary C. Hufbauer, THE FUTURE OF REGIONAL TRADING ARRANGEMENTS IN THE WESTERN HEMISPHERE (Institute for International Economics 1998), http://www.sice.oas.org/ geograph/papers/iie/hufbauer0998.asp, last visited September 26, 2003. *See also Guide*, *supra* note 2, at 9.

[11] Eduardo Mayobre, *The Rules of the World Game in Latin America's Foreign Policy*, 53 CAPITULOS DEL SELA 51, 60 (1998) (commenting on the concept of open regionalism).

actions:[12] first of all, those within the region, sub-regions and bilateral arrangements and secondly, those outside the region, sub-regions and other arrangements, which could be negotiated and agreed in blocs or individually. There is as well a high degree of difficulty as to finding the right balance among the particular concerns and interest of the member countries of the region or sub-regions, and those of the region as a whole in the negotiations with other countries and blocs.

The following sections analyse the contents of the proposed definition against the four features identified along the historical development of the South-South regional and sub-regional integration in Latin America.

II. DIFFERENTIAL TREATMENT AND PREFERENCES

The principle of differential treatment, aimed at balancing the asymmetries present among the countries in the area, has been introduced in almost all South-South agreements in the region. Small and middle size countries react against arrangements that do not consider their different levels of development.

LAFTA (1960) was the first regional attempt to attain economic integration[13] created with the aim of establishing a regional free trade area.[14] It involved countries with diverse levels of development, size, and political interests. Argentina, Mexico and Brazil, as the most industrialised countries within the area, had a clear interest in securing a wider market for their products,[15] while smaller and underdeveloped countries focused on creating industrial development. This imbalance was perceived as a disadvantage of the Treaty of Montevideo 1960 for the less industrialised countries of the region, as the promised benefits failed to reach all countries involved.[16] As

[12] *See* SELA's Permanent Secretariat, *Some Thoughts of the Dynamics on Latin America's and the Caribbean's External Relations*, 55 CAPITULOS DEL SELA 7, 8–9 (1999) (discussing the implications of open regionalism).

[13] The Montevideo Treaty 1960 [hereinafter *MT60*) was signed first by Argentina, Brazil, Chile, Mexico, Paraguay, Peru and Uruguay. Colombia (1961), Ecuador (1961), Venezuela (1966) and Bolivia (1967) joined in latter. *See* Richard Higgott. FROM TRADE LED TO MONETARY-LED REGIONALISM; WHY ASIA IN THE 21ST CENTURY WILL BE DIFFERENT TO EUROPE IN THE 20TH CENTURY 9 (Paper W-2002/1), http://www.cris.unu.edu/Online%20papers/paper%20richard%20higgott.pdf, last visited July 20, 2003.

[14] *See MT60*, Articles 1 and 2.

[15] *See* Barbosa, *supra* note 3, at xiv. *See also* Miguel S Wionczek, *The rise and the decline of Latin America Economic Integration*, IX, No. I, JOURNAL OF COMMON MARKET STUDIES 49, 59 (1970).

[16] *See* Devlin & Estevadeordal, WHAT IS NEW IN THE NEW REGIONALISM IN THE AMERICAS? 23 (Working Paper No. 6, INTAL-ITD-STA 2001), http://www. iadb.org/intal/publicaciones/devlin-estevadeordal_WP6.pdf, last visited July 18, 2003. *See also* Kevin J Middlebrook, *Regional Organizations and Andean Economic Integration*, XVII, No. 1, JOURNAL OF COMMON MARKET STUDIES 62, 64-65 (1978). Also David E. Hojman, *The Andean*

the market forces allocated resources to the countries with important levels of industrial development less developed countries in the area found themselves within an unsustainable situation.[17] Then, they began to 'spill over'.[18]

Sub-regional agreements appeared in the late 1960s and early 1970s as the reaction of small countries against the effects brought upon them by LAFTA. The Andean Pact[19] and the Caribbean Community and Common Market[20] (CARICOM) were established. These agreements, as opposed to LAFTA, were composed of a more homogeneous grouping of countries, territorially linked and with related types of economies.[21]

In 1965, four economists, upon the request of the Chilean President, presented the 'Proposals for the creation of the Latin American Common Market'. They pointed out the need for preferential attention to less developed countries within the region. 'The success of integration depends on all the countries effectively having an equal opportunity to benefit from the establishment of a common market. The relatively less developed countries therefore require preferential attention and special treatment, particularly in three fundamental areas: regional trade policy, technical and financial

Pact: Failure of a model of economic integration, XX, No. 2, JOURNAL OF COMMON MARKET STUDIES 139, 139 (1981). Also William P. Avery and James D. Chochrane, *Innovation in Latin American Regionalism: The Andean Common Market,* 27, no. 2 International organization, (spring 1973) (They present a comprehensive quantitative assessment of LAFTA's fulfilment of the distribution of economic integration benefits, quoted in Middlebrook, page 65, footnote 4).

[17] RICARDO FFRENCH-DAVIS, EL PACTO ANDINO: UN MODELO ORIGINAL DE INTEGRACION [The Andean Pact: An original model of Integration] 32 (Ernesto Tironi (compilator), Lima: Instituto de Estudios Peruanos) (1974).

[18] The following explanation of the concept of 'spill-over' is found in William P Avery & James D. Cochrane, *Subregional Integration in Latin America: the Andean Common Market,* XI, No. I, JOURNAL OF COMMON MARKET STUDIES 85, 86, footnote 3:'Moving to a higher level of integration in order to overcome dissatisfaction is termed 'spill-over' in the neo-functionalist theory of regional integration. The 'spill-over' concept describes a situation in which dissatisfaction, fear, concern, or unfulfilled aspirations at one level of integration or with integration in one economic sector leads the participants or a segment of them, to expand the scope or level of integration, or both, in order to fulfil aspirations, or overcome dissatisfaction, fear or concern.'

[19] The Cartagena Agreement was signed in 1969 setting up the Andean Group or 'Pacto Andino', with the aim of creating a customs union. The Andean Community and the Andean Integration System started operating in 1997, when the Protocol of Trujillo (1996) started to apply. The Andean Community's web site is http://www.comunidadandina.org.

[20] It is a customs union established in 1973 set up among Antigua and Bermuda, Bahamas, Barbados, Belize, Dominica, Grenada, Guyana, Haiti, Jamaica, Montserrat, St. Kitts and Nevis, Saint Lucia, St. Vincent and the Grenadines, Suriname, Trinidad and Tobago. The CARICOM's web site is http://www.caricom.org.

[21] *See* Avery & Cochrane, *supra* note 17, at 102. *See also* Germánico Salgado Peña Herrera, *Viable integration and the economic co-operation problems of the developing world. Part II.* XIX, No. 2, JOURNAL OF COMMON MARKET STUDIES 175, 186 (1980). Also Middlebrook, *supra* note 15, at 65.

assistance and investment policy.'[22] Accordingly, the Cartagena Agreement conceded special treatment to relatively less developed Andean countries such as Bolivia and Ecuador.[23] Differentiated treatment according to levels of development is also established in CARICOM.[24]

As for the region, a new agreement was signed. The Montevideo Treaty 1980, (hereinafter MT80)[25] still in force today, is aimed at establishing a common market through the creation of an Area of Economic Preferences instead of by a Free Trade Area.[26] More than a trade regime, the Treaty created an association, the Latin American Integration Association (LAIA), which gathers bilateral agreements and sub-regional systems under a single set of rules, comprising certain tariff and negotiation aspects. By fostering the development of sub-regional groups and the signing of bilateral or trilateral agreements among its members, the Treaty of Montevideo 1980 has become a legal framework and LAIA an institutional reference for the regional integration process.[27] Differential treatment is established as a principle within the Treaty.[28]

Other arrangements, such as the Central American Common Market, MERCOSUR and the Group of Three, do not formally contemplate differentiated treatment among its member countries on the basis of their level of development. However, either through the treatment of tariffs or considerations established in further Protocols as is the case in MERCOSUR (Ouro Preto 1994), preferential treatment is granted. [29]

To sum up, the lack of differential treatment marked the end of the first regional approach, encouraged sub-regional arrangements and promoted the creation of a zone of economic preferences.

As advocated by ECLAC, open regionalism promotes economic interde-

[22] *See* RAUL PREBISH ET AL., HACIA LA INTEGRACION ACELERADA DE AMERICA LATINA. [Moving towards an accelerated integration in Latin America], 32 (Fondo de Cultura Económica, Mexico) (1965). *See also* Raul Presbish, et al, *Proposals for the creation of Latin American Common Market*, V, No. I, JOURNAL OF COMMON MARKET STUDIES 83, 83–110.

[23] Middlebrook, *supra* note 15, at 64–65. *See also* Avery & Cochrane, *supra* note 17, at 85–102.

[24] *See* Article 3 of the Treaty Establishing the Caribbean Community and Common Market (CARICOM) available at http://www.sice.oas.org/trade/ccme/ccme2.asp, last visited March 17, 2004.

[25] The Montevideo Treaty 1980 [hereinafter *MT80*] ceases LAFTA and establishes the Latin American Integration Association (LAIA) made of the same 11 countries that set up or joined LAFTA. The Member Countries determined to charge each other lower tariffs than those applicable to non-members (Article 5). In this sense, it is a Preferential Trade Agreement.

[26] *See* Barbosa, *supra* note 3, at xvi.

[27] *Guide*, *supra* note 2, at 62-67. *See also* Barbosa, *supra* note 3, at xvii.

[28] Others such as pluralism (*MT80* Article 3, a), convergence (*MT80* Article 3, b), flexibility (*MT80* Article 3, c), and multiplicity (*MT80* Article 3, e) were also included to govern the implementation of the different clauses and the entire evolution of the regional integration process.

[29] SELA, THE TREATMENT OF ASYMMETRIES IN REGIONAL AND SUBREGIONAL INTEGRATION PROCESS. Document available at http://lanic.utexas.edu/~sela/AA2K/EN/ docs/spdddi6-973.htm, last visited March 26, 2004.

pendence at the regional level through preferential integration agreements. 'What differentiates open regionalism from trade liberalization and non-discriminatory export promotion is that it includes a preferential element, which is reflected in integration agreements and reinforced by the geographical closeness and cultural affinity of the countries of the region.'[30]

ECLAC recognises the reality of the general application of the policies based on trade liberalisation throughout the region as a consequence of the external debt crisis. Its view today stresses that open regionalism should take into consideration the problem of equality of opportunities for all countries to obtain the benefits of integration. In this sense, it proposes on the one hand a gradual and progressive tariff reduction process to ease the adjustment of production activities in countries or sectors considered to be less capable of competing within an enhanced market. On the other, it considers the adoption of agreements on special treatment to less developed countries. In addition, it argues that integration in some cases could be facilitated without the need for discriminatory or special measures, i.e. avoiding severe rules of origin or including clauses that enable the greatest number of members to accede to existing agreements. So, sustainable development, balancing economic growth with environmental preservation and social equity will be achieved.[31]

As a consequence, countries unilaterally or through bilateral, sub-regional and regional agreements have become more open to other markets in the region. However, this openness finds Latin American countries engaged in treaties of a different nature and scope. The variety of concessions granted to each other and to non-members generates great complexity. It may restrain trade and bring about legal uncertainty as articulation and convergence have not been attained.

A. Complexity: The Damaging Effect Of The Latin American Area Of Economic Preferences

LAIA establishes an area of economic preferences,[32] which comprises three different mechanisms. 1) A regional tariff preference, which member countries will reciprocally grant to each other. 2) Regional scope agreements in which all member countries participate, and 3) Partial scope agreements in which all member countries do not participate and exclusively bind the signatory member countries or those who may wish to adhere.

Taking into consideration the economic-structural characteristics of the countries and with the purpose of applying the differential treatments fore-

[30] ECLAC, *Open Regionalism, supra* note 9.
[31] *Id.*
[32] *See MT80* at Article 4. *See* Wionczek, *supra* note 14, at 163.

seen in the MT80, LAIA members are considered as follows: Countries at a relatively less advanced stage of economic development: (Bolivia, Ecuador and Paraguay). Intermediate developed countries: (Chile, Colombia, Peru, Uruguay and Venezuela); and other member countries (Argentina, Brazil and Mexico). Uruguay was granted exceptional treatment more favourable than that accorded to the other intermediate developed countries.[33]

B. Mechanisms Used to Grant Differential Treatment and Preferences Among the Laia Members

1. Regional Scope Agreements[34]

There are seven Regional Scope Agreements signed by all LAIA member countries. They are displayed in Table I section A. Article 18 of the MT80 requires member countries to approve negotiated lists of preferable industrial products originating from each relatively less developed country. A total elimination of customs duties and other restrictions would be accorded without reciprocity.

In compliance with this Article, member countries opened their markets to a wide range of products originating from Bolivia, Ecuador and Paraguay, granting the total lift of customs duties and other restrictions on specific products, from April 30th 1983. This Regional Scope Agreements are classified by LAIA as 'Market-Opening Lists' (AR.AM) and numbered AR.AM No.1 (Bolivia), AR.AM No.2 (Ecuador) and AR.AM No.3 (Paraguay).

The forth Regional Scope Agreement is the Regional Tariff Preference Agreement (AR. PAR No. 4). The Regional Tariff Preference (PAR) is established in Article 5 of the MT80. It is determined according to the relative economic development of each country, in conformity with Resolution 6 of the Council of Ministers as referred above. PAR applies to the entire tariff universe, except for a list of products determined by each country. Through this general mechanism member countries grant on a reciprocal basis a reduction of the rate of duties levied on imports from third countries on the importation of products originated in their own countries. The current basic level of PAR is of 20%.[35]

The other three Regional Scope Agreements are related to scientific and technological cooperation (Frame Agreement AR,CYT No. 6), to exchange

[33] *See* Council of Ministers of Foreign Affairs, Resolution 6 of 1980. Document available at http://www.sice.oas.org/trade/Montev_tr/resolute.asp#res6, last visited Sep. 05, 2003.

[34] The objectives and provisions of the treaty apply to these agreements. They may refer to the same matters and include those instruments foreseen for the partial scope agreements. *See MT80* at Article 6.

[35] *See* http://www.aladi.org, last visited March 10, 2004.

of goods and cooperation in cultural, educational and scientific matters (Agreement AR,CEYC No. 7), and the Free Agreement to Trade Promotion by overcoming Technical Barriers to Trade (Agreement AR,OTC No. 8).

2. *Partial Scope Agreements (AAP)* [36]

The aim of these partial scope agreements is to create the conditions necessary to deepen the regional integration process by their progressive multilateralisation[37]. They may refer to trade, economic complementation, agriculture, trade promotion, or adopt several modalities taking into consideration, among others, scientific and technological co-operation, tourism promotion and preservation of the environment.[38]

Partial scope agreements are governed by the following general rules: They are open to accession to the other member countries, prior to negotiation. They contain clauses promoting convergence in order that their benefits reach all member countries and other Latin American countries. They include differential treatments depending on the three categories of countries recognised by the members.[39]

Partial Scope Agreements among member countries have been the instrument to consolidate and deepen their trade relations. It is the will of the participants that determine both scope and intensity.[40] However this mechanism led to a plethora of agreements and differential treatments which should be consolidated through implementing the mechanisms of convergence provided in the Treaty of Montevideo. Tables I, sections B, C and D and Table II all contain Partial Scope Agreements in force at present.

MERCOSUR and the Andean Community are sub-regional arrangements which comprise almost all LAIA members (except from Mexico and Cuba, see Table III). They have reached several agreements aimed at the establishment of a Free Trade Area. Thus, the Secretaries of such sub-regional arrangements and that of LAIA should coordinate and cooperate in order to consolidate all these Partial Scope Agreements. Each one of them has a list of products and determines certain rules to apply the preferences granted. Goods have to be identified according to the national, sub-regional and regional nomenclatures and compared with the unilateral, bilateral, partial scope, sub-regional and regional preferences actually in force and

[36] *See MT80 at* Articles 9–14.
[37] *Id. at* Article 7.
[38] *Id. at* Articles 8 and 14.
[39] *Id. at* Article 9. They may also include, among others, specific rules regarding origin, safeguard clauses, non-tariff restrictions, withdrawal of concessions, re-negotiation of concessions, denouncement, coordination and harmonization of policies. Tariff reductions may be applied to the same products or tariff sub-items and on the basis of a percentage rebate regarding the tariffs applied to imports originating from non-participating countries.
[40] *Guide, supra* note 2 at 65.

granted by the countries in the region. This complexity is certainly not the best incentive for entrepreneurs and indeed creates legal uncertainty.

There are six different types of Partial Scope Agreements. Renegotiation Agreements (AA.PR), displayed in Table I, section B; Commercial Agreements, (AAP.C), Table I, C; Agricultural (AAP.AG), Table I, D; Trade Promotion (AAP.PC), Table I, E; Economic Complementation (AAP.CE), Table II and other Partial Scope Agreements, also in Table II.

(AA.PR) compile the results of the renegotiation of the preferences granted in past negotiations They consist of what is called the 'historic patrimony' of LAIA. Of the original 40 agreements in force by the end of the 1980s, only nine are currently still in force.[41] (AAP.C) are strictly commercial agreements and their scope is restricted to some productive sectors. Currently there are only two commercial agreements in force, of a total of 27 signed during the first decade of the MT80.

(AAP.AG) are Partial Scope Agreements negotiated under Article 12 of the MT80, aimed at promoting and regulating intra-regional trade of agricultural and livestock products. They should take into account the participating countries' socio-economic characteristics of production, establishing flexible mechanisms. These agreements may refer to specific products or groups of products, and may be based on temporary, seasonal, per quota or mixed concessions, or on contracts between State or 'para-State' organisations. (AAP.PC) refer to non-tariff matters and tend to promote intra-regional trade flows.

The following table shows all Regional Scope agreements actually in force and the four forms of Regional Scope Agreements described above (i.e., (AA.PR), (AAP.C), (AAP.AG), and (AAP.PC).

A. Regional Scope Agreements

AR.AM No.1	Market Opening Agreement in favour of Bolivia
AR.AM No.2	Market Opening Agreement in favour of Ecuador
AR.AM No.3	Market Opening Agreement in favour of Paraguay
AR.PAR	Regional Tariff Preference
AR.CYT S	Scientific and Technological Cooperation (Frame Agreement) No information available on the year of signature, prior 1985
AR.CAYC	Exchange of Goods and Cooperation in Cultural, Educational and Scientific Matters
AR.OTC	Trade Promotion by Overcoming Technical Barriers to Trade

41 Information taken from http://www.aladi.org, last visited March 10, 2004.

Table I Regional Scope Agreements and Some Partial Scope Agreements under LAIA

A	Bolivia	Brazil	Chile	Colombia	Ecuador	Mexico	Paraguay	Peru	Uruguay	Venezuela	Cuba
Argentina	AR.AM No 2 1983 AR.AM No 3 1983 AR.PAR No 4 1984 AR.CYT No 6 1993 AR.CEYC No 7 AR.OTC No 8 1997	AR.AM No 1 1983 AR.AM No 2 1983 AR.AM No 3 1983 AR.PAR No 4 1984 AR.CYT No 6 1993 AR.CEY C No 7 AR.OTC No 8 1997	AR.AM No 1 1983 AR.AM No 2 1983 AR.AM No 3 1983 AR.PAR No 4 1984 AR.CYT No 6 1993 AR.CEY C No 7 AR.OTC No 8 1997	AR.AM No 1 1983 AR.AM No 2 1983 AR.AM No 3 1983 AR.PAR No 4 1984 AR.CYT No 6 1993 AR.CEYC No 7 AR.OTC No 8 1997	AR.AM No 1 1983 AR.AM No 3 1983 AR.PAR No 4 1984 AR.CYT No 6 1993 AR.CEYC No 7 AR.OTC No 8 1997	AR.AM No 1 1983 AR.AM No 2 1983 AR.AM No 3 1983 AR.PAR No 4 1984 AR.CYT No 6 1993 AR.CEYC No 7 AR.OTC No 8 1997	AR.AM No 1 1983 AR.AM No 2 1983 AR.PAR No 4 1984 AR.CYT No 6 1993 AR.CEYC No 7 AR.OTC No 8 1997	AR.AM No 1 1983 AR.AM No 2 1983 AR.AM No 3 1983 AR.PAR No 4 1984 AR.CYT No 6 1993 AR.CEYC No 7 AR.OTC No 8 1997	AR.AM No 1 1983 AR.AM No 2 1983 AR.AM No 3 1983 AR.PAR No 4 1984 AR.CYT No 6 1993 AR.CEYC No 7 AR.OTC No 8 1997	AR.AM No 1 1983 AR.AM NO 2 1983 AR.AM No 3 1983 AR.PAR No 4 1984 AR.CYT No 6 1993 AR.CEYC No 7 AR.OTC No 8 1997	AR.AM No 1 1983 AR.AM No 2 1983 AR.AM No 3 1983 AR.PAR No 4 1984 AR.CYT No 6 1993 AR.CEYC No 7 AR.OTC No 8 1997
B											
Brazil						AAP.R No 9 7pa-2000					
Paraguay				AAP.R No 18 1pa-1995		AAP.R No 38 7pa-1993		AAP.R No 20 1pa-1995		AAP.R No 21 1pa-1995	
Uruguay				AAP.R No 23 1pa-1994				AAP.R No 33 1pa-1995		AAP.R No 25 1pa-1994	

Ecuador						AAP.R No 29 1pa-1993					
C											
Uruguay										AAP.C No 5 1982 AAP.C No 13 1982	
D											
Argentina	AAP.AG No 2 1991	AAP.AG No 2 1991	AAP.AG No 2 1991	AAP.AG No 2 1991	AAP.AG No 2 1991		AAP.AG No 2 1991	AAP.AG No 2 1991	AAP.AG No 1 1984 AAP.AG No 2 1991	AAP.AG No 2 1991	AAP.AG No 2 1991
E											
Argentina	AAP.PC No 10 1998 AAP.PC No 11 1997	AAP.PC No 5 1994 AAP.PC No 7 1994 AAP.PC No 8 1994 AAP.PC No 11 1997	AAP.PC No 11 1997	AAP.PC No 11 1997	AAP.PC No 11 1997 AAP.PC No 15 2001	AAP.PC No 11 1997	AAP.PC No 5 1994 AAP.PC No 7 1994 AAP.PC No 8 1994 AAP.PC No 11 1997	AAP.PC No 11 1997 AAP.PC No 12 1988 AAP.PC No 13 1988 AAP.PC No 14 1988	AAP.PC No 1 1992 AAP.PC No 5 1994 AAP.PC No 7 1994 AAP.PC No 8 1994 AAP.PC No 11 1997	AAP.PC No 11 1997	AAP.PC No 11 1997

Table I Continued

A	Bolivia	Brazil	Chile	Colombia	Ecuador	Mexico	Paraguay	Peru	Uruguay	Venezuela	Cuba
Bolivia		AAP.PC No 2 1992					AAP.PC No 16 1994				
Paraguay									AAP.PC No 9 1996		

B. Partial Scope Agreements: Renegotiation Agreements

AAP.R(PA)	ADDITIONAL OR ADOPTING PROTOCOL

C. Partial Scope Agreements: Commercial

AAP.C No 5	Preferences to Chemical Industry
AAP.C No 13	Preferences to Industrial Sector

D. Partial Scope Agreements: Agricultural

AAP.AG	Subscribed under ARTICLE 12 MT80

E. Partial Scope Agreements: Trade Promotion

AAP.PC	Subscribed under ARTICLE 13 MT80

The remaining Partial Scope Agreements are the Economic Complementation Agreements and other modalities of PSA. They are contained in Table II.

Economic complementation agreements[42] (AAP,CE) are aimed, among other objectives, to promote maximum utilization of production factors, stimulate economic complementation, ensure equitable conditions for competition, facilitate entry of products into the international market, and encourage the balanced and harmonious development of member countries.

Besides the sub-regional schemes of integration (Andean Community and MERCOSUR), there are nine agreements of economic complementation, which determine the creation of free trade areas among signatories. These are Chile-Venezuela (AAP.CE No. 23 FTA 1993), Chile-Colombia (AAP.CE No. 24 FTA 1993), Bolivia-Mexico (AAP.CE No. 31 FTA 1994), Chile-Ecuador (AAP.CE No. 32 FTA 1994), Colombia-Mexico-Venezuela, the Group of Tree (AAP.CE No. 33 FTA (G-3) 1994), MERCOSUR-Chile (AAP.CE No. 35 FTA-MS 1994), MERCOSUR-Bolivia (AAP.CE No. 36 FTA-MS 1996), Chile-Peru (AAP.CE No. 38 FTA 1998) and Chile-Mexico (AAP.CE No. 41 FTA 1998).

There are other Economic Complementation Agreements. MERCOSUR-Mexico (AAP.CE No. 54 FTA-MS-M 2002) establishes the framework for a Free Trade Area. The Andean Community and MERCOSUR signed a Partial Scope Agreement under Article 14 MT 80, (AAP.A14TM/11 F-FTA 1998). It is aimed at establishing the frame for a future Free Trade Area. Through several Economic Complementation Agreements, these two sub-regional agreements have been building up an important South American

[42] *See MT80 at* Article 11.

bloc. (AAP.CE No. 48 TFTA-MS 2000, AAP.CE No. 56 TFTA-MS 2002 and the recent AAP.CE No. 59 TFTA-MS 2003).

Other modalities of Partial Scope Agreements (AAP.A14TM) are established under Article 14 of the MT80. They regulate specific matters concerning tariff preferences. It may require cooperation actions aimed at creating favourable conditions for the exchange of goods and services (transport and tourism), for the protection of the environment, the optimum use of road infrastructure or the overcoming of technical barriers to trade.[43]

AAP.CE N° TFTA-MS Economic Complementation Agreement towards a FTA between some Andean countries and MERCOSUR

AAP.CE N° FTA-MS-AS Economic Complementation Agreement comprising a FTA between a single country and MERCOSUR related to automotive sector

AAP.CE N° FTA-MS-M Economic Complementation Agreement comprising a frame for a FTA between a single country and MERCOSUR

Other Partial Scope Agreements

AAP.A14TM Partial Scope Agreement under ARTICLE 14 MT80

AAP.A14TM/11 F-FTA Framework of the future Free Trade Area between Andean Community and Mercosur

AAP.A14TM/12 + CACM 1998Trade Agreement between MERCOSUR and CACM

Table III shows 19 Partial Scope Agreements actually in force (AAP.A25 TM), which some LAIA member countries signed with other Latin American non-members countries and areas of integration.[44] According to Article 19 MT80, the preferences granted in these agreements are automatically extended to the countries of relatively less economic development of the Association.

Finally, to further illustrate the complexity generated by the integration euphoria of the 1990s, the Inter American Development Bank created this graphic which they call the 'spaghetti bowl' of Latin American Regional Integration[45]. It only takes into account trade Agreements signed and under

[43] Information taken from http://www.aladi.org, last visited March 10, 2004.

[44] *See MT80* Article 25.

[45] Figure taken from Antoni Estevadeordal, Regional Integration and Regional Co-operation in Latin America. IADB Capacity Building Workshop, Trade Policy Issues, Singapore February 2002, pages 29–30 at http://www.adb.org/documents/events/2002/ trade_policy/ NRA_pres.pdf last visited July 16, 2003. *See also* IDB. *The New Regionalism*, 19, Latin American Economic Policies, 1, 1 and 5 (2002) at http://www.iadb.org/res/publications/ pubfiles/pubN-19E.pdf, last visited October 28, 2003. *See also* IDB, BEYOND BORDERS: THE NEW REGIONLISM IN LATIN AMERICA 64 (2002). Document available at http://www.iadb.org/res/publications/pubfiles/ pubB-2002E_8462.pdf, last visited March 26, 2004.

Table II Partial Scope Agreements: Economic complementation and others under LAIA

A	Bolivia	Brazil	Chile	Colombia	Ecuador	Mexico	Paraguay	Peru	Uruguay	Venezuela	Cuba
Argentina		AAP.CE No 14 1990	AAP.CE No 16 1991	AAP.CE No 11 1992	AAP.CE No 21 1993	AAP.CE No 6 1993	AAP.CE No 13 1992	AAP.CE No 9 1988	AAP.CE No 1 1985 AAP.CE No 57 2003	AAP.CE No 20 1992	AAP.CE No 45 1999
	AAP.CE No 36 **FTA-MS** 1996 AAP.A14TM/11 **F-FTA 1998** AAP.CE No 56 **tFTA-MS** 2002	AAP.CE No 18 **CM-MS** 1991 AAP.CE No 35 **FTA-MS** 1994 AAP.CE No 36 **FTA-MS** 1996 AAP.CE No 54 **FTA-MS-m** 2002 AAP.CE No 55 **FTA-MS-as** 2002	AAP.CE No 35 **FTA-MS 1994** AAP.A14TM/3 1990	AAP.A14TM/11 **F-FTA 1998** AAP.CE No 48 **tFTA-MS 2000** AAP.CE No 56 **tFTA-MS 2002** AAP.CE No 59 **tFTA-MS 2003**	AAP.A14TM/11 **F-FTA 1998** AAP.CE No 48 **tFTA-MS 2000** AAP.CE No 56 **tFTA-MS 2002** AAP.CE No 59 **tFTA-MS 2003** AAP.A14TM/13 1999	AAP.CE No 54 **FTA-MS-m** 2002 AAP.CE No 55 **FTA-MS-as** 2002	AAP.CE No 18 **CM-MS-1991** AAP.CE No 35 **FTA-MS 1994** AAP.CE No 36 **FTA-MS 1996** AAP.CE No 54 **FTA-MS-m** 2002 AAP.CE No 55 **FTA-MS-as** 2002 AAP.A14TM/11 **F-FTA 1998** AAP.CE No 48 **tFTA-MS 2000** AAP.CE No 56 **tFTA-MS 2002** AAP.CE No 59 **tFTA-MS 2003**	AAP.14TM/11 **F-FTA 1998** AAP.CE No 48 **tFTA-MS** 2000 AAP.CE No 56 **TFTA-MS** 2002 AAP.A14TM/14 1999	AAP.CE No 18 **CM-MS-1991** AAP.CE No 35 **FTA-MS 1994** AAP.CE No 36 **FTA-MS 1996** AAP.CE No 54 **FTA-MS-m** 2002 AAP.CE No 55 **FTA-MS-as** 2002 AAP.A14TM/11 **F-FTA 1998** AAP.CE No 48 **tFTA-MS 2000** AAP.CE No 56 **tFTA-MS 2002** AAP.CE No 59 **tFTA-MS 2003**	AAP.A14TM/11 **F-FTA 1998** AAP.CE No 48 **tFTA-MS 2000** AAP.CE No 56 **tFTA-MS 2002** AAP.CE No 59 **tFTA-MS 2003**	AAP.A14TM/2 1998
	AAP.A14TM/3 1990 AAP.A14TM/8 1992 AAP.A14TM/2 1988 AAP.A14TM/4 1990	AAP.A14TM/11 **F-FTA 1998** AAP.CE No 48 **tFTA-MS** 2000 AAP.CE No 56 **tFTA-MS** 2002 AAP.CE No 59 **tFTA-MS** 2003	AAP.A14TM/8 1992 AAP.A14TM/2 1998 AAP.A14TM/4 1990	AAP.A14TM/2 1998 .A14TM/4 1990	AAP.A14TM/2 1998 AAP.A14TM/4 1990	AAP.A14TM/2 1998	AAP.A14TM/9 1995 AAP.A14TM/3 1990 AAP.A14TM/8 1992 AAP.A14TM/12 +CACM 1998 AAP.A14TM/2 1998 AAP.A14TM/4 1990	AAP.A14TM/3 1990 AAP.A14TM/8 1992 AAP.A14TM/2 1998 AAP.A14TM/4 1990	AAP.A14TM/6 1992 AAP.A14TM/9 1995 AAP.A14TM/3 1990 AAP.A14TM/8 1992 AAP.A14TM/12 **+ CACM 1998** AAP.A14TM/2 1998 AAP.A14TM/4 1990	AAP.A14TM/2 1998 AAP.A14TM/4 1990	

Table II Continued

A	Bolivia	Brazil	Chile	Colombia	Ecuador	Mexico	Paraguay	Peru	Uruguay	Venezuela	Cuba
		AAP.A14TM/6 1992									
	AAP.A14TM/9 1995 AAP.A14TM/3 1990 AAP.A14TM/8 1992 AAP.A14TM/12 + CACM 1998 AAP.A14TM/2 1998 AAP.A14TM/4 1990										
Bolivia	AAP.A14TM/10 1995	AAP.CE No 22 1993 AAP.A14TM/10 1995				AAP.CE No 31 FTA 1994	AAP.A14TM/10 1995	AAP.A14TM/10 1995	AAP.A14TM/1 1968 AAP.A14TM/10 1995		AAP.CE NO 47 2000
Brazil						AAP.CE No 53 2002			AAP.CE No 2 1982–1986 AAP.A14TM/7 1992	AAP.CE No 27 1995 AAP.A14TM/15 1995	AAP.CE No 43 1999 AP.A14TM/15 1995
Chile				AAP.CE No 24 FTA 1993	AAP.CE No 32 FTA 1994	AAP.CE No 41 FTA 1998		AAP.CE No 38 FTA 1998		AAP.CE No 23 FTA 1993	AAP.CE No 42 1999

Colombia	AAP.CE No 33 FTA (G-3) 1994				AAp.CE No 33 FTA 9 (G-3) 1994	AAP.CE No 49 2000
Ecuador		AAP.CE No 30 1994		AAP.CE No 28 1994		AAP.CE No 46 2000
Mexico			AAP.CE No 8 1995	AAP.CE No 5 1999		AAP.CE No 51 2000
Paraguay						AAP.CE No 52 2000
Peru						AAP.CE No 50 2000
Uruguay						AAP.CE No 44 1999
Venezuela						AAP.CE No 40 1999

Table III Partial Scope Agreements with non-members under LAIA

	Guyana	Guatemala	Nicaragua	Costa Rica	El Salvador	Honduras	Panama	CARICOM	Trinidad y Tobago
Brazil	AAP.A25 TM/38 2001								
Colombia		AAP.A25 TM/ 1984	AAP.A25 TM/6 1984	AAP.A25 TM/7 1984	AAP.A25 TM./8 1984	AAP.A25 TM./9 1984	AAP.A25 TM/29 1993	AAP.A25 TM.31 1994	
Cuba		AAP.A25 TM/36 1999							
Mexico		AAP.A25 M/37 1999					AAP.A25 TM/14 1985		
Venezuela	AAP.A25 TM/22 1990	AAP.A25 TM/23 1985	AAP.A25 TM/25 1986	AAP.A25 TM/26 1986	AAP.A25 TM/27 1986	AAP.A25 TM/16 1986		AAP.A25 TM/24 1992	AAP.A25 M/20 1989

AAP.A25TMSubscribed under Article 25 MT80

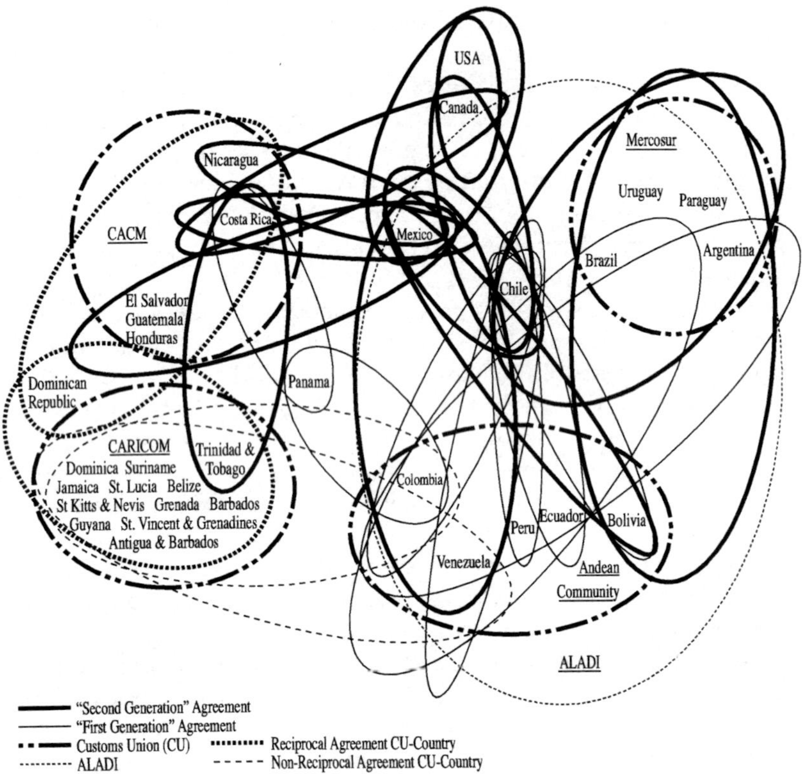

Figure 1 The IDB's 'spaghetti bowl' of Latin American Regional Integration

negotiations in the Americas. It does not consider the bulk of the regional or partial scope agreements signed under LAIA's framework referred to in the last sections and compiled in tables II III and I.

All in all, differential treatment and economic preferences certainly mean complexity. They are conceived as important tools for economic development and integration. Notwithstanding their importance, the lack of convergence among this kaleidoscope of obligations and preferences makes it difficult for the actors of integration to fully understand their implications and scope.

3. *Politically Led Process*

Open regionalism is also based on ECLAC's view that 'unilateral, regional and multilateral liberalization processes can all build upon one another provided that Governments have a clear picture of the interests at stake.'[46] The construction of building blocks for a more open and transparent international economy necessarily requires the leadership of the governments.

The second feature reveals the Latin American integration processes relying on the political will of the local governments. Regional integration is formally reached through International Conventions signed by the Heads of State of the participating countries. The institutions created in order to implement what has been agreed entirely depend on the will of local governments.

Latin American Constitutions present a tendency towards what is called 'Presidencialismo'. This is defined as the inclination to grant enormous powers to the Presidents of the Nations and to provide little accountability. This propensity was very strong within Latin American democracies during the 1970s and 1980s. During this period military dictatorships also appeared in the region. However, the propensity started to decrease in the 1990 but tended to reappear from time to time (i.e. Peru under Fujimori and Venezuela under Chavez Frias).

As for integration, governments lead or undermine the process according to their ideological tendencies and the pressures of the local groups of interest. It happens due to the actual structure of the different sub-regional and regional schemes. Even in cases where there is supranational law, on occasions governments still find it difficult to comply when political circumstances force them to make determinations which protect local interest to the detriment of those of the sub-region. As a consequence, they relax the scope of their commitments and tend to defy the sanctity of the decisions of the supranational bodies according to their national concerns.

LAFTA, for instance, faced serious obstacles in this regard, such as the instability and heterogeneity of the political regimes [military dictatorships (Argentina, Uruguay and Chile, as well as Brazil)] and conflicts between members (Ecuador and Peru) struck the region during the 1960s and 1970s. Ruptures and distancing were the result of episodes of authoritarianism within the region.[47] Changes in governments meant at that time changes in the policies towards sub-regional or regional integration.[48]

As for the Andean Process of integration, the Andean Presidents have played an important role. The leadership of the Andean Presidents has moved forward the Andean scheme in times of crisis or has detained it when

[46] Secretariat of ECLAC, *Globalization and Regionalization: A View from Latin America and the Caribbean*, 58 Capitulos del Sela 51, 63-64 (2000) (discussing the implications of open regionalism to the governments within of the region).

[47] *Guide*, *supra* note 2, at 3.

[48] *See* Rita Giacalone, *La integracion regional en la historia* [Regional integration in history], http://www.comunidadandina.org/bda/docs/VE-INT-0003.pdf, last visited August 05, 2003.

external shocks, lack of understanding or the protection of domestic interests made it necessary. Their involvement has been core in shaping and reshaping the sub-regional scheme. However, the strong politicisation of the Andean bodies was considered one of the causes of its failure at the end of the 1970s. Apart from the different political structures of the members, which became a problem after 1973, governments disrupted the methods of distributing costs and benefits within the bodies of the Andean Pact. By taking advantage of the weakness of its structure and the lack of supranational authority, the manifestation of the political will of the parties was needed in each instance of the process.[49] Due to the remaining politicization of the actual Andean bodies and institutions, the Andean Integration System is highly vulnerable to external shocks such us political changes and misunderstanding among member countries.

Overall, regional integration in Latin America is conceived as a mere action driven by the governments and the institutions established through the integration treaties. In many ways, it has been a 'top down' process, which until recently has taken into account the private actors within the local economies.[50]

ECLAC's hopes for a coordinated and articulated function of the overall regional integration process are far from attained. Especially during the last five years, the simultaneous negotiations within sub-regional, regional, hemispheric and multilateral forums have placed considerable demands on the Latin American countries.

The general impression is that governments are not ready to understand the complexity of the web of treaties created during the last decade and their implications. They do not have a coherent game plan to defend their local interests let alone those of the sub-regions and the region as a whole. This is worsened by the natural tendency of politicians to assess social and economic phenomena with a shortsighted vision and shallow approach. As a result, it makes it more difficult to find a comprehensive and thorough solution to the challenges of integration in the context of globalisation.

In addition, Governments in the region and in the sub-regions (mainly within the Andean Community) do not share the same visions and interests. As the process has taken more than a decade, its continuity has also been affected by the changes in the Heads of States and their international policies. The economic crises still striking the region have weakened the quality and ability of the negotiators and have left the institutions in charge of coordinating integration (i.e SELA, LAIA and Sub-regional Secretariats) with limited technical and financial resources.

49 Rafael Vargas-Hidalgo, *The crisis of the Andean Pact: lessons for Integration among Developing Countries*. XVII, No. 3, JOURNAL OF COMMON MARKET STUDIES 213, 216-217 (1979).

50 Giacalone, *supra* note 48. *See also* Avery & Cochrane, *supra* note 17, at 88 and 89.

III. HIGHLY INSTITUTIONALISED STRUCTURES AND FORUMS

Open regionalism advocates the construction of building blocks aimed at procuring a balanced immersion within the global economy. Consequently, ECLAC's approach poses the challenge of balancing the forces and local interests towards regional integration and global economic immersion.[51] Following Tussie, open regionalism seems to be conducive to more effective multilatelarism.[52] An adequate response to this undertaking implies a certain degree of institutionalism.

The following section introduces both the institutional structures of the six integration schemes in Latin America and the Caribbean and the group of institutions and bodies created with the aim of coordinating and cooperating with the processes of economic integration. After a decade of open regionalism these organs and bodies present a high degree of 'institutional fatigue', duplicity of functions, lack of identity and shortfall of resources. Unless these institutions are rearranged and modernised, the immersion of the region as a bloc in the global economy will face serious difficulties.

A. Institutional Structures

South-South Regional Integration in Latin America has produced a complex web of Institutions and bodies entrusted with different tasks and responsibilities within the region and the sub-regions. The following is a summarised review of the different institutions acting within the structure of the six schemes currently in place including Central America and the Caribbean. It takes into consideration the major bodies with political and executive leadership. Equally, it considers the technical bodies or secretariats. However, it does not refer to jurisdictional, parliamentary or consultative bodies and financial institutions, which are present in almost all arrangements.

At the end of this section there are two tables, which help to correlate and understand at a glance the density of the several bodies, organs and institutions actually in place. Table XII contains the institutions referred to in this section. Table XIII includes those which are not. Vacchino and Noto

[51] Carlos Moneta, *More Than Ever World Reality Requires Coordination and Cooperation Between SELA Member States*, 57 CAPITULOS DEL SELA. 117, 117–119 (1999). *See also* comment on open regionalism at the IDB web page at http://www.iadb.org/exr/topics/integration.htm last visited March 16, 2004.

[52] A 'new multilateralism can emerge from the regional units with countries having a first direct say at the regional rather than multilateral level, as they do now, where power asymmetries are wide and affinities limited.' Diana Tussie, *Multilateralism's New Approach in the Global Economy*, 53 CAPITULOS DEL SELA 29, 43 and 45 (1998).

compiled the information and prepared these two tables for the Permanent Secretariat of Latin American Economic System SELA.[53]

1. Latin American Integration Association (LAIA)

LAIA has a flexible and relatively small Institutional organisation in comparison to the sub-regional schemes. It is established in Chapter VI (Articles 28–42) of the MT80.

The political bodies of the Association are:[54] 1. The Council of Ministers of Foreign Affairs acting as the supreme body of the Association. It comprises the Ministers of Foreign Affairs of the member countries.[55] 2. The Evaluation and Convergence Conference composed of Plenipotentiaries of member countries.[56] 3. The Committee of Representatives, which is the permanent body of the Association.[57]. The technical body of the Association is the General Secretariat.[58]

2. Central American Integration System (SICA)

The Tegucigalpa Protocol[59] created the Central American Integration System in 1991. The governments of Guatemala, El Salvador, Honduras, Nicaragua, Costa Rica and Panama compose SICA. Belize joined in 2000.

SICA contains the following organs: the Presidential Meeting, as the supreme body of the System;[60] the Council of Ministers (the Council of Ministers of Foreign Affairs acting as an organ for coordination and direction);[61] the Executive Committee[62] and the General Secretariat.[63]

[53] The Permanent Secretariat of SELA incorporated these tables into the document '*Proposals for a Regional Integration Articulation and Convergence Program*'. It was published in Permanent Secretariat of SELA, *Democratic Governance and Human Development in LAC*, 67 CAPITULOS DEL SELA (2003), http://www.sela.org/index_e.html, last visited March 15, 2004.

[54] *See MT80 at* Article 28.

[55] *Id.* at Articles 30-32 and 43. The Council of Ministers of Foreign Affairs shall adopt whatever decisions may correspond to the higher governing policy of the economic integration process. Its powers are described in Article 30.

[56] *Id.* at Articles 33–34 and 43. Its powers are established in Article 33.

[57] *Id.* at Articles 35–37 and 43. Its powers and duties are determined in Article 35.

[58] *Id.* at Articles 29 and 38–41.

[59] Available in Spanish at http://www.sgsica.org/sica/documentos/prototegu.pdf. Last visited March 17, 2004.

[60] *See* Articles 12–15 of the Tegucigalpa Protocol. Article 15 defines the activities and scope of the Meeting.

[61] *Id.* at Articles 16–23.

[62] *Id.* at Articles 23 and 24.

[63] *Id.* at Articles 23 and 25–28.

3. Central American Common Market (MCCA)

The General Treaty on Central American Economic Integration between Guatemala, El Salvador, Honduras and Nicaragua was signed in 1960. Costa Rica joined later in 1962.[64] The organs and bodies of the Treaty are established in Chapter IX (Articles XX-XXIV).

The Central American Economic Council[65] is composed of the Ministers of Economic Affairs of the several Contracting Parties. The Executive Council, consisting of one titular official appointed by each Contracting Party, was established for the purpose of applying and administering the Treaty and of undertaking all the negotiations and work designed to give practical effect to the Central American Economic union.[66] A Permanent Secretariat was also instituted.[67]

4. The Caribbean Community and Common Market (CARICOM)

The revised Treaty of Chaguaramas established the Caribbean Community including the CARICOM single market and economy. It was signed by Barbados, Jamaica, Guyana and Trinidad and Tobago and came into effect on August 1, 1973. Another eight Caribbean territories joined later. The Bahamas became the 13th Member State of the Community on July 4, 1983. However, it is not a member of the Common Market.[68]

The principal Organs of the Community[69] are the Conference of Heads of Government acting as the supreme organ of the Community[70] and the Community Council of Ministers[71]. The Council for Finance and Planning[72]; the Council for Trade and Economic Development[73]; the Council for Foreign and Community Relations[74], and the Council for Human and Social Development[75] all assist the principal organs. The Secretariat is the principal administrative organ of the Community.[76]

5. The Andean Community

The Trujillo Procotol 1996 introduced changes to the Cartagena Agreement 1969. This Protocol created the Andean Community and established the

[64] Available at http://www.sice.oas.org/trade/camertoc.asp, last visited March 17, 2004.

[65] *See* Article XX of the General Treaty on Central American Economic Integration [Hereinafter *GT*]. It is main purpose is to integrate the Central American economies and Co-ordinate the economic policy of the Contracting States.

[66] *Id.* at Articles XXI-XXII.

[67] *Id.* at Articles XXIII-XXIV.

[68] For more information visit http://www.caricom.org/.

[69] *See* Article 10 of the Revised Treaty of Chaguaramas [hereinafter *Chaguaramas*].

[70] *Id.* at Article 11. Powers and functions of the Conference are established in Article 12.

[71] *Id.* at Article 13.

[72] *Id.* at Article 14.

[73] *Id.* at Article 15.

[74] *Id.* at Article 16.

[75] *Id.* at Article 17.

[76] *Id.* at Articles 23–25.

Andean Integration System (AIS)[77] in order to promote effective co-ordination between the different bodies and institutions (about 14) that consists of.

The Andean Presidential Council is the highest-level body made up of the Heads of State of the Member Countries.[78] The Andean Council of Ministers of Foreign Affairs is the political leadership body comprising the Ministers of Foreign Affairs of the Member Countries.[79] The Commission of the Andean Community is the main policy-making body encompassing a plenipotentiary representative from each one of the governments of the Member Countries.[80] The General Secretariat of the Andean Community is the executive body of the system.[81]

6. *The Common Market of the South (MERCOSUR)*

The Protocol of Ouro Preto1994[82] modified the Treaty of Asuncion 1991 and established the structure of Mercosur.[83] The highest organ is the Council of the Common Market (CCM). It involves the Ministers for Foreign Affairs and the Ministers of the Economy of the States Parties, or their equivalents.[84] The Common Market Group (CMG) is the executive organ. It consists of four members who must include representatives of the Ministries of Foreign Affairs, the Ministries of the Economy (or their equivalents) and the Central Banks.[85] The Mercosur Trade Commission (MTC) is the body responsible for assisting the Common Market Group. It provides support by monitoring the application of the common trade policy instruments agreed by the States Parties in connection with the operation of the customs union. It also follows up and reviews questions and issues relating to common trade policies, intra-Mercosur trade, and trade with third countries.[86] These three are inter-governmental organs with decision-making powers.[87]

The Joint Parliamentary Commission (JPC) is the organ representing the parliaments of the States Parties within Mercosur.[88] The Economic-Social Consultative Forum (ESCF) is the body representing the economic and social sectors.[89] The Mercosur Administrative Secretariat (MAS) provides administrative support.[90] These institutions are also part of the institutional structure of Mercosur.

As shown in table IV, all the six major bodies considered with political,

[77] Article 6 of the Cartagena Agreement 1969 as amended. Available at http://www.comunidadandina.org/ingles/treaties/trea/ande_trie1.htm, last visited March 21, 2004.

[78] *Id.* at Section A, Articles 11 to 14.

[79] *Id.* at Section B, Articles 15 to 20.

[80] *Id.* at Section C, Articles 21 to 28.

[81] *Id.* at Section D, Articles 29 to 39.

[82] *See* http://www.sice.oas.org/trade/mrcsr/ourop/index.asp last visited March 16, 2004.

[83] *See* Article 1 of the Protocol of Ouro Preto.

[84] *Id.* at Articles 3 to 9.

[85] *Id.* at Articles 10 to 15.

[86] *Id.* at Articles 16 to 21.

[87] *Id.* at Article 2.

[88] *Id.* at Articles 22 to 27.

[89] *Id.* at Articles 28 to 30.

[90] *Id.* at Articles 31 to 33.

*Table IV Comparative Table of Integration Arrangements in Latin America and the Caribbean**

Bodies	ALADI	Andean Community of Nations	Central America Integration System: SICA	Central America Integration System: MCCA	CARICOM	MERCOSUR
Major body/ Political leadership (Presidential level)		Andean Presidential Council	Presidential Meeting		Heads of Government's Conference Conference Table	Summit of MERCOSUR Presidents
(Ministerial level)	Council of Ministers of Foreign Affairs					
Executive leadership/ Adoption of norms (Ministerial level)		Andean Council of Ministers of Foreign Affairs	Council of Ministers of Foreign Affairs	Council of Ministers of Economic Integration Intersectoral Council of Ministers of Economic Integration	Council of Community's Ministers	Common Market Council
					Trade and Economic Development Council	
Sectoral leadership (Ministerial level)		Joint meetings, Commission and sectoral ministers	Council of Ministers	Sectoral Council of Ministers of Economic Integration	Foreign Relations and Community Council Social and Human Development Council Planning and Finance Council	Sectoral Ministerial Meetings

Executive body (Government representatives)	Committeee of representatives	Andean Community Commission	Executive Committee	Executive Committee of Economic Integration		Common Market group Trade Commission
Permanent Secretariat (Technical body)	General Secretariat	General Secretariat of the Andean Community	General Secretariat of the Central American Integration System (SG-SICA	Central American Economic Integration Secretariat (SIECA)	Secretariat of the Community	Administrative Secretariat

* Prepared by Juan Mario Vacchino and Gerardo Noto[91]

** FONPLATA does not belong to MERCOSUR. It was created earlier by specific agreement, however its member countries coincide fully with those of MERCOSUR (Argentina, Brazil, Paraguay and Uruguay are Member States of MERCOSUR, while Bolivia is an Associated State).

ALADI LAIA

[91] Table taken from Permanent Secretariat of SELA, *Proposals for a Regional Integration Articulation and Convergence Program*, 67, CAPITULOS del SELA, (2003), http://www.sela.org/index_e.html, last visited March 15, 2004

executive or technical leadership in the six regional or sub-regional arrangements have a major, if not total, dependency on the governments of each country member. The Ministers of Foreign Affairs are entrusted with important powers and duties. Civil society and private entrepreneurs take little part in the processes.

B. Institutions Created Or Acting With The Aim Of Promoting Articulation, Coordination, Cooperation And Convergence Within The Region

In parallel to the structures, institutions, bodies and organs which comprise the different schemes, organisations already in place, such as LAIA and ECLAC, another set of institutions have been entrusted or established with the aim of promoting articulation, coordination, cooperation and convergence in the region. Some of them have technical purposes. Others are political arrangements. All in all, and due to the increasing tendency of negotiating and establishing North-South agreements, some of these South-South institutions seem to be losing their identity and function.

1. Latin American Integration Association (LAIA)

According to its nature, LAIA is an institution created to promote co-operation and convergence. The kaleidoscope of regional scope agreements, partial scope agreements, renegotiation agreements, commercial, agricultural, trade promotion, other partial scope agreements and agreements with no-members considered above, is the consequence of the intense activity of its member countries.

As stated before, Article 3 of the MT80 establishes, among others, the principle of Convergence upon which member countries would obtain a progressive multilateralisation of the various partial scope agreements by means of periodical negotiations. In this sense, it is clear that if under LAIA's framework a complex web of concessions and obligations was created, the Treaty provides for its convergence. Therefore, LAIA is called to promote this process through the activities and powers of the Council of Ministers of Foreign Affairs and the Evaluation and Convergence Conference. As already pointed out above, the Ministers of Foreign Affairs have a place and important responsibilities not only within LAIA but also in other sub-regional arrangements such as the Andean Community or Mercosur, whose member countries are part of the Association. This circumstance should create the conditions for articulation, cooperation and coordination. However, important work needs to be carried out in this regard.

Table V Comparative Table of Integration Arrangements in Latin America and the Caribbean

Bodies	ALADI	Andean Community of Nations	Central America Integration System		CARICOM	MERCOSUR
			SICA	MCCA		
Foreign trade negotiations					Caribbean Regional Negotiating Machinery	
Jurisdictional body		Andean Justice Tribunal	Central American Justice Court		Caribbean Justice Court	
Parliamentary body		Andean Parliament	Central American Parliament		Assembly of Community's Parliaments	Joint Parliamentary Commission
Economic and social consultative body	Business Advisory Council Consejo Asesor Laboral	Andean Business Consultative Council Consejo Consultivo laboral Andino	Consultation Council		Economic Integration Consultative Council	Economic and Social Consultative Forum

Table V Continued

Bodies	ALADI	Andean Community of Nations	Central America Integration System		CARICOM	MERCOSUR
			SICA	MCCA		
Financial institution		Andean Development Corporation (CAF) Latin American Reserves Fund (FLAR)	Central American Bank of Economic Integration (BCIE)		Caribbean Development Bank	FONPLATA (**)

* Prepared by Juan Mario Vacchino and Gerardo Noto. [92]
** FONPLATA does not belong to MERCOSUR. It was created earlier by specific agreement, however its member countries coincide fully with those of MERCOSUR (Argentina, Brazil, Paraguay and Uruguay are Member States of MERCOSUR, while Bolivia is an Associated State).
ALADI LAIA

92 *Id.*

2. United Nations Economic Commission for Latin America and the Caribbean (ECLAC)

When considering not only the early stages but also the complete process of regional integration in Latin America, it is essential to refer to the comprehensive, influential, and in some cases criticised work of the United Nations Economic Commission for Latin America and the Caribbean (ECLAC). [93]

ECLAC is one of the five regional commissions of the United Nations. It was founded for the purposes of contributing to the economic development of Latin America, coordinating actions directed towards this end, and reinforcing economic relationships among the countries and with the other nations of the world. The promotion of the region's social development was later included among its primary objectives.[94]

ECLAC, being a UN institutution, is independent from all regional and sub-regional arrangements. It still plays a key role in the region not only by providing assistance and meaningful research but also proposing policies aimed at gaining sustainable and balanced development for the Latin American countries.

3. The Latin American Economic System (SELA)

In 1975, the heads of States present at the Panama Convention considered it imperative to promote greater unity among Latin American countries. They found it essential to carry out concerted actions in the field of intra-regional economic and social cooperation. At the same time, it was considered fundamental to increase the bargaining power of the region and to ensure that Latin America occupies its rightful position in the international community.

To that end, they established the Latin American Economic System (SELA). It is a permanent regional body for consultation, coordination, cooperation and joint economic and social promotion.[95] SELA has two fundamental purposes: a) To promote intra-regional cooperation in order to accelerate the economic and social development of its members. b) To provide a permanent system of consultation and coordination for the adoption of common positions and strategies on economic and social matters in

[93] The United Nations Economic and Social Council through Resolution 106 (VI) of 25 February 1948 originally established it. Caribbean countries were included later on by Resolution 1984/67 of 27 July 1984, changing its name to the Economic Commission for Latin America and the Caribbean (ECLAC). For more information on the ECLAC *See* http://www.eclac.cl/acerca/default-i.asp, last visited July 28, 2003. *See* also Balassa, *supra* 8, at 59 and 60.

[94] Taken from http://www.eclac.cl/acerca/default-i.asp, last visited March 09, 2004.

[95] Article 2 of the Panama Convention 1975, document available at http://www.sela.org/index_e.html, last visited March 09, 2004.

international bodies and forums as well as before third countries and groups of countries.[96]

This institution provides important research and is a core forum for discussion among its members. CAPITULOS is a serious publication, which offers meaningful contributions to scholars and the public in general. However, as a consequence of the establishment of additional forums such as the group of Rio, its influence in the region has been undermined.[97]

C. Association of Caribbean States (ACS)

The Convention Establishing the ACS was signed on 24 July 1994 in Cartagena de Indias, Colombia, with the aim of promoting consultation, cooperation and concerted action among all the countries of the Caribbean[98]. It comprises 25 member States as follows: Antigua and Bermuda, Bahamas, Barbados, Belize, Colombia, Costa Rica, Cuba, Dominica, Dominican Republic, El Salvador, Grenada, Guatemala, Guyana, Haiti, Honduras, Jamaica, Mexico, Nicaragua, Panama, St. Kitts and Nevis, St Lucia, St Vincent and the Granadines, Suriname, Trinidad and Tobago, Venezuela. There are also three associate members: Aruba, France (on behalf of French Guiana, Guadeloupe and Martinique). Eight other non-independent Caribbean countries are eligible for associate membership

Among other activities, the Association promotes gradually and progressively among its members: 1. Economic integration, (including the liberalisation of trade, investment, transportation and other related areas). 2. Discussion on matters of common interest for the purpose of facilitating active and coordinated participation by the region in the various multilateral forums. 3. Consultation, cooperation and concerted action in such other areas as may be agreed upon.

D. Rio Group

The Rio Group is the Permanent Mechanism of Political Consultation and Coordination created in 1986. The members of this group are Argentina, Bolivia, Brazil, Chile, Colombia, Costa Rica, Dominican Republic, El Salvador, Guatemala, Honduras, Ecuador, Mexico, Nicaragua, Panama, Paraguay, Peru, Uruguay, Venezuela and Guyana, on behalf of CARICOM.

The Mechanism is the result of the fusion of the Contadora Group (Mexico, Colombia, Venezuela and Panama) and the Support Group

[96] *Id.* at Article 3.

[97] SEBASTIAN ALLEGRETT, IS THE CRISIS IN SELA OR IN LATIN AMERICA? (A SELA publication 2002).

[98] Article III Convention Establishing the Association of Caribbean States available at http://www.acs-aec.org/convention.htm#PREAMBLE, last visited March 09, 2004.

(Argentina, Brazil, Uruguay and Peru), which met previously to analyse and propose solutions to the political crises in Central America.[99]

The Declaration of Rio de Janeiro (1986) established the main objectives of the Group, as follows: 1. To expand and systematise political cooperation among the member states. 2. To examine international issues which may be of interest and coordinate common positions on these issues. 3. To promote more efficient operation and coordination of Latin American cooperation and integration organisations. 4. To present appropriate solutions to the problems and conflicts affecting the region. 5. To provide momentum, through dialogue and cooperation, to the initiatives and actions undertaken to improve inter-American relations; 5.) To explore jointly new fields of cooperation which enhance economic, social, scientific and technological development.

In March 1999, member countries signed the Veracruz Act, assessing, among other issues, those related to regional institutionalism and regional integration.[100]

In relation to regional institutionalism, the Heads of States pointed out the need for enhancing efficiency, avoiding duplication of efforts and procuring effective use of the resources available. Due to the new perspectives regarding hemispheric integration, they considered it important to strengthen cooperation and coordination mechanisms aiming at rationalising the functioning of the different regional organisms.

The Rio Group also considered regional integration as a core political commitment and supported all integration processes of regional, sub-regional, multilateral and bilateral scope, based upon the principle of open regionalism, and was conducive to harmonious development.

Table VI relates all countries, which compose Central America, the Caribbean and South America, to the regional or sub-regional South-South agreements they belong to such as LAIA, MERCOSUR, ANDEAN COMMUNITY, SICA, MCCA and CARICOM. At the same time, it features the institutions set up and aimed at coordinating and cooperating with the process of regional or sub-regional economic integration. To that end, firstly it displays technical institutions such as ECLAC and SELA. Secondly, it shows the political organisations created with the purpose of enhancing cooperation and coordination among the countries in the region, *i.e.* the Association of Caribbean States (ACS) and the Rio Group.

The effect of this tendency towards setting up heavy institutionalised schemes is two-folded. On the one hand, the propensity towards crowded internal structures present among the various arrangements creates bureau-

[99] For more information on the Rio Group *See* http://www.mre.gov.br/ingles/politica_externa/grupos/grupo_rio/index.asp, last visited March 26, 2004.

[100] Find more information on the Veracruz summit in Spanish at http://zedillo.presidencia.gob.mx/pages/grio/2_info/2_actver.html, last visited March 24, 2004.

cracy and does not allow enough room for convergence. On the other, governments seek other forums different from those already created within the regions or sub-regions, duplicating efforts and making the use of resources inefficient.

It is argued that Latin American South-South regional integration has been a politically led process. All mayor schemes have been either affected by the lack of commitment of the governments involved or boosted in periods of integration euphoria. As can be derived from the different institutional structures, the leadership of the different processes has been placed on the Presidents or the Ministers of Foreign Affairs of the member countries. In this sense, articulation, convergence, cooperation and coordination should come from the governments, as it has been a 'top down' process.

The lack of a clear, concerted and committed external policy among the governments of the region and within the sub-regional arrangements constitutes one of the main causes of the dysfunctional operation of their institutional networks.Table VI Central American, Caribbean and South American countries and their participation in regional, sub-regional and other institutions

IV. ANTITHETIC POLICIES AND POSITIONS TOWARDS EXTERNAL MARKETS

A. From Import-substitution Policies to Neo-liberal Policies and Still Fragile

ECLAC's definition sustains that open regionalism promotes economic interdependence at the regional level through various policies in a context of liberalization and deregulation, geared towards enhancing the competitiveness of the countries of the region.

The early regional integration and sub-regional attempts (i.e., LAFTA and Andean Pact) were conducted within the framework of the import substitution industrialisation policy.[101] By impeding manufactured imports through the establishment of high tariffs on them it was expected that member countries would develop their own industries, reducing with it their dependency on industrialised countries. Production sharing arrange-

[101] This policy was based on ECLA's model. At that time, it argued consistently that Latin American countries were peripheral to the more industrialised economies, which were considered the centre. To transform this relationship, Latin American economies must develop industrialisation programs led by the States in order to limit their role as mere exporters of raw materials to the centre. By temporally introducing tariffs, selectively and moderately to those elaborated goods produced by the countries in the centre, industrialisation through import substitution would achieve economic development. *See Guide*, *supra* note 2, at 6–7. *See* also F.A.G KEESING & and P.J. BRAND, POSSIBLE ROLE OF A CLEARING HOUSE IN THE LATIN AMERICAN REGIONAL MARKET 390, 411–413 (IMF Staff Papers Vol. 10 1963).

Table VI Central American, Caribbean and South American countries and their participation in regional, subregional and ther institutions

Bodies	ALADI	Andean Community of Nations	Central America Integration System		CARICOM	MERCOSUR
			SICA	MCCA		
Foreign trade negotiations					Caribbean Regional Negotiating Machinery	
Jurisdictional body		Andean Justice Tribunal	Central American Justice Court		Caribbean Justice Court	
Parliamentary body		Andean Parliament	Central American Parliament		Assembly of Community's Parliaments	Joint Parliamentary Commission
Economic and social consultative body	Business Advisory Council Consejo Asesor Laboral	Andean Business Consultative Council Consejo Consultivo laboral Andino	Consultation Council	Consultative	Economic Integration Council	Economic and Social Consultative Forum
Financial institution		Andean Development Corporation (CAF) Latin American Reserves Fund (FLAR)	Central American Bank of Economic Integration (BCIE)	Development	Caribbean Bank	FONPLATA (**)

ments were also put in place dividing the production process across the region. As local markets would become too small for the production, regional integration was required in order to allow economies of scale, creating larger markets for regionally manufactured products.[102]

Notwithstanding the import substitution model, countries carried on relying on exports of primary products. Even though the composition of imports changed, the quantity as a whole did not diminish. At the same time, the industrialisation process was based on strongly protected national markets, which generated interest groups in national economies opposed to opening up the local markets to other countries in the region. As a result, countries started to present imbalances in the external sector, which were resolved through external financing. The availability of 'eurodollars' as a consequence of the boom in the oil industry in the 1970s triggered unprecedented external borrowing from Latin American countries. It badly affected the whole region when policies of developed countries changed in order to control their internal inflation.[103] The increasingly onerous financial conditions forced the countries to create surpluses in order to service the external debt by contracting imports, therefore closing their markets to other countries.[104]

These international economic factors as well as the first petroleum crisis in 1978 and the increasing external debt of the Latin American countries made the economies of the region more dependent on international markets. This escalating reliance on external funding and the consequent external debt crisis of the 1980s changed the attitudes of these countries towards regional integration.[105]

On 20 August 1982, Mexico announced the unilateral suspension of principal payments on its foreign debt. Then, the external debt crisis started. New loans and rescheduling of private sector's current obligations and official debts were the immediate actions taken by the international lenders.[106]

The rescheduling of official debt was managed through the so-called 'Paris Club'[107], which usually required the acceptance of an IMF structural

[102] *See* HUFBAUER AND KOTSCHWAR, THE FUTURE OF REGIONAL TRADING ARRANGEMENTS IN THE WESTERN HEMISPHERE. (Institute for International Economics 1998), http://www.sice.oas.org/geograph/papers/iie/hufbauer0998.asp, last visited August 29, 2003.

[103] *See* ECLAC. MARCO HISTORICO DE LA INTEGRACION LATINOAMERICANA [Historic framework of the Latin American Integration], in Spanish version at http://www.eclac.cl/publicaciones/Comercio/0/lcr1820/capi.htm, last visited March 26, 2004.

[104] *Guide*, *supra* note 2, at 8.

[105] Barbosa, *supra* note 3, at xiv.

[106] ROSS P. BUCKLEY, EMERGING MARKETS DEBT. AN ANALYSIS OF THE SECONDARY MARKET 29–44 (Kluwer Law International, Vol. 8, 1999).

[107] *Id.* It meets any time a rescheduling of official debt is needed. As its members are the major creditors of the requesting nation, it has not fixed members, no office, no administrative bodies. *Id.* at 30.

adjustment programme before rescheduling. The same was applied to the rescheduling of commercial debt. The IMF started to play a supervisory role conditioning its loans both on the commitment of new funds from commercial banks and on the economic policy reform of the debtors.[108]

The IMF reform programmes[109] were aimed at generating enough resources to allow debtors to pay back international loans. Apart from reducing the size and role of local governments, IMF structural adjustments were also focused on curtailing protectionism as opposed to the Washington consensus by which 'economic growth is promoted through unilateral tariff cuts and reduction in import restrictions.'[110]

The structural reforms implemented were based on policies which clashed with those supporting the regional and sub-regional integration schemes in place at that time, induced a general non-compliance with the sub-regional or bilateral obligations.[111] For some commentators, the eighties constituted 'the lost decade for integration'[112]. As the sub-regional integration effort seemed meaningless, member countries opted for a pragmatic approach, easing the obligations originally contracted.[113]

The end of the Cold War in 1989 brought fears within the region that international capital flows might be allocated in the former Soviet countries. Therefore, it was essential for all Latin American economies to participate and be competitive in the world economy. [114] Neo-liberal policies introduced in the domestic context geared up to the opening of the Latin

[108] *Id.* at 31.

[109] According to Buckley, policies proposed included: 1. Reduction in the budget deficit to limit inflation, local interest rates and the need for foreign borrowing. 2. Limits on domestic credit expansion to control inflation. 3. Exchange rate devaluations to discourage imports and encourage exports. 4) Limits on borrowing consistent with the debtor's capacity to pay. Other structural adjustments included, 5) Higher income and sales taxes. 6) Higher charges for state-produced goods and services such as electricity and water. 7) Privatisation of state-owned companies. 8) Deregulation of the labour market. 9) Reform of tariffs and import quota regimes. *Id.* at 32

[110] *Id.* at 32

[111] A report by the Board of the Cartagena Agreement at that time refers that 'Today the Andean Group is being subjected to adverse forces that significantly hold back its progress and seriously jeopardize the community structures built with so much effort. Currently there are problems in the field of trade liberalization, difficulties that prevent the industrialization programmes from being implemented, lack of definition on issues like the common external tariff and many instances where the commitments made in the field of legal regulations have not been fulfilled'. Quoted in SELA, LATIN AMERICA AND CARIBBEAN INTEGRATION SCHEMES IN THE FACE OF THE INTERNATIONAL CRISIS (1999), http://lanic.utexas.edu/~sela/AA2K/EN/docs/spclxxvdi9-2.htm, last visited March 10, 2003

[112] *Id. See* also Barbosa, *supra* note 3, at page xviii.

[113] *Guide*, *supra* note 2, at 45. *See* also Barbosa, *supra* note 3, at xi–xii.

[114] *Guide*, *supra* note 2, at 8–9. *See* also Bela Balassa, *The Process of Industrial Development and Alternative Development Strategies,* ESSAYS IN INTERNATIONAL FINANCE, No. 141, Dec. 1980 at 6–12. (International Finance Section, Department of Economics, Princeton University).

American markets,[115] eliminating the 'anti-exportation bias' inherent to the inward-oriented industrial development strategies. [116]

The 'lost decade' of the 1980s, instead of ending the on-going process of regional and sub-regional integration, encouraged it under new policies, which promoted the opening of the markets to foreign trade. The resultant need to do so invigorated integration schemes during the 1990s.

This 'new regionalism'[117] is based upon a different policy framework that promotes open and competitive private market-based economies within a democratic institutional setting. It involves the following premises: 'Deepening grade liberalisation and lock-in reforms, market driven and attraction of foreign direct investment, creating and diversifying trade and dynamic productive transformation, geopolitics, institutional modernisation and enhanced regional co-operation. At the same time, it applies simple liberalisation programs, irreversible commitments, GATT/WTO rules of liberalisation, it is highly reciprocal and uses automatic schedules to liberalise trade with limited negative lists.'[118]

As countries in the region shared the same market-oriented economic policies, 'the impact of concessions given to each other was not very different from the concessions given to third countries.' [119] Consequently, bilateral and trilateral arrangements appeared, as well as several preferential trading arrangements. As referred above, the Partial Scope Agreements provided for in the MT80, brought about MERCOSUR.[120] Reciprocal free trade areas were negotiated mainly by Chile and among sub-regional schemes. The establishment of the G-3 between Colombia, Mexico and Venezuela is another example. It also allowed the establishment of North-

[115] Barbosa, *supra* note 3, at xviii. *See* also *Guide*, *supra* note 2, at 45. RENATO BAUMANN ET AL., LOS PROCESOS DE INTEGRACION DE LOS PAISES DE AMERICA LATINA Y EL CARIBE 2000-2001: AVANCES, RETROCESOS Y TEMAS PENDIENTES. (The proccesses of integration of the Latin American and Caribbean Countries 2000-2001: gians, drawbacks and issues to define) 30-31 (CEPAL, División de Comercio e Integración 2002), http://www.sice.oas.org/geograph/westernh/eclac02.pdf, last visited June 10, 2003.

[116] *See* ECLAC, *Open Regionalism, supra* note 9, at 1.

[117] *See* Devlin & Estevadeordal, *supra* note 15.

[118] *See* Devlin & Estevadeordal, TRADE AND COOPERATION: A REGIONAL PUBLIC GOODS APPROACH, (2002), http://www.netamericas.net/Documents/Presentations2/Presentation_NET%20AMERICAS%20OAS%202002_1.ppt, last visited March 19, 2004. *See* also Antoni Estevadeordal, REGIONAL INTEGRATION AND REGIONAL COOPERATION IN LATIN AMERICA 12–13, (2002), http://www.adb.org/documents/events/2002/ trade_policy/NRA_pres.pdf last visited July 16, 2003. Also Devlin & Estevadeordal, *supra* note 15 and Devlin & Castro, REGIONAL BANKS AND REGIONALISM: A NEW FRONTIER FOR DEVELOPMENT FINANCING 3, (Integration and Regional Programs Department, Working Paper No. 13, IDB, INTAL-ITD-STA 2002), http://www.iadb.org/ intal/publicaciones/Devlin-Castro_WP13.pdf or http://www.iie.com/ publications/papers/ devlin-castro0202.pdf.

[119] *Guide, supra* note 2, at 24.

[120] *See* ECLAC, *Open Regionalism, supra* note 9, at 5. *See* also THOMAS ANDREW O'KEEFE, LATIN AMERICAN TRADE AGREEMENTS (Transational Publishers, Inc. New York. 2001).

South agreements such as NAFTA and the consequent Free Trade Agreement signed between USA and Chile. Furthermore, the whole South-South agreements started to shake as a consequence of the negotiations towards the establishment of the Free Trade Area of the Americas (FTAA).

The inward-looking model, which tried to protect the region from external pressures and allow it immersion in the international economy of the time was strongly affected, and failed, among other factors, due to the external debt crises. An antithetic outward oriented strategy was embraced and it is currently in place. As a result of the economic liberalisation and structural adjustment programs and the tremendous effect of neo-liberal policies on the approach of the countries towards regional integration, a worrying degree of vulnerability from external forces is still present in all schemes.

Mid and late 1990s witnessed the Tequila crisis of 1994 (the first time that Latin America experienced an important impact generated by financial globalization[121]), the transnationalisation of finance, the tele-information revolution, the Asian (1997) and Russian (1998) crises, and also the Brazil and Argentinean crises (starting in 1999). All of them evidenced the fragility of the region form externalities.[122]

Notwithstanding the structural and second generation reforms placed in the region, the impact of the circumstances affecting the international economy and the local economic crisis led ECLAC again to speak of the 'lost half decade' of the Latin American and Caribbean region[123]. Until recently, sub-regions such as MERCOSUR and the Andean Community had started to work on the establishment of harmonised macroeconomic policies, particularly exchange, financial and fiscal policies. To sum up, regional integration in Latin America has been based on policies which underlined trade in goods and do not prepare the region for the changes and effects of the international economy, leaving it vulnerable to external factors.

B. Are the Economies in the Region Really Open?

In order to assess the question about the degree of openness of the

121 Juan F. Rojas Penso, *The Effects of the Crisis on Integration*, 57 CAPITULOS DEL SERA 33, 33 (1999).

122 *See* SELA & AECI, THE ECONOMIC LABYRINTH. THE AGENDA OF LATIN AMERICA AND THE CARIBBEAN TO COPE WITH THE INTERNATIONAL FINANCIAL CRISIS (Ediciones Corregidor, 1999).

123 ECLAC, PRELIMINARY OVERVIEW OF THE ECONOMIES OF LATIN AMERICA AND THE CARIBBEAN 2003, (December 2003), http://www.eclac.cl/publicaciones/ DesarrolloEconomico/ 3/LcG2223PI/lcg2223-i.pdf, last visited March 20, 2004. *See* also NORMAL GIRVAN, THE LOST HALF DECADE IN LATIN AMERICA AND THE CARIBBEAN, http://www.acs-aec.org/column/ index66.htm, last visited March 20, 2004.

economies of the region, this section compares the 12 LAIA country members during the period in which open regionalism has been in place. To that end, it takes the *Index of Economic Freedom* issued by The Heritage Foundation and The Wall Street Journal.[124] The *Index* uses a methodology[125] which measures the degree of economic freedom in a considerable number of countries around the globe.

According to the *Index*, economic freedom is defined as ' the absence of government coercion or constraint on the production, distribution, or consumption of goods and services beyond the extent necessary for citizens to protect and maintain liberty itself.'[126] To measure economic freedom and rate each country, the authors of the *Index* established 10 broad categories or factors of economic freedom, which are weighted equally.

These categories comprise Trade policy, Fiscal burden of government, Government intervention in the economy, Monetary policy, Capital flows and foreign investment, Banking and finance, Wages and prices, Property rights, Regulation, and Informal market activity.

Each factor is graded according to a unique scale, which runs from 1 to 5: A score of 1 signifies an economic environment or set of policies that are most conducive to economic freedom. A score of 5 signifies a set of policies that are least conducive to economic freedom. The four broad categories of economic freedom in the *Index* are as follows: FREE: countries with an average overall score of 1.99 or less. MOSTLY FREE: countries with an average overall score of 2.00 to 2.99. MOSTLY UNFREE: countries with an average overall score of 3.00 to 3.99; and REPRESSED: countries with an average overall score of 4.00 or higher.

Table VII shows the overall score of the LAIA member countries during the last 10 years. Chile is the single country in the region which has scored (2002 and 2004) within the category of those regarded as 'Free' countries by the Index. Chile is a member of none of the sub-regional arrangements in Latin America, as it adopted an independent model of development. The country has engaged individually in numerous trade treaties not only with countries in the region but also with the US. In this sense, the index reflects the effects of the coherent external policy of the country and the implementation of the reforms required to immerse Chile in the global economy. However, the average score of the last 10 years reveals it as a 'Mostly Free' country.

[124] For more information *See* http://www.heritage.org/research/features/index/, last visited March 20, 2004.

[125] The methodology is explained by The Heritage Foundation and The Wall Street Journal in the document *Index of Economic Freedom 2004*, [hereinafter *Index*], Chapter 5, at 49–70, http://www.heritage.org/research/features/index/countryFiles/English/2004Index.pdf, last visited March 20, 2004.

[126] *Id.* at 50.

The first four countries within the table comprise MERCOSUR. Argentina and Uruguay present an average, which define them as 'Mostly Free countries' whereas Brazil and Paraguay are among those regarded as 'Mostly Unfree countries' by the *Index*. During the last three years all these countries present a tendency to increase their score, which reveals an inclination to close their markets. Comparing their score in 1995 and the average score of the last 10 years, excepting Paraguay, the other MERCOSUR member countries display an overall tendency towards opening their markets.

The next five countries encompass the Andean Community. Two members, Bolivia and Peru are considered among the 'Mostly Free countries' according to the average of the last ten years. Colombia, Ecuador and Venezuela rank as 'Mostly Unfree countries'.

Mexico, being a member of NAFTA, registers an average which categorises it as a 'Mostly Unfree' country. Only during the last three years has its score defined Mexico as a 'Mostly Free' country. However, there is a slight tendency towards increasing the score.

Table VIII displays the first one of the 10 categories or factors included in the *Index,* as it is considered a key factor in measuring economic freedom: the trade policy.[127] It is 'The trade policy score is based on a country's weighted average tariff rate—weighted by imports from the country's trading partners. The higher the rate, the worse (or higher) the score.'[128]

Score 1 indicates that the level of protectionism is 'very low'. The weighted average tariff rate is less than or equal to 4 percent. In score 2, the level of protectionism is 'low'. The weighted-average tariff rate is greater than 4 percent but less than or equal to 9 percent. As for score 3, the level of protectionism is 'moderate'. The weighted average tariff rate is greater than 9 percent but less than or equal to 14 percent. Score 4, the level of protectionism is 'high'. The weighted average tariff rate is greater than 14 percent but less than or equal to 19 percent. Finally, in score 5 the level of protectionism is 'very high' as the weighted average tariff rate is greater than 19 percent.

Comparing the level of protectionism as it was evaluated in 1995 to the average of each country during the last ten years, all countries except for Bolivia, register a reduction in the score. It indicates an overall tendency towards reducing protectionism. However, during the last three years the inclination of the countries has been either to preserve the level of protectionism in place in 2002 or to augment it. Argentina, Brazil, Paraguay, Ecuador, Venezuela, Chile and Mexico kept the same score. Bolivia, Colombia and Peru, all members of the Andean Community, increased it.

When examining the countries according to the sub-regional schemes,

[127] *Id.* at 52–53. [128] *Id.* at 52.

Table VII Overall Score

Country	1995	1996	1997	1998	1999	2000	2001	2002	2003	2004	Average
Argentina	2.85	2.63	2.75	2.53	2.28	2.23	2.29	2.58	3.04	3.48	2.666
Brazil	3.46	3.56	3.28	3.36	3.19	3.46	3.21	3.06	3.01	3.10	3.269
Paraguay	2.94	2.89	2.91	3.04	3.00	3.01	3.39	3.28	3.40	3.39	3.125
Uruguay	3.03	2.85	2.60	2.59	2.60	2.50	2.30	2.51	2.45	2.55	2.598
Bolivia	3.21	2.61	2.56	2.61	2.61	2.61	2.31	2.66	2.59	2.59	2.636
Colombia	3.10	3.15	3.23	3.19	2.99	3.14	3.00	2.94	3.10	3.13	3.097
Ecuador	3.39	3.33	3.21	3.10	3.09	3.14	3.51	3.60	3.58	3.60	3.355
Peru	3.59	3.06	3.03	2.96	2.66	2.64	2.61	2.88	2.86	2.83	2.912
Venezuela	3.28	3.63	3.58	3.43	3.48	3.43	3.78	3.88	3.71	4.18	3.638
Chile	2.60	2.61	2.26	2.10	2.13	2.04	2.03	1.88	2.01	1.91	2.157
Mexico	3.10	3.31	3.35	3.41	3.25	3.09	3.05	2.96	2.81	2.90	3.123
Cuba	4.95	5.00	4.90	4.95	4.90	4.88	4.88	4.88	4.43	4.08	4.785

the biggest countries within MERCOSUR display a tendency towards high protectionism. Argentina fluctuates between moderate and high scores whereas Brazil ranks among high and very high protectionism. On the contrary, the smallest countries are disposed towards low protectionism. The same score found in 1995 is present in all countries in 2002. Except Uruguay, whose average declined one point in 2004, the other three MERCOSUR countries have the same score.

The principle of open regionalism relies primarily on the fact that countries open their markets to members and no-members to trade. The *Index* shows that the actual level of protectionism is the same as the one registered in 1995. Therefore, the *Index* suggests that open regionalism has made little impact in the sub-region during the last ten years as far as trade policy is concerned.

In the case of the Andean Community, member countries show an overall reduction in the score comparing the average of the last then years with that registered in 1995. Bolivia increased its score as in 1995 it ranked 'low' protectionism but it has moved to 'moderate' within the last to years. Colombia, Ecuador and Venezuela are countries inclined to preserve the same level of protectionism recorded by the *Index* in 1995. Peru, which scored 'very high' on the scale in 1995, reached a 'low' level for three years (1998–2000). However, its tendency during the last four years is for a high level of protectionism. As evidenced in the MERCOSUR countries and based on the *Index*, trade policy in the Andean countries does not reflect the effects that the implementation of open regionalism should produce.

Chile registers an important reduction of its position on the scale. In 1995 its level of protectionism was considered 'high'. Since 1997 it has recorded a 'low' level. The results are in accordance with the market-oriented strategy of the country. Mexico has also decreased its score from moderate (1995) to low (1999), excepting year 2000 when it ranked 'high' turning into 'low' again the following year.

After more than a decade of implementing policies and carrying out structural reforms it seems that Latin American economies are not that open and integration with countries and schemes out of the region have not been accomplished yet. Furthermore, there is a threatening tendency towards protectionism within a certain degree of political populism, which may constitute some hindrance to the real efforts towards South-South and North-South integration.

V. CONCLUDING REMARKS

The propagation of regional, sub-regional and bilateral treaties, institutions and arrangements has responded to the valid aspiration of the Latin

Table VIII Trade policy score

Country	1995	1996	1997	1998	1999	2000	2001	2002	2003	2004	Average
Argentina	4	4	4	4	3	3	3	4	4	4	3.7
Brazil	4	4	4	4	4	5	4	4	4	4	4.1
Paraguay	3	2	2	2	2	2	3	3	3	3	2.5
Uruguay	3	3	2	2	2	2	1	3	3	2	2.3
Bolivia	2	2	2	2	2	2	2	2	3	3	3.5
Colombia	4	4	4	3	3	3	3	3	4	4	3.5
Ecuador	4	4	3	3	3	3	4	4	4	4	3.6
Peru	5	4	3	2	2	2	3	3	4	4	3.2
Venezuela	4	4	4	3	3	3	4	4	4	4	3.7
Chile	4	4	2	2	2	2	2	2	2	2	2.4
Mexico	3	3	3	3	2	4	2	2	2	2	2.6
Cuba	5	5	5	5	5	5	5	5	3	3	4.6

American and Caribbean countries to explore the structures and policies which better suit and represent the needs of their overall population and interest groups.

This chapter has discussed South-South Latin American regionalism from the perspective of its main features and their correlation with open regionalism. Granting of differential treatment and preferences has brought about complexity, confusion and legal uncertainty in the region. At the same time, integration being a politically led process, political intrusion, lack of understanding, improvisation and incoherent strategies have affected the process of integration as a whole, as the structures created to implement it depend entirely on the political will of the governments.

Equally, the heavily institutionalised structures and forums have become dysfunctional. As Latin American regionalism has the propensity towards crowded internal structures, bureaucracy is a damaging consequence. In addition, governments seek other forums different from those already created within the regions or sub-regions. It duplicates efforts and makes inefficient use of the limited resources. Furthermore, regional integration in Latin America has been based on policies which underlined trade in goods and do not prepare the region for the changes and effects of the international economy leaving it defenceless against external factors.

As the definition of Open regionalism contains the features present in the Latin American processes of integration, their weaknesses affect not only the region but also its relationships with other countries and blocs.

Regional Integration in Latin America is akin to an organic process. Its common elements interact together affecting each other organically. Therefore all must be fine-tuned. By strengthening their weaknesses, open regionalism will conduct to the construction of building blocks aimed at procuring a balanced immersion within the global economy.

In this regard, there is a need to articulate the various regional, sub-regional trilateral and bilateral treaties in order to direct open regionalism towards more effective multilateralism. Convergence should be attained through the different mechanisms established within LAIA and by the political will of the governments of the member countries aimed at clarifying and establishing a common treatment to the products within the region, bearing in mind the principle of differential treatment. The implementation of the agreed Free Trade Area between the Andean Community and MERCOSUR should end the complexity created by the Regional and Partial Scope Agreements actually in force.

The recent developments within the region and the negotiations towards a hemispheric agreement require the governments to use, sustain, modernise and consolidate the regional institutions, bodies and organs in charge of providing articulation and coordination. It implies a serious effort of coordination among domestic government officials, decision-making bodies and organs of consultation.

The evolution and dynamism of the process have produced a complex network of bodies, institutions and organs, which have lost their influence in procuring the required convergence, coordination and cooperation. By re-examining the Latin American and the Caribbean integration framework and correcting the weaknesses present in the features discussed, the region as a bloc will find a balanced immersion in the global economy. As all this requires a major political commitment, much work needs to be done in order to put pressure on the Latin American governments to plan, carry out and comply with the reforms needed.

CHAPTER FOURTEEN

Expanding Trade Remedies Unilaterally: The Byrd Amendment *Case and the United States Against the World*

*by Raj Bhala**

CHAPTER OUTLINE

I. America Against the World
II. Points of Contention
III. The Bottom Line
IV. 'Specific' and the Constituent Elements Test
V. 'Against' and the Adverse Bearing Test
VI. Why Fight this Case?
VII. Non-Compliance?

I. AMERICA AGAINST THE WORLD[1]

It is only a modest exaggeration to characterize the *Byrd Amendment* controversy as yet another international trade case pitting the United States

* Rice Distinguished Professor, The University of Kansas, School of Law, Green Hall, 1535 West 15th Street, Lawrence, KS 66045-7577 U.S.A. Tel. 785-864-9224. Fax. 785-864-5054. www.law.ku.edu. J.D., Harvard (1989); M.Sc., Oxford (1986); M.Sc., London School of Economics (1985); A.B., Duke (1984). Marshall Scholar (1984-86). Author of *Trade, Development, and Social Justice* (Carolina Academic Press 2003) and *GATT Law* (Sweet and Maxwell, forthcoming 2005). This Chapter is modified from the *WTO Case Review 2003*, 21 ARIZONA JOURNAL OF INTERNATIONAL AND COMPARATIVE LAW spring 2004 (co-authored with Professor David Gantz), in which the discussion of the *Byrd Amendment* case first appeared.

[1] The discussion of the facts of the case is drawn from World Trade Organization, *Update of WTO Dispute Settlement Cases*, WT/DS/OV/16, at 115–17 (17 Oct. 2003) (available on the WTO web site, www.wto.org); Report of the Panel, *United States—Continued Dumping and Subsidy Offset Act of 2000*, WT/DS217/R, WT/DS234/R, at ¶¶ 1.1–2.7 (issued 16 Sept. 2002, adopted as modified by the Appellate Body 8 Jan. 2003).

The Appellate Body Report in the case is *United States—Continued Dumping and Subsidy Offset Act of 2000*, WT/DS217/AB/R, WT/DS234/AB/R (issued 16 January 2003, adopted 27 January 2003) (joint complaint by Australia, Brazil, Chile, European Communities, India, Indonesia, Japan, Korea, and Thailand, and joint complaint by Canada and Mexico). Like all

against the world. Obviously, several, but not all, Members of the World Trade Organization ('WTO') were complainants against the United States. What is hardly an exaggeration at all is to characterize this case as a unilateral attempt by the United States to expand antidumping ('AD') and countervailing duty ('CVD') remedies beyond the boundaries permitted by applicable WTO agreements. The purpose, then, of the present Chapter is not only to review the important facts, holdings, and rationales of the *Byrd Amendment* case, but also to set this case in the American and international political and economic contexts in which it arose.

The *Continued Dumping and Subsidy Offset Act of 2000*, sometimes referred to by its acronym '*CDSOA*,' but more typically as the '*Byrd Amendment*' (after its legislative sponsor, Senator Robert Byrd (D-W.Va.)), is an addition to title VII of the United States Tariff Act of 1930.[2] From its inception, this *Amendment* generated heated rhetoric, even from *The Economist*, which wrote:

> Could Robert Byrd be taking lessons from Ariel Sharon? . . . Only days after Mr. Sharon inflamed Israeli-Palestinian tensions, the cantankerous former majority leader of the Senate pushed through a piece of legislation that could torpedo the fragile transatlantic détente on trade.

Mr. Byrd has become something of a loose cannon in the Senate of late, but little could compare with his latest antics.[3]

Not surprisingly, even the way in which the *Amendment* came about was controversial—it was an attachment to an $80 billion agriculture appropriations bill.[4] That bill—the 'Agriculture, Rural Development, Food and Drug Administration, and Related Agencies Appropriations Act for FY 2001'—extended the dairy price support program and provided for direct market loss payments to American farmers, funded the export loan

WTO reports, the Panel and Appellate Body decisions in the *Byrd Amendment* case are available on the web site of the WTO, www.wto.org. The texts of the WTO agreements discussed in this Chapter are available on this web site, and published in a variety of sources, including Raj Bhala, *International Trade Law Handbook* (2nd ed. 2001).

To minimize footnotes in this Chapter, citations are provided to indicate sources from which the sections of the Chapter are drawn.

[2] The *Byrd Amendment* is part of Public Law 106–387, 114 Stat. 1549, 28 Oct. 2000, §§ 1001–1003, codified at 19 U.S.C. § 1675c. Section 1675c is entitled 'Continued Dumping and Subsidy Offset,' and in 2001, the United States Customs Service (now formally called the 'Customs and Border Patrol') promulgated regulations implementing this Section. *See Distribution of Continued Dumping and Subsidy Offset to Affected Domestic Producers*, 66 FED. REG. 48,546 (21 Sept. 2001), codified at 19 C.F.R. §§159.61–159.64. Interestingly, Public Law 106–387 is not a trade bill, but rather a bill dealing with agriculture and agriculture-related issues, and is entitled the *Agriculture, Rural Development, Food and Drug Administration and Related Agencies Appropriations Act, 2001*.

[3] *For the Byrds*, THE ECONOMIST, Oct. 21, 2000, at 88.

[4] Edward Alden & Guy de Jonquières, *Dumping Move Attracts EU Ire*, FINANCIAL TIMES, Oct. 10, 2000, at 4 (mentioning the spending bill).

program of the Commodity Credit Corporation, and eased sanctions on food and medicine for Cuba, Libya, North Korea, and Sudan (and codified restrictions on travel to Cuba).[5] By tossing the *Amendment* into a bill of this nature, the likelihood of a Presidential veto was reduced.

Swift opposition to the *Amendment* came not only from the Clinton Administration, which explained the ideas contained in the *Amendment* were considered and rejected by Congress during the debate about the Uruguay Round agreements, but also from the National Taxpayers Union, which was concerned that American companies might engage in 'bounty hunting' at government expense (*i.e.*, they might file 'frivolous' trade remedy actions because they have nothing to lose).[6] The incentive would be particularly strong for small companies, which typically feel stymied from using trade remedies because of the high legal costs in bringing a case.[7] In turn, the basic tests used in antidumping ('AD') and countervailing duty ('CVD') cases to ensure a domestic industry supports a petition—the 25 percent and 50 percent tests[8]—would be adulterated by this incentive, as companies registered support in the hopes of receiving payments in a successful case.

What, exactly, does the *Byrd Amendment* say? The *Amendment* applies to all AD and CVD orders issued in the United States on or after 1 October 2000. The essence of the *Amendment* is it gives the duties collected in these trade remedy cases 'to the companies that the duties are designed to protect.'[9] The key part of the *Amendment* states:

> *Duties assessed pursuant to a countervailing duty order, an antidumping duty order*, or a finding under the Antidumping Act of 1921, *shall be distributed* on an annual basis under this section [Section 754, 19 U.S.C. § 1675c] *to the affected domestic producers for qualifying expenditures*. Such distribution shall be known as 'the continued dumping and subsidy offset.'[10]

In turn, the definition of 'affected domestic producers' divides the universe into entities 'for' and 'against' the petition, and shows a distinct preference for the first category.

This definition encompasses essentially any successful petitioner, or

[5] *See President Signs Controversial Agriculture Appropriations Bill*, 17 International Trade Reporter (BNA) 1687 (Nov. 2, 2000) (also reporting the appropriations value as $78 billion).

[6] *For the Byrds*, THE ECONOMIST, Oct. 21, 2000, at 88, 89.

[7] *See* Edward Alden & Guy de Jonquières, *Dumping Move Attracts EU Ire*, FINANCIAL TIMES, Oct. 10, 2000, at 4 (mentioning these costs).

[8] These tests for standing to file a petition are explained in Raj Bhala, *International Trade Law: Theory and Practice* 888 (2nd ed. 2001). In brief, at least 25 percent of total production of the like product of the domestic industry, and more than 50 percent of domestic like product production expressing a view (either support for or opposition to) the petition, must support the petition.

[9] *For the Byrds*, THE ECONOMIST, Oct. 21, 2000, at 88, 89.

[10] 19 U.S.C. §1675c(a) (emphasis added).

supporter of a successful petitioner. It obviously excludes opponents of the petition, but also goes on to cut out successor entities related to any opponent of the initial AD or CVD investigation:

> [An 'affected domestic producer' is] a manufacturer, producer, farmer, rancher, or worker representative (including associations of such persons) that –
> (A) was a petitioner or interested party in support of the petition with respect to which an antidumping duty order, a finding under the Antidumping Act of 1921, or a countervailing duty order has been entered, and
> (B) remains in operation.

Companies, businesses, or persons that have ceased the production of the product covered by the order or finding or *who have been acquired by a company or business that is related to a company that opposed the investigation shall not be an affected domestic producer.*[11]

What are the 'qualifying expenditures' on which an 'affected domestic producer' can spend the offset? The *Byrd Amendment* allows for ten uses of the offset: (1) manufacturing facilities; (2) equipment; (3) research and development; (4) personnel training; (5) technology; (6) employee health care benefits (if they are paid for by the employer); (7) employee pension benefits (again, if they are paid for by the employer); (8) environmental equipment, training, or technology; (9) raw materials and other inputs; and (10) working capital or other funds necessary to maintain production.[12]

In practice, the offset is collected (like any other AD duty or CVD) by the Customs and Border Protection (the new name for the United States Customs Service, following its placement under the Department of Homeland Security). However, unlike the logistics in pre-*Byrd Amendment* AD or CVD practice, the Customs Service deposits the offset into a special account held at the United States Department of the Treasury. (As of October 2000, when the *Byrd Amendment* was enacted, one report stated the Treasury Department collects about $40 million annually in AD duties and CVDs, though a different report put the figure at $125 million.[13]) The Customs Service also receives from the International Trade Commission ('ITC') a list of 'affected domestic producers,' in connection with each AD or CVD order, who are eligible to receive the offset.[14]

Upon certification by an affected domestic producer it is eligible to receive the offset and it desires the offset for a qualifying expenditure incurred since the AD or CVD order was issued, the Customs Service disburses the offset to that producer. The Customs Service makes the distri-

[11] 19 U.S.C. § 1675c(b)(1) (emphasis added).

[12] *See* 19 U.S.C. § 1675c(b)(4) (listing the 'qualifying expenditure[s]' in items (A)–(J)).

[13] *See* Sebastian Mallaby, *Byrd Poison*, WASHINGTON POST, Oct. 23, 2000, at A23 (mentioning the $125 million statistic); Edward Alden & Guy de Jonquières, *Dumping Move Attracts EU Ire*, FINANCIAL TIMES, Oct. 10, 2000, at 4 (mentioning the $40 million statistic).

[14] *See* 19 U.S.C. § 1675c(d)(1).

butions from all assessed AD duties and CVDs (including interest earned thereon) it obtained in the preceding fiscal year, and does so within 60 days of the beginning of the subsequent fiscal year. If the sum total of certified claims equals or is less than the total amount of offset available, then each affected domestic producer with a certified claim is paid in full. If the sum of certified claims exceeds the total available offset, then each claimant is paid a *pro rata* amount calculated on the basis of its claim. Shortly after an AD or CVD order is terminated, and all merchandise subject to the order has been liquidated and duties assessed have been collected, the special account into which offset monies had been deposited also is terminated.

Put succinctly, one way to characterize the *Byrd Amendment* is it establishes a 'victim's compensation fund' for petitioners in AD or CVD cases who have proved themselves to have been materially injured by dumping or subsidization (or threatened with material injury). The *Amendment* channels duties collected in these cases to the victims—the 'affected domestic producers' of dumped or subsidized imports. The victims then may spend the funds on programs that might help them recover from these unfairly traded imports. Characterized in this noble-sounding manner, how could the Congress reject the idea? The measure passed the House of Representatives on 11 October 2000, and the Senate on 18 October.[15] Not wanting to delay the rest of the legislation to which the *Byrd Amendment* was attached (including essential spending), President Clinton signed the *Amendment* into law on 28 October 2000.[16] As he told reporters, 'I decided on balance this bill advances the interests of the American people. That's why I signed it, and that's how progress is made, when we work together and have honorable compromise. No one gets everything he or she wants.'[17]

Of course, the noble characterization was not the one adopted by most of America's trading partners, and even by many American observers, and the President's pragmatic justification was unpersuasive to them. Member after Member of the WTO accused the United States of flagrantly violating its multilateral trade law commitments, particularly under the *General Agreement on Tariffs and Trade* ('*GATT*') and Uruguay Round *Agreement on Implementation of Article VI of the General Agreement on Tariffs and Trade 1994* (the '*Antidumping Agreement*,' or '*AD Agreement*'), the Uruguay Round *Agreement on Subsidies and Countervailing Measures* ('*SCM Agreement*'). The spokesman for the European Union ('EU'),

[15] Rossella Brevetti *et al.*, *EU, Japan Weighing WTO Challenge to Byrd Amendment Dumping Provision*, 17 International Trade Reporter (BNA) 1682 (Nov. 2, 2000).

[16] *For the Byrds*, THE ECONOMIST, Oct. 21, 2000, at 88, 89.

[17] President Bill Clinton, *quoted in* Rossella Brevetti *et al.*, *EU, Japan Weighing WTO Challenge to Byrd Amendment Dumping Provision*, 17 International Trade Reporter (BNA) 1682 (Nov. 2, 2000).

Anthony Gooch, said '[i]t isn't just a U.S.-EU problem but a rest-of-the world trading problem. The U.S. will have problems with everyone.'[18] The Japanese Vice Minister of International Trade, Katsusada Hirose, offered the same point: 'This is a problem of concern to many countries around the world, not just Japan alone.'[19]

In brief, the critics charged the WTO agreements already set AD duties and CVDs to offset unfair foreign pricing and subsidization, respectively, and 'handing them [the duties] over as subsidies to domestic firms adds a second layer of protection.'[20] In other words, the EC and many other WTO Members accused the United States of concocting 'a double protection for domestic U.S. industry.'[21] They urged 'WTO rules allow only for governments to impose tariffs against dumped [or illegally subsidized] products, not to pass those monies on to domestic competitors.'[22] One American observer added:

> The most charitable view of Byrd's law is that it is simple pork, provided for the benefit of the steel industry in his native West Virginia [a major user of AD and CVD law]. . . .

Protectionists in the Senate have been pushing cash prizes for years, but the idea was always defeated on the merits. For one thing, the scheme may well be illegal under World Trade Organization rules; and if it isn't, other countries will copy the idea to keep out U.S. products. For another, the whole body of anti-dumping law penalizes U.S. firms that depend on competitive imports. There is not much sense protecting steel when steel-using industries—cars, industrial machinery, construction and so on—employ many times as many workers.[23]

[18] *Quoted in* Rossella Brevetti *et al.*, *EU, Japan Weighing WTO Challenge to Byrd Amendment Dumping Provision*, 17 International Trade Reporter (BNA) 1682 (Nov. 2, 2000).

[19] *Quoted in* Rossella Brevetti *et al.*, *EU, Japan Weighing WTO Challenge to Byrd Amendment Dumping Provision*, 17 International Trade Reporter (BNA) 1682 (Nov. 2, 2000).

[20] *For the Byrds*, THE ECONOMIST, Oct. 21, 2000, at 88, 89.

[21] Guenter Burghardt, Ambassador from the European Union to the United States, *quoted in* Edward Alden & Guy de Jonquières, *Dumping Move Attracts EU Ire*, FINANCIAL TIMES, Oct. 10, 2000, at 4. *See also* Daniel Pruzin, *WTO Members Denounce Adoption of Byrd Amendment by United States*, 17 International Trade Reporter (BNA) 1699 (Nov. 9, 2000) (reporting on the opposition from Australia, Brazil, Canada, Chile, India, Mexico, New Zealand, South Africa, and South Korea, and the Brazilian characterization of the offset as 'triple protection'—targeted companies pay, American firms profit, and American firms receive an unfair subsidy to the detriment of foreign competitors).

[22] Edward Alden & Guy de Jonquières, *Dumping Move Attracts EU Ire*, FINANCIAL TIMES, Oct. 10, 2000, at 4 (mentioning this statistic).

[23] Sebastian Mallaby, *Byrd Poison*, WASHINGTON POST, Oct. 23, 2000, at A23. Not surprisingly, among the American groups opposed to the *Byrd Amendment*, and vowing to help seek its repeal, were the Consuming Industries Trade Action Coalition and the National Foreign Trade Council. *See* Gary G. Yerkey *et al.*, *EU Could Move Against 'Byrd Amendment' in WTO as Early as this Week, Official Says*, 17 International Trade Reporter (BNA) 1626.

Fortunately, the controversy did not descend to the level of other WTO Members unilaterally enacting *Byrd Amendment* analogs. However, when the consultation phase of WTO dispute proceedings failed, 11 Members eagerly filed actions against the United States (in two joint complaints, filed in July and August, 2001). Even formation of a panel was difficult. The WTO Director-General stepped in to determine its composition, at the request of the complaints, pursuant to Article 8:7 of the WTO *Understanding on the Rules and Procedures Governing the Settlement of Disputes* ('*DSU*').

II. POINTS OF CONTENTION[24]

The Panel, established in October 2001, took until the following September to issue its report. When it did, the United States was faced with a stark choice: repeal the *Byrd Amendment*, as the Panel recommended, or appeal. The Panel held the *Amendment* violated Articles 5:4, 18:1, and 18:4 of the *AD Agreement*, Articles 11:4, 32:1, and 32:5 of the *SCM Agreement*, and Articles VI:1-2 of *GATT*.[25] The United States took little time in making its choice: in October 2002, it chose to fight on. What were the grounds for the appeal? The United States argued the Panel had erred in all of these holdings.

Specifically, the United States argued the *Byrd Amendment* is a permissible, specific action against dumping or subsidization, and thus is consistent with Article 18:1 of the *AD Agreement* and Article 32:1 of the *SCM Agreement*. Both provisions deal with the range (or lack thereof) of permissible remedies. Article 18:1 of the *AD Agreement* states simply: 'No *specific* action *against* dumping of exports from another [WTO] Member can be taken except *in accordance with* the provisions of GATT 1994, as interpreted by this Agreement [emphasis added].' (A footnote to the provision clarifies that Article 18:1 does not preclude action under other relevant WTO agreements.) Article 32:1 of the *SCM Agreement* is nearly a *verbatim* text: 'No *specific* action *against* a subsidy of another [WTO] Member can be taken except *in accordance with* the provisions of GATT 1994, as interpreted by this Agreement [emphasis added].' (A footnote nearly identical to that for Article 18:1 follows this provision.)

[24] This discussion is drawn from World Trade Organization, *Update of WTO Dispute Settlement Cases*, WT/DS/OV/16, at 115–17 (17 Oct. 2003) (available on the WTO web site, www.wto.org); Report of the Panel, *United States—Continued Dumping and Subsidy Offset Act of 2000*, WT/DS217/R, WT/DS234/R, at ¶¶1.1–2.7 (issued 16 Sept. 2002, adopted as modified by the Appellate Body 8 Jan. 2003).

[25] The Panel also ruled the *Byrd Amendment* violated Article XVI:4 of the Uruguay Round *Agreement Establishing the World Trade Organization* ('*WTO Agreement*'), and agreed it nullifies or impairs benefits accruing to the complaints under the relevant agreements.

Moreover, because the *Byrd Amendment* is consistent with these provisions, the United States argued on appeal it does not run afoul of Article 18:4 of the *AD Agreement*, nor of Article 32:5 of the *SCM Agreement*. These provisions amount to guarantees provided by each WTO Member that its laws comply with the respective accords. Article 18:4 of the *AD Agreement* says: 'Each Member shall take all necessary steps, of a general or particular character, to ensure, not later than the date of entry into force of the WTO Agreement for it, the conformity of its laws, regulations and administrative procedures with the provisions of this Agreement as they may apply for the Member in question.' In parallel fashion, Article 32:5 of the *SCM Agreement* says: 'Each Member shall take all necessary steps, of a general or particular character, to ensure, not later than the date of entry into force of the WTO Agreement for it, the conformity of its laws, regulations and administrative procedures with the provisions of this Agreement as they may apply to the Member in question.'

III. THE BOTTOM LINE[26]

The Appellate Body rejected all of the arguments central to the American appeal. (The United States was successful in only one substantive aspect of its appeal—namely, that the *Byrd Amendment* itself was consistent with Article 5:4 of the *AD Agreement* and Article 11:4 of the *SCM Agreement*.[27]) The Appellate Body upheld the finding of the Panel. Specifically, the Appellate Body held the *Byrd Amendment* creates a non-permissible specific action against dumping and subsidization, in violation of Article 18:1 of the *AD Agreement* and Article 32:1 of the *SCM Agreement*, respectively.

[26] This discussion is drawn from World Trade Organization, *Update of WTO Dispute Settlement Cases*, WT/DS/OV/16, at 115–17 (17 Oct. 2003) (available on the WTO web site, www.wto.org); Report of the Appellate Body, *United States—Continued Dumping and Subsidy Offset Act of 2000*, WT/DS217/AB/R, WT/DS234/AB/R, at ¶¶224–274, 318 (issued 16 Jan. 2003, adopted 27 Jan. 2003) (hereinafter, '*Byrd Amendment* Appellate Body Report').

[27] Consequently, the Appellate Body agreed with the United States it had acted in good faith with respect to its commitments under Article 5:4 of the *AD Agreement* and Article 11:4 of the *SCM Agreement*, and reversed the Panel's finding to the contrary. *See Byrd Amendment* Appellate Body Report, *supra*, at ¶¶223(b), 275–99, 318(d)–(e).

In brief, Article 5:4 forbids the initiation of an AD investigation unless the authorities first determine the petition is supported by or on behalf of a domestic industry producing a product like that of the allegedly dumped merchandise. In making this determination, Article 5:4 obligates the authorities to make use of the 50 percent and 25 percent tests, *i.e.*, to check if the petition is supported by domestic like product producers whose collective output (1) is more than 50 percent of total production of the like product made by domestic firms expressing a view about the petition (either support or opposition), and (2) is 25 percent or more of total output of the like product by the entire domestic industry. Article 11:4 has the same requirements for CVD investigations.

As usual, the Appellate Body's recommendation was couched in the polite diplomatic phrases of public international law jargon. It requested the United States to bring the *Byrd Amendment* into conformity with WTO obligations. However, from an American perspective, in practice what that recommendation really said—and indeed, could only say, given the nature of the *Byrd Amendment*—was to repeal the law.

The Appellate Body based its reasoning on a straightforward interpretation of the ordinary meaning of the words in Articles 18:1 and 32:1 of the *AD* and *SCM Agreements*, respectively. Two words, in particular, are important: 'specific' and 'against.' The Appellate Body interpreted these words as pre-conditions for the application of the Articles to an AD or CVD measure.

That is, the Appellate Body held a measure must be 'specific' to dumping or subsidization, and it must be directed 'against' dumping or subsidization. Otherwise, the measure is not governed by the rules of Article 18:1 or 32:1. Assuming both conditions precedent exist, then the measure falls within the disciplines of these Articles. In that event, the measure is to be analyzed under them, which means it must be asked whether the measure was taken in accordance with the provisions of *GATT 1994*, as those provisions are amplified by the *AD* and *SCM Agreements*. Only if the scrutinized measure is not taken in accordance with these provisions does it run afoul of Article 18:1 or 32:1. In brief, the Appellate Body interpreted these Articles as creating a two-step test: first, is a measure subject to discipline under them, which is to say, is the measure a specific action against dumping or subsidization, and if so, then second, is the measure consistent with the *GATT*, *AD Agreement*, and *SCM Agreement*.

IV. 'SPECIFIC' AND THE CONSTITUENT ELEMENTS TEST[28]

In the first step of the test, the Appellate Body rested on its own precedent—the *United States—1916 Act* case.[29] The Appellate Body quoted from its earlier report:

> the ordinary meaning of the phrase 'specific action against dumping' of exports within the meaning of Article 18:1 is action that is taken in response to situations presenting the constituent elements of 'dumping.' 'Specific action against dumping' of exports must, at a minimum, encompass action that may be taken *only* when the constituent elements of 'dumping' are present.[30]

[28] This discussion is drawn from World Trade Organization, *Update of WTO Dispute Settlement Cases*, WT/DS/OV/16, at 115–17 (17 Oct. 2003) (available on the WTO web site, www.wto.org); *Byrd Amendment* Appellate Body Report, at ¶¶224–274, 318.

[29] *See* Raj Bhala & David Gantz, *WTO Case Review 2000*, 18 ARIZONA JOURNAL OF INTERNATIONAL & COMPARATIVE LAW 44 (2001) (discussing this case).

[30] *United States—1916 Act*, ¶122 (emphasis original), *quoted in Byrd Amendment* Appellate Body Report, ¶238.

In the earlier case, the United States argued unsuccessfully its Antidumping Act of 1916 did not fall within the scope of *GATT* Article VI because it was aimed at predatory pricing, not dumping. The Appellate Body rejected this argument, holding the 1916 Act was 'specific action against dumping.' It reasoned that the constituent elements of dumping were built into the essential elements for civil and criminal liability under the 1916 Act, and the way in which the Act is worded made clear liability could occur only if the constituent elements were present.

In the *Byrd Amendment* case, the Appellate Body simply applied the 'constituent elements' test. The Appellate Body held that a remedial measure may be imposed only when the constituent elements of dumping or a subsidy are present in a 'specific action' in response to dumping within the meaning of Article 18:1 of the *AD Agreement*, or in a 'specific action' in response to subsidization within the meaning of Article 32:1 of the *SCM Agreement*. What are those constituent elements? They are, as the Appellate Body reminded in its *Byrd Amendment* report, none other than the requirements for commencing an AD investigation set forth in Article VI:1 of *GATT* and elaborated on in Article 2 of the *AD Agreement*, and for commencing a CVD investigation set forth in Article 1 of the *SCM Agreement*.

Did the Appellate Body introduce any innovations with respect to the 'constituent elements' test it had established in the 1916 Act case? The answer is 'yes.' It introduced three innovations, though the first 'innovation' was hardly much of one. First, noting the nearly identical language in Article 18:1 of the *AD Agreement* and Article 32:1 of the *SCM Agreement*, the Appellate Body said the test applies to both texts.

Second, the Appellate Body squarely rejected the American argument that under the 'constituent elements' test, the elements of dumping or subsidization had to be mentioned in the statute being challenged. The United States urged, unsuccessfully, that a trade remedy could not be aimed specifically against dumping or subsidization unless the constituent elements of dumping or subsidization were among the essential components of the remedy. The Appellate Body found the American interpretation and application of the *1916 Act* case too narrow. It explained its *1916 Act* precedent does not require a statute to refer explicitly to the elements of dumping or subsidization, nor does it require those elements to be essential components in the statute, for that statute to be 'specific' to dumping or subsidization. Rather, what matters is the strength of the link, or degree of correlation, between the remedy and dumping or subsidization.

The question of linkage leads to the third noteworthy innovation in the Appellate Body's *Byrd Amendment* holding. It amplified on the 'constituent elements' test by clarifying that the connection between (1) the elements of dumping or subsidization and (2) the application of the measure must be strong. As the Appellate Body put it, so long as the measure is 'inextricably linked to,' or has 'a strong correlation with,' the constituent elements of dumping or a subsidy, then it is a 'specific action' subject to the discipline of these Articles. In the *1916 Act* case, the remedy could be applied only in an instance of conduct that includes the constituent elements of dumping—hence, the link was strong. A strong link can occur whether the constituent elements are expressly or implicitly referred to in a statute. The Appellate Body added that even if it were to put some stock in the narrow interpretation urged by the United States—namely, that an express link must be found in the statute—that interpretation would not help the American case. The *Byrd Amendment* clearly implies the presence of the constituent elements of dumping by expressly referring to duties assessed pursuant to an AD or CVD order.

Why, then, did the Appellate Body conclude the *Byrd Amendment*, itself, creates a 'specific' action aimed at dumping or subsidization? Put directly, because 'offset payments are *inextricably linked to*, and *strongly correlated with*, a determination of dumping, as defined in Article VI:1 of the GATT 1994 and in the *Anti-Dumping Agreement*, or a determination of a subsidy, as defined in the *SCM Agreement*.'[31] Indeed, the Appellate Body had no trouble applying its 'constituent elements' test to the Amendment. Offset payments could be made only after AD or CVD duties had been collected, these duties could be collected only pursuant to an AD or CVD order, and an order could be imposed only following a determination of dumping as defined in *GATT* and the *AD Agreement* or subsidization as defined in the *SCM Agreement*. What more of a clear, direct, and unavoidable connection between dumping or subsidization, on the one hand, and offset payments on the other hand, could possibly exist?[32]

[31] *Byrd Amendment* Appellate Body Report, ¶242 (emphasis added). The Appellate Body ought to have used the disjunctive ('or'), not the conjunctive ('and'), because an inextricable link surely would mean a strong correlation, but not *vice versa*.

[32] The Appellate Body also rejected the American argument that footnote 24 of the *AD Agreement*, and footnote 56 of the SCM Agreement, permit (respectively) dumping and subsidy remedies that are not 'specific actions' within the meaning of Article 18:1 of the *AD Agreement* or Article 32:1 of the *SCM Agreement*. In other words, urged the United States, the footnotes authorize any measure that is not a 'specific action' within the ambit of those Articles. The Appellate Body said the American argument essentially treated the footnotes as primary textual provisions, and accorded the Articles a residual status. In truth, the footnotes are accessory, and are designed to clarify the Articles. The clarification is simply that if an action is not 'specific' under Article 18:1 or 32:1, under the constituent elements test from the *1916 Act* case, but is related to dumping or subsidization, then these Articles do not prohibit the action. *See Byrd Amendment* Appellate Body Report, ¶¶260-62.

V. 'AGAINST' AND THE ADVERSE BEARING TEST[33]

As indicated earlier, there are two conditions precedent in Article 18:1 of the *AD Agreement* and Article 32:1 of the *SCM Agreement*—a measure must be both 'specific' to dumping or subsidization and 'against' dumping or subsidization. In the *1916 Act* case, the Appellate Body did not have to opine on the word 'against.' But, in the *Byrd Amendment* case it could not avoid interpreting what the word means.

The United States constructed a hypothetical scenario in which it decides to spend *Byrd Amendment* funds to cover international emergency relief. It argued that if spending the offset on a foreign relief project were impermissible under Article 18:1 and Article 32:1, then any expenditure of duties collected in dumping or subsidy cases would be illegal under WTO obligations. At first glance, the argument sounds like a scary slippery slope, in that the United States is challenging the Appellate Body not to over-reach and regulate every expenditure of collected duties. However, the Appellate Body stood its ground, pointing out a fatal flaw in the American argument: spending money for international emergency assistance would not be 'against' dumping or subsidization. Indeed, that expenditure would have no effect at all on the unfair trade practice. That is, the American argument ignored the second condition precedent.

How, then, did the Appellate Body analyze the word 'against'? The Panel defined 'against' as 'adverse bearing,' and held that duties collected in an AD or CVD case are 'against' dumping or subsidization if they have a direct or indirect 'adverse bearing on dumping or subsidization,' even if the remedy does not apply directly to the imported good or to the entity responsible for that good. In effect, the Panel likened 'against' to a burdensome effect on dumping or subsidization. The United States called for a more rigorous definition than what the Panel offered, saying 'against' means the remedy must come into contact with the wrongful act or wrongdoer, and pointing to the *New Shorter Oxford English Dictionary* ('*OED*') definition of 'against,' which lists 'in contact with' as a meaning. Even more specifically, argued the United States, the word 'against' means active, hostile opposition, and presumes that the remedy operates directly on the imported dumped or subsidized merchandise, or the entity responsible for that merchandise.

The United States was right to turn to the favorite lexicographic source for the meaning of 'against.' It might well have expected a more favorable ruling from the Appellate Body on this issue, as the Appellate Body on

[33] This discussion is drawn from World Trade Organization, *Update of WTO Dispute Settlement Cases*, WT/DS/OV/16, at 115-17 (17 Oct. 2003) (available on the WTO web site, www.wto.org); *Byrd Amendment* Appellate Body Report, at ¶¶224–274, 318.

countless previous occasions had looked to the *OED*. Not so, however, as the Appellate Body (amazingly, perhaps) said '[i]t should be remembered that dictionaries are *important guides to*, *not dispositive statements* of, definitions of words appearing in agreements and legal documents.'[34] Fair enough, but was the Appellate Body then guilty of cafeteria plan lexicography, using the *OED* in cases in which it found that dictionary helpful to the result it sought?

Leaving that uncertainty aside, the Appellate Body opined that 'in contact with' refers to physical contact between two objects, *i.e.*, tangible things touching one another. That context is entirely irrelevant to duties imposed in an AD or CVD case. In turn, the American view that the duties must have direct contact with imported merchandise or the entity responsible for that merchandise is unsustainable. The Appellate Body put the *OED* aside, turned to the *Vienna Convention on the Law of Treaties*, and looked at the text of Article 18:1 of the *AD Agreement* and Article 32:1 of the *SCM Agreement*. Its textual analysis uncovered no express requirement in either provision that a dumping or subsidy measure act directly against the imported merchandise, or the producers or importers of the merchandise.

Likewise, reasoned the Appellate Body, the object and purpose of these provisions do not support the incorporation into them, through the term 'against,' of a requirement that a dumping or subsidy remedy must come into direct contact with imported merchandise or the entity responsible for the merchandise. Both provisions are designed to circumscribe the range of actions a WTO Member can take unilaterally to counteract dumping or subsidization. Under the American interpretation, any measure not coming into direct contact with the imported merchandise or responsible entity would not be subject to the discipline of Article 18:1 or Article 32:1. In other words, WTO Members would be free to apply indirect measures against dumping and subsidization—and that freedom would undermine the object and purpose of these provisions.

What, then, does 'against' mean? The Appellate Body upheld the Panel's definition. The word meant an AD or CVD measure has an adverse bearing on the practice of dumping or subsidization, in the sense of dissuading these practices, or creating an incentive to terminate them. In design and structure, the *Byrd Amendment*, said the Appellate Body, has exactly these effects.

Why? First, because the Amendment compels a transfer of financial resources from a producer or exporter of dumped or subsidized merchandise to the domestic competitor of that merchandise. The offset payments come from AD duties and CVDs ultimately paid by foreign producers and exporters. The offset is paid to 'affected domestic producers,' *i.e.*, competitors

[34] *Byrd Amendment* Appellate Body Report, ¶248 (emphasis added).

of the foreign entities that petitioned for relief or supported the petition. Second, the offset must be spent on a 'qualifying expenditure,' which are related to the production of the same product that is the subject of the AD or CVD order (*i.e.*, the like domestic product). Third, the affected domestic producers are free to spend the offset on their production of a like product as they deem appropriate, which means they may use the funds to improve their competitive position relative to their foreign competitors whose products are subject to an AD or CVD order.

The Appellate Body inferred from these three facts about the operation of the *Byrd Amendment* that the offset has an adverse bearing on foreign producers and exporters of subject merchandise. Because producers in the United States of a like product compete with these foreign entities, and because the producers in the United States not only are eligible for the offset, but also can use it to bolster their competitive position, the foreign entities have an incentive not to engage in the practices of dumping or subsidization, and to terminate these practices. What more obvious illustration could there be of a measure 'against' dumping or subsidies?

Having held the *Byrd Amendment* to be a 'specific' action 'against' dumping and subsidization, the Appellate Body needed to address one final substantive point: did it run afoul of the discipline of Article 18:1 of the *AD Agreement* and Article 32:1 of the *SCM Agreement*? That discipline is contained in the language of these Articles, namely, that a measure 'be taken . . . in accordance with the provisions of *GATT 1994*, as interpreted by. . .' the *AD* or *SCM Agreement*. Obviously, there was always the chance the American legislation was both subject to and satisfied the discipline, by being consistent with *GATT 1994*. Of course, that was not the final outcome in the case.

With respect to AD actions, the Appellate Body found the *Byrd Amendment* inconsistent with *GATT 1994*. Indeed, the Appellate Body needed only two paragraphs to explain why. First, the Appellate Body reminded the United States that the reference in Article 18:1 of the *AD Agreement* to '*GATT 1994*' was to Article VI:2 of *GATT*, which authorizes a WTO Member to levy an AD dumping up to the amount of the dumping margin. The Appellate Body cited its report in the *1916 Act* case for the proposition that '*GATT 1994*' in Article 18:1 means Article VI:2. Second, the Appellate Body pointed out that the *Byrd Amendment* offset was not a definitive or provisional duty, nor was it a price undertaking. Here, too, the Appellate Body cited its *1916 Act* Report, in which it had held *GATT* Article VI:2, when read in conjunction with the *AD Agreement*, limits the permissible remedies against dumping to a definitive AD duty, a provisional measure, and a price undertaking.

With respect to CVD actions, the Appellate Body could not rely on the *1916 Act* precedent, because that case involved a dumping statute. The

United States said the reference in Article 32:1 of the *SCM Agreement* to *GATT 1994* was to *GATT* Article VI:3, which authorizes imposition of a duty up to the amount of the estimated subsidy granted. The Appellate Body agreed with this point. But, it disagreed with the broader proposition put forth by the United States that *GATT* Article VI:3, when read in conjunction with the *SCM Agreement*, does not limit the permissible remedies for a subsidy to just one kind of measure—a CVD.

The American argument has a sound textual basis. In the *AD Agreement*, Article 1 refers to antidumping 'measures.' That, said the United States, is a generic term encompassing all remedies against dumping—not just an AD duty, a provisional measure, or a price undertaking. In contrast, Article 10 of the *SCM Agreement* refers to countervailing 'duties.' The term 'duty' captures a CVD, and a provisional measure or price undertaking—but, nothing more, unlike the broader term 'measure.' Therefore, urged the United States, while the *AD Agreement* governs all measures against dumping, the *SCM Agreement* governs only duties against subsidization.

The Appellate Body was not persuaded. It turned again to its *1916 Act* Report, plucking language from it to the effect that its decision in that case was based not on any one provision in the *AD Agreement*, but the *AD Agreement* as a whole. Then, the Appellate Body reminded the United States of the identical terminology and structure in Article 18:1 of the *AD Agreement* and Article 32:1 of the *SCM Agreement*. In a paragraph that is nothing short of judicial interpretation to fill a void from the Uruguay Round, the Appellate Body stated:

Article VI of the GATT 1994 and the *Anti-Dumping Agreement* identify three responses to dumping, namely, definitive anti-dumping duties, provisional measures and price undertakings. No other response is envisaged in the text of Article VI of the GATT 1994, or the text of the *Anti-Dumping Agreement*. Therefore, to be in accordance with Article VI of the GATT 1994, as interpreted by the *Anti-Dumping Agreement*, a response to dumping must be in one of these three forms. *We confirmed this in U.S.—1916 Act. We fail to see why similar reasoning should not apply to subsidization.* The GATT 1994 and the *SCM Agreement* provide four responses to a countervailable subsidy: (i) definitive countervailing duties; (ii) provisional measures; (iii) price undertakings; and (iv) multilaterally-sanctioned countermeasures under the dispute settlement system. No other response to subsidization is envisaged in the text of the GATT 1994, or in the text of the *SCM Agreement*. Therefore, to be 'in accordance with the GATT 1994, as interpreted by' the *SCM Agreement*, a response to subsidization must be in one of those four forms.[35]

[35] *Byrd Amendment* Appellate Body Report, ¶269 (emphasis added).

The italicized sentences articulate the two crucial steps in the reasoning of the Appellate Body. In the first sentence, the Appellate Body explains its precedent from an AD case. In the second sentence, the Appellate Body extends this precedent to CVD cases. Skillful as the American textual argument was, it was insufficient to overcome these steps.

The Appellate Body then took the third and final step. It applied this reasoning to the facts of the *Byrd Amendment* in a straightforward matter. The offset was not a definitive CVD, a provisional measure, or a price undertaking. Therefore, the offset was not a permissible remedy. Lest there be any doubt about these steps, the Appellate Body added a point about statutory construction and the untoward consequence of the American argument.

The Appellate Body said the American argument would render ineffective Article 32:1 of the *SCM Agreement*. Why? The United States defined Article VI:3 of *GATT* and Part V of the *SCM Agreement* (which encompasses Articles 10-23 and, ironically, is entitled 'Countervailing Measures') to cover only countervailing 'duties.' Were that so, then Article 32:1 would be redundant, because it would not provide any additional discipline beyond Article VI:3 or Part V. The American argument also would render Article 32:1 inutile, because any specific action against subsidization, other than a duty, would not violate Article 32:1. In other words, it would be impossible to find a violation of Article 32:1 in cases of remedies aside from a CVD.

In sum, the Appellate Body concluded that *GATT* Article VI:3 and the *SCM Agreement* encompass all measures taken against subsidization, just as *GATT* Article VI:2 and the *AD Agreement* cover all measures against dumping. The two schemes are symmetrical and comprehensive in the discipline they impose on remedies against unfair trade practices.

VI. WHY FIGHT THIS CASE?

Why did the United States bother to argue the *Byrd Amendment* was not a 'specific action' that was 'against' dumping'? Surely, the United States was aware that fighting the case would exacerbate trade relations with many WTO Members. It would take a stunning lack of empathy by the United States for it not to appreciate that, from the perspective of other Members, the Byrd Amendment was a unilateral effort to re-draw the boundaries around permissible AD and CVD remedies. Perhaps, on policy grounds, those boundaries ought to be re-drawn—but not by one Member acting along.

On legal grounds alone, why the United States fought the case is worth asking. Indubitably, the United States was aware of the 'constituent elements' test from its loss in the *1916 Act* case. If a statute (the 1916 Act) aimed at predatory dumping qualified as a measure against dumping, then *a fortiori* the *Byrd Amendment* does too, because it is set squarely within the principal American AD (and CVD) statute, which makes no pretence of targeting predatory pricing or any other bad behavior. Put bluntly, why did the United States not heed the advice, reported in November 2000, that it was unlikely to win the case in light of the 1916 Act precedent?[36]

One answer to 'why fight?' is the United States adheres to the view that nothing the Appellate Body decides has any precedential value beyond the case in which it renders the decision. So, why not re-litigate the same questions, however self-evident the answers may be, and however helpful it might be to the WTO to conserve judicial resources for questions for first impression?

A second answer, suggested by the Appellate Body in its Report, is the United States wanted to make a distinction between a statute that refers expressly to the constituent elements of dumping or subsidization (like the 1916 Act) and one that does not do so (like the *Byrd Amendment*).[37] As discussed above, the Appellate Body found this distinction too fine for its liking.

A third answer is there were aspects of the Panel's reasoning the United States wanted to challenge and, it hoped, persuade the Appellate Body to overturn. If that is an, or the, answer, then perhaps the United States cannot be faulted for litigating the case. On one key point, the Appellate Body did side with the United States.

The Panel had found the *Byrd Amendment* creates a financial incentive for a domestic producer to file, or support, an AD or CVD petition. In turn, this incentive likely will lead to more such petitions. The United States disagreed with the Panel's reasoning, finding it overly broad, and arguing it is not a permissible ground to conclude the *Amendment* 'against' dumping or a subsidy. The Appellate Body agreed with the United States. The basic logic of both the Appellate Body and the United States is a measure must not be held to be 'against' dumping simply because it facilitates, or induces, the exercisc of a right that is consistent with WTO obligations. Why not?

One response, in support of the Panel, would be the *Byrd Amendment* is analogous to a lottery. Producers in the United States have an incentive to file petitions, in the hope they might 'win the lottery,' meaning they get a

36 In November 2000, the *International Trade Reporter* wrote: 'Trade officials said it was *highly doubtful* that the Byrd amendment would survive a formal dispute challenge at the WTO, noting that the trade body *ruled earlier this year against the U.S. 1916 Antidumping Act* because it went beyond Antidumping Agreement provisions limiting penalties in dumping cases to the imposition of antidumping duties [emphasis added].' Daniel Pruzin, *WTO Members Denounce Adoption of Byrd Amendment by United States*, 17 International Trade Reporter (BNA) 1699, 1700 (Nov. 9, 2000).

37 *See Byrd Amendment* Appellate Body Report, ¶¶243–44 (discussing this argument).

pay out if their petition is successful. In turn, the greater the number of petitions filed, the greater the disincentive to engage in dumping or receive a subsidy—generally speaking, and in respect of any particular class of foreign merchandise. However, a contrary response is that the better analogy is not to a lottery but to a victim's compensation fund. As Senator Max Baucus (D-Mont.) put it:

> [The *Byrd Amendment* is] good, common–sense trade policy. It simply states that the duties collected on unfairly traded imports should be redistributed to the industries injured by those imports. It is now benefiting industries in all 50 states.[38]

In other words, not unlike some successful criminal prosecutions or tort claims, in an AD or CVD case the *Byrd Amendment* simply calls for channeling funds to the 'victims' of dumping or subsidization—the petitioners.

In its Report, the Appellate Body clearly indicated its appreciation for this characterization. It asked the following hypothetical question: would a legal aid program designed to help small domestic producers in AD or CVD investigations be a measure 'against' dumping? The answer should be 'no.' But, under the Panel's reasoning, the answer would be 'yes,' because the Panel would view legal aid as a financial incentive likely to result in a greater number of petitions, investigations, and orders. In sum, the Appellate Body agreed with the United States that whether a dumping or subsidy remedy creates an incentive to file a petition is not, itself, an appropriate basis on which to conclude the remedy is 'against' dumping.

Is there another explanation for why the United States fought the *Byrd Amendment* case? Perhaps WTO Members appreciate in advance they will lose a case, but fight it anyway. Indeed, maybe they hope to exhaust WTO adjudicatory procedures and suffer defeat. They can use the consequent Appellate Body Report as a hammer with which to hit recalcitrant, protectionist legislatures in their national assemblies. That would imply the Appellate Body is not just an end in itself, but also a means, toward freer trade.

VII. NON-COMPLIANCE?

To be sure, that appreciation (namely, of the value of a loss as a catalyst for reform) must have been small comfort to the United States. It still had an international legal obligation to repeal the *Byrd Amendment* (or otherwise meet the Appellate Body's recommendation). President Bush tried to do just that, proposing repeal of the *Amendment* in the federal budget bill for fiscal

[38] *Quoted in* Rossella Brevetti, *Bush Administration Proposes Repeal of Byrd Amendment in FY 2005 Budget*, 21 International Trade Reporter (BNA) 221, 222 (Feb. 5, 2004).

year 2004, and then again in the budget bill for fiscal year 2005.[39] The President's first attempt met with a stern letter from 70 senators telling him—diplomatically—to back off. Not surprisingly, the Senate bill to repeal the *Amendment* (S.1299, sponsored by Senators Olympia Snowe (R-Maine) and Lisa Murkowski (R-Alaska)) never was debated in the Senate, and the United States missed the deadline of 27 December 2003 for compliance with the Appellate Body's Report. In January 2004, eight senators wrote to their colleagues in the House of Representatives exhorting them not to rescind the *Amendment*, and instead to push for changes in WTO rules that would allow for offset payments.

The Bush Administration has been a bit more successful in working toward repeal of the Antidumping Act of 1916. In January 2004, the Judiciary Committee in the House of Representatives voted in favor of repeal.[40] In February 2004, a WTO arbitration panel rejected the EC's proposed retaliation against the United States for failing to repeal the 1916 Act.[41] As more evidence of the seemingly endless tit-for-tat immaturity infecting trans-Atlantic trade relations, the EC proposed to adopt a regulation mimicking the 1916 Act. Under the proposal, the EC would impose treble damages against American companies dumping in the EC if specific intent requirements analogous to the 1916 Act criteria are proven. The United States countered this level of suspension, or retaliation, would exceed the level of nullification or impairment, *i.e.*, of harm to the EC from the 1916 Act, because there have been no final judgments against EC companies under the Act, and settlements in such cases have been kept confidential. The arbitration panel agreed with the United States, though it held open the possibility of future retaliation by the EC, equal to the sum of any final judgments and publicized settlements (but excluding legal fees).[42] Interestingly, in December 2003, the first successful prosecution under the 1916 Act occurred. In December 2003, a United States District Court for the Northern District of Iowa ruled an importer of printing presses from Japan had violated the 1916 Act, and ordered it to pay over

[39] This discussion of compliance and retaliation is drawn from Rossella Brevetti, *Bush Administration Proposes Repeal of Byrd Amendment in FY 2005 Budget*, 21 International Trade Reporter (BNA) 221, 222 (Feb. 5, 2004); Daniel Pruzin, *U.S. Initiates WTO Arbitration on Byrd Sanctions, Hits Out at Trading Partners*, 21 International Trade Rep. (BNA) 204 (Jan. 29, 2004).

[40] *See* Rossella Brevetti, *House Judiciary Committee Approves Bill to Repeal 1916 Antidumping Act*, 21 International Trade Reporter (BNA) 229 (Feb. 5, 2004) (also reporting the House bill was introduced on 4 March 2003, and similar legislation is pending in the Senate).

[41] *See* Office of the United States Trade Representative, Statement of Richard Mills, USTR Spokesman, Regarding the 1916 Act Arbitration Award (Press Reslease, Feb. 24, 2004), available at www.ustr.gov.

[42] *See* Frances Williams, *WTO Allows Trade Sanctions on U.S.*, FINANCIAL TIMES, Feb. 25, 2004, at 3 (summarizing the ruling).

$31 million in damages (*i.e.*, treble the $10.5 million in damages, as called for under the Act) to its American competitor, Goss International.[43] The ruling is on appeal.[44]

As for the *Byrd Amendment*, the official Bush Administration position remained one of commitment to repeal. But, that position hardly deterred the successful complainants in the WTO action from obtaining authorization to retaliate against the United States because of its compliance failure. The Administration thus faced two battles—in Congress, to secure repeal, and in the WTO, on the appropriate amount for retaliation. The complainants made the plausible argument they should be entitled to retaliatory payments equal to whatever the United States disbursed as offset payments. They estimated the amount at $245 million for 2003, and as much as $1.7 billion for 2004 (the increase being due largely to cash deposit collections from the Canadian softwood lumber case). The Administration projected offset disbursements of $293 million in 2004, and $885 million in 2005. However, the differences in estimates masked the real battle in the WTO.

In January 2004, the United States sought arbitration on whether the complainants had a right to impose retaliation. The United States argued the offset disbursements had no negative impact on their trade with the United States. The United States pointed out that under Article 22:4 of the *Understanding on Rules and Procedures Governing the Settlement of Disputes* ('*Dispute Settlement Understanding*,' or '*DSU*'), the right to retaliate 'shall be equivalent to the level of nullification or impairment' of benefits associated with the offending measure. If there was no nullification or impairment of benefits, then there could be no retaliation.

[43] *See Goss International Corp. v. Tokyo Kikai Seisakusho Ltd.*, No. 00-CV-0035-LRR (N.D. Iowa, Dec. 3, 2002); *Federal Jury Awards U.S. Firm Damages Under 1916 Dumping Act*, 20 International Trade Reporter (BNA) 2072 (Dec. 18, 2003).

[44] *See* Tobias Buck, *Brussels Awaits WTO Dumping Ruling*, Feb. 24, 2004, at 6 (discussing this case).

CHAPTER FIFTEEN

The Multilateralism of Bretton Woods Revisited: The Crucial Role of the WTO in the Integration of Transition Economies

*by J.H. Hoogmartens**

CHAPTER OUTLINE

I. Bretton Woods, Free Trade and the World
   A. Managing the World Economy
   B. Post-Cold War Challenges
II. The Role of the WTO
III. The Process of Integration
   A. Different Types of Market Economy
   B. Towards Integration in the World Economy
IV. Legal System
   A. Capitalism and the Rule of Law
   B. Integration into the International Legal System
V. Final Observations

In 1944 allied forces met in Bretton Woods, New Hampshire, to discuss an international monetary and economic system to rebuild and maintain economic and financial order to establish long-term peace: out of this a system of multilateral institutions were established (the Bretton Woods System). Today, the international economic order is substantially different from that of the immediate post-war years), the International Monetary Fund (IMF), the World Bank (Bank) and their long-lost sister the World Trade Organisation (WTO) remain influential in allocating financing, capital, trade and economic growth. The monetary affairs, development/investment and trade policies under their influence go hand-in-hand. After all, imposing creditworthiness and financial stability entails monetary and

* PhD (London). Legal Adviser, Office of the Vice Prime Minister, Brussels, Belgium.

fiscal discipline next to emphasising export expansion and productivity improvement. Therefore these multilateral organisations continue to play an important role in balancing the economic system.

Nowadays, our international economic order faces the challenge of emerging markets joining and especially the former communist societies, which may be considered a special group of emerging economies, namely transition economies.

In integrating these transition economies, the WTO (as a working multilateral organization) plays a crucial role, because IMF and World Bank membership do not require domestic policy reforms as profound as are required for WTO membership. These reforms emphasise the two premises upon which all three Bretton Woods institutions are built: a capitalist market economy and a Western rule of law. These two pillars are crucial in the process of integration of transition economies. This integration process should transcend the agenda of the New International Economic Order movement (NIEO) rooted in the Developing World's strident self-consciousness, which begged for special and differential treatment, but should focus on economic and legal co-operation and assistance to transform and develop transition economies to make them responsible members of the international economic and financial order. However, it is important that this universalism pays due regard to the many cultural differences, which need to be interfaced. After all, variations in legal and economic systems may be good for global competition in attracting capital and foreign investment. Though harmonisation and standardisation in certain areas should provide for the necessary bridges.

This article will begin with sketching the international economic and financial order and the challenges represented by transition economies. It will then move on to discuss briefly the role of the WTO, as a multilateral institution, in integrating these economies into the global economy. Subsequently much time is devoted to the process of integration, which involves the adoption of a market economy and a functioning legal system.

I. BRETTON WOODS, FREE TRADE AND THE WORLD

At the end of World War II two worlds ideologically and militarily confronted each other, thereby espousing two different approaches to achieve prosperity and social change. Each side was drawing its own lessons from the terrible consequences of the economic disasters of the inter-war years. On one side of the spectrum, liberals considered economic interdependence to create positive bonds among peoples and to promote harmony of interest among societies. On the other side nationalists and Marxists regarded trade as pernicious, because economic specialisation and interdependence would make states insecure and vulnerable.[1] The memory of this event impresses upon us how closely the fortune of free trade remains tied to prospects for peace and how international politics affects international trade.[2] A glance along the horizon from Korea to the Balkans to Rwanda and the Middle East will remind us how far we still are from the ideal of an international civil society, and how important it is that steady, sustained efforts in that direction be made.[3] According to liberals the promotion of peace should encompass the promotion of international trade.[4]

As a result of this ideological split between a liberal capitalist and a socialist bloc, international economic law reflected for many years a bipolar character to guarantee international stability.[5] Since the end of the Cold War the current international system is described as:

'[A] liberal international order, which comprises a degree of order, but no over-arching governmental structures; a continued diversity of types of States and political systems; a broad consensus, but not unanimity, on market economies; and a degree of consensus on democracy, but without general agreement on the forms and true content that it should assume'.[6]

Within this international system the pace of international economic activity and the interdependence of national economies is head spinning. Because this activity often crosses borders it escapes the reach of much of

[1] About these two theories of international trade, *See* R. Gilpin, THE POLITICAL ECONOMY OF INTERNATIONAL RELATIONS 172 (Princeton University Press 1987).

[2] *See e.g.* J. Delors, *The Future of Free Trade in Europe and the World*, 18 FORDHAM INT'L L.J. 715–25 (1995).

[3] *See e.g.* M. Albright, *International Law Approaches in the 21st Century: A US Perspective on Enforcement*, 18 FORDHAM INT'L L.J. 1595–1606 (1995); THE UN AND THE BRETTON WOODS INSTITUTIONS—NEW CHALLENGES FOR THE 21ST CENTURY (M. Ul Haq & R. Jolly et al. eds., St. Martin's Press, 1995). R. Boardman, POST-SOCIALIST WORLD ORDERS: RUSSIA, CHINA AND THE UN SYSTEM (St. Martin's Press 1994). About the direct role of Bretton Woods institutions in international peace and security, *See* J. Ciorciari, *A Prospective Enlargement of the Roles of the Bretton Woods Financial Institutions in International Peace Operations* 22 FORDHAM INT'L L.J. 292–354 (1998).

[4] Gilpin, *supra* note 1, at 172. *See also* F. Fabricius, *The Universal and Regional Harmonisation of International Trade Law as a Means of Maintaining World Peace*, in INTERNATIONAL ECONOMIC AND TRADE LAW—UNIVERSAL AND REGIONAL INTEGRATION 201–25 (C. Schmitthoff & K Simmonds eds. 1976).

[5] *See e.g.* FABRICUS, id, at 202-03. The author notes that international trade law must harbour the germ of conflicts and that to maintain peace is the dominant aim of a legal system. This delicate balance in international trade law can also be found in A. Lowenfeld, TRADE CONTROLS FOR POLITICAL ENDS (Matthew Bender 1983) (dealing with the controls on trade with communist countries and the patterns of evolution in East-West trade). For further reference *See also*, T. WOLF, US EAST-WEST TRADE POLICY (Lexington Books 1973) and R. Pollard, ECONOMIC SECURITY AND THE ORIGINS OF THE COLD WAR 1945–1950 (Columbia University Press 1985).

[6] R. Higgens, *International Law in a Changing International System*, 58 Cambridge L. J. 78–95, 81–82 (1999).

national government control.[7] This phenomenon is often referred to as globalisation.[8] A broad inventory of subjects as diverse as insurance, brokerage, product health and safety standards, environmental protection, banking, securities and investment, professional services such as medical and law, and many more, can be covered by international economic law. Notwithstanding this very broad inventory, the core aspects of international economic regulation are found in the three Bretton Woods institutions:[9] the International Monetary Fund (IMF),[10] the World Bank Group (the World Bank or just the Bank)[11] and latecomer the WTO,[12] which emerged from a

[7] *See e.g.* J. H. Jackson, *Interdisciplinary Approaches to International Economic Law: International Economic Law: Reflections on the 'Boilerroom' of International Relations* 10 AM. U. J. INT'L & POL'Y 595 (1995). Illuminating in this regard is also M. Stewart, THE AGE OF INTERDEPENDENCE 28–29 (MIT Press 1984) (discussing the impact of greater interdependence). *See also* O. Schachter, *The Erosion of State Authority and Its Implications for Equitable Development*, in INTERNATIONAL ECONOMIC LAW WITH A HUMAN FACE 31–44 (F. Weiss et al. ed., Kluwer Law 1998) (noting that capitalism and global markets may be stateless, but that markets in one way or another need regimes that may go beyond the province of the state. Nevertheless, states will continue to play a major role in the creation and application of these legal and quasi-legal regimes); and P. Malanczuk, *Globalisation and the Future Role of Sovereign States*, in INTERNATIONAL ECONOMIC LAW WITH A HUMAN FACE 45–65 (F. Weiss et al. eds., Kluwer Law 1998) (noting that sovereignty still is the cornerstone of international law).

[8] For some meanings of globalisation, see G. Walker & M. Fox, *Globalisation: An Analytical Framework* 3 Global Legal Studies J., No.2, at www.law.indiana.edu/glsj/vol3/no2/ walker.html (last visited 4 August 2000). Authors note that globalisation differs from internationalisation because the erosion and irrelevance of national boundaries in markets only underlies the former concept. Because of technological progress geographical constraints recede and this adds to a sense of increased interconnectedness. For similar views see also J. Delbruck, *Globalisation of Law, Politics, and Markets—Implications for Domestic Law: A European Perspective* 1 Global Legal Studies J., at www.law.indiana.edu/glsj/vol1/ delbruck.html (last visited 4 August 2000). For further reference see also, D. RODRIK, HAS GLOBALISATION GONE TOO FAR? (Institute for Int'l Econ. L. 1997); J. FOREMAN-PECK, HISTORICAL FOUNDATIONS OF GLOBALISATION (Edward Elgar Publishing 1998); and ECONOMIC GLOBALIZATION, INTERNATIONAL ORGANIZATIONS AND CRISIS MANAGEMENT (R. Tilly & P. Welfens eds., Springer 2000).

[9] Called after the conference held at Bretton Woods, New Hampshire, in July 1944. *See* UNITED NATIONS MONETARY AND FINANCIAL CONFERENCE, Bretton Woods, New Hampshire, July 1–22, 1944, Department of State, Vol. I–II (proceedings and documents). *See also* A. VAN DORMAEL, BRETTON WOODS—BIRTH OF A MONETARY SYSTEM (Macmillan Press 1978).

[10] *See e.g.* J. GOLD, MEMBERSHIP AND NONMEMBERSHIP (IMF 1974), and J. GOLD, INTERPRETATION: THE IMF AND INTERNATIONAL LAW (Kluwer Law 1996). *See also* J. GOLD, LEGAL AND INSTITUTIONAL ASPECTS OF THE INTERNATIONAL MONETARY SYSTEM: SELECTED ESSAYS (IMF 1984); and M. DE VRIES, THE IMF IN A CHANGING WORLD, 1945–1985 (IMF 1986).

[11] The World Bank Group comprises the IBRD, IDA, IFC, MIGA and ICSID. *See e.g.* WORLD BANK OPERATIONS (John Hopkins University Press 1972); E. MASON & R. ASHER, THE WORLD BANK SINCE BRETTON WOODS (The Brookings Institution 1973); I. SHIHATA, THE WORLD BANK IN A CHANGING WORLD (Kluwer Law 1995); THE WORLD BANK—ITS FIRST HALF CENTURY, Vol.1–2 (D. Kapur et al. eds., *the* Brookings Institution 1997)

[12] The charter establishing the World Trade Organisation was signed at a ministerial meeting in Marrakesh on 15 Apr. 1995. *See* J. H. JACKSON, THE WORLD TRADING SYSTEM—LAW

transformed General Agreement of Tariffs and Trade (GATT), and was originally conceived as the International Trade Organisation (ITO).[13] Of course the WTO or the three Bretton Woods institutions cannot deal with all these matters in a comprehensive way. Consequently initiatives have emerged from diverse sources such as the Organisation for Economic Co-operation and Development (OECD).

A. Managing The World Economy

International lawyers and scholars have helped elucidate the crucial compromises during the formative era of Bretton Woods institutions, the institutions' evolution through post-war reconstruction, economic recovery, and the trend toward more equal collaboration among developed countries, allied in the OECD, and developing countries.[14] The recent post-Cold War

AND POLICY OF INTERNATIONAL ECONOMIC RELATIONS 45–46 (MIT Press 2d ed. 1997). The same story line can also be found in the beginning chapters of J. H. JACKSON, THE WORLD TRADE ORGANIZATION—CONSTITUTION AND JURISPRUDENCE (Royal Institute of International Affairs 1999). The WTO was designed after negotiations were launched with the ambitious Punta del Este Declaration in the Uruguay-Round (1986–1995). By 1990 Canada proposed a new institution bearing the present name. The European Community supported the idea of a 'Multilateral Trade Organisation' (MTO). This proposal ended up in the Dunkel Draft, called after then GATT director-general Arthur Dunkel, and led after intense negotiations in 1993 to a draft charter acceptable to the U.S. as well. *See also* T. Dillon, *The World Trade Organization: A New Legal Order for World Trade?* 16 MICH. J. INT'L L. 350–402 (1995); AND R. VERNON, *THE WORLD TRADE ORGANISATION: A NEW STAge in International Trade and Development* 36 HARV. INT'L L.J. 329–40 (1995).

[13] This history starting with the Bretton Woods system in 1944 is clearly depicted in Ch. 2 of JACKSON, *supra* note 12, at 31–46; and JACKSON, *supra* note 12, Ch. 1–2, at 1–35. Next to the International Monetary Fund (IMF) and the World Bank, the Bretton Woods system, devised to safeguard monetary and economic stability after the disaster of World War II, was supposed to comprise a third leg *viz.* the International Trade Organisation (ITO). Basically because the war momentum had faded away by 1947, only the precursor to the ITO, the GATT, came into existence. This temporary solution provided for in the Provisional Protocol of Accession (PPA), became a permanent *de facto* organisation until the Marrakesh meeting *supra* note . About the GATT, see also K. DAM, THE GATT LAW AND INTERNATIONAL ECONOMIC ORGANISATION (University of Chicago Press 1970); O. LONG, LAW AND ITS LIMITATIONS IN THE GATT MULTILATERAL TRADE SYSTEM (Martinus Nijhoff 1987); and R. HUDEC, THE GATT LEGAL SYSTEM AND WORLD TRADE DIPLOMACY (Butterworths, 2d ed. 1990). Interesting literature in this regard is also, G. Bronz, *An International Trade Organization: The Second Attempt*, 69 HARV. L. REV. 440–82 (1956); M. Hansen & E. Vermulst, *The GATT Protocol of Provisional Application: A Dying Grandfather*? 27 COLUM J. TRANSNAT'L L. 263–308 (1989); P. Demaret, *The Metamorphosis of the GATT: From the Havana Charter to the World Trade Organisation*, 34 COLUM J. TRANSNAT'L L. 123–71 (1995); and P. Moore, *The Decisions Bridging the GATT 1947 and the WTO Agreement*, 90 AM. J. INT'L L. 317–28 (1996).

[14] *See generally* A. VAN DORMAEL, BRETTON WOODS—BIRTH OF A MONETARY SYSTEM (Macmillan 1978); DE VRIES, *supra* note 10; R. MIKESELL, THE BRETTON WOODS DEBATES (Princeton, Essays in International Finance, No. 192, 1994); E. HELLEINER, STATES AND THE REEMERGENCE OF GLOBAL FINANCE: FROM BRETTON WOODS TO THE 1990s (Cornell University Press 1994); A RETROSPECTIVE ON THE BRETTON WOODS SYSTEM: LESSONS FROM INTERNATIONAL

era has caused scholars to focus on challenges including uneven economic development, wide income disparities, growing environmental concerns, extensive underemployment, expanding global investment and trade, exchange rate instabilities, trade imbalance, current account problems etc.[15]

Our story of managing the world economy starts in the first heydays of Bretton Woods when the world benefited from a fixed dollar-gold exchange standard (1945–71). But when the US no longer was the most stable and predominant economy, the IMF soon became a crucial forum for managed floating.[16] Major OECD countries comprising the US, UK, Germany, Japan, France and later also Italy and Canada informally gathered in the G-5, enlarged to G-7. This group of strong economies gave some general leadership and guidance to the world economy. IMF and World Bank provided essential adjustment assistance and 'soft' loans to many developing countries (and to some developed countries until 25 years or so ago) with no access to commercial banks and capital markets.[17] Notwithstanding the IMF 's controversial conditionality discipline,[18] its co-operation with the OECD nations and its major international banks fostered responsibility to

MONETARY REFORM (M. Bordo & B. Elchengreen eds., Chicago University Press 1993); J. SHELTON, MONEY MELTDOWN: RESTORING ORDER TO THE GLOBAL CURRENCY SYSTEM (Free Press 1994); BEYOND BRETTON WOODS: ALTERNATIVES TO THE GLOBAL ECONOMIC ORDER (J. Cavanagh et al. eds., Transnational Institute 1994); PERPETUATING POVERTY: THE WORLD BANK, THE IMF AND THE DEVELOPING WORLD (D. Bandow & I. Vasquez eds., Cato Institute 1994); MANAGING THE WORLD ECONOMY: FIFTY YEARS AFTER BRETTON WOODS (P. Kenen ed., Institute for International Economics, 1994); H. JAMES, INTERNATIONAL MONETARY COOPERATION SINCE BRETTON WOODS (Oxford University Press 1996); THE BRETTON WOODS–GATT SYSTEM—RETROSPECT AND PROSPECT AFTER FIFTY YEARS (O. Kirshner ed., M.E. Sharpe 1996); 1–5 RETHINKING BRETTON WOODS (J. Griesgaber & B. Gunter eds., Pluto 1996); and BRETTON WOODS: LOOKING TO THE FUTURE (Bretton Woods Committee 1994). For an introduction to public financial management see P. STEPHAN & D. P. WALLACE ET AL., INTERNATIONAL BUSINESS AND ECONOMICS—LAW AND POLICY (Michie 1993).

[15] *See e.g.* N. RAFTS, GLOBALISATION AND GROWTH IN THE TWENTIETH CENTURY 10 (IMF 2000) (noting mainly that the gap between rich and poor has widened enormously).

[16] *See e.g.* GOLD, *supra* note ; and M. DE VRIES, THE INTERNATIONAL MONETARY FUND, 1966-1971: THE SYTEM UNDER STRESS (IMF 1976).

[17] *See generally* 'The IMF at a Glance' at www.imf.org, which lists the available IMF financial facilities. Similar development information on soft loans, usually a responsibility of the International Development Association (IDA) and an overview of World Bank Group activities can be found at www.worldbank.org. *See* for further reference also D. Driscoll, WHAT IS THE INTERNATIONAL MONETARY FUND? (IMF 1992); D. DRISCOLL, THE IMF AND THE WORLD BANK—HOW DO THEY DIFFER? (IMF 1992); M. GUITAN, THE UNIQUE NATURE OF THE RESPONSIBILITIES OF THE INTERNATIONAL MONETARY FUND (IMF 1992); I. Shihata, *Development Policies and Strategies—With Emphasis on the World Bank Group*, in Shihata, *supra* note , at 33–69; and other publications like the WORLD BANK INFORMATION BRIEFS (World Bank).

[18] On IMF conditionality see generally IMF CONDITIONALITY (J. Williamson ed., MIT Press 1983); E. DENTERS, LAW AND POLICY OF IMF CONDITIONALITY (Kluwer Law 1996); and A. QURESHI, INTERNATIONAL ECONOMIC LAW (Sweet & Maxwell 1999). *See also* GOLD, *supra* note 10.

creditors and broader capital markets. Hence the system encouraged international investment, trade and the development of a global marketplace. The foundation for a more stable reliable economic regime and more market-friendly state practices among developing nations was cast.

OPEC oil and other price shocks hurt many economies in the 1970s.[19] Worldwide flows of petroleum dollars, recycled through expanding Eurocurrency banking and capital markets, were used to expand loans and international debt leading in turn to a worldwide inflationary surge. To crack down inflation, interest rates increased greatly, bringing widespread recession and rising unemployment. Latin American countries suffering from serious debt overloads failed to service increased interest obligations by the early 1980s.[20] The IMF, the World Bank and the Paris Club of private multinational banks responded with a mix of rescheduling, additional credits and limited relief. Creditworthiness was gradually restored by accepting stronger fiscal discipline, emphasising export expansion, and stressing productivity improvement.[21] Successful rescheduling called for confidence in expanding global trade. Yet a rising trend of protectionism, subsidies and trade barriers could abort the recovery process by the mid-1980s.

To fight a greater slump in the global economy the Uruguay Round of the GATT was launched in 1986. Its multifaceted agenda comprised additional tariff reductions, especially among newly industrialised countries (NIC), market opening for agriculture, services and financial markets and stronger intellectual property rights. It hoped to limit protectionism on trade flows by addressing antidumping and countervailing duty proceedings, safeguard relief and such other equivalents in national law. The negotiations were difficult and slow, but nonetheless by accepting most of the Dunkel Draft provisions in late 1993 the world accepted a stronger version of the WTO than many had expected.

B. Post-Cold War Challenges

Adding three billion people who currently live in transition economies to the international system in which the Bretton Woods institutions operate is rightly called a challenge.[22] There probably will not be a successor conference to the Bretton Woods one of 1944. Instead international governance is

[19] *See e.g.* J. SPERO & J. HART, THE POLITICS OF INTERNATIONAL ECONOMIC RELATIONS 172 (Routledge, 5th ed. 1997).

[20] *Id.* at 179–182, 186.

[21] *See e.g.* SPERO and HART, *supra* note 19, at 189; see also, STEPHAN *et al*, *supra* note 14, at 283–287.

[22] D. Hale, *Global Economic Integration After the Cold War*, in THE FINANCIAL SYSTEM UNDER STRESS 81–131 (M. Uzan ed., Routledge 1996). *See also* J. Bello & F. Holmer, *After the Cold War: Whither International Economic Law?* 32 (2) HARV. INT'L L.J. 323–29 (1991).

taken up by the existing international organisations and *ad hoc* meetings such as the G-7, which with the support of Russia continues its work.[23]

In the post-Cold War era the Bretton Woods institutions face a wider range of controversies. The IMF, the World Bank and the WTO are on the one hand appreciated and on the other hand criticised for influencing the allocation of financing, capital, trade and economic growth among nations during recent crises such as in Mexico and Asia.[24] However, the rational for Bretton Woods institutions has not changed fundamentally. Sustained trade/current-account imbalances have long been a concern,[25] and still need to be addressed in emerging markets. The lessons prescribed for deficit countries have remained and emphasise fiscal discipline, budget retrenchment, improved competitiveness, export enhancement and devaluation or import restrictions, if necessary. Surplus nations must expect currency appreciation and reduced exports.[26]

But what have changed since 1944, are the composition of the world and the process of international economic law. Whereas Bretton Woods was very much a dialogue between United States' Harry Dexter White and the British Empire, with ideas represented by John Maynard Keynes, today's world counts many voices more. More members classified according to stereotypes such as Less Developed Countries (LDC), NIC and divisions between North-South and East-West, means different needs.[27] This has caused Bretton Woods institutions to pay more attention to development. Therefore many believe the interests of poorer nations deserve more sympathetic attention and that environmental and population concerns demand more respect internationally.[28] But also the process of international

[23] *See e.g.* Report of G-7 Finance Ministers to the Köln Economic Summit, Cologne, Germany, 18–20 June, 1999 (discussing *inter alia* the strengthening and reforming of international financial institutions and arrangements, strengthening macroeconomic policies in emerging markets, debt management and crisis prevention).

[24] *See e.g.* T. Canova, *Banking and Financial Reform at the Crossroads of the Neoliberal Contagion*, 14 AM. U. IINT'L L. REV. 1571–1645 (1999); and also B. EICHENGREEN, TOWARD A NEW INTERNATIONAL FINANCIAL ARCHITECTURE: A PRACTICAL POST-ASIA AGENDA (Institute for International Economics 1999).

[25] *See e.g.* MAINTAINING AND RESTORING BALANCE IN INTERNATIONAL PAYMENTS (W. Fellner et al. eds., Princeton University Press 1966).

[26] F. Machlup, *In Search of Guides for Policy*, in MAINTAINING AND RESTORING BALANCE IN INTERNATIONAL PAYMENTS, *supra* note 25, at 33–84.

[27] For definitional matters and an overview of the heterogeneous developing world, see R. SARKAR, DEVELOPMENT LAW AND INTERNATIONAL FINANCE 1 (Kluwer Law 2000).

[28] *See e.g.* 50 YEARS IS ENOUGH—THE CASE AGAINST THE WORLD BANK AND THE IMF (K. Danaher ed., South End Press 1994); more moderate are in INTERNATIONAL ECONOMIC LAW WITH A HUMAN FACE, *supra* note 7; and FAIR TRADE AND HARMONIZATION (J. Bhagwati & R. Hudec eds., MIT Press 1996), which pay attention to labour, environmental and human rights concerns in the international economy. These issues played an important role in the streets outside the Seattle Ministerial Conference of WTO in December 1999. *See* D Gantz, *Failed Efforts to Initiate the 'Millennium Round' in Seattle: Lessons for Future Global Trade Negotiations*, 17 ARIS. J. INT'L & COMP. L. 349–369 (2000).

economic law has changed dramatically. International economic law, especially in the case of the WTO, has become more rule-oriented.

This process of international economic law weighs heavily on the integration of transition economies and needs a mix of rigidity and flexibility. Rigidity means the need for a firm foundation based on rules to cabin the risks and the costs of the integration. At the same time a sufficient amount of flexibility is needed to make swift adjustments to changing circumstances possible and to find compromises when necessary.[29] The WTO definitely has the advantage of being a rule-based organisation, but does it still have enough flexible muscle to manoeuvre?[30] This will in large part depend on its safeguard and dispute settlement mechanisms.

II. THE ROLE OF THE WTO

The most important objectives that the WTO like its predecessor the GATT keeps in mind are: (1) to provide a forum to negotiate trade liberalisation, and to monitor and improve policy transparency; and (2) to settle trade disputes between members.[31] But principal objectives include also raising standards of living, ensuring full employment, expanding production and trade, and allowing optimal use of the world's resources.[32]

To realise these objectives the technical purpose of GATT/WTO is to remove trade barriers like tariffs, quotas, customs procedures, state trading and subsidies to pave the way for liberal trade.[33] Tariffs distort competition and attribute monopoly rents to producers in countries that uphold them.[34]

[29] *See e.g.* I Patel, *The Adjustment Problem*, in TRADE POLICIES FOR A BETTER FUTURE—THE 'LEUTWILER REPORT', THE GATT AND THE URUGUAY ROUND 87–94 (Martinus Nijhoff 1987).

[30] A dose of flexibility is needed to serve economics and economists. QURESHI, *supra* note 18, at 102 (noting that sometimes an 'imaginative approach' is preferred in international economic law).

[31] *See e.g.* A. Lowenfeld, *Remedies Along with Rights: Institutional Reform in the New GATT*, 88 AM. J. INT'L L. 477–88 (1994); P. Nichols, *GATT Doctrine*, 36 VA. J. INT'L L. 379–466 (1996); and J. H. Jackson, *The WTO Dispute Settlement Understanding—Misunderstandings on the Nature of Legal Obligations*, 91 AM. J. INT'L L. 60–64 (1997) (noting that the WTO has teeth to enforce international legal obligations); and E. PETERSMANN, THE GATT/WTO DISPUTE SETTLEMENT SYSTEM (Kluwer Law 1997).

[32] Read the preamble of the Marakesh Charter, Final Act of the Uruguay Round, *supra* note 12.

[33] *See generally* GILPIN, *supra* note 1. Since Medieval times countries tried to amass as much gold and silver by selling more than buying from neighbouring empires. This mercantilism came under attack from ADAM SMITH'S AN INQUIRY INTO THE WEALTH OF NATIONS, 1776. His theory of the 'absolute advantage' was refined by DAVID RICARDO in THE PRINCIPLES OF POLITICAL ECONOMY of 1817, who introduced the notion of 'comparative advantage', meaning that each country, in order to increase overall prosperity, should produce and trade in those sectors of the economy, which have more abundant factors. *See also* M. TREBILCOCK & R. HOWSE, THE REGULATION OF INTERNATIONAL TRADE 2–4 (Routledge 1995).

[34] JACKSON, *supra* note 12, at 140.

Quotas usually do not yield more profit for domestic producers, but may yield corruption instead,[35] just like discriminatory licensing.[36]

Rules to govern international trade protect the welfare of small and weak nations against discriminatory trade policy actions of large and powerful nations. Fairness rules such as GATT Article I, the Most Favoured Nation clause,[37] and Article III, the National Treatment clause,[38] are fundamental to instilling confidence in the world trading system and to support the evolution towards more legality in global markets. Large economies have the potential to exploit their monopoly power by taxing their trade, but make the world worse off by such trade taxes. Thus without international trade regulation welfare reductions are rampant. Multilateral rules disciplining trade policy are also beneficial in that they help governments ward off domestic interesting groups asking special favours.[39] A more cynical, and perhaps more realistic point of view,[40] does not naively believe in the increase of WTO authoritativeness. It questions the exceptions fashioned in agriculture and textiles, two domains in which subsidies and protectionism have survived. It also draws our attention to many escape routes that lead away from basic free trade principles. China's accession to the WTO cannot drag us away from this constant tension between the

[35] Bribes can also be considered as tariffs or tariff surcharges, see P. Nichols, *Corruption in the World Trade Organisation: Discerning the Limits of the World Trade Organisation's Authority*, 28 N.Y.U. J. INT'L L. & POL. 711–84 (1996).

[36] JACKSON, *supra* note 12, at 140, 153, 164. Concerning quantitative restrictions it is important that not only imports of a certain product from all countries is restricted, but that it is also done in a non-discriminatory manner, see R. Hudec, Tiger, *Tiger in the House: A Critical Appraisal of the Case Against Discriminatory Trade Measures*, in THE NEW GATT ROUND OF MULTILATERAL TRADE NEGOTIATIONS 177 (E. Petersmann & M. Hilf eds., 2d ed. 1991). Article XIII GATT thereto states that licensing must happen either on a first-come-first-serve basis or with global licenses to local importers or with country-specific quotas based on historic market shares or expected market share. Article XIV GATT, however, provides for discriminatory quantitative restrictions in case of Balance of Payment difficulties.

[37] *See* WTO, GUIDE TO GATT LAW AND PRACTICE 23–61(WTO 1995) (hereinafter GATT Analytical Index). *See also* JACKSON, *supra* note 12, at 157. *See also* UN, 'First Report on the Most-favoured-nations Clause', 18 April 1969, Document A/CN.4/23 and UN, 'Second Report on the most-favoured-nations clause', 9 March and 18 May 1970, Document A/CN.4/228 and Add. 1. For an analysis, see also W. Schwartz & A. Sykes, *The Economics of the Most-favoured-nations Clause*, in ECONOMIC DIMENSIONS IN INTERNATIONAL LAW 43-79 (J. Bhandari & A. Sykes eds., Cambridge University Press 1997).

[38] *See* JACKSON, *supra* note 12, at 213.

[39] On the debate for and against free trade, see generally GILPIN, *supra* note 1; R. BHALA, INTERNATIONAL TRADE LAW (Michie 1996), chapter I; and J. H. JACKSON et al., LEGAL PROBLEMS OF INTERNATIONAL ECONOMIC RELATIONS (West Publishing 1995).

[40] This point of view is called realistic in the sense that it also points out the immanent and inherent objections to free trade like the impact on wages and employment. Free trade may hurt domestically vulnerable industries, even if the overall net effect is positive. Free trade has an impact on social policies as well. However, if trade liberalisation increases overall prosperity, it will also enable social policies to redistribute wealth. Other objections include the impact on cultural diversity with the creation of homogeneity and materialism and the impact on domestic sovereignty. *See* TREBILCOCK, *supra* note 33, *at* 11–14.

further institutionalisation and rationalisation over the creation of free trade and the empirical reality of global protectionism by devising exceptions to address domestic concerns.

One of the lessons is that an economy unable to influence its international terms of trade cannot maximise its national income without allowing free trade in all goods and services. Still countries do restrict their trade even when it is actually in their interest to liberalise unilaterally. A compelling explanation is the national income re-distributive feature of trade policies, the gains can be concentrated in the hands of a few who are prepared to support politicians who favour protection. The gains from reciprocal and multilateral trade negotiations will tend to be greater the larger the number of countries involved and the broader the product and issues coverage of the negotiations.

According to GATT Article II tariff concessions[41] are formalised in tariff bindings after negotiation rounds.[42] Sometimes countries are permitted to depart temporarily from bindings, called waivers, or may decide to withdraw certain concessions, in which case compensation and renegotiation must be offered to trading partners in an attempt to rebalance.[43]

Apart from tariffs there exist plenty of Non-Tariff Barriers (NTBs). It is the purpose of GATT Article XI to eradicate these trade-restricting measures. But human creativeness seems to be boundless here.[44] Efforts to remove these have proven to be more difficult.[45] Important is also that these NTBs are not always in line with National Treatment. Once goods have entered the internal circuit of commerce, imported goods should not be treated differently from national products, unless this equal treatment would provoke *de facto* or implicit discrimination.[46] This might be true for taxes, licensing requirements, technical standards, inspections etc.

When it comes to the escape routes many good reasons can be found in national security, health and welfare, Balance-of-Payment exceptions and currency obligations to name the most important ones.[47] The Uruguay

[41] GATT Analytical Index, *supra* note , at 63–119. *See also* D. Tarullo, *Law and Politics in Twentieth Century Tariff History*, 34 UCLA L. REV. 285–370 (1986).

[42] *See* JACKSON, *supra* note 12, at 142. *See also* DAM, *supra* note 37, at 79. On the negotiation process, see also D. Mcrae & J. Thomas, *The GATT and Multilateral Treaty Making: The Tokyo Round*, 77 AM. J. INT'L L. 51–83 (1983).

[43] Article XXVIII GATT, see JACKSON, *supra* note 12, at 143.

[44] Human creativeness is boundless in many policies trying to evade international obligations to liberalise trade. *See* again JACKSON, *supra* note 12, at 139, 229.

[45] Again JACKSON, *supra* note 12, at 153.

[46] *Id.* at 216.

[47] On Safeguards, see M. BRONCKERS, SELECTIVE SAFEGUARD MEASURES IN MULTILATERAL TRADE RELATIONS (Kluwer Law 1985). *See also* JACKSON, *supra* note 12, at 175, 241 for Balance-of-Payments exceptions. *See* in this regard GATT Article XXVIII, as the main provision to free oneself from tariff bindings. *See* GATT Article XIX, the escape clause, also at GATT Analytical Index, at 515–539, and GATT Article XII, for restrictions to safeguard the balance of payments, also at GATT Analytical Index, *supra* note 37, at 355–391. General

Round[48] came up with a very ambitious new safeguard agreement. If liberal trade policies and practices did not exist, then there would be perhaps no need to consider safeguards as such, economic adjustment needs and practical politics, however, demand otherwise.[49] The reality of comparative advantage provides little consolation to a suffering economy.[50] The economic costs of liberalisation are immediately felt by the industry affected, while the gains over time are diffuse.

In support of these safeguard mechanisms, a non-market economy like China may create stress vis-à-vis market-oriented trading partners.[51] By the very difference in economic nature, parties may interpret certain behaviour as unfair. GATT safeguards might therefore serve as a buffer zone between two opposite economic systems. The risk of damage to liberal trade, however, remains immanent. Perhaps therefore the WTO should put more effort in becoming an interface for all trading nations, whatever their economic background may be, and depart from being solely a market-oriented organisation.[52]

III. THE PROCESS OF INTEGRATION

Earlier the international system, of which the three Bretton Woods institutions are an inalienable part, has been defined as a consensus without unanimity.[53] A large consensus in many transition economies exists that the

exceptions can be found in GATT Article XX, GATT Analytical Index, at 561–597. On the recent controversy whether unilateral measures to protect life and health in the context of sustainable development should be considered by Article XX, see *e.g.* P. De Waart, *Quality of Life at the Mercy of WTO Panels: GATT's Article XX an Empty Shell*?, in INTERNATIONAL ECONOMIC LAW WITH A HUMAN FACE, *supra* note 7 at 108–131.

[48] On the achievements of this trade negotiations round, see *e.g.* J. Bello & M. Footer, *Symposium: Uruguay Round—GATT/WTO*, 29 Int'l Law 335–43 (1995) (gives a good chronology of events and the American perspective). *See also* D. Leebron, *An Overview of the Uruguay Round Results*, 34 COLUM. J. TRANSNAT'L L. 11–35 (1995). A more elaborate study is from K. Kennedy, *The GATT-WTO System at Fifty*, 16 WIS. INT'L L.J. 421–528 (1998).

[49] JACKSON, *supra* note 12, at 175.

[50] *See* D. Trubek, *Protectionism and Development: Time for a New Dialogue*? 25 N.Y.U. J. INT'L & POL. 345, 353. For some of the objections against free trade see also *supra* note 40.

[51] *See e.g.* W. Cai, *China's GATT Membership: Selected Legal and Political Issues*, 26 (1) *J.W.T.* 44 (1992) (who contends that China's potential competitiveness in international markets and its volume of low-cost labour-intensive products might constitute a threat to developed domestic industries).

[52] *See* JACKSON, *supra* note 12, at 319. The urgency to improve GATT rules for trade between the nonmarket economies and other Contracting Parties was already noted in 1986 by E. Patterson, *Improving GATT Rules for Nonmarket Economies*, 20 (2) J.W.T. 185–205 (1986). However, Patterson still emphasises one way compliance with GATT/WTO standards, whereas it may be necessary for the WTO to adapt itself also to the accession of non-market economies.

[53] *See* Higgens, *supra* note 6 and accompanying citation.

integration in the world economy presupposes the presence of two fundamental premises, upon which also IMF, World Bank and WTO are actually founded, i.e. a market economy and a functioning legal system.[54] Since this consensus in the international system does not insist on unanimity, many differences indeed remain as is exemplified by the different capitalism that is practised in Japan, the EU and the US. Nevertheless countries of transition are well aware of the need to embrace a thorough process of restructuring.

But apart from the differences it is the amount of co-operation that counts, to accommodate some of the differences and difficulties, and to form a proper interface for these variances.[55] There is no all-round, all-weather scenario to reach harmony or consensus in creating an interface, but the co-operation between IMF, World Bank and WTO thus far has developed a set of paradigms about the relative roles of the public and private sectors in the global restructuring process. Such co-operation leads to an idea of international governance,[56] which is built upon a shared common interest combined with setting priorities to reach sustainable development.[57] It is therefore appropriate to address here some theoretical perspectives on development and the important role of law and economy therein.

[54] Although WTO and IMF do not require a market economy, the Bretton Woods Institutions still treat market economies accompanied with a legal system as the norm and their policy recommendations usually follow these prescriptions. However, the IMF and World Bank have studied differences between market and planned economies for Fund or Bank relationships with member countries that had different systems. But this initial curiosity disappeared from publications, as is noted by JACOBSON & M. OKSENBERG, CHINA'S PARTICIPATION IN THE IMF, THE WORLD BANK AND GATT: TOWARDS A GLOBAL ECONOMIC ORDER 134 (University of Michigan Press 1990). *See also e.g.* T. Wolf, *Economic Stabilisation in Planned Economies: Toward an Analytical Framework*, 32 (1) IMF Staff Papers 78–131 (1985). *See also* Schachter, *supra* note 7, at 33 (noting that on the intellectual level the superiority of market to state control is almost universally accepted even in China and Vietnam. The market is viewed as an engine of development). Whether this foundation reflects solely the predominance of the West, see A. Carty, *Liberal Rhetoric as an Obstacle to the Democratisation of the World Economy*, 98 Ethics 724–56 (1988). Illuminating in this regard is also the history of the U.S.S.R. at the time of the Bretton Woods conference. According to the White Plan, dated April 1942, no restrictions as to membership should be imposed on grounds of the particular economic structure adopted by any country. But nothing in the commentary indicates how White saw membership for a 'socialist economy'. The Keynes Plan stated that the position of Russia would require special consideration, but there was no comparable statement in the final version of 8 April 1943. *See* J. GOLD, MEMBERSHIP AND NONMEMBERSHIP IN THE INTERNATIONAL MONETARY FUND 129 (IMF 1974); and J. HORSEFIELD *et al.*, 3 THE INTERNATIONAL MONETARY FUND, 1945–1965: TWENTY YEARS OF INTERNATIONAL MONETARY CO-OPERATION 15 (IMF 1969).

[55] *See* in this regard J. H. Jackson, *United States Policy Regarding Disruptive Imports from State Trading Countries or Government Owned Enterprises*, in INTERFACE ONE (D. Wallace et al. eds., Institute for International and Foreign Trade Law 1980).

[56] *See, e.g,* Prof. Joel Trachtman believes with other New Economic Institutionalists that the international legal system is the fruit of endogenous co-operation, starting from a prisoner's dilemma analysis)

[57] E. Zoller, *Institutional Aspects of International Governance*, 3 (1) Global Legal Studies J., at *www.law.indiana.edu/glsj/vol3/no1/zoller.html*.

Neo-classicist thinkers such as Rostow assume that every country is capable of 'modernisation' or, in other words, is capable of gradually transforming itself into the model of a Western-style modern capitalist state.[58] According to 'modernisation' theory non-western peoples should incorporate Western values, institutions and laws because such values should be considered universal in nature. This Western 'universalism' is built on individualism, the rule of law, a free market economy, and democracy. These are in turn to be believed the foundations for 'modern' development. The lack of a Western-style legal infrastructure is often cited as an impediment to the development of a fully functioning market system. This modernisation theory came under attack by the Critical Legal Studies (CLS) movement of the 1970s and the Marxist school of dependency theorists.[59]

The CLS warned against the dangers of exporting Western laws and legal institutions to the developing world, which considered it too Eurocentric, too conservative, and too naive. At that time it was definitely not so that all developing countries desired a capitalist society. As cultural relativists they believed the consequence of Western universalism had to be imperialism and that no universal norm for human development could exist.[60]

Marxists had their own brand of analysis. These dependency theorists believed that colonialism and economic domination was to be blamed for underdevelopment. They advocated nationalisation, import substitution and other forms of protectionism. They were convinced that ultimately the neo-classical economic prescriptions were imposed by the IMF to let developing economies suffer under the weight of heavy sovereign debts. For Marxists economics rather than law was the focal point of their analysis. In the 1970s their advocating led to such changes as preferential trade relations with developing countries. Many of these principles were articulated into a series of UN resolutions, declarations, reports and other documents better known as an initiative called 'New International Economic Order'.[61]

Although the dependency theory, culminating in a 'New International Economic Order' initiative, may have provided an explanation of certain economic imbalances, it does not resolve them as the demise of the Soviet-style approach to economics, politics and law shows. The integration process of transition economies should transcend the tradition of the NIEO

[58] SARKAR, *supra* note 27, at 19, who goes back to W. ROSTOW, THE STAGES OF ECONOMIC GROWTH: A NON-COMMUNIST MANIFESTO 4–16 (Cambridge University Press, 3d ed 1990). On Modernisation theory, see also SARKAR, *supra* note , at 20–22.

[59] Prominent scholars in this school were David Trubek and Marc Galanter. *See e.g.* D. Trubek & M. Galanter, *Scholars in Self-Estrangement: Some Reflections on the Crisis of Law and Development Studies in the United States*, WIS. L. REV. 1062 (1974).

[60] SARKAR, *supra* note 27, at 22

[61] For more details, see *e.g.* M. Bulajic, *A Changing World Calls for International Development Law*, in LEGAL ISSUES IN INTERNATIONAL TRADE 1–22 (P. Sarcevic & H. Van Houtte eds., Martinus Nijhoff 1990).

agenda. Preferred access to credit, development assistance, trade relations, and technology transfers have created differential treatment, which separated developed countries from developing countries. These differential norms, which provide presumably more advantageous treatment for one set of states, will not advance the fate of transition economies. In order to develop these states the way they themselves have decided to embrace the free market and a legal system, a paradigm, as a structure of fundamental assumptions, is needed. The reigning paradigm at this time would be a consensus about the appropriate methods and about the legitimate problems in integrating these economies.

Countries of transition have accepted that the creation of a market economy is the only way to improve their economic performances. Communism created in this sense a paradox, because the only way to improve economic performance was to adopt capitalist institutions. By consequence the evolution of communism consisted in converging toward capitalism and to integrate into the world economy. The initial economic conditions in these countries may be somewhat different but after all there are also clear similarities.[62]

A. *Different Types of Market Economy*

Most of the countries of Eastern Europe, having attempted various reforms, and having failed,[63] have set their sights on a transition from command socialist economies to genuine market economies after the Western pattern.[64] A market involves the exchange of goods and services in a public way. A true market entails such exchanges on the basis of economic freedom that both parties enjoy in the transaction. It simply means that both parties can and do decide whether or not to give away what she or he has in exchange for what the other party offers, only on the economic merits each perceives. If one or both parties think otherwise, the deal is off.[65]

Schematically there are three main 'models' such as the social market

[62] *See* S. Fisher & A. Gelb, *Issues in Socialist Economy Reform*, in THE TRANSITION TO A MARKET ECONOMY 184–201 (P. Marer & S. Zecchini eds., OECD 1991).

[63] *See e.g.* B. Kaminski, *The Legacy of Communism*, in EAST-CENTRAL EUROPEAN ECONOMIES IN TRANSITION 9–24 (Joint Economic Committee Congress of the United States, Study Papers, 1994) (noting that during the last few years before the collapse of communism, the Hungarian and Polish authorities introduced changes effectively overhauling some important components of the central planning system and indicating their willingness to move to a market economy).

[64] H. Gabrisch & K Laski, *Transition from Command to Market Economies*, in DISMANTLING THE COMMAND ECONOMY IN EASTERN EUROPE 15 (P. Havlik ed., the Vienna Institute for Comparative Economic Studies Yearbook III, Westview 1991).

[65] *See generally* M. FRIEDMAN, CAPITALISM AND FREEDOM (University of Chicago Press 1962). *See also* J. Buchanan, *General Implications of Subjectivism in Economics*, in WHAT SHOULD ECONOMISTS DO? 81–91 (J. Buchanan ed., Liberty Press 1979) (who notes that the most important central principle in economics, the principle of spontaneous order. It is the idea that individuals seeking their own gain in a system of private ownership and free markets bring

economies of Western Europe, the consumer-directed market economy of the US and the Japanese administratively-guided market economy. Although there are vast differences among countries in Western-Europe, the social market economy is characterised not only by its commitment to the predominance of market forces, but also to the responsibility of the state for sound monetary and fiscal policies, for efficient infrastructure, the environment, adequate health care, education and housing to help the unemployed and the poor. The basic idea is a humane capitalism sustained by social democratic values, but not to interfere with market forces as to lose too much efficiency gains.[66]

The US model thrives on a vigorous entrepreneurial spirit and the mobility of the factors of production is high. The efficiency of the market is praised and government interference widely criticised. Corporations often think short-term and regulation and deregulation by the government target the consumer as the beneficiary. There generally is an underprovision of social investment. A large underclass, with no stake in the prevailing social and economic order, has emerged and is being perpetuated.[67]

In Japan another successful blend of features exists, rooted in intense domestic competition for greater market shares rather than for short-term profits. Long-term thinking and continuous improvements in efficiency, productivity and cost-competitiveness are counted among the results. Domestic markets have been protected from foreign competition until firms in an industry have matured and become competitive internationally. Japan has allowed the rate of growth of consumption to lag behind its rate of growth of production.[68]

Whatever interpretation of market economy former centrally planned economies may follow, the assimilation of their economies into the world economy crucially depends on a radical change of their previous systems into a market system. A third road, in between plan and market, a 'socialist market economy',[69] may seem unrealistic.[70] However, on their way to a non-socialist economy a shorter or longer transitional period of cohabita-

about mutually beneficial exchanges, and that competitively determined prices co-ordinate economic decisions without central planning).

[66] *See* P. Marer, *Models of Successful Market Economies*, in THE TRANSITION TO A MARKET ECONOMY 108 (P. Marer & S. Zecchini eds., OECD 1991).

[67] *Id*, at 109.

[68] *Id*, at 110.

[69] This term is specifically relevant for China. On the notion of a 'socialist market economy', see S. GAO & F. CHI, THEORY AND REALITY OF TRANSITION TO A MARKET ECONOMY 19 (Foreign Languages Press 1996) (noting that China's socialist market economy is an operating system which integrates both planning and the market, with the market mechanism mainly playing a regulatory role in microenonomic sectors. Planned regulation must continue to play its role in the macroeconomic sphere). Read also further on in the text and the accompanying footnotes.

[70] *See* J. Dorn, *China's Future: Market Socialism or Market Taoism*, in CHINA IN THE NEW MILLENNIUM: MARKET REFORMS AND SOCIAL DEVELOPMENT 101 (J. Dorn ed., CATO 1998)

tion of state enterprises and market mechanisms is inevitable.[71] But these countries can still retain distinctive features in the structure and operation of their economic systems while strengthening their economic ties with the West by interacting more closely through trade or labour and capital movements or technology transfers.[72]

In China the 14th Party Congress[73] clearly defined the country's reform objective as being the establishment of a 'socialist market economy'. The market is established as the main instrument for resource allocation as is enshrined in the Constitution.[74] However, what constitutes a socialist market economy is a much-debated subject. It seems to be generally agreed that a socialist market economy, while allowing market forces to play the major role in market allocation,[75] additionally incorporates two fundamental socialist principles.[76] First, public ownership would be the mainstay in the economy, supplemented by private ownership.[77] Second, it would adopt measures to prevent an 'unfair' income distribution and emphasise the elimination of remaining poverty.[78]

China's economic approach points out some parallels with the modern

(who notes that building a socialist market economy is a grand illusion. The market and its supporting institutions, notably private property and the rule of law, cannot be grafted onto socialism. Markets are based on voluntary exchange. Socialism, however, destroys the spontaneous nature of markets and substitutes government control for individual responsibility. Market socialism, even with Chinese characteristics, is an unnatural and artificial system and therefore destined to fail like the Yugoslav experiment. In citing Alexander Tsypko at 103, the author notes that there is no third way between modern civilisation and socialism as it is. The five wasted years of perestroika have shown that the market cannot be combined with public ownership of the means of production).

[71] Gao & Chi, *supra* note 69, at 15–18.

[72] *See* S. Zecchini, *Assimilating Central and Eastern Europe into the World Economy*, in THE TRANSITION TO A MARKET ECONOMY, *supra* note 66, at 27.

[73] The 13th Congress in 1987 characterised the new economic system as one in which the state regulates the market, and the market guides the enterprises, but it did not indicate whether planning or market should be the main method of resource allocation. *See also* P. HARROLD & R. LALL, CHINA: REFORM AND DEVELOPMENT IN 1992–93, 30 (World Bank 1993).

[74] The constitutional amendment of 29 March 1993 replaced the text 'Planned economy under public ownership' with the words 'socialist market economy'.

[75] Gabrisch & Laski, *supra* note 4, at 18, who define market socialism as a market economy with prevailing collective (mostly state) ownership of the means of production but without any form of directive planning.

[76] Gao & Chi, *supra* note 69, at 18, (noting that the market economy does not only exist under the capitalist system where it plays its due role in economic regulation, but also exists and plays the same role under socialism. Therefore the socialist market economy is in fact a market economy operating under socialist conditions).

[77] *Id* (noting that the socialist economy is characterised by the public-owned economy and is better equipped than capitalism to amass quite a large proportion of GNP under state control. On page 19–20 they continue to say that the question what a socialist market economy in fact means, is a simple one, but that the reality is quite the opposite. So to a certain extent, the Chinese themselves seem not to know what it should mean in practice).

[78] Harrold & Lall, *supra* note 3, at 30. And also GAO & CHI, *supra* note 69, at 19, (agreeing and holding that the socialist market economy means a combination of social fairness and market efficiency).

market economy in France. But France's large public sector and state planning have always operated in the context of a competitive private sector. State enterprises have been expected to be competitive, and have operated under contractual relations with the state.[79] Second, the French planning system has been neither complete nor compulsory, but rather has been principally a process within which the public and private sectors have co-ordinated their expectations and plans. Pervasive state interventionism was rejected from the beginning, but important is the process of building a social consensus, the attempt to develop a common view among civil servants, business leaders and labour groups.[80] Parallels also exist between China and the economies of Japan and South Korea where managed trade plays a large role in development strategy.

It is clear that in obtaining a Western-type market economy different scenarios exist. In any event China and the other transition economies will have to duplicate those basic features and policies that seem to account for much of the successes of the well-performing market economies.[81] Only practice can prove whether China's scenario with enterprises mostly state-owned and instructed to act in a market-conforming manner next to a real market would represent a viable transitional solution.[82]

B. Towards Integration in the World Economy

Once transition economies have chosen their kind of market-economy and have embarked on a path to pursue their target, the price liberalisation inside the country should sooner or later be linked with foreign trade liberalisation,[83] to adjust the internal price and output structure to the world market conditions. Liberalisation is accompanied by a full convertibility of the currency, the abandonment of the central foreign exchange control, the foreign trade monopoly and the introduction of appropriate tariff policies.

[79] J. Helliwell, *Creating Market Economies in Central and Eastern Europe: Lessons from the West*, in THE TRANSITION TO A MARKET ECONOMY, *supra* note 66, at 119.

[80] *Id.* at 119–20.

[81] *See* Zecchini, *supra* note 72, at 27. Those features comprise according to Marer, *supra* note 66, at 111–13, the rule of law; private ownership; competition and trade; sound currency; savings, taxation, financial intermediation; infrastructure and the environment; political and economic freedom to seek personal fulfilment.

[82] Gabrisch & Laski, *supra* note 64, at 18. And also Gao & Chi, *supra* note 69, at 19 (also asking the question whether socialism can coexist with the market economy. Viewed in a traditional way, socialism is incompatible with the market economy. Socialism can be regarded as a social system, a policy, or a moral. Nevertheless, the final objective is to attain social fairness combined with market efficiency).

[83] K. Crane, *The Costs and Benefits of Transition*, in EAST-CENTRAL EUROPEAN ECONOMIES IN TRANSITION 40 (Joint Economic Committee Congress of the United States, Study Papers 1994) (noting that the centrally planned economies suffered from the most complete trade protection in the world. Despite the rapid change in trade policies, trade liberalisation has been only partial).

Governments may opt to assist some exporting industries and to protect some sectors, so as not to expose the economy to the pressures of world competition all too sudden.[84]

A central problem to be mastered in the search for new ways towards integration in the world economy and world trade is the expansion of exports.[85] The expansion of exports is the only factor in the long run, which determines the import prospects of any economy.[86] The chances for a successful restructuring of the economy, improving efficiency and raising living standards are not very encouraging if exports cannot be expanded. This expansion is difficult given the outdated production structures, the lack of investment funds and the old management lacking entrepreneurial acumen and experience. In this regard foreign direct investment is absolutely necessary, what in turn presupposes the removal of barriers to the entry of foreign capital. Integration in the world economy thus necessitates also integration into the international capital flows.

The Bretton Woods institutions and their Western members are faced with the question how to support the transition economically and also in other respects such as technical assistance, training, counselling, know-how. It would be a mistake for Western countries to take the opening of the East to be nothing but an opportunity for increasing exports. The attitude of the European Community and the United States vis-à-vis transition economies is sometimes dangerous for further trade liberalisation.

The validity and stability of the new international economic order largely depends on the effectiveness of the WTO. To be a truly universal system, the WTO should incorporate all the leading economic powers. Looking at the history of the GATT/WTO, we have no difficulty to find that China experienced a more complex process and faced higher entry barriers than many other countries. Poland and Romania have proven that a full market economy apparently is not a necessary condition for accession. In terms of importing goods and attracting investment, China is more liberal than these countries at the time of accession. But economically China is growing too fast and becoming too important and politically the country is still led by a Communist party.

It is true that China is a large exporting country, but should it be penalised for its good performance?[87] Western safeguard options and

[84] *Id.* (noting that transition economies continue to employ high tariffs, strict quotas, and other nontariff barriers to trade to protect domestic industries. These protectionist measures impose all the attendant associated costs on the economy).

[85] The success of most transition economies in increasing exports to the West has been one of the most pleasant surprises of transition, as is noted by Crane, *supra* note 83, at 41.

[86] *See e.g.* R. COOPER & J. GACS, TRADE GRWOTH IN TRANSITION ECONOMIES (Edward Elgar 1997) (noting that Eastern and Central Europe are a reference to prove that exports are necessary to pay for imports. Good export performance is necessary for general economic progress).

[87] H. Wen, *The WTO and China's Objectives as a World Trading Power*, in Dorn, *supra* note 70, at 183.

dumping charges may undermine the objective of China's WTO accession. In China trade policy reform is a very important part of China's transition to a market economy. Liberalisation and rationalisation of its import regime are moving much slower than liberalisation and decentralisation of exports. Some Chinese authors too seem to admit that a unified socialist market means a thriving and vigorous competitive market linked with the international market to ensure commercialisation. But they stress the free circulation of domestic resources, free from regional trade restrictions. They hope to exhibit the unique strong points and advantages of Chinese localities, industries and enterprises in economic development, promote extensive communications and co-operation between China and countries throughout the world, accelerate China's modernisation process and achieve higher production efficiency. Realising such a market mode requires the emancipation of Chinese thinking, the renewal of ideology and the deepening of reform.[88] The rapid increase in exports has made developed countries nervous about the future challenge. Nobody knows for sure whether China will become another Japan. Before this concern becomes a reality, developed countries want to learn a lesson from the past.

IV. LEGAL SYSTEM

In this section it is discussed that the development of a market economy in countries of transition also entails the creation of a legal system. Traditional Western capitalism is firmly built on the rule of law philosophy. By consequence also integration into the WTO requires the adoption of the necessary legal infrastructure to support the free market economy. The need for legal institutions can be found in several articles of different WTO texts. The WTO Agreements cover a large number of provisions requiring the availability of judicial, arbitral or administrative tribunals and independent domestic review procedures.[89] Some of the covered agreements provide specific means for the enforcement of WTO rules by national administrative and judicial bodies.[90] The general principle of legal transparency, however, is reflected in GATT Article X.[91]

The status of international economic law in domestic law has a bearing on the adherence to certain fundamental international economic norms.

[88] Gao and Chi, *supra* note 69, at 160.

[89] GATT Article X, Article 13 of the Antidumping Agreement, Article 11 of the Agreement on Custom Valuation, Article 2 (j) of the Agreement on Rules of Origin, Article 4 of the Agreement Pre-shipment Inspection, Article 23 of the Subsidies Agreement, Article VI of the GATS, Article 41–50 and Article 59 of the TRIPS, and Article XX of the Government Procurement.

[90] *See,e.g,*. Article 70.8 (a) of the TRIPS

[91] *See* S. Ostry, *China and the WTO: The Transparency Issue*, 3 UCLA J. INT'L L. & FOREIGN AFF. 1–19 (1998).

Whatever system a state adopts, monism or dualism, incorporation or transformation, the presumption in all states should exist that domestic legislation is to be interpreted in such a manner so as to avoid conflict with international law and thus WTO law.[92]

It must be noted that in comparison with the different types of market economy, also different and culturally dependent attitudes to law exist. The view is defended here that formal adherence to the rule of law philosophy, which is culturally dependent on the West, is not absolutely required for WTO integration, but that a legal system is desired that plays part of a methodology to assist in the further liberalisation of emerging markets and transition economies.

It is equally important to link integration efforts through legal reforms with the development of transition countries. Besides, to provide these countries with legal institutions is necessary for their development. Development and WTO integration should go hand in hand. Integration into the WTO is therefore a lesson in development theory as well. The next paragraphs will first explain the intricate relationship between the capitalist free market and the rule of law, to demonstrate an important Western premise of the Bretton Woods institutions, but also to conclude with many great thinkers that markets need legal institutions. However, just as different attitudes exist towards the adoption of a market economy, also different cultural attitudes towards law exist, which need to be interfaced. Harmonisation and standardisation of legal rules may be a solution to smoothen the process of change from commercial institutions in transition countries based on a relational orientation to a formal orientation. A formal orientation allows businesses and businesspersons in emerging economies to enter into commercial relations with persons and entities outside of their own polity.[93] But the adoption of foreign legal models and the process of harmonisation itself are not without difficulty. Therefore tensions will remain. It must be taken into account that building a legal framework to interface the different trade policies cannot escape the environment that is replete with existing institutions as will be exemplified by the Chinese situation afterwards.[94]

A. Capitalism and the Rule of Law

With the economic failure of communism, it also became clear that the socialist legal system was ill prepared for the changes needed to suit an open

92 QURESHI, *supra* note , at 85–88.

93 *See* in this regard P. Nichols, *A Legal Theory of Emerging Economies*, 39 VA. J. INT'L L. 229–300 (1999).

94 *Id.*

market economy.[95] In New Institutional Economics,[96] it is generally accepted that law plays a fundamental role in facilitating the development of markets and entrepreneurship. To this end the implementation, acceptance and legitimacy of a new legal system has to take place alongside the creation of a market economy in transition countries.

According to neo-classical economists of the Chicago school a link exists between economic returns and the autonomy in using and operating property, because a legal system is the necessary complement of an open market economy. This link depends on legal rights, especially ownership. Therefore in neo-classical economics it is thus believed that institutions of formal and well-defined property rights are the precondition for economic prosperity and are set up to reduce transaction costs.[97] Because the true owners have the power and incentives to stop losses and encourage profitability, true

[95] The aim of socialist law is not to define standards of conduct in the private or public sphere, and therefore laws need not be clear or accessible to ordinary citizens. Structural limits on governmental entities are considered artificial and contrived. The communist ideal is the development of a society in which government and law are completely unnecessary. In practice, socialist law operates according to the dictates of political expediency. *See* ENCYCLOPEDIA OF SOVIET LAW 706 (2d ed.,1985). For discussion of the development of the rule of law in the Soviet Union, see V. Karatashkin, *Human Rights and the Emergence of the State of the Rule of Law in the USSR*, 40 EMORY L.J. 889 (1991); H. Berman, *Counterrevolution of Transition: A Response to Human Rights and the Emergence of the State of the Rule of Law in the USSR*, 40 EMORY L.J. 903 (1991).

[96] New Institutional Economics is built upon *inter alia* the ideas of both the Chicago and Virginia schools of law and economics (Coase, Demsetz, Posner, Buchanan, Tullock, Krueger), the Austrian theory on institutions and entrepreneurship (Hayek, Menger and Kirzner), and the new economic history of Douglas North. These ideas are amplified in subsequent paragraphs. In short it defends the position that the emergence of markets and entrepreneurship is promoted by institutions such as for the protection of property rights and the enforcement of contracts. It is relevant for our discussion here, that postcommunist market building must coincide with the creation of an appropriate legal system. Sociological institutionalism offers perhaps the broadest definition of institutions of any of the new forms of institutionalism. The definition includes formal and infomal rules, symbols, cognitions, norms, and any other templates that organise or give meaning to the human condition. International law scholarship in particular has embraced two iterations of institutionalism. *See e.g.* A. Slaughter-Burley, *International Law and International Relations Theory: A Dual Agenda*, 87 AM. J. INT'L L. 205–39 (1993); J. Setaer, *An Iterative Perspective on Treaties: A Synthesis of International Relations Theory and International Law*, 37 HARV. INT'L L.J. 139–229 (1996); and A. Slaughter et al., *International Law and International Relations Theory: A new Generation of Interdisciplinary Scholarship*, 92 AM. J. INT'L L. 367–97 (1998). For the most part institutionalism as used by legal scholars either borrows from other disciplines or refers to the judiciary and other political entities. It is not just courts and political agencies, but also the law itself is considered an institution.

[97] *See e.g.*, R. Coase, *The Nature of the Firm*, 4 Economica 386–405 (1937); R. Coase, *The Problem of Social Costs*, 3 J.L. & ECON. 1–44 (1960). Transaction costs, unlike costs of production, are defined as those costs that are incurred in the process of exchange such as the costs of searching for prices and/or trading partners, the costs of negotiation and enforcement of contracts, and the costs of breach. Coase argues that, in a real world with positive transactions costs, institutions including the state have important roles to play, in economising on transaction costs.

private property blocks the inefficiency, which is characteristic of the old socialist economic system.[98]

Also the Virginia 'School' of Law & Economics defends that the emergence of markets and entrepreneurship depends on the creation of formal laws and institutions for the protection of property rights and the enforcement of contracts. In their approach laws/legal norms of the state conceptually emerge endogenously via a *public choice* or *contractarian* process.[99] Property rights and contracts in a market economy must therefore be protected by the 'protective state'.[100] Other prominent economists such as Williamson emphasise the importance of different forms of private ordering,[101] of which relational contracting is a prime example. Williamson emphasises the importance of *ex post* monitoring of contracts, that is, how contracts are to be protected from 'opportunism'.[102]

Profit making needs predictability and calculability according to sociologist Max Weber.[103] This is enhanced by clear rules of property and ownership. The more property, capable of being privately owned, becomes alienable, the more transactions in the market will take place. And exchange is the key of capitalism. Rules of contract, especially the freedom of contract, take a very important place. Fairness, impartiality and equality also become overly important because they are necessary to manage and to calculate commercial risks.

The rule of law may be inextricably linked with, but does not necessarily equal an operational and workable infrastructure that promotes foreign direct investment and international trade and in so doing enhances the functions of the Bretton Woods institutions.[104] Therefore the legal system for our purpose here is the regulatory framework supporting the development

[98] *See e.g.* Y. BARZELL, ECONOMIC ANALYSIS OF PROPERTY RIGHTS (Cambridge University Press 1989).

[99] *See e.g.* J. BUCHANAN & G. TULLOCK, THE CALCULUS OF CONSENT: LOGICAL FOUNDATIONS OF CONSTITUTIONAL DEMOCRACY (University of Michigan Press 1962); J. BUCHANAN, THE LIMITS OF LIBERTY: BETWEEN ANARCHY AND LEVIATHAN (The University of Chicago Press 1975).

[100] *Id.* at 95–96.

[101] Unlike the Chicago and Virginia schools, which follow the Hobbesian legalist centralist tradition emphasising the importance of the state in achieving social order via its role in protecting property rights and enforcing contracts, Williamson emphasises 'private ordering'. *See* O. WILLIAMSON, THE ECONOMIC INSTITUTIONS OF CAPITALISM: FIRMS, MARKETS, RELATIONAL CONTRACTING (The Free Press 1985). *See also* P. Rubin, *Growing a Legal System in the Post-Communist Economies*, 27 CORNELL INT'L L.J. 1–47 (1994) (who demonstrates that private ordering and government involvement are complementary in growing a legal system).

[102] WILLIAMSON, *id*, at 61.

[103] *See e.g.* MAX WEBER ON LAW IN ECONOMY AND SOCIETY (M. Rheinstein ed., Harvard University Press, 1954).

[104] In this regard it is often referred to economies such as Singapore and Hong Kong. *See* on the link between politics and economics in the so-called 'little dragons': C. Johnson, *Political Institutions and Economic Performance: The government-business relationship in Japan, South Korea and Taiwan*, in ASIAN ECONOMIC DEVELOPMENT—PRESENT AND FUTURE (R. Scalapino et al. eds., Institute of East Asian Studies, Berkeley 1985).

and maintenance of a transparent and stable economic environment conducive to efficient private sector activities, which comes close to what the IMF understands to be an important facet of good economic governance.[105] Nevertheless the socio-cultural legacy of the three Bretton Woods institutions gives away all the characteristics of the Western rule of law, also because it is very difficult to separate the economic aspects of governance from the political aspects. This is true also for the WTO.

But creating a legal system is more than legislative activity, it must also permeate the legal consciousness of the people living in the region under transition. Western influence raises the concern of 'transplantability' of Western social and political institutions and post-communist state building.[106] Moreover economic troubles often compound the problem of popular acceptance to establish a rule of law in transition economies.[107] It is, however, not questioned that the economic transformation of transition economies inevitably entails legal reform and legal system development.

B. Integration into the International Legal System

Integration into the WTO as part of the larger international legal system in the Bretton Woods order is not just an economic process, but also presupposes profound domestic law reform, for the reason indicated earlier that law facilitates the market as a means to development and finally may lead to more prosperity. At the same time integration may need some degree of legal convergence on the international level, to foster the domestic law reform process. So basically there are two interrelated tendencies. On the one hand there is the restructuring of the world economy on a regional and global scale through transnational legal co-operation from above. On the other hand and simultaneously there are domestic social and legal forces working from below. It is important, however, that each level is receptive of what happens at the other level.

Yet, the implementation of international WTO obligations in a domestic legal system is influenced by the different political systems, constitutions and legal traditions of member states and continue to be widely regarded as a domestic matter.[108]

[105] *See* GOOD GOVERNANCE—THE IMF'S ROLE (IMF 1997).

[106] A. Chua, *Markets, Democracy, and Ethnicity: Toward a New Paradigm for Law and Development*, 108 YALE L.J. 1, 5. (noting that entrenched ethnic divisions permeate most developing countries, and these divisions bear a distinctive and potentially subversive relationship to the project of marketisation and democratisation).

[107] K. Storin Doty, *Economic Legal Reforms as a Necessary Means for Eastern European Transition in to the Twenty-first Century*, 33 INT'L LAW. 195–97 (1999). For a discussion, see also Recent Development Symposium, 26 September 1996, in *Constitutional 'Refolution' in the Ex-Communist World: The Rule of Law*, 12 AM. U. J. INT'L L. & POL'Y 45–143 (1997).

[108] E. Petersmann, *Strengthening the Domestic Legal Framework of the GATT Multilateral*

The international level can be quite useful to tackle the domestic problems,[109] which in a globalised context push nations towards greater co-operation. These co-operative efforts raise several general questions, such as whether this co-operative approach should be voluntary, or binding;[110] whether the emphasis should be on procedural rather than substantive rules; and whether with respect to substantive rules some sort of minimum standards as the basis of a rule should apply.[111]

Globalisation and interdependence will definitely influence the techniques of this co-operation and integration. Harmonisation is a first technique that gradually induces nations towards uniform approaches to a variety of economic regulations and structures.[112] A second technique is a system of continuous 'trades' or 'swaps' of measures to liberalise (or restrict) trade, which is referred to as reciprocity. Finally, what is termed 'interface' by John Jackson, is a technique which recognises that different economic systems will always exist in the world and tries to create the institutional, legal means to ameliorate international tensions caused by those differences, perhaps through buffering or escape clause mechanisms.[113] These techniques are of course not mutually exclusive, but the question exists as to what the appropriate mixture is.[114]

The integration of transition economies into the WTO and the larger international and global environment in which the Bretton Woods institutions operate also raises a series of very basic legal questions that are not

Trading System: Possibilities and Problems of Making GATT Rules Effective in Domestic Legal Systems, in the NEW GATT ROUND OF MULTILATERAL TRADE NEGOTIATIONS, *supra* note 36, at 37.

[109] A common argument is that the international level may help countries to commit to their reform efforts and in so doing in the case of transition economies ideally provide guidance for the domestic social forces working from below.

[110] *See* J. H. Jackson, *Global Economics and International Economic Law*, 1 J. INT'L ECON. L. 1, 21 (1998). *See* in this regard also *e.g.* C. Chinkin, *The Challenge of Soft Law: Development and Change in International Law*, 38 I.C.L.Q. 850–66 (1989).

[111] *See* Jackson, *id*, at 21.

[112] An example in the WTO context could be the uniformity of procedures for applying countervailing duties or escape clause measures. On harmonisation, see D Leebron, *Lying Down with Procrustes: An Analysis of Harmonisation Claims*, in FAIR TRADE AND HARMONIZATION, *supra* note 28, at 41–117 (noting at 62 that harmonisation is at best a crude tool to deal with systemic and structural trade imbalances. Harmonisation raises significant resource allocation and efficiency questions). *See also* F. Roessler, *Diverging Domestic Policies and Multilateral Trade Integration* in *id*, at 21–56 (noting that GATT focuses on the reduction of trade barriers and not on the harmonisation of competitive strategies or conditions in the market. The Agreement on Technical Barriers to Trade is a first effort to harmonise, and demands are increasing; and at 37 questioning how an agreement on minimum standards can be achieved among so many countries with different values and resources without a clever mix of carrots and sticks).

[113] Roessler, *id*, at 41 (noting that the more safeguards and impairment procedures are adopted, the less need will be felt for domestic policy harmonisation and *vice versa*).

[114] *See* Jackson, *supra* note 110, at 21.

new to international legal scholars. In the context of the WTO and John Jackson's research in international economic law, these questions involve rule-making at the international level (rule-oriented system) and whether scientific and moral concerns should be taken into due consideration in international trade.[115] They involve questions of international dispute settlement resolution and to what extent they should adequately consider opposing policy goals, or provide for appropriate advocacy from interested authorities and citizen groups. This also leads to questions of transparency and democratic processes. Also important is the relationship between international rules and domestic constitutional and other laws and problems of regulatory competition.

The supply of ready-made law in the form of international standards or the transplantation of Western laws and institutions must be approached cautiously.[116] Similar to the supply of technical equipment by donor countries, the supply of legal norms must be accompanied by modes of instruction or better a full learning process. Rather than to supply the fish, it is better to teach how to fish. And therefore for transition economies and other countries of reform it is better to subject their law makers to the art of how to gain experience in the process and debate of law making.[117] The acquisition of this experience may thus be harmed if only ready-made laws are imported.

The efficacy of international economic rules will depend to a large extent on the ability of different countries to enforce them. The enforcement of legal standards thus introduced depends on substantial domestic support as well as additional institutional changes. By shifting jurisdiction to a supranational body, such as the dispute settlement body, it may be possible to solve the political stalemate to a certain extent.[118] Voluntary compliance is the preferred method.

Developing and transition countries with limited resources available for law reform clearly need to make a choice and target their reforms to areas that will bring the highest returns. But the adoption of legal standards in any area of the law is not enough to create an effective institutional framework to enhance a country's ability to attract foreign investment. Good

[115] *See* in this regard the question whether any country can afford a moral foreign policy. *See* T. KOH, THE QUEST FOR WORLD ORDER: PERSPECTIVES OF A PRAGMATIC IDEALIST (Times Academic Press 1998).

[116] There are several reasons for copying ready-made models. First, because they are successful in their own environment and second, because they can speed up reforms. But comparative law studies of industrialised countries are necessary to facilitate much needed economic reform. *See* J. NORTON, FINANCIAL SECTOR LAW REFORM IN EMERGING ECONOMIES 130 (British Institute of International and Comparative Law 2000).

[117] *See* in this respect *e.g.* LEGISLATIVE DRAFTING FOR MARKET REFORM: SOME LESSONS FROM CHINA (A Seidman ed., Macmillan 1997).

[118] However, in this regard constitutional problems within the WTO may arise and punishing non-conforming countries might be costly.

laws on the books may serve as an important signal to foreign investors, but only if this infrastructure is perceived to be effective foreign investment and international trade will be enhanced. Institutional reforms take time to materialise. Developing countries need time to develop the capacity to enforce the newly adopted laws and in fact to demonstrate this capacity. The effectiveness of legal institutions has a large impact on the creation of markets and vice versa. Thus the key to success for any given country will be the establishment of effective legal institutions.

V. FINAL OBSERVATIONS

The integration of transition economies into the economic and legal international order presents challenges to the Bretton Woods institutions. Our focus was not so much on the institutional questions that membership raises but rather on the presence of a market economy and a legal system as substantial and presupposed requirements. These two fundamental building blocks serve a double goal. On the one hand they must facilitate the integration into the international community and on the other hand enhance the development of the countries concerned.

But governments differ widely in the practical application of legal and economic principles within these building blocks. Therefore one of the most important challenges is to interface the relationship between the WTO system of multilateral rules and the domestic regulatory systems of its members, especially if they previously adhered to a planned economy. It was discussed that profound reforms are needed thereto and that there exists no all-round weather scenario for these reforms. Moreover the creation of legal institutions cannot escape the historical and cultural environment that is filled with pre-existing social institutions already, as we tried to show in the Chinese example.

The engine behind this integration process is to a large extent the globalisation of the economy, which results in an ambiguous form of homogenisation. First it awakens a shared common interest and hence leads to larger co-operation and harmonisation or standardisation. But in second instance the domination of liberal norms in the Bretton Woods institutions may result in the imposition of outside ideas, hence fuelling nationalism and protectionism. It is therefore essential to recognise the differences and in so doing to prevent them from inhibiting international co-operation. The WTO as a rule-oriented institution has many advantages in this respect, but it is too optimistic to think that rules can solve every issue. The WTO needs flexible muscles and therefore needs diplomacy and negotiation. The latter techniques are necessary as well to deal with the supra-national aspirations of the WTO *vis-à-vis* the member states' sovereignty. This debate is ongoing and the appellate body is trying to strike a fine balance. These tensions further indicated that the integration debate is linked with fundamental questions in international public law.

But already the beginning of the article warned for the revival of protectionism as one of the possible dangers of integration. The expansion of exports is often seen as the only factor in the long run which determines the import prospects of any economy and the low cost structure of emerging and transition economies as a threat to more mature economies may slow down international co-operation. The validity and the stability of the international economic system largely depend on WTO effectiveness, and I use this term to include also the legal effectiveness of WTO law on the domestic level and not just the international policy formulation, harmonisation and enforcement on the international level.

CHAPTER SIXTEEN

Multilateralism versus Unilateralism in the Sovereign Debt Restructuring Context: Will Either Approach Prevent Default?

*by Kristin McFetridge**

CHAPTER OUTLINE

I. Introduction
II. Background
  A. Financial Markets In the 20th Century
  B. The Use of Bonds in Raising Equity
  C. Life after Brady Bonds—Recent Events in Latin America
  D. Further Examples of Bond Usage
  E. Summary of the International Financial Architecture
  F. The Role of the IMF
III. The Multilateral Approach: The IMF's Proposal of a Sovereign Debt Restructuring Mechanism
  A. Background
  B. The SDRM in Brief
  C. Claims under the SDRM
  D. Activation
  E. Stay of Claims
  F. Administration
  G. Benefits
  H. Criticisms
IV. The Unilateral Approach: Collective Action Clauses
  A. Background and Mechanics of CACs
  B. Complementary Use of Exit Consents in Current Bond Agreements
  C. Recent Developments in CAC Usage

* JD (SMU); member Weil Gotshal & Manges LLP, New York City.

D. Benefits
E. Criticisms
V. Conclusion

I. INTRODUCTION

The invasion of Iraq by the United States in the spring of 2003, absent a mandate by the United Nations, launched a new discourse over the age-old issue of the efficacy of the multilateral approach to resolving international issues. Effectively spurning the mechanisms in place to address international crises, the United States opted instead to act unilaterally and proceeded to invade, supported openly by only the United Kingdom and Spain. This is but one example, albeit the most salient in today's political climate, of the United States rejecting a unified multilateral resolution. In the context of sovereign debt, the United States has acted in concert, withdrawing any support for an international bankruptcy type scheme in early 2003. Instead, the United States has urged the use of Collective Action Clauses ('CACs') by the financial community as a preferable alternative, espousing the concept of the 'freedom of contract.' Yet, the question remains whether this is indeed the optimal solution for creditors and debtors alike and whether the use of these clauses will prevent further crises or eradicate current issues in restructuring. Therefore, despite the United States' essential declaration that a multilateral approach is null, it is still necessary in a thorough analysis of potential resolutions to examine the now defunct proposal of the Sovereign Debt Restructuring Mechanism ('SDRM') by the International Monetary Fund ('IMF') and its strengths and weaknesses as compared to the current prevailing recommendation of using CACs. This paper sets out to describe the two most prevalent, and conflicting, recommendations for managing the past, current, and potential sovereign restructuring issues and to analyze the viability of each: (1) the SDRM proffered by the IMF; (2) the incorporation of CACs; and (3) the complementary use of exit consents in individual debt offerings. The multilateral versus unilateral framework encompasses this analysis. More specifically, the focus is whether an internationally unified and standard method is superior or inferior to an 'efficient market' driven theory, whereby individuals are free to contract and will, therefore, include covenants and clauses recognizing the potential for default and adjust pricing and terms accordingly.

Before one can theorize on the ideal solution to a problem, a full understanding of the scope of the problem is necessary. To that end, Part II of this paper begins with the relevant background information concerning the events of the last thirty years giving rise to the need for a restructuring solution, including a discussion of the relevant players in the international financial community. Parts III and IV, respectively, examine in depth the SDRM proposal and the use of CACs, including the status of both and the benefits and criticisms of each. Finally, the conclusion compares the two approaches and exposes the shortcomings of each, suggesting that a combination of both is really the ultimate solution.

II. BACKGROUND

A. Financial Markets in the 20th Century

Example: The Latin American Debt Crisis

The unique problem with regard to sovereign debt did not occur in a vacuum. Certain events led to changes in the international financial arena which precipitated the crises of the past thirty years, beginning with the Mexican peso crisis in the 1980s. In order to fully comprehend the suggested solutions, it is helpful to place them in the context of the entire situation. This section begins wth an examination of the changes in the capital markets and their implications in sovereign indebtedness.

In the late 1970s, commercial banks in the United States were in search of borrowers, as economic conditions in the United States had curtailed the need for capital.[1] Additionally, strong export prices for Latin American countries and the high inflation rate in the United States indicated minimal risk for the borrowing nations despite high interest rates.[2] These factors led many U.S. banks to invest heavily in Mexico and other Latin American countries with perhaps less scrutiny in terms of risk analysis than would have been pragmatic.[3] This heyday came to a crashing halt in 1979. The oil crisis forced debtor nations to increase their borrowing to compensate for higher fuel prices and the United States Federal Reserve Board raised interest rates.[4] This led to a significant exchange rate disparity and trade imbalance between Mexico and the United States (its largest trading partner), with Mexico carrying debt equal to 53 percent of its Gross Domestic Product (GDP) in 1982.[5] The debt burden became unsustainable for Mexico and in the same year, the country announced its inability to meet its loan payments.[6] Other Latin American nations were suffering under

[1] Phillip J. Power, Note, *Sovereign Debt: The Rise of the Secondary Market and its Implications for Future Restructurings*, 64 FORDHAM L. REV. 2701, 2707 (1996).

[2] *Id.* at 2707. [3] *Id.* [4] *Id.* at 2708.

[5] Raphael Bergoeing et. al., *Decades Lost and Found: Mexico and Chile since 1980*, 26 FED. RES. BANK OF MINN. Q. REV. 1, 4 (2002), *available at* http://www.utdt.edu/~summer/Kehoe.pdf.

[6] Power, *supra* note 1, at 2708.

similar conditions, and shortly after Mexico's announcement, Argentina, Bolivia, Brazil, and Venezuela followed suit.[7]

Through creative refinancing measures, the U.S. banks took action to stem the onslaught of default and the crisis was averted temporarily.[8] These measures consisted primarily of extending 'bridge loans' that permitted the debtor nations to borrow more money to service the interest payments on their outstanding loans.[9] Bridge loans were attractive to the banks and the debtor-nations, as it allowed them to represent the outstanding loans as performing loans on their balance sheets.[10] Additionally, the creditor committees representing the banks in negotiating restructuring terms used strong pressure to induce all of the lenders in the class to accept the revised terms.[11] The IMF also exerted pressure on the commercial banks, conditioning the dispersal of funds to assist debtor nations on the cooperation of the banks.[12]

Even with this assistance, the Latin American nations found themselves unable to stabilize and instead struggled with their growing debt burden.[13] The next ten years in Latin America were referred to as the 'Lost Decade,' due to the stunted economic growth and excessive inflation.[14] After several failed proposals, a resolution was suggested by then United States Secretary of the Treasury, Nicholas Brady.[15] Brady suggested uniting the banks that had lent to each particular country by pooling the outstanding loans and repackaging them as bonds, which could then be sold on the secondary market to individual investors.[16] This appealed to the banks, allowing them to remove the liabilities of the loans from their balance sheets, and to the debtor-nations, as the new bonds included a reduction in either the principal or the interest rates and were backed by U.S. Treasury zero coupon bonds.[17] Once this securitization into the 'Brady Bonds' occurred, the relationship between the debtor nations and the banks was effectively terminated, with all future debt payments made to a trustee, who forwarded the coupon payments to the bondholders.[18] Thus began a new trend in raising capital for indebted nations.

By 1994, the amount of eligible debt converted into Brady Bonds was in excess of $190 billion, with $61 billion total forgiven.[19] All of the Brady Bonds were issued with a choice of law clause selecting New York law[20]

[7] *Id.* at 2710. [8] *Id.* [9] *Id.*

[10] *Id.* At the time, loans were only shown as non-performing if the borrower was in default on the interest payment, not the principal. Non-performing loans adversely affect the balance sheet of lending banks.

[11] *Id.* at 2711–12. [12] *Id.* at 2712. [13] *Id.* at 2714.

[14] Bergoeing, *supra* note 5, at 1. [15] Power, *supra* note 1, at 2720.

[16] *Id.* at 2721. [17] *Id.* [18] *Id.* at 2720.

[19] William Cline, *Managing International Debt: How One Big Battle was Won*, ECONOMIST, Feb. 18, 1995, at 17.

[20] Rory MacMillan, *The Next Sovereign Debt Crisis*, 31 STAN. J. INT'L L. 305, 353 (1995).

and two important implications: first, the agreements were subject to the Foreign Sovereign Immunities Act;[21] and second, amendments to the payment terms (including amount and schedule) often required a unanimous vote by all bondholders.[22] The Foreign Sovereign Immunities Act holds that generally, sovereigns are immune from suit in a U.S. court.[23] However, exceptions to this include waiver or when the foreign sovereign has engaged in a commercial activity.[24] Both of these exceptions were applicable in this case and bondholders did (and do) have legal recourse within the United States in the event of a default by a debtor nation.[25] The options for these debtor-nations to restructure were severely constrained, as bonds issued under New York law tended to require unanimity to effect changes to the payment terms of the bond agreements.[26]

B. The Use of Bonds in Raising Equity

Following the use of Brady Bonds in the Latin American crisis of the 1980s, more and more debtor-nations turned to bond issuances as an alternative to higher interest bank loans. The conversion of Brady Bonds also became a popular option, with Mexico initiating a $2.5 billion dollar swap in 1996. In this new issuance, the bonds were absent one noticeable item: collateral.[27] These new dollar-denominated bonds were issued at a 30-year maturity and the proceeds were used to pay off short-term debt that was coming due.[28] Argentina quickly leapt on the bandwagon, issuing three and fifteen-year Deutschemark-denominated bonds.[29] In September 2002, Mexico issued a twenty-year $1.75 billion bond and used the proceeds to buy back $1.3 billion worth of Brady Bonds.[30]

One commonality between the Brady bonds and other non-collateralized bonds is that, unlike bank syndicated loans, which are contractually held by large easily identifiable financial institutions, bonds are highly mobile,

[21] Foreign Sovereign Immunities Act of 1976, 23 U.S.C. §§ 1330, 1332, 1391, 1441, 1602 et seq. (2003).

[22] The use of unanimity clauses in the United States has historical roots, tracing back to the Stock Market Crash of 1929. After the crash, shareholders of companies would buy bonds from their companies and then vote to forgive to debt, freeing up capital for the shareholders. In response to this, the U.S. government passed The Trust Indenture Act of 1939 with the provision that bond payments could only be restructured by a unanimous vote or in an official bankruptcy proceeding. While this Act does not apply to sovereign debt agreements, it establishes a drafting precedence that is followed in practice. *See* Lee C. Buchheit & G. Mitu Gulati, *Exit Consents in Sovereign Bond Exchanges*, 48 UCLA L. REV. 59, 66-67 (2000).

[23] 23 U.S.C. §§ 1330, 1332, 1391, 1441, 1602.

[24] *Id.*

[25] MacMillan, *supra* note 20, at 353.

[26] The majority of bond agreements governed by New York Law adopt the unanimity as a matter of standard drafting convention. For a complete discussion of the background and reasons for this, *see* Buchheit, *supra* note 22, at 1329–30.

[27] *Warranted: Mexican Debt*, ECONOMIST, May 4, 1996.

[28] *Id.*

[29] *Id.*

[30] *Id.*

issued in a number of different jurisdictions, and sold to a plethora of different investors.[31] This presents a unique problem for debtors wishing to revise the terms of the bond agreements—locating the bondholders to achieve their consent, and depending on the structure and jurisdiction of the bond agreements, agreement by majority or unanimity may be required.[32] Additionally, unlike in large syndicated loans, creditors in bond packages do not know the identity of each other and have no relationship or incentive to collaborate in the event of a restructuring.[33] As one scholar described it:

> Bond investors are like patrons in a theater audience: each one has decided to see a particular play on a particular night, but none has any idea who she will be seeing it with. If you wish to carry the analogy further, the tradable nature of bonds means that fellow patrons are constantly leaving and entering the theater throughout the performance.[34]

This is a good illustration of the anonymous nature of the relationship between the bondholders. In the situation of a performing debtor, the relationship is irrelevant. In the case of a need to restructure, a myriad of problems erupts, primarily that of the 'hold-out creditor' who refuses to restructure, jockeying instead for a preferential settlement.[35]

C. Life after Brady Bonds—Recent Events in Latin America

Following the Brady Bond bailout, the Latin Ameican region witnessed a period of comparative stability. However, for some countries, the foreign currency-denominated bonds were a ticking time bomb waiting to erupt. The market for emerging economy debt at its height in 1998, with $88 billion being raised,[36] began to wane shortly thereafter in 1998–99, as a

[31] International Monetary Fund, *The Design of the Sovereign Debt Restructuring Mechanism—Further Considerations*, at 5 n. 3 (Nov. 27, 2002), *available at* http://www.imf.org/ external/np/pdr/sdrm/2002/112702.pdf [hereinafter *International Monetary Fund, SDRM Proposal of November 2002*].

[32] According to the IMF, roughly 25 percent of the international and Brady Bonds are issued under English law, which permits a majority vote to approve changes to the payment terms. The remaining bonds are issued under New York law, generally requiring unanimity for amendments to payment terms. *See* The International Monetary Fund, *Resolving and Preventing Financial Crises: The Role of the Private Sector* (Mar. 26, 2001), *available at* http://www.imf.org/external/np/exr/ib/2001/032601.htm [hereinafter *Resolving and Preventing Financial Crises*].

[33] Lee C. Buchheit & G. Mitu Gulati, *Sovereign Bonds and the Collective Will*, 51 EMORY L. J. 1317, 1320 (2002).

[34] *Id.*

[35] Samuel E. Goldman, Comment, *Mavericks in the Market: The Emerging Problem of Hold-Outs in Sovereign Debt Restructuring*, 5 UCLA J. INT'L. L. & FOREIGN AFF. 159, 164 (2000).

[36] *A Better Way to go Bust*, ECONOMIST, Feb. 1, 2003, *available at* 2003 WL 6244817.

result of the Asian and Russian troubles. As the U.S. economy started to turn south at the millennium, the effects were felt profoundly in terms of exchange rates and trade in countries with significant financial relations with the United States. Brazil suffered a currency devaluation in 1999, and Argentina's dollar-pegged currency, which caused their exchange rate to be overvalued, was stifling exports and stimulating imports.[37] Some argue the Brazilian devaluation of the Real also adversely affected Argentina, a primary trading partner in Mercosur,[38] as the Argentine dollar-pegged peso remained strong in comparison.[39]

Argentina's trade imbalance led to a dearth of foreign capital greatly needed to make payments on the outstanding foreign currency denominated bonds.[40] With $30 billion due in 2002, and total debt equal to 50 percent of the Gross Domestic Product as of 2001,[41] Argentina halted all payments on its $141 billion debt in the spring of 2003.[42] This default resulted in a lengthy and painful process, with payments still in arrears and Argentina facing over $750 million in lawsuits, the most recent of which is the first certified class action suit against a sovereign in a U.S. court.[43] Negotiations between the bondholders and Argentina are still underway, but the prognosis is not positive. Peter Allen, the financial advisor to the Argentina Bondholders' Committee, commented, 'Unfortunately, there is really very little good faith between the government and the foreign bond holders at the moment.'[44] Further complicating the restructuring is the complexity of Argentina's debt, including over 100 bonds denominated in dollars, yen, euros, pounds sterling, and Swiss francs, largely owned by European retail investors.[45]

[37] Martin Feldstein, *Argentina's Fall, Lessons from the Latest Financial Crisis*, 81 FOREIGN AFF. 8 (2002).

[38] MERCOSUR, or Mercado Común del Sur, is a free trade and common market agreement between the following countries: Brazil, Uruguay, Paraguay, and Argentina, with Chile and Bolivia as associate members. The treaty, or Tratado de Asunción, was signed in March of 1991, and has the unique aspect of focusing on cultural alignment as well as economic growth, representing the 4th largest economic coalition in the world, with 80 percent of Latin American companies located within the MERCOSUR nations. The agreement has stimulated trade between members, with growth exceeding 300 percent in the years between 1991 and 1999. *See* Jerry Haar, *Bring Back Competitiveness*, LATINFIN., Mar. 2002, at 39. For more information *see* http://www.mercosur.org.uy/espanol/sinf/varios/introduccion.htm.

[39] *Don't Cry for Argentina*, WALL ST. J., Dec. 4, 2001, at J18.

[40] Feldstein, *supra* note 37, at 8.

[41] *Id.*

[42] John Barham, *Heading out of the Storm*, LATINFIN., Feb. 2003, at 16.

[43] *US Ruling a Setback for Argentina*, WALL ST. J., Jan. 2, 2004, at B4.

[44] Paivi Munter, *Argentina Faces a Restructuring Challenge: After a Dollars 95bn Default, Settlement With its Creditors Will Take Years*, FIN. TIMES LTD., Mar. 5, 2003, at 35.

[45] *Id.*

D. Further Examples of Bond Usage

Latin American countries are not the only nations have have turned to sovereign bonds to raise capital and then faced surmounting debt problems. The Ukraine, Pakistan, Ecuador, Russia and Peru also utilized these financing vehicles, later dealing with the reality of disparate creditors and unmanageable payment schedules.[46]

Following years of struggle after the demise of the Soviet Union, in 1993, Russia issued five dollar denominated bonds as domestic debt.[47] Again in 1996, in an attempt to raise equity, Russia issued short-term treasury bonds, and in the two years subsequent, issued several Eurobonds.[48] In 1997, when the oil market suffered a drop in prices, representing 25 percent of Russia's exports at the time, Russia's credibility was diminished and fears of currency devaluation led the IMF to offer an $11.2 billion bailout.[49] Unfortunately, this aid failed to stave off a default.[50]

Similarly, the Ukraine, Pakistan, and Ecuador all utilized foreign currency denominated bonds as a means of raising capital and subsequently were forced to restructure their debts.[51] Fortunately, Pakistan and the Ukraine were able to swap their bonds for new issuances with more favorable payment terms, without facing litigation from any of the bondholders.[52] Ecuador was also able to reach a workout with its creditors when the country announced in 2000 that it would have to restructure $ 6.65 billion in bonds.[53] Following an offer of a swap for thirty and twelve-year bonds, 98 percent of the bondholders accepted.[54] While these countries have all been able to facilitate ad-hoc restructurings, the number and frequency of nations increasingly encountering financial difficulties provided incentive for the international financial community to devise a standardized, predictable manner of dealing with potential default.

E. Summary of the International Financial Architecture

Analyzing the existing international financial framework under which these debt instruments were issued is crucial to fully comprehending the implica-

[46] *Resolving and Preventing Financial Crises, supra* note 32.

[47] Frederico Sturzenegger, Universidad Torcuato Di Tella, *Default Episodes in the 90s: Factbook and Preliminary Lessons*, at 22 (June 2002), *available at* http://www.utdt.edu/~fsturzen/Publications.htm (prepared for the World Bank).

[48] *Id.* at 24.

[49] *Id.*

[50] Christopher Mailander, *Financial Innovation, Domestic Regulation and the International Marketplace: Lessons on Meeting Globalization's Challenge Drawn from the International Bond Market*, 31 GEO. WASH. J. INT'L L. & ECON 341, 388 (1998).

[51] *See generally* Sturzenegger, *supra* note 47.

[52] *Resolving and Preventing Financial Crises, supra* note 32.

[53] *Id.*

[54] *Id.*

tions of any resolution to the issue of sovereign debt. The international financial architecture has been the subject of countless debates, articles, studies, and research, and is generally thought to be comprised of a variety of international financial institutions with varying initiatives, membership, and degrees of authority.

Following the Mexican peso crisis, seven representatives of the major industrial nations convened to address the issues in Lyon, France, in 1996.[55] At this summit, the 'Group of Seven (G-7)'[56] requested that the major international financial institutions develop standards for the international financial community, as well as viable solutions to avert similar crises in the future.[57] Following that meeting, in 1998, the finance ministers and Central Bank Governors of twenty-two nations set up working groups to investigate certain aspects of international finance, including crisis management.[58] Out of this effort came a report endorsed by the G-7, which requested the IMF, the World Bank, the Basle Committee on Banking Supervision, and other international bodies to develop international standards.[59]

The IMF became heavily involved in the structuring of the international financial architecture, in concert with the World Bank and the Basel Committee on Banking Supervision.[60] In addition to exploring an international set of standards and rules governing the global economy, the IMF sought out to examine a possible resolution to the financial crises of its member nations. [61] The result of that examination is the SDRM.

F. The Role of the IMF

Through its nature of involvement in financial crises, the IMF has been at the heart of the sovereign debt discussion. The IMF is a supranational organization, founded in 1944 at the Bretton Woods conference, and has grown

[55] Joseph J. Norton, *A 'New Financial Architecture'—Reflections on the Possible Law Based Dimension*, 33 INTL LAW. 891, 899 (1999).

[56] The G-7, now known as the G-8, is a supranational organization that meets annually with leaders from each of its member nations to address key economic, political and social issues in the international arena. The G-8 representatives are leaders from the following nations: Canada, France, Germany, Italy, Japan, Russia, the United Kingdom, the United States and a member of the European Union. For more information, *see* http://www.g8.gc.ca/menu-en.asp.

[57] Norton, *supra* note 55, at 901.

[58] Herbert V. Morais, *The Quest for International Standards: Global Governance vs. Sovereignty*, 50 KAN. L. REV. 779, 789 (2002).

[59] *Id.* at 790.

[60] Horst Kohler, Reform of the International Financial Architecture, Address Before the Central Bank Governor's Symposium (July 5, 2002), *available at* http://www.imf.org/external/np/speeches/2002/070502/htm.

[61] *Id.*

from forty-five member countries to 184 members today.[62] In the Articles of Agreement of the International Monetary Fund, the members elucidated the purposes of the IMF to 'promote the stability of exchange rates, the financing of balance of payment deficits, and the liberalization of payments for current international transactions.'[63] The IMF does not see itself as a lender or as a financial institution that serves to assist debt-ridden nations.[64] The funds received by these nations are delivered through currency exchange transactions, whereby the IMF purchases a nation's currency with an alternate currency in order to facilitate a restoration of the balance of payments.[65] However, as of June 2002, the IMF had approximately $88 billion in loans and credits outstanding to 88 countries.[66]

The IMF has a long history of involvement with financial crises, from the Mexican Peso Crisis of the 1980's, to the East Asian Crisis in 1997. The IMF has been the source of much controversy, not the least of which focuses on the IMF's role in perpetuating globalization. Not everyone favors the liberalization of capital markets and globalization like the financial world does. In fact, opponents of globalization compare it to the colonialism and imperialism of times gone by, actually damaging the human rights of inhabitants of the historically known 'Lesser Developed Countries (LDCs).'[67] Specifically, it is argued that the repayment of debt to the IMF and World Bank prohibits domestic healthcare and education spending.[68]

Further criticism of the IMF centers on its perceived expansion of its original role in the international financial community. As one scholar notes:

> It is far from evident that the IFIs[69] are operating in accordance with these provisions. Commentators have pointed out that, in recent times, the IFIs are playing an extraordinarily intrusive role in establishing national economic policy. They have expanded their mandate to deal with an enormous range of issues which seem far removed from the core functions they are required to perform by their Articles of

[62] International Monetary Fund, *The IMF at a Glance: Factsheet* (Aug. 21, 2002), *available at* http://www.imf.org/external/np/exr/facts/glance.htm [hereinafter *Factsheet*].

[63] Francois Gianviti, *Evolving Role and Challenges for the International Monetary Fund*, 35 INT'L. LAW. 1371 (2001). *See also* The International Monetary Fund, *Articles of Agreement of the International Monetary Fund*, *available at* http://www.imf.org/external/pubs/ft/aa. (last visited March 12, 2003.)

[64] Gianviti, *supra* note 63, at 1371. [65] *Id.* [66] *Factsheet*, *supra* note 62.

[67] Antony Anghie, *Time Present and Time Past: Globalization, International Financial Institutions, and the Third World*, 32 N.Y.U. J. INT'L L. & POL. 243, 252–253 (2000).

[68] For example, in Tanzania in 2000, debt repayment was six times that of the healthcare budget, while in Ethiopia it is 4 times the public spending on healthcare. And, in the continent of Africa as a whole, nations spend 4 times more on debt repayments than they do on education or healthcare. *See* Anghie, *supra* note 67, at 253; *see also* The International Monetary Fund, *Debt Relief Under the Heavily Indebted Poor Countries (HIPC) Initiative: A Factsheet*, *available at* http://www.imf.org/external/np/exr/facts/hipc.htm (last visited Mar. 22, 2003) [hereinafter *HIPC*] (for a through discussion of the IMF's initiatives in this area).

[69] The use of IFIs refers to International Financial Institutions, in this instance, the International Monetary Fund and the World Bank.

Agreement. Furthermore, contrary to their Articles of Agreement, the decision making of both these institutions appears to be based on the interests of the majority shareholders rather than on the technocratic considerations contemplated by the Articles of Agreement.[70]

In addition to an alleged abuse of powers, the IMF has been criticized for making assumptions about economies that have led to these financial crises. Specifically, in encouraging globalization, the IMF anticipated that these markets 'had already achieved what foreign aid is allegedly allocated to help them become: capitalist economies able to receive money and allocate it according to market principles, free from patronage, and accountable creditor expectations.'[71]

Despite the controversy surrounding the IMF, efforts continue to work with the troubled economies of debtor nations. However, this criticism has cast a shadow on any resolutions that the IMF has posited, especially the SDRM.

III. THE MULTILATERAL APPROACH: THE IMF'S PROPOSAL OF A SOVEREIGN DEBT RESTRUCTURING MECHANISM

A. Background

At the request of the International Monetary and Financial Committee (IMFC), an advisory committee on the international monetary and financial system to the IMF,[72] Anne Krueger, First Deputy Managing Director of the IMF, first introduced the proposal for the SDRM in November 2001.[73] Subsequently, the IMF explored varying approaches with the international financial community and promulgated an official draft on November 27, 2002.[74] On January 22, 2003, the IMF held a conference to discuss the SDRM proposal and elicit feedback from the international community.[75] Shortly thereafter, the United States indicated its unwillingness to support the proposal, despite strong support by the United Kingdom and other

70 Anghie, *supra* note 67, at 266.

71 James Soemijantro Wilson, *Why Foreign Aid Fails: Lessons from Indonesia's Economic Collapse*, 22 LAW & POL'Y INT'L BUS. 145, 169 (2001).

72 International Monetary Fund, *A Brief Guide to Committees, Groups, and Clubs: A Factsheet*, *available at* http://www.imf.org/external/np/exr/facts/groups.htm#IC (last visited Mar. 22, 2003).

73 Anne Krueger, International Monetary Fund, *Sovereign Debt Restructuring Mechanism-One Year Later* (Dec. 10, 2002), *available at* http://imf.org/external/np/speeches/2002/121002.htm (address before the European Commission).

74 *International Monetary Fund, SDRM Proposal of November 2002, supra* note 31.

75 International Monetary Fund, *A New Approach to Sovereign Debt Restructuring: an IMF Proposal*, (Jan. 22, 2003), *available at* http://www.imf.org/external/np/exr/ecforums/2003/012203.htm.

members of the European Union, and the SDRM was essentially shelved in lieu of the CAC approach.[76] While it is no longer being actively pursued, the lessons from the exercise and the learning garnered should still be utilized in the sovereign debt context, and the IMF and United States have urged the international community to do just that.

It bears mentioning that the SDRM was not applicable to countries with extemely low income and excessive debt. Under the Heavily Indebted Poor Countries (HIPC) initiative, the IMF endeavors to provide a form of debt forgiveness for those nations with unsustainable levels of debt, dangerous levels of poverty, and poor social and economic health.[77] Countries included in the HIPC initiative tend to be in Africa and had to qualify for assistance under this program following a debt sustainability analysis.[78] Following this analysis, if a country's external debt ratio exceeded 150 percent of the net present value of its debt to exports, the country was considered for eligibility and was then required to adhere to various IMF/World Bank economic and financial programs in order to receive full benefit of the initiative.[79]

B. The SDRM in Brief

The IMF designed the SDRM under the guidelines of eleven principles:

The SDRM should only be used for debts that are unsustainable and should not be used in such a way as to encourage default;

The SDRM should include incentives for nations to quickly effectuate a restructuring;

- Conflicts with contractual obligations should be kept to a minimum and should be limited to measures that serve the best interests of the collective creditors;
- The SDRM should promote transparency in the manner of restructuring;
- Early and active creditor involvement should be encouraged.

There should be no interference with the sovereignty of a debtor state.

- To that end, activation can only be made at the sovereign's request;
- The SDRM should only provide mechanisms to incent negotiation, and will not be a concrete plan for the restructuring process;
- Flexibility and simplicity are essential in order to provide endurance of the structure over time;

[76] Alan Beattie, *US Set to Block 'Sovereign Chapter 11' Proposals*, FIN. TIMES LTD., Mar. 31, 2003, at 13.

[77] *HIPC*, supra note 68.

[78] *Id.*

[79] *Id.*

- The SDRM should not supersede domestic insolvency structures already in place and applicable to any claims;
- Dispute resolution would be facilitated in an effective, impartial, and expedient manner; and,
- The IMF's role in the SDRM should be limited to its existing powers and must not be enlarged in any way.[80]

C. Claims under the SDRM

Claims that fell under the SDRM included 'all rights to receive payments relating to the commercial activities of the sovereign.'[81] A claim could be included in the restructuring when there was a clear contractual obligation to provide payment in either currency or goods, in association with commercial activities.[82] 'The central government would have the option to include its own debt and, subject to the consent of the debtor in question, claims on: (i) the central bank and (ii) public entities or subnational governments that are not subject to a domestic insolvency framework.'[83] There are often occasions where a central government has guaranteed funds for a third party or holds another contingent obligation, and these claims would not have automatically fallen under the bailiwick of the SDRM.[84] However, had the claims underlying any sovereign guarantees entered into default, or the contingent claims either matured or could easily be valued at market conditions, these claims would also have been included in the restructuring.[85]

Claims excluded from the framework included domestic debts governed by the applicable insolvency laws of the debtor nation and debts owed to international organizations, including the IMF.[86] Although claims by international organizations and domestic lenders would not have fallen under the auspices of the SDRM, the handling of these claims would have been provided in the name of transparency.[87]

Perhaps the most controversial aspect of the SDRM was the exclusion of international organizations from the class of creditors to be restructured. The proposal clearly defended this position, stating:

> . . . multilateral development banks provide both adjustment lending and financing for investment in human and physical capital at lower costs than could be obtained from international capital markets. The financing of such public goods and capital formation promotes both financial stability and economic growth, and thereby

[80] *International Monetary Fund, SDRM Proposal of November 2002, supra* note 31, at 7–9.

[81] *Id.* at 17.

[82] *Id.*

[83] *Id.* at 8.

[84] *Id.* at 20.

[85] *Id.*

[86] *Id.* at 9.

[87] *Id.* at 10.

enhances the value of private creditors' claims. The ability of these institutions to provide financing at the current cost structure depends critically on the assurance that their claims would not be captured in a sovereign debt restructuring.[88]

The proposal also stated that restructuring of these outstanding debts would not be expected. Interestingly, claims of the Paris Group[89] or other official bilateral groups would have been restructured either within the SDRM, as a separate class, or in tandem with it.[90] The SDRM proposal went on to explain creditor classification, placing all unsecured claims in the same class and allowing secured claims and official bilateral creditors to be in separate classes.[91]

D. Activation

The proposal also left open the question of whether a sovereign could unilaterally initiate the mechanism or whether independent validation would have been required, and if so, by whom.[92] Once activated, the SDRM outlined a process whereby creditors were notified of all outstanding claims, including those that would have been structured in tandem, but not under the SDRM, and those that would not have been restructured at all.[93] Once notified, all creditors were required to register their claims within a certain time period or they were declared null and void.[94] After notification to all of the creditors, a creditor's committee would have been created with representation from the creditors, and approval of any measures would have required a vote of 75 percent of the outstanding principal claims.[95] This vote also empowered the creditors to reject the usage of

[88] *Id.* at 22.

[89] The Paris Club is a group of informal creditors who work to find solutions to unsustainable debts by debtor-nations, beginning in 1956 with a meeting between Argentina and its creditors at the time. A completely informal arrangement, the Club has managed to work through 366 arrangements with over seventy-five countries, with a total debt of $410 billion, since its inception. The unique aspect of the Paris Club is that it has no legal basis, status, or authority in the international arena, yet the creditor nations have agreed upon a set of guidelines to be followed. Meetings are held several times a year, always in Paris and the group is committed to finding ways to restructuring debt, including rescheduling or reducing debt obligations. The creditor member countries are: Austria, Australia, Belgium, Canada, Denmark, Finland, France, Germany, Ireland, Italy, Japan, the Netherlands, Norway, the Russian Federation, Spain, Sweden, Switzerland, the United Kingdom and the United States. Other official creditors who have been invited to attend meetings, but are not members are: Abu Dhabi, South Africa, Argentina, Brazil, Korea, Israel, Kuwait, Mexico, Morocco, New Zealand, Portugal, Trinidad and Tobago, and Turkey. For more information, *see* http://www.clubdeparis.org/en/.

[90] *International Monetary Fund, SDRM Proposal of November 2002, supra* note 31, at 23–4.

[91] *Id.* at 49–51. [92] *Id.* at 9. [93] *Id.* at 29.

[94] *Id.* [95] *Id.* at 10.

the SDRM, as an option existed for the creditors collectively to vote to terminate the mechanism once the process was activated.[96]

E. Stay of Claims

Once activated, no stay of claims existed, as in the U.S. Bankruptcy laws. Rather, any monies collected through litigation would be subtracted from any amount apportioned to that creditor through the restructuring agreement.[97] This exclusion of the traditional insolvency concept was justified on the basis that it interfered with the contractual rights of parties who were already at a disadvantage in terms of bargaining power with the sovereign borrowers.[98] Following notification, creditors with secured claims would have the option of seizing any collateral to the extent afforded by their contractual rights.[99] Unsecured creditors could have at their choosing initiated any action within their rights; however, judgments awarded, but not received, would also be subject to the SDRM as an additional liability and could thus be altered by a majority vote of the creditors.[100] In an effort to further discourage holdout creditors and litigation, judgments that were received would be subject to the 'hotchpot' rule.[101] The hotchpot rule, derived from English bankruptcy law, effectively reduces any subsequent settlement by the amount received in litigation, thereby ensuring equitable distribution of payments.[102] A drawback to this approach arose where the creditor was able to receive a larger judgment than that which would have been apportioned under the SDRM. While there was no method to rectify this potential inequity, the IMF believed that the lengthy process of litigation and remuneration would have far exceeded the time required to effectuate the SDRM, thereby eliminating any potential value to the holdout creditor.[103] Rather, the creditor ended up receiving the amount to which he was entitled under the SDRM, but with the added loss of legal expenses.

Another insolvency concept excluded from the SDRM involved interest payments. In some jurisdictions, interest payments cease to accrue upon commencement of restructuring.[104] The SDRM did not recommend this

[96] *Id.* at 26. [97] *Id.* at 9. [98] *Id.* at 33.
[99] *Id.* at 38. [100] *Id.* at 34. [101] *Id.* at 36.
[102] *Id.* at 37. For example, if Creditor A is owed $10 million dollars and receives a judgment for $5 million, that award will reduce any amount apportioned to Creditor A under the SDRM. Hence, Creditor A's claim is still valued at $10 million and not the reduced $5 million, so a percentage of recovery is based on the original amount. If, under the SDRM, Creditor A is entitled to 75 percent of the debt, Creditor A will receive $7.5 million, minus the $5 million already received, rather than 75 percent of the remaining $5 million. Creditor A will receive $2.5 million from the restructuring, not $3.75 million.
[103] *International Monetary Fund, SDRM Proposal of November 2002, supra* note 31, at 38.
[104] But, compare with the U.S. Chapter 11 procedure, which does not halt the accrual of interest. *See* 11 U.S.C. § 362 (1994).

action, but instead allowed any additional debt accumulated as interest to be included in the restructuring.[105]

Additionally, any new financing was not given priority over existing claims, as is a common practice.[106] Rather, if a qualified majority of the creditors approved, any new financing could be excluded from the restructuring. [107]

F. Administration

Overseeing all of these procedures was the Sovereign Debt Dispute Resolution Forum (SDDRF), consisting of twelve to sixteen appointees with judicial experience in debt restructing matters.[108] These individuals would operate from their home nations and would comprise a pool from which judges were impaneled in the event of a crisis.[109] For each incident, fours judges were to be appointed—one to oversee the process and three to serve as an appellate forum.[110]

The legal basis for this process involved amending the IMF's Articles, which requires a 3/5 approval by the members holding 85 percent of the voting power.[111] As this amendment implicates international treaty terms, many nations, including the United States, would require legislative endorsement and possibly a revision of certain domestic laws and policies.[112] Following that, a verification process would be needed where creditors and claims would be finalized, with any disputes being managed by the SDDRF.[113]

G. Benefits

The most obvious benefit of the SDRM was the potential simplification and standardization of having an international mechanism. Removing the uncertainty would have helped to reassure creditors and debtors alike. As the current situation stood then and continues now, any potential default is handled on an ad-hoc basis, often with the IMF stepping in with significant bailout packages (as in the case of Argentina).[114]

The availability of a structured approach would also have likely encouraged more open communication between debtor-nations and creditors, possibly eliminating the need for costly and painful defaults, such as the one Argentina has recently experienced. When comparing Argentina's experi-

[105] *International Monetary Fund, SDRM Proposal of November 2002, supra* note 31, at 42.
[106] *Id.* at 47. [107] *Id.* [108] *Id.* at 11.
[109] *Id.* [110] *Id.* [111] *Id.* at 12.
[112] *Id.* [113] *Id.* at 33.
[114] Alan Beattie, *Argentine 'Blackmail': As the IMF Prepares a $6bn Debt Roll-over, Doubts About the Fund's Credibility Resurface*, FIN. TIMES, Jan. 21, 2003, at 11.

ence with Brazil's, it is clear that voluntary submission to re-organization bodes far better for a quick economic recovery.[115]

H. Criticisms

The SDRM was subject to significant criticism from the international financial community and IMF member nations. In the spring of 2003, the announcement was made to discontinue any efforts to establish the multilateral approach espoused in the mechanism.[116]

A very vocal criticism of the SDRM focused on the impartiality, or rather, lack thereof, of the IMF in instituting a solution. As one scholar, Christopher Paulus, has pointed out, in referring to the IMF and World Bank and their ability to oversee an international insolvency proceeding, '. . .these institutions are too allied with the creditors (even if this were true only from the debtor's perspective) because they themselves are in fact also creditors.'[117] This was a commonly held concern, exacerbated by the SDRM's exclusion of IMF claims in any restructuring. As William Rhodes, the senior Vice-Chairman of Citigroup, Citicorp, and Citibank, stated:

> It should be noted that, while private sector creditors frequently take losses in country workouts—40 percent with Ecuador recently, on top of an earlier 45 percent under the Brady Plan—the international financial institutions, including the IMF and Paris Club of government lenders reduce their claims only for the so-called highly indebted poor countries. [118]

Mr. Rhodes also felt that the institutionalizing of a formal bankruptcy standard would have:

> . . . encourage[d] more restructurings, thereby further damaging emerging markets as a group and threatening contagion. One result would be reduced private capital flows and a greater need for public sector finance. At the same time, countries that are successfully meeting their debt obligations but face temporary liquidity problems might come under domestic political pressure to file for bankruptcy protection, worsening market sentiment and delaying a return to growth.[119]

He was not alone in his sentiments. Although the SDRM has been criticized

[115] William Rhodes, *The Drawbacks of Orderly Rescue: A Formal Bankruptcy Procedure for Countries Facing Economic Crisis Would be Inefficient and Damaging*, FIN. TIMES, Mar. 22, 2002, at 13.

[116] International Monetary Fund, *The Restructuring Of Sovereign Debt—Assessing the Benefits, Risks, and Feasibility of Aggregating Claims*, at 4 (Sept. 3, 2003), *available at* http://www.imf.org/external/np/pdr/sdrm/2003/090303.pdf [hereinafter *International Monetary Fund, Aggregating Claims*].

[117] Christopher G. Paulus, *Some Thoughts on an Insolvency Procedure for Countries*, 50 AM. J. COMP. L. 531, 541 (2002).

[118] Rhodes, *supra* note 115.

[119] *Id.*

as being too pro-creditor, many bankers and investors were also displeased with the efforts of the IMF.[120] Their concern prior to the issuance of the SDRM appeared to be that the proposal would permit sovereigns to halt payments through a stay on creditor claims.[121] Voicing those concerns was Sir David Walker, a senior advisor at Morgan Stanley, stating 'If the market thinks a mechanism will be put in place where a sovereign borrower in trouble can pull the trigger and stop paying its debts, it will react by tightening up those debt contracts before it happens.'[122]

Clearly, the IMF listened to these concerns, as evidenced by the exclusion of the stay on creditor enforcement and priority financing. However, this met with a backlash from others in the international financial world arguing that a stay on enforcement is imperative, as is the need for priority treatment for any new debt issued subsequent to commencement of an insolvency procedure.[123]

Finally, some parties felt that the need for complete overhaul of the international financial crises management was unnecessary and unrealistic. Experts at the International Institute for Economics claim that most sovereign debtors pay their debts in a timely fashion and the challenges posed by instituting the SDRM far exceeded any benefit that would be derived.[124] The process for instituting this measure, including amending the IMF's Articles of Agreement and then requiring a large part of the membership to adopt domestic legislation in support of it, was considered by some to be insurmountable,[125] especially given that a significant factor behind the financial crises of the past was weak domestic bankruptcy laws.[126]

The nail in the coffin of the SDRM was the very public withdrawal of support by the United States. At a statement to the International Monetary and Financial Committee of the IMF in April 2003, U.S. Treasury Secretary John Snow publicly rejected the use of the SDRM, stating, '[t]he source of these problems lies in the relationships and agreements of debtors and their creditors. It is these parties, not an international organization that must

[120] Alan Beattie & Peronet Despeignes, *IMF Fighting to introduce new sovereign debt rules*, FIN. TIMES, Sept. 30, 2002, at 9.

[121] *Id.*

[122] *Id.* It bears noting that with or without a sovereign debt mechanism, countries have chosen to cease payments on their debt, including Argentina, Ecuador, and Russia. *See* Rhodes, *supra* note 114.

[123] Christopher G. Paulus, *supra* note 117, at 547.

[124] Business Week Online, *The IMF Mess: Can the Treasury Dept. Push the Sort of Real Reforms That Will Help Deadbeat Nations and Their Creditors Come to Terms?* (Sept. 20, 2002), *available at* http://www.businessweek.com.

[125] Barry Eichengreen, *Bailing in the Private Sector: Burden Sharing in the International Financial Crisis Management*, 23 FLETCHER F. WORLD. AFF 57 (1999).

[126] Sean Hagan, *Insolvency Reform and Economic Policy*, 17 CONN. J. INT'L L. 63, 69 (2001); *see also* E. Bruce Leonard, *Bankruptcy—Indonesian Style*, 21 AM. BANKR. INST. J. 26 (2002) (for a thorough discussion of the Indonesian bankruptcy system).

assume responsibility for the solution. Therefore it is neither necessary nor feasible to continue working on the SDRM.'[127]

In the same speech, Secretary Snow also called for the inclusion of Collective Action Clauses ('CACs') as an alternative and preferable approach to the sovereign debt restructuring issue, challenging the IMF to focus on encouraging the widespread use of CACs, as well as improving transparency and open disclosure.[128] Subsequent to this dismissal of the SDRM by the United States, focus did indeed turn towards the inclusion of CACs in new bond agreements and the viability of their usage in correcting existing agreements drafted under conventional unanimity terms.

IV. THE UNILATERAL APPROACH: COLLECTIVE ACTION CLAUSES

A. Background and Mechanics of CACs

Since the abandonment of the SDRM, the international financial community has concentrated efforts in the area of debt restructuring on the usage of CACs as a means to eradicate default. Long used in English bond contracts, CACs allow a majority of creditors to amend clauses, including those regarding payment terms of existing agreements, provided a minimum number of creditors approve the changes.[129] The 'Group of Ten' (G-10)' [130] issued a working report on September 26, 2002, regarding the use of contractual clauses in remedying the sovereign debt solution and proffering recommended terms to be included in bond agreements.[131] Among the clauses recommended by the G-10 for inclusion in sovereign debt agreements were CACs, termed 'majority amendment clauses,' which would permit a majority of bondholders to amend the payment terms; or alternatively, a majority clause to approve an exchange for a new offering.[132] In both cases, determining the threshold for participation would be measured by either a percentage of the outstanding principal amount or based on a quorum system, whereby a quorum of bondholders must be reached before

[127] Press Release, Secretary John Snow, U.S. Department of Treasury, Statement to the International Monetary and Financial Committee of the IMF (Apr. 12, 2003), *available at* http://www.treas.gov/press/releases.

[128] *Id.*

[129] Jack Boorman, Sovereign Debt Restructuring Mechanism: Where Stands the Debate?, Speech to the Economist and Cato Institute (Oct. 17, 2002), *available at* http://www.imf.org/external/np/speeches/2002/101710.htm. [hereinafter Where Stands the Debate?].

[130] The G-10 Working Group on Contractual Clauses is comprised of representatives of the central banks from the European Union and the following countries: Belgium, Canada, France, Germany, Italy, Japan, the Netherlands, Switzerland, Sweden, the United States and the United Kingdom.

[131] Group of Ten, *Report of the G-10 Working Group on Contractual Clauses* (Sept. 26, 2002), *available at* http://www.bis.org/publ/gten08.htm [hereinafter *G-10 Report*].

[132] *Id.*

the requisite percentage approval vote should go into effect.[133] With regard to changes in payment terms, the G-10 recommended the maximum level be 75 percent, while lowering that level to 66 2/3 percent for terms not relatred to payment.[134]

In addition to payment clauses, the G-10 set out detailed recommendations for altering other terms of bond agreements, including the election of a bondholder representatives, who is similar to a trustee and would serve as the liaison for bondholders in communications with the debtor.[135] This bondholder representative would negotiate restructuring terms with the debtor and would have power to take legal action and distribute any recovery to the bondholders.[136] The need for improved disclosure and transparency also calls for additional financial covenants, requiring the debtor to provide timely and specific information regarding financial and economic status.[137] In an effort to limit disruptive acceleration of claims and litigation, clauses would be added to provide for a majority vote to approve a stay of claims.[138]

The examples proffered by the G-10 were soundly endorsed by the United States. John B. Taylor, U.S. Secretary of Treasury for International Affairs, outlined the American proposal in a speech to the Institute for International Economics in April 2002, calling for a majority vote, binding on all bondholders, to agree to a restructuring, a bondholder representative, and an activation process by which the sovereign could enter into restructuring negotiations while staying any litigation or claims as necessary.[139]

Following the U.S. lead, the IMF also shifted gears and issued multiple working papers and reports on the progress and surrounding issues of the use of CACs.[140] Since the United States' effectual 'ruling' on the SDRM, the IMF has explored the use of CACs in depth. The IMF has examined whether an aggregation of claims could be incorporated into the approach, so that creditors across the board could be considered on any vote to

133 *Id.* at 5.
134 *Id.*
135 *Id.* at 2.
136 *Id.*
137 *Id.* at 3.
138 *Id.*

139 John B. Taylor, Sovereign Debt Restructuring: A US Perspective, Speech at the Conference 'Sovereign Debt Workouts: Hopes and Hazards' (Apr. 2, 2002), *available at* http://www.iie.com/publications/papers/taylor0402.htm.

140 International Monetary Fund, *Progress Report to the International Monetary and Financial Committee on Crisis Resolution* (Sept. 5, 2003), *available at* http://www.imf.org/external/np/pdr/cr/2003/eng/090503.pdf [hereinafter *International Monetary Fund, Progress Report*]; International Monetary Fund, *Collective Action Clauses: Recent Developments and Issues* (Mar. 25, 2003), *available at* http://www.imf.org/ external/np/psi/2003/032503.pdf [hereinafter *International Monetary Fund, Collective Action Clauses: Recent Developments and Issues*]; International Monetary Fund, *Reviewing the Process for Sovereign Debt Restructuring within the Existing Legal Framework* (Aug. 1, 2003), *available at* http://www.imf.org/external/np/pdr/sdrm/2003/080103.pdf [hereinafter *International Monetary Fund, Reviewing the Process*]; *International Monetary Fund, Aggregating Claims*, *supra* note 116.

restructure, mimicking an all-encompassing bankruptcy style forum.[141] While ultimately deciding that aggregation should not be pursued, the analysis did shed light on the areas for improvement and continued exploration.[142] Additionally, the IMF has published information regarding the status and prevalence of CAC usage in the sovereign bond context.[143]

B. Complementary Use of Exit Consents in Current Bond Agreements

While the use of CACs is a viable option to prevent default in new bond contracts, the issue remains of the billions of dollars already in existence, governed by agreements that are absent these provisions, and structured such that payment terms cannot be altered at all. As a complementary solution, debtors may have the option of swapping existing agreements for new ones that do include CACs, and using the exit consents of the old offering to provide protection from any bondholder who refuses to submit to the swap.

Should a debtor choose to offer a new bond to its existing creditors, any of the bondholders have the option of accepting or refusing the new contracts. The danger lies with the creditors who refuse the new agreements because once these 'hold outs' remain, they will comprise the majority of the bondholders and depending on the terms of the agreement, could even accelerate payment in the event of a default.[144] To combat this problem, debtors can utilize the clause in bond agreements that allows for non payment-related alterations to the bond.[145] Typically, these clauses require a 1/2 or 2/3 vote of the bondholders and permit changes to the agreement.[146] The intent is that by using these clauses in exchange for new debt instruments, bondholders will amend the agreement such that it is rendered invaluable to any potential holdout creditors.[147] The old bond agreements can then be swapped for new agreements with revised payment terms, effectively restructuring the debt. Examples of the types of clauses that can be removed through this manner are financial covenant clauses, which reduce the secondary market value of the bond, and other clauses that impair the likelihood of repayment, hamper efforts to accelerate debt, or limit the rights to pursue litigation in the event of a default.[148]

141 *International Monetary Fund, aggregating claims, supra* note 116, at XX.

142 *Id.*

143 *Id.*

144 Most bond agreements include language that permits acceleration of unmatured principal in the event of a default. A default is also not necessarily a failure to pay on that particular instrument; it can also be the failure to adhere to certain financial covenants related to solvency, liquidity etc. or a default on another loan or bond. Lee C. Buchheit & G. Mitu Gulati, *Exit Consents in Sovereign Bond Exchanges*, 48 UCLA L. REV. 59, 65 (2000).

145 *Id.* at 60.

146 *Id.*

147 *Id.*

148 *Id.*

The use of exit consents to effect a swap of old agreements to new is illustrated by the recent restructurings of Uruguay and Ecuador. Following the Argentine crisis, Uruguay was faced with a debt totaling over U.S. $11 billion and restructured close to half of that in 2003.[149] Ecuador was the first nation to use exit consents to impair old bonds in lieu of the new issues.[150] In the case of Uruguay, the old agreements were modified to affect the waiver of sovereign immunity, and bondholders were given the option to 'opt out' of the exit.[151] For those who did agree to the exchange, they approved consents that limited the 'holdout creditors' from enforcing the debt obligation part of the bond.[152]

C. Recent Developments in CAC Usage

The IMF has undertaken several reports to measure the usage of CACs, since the focus of the international financial community shifted from the SDRM. Mexico has been lauded as leading the way with $1 billion offering in February 2003, governed by New York law and including a 75 percent majority action clause.[153] In keeping with the recommendations made by the G-10, the Mexico bond measured the threshold in terms of outstanding principal and excluded from the voting any bondholders who are directly or indirectly controlled by the government, but rejected the use of activation and transparency clauses, and chose to rely instead on market drivers to establish best practices.[154] The IMF reported this offering as successful, as there was no evidence of a yield premium in either the initial offering or secondary market.[155] However, whether that is more of a reflection of Mexico's investment grade is still an open question. Whether a lower grade sovereign would enjoy the same result remains to be seen. In terms of creditor action following a default, the Mexican bond did include a threshold of 25 percent outstanding principal minimum vote before acceleration of payments could begin, and more than 50 percent outstanding principal vote to de-accelerate payments.[156] With the absence of a clause representing a

[149] *International Monetary Fund, Reviewing the Process*, *supra* note 140, at 32.
[150] *Id.*
[151] *Id.* at 24.
[152] *Id.* at 32.
[153] Intergovernmental Group of Twenty Four, *G24 Secretariat Briefing Paper on Sovereign Debt Restructuring* (Apr. 4, 2003), *available at* http://www.g24.org/debt.pdf. The Intergovernmental Group of Twenty Four consists of representatives from developing nations to convene over matters of international monetary and fiscal policy. The member countries are: Algeria, Cote D'Ivoire, Egypt, Ethiopia, Gabon, Ghana, Nigeria, South Africa, Democratic Republic of Congo, Argentina, Brazil, Colombia, Guatemala, Mexico, Peru, Trinidad and Tobago, Venezuela, India, Iran, Lebanon, Pakistan, Philippines, Sri Lanka, and Syrian Arab Republic. *See* http://www.g24.org/about.htm.
[154] *International Monetary Fund, Collective Action Clauses: Recent Developments and Issues*, *supra* note 140, at 21.
[155] *Id.* at 22.
[156] *Id.* at 24.

bondholder representative, the agreement was silent as to the result of any bondholder litigation.[157]

Following the Mexican offering, several other sovereign nations issued bonds governed by New York law and included CACs. In the offerings by Brazil, South Africa, the Republic of Korea, Belize, and Guatemala, the IMF found no showing of a pricing disadvantage attributable to the use of CACs.[158] The threshold for restructuring was set at 75 percent for the Korean and South African issuances, while the Brazilian, Guatemalan, and Belizean bonds upped the percentage to 85 percent.[159] All of the bonds included a 25 percent acceleration clause, and the Korean and South African bonds followed suit with Mexico by including a 50 percent de-acceleration threshold, while the remaining three countries opted for 66 2/3 percent.[160]

In total, the number of bonds issued with CACs has increased. In February 2003, the IMF reported that 33 percent of bonds issued included CACs.[161] The European Union Finance Ministers have also stated that any bonds issued for EU members that are governed by foreign law or subject to a foreign choice of forum clause will include CACs.[162] Despite the small percentage of these issuances, this statement heralds public support for the use of CACs. In terms of actual numbers of bonds issued in the first three quarters of 2003 in the emerging markets sector, of the forty nine issuances, twenty seven included CACs, nine of which were governed by New York law.[163] Contrast this with the numbers reported in 2001 (ninety-three issuances and less than two were issued under New York law) with CACs, and it is clear that the United States' push for CACs is having an impact on market practices.[164]

D. Benefits

The primary benefit of using CACs and exit consents, and the reason the United States is so firmly in support of such tools, resides in the ability of individual debtors and creditors to fashion their own mutually acceptable terms and covenants. This freedom of contract is a fundamental principle in U.S. law and is evidenced in the market driven policies of the American financial community. In fact, even U.S. securities regulation is premised on disclosure rather than merit, facilitating independent decision-making on the parts of investors.

157 *Id.* at 32.
158 *International Monetary Fund, Progress Report, supra* note 140, at 3.
159 *Id.* at 7.
160 *Id.* at 8.
161 *International Monetary Fund, Collective Action Clauses: Recent Developments and Issues, supra* note 140, at 15.
162 *Id. at* 19.
163 *International Monetary Fund, Progress Report, supra* note 140, at 4.
164 *Id.*

A second, but no less prevalent, advantage of CACs and exit consents is the relative ease with which this change can take place. Rather than requiring multilateral treaty amendments and subsequent domestic legislation overhauls, parties can begin, and indeed have begun, implementing these changes immediately.

Finally, the fact remains that the United States and international financial community have pledged their support of the use of CACs in lieu of a SDRM type structure. Regardless of whether CACs are the ideal solution, or whether debtor nations would prefer an international forum for resolution, as the parties who hold the purse strings, the United States and other creditors will ultimately dictate the path chosen.

E. Criticisms

Obviously, while the merits of utilizing CACs and exit consents is that, in tandem, the two could prove immediately effective (i.e. using the exit clause to entice creditors to accept new agreements containing CACs), the problem still remains that the creditors must be willing to accept the terms of the new agreements. They must believe that what is in the best interest of the debtor is in their best interest as well. This common economic predicament is referred to as the 'Prisoner's Dilemma,' where one party must trust that their sacrifice is truly the most advantageous for all. In terms of hold out creditors, this poses a daunting challenge. For exit consents to help reduce the number of hold out creditors, there must first be a significant number of creditors willing to approve the use of the bond altering exit consents. The IMF reports that persuading these creditors to accept the new arrangement may be more likely when a default is already imminent, defeating the purpose of including CACs and exit consents to avert default.[165] Contributing to this concept is the ever-present concern of moral hazard and the historical bail-out packages provided by the IMF. As evidenced by recent restructuring attempts, creditors are much more likely to hold out if the option of an IMF bail out package seems imminent.

Locating and assembling a significant enough number of creditors to utilize this option also remains a formidable task. As described above, bondholders are numerous and varied, and a mechanism would have to be instituted to capture data on the individuals or institutions empowered to vote on any collective action. This could be accomplished with the G-10's recommendation of appointing a bondholder representative. But, as evidenced by the Mexican offering, this clause may not be included. The IMF has also recommended a method for tracking bondholders through a

[165] *International Monetary Fund, Reviewing the Process*, *supra* note 140, at 22.

voluntary registry system.[166] Notwithstanding the fact that there is no forum to maintain this type of information, even if this was feasible it would only affect new issuances. Locating and assembling data on current bondholders would be a significant and costly challenge.

What if exit consents are not an option? The use of CACs alone will do nothing to eliminate the burden on nations currently, as it can only be applied to agreements issued here forthwith. It still stands that the majority of current bond contracts cannot be amended to include this type of provision.

Additionally, Jack Boorman, Special Advisor to the Managing Director of the IMF, criticizes the use of CACs in that the application of law among the varying jurisdictions would be inconsistent by virtue of the fact that each jurisdiction maintains their own legal idiosyncrasies.[167] This is most troubling for debtor nations who could face disparate legal treatment among jurisdictions, possibly from the same bond indenture where legal action may be initiated by diverse bondholders. Although choice of law and forum clauses are inevitably included in each agreement, it is not atypical for sovereign debtors to hold multiple bonds denominated in various currencies and governed by different nations.

Market concerns about the 'signaling effects' of the uses of CACS also can not be discounted, despite the comments by the IMF regarding the Mexican issuance. Noted economist, Barry Eichengreen, outlined this concern in an article published in advance of his book on the International Financial Architecture.[168] Mr. Eichengreen pointed out that any nation choosing to include these types of clauses in their debt instruments may be the victim of the 'adverse signaling effect,' whereby choosing to use these clauses indicates the likelihood of default and the need for rescheduling.[169] He analogizes the use of these clauses to the use of a prenuptial agreement by a bride and groom.[170] Until, and unless, the inclusion of these clauses becomes standard drafting techniques, the likelihood of making creditors wary may be counterproductive.

The implication of U.S. securities laws is also a factor that must be recognized. In bonds issued by Egypt, Lebanon and Qatar, in 2000 and 2001, the exemption under Rule 144A was perfected, allowing the issuers to sell only to qualified institutional buyers, thus avoiding the complex and tedious registration process.[171] However, whether any discussions between creditors and debtors regarding a swap or new issuance would violate securities regulation preventing 'market conditioning' is as of yet still undetermined.

[166] *Id.* at 16.
[167] Where Stands the Debate, supra note 129.
[168] Eichengreen, *supra* note 125, at 57.
[169] *Id.*
[170] *Id.*
[171] *International Monetary Fund, Collective Action Clauses: Recent Developments and Issues*, *supra* note 140, at 19.

This communication between potential investors and the issuer or underwriter could be construed as an offer to sell, and, absent a statutory prospectus, would be a violation of Sec. 5(c) of the 1933 Securities Act.[172] Indeed, Ecuador and Uruguay both determined that the details of their respective debt exchanges could not be disclosed until the proper filings were made with the U.S. Securities Exchange Commission.[173]

Finally, the inclusion of CACs in each bond agreement fails to address the restructuring in its entirety, unless a type of aggregation is included in the agreement. So, while a single bond may be revised, absent a clause to the contrary, each individual debt agreement would have to be modified independently through a costly and complex process. The IMF drafted a report on the use of aggregation in the CAC context, and while finding merit in the efficacy, ultimately determined that the challenges and potential negative reaction of the market indicated that it 'would not be appropriate for the Fund to endorse a particular set of aggregation provisions at this time.'[174] Uruguay did include a form of aggregation in their recent debt swap, in that payment terms could be modified for multiple bonds via an aggregate voting mechanism.[175] Specifically, the 75 percent threshold would drop to 66 2/3 percent on each individual bond, upon a vote to restructure by 85 percent of the bondholders of the aggregated outstanding principal amount.[176] However, this aggregation was limited, as it only applied to new bonds issued under the same trust agreement and governed by New York law.[177] Any past issuance or other forms of sovereign debt would not be eligible for aggregation. The G-10 also touched on the potential for aggregation among creditors for voting purposes and came to the same conclusion as the IMF, stating that while '. . .desirable, is not practicable within a contractually based mechanism.'[178]

V. CONCLUSION

A. Comparison of Methods

It is not enough to merely analyze the differing proposals for sovereign debt in and of themselves, absent the underpinning motivation of the resolution. Different nations and cultures strive for varied goals in the resolution of solvency issues. For example, the United States tends to encompass a more debtor-friendly approach, encouraging the debtor to re-organize and the

[172] 1933 Securities Act, 15 U.S.C § 77(a) (2003).
[173] *International Monetary Fund, Reviewing the Process, supra* note 140, at 11.
[174] *International Monetary Fund, Collective Action Clauses: Recent Developments and Issues, supra* note 140, at 30.
[175] *Id.* at 6. [176] *Id.* [177] *Id.*
[178] *G-10 Report, supra* note 131.

creditor to be more accommodating.[179] In contrast, Germany tends to emphasize creditor rights, and France focuses on the labor force affected by the financial distress.[180] While these generalities apply to corporate bankruptcy, in cases of nations where total liquidation or external management is not an option, some or all of these may still be applicable.[181]

So, while economic efficiency is certainly not a component in evaluating a solution, whether a plan for reorganization is designed more to protect the rights of the creditors, or encourage a 'fresh start' for the debtor is an important factor. The use of the SDRM, exit consents, and CACs all tend to favor the creditor, an irony that cannot be overlooked, given these proposals have come from supranational organizations that tend to serve as creditors. Ideally, given the context of sovereign debt, a plan for re-organization would mimic the more debtor friendly policies of the United States.

Leading economists, politicians, and legal authorities have grappled with the issue of sovereign debt for years and have failed to come up with a solution that pleases all parties. The recommendations today are no exception. Notwithstanding the current status of the multilateral approach, it is arguable that for purposes of consistency, credibility, and simplicity, the best solution is still to institute an international sovereign debt restructuring mechanism. However, the SDRM falls well short of an ideal proposal. The criticisms of the SDRM are valid, but rather than completely disengaging from the multilateral perspective, the international financial community should use the lessons learned from that exercise to create a more equitable and balanced scheme.

The apparent creditor friendly framework of the SDRM leaves the debtors smarting, while the creditors feel as though this mechanism possesses the power to alienate them from property which they are rightfully due. Neither party wants to admit that the option of default exists—the creditors because they feel that will entice debtors into a restructuring; and the debtors because of the potential impact on capital flows to their home states. However, default does exist and the SDRM is a good foundation for an overarching scheme to deal with it. The SDRM fails though in its crippled and weak state. The exclusion of a stay on creditor claims and actions, the accumulation of the interest, and the enlarged power of the IMF, all expose the limits of consensus philosophy in multilateral solutions. It succeeds in the aggregation of claims and the consistency and applicability of an international structure and forum. The use of CACs alone will never accomplish that same uniformity and clarity.

Structurally speaking, the use of CACs essentially provides the same majority approval process that the SDRM proposed, but manages the resolution on a micro-contractual level, retaining any choice of law/forum

[179] Paulus, *supra* note 117, at 540. [180] *Id.* [181] *Id.* at 534.

agreements included in the individual bond contract.[182] In contrast, the SDRM incorporated a more macroeconomic structure, subjugating all agreements to an overarching international insolvency scheme.[183] A balance between the two is the ideal solution, for although the U.S. definitely favors the 'freedom of contract,' contract terms and conditions do not exist in a vacuum. Rather, there is an entire code, the Uniform Commercial Code, as well as a surfeit of case law dedicated to eliminating ambiguity and inconsistency in contract law application. Debtors and creditors should still have the freedom to negotiate terms acceptable to both, but there should be an international forum to which nations can turn in the event of a breakdown. As the past decade has taught us, default is inevitable and pretending that it will not occur is not only harmful to all parties, but foolish and naïve.

Social contract theory tells us that communities make laws to eliminate uncertainty. In a truly global economy where nations enter into financial agreements with each other, all states are essentially a member of the same community. Adopting a non-regulatory laissez faire style ignores the reality that default and restructuring is an inevitable result and, absent a regulatory structure, leads to the type of stand-off we are seeing in Argentina today.

Critics of the SDRM, or a similar program, point to the challenges in implementation as support for abandoning the approach. While the logistics of implementing the SDRM appear unfathomable, requiring not only an amendment to the Article's of Agreement, but also for each member nation to adopt a legal structure that fits in with the regulatory concepts of the SDRM, the fact that a task is daunting is a poor excuse for failing to endeavor.

Is the IMF really the correct proponent of this type of mechanism? As a controversial international institution, the IMF appears to be struggling with an identity crisis regarding its role in the financial community. It touts itself as being an agency to correct balance of payments problems, yet admits that most see it as a lender of last resort. It even goes so far as to exclude itself from debt restructuring because of its position as a creditor who will provide capital when all others refuse. If that does not define it as a 'lender of last resort,' then the concept behind that is clearly misunderstood. While the IMF appeared to be limiting its power on the surface by making outright declarations that the SDRM did not enlarge its power, it is truly incredible to see how the SDRM did quite the opposite. Not only did it safeguard the IMF loans from restructuring, but it put into place a quasi-judicial body to oversee the restructurings that would be hand selected by the IMF. Additionally, with the IMF's historic policy of requiring indebted

182 Where Stands the Debate?, supra note 129. 183 *Id.*

nations to institute social and economic policies as dictated by the IMF, there can be no question of the lack of impartiality or neutrality in its position with regards to these debtor nations.

While the concept of an international bankruptcy scheme is a good one in theory and by all rights, an obviously necessary one given the status of the multilateral approach, the likelihood of getting stubborn, fiercely independent nations and parties to succumb to a supranational power appears dismal at best. One only need look at the current state of affairs in the United Nations, the trade squabbles in the World Trade Organization, or the impaired jurisdiction of the International Criminal Court to realize that.

Nobel Prize winning economist Joseph Stiglitz says it best:

> . . . it is good news that the IMF, after the failure if six bailouts in as many years, finally recognized that an alternative approach was needed, and that some sovereign debt restructuring mechanism was desirable. They are right, too, that one cannot rely on market-based approaches (a fact which they failed to recognize in east Asia), that some version of a statutory approach was desirable. It should have been obvious that in any bankruptcy procedure which is viewed as fair, a major creditor (such as the IMF) cannot simultaneously play the role as the bankruptcy judge, nor even have a central role in the process, other than as one of the claimants. To many, the IMF's attempt to give itself such a central role says much about its political insensitivities.[184]

Yet, CACs do not present a viable alternative. As Professor Sitglitz has pointed out, it is evident that market efficiency based approaches are also not satisfactory:

> . . . the long debate about bankruptcy reform in the United States should have made it clear that there is not a single 'best' bankruptcy code. The fact that every government among the advanced industrial countries has taken a statutory approach (rather than relying on market mechanisms, modified, by, for instance, mandatory collective action clauses) should have made it clear that the position of the U.S. Treasury (which seemed to claim that all that was required was collective action clauses) makes little sense, reinforcing the results of theoretical and empirical research on bankruptcy and bargaining. [185]

In line with Prof. Stiglitz's thinking, the CAC/exit consent approach suffers its own weaknesses by relying on market actions to rectify an already tenuous situation. An impromtptu, ad-hoc solution at best, it can be analogized to the little Dutch boy and the dike. No matter how often you plug the hole, water will seep from somewhere. Rather than focusing on the

[184] Joseph E. Stiglitz, *Development Policies in a World of Globalization* (Sept. 12-13, 2002), *available at* http://www.gsb.Columbia.edu/faculty/jstiglitz/dowload/developmentglobalization.pdf (paper presented at the seminar New International Trends for Economic Development),

[185] *Id.*

leaks, the best bet of the international financial community is to create a consistent and all-encompassing resolution and attack the problem from a new angle. Utilizing loopholes in existing agreements does nothing to further strengthen investors confidence, national stability, or fiscal soundness. These three components for sovereign solvency should be the focus of the many hours and energies spent in dissecting the problems with sovereign debt; creating an international forum for conflict resolution promotes these three concepts. It is far better to treat the illness than the symptom.

B. Conclusion

In conclusion, the best solution to alleviate the pressure of default is a combination approach of using unilateralism and multilateralism; or, in other words, maintaining the freedom to contract, but shrouded in the safety of an international bankruptcy scheme to encompass externalities. While the SDRM is an admirable effort and mimics in many ways the successful bankruptcy practices of developed nations, several aspects render it lame. Primarily, without the credibility and authority of a supranational body, netural and empowered to ensure its enforcement, it remains as idealistic, yet ineffective as the intergovernmental institutions in place today. Additionally, an international endorsement will not be forthcoming without the United States altering its position on the preferred solution to debt restructuring. The dogged determination of the U.S. to unilaterally claim that CACs are the panacea for all the ails of the current financial crises stultifies any multilateral efforts. Even if the weaknesses of the SDRM were addressed and the process fortified with more debtor-friendly and equitable elements, such as priority for debtor financing, stays on claims and interest, and a more neutral adjudicating body than the IMF, without U.S. support any efforts appear to be moot.

Having said that, the use of CACs will not alone eradicate the current economic situation, for there are too many unresolved issues, such as an absence of aggregation, challenges inherent in the volume of outstanding issuances without CACs, difficulty in locating and assembling the diverse investors, and concerns regarding U.S. securities law implications. Inevitably, the international financial community will realize this when the next Argentine-style default occurs, and discourse will erupt again over the optimal solution. It can only be hoped that at this point, the lessons from the SDRM will be better utilized and a consensus will be reached establishing a regulatory framework that is economically efficient, equitable, and effective.

CHAPTER SEVENTEEN

Legal Development Co-operation: Conditions, Principles and Methods

*by Claes Sandgren**

CHAPTER OUTLINE

I. Background, Development and Theory
   A. Background
   B. Development
   C. Why Legal Development Co-operation?
   D. The Law, Democracy and Economy
II. Judicial Functions and Legal Development Co-operation
   A. Attitudes of the Law
   B. General Functions
   C. Functions of the Rule of Law and the Market Economy
III. The Judicial Sector and Legal Development Co-operation
   A. Delimiting and Defining
   B. The Sections of the Sector
   C. Judicial Pluralism
   D. Civil Society
   E. State and Private
IV. Legal Development Co-operation
   A. Special Requirements for Legal Development Co-operation
   B. Principles for Legal Development Co-operation
   C. Transfer of Regulations?
   D. Legal Development Co-operation to 'Difficult Countries'
   E. Legal Development Co-operation to Countries After Conflicts
V. Methods For Legal Development Co-operation
   A. Method for Legal Development Co-operation
   B. Need for Development of Competence

This chapter is an attempt to paint a broad picture of legal development co-operation by emphasising the particular requirements of legal assistance, its

* Dean, and Professor of Law, Faculty of Law, Stockholm University <claes.sandgren@juridicum.su.se>

principles, and methods. This means that a considerable number of general, policy, and technical issues related to legal development co-operation are left aside.

I. BACKGROUND, DEVELOPMENT AND THEORY

A. Background

For the past two decades a very large number of countries in the South and in eastern Europe have been undergoing a transformation. One-party states are becoming democracies and controlled economies are changing into market economies.[1] Assets held in collective ownership—whether state or other kinds of societal ownership—are being privatised. Many economies that formerly had high inflation rates are being stabilised. Closed economies are opening to the surrounding world and becoming internationalised. There is also a form of 'modernisation' of many cultures; this modernity affects the values, life style, and even identity of many people. This is a process that not only embraces countries in transition in the former communist world, but also a number of countries in Africa, Asia, and Latin America which have suffered from economic stagnation and/or political totalitarianism. The process opens these countries' legal systems to far-reaching demands for reform.[2]

1. Conclusions For Legal Development Co-Operation

In countries in transition, it is the issue of a transformation that requires judicial reform on a broad front. For countries in the process of liberalisation, e.g., India and in Latin America, they are largely concerned with deregulation[3] and repromulgation of the body of laws governing the market economy. The legal system is influenced by this transformation and creates a basis for it, but can also be a means of keeping a tight rein on its negative effects. This also implies that the law will come into focus for a donor more clearly than in the past.

[1] Janine S. Hiller & Snjezana Puselj Drezga, *Progress and Challenges of Privatization: The Croatian Experience*, 17 U. PA. J. INT'L ECON. L. 383, 383–84 (1996).

[2] *See, e.g.*, Joseph J. Norton, FINANCIAL SECTOR REFORM IN EMERGING MARKETS (BIICL 2000).

[3] Barry R. Weingast, *The Economic Role of Political Institutions: Market-Preserving Federalism and Economic Development*, 11 J.L. ECON. & ORG. 1, 1–2 (1995).

B. Developments

1. Previous Developments

Judicial issues are not completely new in the context of development co-operation. The so-called Law & Development Movement, which had its beginning in the USA, was very popular in the 1960s, but only achieved limited results. The movement, which was based on a 'modernisation theory' popular at the time, had an evolutionary approach to development, namely that it occurred (and ought to occur) in a chain of given steps which result in the same values and institutions as in the west. It also had ethnocentric features, that is familiarity with and respect for the culture of the rule of law, and assumed that the social context in recipient countries was imperfect. In the third world, however, there was a widespread scepticism of the values and judicial models which were characteristic of legal development co-operation at the time. The movement thus passed into a twilight phase, which did not prevent many developing countries from cautiously trying to reform their legal systems on the basis of their own conditions and with some inspiration from industrialised countries. Though inputs for legal development co-operation have thus been in a backwater for some time, there was an upswing during the latter part of the 1980s and that continued to accelerate throughout the 1990s.[4]

2. Legal Development Co-Operation Today

Legal development co-operation continues to grow today, even if it is from a relatively low level. Vietnam is one example of these rapid developments. The United Nations Development Programme (UNDP) existed first (1992) and was soon followed by Sweden and France. Apparently, Vietnam now has 30 donors in the field of legal development co-operation, which implies that the country may be over-financed. In general, most donors and lenders are increasing their activities in the judicial sector. The World Bank[5] and UNDP, as well as the Inter-American Development Bank (IDB) and Asian Development Bank (AsDB), are very active and the International Monetary Fund (IMF) consistently maintains the need for judicial reforms. In the past, judicial projects were financed through grants, but in recent years an increasing number of countries have taken loans from international financial institutions for broad judicial programmes. Policy work is also underway in several places—*e.g.*, in the United Kingdom's Department for

4 Matthew M. Getter, *Yugoslavia and the European Economic Community: Is a Merger Feasible?*, 11 UPAJIBL 789 (1990).

5 See Judicial Reform Program, *available at* http://www4.worldbank.org/legal/leglr/ (last visited March 2003).

International Development (DFID) and UNDP—even if the thinking is not nearly as sophisticated as policy development in the mature development co-operation sectors.

3. Legal Development Co-Operation In Eastern Europe

Significant inputs are being made in eastern Europe by European Bank for Reconstruction and Development (EBRD), the European Union (EU), the World Bank and others. Here, legal development co-operation is closely related to EU expansion, since it requires far-reaching judicial reforms in the countries in transition that are now applying for membership. Recently, there has been an increase in consciousness of the sector 'justice and home affairs' and the major problems that can arise in the negotiations. Candidate countries have increasingly been forced to devise strategies for a reformation of the entire judicial sector. In other countries in transition, including Russia, and post-conflict countries, like former Yugoslavia, need also exists for judicial reform for which knowledge and resources are lacking.

4. Conclusions For Legal Development Co-Operation

Developments uniformly indicate a continued expansion of legal development co-operation. Thus, it is apposite for a donor to closely follow the rapid developments that are underway, systematically to make use of the experiences that have been gained and the development of competence that is undertaken.

C. Why Legal Development Co-operation?

1. The Importance of the Institutions

Socio-economic research has shown how important institutions are for both economic growth and for poor and other vulnerable groups. One category of institutions is the judicial in a broad sense which includes both state and private organisations and the judicial framework Characteristic of the market economy are the institutions—regulations and organs that are taken for granted in the west—which control the activities of the actors on the market.

2. The Importance of the Costs of Transactions

The cost of transactions is typically large in a developing country and as a consequence, companies are reluctant to invest or to embark on risky transactions including long-term commitments. This restricts economic growth and necessitates a reliable and efficient judiciary, since it can reduce these costs.

3. *Globalisation*

Globalisation has many dimensions.[6] Here, it is natural to point out that a country can use the law as an instrument to embrace the opportunities that globalisation offers, *e.g.*, to participate in international trade and attract investments. It can also counteract its negative effects. Not least, many of the losses of suzerainty of weaker states that may follow in the wake of globalisation can be offset through agreements on the global plane, *e.g.*, control of financial activity and organised crime. Human rights are also included in this pattern as an integrated part of trade treaties.

4. *'Modern Development Co-operation'*

Development co-operation that regards its task as creating *preconditions* for growth has good reasons to give priority to legal development co-operation. This can lead to an increased exchange of resources and development processes within many social sectors. A well-functioning judicial system also improves the outlook for development co-operation and for other efforts being made in many sectors.

5. *Perspective*

(a) *The concept of development.* Already, the concept of 'development' implies that a society has a minimal rule of law.[7] If people are arbitrarily imprisoned, if 'justice' can be bought, if the spread of crime is unchecked, if agreements are not honoured, or if sentences are not enforced, serious problems abound in society. The quality of a system of justice in a society consequently has a value of its own and it has a place in the concept of development.

[6] Stanley, Aronowitz, Heather Gautney, and Clyde W. Barrow. *Implicating Empire: Globalization and Resistance in the 21st Century World Order* (New York: Basic Books 2003); Neil Brenner, *State/Space: A Reader* (Oxford: Blackwell Pub. 2003); Will Hutton, *A Declaration of Interdependence: Why America Should Join the World* (1st American ed. New York: W. W. Norton 2003); Jan Nederveen Pieterse, *Globalization and Culture: Global Melange* (Lanham: ROWMAN & LITTLEFIELD 2004); George Ritzer, *The Globalization of Nothing* (Pine Forge Press 2004). See also Heba Shams, *Law in the Context of Gloablization: A Framework of Analysis*, 35 INT'L LAW. 1589–1626 (2001).

[7] Boniface Ahunwan, *Globalization and Corporate Governance in Developing Countries: A Micro Analysis of Global Corporate Interconnection between Developing African Countries and Developed Countries*. Series on International Law and Development (Transnational Publishers 2003); World Bank, Legal Vice Presidency. 'The World Bank Legal Review: Law and Justice for Development.' Washington, DC, The Hague; New York: World Bank;Kluwer Law International, 2003.

(b) *Poverty*. Human rights and freedoms are of great importance for the poorest of the poor. Such an approach emphasises the individual's own capabilities and counteracts the reduction of the poor to victims or clients. It is also the poorest who are most affected by high crime rates. Projects that include education on rights, legal aid, mechanisms of appeal, crime prevention, etc. have a clear poverty profile. The judicial framework can also help the poor to organise themselves, *e.g.*, in water-user co-operatives and similar types of organisations. A poverty approach also has positive effects on gender equality.

(c) *Human Rights*. Human rights are to an increasing degree a general starting point for development co-operation. Such a human rights perspective assumes that a system of justice exists which can guarantee respect for these rights, *i.e.* regulations governing rights and institutions which ensure that the rights can have substance and form the basis of the growth of a 'culture of human rights.'[8] The judicial system is particularly important for the poor, as they do not have recourse to other means of asserting their rights. Similarly, the judicial system, *e.g.*, laws on procurement and transparency, can contribute to combating corruption; and laws, which entail a liberalisation of the economy, can remove the grounds for certain forms of corruption.

(d) *Equality*. Sexually related violence ought to be dealt with in a judicial way, like rape and other assault, trade in women, prostitution, child marriage, female circumcision etc. Equality in the woman's economic position can also be reinforced via the judiciary, particularly through counteracting discrimination in the work place and strengthening her right to own property, including rights of inheritance. Constitutional reforms can reinforce women's position in political life.

(e) *Environment*. Legislation to protect the environment has with time come to be a central feature of inputs to safeguard the environment.[9] It is not only concerned with ecological protection in a narrow sense—protec-

[8] Kenneth W. Hunter, and Timothy C. Mack, *International Rights and Responsibilities for the Future* (Praeger 1996); Robert G. Patman, *Universal Human Rights?* (New York: St. Martin's Press 2000); Joseph Wronka, *Human Rights and Social Policy in the 21st Century: A History of the Idea of Human Rights and Comparison of the United Nations Universal Declaration of Human Rights with United States Federal and State Constitution.*

[9] Borgese, Elisabeth Mann, et al. *Marine Issues: From a Scientific, Political and Legal Perspective*, The Hague; New York: KLUWER LAW INTERNATIONAL, 2002. Geradin, Damien, *The Liberalization of Electricity and Natural Gas in the European Union*, European Monographs; 27. The Hague; London; Boston: Kluwer Law International, 2001. Law of the Sea Institute. Conference (29th: 1995: Denpasar Indonesia), et al. Sustainable Development and Preservation of the Oceans: The Challenges of Unclos and Agenda 21. Honolulu: Law of the Sea Institute, William S. Richardson School of Law, University of Hawaii, 1997. Sand, Peter H. Transnational Environmental Law: Lessons in Global Change. International Environmental Law and Policy Series; V. 53. The Hague; Boston: Kluwer Law International, 1999.

tion against pollution of air, water etc.—but also the legislation that regulates agriculture, industry, and other environmentally sensitive commercial activities.

6. *Conclusions for Legal Development Co-operation*

Judicial reform facilitates reforms in many sectors. In numerous cases, it is a prerequisite for better use of resources. Legal development co-operation can contribute to such judicial reform. It can also strengthen the judicial system in a country, which can be a great support for all those who seek to assert their rights, not least, those without property, minorities, and others who cannot maintain their rights in any other way.

D. The Law, Democracy and Economy

1. *The Law and Democracy*

The law and democracy are related. Politics and the judiciary are thus not two separate spheres. Judicial reforms are political—human rights,[10] for instance, offer the individual greater safeguards against the state and in this way limit its powers. On the other hand, judicial reforms often are reliant on political reforms—independence for the courts, for example, requires adopting a political stance.

2. *The Law and the Economy*

Functioning markets and the rule of law also impact one another in various ways. Judicial reforms are largely economic reforms. In many cases bankruptcy legislation, for instance, leads to the restructuring of (state) companies. Conversely, a number of judicial reforms require economic reforms, *e.g.*, privatisation, while at the same time privatisation of state enterprises requires a well-functioning legal system. A close correspondence between judicial reforms and economic policies must exist. The law can play an important role for economic developments, at least if the government has sound economic policies.

[10] Biebesheimer, Christina, Francisco Mej,ia, and Inter-American Development Bank. Justice Beyond Our Borders: Judicial Reforms for Latin America and the Caribbean. Washington, D.C.: Distributed by the Johns Hopkins University Press for the Inter-American Development Bank, 2000. Burnell, Peter J. Democracy Assistance: International Co-Operation for Democratization. [Democratization Studies,. London; Portland, OR: F. Cass, 2000. Shihata, Ibrahim F. I., Sabine Schlemmer-Schulte, and Keyong Dong. Liber Amicorum Ibrahim F.I. Shihata: International Finance and Development Law. The Hague [The Netherlands]; Boston: Kluwer Law International, 2001. Solomon, Peter H. Courts and Transition in Russia: The Challenge of Judicial Reform. Boulder, CO: Westview Press, 2000.

3. *Conclusions for Legal Development Co-operation*

The three spheres of politics, economy, and law are closely related. Judicial reforms that do not harmonise with political and economic reforms lose a degree of efficacy. Those who design legal development co-operation must keep an eye on the judicial interplay with politics and the economy; otherwise, there is a risk that the inputs become inoperative. There are also reasons to direct inputs to areas where the law has particular significance for economic developments.[11] An example is the private sector in general and capital markets. Within the sphere of the rule of law, one can point out that the law is central to combating discrimination and corruption.

II. JUDICIAL FUNCTIONS AND LEGAL DEVELOPMENT CO-OPERATION

A. *Attitudes to the Law*

1. *Instrumental Approach*

To a large degree, the law is a tool of those in power; that is, it is primarily the tool of the political powers. This is how it functions in all types of regimes. In totalitarian regimes, the law tends only to be regarded as such a 'tool,' and the regime as per definition good.

2. *Intrinsic Value and Counterbalance*

In democracies, the law also has an intrinsic value and can even provide a counterbalance that limits the authority of those in power in favour of certain basic values. Human rights fulfil such a function irrespective of whether they are laid down in the constitution or backed up by international agreements. This means that not even a popularly elected parliament can legitimately take decisions exactly as they wish. Among other things, minorities have the law to protect them.

3. *The Framework of the Market Economy*

Law can also fulfil a third function; namely, to be a framework for

[11] Council of Europe. Evaluation of Legislation: Proceedings of the Council of Europe's Legal Co-Operation and Assistance Activities (2000-2001). Strasbourg: Council of Europe Pub., 2001.—Information and Legal Co-operation Concerning 'Information Society Services': Convention Ets No. 180 Opened for Signature in Moscow on 4 October 2001 and Explanatory Report. Legal Issues. Strasbourg [Croton-on-Hudson, NY: Council of Europe Pub.; Manhattan Pub. Co., distributor], 2001 Council of Europe. European Committee on Legal Co-operation, and Council of Europe.

economic transactions. Its aim is primarily to reduce the costs of transactions in a market economy. In such cases, regulations are typically neutral in relation to the state's interests. In the first place, in cases where they negotiate on such issues, economic actors should agree on the content of the regulations with the addition of certain protective mechanisms.

4. Conclusions for Legal Development Co-operation

In all the countries now leaving one party rule and planned economies, there is a need also to deal with the instrumental approach to the law which prevailed previously. For political reasons, it is a painful process for politicians and others. The culture of the rule of law is also a restriction in the sense that the instrumental view is so deeply rooted even among lawyers that they find it difficult to liberate themselves from it. Such an approach blocks both legal development co-operation that would like to promote reforms of the rule of law, and deregulation that robs the state and state enterprises of a favoured position in economic life.

B. General Functions

1. Functions

The law fulfils a number functions in all societies. One can broadly distinguish between the following functions, each of which is carried out by one or more institutions:

- Creating the law (done by law-makers and precedence setting bodies);
- Conflict-resolution (courts, arbitration councils, extra-judicial organs, direct negotiations);
- Control of the implementation of rules and agreements (police, public prosecutors, courts);
- Representatives of the parties (legal aid organisation, advocates, paralegals and other non-professional representatives);
- Execution (executive authorities, prison and correctional services, tax authorities);
- Checks on the system (ombudsmen, norm-testing organs, human rights organisations, media); and
- Morale formation (all).

2. Conclusions for Legal Development Co-operation

This catalogue indicates that the legal system as a whole that functions more or less well. The catalogue thereby also becomes a tool for analysis of legal support, both ex-ante and ex-post. It is a reminder that legal support should not routinely be chosen to top the list. If weaker parts of the system are found lower down on the list, this can be reason to direct attention to them, which is often important from a poverty perspective.[12]

C. *Functions of the Rule of Law and the Market Economy*

If one turns to the contents of legal support, one can differentiate between two main categories of inputs, namely support to the rule of law (C.1) and inputs directed at the market (C.2).

1. *Rule of Law Inputs*

a. Monitoring Function

Support to the rule of law has the aim of strengthening the constitutional state ('rechtsstaat', 'rättsstat'). Not unusually, the attempt to create 'increased justice' is in some sense regarded as a monitoring function for inputs of this type. It is a diffuse concept, but is nevertheless important when evaluating inputs of this type, with the result that one should attempt to clarify the goal for the inputs as far as possible. There are, for instance, reasons to distinguish between formal and material justice, and between the rule of law (more or less, security of life and property) and rule BY law (more or less, subjection to the law).[13] Of greatest operative value is perhaps the distinction between security of life and property, equality before the law, security before the law, and accessibility of the law.

b. Functions

(a) Rule of law, or security of life and property, is a concept that is used in the most varied contexts, including development co-operation. Thus, one ought to clarify what is entailed. Lawfulness, predictability, and perhaps other things may be considered. One ought also to pose the question if it is only due process which is referred to, or whether the concept of the rule of

[12] Project Group on Administrative Law. The Status of Public Officials in Europe: Recommendation No. R (2000) 6. Legal Issues. Strasbourg Croton-on-Hudson, NY, USA: Council of Europe Pub.; Manhattan Pub. [distributors], 2000. Demo-Droit Programme., Themis (Project), and Council of Europe. The Training of Judges and Prosecutors: In Matters Relating to Their Professional Obligations and Ethics. Strasbourg Croton-on-Hudson, NY, USA: Council of Europe Pub.; Manhattan Pub. [distributor], 1997. Kronenberger, Vincent, and T.M.C. Asser Instituut. The European Union and the International Legal Order: Discord or Harmony? The Hague Norwell, MA: T.M.C. Asser Press; Sold and distribted in North, Central and South America by Kluwer Law International, 2001. Sevastik, Per. Legal Assistance to Developing Countries: Swedish Perspectives on the Rule of Law. Dordrecht, the Netherlands; Cambridge, MA: Kluwer Law International, 1998.

[13] Themis (Project), Demo-Droit Programme., and Council of Europe. Judicial Control of Administrative Acts: Multilateral Seminar, Madrid, 13–15 Nov. 1996. Strasbourg Croton-on-Hudson, NY, USA: Council of Europe Pub.; Manhattan Pub. [distributor], 1997.

law also entails a certain minimum material standard in the form of human rights.

(b) Equality before the law is often regarded as part of the rule of law, but it also has connections with the accessibility of the law. It requires equality before the law, non-discrimination, as well as equality between parties in conflict.

(c) Security before the law is directed at the individual's security. In contrast to security of life and property, security before the law is not pointedly directed against encroachment by the state. On the contrary, it demands action by the police and other state organs against crime, damage, transgressions, and the exercise of gratuitous violence on the part of the state, etc. Here, however, there is a link to human rights: the failure on the part of the state to move against serious crimes against an individual can be a violation of the rights of an individual.

(d) Accessibility of the law ('access to justice') is a prerequisite for giving substance to regulations about security of life and property, equality before the law, and security before the law. This includes reasonable costs, legal aid, clearly written and easily available laws, other legal sources and information material, rapid process, and physical access to courts and other judicial institutions.

All four functions have significance for the poor, perhaps particularly accessibility of the law. Examples in the area of rule of law inputs are constitutional reforms, criminal-political reforms, reinforcement of the courts, human rights, guarantees for freedom of expression, and transparency, combating corruption, and legal aid.

2. *Market Economy Inputs*

a. Functions

(a) Definition of property. Regulations should offer comprehensive property security, including non-material rights, *e.g.*, through safeguards against confiscation, and the creation of a system for registering fixed property and businesses, *etc.* Through this, conditions for land reform and for credit institutions are created, which in turn form the basis for investments.

(b) Exchange of rights. Contractual rights, and rights of purchase, transport, public procurement and various other topics are included here.

(c) Entrance to and exit from the market. It encompasses the law of association, banking law, financial market law, credit legislation, bankruptcy law, fair/unfair competition law, etc.

(d) Compensation for damage. Regulations that define what is unlawful damage and that stipulate compensation to one who has suffered unlawful damage.

(e) The market structure and the actors' actions on the market. Here competitive legislation, disloyal competition and legal safeguards are meant (rental law, labour law, consumer safeguards, etc.).

Examples in the area of market economy inputs are privatisation of telephone, electricity, and other state enterprises (which usually involve serious losses for the state); the capital market and mortgage system; insolvency (debt recovery, bankruptcy, collection of claims); central parts of commercial law, among others those highlighted by the World Trade Organisation (WTO); environmental protection and conflict resolution.[14] The areas mentioned here also require competent institutions to apply the regulations, like registration authorities, free competition bodies, boards of executors, courts and arbitration councils *etc*. For the poorest, regulations about the right to land and other property safeguards, credit and insurance, and protective legislation are of immediate relevance.

3. Conclusions for Legal Development Co-operation

Rule of law (7.1) and market economy (7.2) inputs have different directions and goals in principle, but they also interact: property safeguards, independent courts, security of life and property, equality before the law, and security before the law are characteristic of the rule of law, and at the same time are prerequisites for the development of the market economy. Predictability is a common denominator. In a corresponding way, market economy reforms contribute to a strong judicial state, *e.g.*, in the form of increased public access and freedom of expression, and greater independence from the state. Not least important is that a constitutional state must be largely financed by taxes, which is why a sound economy is an advantage in a constitutional state.

III. JUDICIAL SECTOR AND LEGAL DEVELOPMENT CO-OPERATION

A. Delimiting and Defining

1. Definition of Legal Development Co-operation

One can work with a judicial *legal concept* or with a sociological one where the latter is broader than the former. Both have their place within legal development co-operation. This also concerns traditional law, since the poorest can to a limited extent gain advantages from the official law.

[14] Lee, Yong-Shik. *Safeguard Measures in World Trade: The Legal Analysis*, The Hague; London; New York: Kluwer Law International, 2003; Pauwelyn, Joost. *Conflict of Norms in Public International Law: How WTO Law Relates to Other Rules of International Law*, Cambridge Studies in International and Comparative Law, Cambridge: Cambridge University Press, 2003; World Trade, Forum, *Role of the Judge in International Trade Regulation: Experience and Lessons for the WTO*, Ann Arbor: UNIV OF MICHIGAN PRESS, 2003.

No judicial areas ought to be excluded from legal development co-operation even if certain these areas can be more delicate or less meaningful than others. It should, however, be noted that human rights, corruption, administration, *etc.* are transverse processes and, when dealing with them, they also belong to other 'spheres of development co-operation.'

Institutional delimitation is also not completely clear, nor does it need to be. The institutions which can be given space within legal development co-operation—alongside the judicial organs in a narrow sense—include the following:

- The public sector, including the central authorities, tax authorities, registration of property etc.;
- Parliament, the electoral commission;
- Civil society (non-governmental organisations, informal conflict-resolution organisations, chambers of commerce, auditing agencies, etc.); and
- The media.

It should be noted that the concept of the judicial sector as well as the rule of law can have extremely varied substance. The UN, for example, includes media and the military in the concept of the rule of law.

Nor is the relationship to *good governance* unambiguous. It is simplest to see legal development and good governance as two parallel processes that partly overlap, which is why some legal support can very well be regarded as support of good governance. Examples are inputs that aim at transparency, accountability, and combating corruption. Honesty and efficiency in an administration can be of particular importance for the poor.

Support to *human rights* can be included in legal development co-operation. It ought, however, be observed that human rights are sometimes seen as a concept that is broader than the judicial sector. Support for human rights occurs in the most diverse projects, and particularly, references are perhaps made to human rights as support for a certain project. One ought to be clear about these conceptual differences when choosing terminology and designing inputs. If one talks about human rights projects it ought to be clear whether it is the project's goal that motivates the name—projects related to (the right to) health, education, etc., can then be included—or whether it is the institutions themselves that are given support when it may be natural to draw boundaries at the human rights institutions in the strict sense.

2. *Conclusions for Legal Development Co-operation*

Legal development co-operation requires a clear understanding of the law and the phenomena related to it. It probably does not matter so much that many of the concepts, which have just been mentioned, are used in a different sense in various contexts. Nor is it a problem that legal support is not clearly defined, as long as it is based on a sound analysis.

B. The Sections of the Sector

Legal development co-operation can be allocated to all parts of the judicial sector. A brief review of these sections follows.

1. Legal Sources

Legal development co-operation is usually completely focused on the official, national body of law. Here, legislation is central, possibly including the requisite preparatory work for each law. Legal precedence (judiciary) and literature (doctrine) are also legal sources. In many areas the informal (traditional) law is of great significance, which is why planning of projects must also take the latter into account and perhaps also seek to build on the resource which it entails.

2. Institutions

There are a large number of 'institutions' in the judicial arena that can be encompassed by legal development co-operation:

- Legislators (ministries, committees, parliament etc.);
- The courts and other organs for conflict-resolution (formal and informal);
- Executive organs (board of executors, prisons and correctional services, tax authorities);
- Representatives (advocates, bankruptcy administrators, paralegals, public prosecutors);
- The police;
- 'Judicial authorities' (management of competition, registration of companies and non-material rights, property registration, consumer safeguards etc.);
- Legal aid institutions (state; private);
- Educational and research institutions;
- The legal profession as a whole (administrative jurists, company lawyers, etc.);
- Supervisory organs (Justice Ombudsman institutions, advocates, associations of advocates and other professional bodies, *e.g.*, auditors, human rights organisations, public authorities, *e.g.*, finance inspectorate, consumer associations, the media);
- Functionaries (personnel well-versed in the law, administrative officials, 'informal decision-makers' (village headmen and the like)); and

- 'Users' (the public seeking justice, parties in civil law conflicts, the accused, sentenced and imprisoned, victims of crimes and other plaintiffs, human rights organisations).

3. *Infrastructure*

(a) Buildings, material, Information Technology (IT) and other equipment;
(b) Collections of laws and sentences, literature and information systems;
(c) Administration and methods of work.

4. *Legal Culture*

The traditions, values, ways of thinking, methods, unwritten regulations, professional standards and ethics, *etc.* that are features of the legal system and judiciary in a country are part of the judicial culture. One can also include the position of the legal system in society and the approach of the public and the powers that be on the system and the knowledge about it. Attention has increasingly focused on the legal culture and its significance. This factor is difficult to grasp, but important, as it can jeopardise many reforms. It is for this reason alone an eye ought to be kept on it in legal development co-operation.

5. *Conclusions for Legal Development Co-operation*

The 'judicial sector' is broad and heterogeneous. Those sections of the sector to receive support are often selected in a routine-like way. Goals and perspectives for inputs ought to guide the selection to some extent, which can lead to a more appropriate choice of those parts of the sector on which inputs focus. Both a poverty perspective and an egalitarian perspective naturally focus on the users and perhaps lead to attention being paid to the knowledge and attitudes of the public.

C. *Judicial Pluralism*

1. *Judicial Normative Systems*

Several competitive and interactive normative systems should be taken into account in the framework of legal development co-operation:

- Domestic state law (formal law; official law, including transplanted 'modern law');
- Law, custom, judicial praxis;
- Internationally binding norms, particularly international agreements, *e.g.*, WTO's regulations and EU law (formal law);

- Colonial law (usually with traces of local law);
- Religious law, *e.g.*, sharia;
- Informal law (traditional law), usually in the form of local customs;
- Socialist law, including planned economies (more an approach than legislated in the South);
- Traditions of common law and civil law;
- Norms not prescribed by law: prestige, contacts, ethnic links, family ties; and
- 'Non-legal': more or less illegal methods, *e.g.*, bribery, threats, violence (c.f. the controls exercised by the mafia).

2. *Traditional Law and the Relation Between Normative Systems*

Normative systems compete, interact, and affect one another. Official law and traditional law are rivals, but they also interplay with each other. Local customs and religious laws can be sources of justice for the official law, thereby giving legitimacy to both of these normative systems. The law is also continuously changing: normative systems develop,[15] and even traditional law is affected by modern influences and other impulses. Traditional African societies are more open, more inclined to change and more conflict-ridden than westerners previously believed. Many 'chiefs' who judge according to traditional law wish to educate themselves in the official law. Here, a possibility emerges of utilising traditional institutions to supply legal aid. It can, however, also be mentioned that traditional courts in many cases have not proved to be suitable for resolving one of the most common types of conflict, namely land conflicts.

Judicial pluralism not only depends on different normative systems but also relies on different values, traditions, and 'forms of rationality'[16] to contribute to pluralism. The same is true of the different organs that 'administrate' normative systemsóinternational organs, official courts, private and alternative forms of conflict-resolution, religious leaders, local chiefs *etc*.

A particular range of problems is competition between common law and

[15] Alchourrâon, Carlos E., Eugenio Bulygin, and Ernesto Garzâon Vald,es, *Normative Systems in Legal and Moral Theory: Festschrift for Carlos E. Alchourr,on and Eugenio Bulygin*, Berlin: Duncker & Humblot, 1997; Franck, Thomas M. Fairness in International Law and Institutions. OXFORD NEW YORK: CLARENDON PRESS; OXFORD UNIVERSITY PRESS, 1995.

[16] Kerchove, Michel van de, and François Ost. *Legal System between Order and Disorder*, OXFORD; NEW YORK: OXFORD UNIVERSITY PRESS, 1994; Martino, Antonio Anselmo. *Expert Systems in Law*, Amsterdam; New York: North-Holland, 1992; Moreso, Josep J. *Legal Indeterminacy and Constitutional Interpretation*. Law and Philosophy Library; V. 37. DORDRECHT; BOSTON: KLUWER ACADEMIC PUBLISHERS, 1998.

civil law. Opinion is divided on the possibilities of merging both of these traditions, as in the EU, and how it should be implemented, in that case.

3. *Conclusions for Legal Development Co-operation*

A donor can have reasons to take all normative systems and the relations between them into account. Judicial pluralism means that the formal (official law) ought not automatically to be given precedence before the informal, which may emphasise a bottom-up perspective and other 'alternative perspectives,' *e.g.*, minority rights, life-style and identity. An alternative perspective can also create awareness of judicial limitations. In certain 'judicial cultures' the official law is accorded little weight by comparison with family ties, ethnic links, prestige, contacts, and similar means of manipulating the law. At the same time, it is important not to be seduced by traditional and informal law. It can have repressive features and also be unserviceable to promote commerce and development.

D. *Civil Society*

1. *Developments*

Civil society has a large role to play in legal development co-operation. It can encompass non-governmental organisations, informal groups, and sometimes also the media. To be included in this context, it is desirable for an organisation to be independent, transparent, and have democratic roots and a democratic way of working. Not infrequently, one must resign oneself to more modest demands; even in relatively developed countries in eastern Europe, where civil society has remained weak.

2. *Judicial Organisations*

One can generally differentiate between two categories of non-governmental organisations in the field of legal development co-operation:

Organisations that provide social services; in this case, primarily the organisations that offer or supply legal aid are of interest;

Opinion-forming organisations; here the issue may be to monitor respect for human rights in a more general way, influence the work of legislation and international setting of norms, prosecuting pilot cases, observing trials, spreading information (about constitutional rights or new legal cases) *etc.*

3. *Conclusions for Legal Development Co-operation*

Consideration of support to judicial organisations depends on several circumstances, *e.g.*, what is permitted, the needs and resources (economic, competence etc.). Support to the former (a, above) is usually more expensive than to the latter (b, above). Judicial access may, however, improve substantially, thanks to the former. Experience of the latter category of organisation is good on the whole. There is usually no reason for donors to exclude support to civil society for the reason that bilateral legal co-operation is being undertaken with the country in question.

E. The State and the Private Sector

1. The Relationship Between the State and the Private Sector

Features of the relationship between the state and the private sector include both co-operation and rivalry. The state and civil society require, support, and keep checks on each other and in some cases they compete with each other. From the viewpoint of a private actor, the state may be both the problem and the solution.

Certain functions can only be undertaken by state institutions and should be performed without being affected by irrelevant considerations. To some extent such institutions are a prerequisite for the private sector. They provide guarantees for non-governmental organisations, against injustices for instance, and also—paradoxically enough—against unfair treatment by state institutions. The state is also a guarantor of certain private mechanisms, like the carrying out of arbitration and alternative conflict-resolution mechanisms. At the same time, in certain cases the state is the supervisor of non-governmental organisations like bar associations, as well as the opposite party, in policy issues and conflicts for instance. The state can function as financier, concession granter, and public prosecutor, sometimes in relation to one and the same organisation.

Conversely, private organisations are a prerequisite for the state's way of functioning. They keep an eye on and influence the state, train state personnel, inform the public about the state's work, and carry out tasks on behalf of the state. Many tasks can be performed by both the state and private agencies (like education, legal aid, conflict-resolution, information dissemination, influencing public opinion).

2. The Informal Sector

The informal sector is variegated (one can differentiate between illegal, non-registered and non-reported companies and transactions). The sector is problematic from the viewpoint of legal development co-operation. On the one hand, it often functions fairly well and is extensive, in many countries being 50–75 % of the economy. Legal development co-operation ought not to harm this sector, particularly as the poor work within it. On the other hand, it is a grey area with illegal aspects that can hardly be directly supported by a donor. High transaction costs inhibit the expansion of informal businesses and corruption flourishes in this grey area.

3. Conclusions for Legal Development Co-operation

Legal development co-operation ought to build on the insight that while certain functions can be carried out only by the state, others can only be done by civil society. In addition, private actors can give support to the state and vice versa. State measures can sometimes be the best way of facilitating the growth of non-governmental organisations. Legal development co-operation can achieve an increased degree of efficiency if donors utilise their opportunities to combine support to the state and the private sector. Donors may even sometimes have reason to talk of the violation of human rights while at the same time giving assistance to the very institutions of the state that are responsible for the violations.

The planning of legal support is sometimes done as if the informal sector did not exist. This is a pragmatic approach to the problem, but is debatable. The long term goal ought to be to design a system of justice so that these enterprises become a part of the regular economy. It would lay the basis for the expansion of many small businesses, thanks to lower transaction costs and thereby give the state increased revenue from taxation. It would also reduce the opportunities for corruption.

IV. LEGAL DEVELOPMENT CO-OPERATION

A. Special Requirements for Legal Development Co-operation

1. Central Powers

The law and the central powers are closely linked. A system of justice is the responsibility of the state and judicial reforms are dependent on the support of those in power. They must be built on the central state institutions which make up the core of the judiciary, like courts, prosecutors, and the executive. If these conditions for support do not exist, development co-operation cannot build a functioning judiciary.

Judicial reforms may threaten the position of those in power, for example, because the party and the state are no longer synonymous and the state's power is restricted; new centres of power may arise that compete with the political powers; respect for minorities is enforced; critical reviews become possible, and the law, and thus the lawyer, each gain new roles.

2. *Demand*

Sometimes there is a lack of genuine demand for judicial reform, not only because it might lead to undesirable consequences for many of the interested parties, but also because old ways of thinking remain in post-communist societies. The aforementioned is relevant not only to politicians but also to businessmen who are used to a 'rent-seeking-culture' and to the legal profession which is at risk because its knowledge may become outdated. Many proponents of the profession may have 20–30 remaining years at their posts and may have good reason and opportunity to object. To the extent that re-schooling is impossible, dismissal may provide the only accessible route.

3. *Vulnerability*

Legal development co-operation projects are vulnerable not only because there may be a change for those who hold power. Unlike, for instance, the physical infrastructure, legal reforms can easily be obliterated or undermined. They are more vulnerable than many other projects also because the legislation to implement the reforms or the institutional build-up is often delayed, which is why nothing happens although a law is adopted or another measure has been taken with the help of development co-operation. Often the donor does not have a role to play in this part of the implementation nor has any insight into it.

4. *Point of Departure*

For other reasons, developing countries are often characterised by a lack of reliable information, poor communications, and a high cost of transactions. In addition, the judicial sector is often neglected and functions poorly as a result of other sectors having higher priority. It may be characterised by small resources and low educational levels. Institutions are often so rundown that one cannot build on them because the parties that should be involved are often too weak to be able to co-operate with them. The system is more or less corrupt and compromised, and people in general have no confidence in it.

5. *The Culture of Justice, etc.*

The law is culturally and historically conditioned and great differences exist between different regions and countries. In many cases, the developing world has rudimentary systems of justice where informal law is central, while many east European countries can build upon a previous, often well-developed, system. Clear differences also exist between east European countries, just as between developing countries in various regions. This is true of legal-cultural differences (approach to the law and the role of lawyers, systems, concepts, sources of jurisprudence, the study of legislation etc.). Legal-cultural differences, like language problems and other factors, have shown themselves to lead to serious communication problems in the legal arena, even in co-operation with the east, though these countries are relatively well-developed.

6. *Standards*

Judicial reform and thus legal development co-operation has certain given points of departure. These concern international agreements that set a standard for human rights as well as the entire body of commercial law (WTO, ASEAN, international treaties, praxis, codes, lex mercatoria etc.) which must have a specific content to create the environment to promote trade and investment. For certain countries, a 'treaty' enforced by the international community exists, like the Dayton agreement for Bosnia and Hercegovina, or a more traditional form of peace accord, like in Central America. For presumptive members of the EU, the judicial content is also largely givenóthe system of justice must meet a 'west-European standard'[17] (c.f. Copenhagen criteria, acquis, etc.). In addition, there are organs that keep an eye on whether the above-mentioned standards are achieved, which is why legal development co-operation must also pay attention to the institutional side. In the third world there are, however, strong forces that question the legitimacy of the donor community to assert these standards and other 'universal values,' to the extent that they conflict with traditional values and life-styles.

7. *The Process of Change*

When the law in the south is reformed, traditional laws may lose their functionality, without new ones becoming effective. Such a vacuum can only be avoided if judicial modernisation is undertaken with great sensitivity to the role of the traditional judiciary. Legal development co-operation in eastern Europe must also be designed to take into account that 'transitional law' has particular features that in many ways are unknown to western jurists. The process of change may create space for misuse since control mechanisms are

[17] Cappelletti, Mauro, Monica Seccombe, and Joseph Weiler, *Integration through Law: Europe and the American Federal Experience*, Berlin; New York: W. de Gruyter, 1985; Micklitz, Hans- W., and Stephen Weatherill, *European Economic Law, Tempus Textbook Series on European Law and European Legal Cultures*, Aldershot, Hants, England; Brookfield, Vt., USA: Ashgate/Dartmouth, 1997.

not necessarily developed at the same pace as the transition. To make the choice of the speed and sequence for judicial reforms requires specialised knowledge.

8. *The Independence of Institutions*

Several judicial institutions enjoy an entrenched independence that has no equivalent in other social sectors. They are also more closely linked to national sovereignty than, for instance, the social sector or the infrastructure. The courts, the public prosecutor, and certain other institutions may be involved. They cannot simply be 'reformed' and thus advice and dialogue may need to occur in more restrained forms than currently.

9. *Formalisation*

A formalisation of the judicial system may have advantages, in the form of higher levels of knowledge, more uniform application of justice, etc. It is not unusual for village headmen and other practitioners of traditional law to desire to raise their level of knowledge by schooling themselves in 'modern law.' A formalisation can, however, also contribute to the system becoming more expensive and more complex. This may lead to para-legals being pushed aside, with the result that accessibility for the poor deteriorates.

10. *The Resource Base*

The resource base in donor countries is more limited in the field of legal development co-operation than in most others. This is not only because the area is new, but also because many jurists do not have the relevant knowledge: their knowledge is limited about developing countries and they have not assimilated the experiences that have been gained in other areas of development co-operation. They also have limited knowledge of comparing the law and 'transitional justice' (transition from one system to another). They gladly yield to the temptation to teach about their domestic law and automatically recommend their own administrative and organisational solutions. Thus, the resource base may restrict what can be achieved in the short term. Increased co-operation of experts from several countries would be healthy.

11. *Conclusions for Legal Development Co-operation*

In the preceding, a number of circumstances peculiar to legal development co-operation are pointed out though some of these may also play a role in other areas in a less accentuated way. Taken together, these circumstances involve a number of restrictions that require detailed planning of legal development co-operation projects. A good quality risk and an interest analysis are required as part of the preparations, as are a clear and long-term vision and a preparedness to allocate resources.

B. Principles for Legal Development Co-operation

1. To Learn From Experience

Donors have hitherto acted pragmatically, as they did not have a theoretical and consistent model for legal development. The experiences mentioned above ought naturally to be taken into account. One ought to avoid an evolutionist, instrumental, and ethnocentric approach to the law. However, the conditions for legal development co-operation are now more favourable than in the past. Not only is there more knowledge about legal development co-operation, but conditions have also improved. In addition, there is a better understanding of the importance of the judiciary, as a result of the process of change which was mentioned at the beginning, and in many countries, e.g., in Latin America, there is now a stability which makes them better equipped for judicial reform.

2. National Resources

Many of the problems which are a feature of the legal systems in the south and in eastern Europe are caused by a scarcity of resources and the evil circle this creates. It relates to corruption, lack of competent personnel, inefficient ways of working, drawn-out procedures, citizens' lack of trust in the system, inadequate access for the poor, bad premises, out-dated equipment, etc. In dialogue, a central task for donors should be to point out the necessity for the government to allocate resources to the judicial system. If it does not, its commitment can be called into question. The forms for judicial reform may influence the government in the correct direction. If it proceeds through a well-rooted process, this may improve the prospects for the government to allocate the means required for a reformation.

3. System Approach (holistic view)

One of the few recognised principles for legal development co-operation is probably the need for a system approach. First, conditions in sectors other than the judicial affect the latter and the reverse. A weak school system, for example, has an impact, since illiterate people have difficulty in asserting their rights with the assistance of the legal system.[18] The legal system can protect the media from interference while, at the same time, the media can combat corruption in the legal system. Second, a system approach encapsulates demands on agreement between economic policies and judicial reforms as well as between political developments and judicial reforms. Both of these system approaches (which can be said to have an external perspective) in general agree with development co-operation trends to emphasise the general policy environment in partner countries and to adopt an integrated approach as a basis for co-operation.

Third, in a system approach the various parts of the legal system hang together and must be taken into account—both regulations and institutions (internal perspective). Civil society should be accorded its rightful place and informal (traditional) law and informal institutions must be brought into the picture. Here, the elements that are more difficult to grasp can be found, like attitudes to the law and other parts of the culture of justice.

Fourth, reforms should be implemented on the basis of well-founded priorities, in a sequence and with a speed that suits the conditions in the concrete case, for both the first mentioned (external) and the third (internal). A system approach entails that not everything needs to be done at one and the same time.

The demand for a holistic view is particularly apparent during structural reform of the legal system (see 14.9 below) and one ought to avoid introducing a very broad programme which lacks clear focus. If the judicial reformation is part of a sectoral reform, there is also a demand for a holistic view, though it may be less stressed, while many isolated inputs require a less ambitious framework.

4. *Developing Capacity*

In agreement with the need for a system approach, capacity development should be as much of a catch-word in the field of legal development co-operation as in most other sectors. The legal system as a whole ought to be purposefully organised, including the relations between and tasks of its institutions. Judicial institutions ought to be given the competence, tools, and other resources, organisation and methods of work,[19] etc. which are

[18] See UN Conference on Financing for Development available at http://www.un.org/esa/ffd/ (the Monterrey Consensus and its new 'holistic' approach to development)

[19] Capacity Building for Environmental Law in the Asian & Pacific Region; V. Ii: Approaches and Resource. Manila: ASIAN DEVELOMENT BANK, 2002; Al-Nauimi, Najeeb M., and Richard Meese, *International Legal Issues Arising under the United Nations Decade of International Law*, The Hague; Boston Cambridge, MA, U.S.A.: MARTINUS NIJHOFF PUBLISHERS; Sold and distributed in the U.S.A. and Canada by Kluwer Law International, 1995; Law of the Sea Institute, Conference (29th: 1995: Denpasar Indonesia), et al.

required for them to be able to fulfil their role. In this context, capacity refers to all parts of the system, not only to the key organs, but also to institutions like those for education and further education. If such capacity is built up, not only the legal system as such is favoured, but it also contributes to the general attempt to strengthen governance of society.

5. *Long-term Perspective and Resources*

System changes require firm establishment, a long-term vision with corresponding programming, sustainability and resources, so that judicial reforms can be implemented. Smaller, isolated projects may be justified, but if possible, ought then to act as a stimulus to the system changes.

6. *Money or Ideas?*

The poorer the policy environment, the greater the reason to focus on the ideas. To the extent that development co-operation is utilisable, the reasons to do so are reinforced. Conditions at central level have small chance of influencing the recipients to a similar degree as legal development co-operation concerns the interests of the central powers. At the local level, conditionality may often be more effective. One should add that co-operation with the east should in principle be based on utilising legal knowledge to build up capacity, so that funds for the legal area are not used to finance investments in, for example, infrastructure.

7. *Reform Process*

Experience indicates that the approach to judicial reform has considerable significance, sometimes as great as the material content of the reforms. It requires a broad process that involves the interested parties and includes education about the judicial reforms and spreading information on them. Such a process can create the clarity, predictability, and legitimacy required for the acceptance of the regulations and have the intended effects. It can also clarify which parties are most favoured by a certain input.

8. *Comparative Advantages*

A donor's comparative advantages may affect the choice of countries for legal development co-operation, the choice of areas of input, and the choice

Sustainable Development and Preservation of the Oceans: The Challenges of Unclos and Agenda 21. Honolulu: Law of the Sea Institute, William S. Richardson School of Law, University of Hawaii, 1997; World Trade Organization. The WTO: Capacity Building and Development: A Proposal.: WTO, 2001.

of methods. It may seem easier to specialise in certain types of inputs, for example, the development of organisations in the ministry of justice or accessibility of the law; however, the disadvantages of such a selection procedure (c.f. 18.2 below) are tangible as long as they do not rest on a firm foundation, *e.g.*, the standards for legal development co-operation (see 13.6 above).

9. *Choice of Approach and Ambitions*

It is desirable for a donor to have a clear understanding of the ambitions—and thereby the resources and the time perspective—which should form the basis for legal development co-operation in any concrete case. One can differentiate between support to structural reform, 'integrated inputs,' and clearly limited inputs:

(a) If the object is to give support to a *structural reform* of the judicial sector, the ambition is set high. Resources and time horizons must be adapted to this, since it concerns contributing to a change of basic conditions, including the legal culture and other supports.

(b) If the object is to support judicial reform in a *sector*, the ambition is typically set lower. Judicial reform is here usually integrated in a more extensive reform, *e.g.*, of the state administration, a social sector, the financial market or an industry. Judicial reform which is a part of structural adaptation can also be regarded as an integrated input. This type of integration can become an effective way of giving substance to development co-operation based on human rights.

(c) One can also conceive of *limited projects* of varying kinds, like seminars, field studies, individual legislative measures, buying literature, etc. The choice of ambition and approach has consequences not only on the need for resources and the time perspective, but it also affects the risks and relevance of the inputs. Assessment of the relevance of the inputs and how they can be implemented becomes easier the lower down the ladder one goes and in a correspondingly, the vulnerability and risks of the inputs is reduced. Methodologically, the same thing can be achieved by departing from a clear and well-defined problem which the recipient is well-aware of (bottom-up), after which the programme can be extended. Alternatively, one can take a holistic view from the beginning (top-down), but it is theoretically more satisfying but usually riskier.

10. *Prerequisites and Timing*

Not only the needs of the recipient country and the donor's resources ought to determine which level of ambition and approach are suitable. At least as important are the conditions and the timing. If the prerequisites for large reforming projects are missing, *e.g.*, because the political will is not there, the ambitions must be adapted to this reality, irrespective of which urgent needs are apparent. Similarly, one must be cautious in delicate situations, even if the political will to reform is strong; in the legal area it is the rule rather than the exception that recipient capacity is weak.

11. Target Groups

Most legal development co-operation projects are probably of use to both the citizens in general and to certain individuals. A mortgage system, for instance, fosters general economic development, but is also of use to the agriculturist who can get credit. Freedom of the press can be of general use, *e.g.*, if it counteracts corruption, at the same time as it can protect an individual whose rights are violated.

Sometimes it is said that inputs should start with the people or the individual. Yet it is not so easy to see in which way an *individual perspective* could lead to any assistance other than to the development of institutions. If, for example, one strengthens the office of the public prosecutor or legal aid and reforms the rest of the system, one may reduce awaiting trial times to the advantage of the detainees.

An individual perspective may, however, serve as a reminder that institutions are simply means to strengthen an individual's abilities. If a poor person cannot utilise her/his rights because s/he cannot read, one ought to admit that her/his rights are not realised, rather than assert that s/he has not made use of the law. An individual perspective may also be a good tool of analysis. One can analyse which effects an input has on a certain category of individual and can also analyse the legal system by following an individual through the system, for example, a woman who has been raped or a citizen who has a claim or wants to establish a business. In this way, a poverty or an egalitarian perspective can hopefully make a greater impact in the planning of the project. An individual perspective can also be a starting point for co-operation based on human rights.

12. Conclusions for Legal Development Co-operation

Principles and methods for legal development co-operation must be adapted to the particular prerequisites of legal development co-operation (see 13 above). This means that the lack of resources in the sector must be taken into account, that a holistic view is required, and that the principles, which have been referred to in the preceding, must be upheld. Since legal development co-operation is relatively new and principles and methods less tested than is desirable, particular care has been devoted to the aspect of the principles.

C. *Transfer of Regulations?*

1. *Transfer of Regulations or Capacity*

A large number of legal development co-operation projects are made up of the transfer of legislation, judicial institutes, and institutions from the donor's national system. It is not beyond the bounds of possibility that such transfers may have positive effects, but the angle of approach is ethnocentric, with the result that attention is diverted from the context in the recipient country, like its traditions and legal culture, and the need for accepting the legislation. Particularly in countries where the law only has a small role to play as a means for controlling society, such transfers may have difficulty in becoming established. Alternatives that have already been mentioned include capacity development with the aim of strengthening the recipient country's capacity to analyse its needs, design its legislation and judicial institutes, and build institutions.

2. *Regulations and Institutions*

Building up capacity is both costly and requires time. As we saw, in certain respects there is an answer to the question of when is 'the law correct' (see 13.6). Then it is legitimate to participate in ensuring that such regulations and institutes are introduced, but only to the extent that the local context is taken into account. This includes the implementation of international agreements and certain generally accepted principles of the market economy, and the standards set by the EU.

3. *Models*

To the extent that regulations and institutes are transferred, there are reasons to prefer models that have shown themselves to work in different contexts. Examples are Unidroit's, UNCITRALS' and ICC's well-established work with models.[20] Similarly successful national codification can be

[20] Ali, Paul A. U., *The Law of Secured Finance: An International Survey of Security Interests over Personal Property*, Oxford; New York: OXFORD UNIVERSITY PRESS, 2002; Alvarez, Henri C., David W. Rivkin, and Neil Kaplan, *Model Law Decisions: Cases Applying the Uncitral Model Law on International Commercial Arbitration* (1985–2001). The Hague; New York: KLUWER LAW INTERNATIONAL, 2003; Bhatia, V. K., Christopher Candlin, and Maurizio Gotti, *Legal Discourse in Multilingual and Multicultural Contexts: Arbitration Texts in Europe*, LINGUISTIC INSIGHTS, V. 6. Bern; New York: P. Lang, 2003; Campbell, Dennis, *United Nations Commission on International Trade Law*, and United Nations Commission on International Trade Law. Working Group VI (Security Interests). International Secured Transactions. Dobbs Ferry, NY: Oceana Publications, 2003; Ferrari, Franco, et al. *The Draft Uncitral Digest and Beyond: Cases, Analysis and Unresolved Issues in the U.N. Sales Convention*: Papers of the Pittsburgh Conference Organized by the Center for International Legal Education (Cile). London: Sweet & Maxwell, 2004.

employed, *e.g.*, the Netherland's and Quebec's codifications which have been successfully used recently in eastern European countries like Russia, and Latin American countries like the Argentine. The AsDB has created a system for disseminating comparative legal material to be used in the work of judicial reform. To the degree that the legal development co-operation of a country encompasses transfers, it thus need not necessarily be concerned with certain perhaps peculiar regulations of this country. A different matter is that legal institutes of any country may provide impulses for judicial reform or that national 'experts' of the country are perhaps not familiar with the relevant regulations.

4. *Conclusions for Legal Development Co-operation*

The transfer of regulations and institutes are often linked to tremendous difficulties and are usually a less efficient form of development co-operation than building up capacity. To the extent that regulations and institutes are implanted, there are reasons to select models that have already shown themselves to work in different contexts.

D. *Legal Development Co-operation to 'Difficult Countries'?*

1. *'Difficult Countries'*

One of the main problems for legal development co-operation may be that those in power do not have a genuine interest in judicial reforms. A repressive structure, attitudes to the law, the effects of the communist heritage, and corruption, organised crime and other factors, may each play a role.

2. *Influence of Attitudes*

The dialogue may provide space for influencing attitudes. Even in the most difficult environments, it is usually possible to give support to forming public opinion and perhaps consensus, *e.g.*, convincing the public of the value of judicial reforms or about humane criminal policies. This may occur in the form of support to non-governmental organisations and the private sector (bar council, commercial organisations, media that work for judicial reforms, etc.). Such support can in any case give visibility and safeguards in authoritarian environments. At best, networks are created which have a multiplicatory effect.

3. *Education, Further Education, and Research etc.*

The education of teachers of jurisprudence can be a way of proceeding, even in difficult countries. The development of curricula, didactics, and literature can be added to the list. Similarly, the further education of practising lawyers may be promising as well as participation in regional conferences and similar events. For both of these categories of lawyers, an exchange with colleagues in other countries may be of great value. New knowledge and feelings of collegiality create self-confidence and can sow the seeds of renewal. Depending on the choice of subject matter, judicial research may be more sensitive, but usually it is recognised that there is a dearth of knowledge.

4. A New Generation

In nearly all 'difficult countries,' there is a younger generation that is knowledgeable and inclined to seek change. There may be reasons to direct tailor-made inputs to this category, *e.g.*, to contribute to making contacts in foreign countries which can function as a stimulus to their efforts.

5. Conclusions for Legal Development Co-operation

Not unusually there is good reason to refrain from legal development co-operation to regimes which are repressive or at least 'difficult.' If there are strong reasons nonetheless to make an input, great care must be devoted to designing it. Otherwise, there is a substantial risk that the input may legitimise undemocratic structures and produce meagre results.

E. Legal Development Co-operation to Countries After Conflicts

Increasing attention has been drawn to the fact that the law can not only play a role in preventing conflict. It is also an important instrument in 'post-conflict situations,' *e.g.*, Bosnia, Haiti, Cambodia, Kosovo, Serbia, eastern Europe, East Timor, as well as South Africa and several other African countries.

1. Reconciliation, Truth, and Legal Proceedings

There are always reasons to attempt to bring clarity to what has happened. It is a psychosocial concern and may contribute to reconciliation. To bring war criminals to justice and demand other kinds of accountability is normally desirable, but in certain cases amnesty may be motivated (*e.g.*, if a referendum has been held or 'both sides' are agreed on ignoring the past). Truth commissions do not exclude trials, since the latter typically encompass fewer people and take more time.

2. *Restitution and Compensation*

Normally, a well-functioning judicial system is required for restitution and compensation to be possible. It includes restitution of housing, land, other property, and of jobs and additional economic recompense in those cases where restitution is not possible. Compensation for non-payment of earnings and compensation for psychological suffering are also on the list.

3. *Protection of Minorities*

Many conflicts have an ethnic background, which is why effective safeguards of minority rights are a precondition for a sustainable peace. It is concerned with judicial safeguards from discrimination at all levels[21]—from the constitution to local bye-laws—and in many areas, like protection against discrimination in the work place, at school, by the police, and the judicial system.

4. *Support to Returnees*

It should be a central part of a post-conflict policy to facilitate the situation for returning exiles, which not only requires strong support from the legal system in several respects which have already been mentioned, but also the right to get credit for time spent abroad when the rate of pay is set, a law to validate foreign examinations, and a law to get documents.

5. *Support to Civil Society*

Different phases in a country require different sorts of support to civil society. After a conflict, organisations that deliver social services of various kinds are needed, *e.g.*, legal aid, but also organisations which build public opinion regarding issues like those mentioned in E.1–E.4. Support to civil society may, however, not take the place of inputs to state institutions, since a number of functions can only be undertaken by them.[22]

[21] *See* United States. Dept. of Justice. Civil Rights Division. Federal Protections against National Origin Discrimination. [Washington, D.C.?]: U.S. Dept. of Justice, Civil Rights Division, 2001; Protecciones Federales Contra La Discriminaciâon Por Origen Nacional. [Washington, D.C.?]: Departamento de Justicia de los EE.UU., Divisi,on de Derechos Civiles, 2001.

[22] Fineman, Martha, *The Autonomy Myth: A Theory of Dependency*, New York: New Press, 2004; Howard, Marc Morjâe. *The Weakness of Civil Society in Post-Communist Europe*, Cambridge, U.K.; New York, NY: Cambridge University Press, 2003; Kopeckây, Petr, and Cas Mudde, *Uncivil Society?: Contentious Politics in Post-Communist Europe*, Routledge Studies in Extremism and Democracy; 1. London; New York: Routledge, 2003; Segesvary, Victor, World State, Nation States, or Non-Centralized Institutions?: A Vision of the Future in Politics, Lanham, MD: University Press of America, 2003.

6. Conclusions for Legal Development Co-operation

After a conflict it is necessary to build up the legal system again, since a number of urgent needs can only be met if there is a well-functioning system of justice. Thus it is desirable for an identification of needs to be done as soon as possible. What has been said here about 'post-conflict countries' is largely also applicable in countries that have been hit by natural disasters, even if the views put forward in 17.1 and 17.3 usually are assumed to have less relevance.

V. METHODS FOR LEGAL DEVELOPMENT CO-OPERATION

A. Methods for Legal Development Co-operation

1. General

It is apparent that there are a number of conditions that apply specially to legal development co-operation (see 13 above), but one can nevertheless assume that what is good methodology for development co-operation as a whole is good practice also for this form. For reasons touched on in the preceding, legal development co-operation may, however, be both more sensitive and more vulnerable than development co-operation in many other areas. Thus, particular care ought to be devoted to accountability, sustainability, building capacity, and similar factors.

2. Accountability of the Recipient

The accountability of the recipient (ownership) is central, since in many cases the institutions in the legal area are weak and there may be pockets of resistance to the desire to reform. The more ambitious the reforms (see 14.9 above), the greater the demand for accountability of the recipient. A factor that may affect accountability—and thus is one of its indicators—is the political will which can advantageously be manifested in a strategy for the sector. Other positive factors are the division of costs, loan financing, the strength of the partners in co-operation, problem and need orientation (which counteracts the control of what is on offer), and interactive ways of working which start with the recipient's problems. It is desirable for accountability to be based on a genuine partnership both between parties in development co-operation and between the government of the partner country and those with interests in the projects. There may be a need for an analysis of interests to reveal the attitudes of key actors to the projects. In the case where the recipient is not prepared to shoulder responsibility, the idea should be set in the foreground and the volume of co-operation be restrained. This suggests that partners in co-operation, for instance the ministry of justice, may need to be strengthened and perhaps also that non-governmental organisations become involved.

3. Sustainability

A clear shouldering of responsibility makes for a good prognosis for sustainability. In addition, sustainability is furthered by a long-term perspective, mutual trust, capacity building, and integration of the work in the national budget. It should be observed that sustainability does not always need to be institutional, but can be supported by individuals who circulate in the 'judicial sector.' Many organisations may never become self-sustaining and often it is healthy for civil society to be restructured.

4. Building Capacity

It has been pointed out that building capacity may have many different aspects, but analytically, capacity is a key factor. It should be noted that one cannot casually build on existing judicial institutions, irrespective of how tempting this may be in a short-term perspective. Some parts of the legal system will be so compromised and in other ways run-down that one is paving the way for problems if one does not build up something new. Perhaps the ministry of justice is an exception; there is no alternative if one wants to deal with this central institution, for instance, because its analytical capacity must inevitably be strengthened. The legal area is well-suited to co-operation between partners ('twinning') or other forms of fraternal collaboration as a method of building up capacity, and is not limited to eastern Europe, where the EU is working for such co-operation on a large scale in candidate countries.

5. Planning, Follow-up and Evaluation

Legal support often needs more careful planning and follow-up than other areas. A system approach (see 14.3 above) requires planning on the part of the donor so that it does not remain a reaction to isolated wishes on the part of the donor. Such planning requires good knowledge of the system in its entirety. If such knowledge cannot be gained, there may be reasons to limit the ambitions and perhaps to prefer a 'bottom-up' approach. In eastern Europe, the situation may permit a freer view as a result of the Copenhagen criteria largely prescribing what should be done.

The goal for legal support can be based on functions, standards, and other aspects that have been touched on in the preceding, particularly those that permit operationalisation and can be translated into indicators for measurement. A logical framework approach (so-called LFA) may be an excellent tool for the design of these projects. It is, however, not always so easy to define the precise goal and the target groups, or to assess the effects of the interventions at different levels. But the framework approach ought to be a useful method if one wants to find out what the result is at the end, since it requires a holistic view that also takes into account the circumstances beyond the legal system (see 14.3 above).

One ought to be open to the need for a complementary approach. It reveals itself in that inputs in this area—similarly to inputs in other difficult areas—are often changed during the course of the programme, with the result that the original goal becomes less relevant. Follow-up and evaluation may thus need to take place using a somewhat different yardstick than the original objectives. A process-oriented approach may then be required. One can also pay attention to the way the system functions rather than its results. This indicates that evaluations of inputs of this type ought to include the rationality of the inputs (relevance) and not remain with efficiency and goal achievement.

6. *Coordination*

As might be expected, coordination of legal support is far from perfect. Among other things, it is notoriously weak between ministries of justice in recipient countries. In eastern Europe, coordination has broken down and the EU as the dominant actor has neglected other donors. Increased coordination and exchange of experiences is desirable. Experiences from other areas of development co-operation indicate that efficient coordination is simplified if a common programme for reform exists; the above-mentioned standards may fulfil such a function to some extent. Preferably there ought to be an institutional structure for coordination.

Does it cause damage if a recipient is given conflicting advice? This usually happens, but it is not inevitable, if the recipient has the capacity to evaluate all the advice and combine it in an insightful way as, for example, Vietnam appears to be trying to do. It remains to be seen if the hybrids of common and civil law that are now evolving have a future. Coordination ought preferably to include inputs made through non-governmental organisations, since they often go together with the inputs made between states.

7. *Dialogue*

A donor may have legitimate grounds for expressing critical views, especially if they are based on standards for human rights. Since a well-functioning legal system is a prerequisite for citizens to be able to assert their rights, it is legitimate for a donor not only to take up violations of human rights, but also anomalies in the system of justice. On the other hand, there may be faults in the central functions which is why criticism may touch on national sovereignty. This is a cogent argument for being tactful in the dialogue.

8. Focus on Eastern Europe

West-European countries' self-interest not only creates a good basis for co-operation with their neighbours, but also a 'pressure to offer supplies.' It is thus relevant whether the principle of division of costs can be maintained, so that the co-operation can become firmly established and safeguarded in the partner country. If a division of costs cannot be achieved—it may, for instance, be difficult in Russia, Latvia or Lithuania—the establishment should be safeguarded in another way. One example is a clearly articulated account by the partner country of its needs and priorities in the legal area. Not uncommonly, the donor side has sought this in vain. Causes are lack of competence on the part of the recipient and linguistic problems. It is also possible that one can reduce the demands moderately in those cases where projects relate directly to an EU requirement or alternately to very strong self-interests of the donor country. In the latter case, it is then desirable that the 'donor country interests' make their own contributions. In other cases one should design the co-operation to be more in line with the methodology that is traditionally applied in development co-operation with the south.[23] It should also be noted that there may be a great need in a certain sector, *e.g.*, the judicial, but that there is a lack of projects, which is why the partner country may have good reason not to allocate means.

9. Focus on Development Co-operation After Conflicts

After a civil war or disaster it is often the public institutions that are incapable of taking responsibility. This may be an argument for rapid measures from the donor community and perhaps also for generous financing of running costs and other local expenses. At the same time, there may be a need to set up conditions for development co-operation, for example, to protect minorities or to adopt anti-corruption measures. The result may be strongly donor-controlled assistance with little opportunity for accountability by local politicians and authorities. This is a disadvantage for efficient development co-operation and undermines the democratic process.

[23] Baker, Gideon, Civil Society and Democratic Theory: Alternative Voices. Routledge Innovations in Political Theory 9. London; New York: Routledge, 2002; Diamond, Larry Jay, and Marc F. Plattner, Democracy after Communism. A Journal of Democracy Book. Baltimore, MD: Johns Hopkins University Press, 2002; Feldbrugge, F. J. M. Law in Transition. Law in Eastern Europe; No. 52. The Hague; New York: M. Nijhoff, 2002.

This dilemma requires the donor to go forward in stages, to involve local actors and to be flexible.

10. Conclusions for Legal Development Co-operation

The role of the development co-operation authorities in the field of legal development co-operation is demanding. Strategic planning, design of inputs, follow-up are among the factors involved here and are difficult to assess and in other ways the inputs are risky. Probably the basis for decisions is in many cases poorer in this area than in many others. In addition, a holistic view is desirable at the same time as the level of knowledge remains rudimentary. Caution and methodical care are required. Legal support may be required in many 'factual areas'—*e.g.*, environment, capital markets, infrastructure—which is why a donor must combine such professional knowledge with legal expertise.

B. Need for the Development of Competence

1. Lack of Knowledge

Development co-operation in the legal area takes place in a theoretical vacuum compared to many other areas. There is no established theoretical framework to form the basis for inputs. Not least, there is hardly any research on the legal system of societies in transition. It presumably needs an inter-disciplinary approach that combines traditional legal studies with judicial philosophy, legal anthropology and general theoretical development thinking. Similarly, studies are required of the conditions necessary to develop and support traditional law and its institutions and the opportunity to combine traditional and official law as well as their respective institutions. The methodology of development co-operation also needs to grow so that it can be adapted to the conditions in the legal area. This requires *inter alia* the systematic documentation and application of experiences.

2. Conclusions for Legal Development Co-operation

The vacuum that exists argues for things like a careful approach and flexibility in the area of development co-operation, projects that are not too large, careful planning, and sometimes, a bottom-up approach.

CHAPTER EIGHTEEN

'Club Multilateralism' and Global Supranationalism: The Case of FATF

*by Heba M. Shams**

CHAPTER OUTLINE

I. Introduction
II. The Financial Action Task Force: Origin, Mandate and Nature
III. Membership
IV. Structure of Governance
V. Functions
 A. Rulemaking
 B. Enforcement
VI. FATF Supranationalism: Analysis and Critique
VII Conclusion

I. INTRODUCTION

The processes of globalization, which have intensified since the 1970s, posed a challenge to state-based governance. Scores of political and economic phenomena have assumed transnational dimensions. Capital markets and the operations of multinational enterprises are but two examples. The transnational features of economic activities were not confined to legitimate enterprises. Instead, criminal economic activities also increasingly make use of the cross-border channels of commerce. With a territorially organised state-based governance, the challenges of these cross-border activities to governance are self-evident.

As a response to this state of affairs, there is a growing trend towards creating structures of supranational governance based on the sovereign

* LLB, LLM, PhD. Shihata Lecturer in International Economic Law, CCLS, Queen Mary, University of London; Head of the Secretariat of the London Forum for International Economic Law and Development; Member, Financial Integrity Sector, World Bank, Washington, DC.

participation of a small group of countries in a multilateral process of standard-setting and decision-making. The outcome of these multilateral processes is imposed globally through elaborate processes of persuasion based on incentives and sanctions. Examples of this type of multilateralism/supranationalism abound in the area of global financial regulation. This Chapter is concerned with demonstrating critically the dynLLB, LLM, PhD. Shihata Lecturer in International Economic Law, CCLS, Queen Mary, University of London; and Head of the Secretariat of the London Forum for International Economic Law and Development. amics of this form of governance through discussion of the development and operations of the Financial Action Task Force.

Before one delves into the discussion of the particular case at hand, a clarification of the content of the concept of supranationalism is necessary. Supranationalism is a term loosely used. It has not developed into a specific legal doctrine. Its history goes back to the 1950s and specifically to the formation of the European Coal and Steel Community. The treaty instituting this Community is probably the first international legal instrument to use 'supranational' as a legal term.[1] Despite the diversity of usage, a minimum common denominator could be established. Whenever the term is used it denotes an institutionalised exercise of power or authority over the State not by another State but by an international organisation or organ. The powers typically exercised are either judicial or prescriptive. That is to say that the supranational character has been attached to international organisations or organs that are either adjudicating disputes between States or prescribing rules of conduct to be followed by States.

One international scholar analysing the term 'supranational' has identified a number of traits that would give a certain organ a supranational character. This taxonomy included, amongst others, the following practices:[2]

- an international organ or the organisation is empowered to make decisions binding on its Member States by majority voting;
- a non-representative international organ of an organisation is empowered to make decisions binding on all the members of the organisation including those that are not represented in the organ; and
- an international organ or organisation composed of individuals acting independently from their governments is empowered to make binding decisions on its member governments.

[1] Art. (9) Paras. 5 & 6. Verzijl, J., *International Law in Historical Perspective Vol. I* (1968), at 285.

[2] *Id.* at 287 *et seq.*

The common feature of these various practices as indicative of a supranational character is that they all depart from the principle of voluntariness and consent that govern the sources of international law and underlie the operations of international organisations.[3] In that sense suprnataionalism is a departure from the doctrine of external sovereignty towards establishing structures of superior authorities in the international system. Sometimes this session of sovereignty is voluntary but at other occasions it is coercive or at least not based on genuine consent.

This Chapter will discuss the governance structures and operations of the Financial Action Task Force. In doing so, it will seek to demonstrate the contrast the multilateral nature of the group as it operates internally i.e., *vis-à-vis* its membership, and the supranational nature of its operations *vis-à-vis* non-members.

II. THE FINANCIAL ACTION TASK FORCE: ORIGIN, MANDATE AND NATURE

The FATF was created in 1989 by the G7 Summit in Paris. Its mandate consists of one paragraph in the Summit's declaration on 'Drug Issues.' Following a preamble on the seriousness of the drug problem, the Summit resolved as one of a variety of measures to convene a financial action task force from Summit participants and other countries interested in these problems. Its mandate is to assess the results of cooperation already undertaken in order to prevent the utilization of the banking system and financial institutions for the purpose of money laundering, and to consider additional preventive efforts in this field, including the adaptation of the legal and regulatory systems so as to enhance multilateral judicial assistance. The first meeting of this task force will be called by France and its report will be completed by April 1990.[4]

Following its creation by the Summit, the FATF assumed a life of its own, without any limitations of mandate or timeframe. It is left to the FATF to decide its own destiny and to define its own mission. According to the Summit's practice and according to the standard operation of such entities, this body becomes independent of the Summit and no longer associated with it. Although what exactly this independence means is not entirely clear.

The FATF was called into meeting by France and it produced its first report ahead of the deadline in February 1990.[5] Its existence was subject to periodic review and was repeatedly extended for periods of five years. The last review took place in 1997–1998 and the operation of the FATF was

[3] *See id.* at 286.

[4] G7 Summit, Paris, July 14–16, 1989 Declaration on Drug Issues para. 53 (*available at* www.library.utoronto.ca/g7.). Last Visited Mar. 1, 2000).

[5] FATF, *Report* (February 7th, 1990).

determined to continue until 2004.[6] In the second year of its operation 1990-1991, the FATF agreed upon its mandate. The mandate was set in terms of four tasks for the FATF to accomplish:[7]

- self- reporting and mutual assessment (monitoring and surveillance) on the adoption and implementation of FATF recommendation by all members;
- coordination and oversight of efforts to encourage non-members to adopt and implement the recommendations;
- making further recommendations and evaluations of countermeasures while serving as a forum for considering developments in money laundering techniques domestically and worldwide; and for the exchange of information on enforcement techniques to combat money laundering; and
- standing ready to facilitate cooperation between organizations concerned with combating money laundering and between individual countries or territories.

This mandate was later translated into three priorities for the Task Force's work:[8]

(1) to define and carry out a systematic verification of the degree of implementation of its forty recommendations;
(2) to undertake in-depth assessment of laundering techniques and their implications for the recommendations; and
(4) to develop a well-focused and comprehensive external profile.

These three priorities, set in accordance with the FATF's 1991 mandate, continued unchanged in subsequent reviews. What has changed, however, is the order of these priorities.

In reviewing its operations and extending its existence in 1997–1998, the FATF revised its order of priorities and set as its main priority to 'establish a world-wide anti-money laundering network and to spread the FATF's message to all countries and regions of the globe.'[9] The other two priorities of monitoring compliance with the forty recommendations and continuing the review of money laundering trends and countermeasures remained but in secondary place to this primary worldwide lobbying function.

Following the September 11th event, the FATF held an extraordinary

[6] FATF, *Annual Report 1997–1998* (June 1998), *available at* www.oecd.org/fatf. (last visited Apr. 29 2002).

[7] FATF, *Report 1990–1991* (May 13, 1991), at 3.

[8] FATF, *Annual Report 1991–1992* (June 25, 1992), at para.1, *available at* www.oecd.org/fatf. (last visited Apr. 29 2002).

[9] FATF, *Annual Report 1997–1998* (June 1998), para.16–17, *available at* www.oecd.org/fatf. (last visited Apr. 29 2002).

plenary meeting on October 31 2001.[10] In this meeting, the FATF expanded its mandate beyond money laundering to include terrorist financing.[11] The FATF's action plan as set in this extraordinary meeting indicate that the Task Force will extend the same set of activities it conducts with respect to money laundering to include terrorist financing. This includes developing countermeasures, monitoring compliance, studying trends and spreading the system worldwide.[12]

The FATF is of a fluid nature. This fluidity is even felt in the search for the right words to describe its operation and its actions. It does seem to express some form of collective will distinct from its members. It, however, does not possess any constitution and, apart from a small secretariat of four individuals, it does not possess any permanent organs separate from the members. Its entire work is conducted through plenary meetings deciding by consensus and *ad hoc* working groups of experts or is distributed amongst its members and carried out through their own domestic institutions. It is clear from the declaration that created the FATF, from subsequent practice and from explicit statements in FATF reports that its members do not wish to secure for it any legal personality or international organisation status. This leads to the inevitable conclusion that the FATF is not an international organisation.

It describes itself as an intergovernmental body defined by its purpose. According to the dictionary definition, a task force is: 'a unit specially organised for a task'[13] the FATF remains committed to this specific nature as it defines its mission and role in annual mandates geared towards clear goals.[14] This fluid nature of the FATF is something that it takes pride in. It promotes this *informality* as one reason of its success in building consensus and spreading money laundering control regime all over the world.

III. MEMBERSHIP

The FATF is not an open intergovernmental body. Its membership is restrictive and any extension of the membership is thoroughly calculated. Created by the G7 Summit, its core membership consists of the members of this group: United States, Japan, Germany, France, United Kingdom, Italy, Canada, and the Commission of the European Communities. Recognising

[10] FATF, *FATF Cracks on Terrorist Financing*, Press Release (Washington, 31 October 2001), *available at* www.oecd.org/fatf. (last visited Apr. 29, 2002).

[11] *Id.*

[12] *Id.*

[13] The Concise Oxford Dictionary (8th ed. 1990)

[14] 'In keeping with the FATF's function as a task force, this work should be directed through annual mandates towards clear goals in each area.' FATF, *Annual Report 1993–1994* (16 June 1994), at para. 17, *available at* www.oecd.org/fatf. (last visited Apr. 29, 2002).

the importance of wider participation in this effort, the Summit Participants invited a number of other countries to join the Task Force. The extension of the invitation was based on either the country's concern with the problem of money laundering or the country's special expertise in the fight against money laundering.[15] Accordingly the invitation was extended to Sweden, the Netherlands, Luxembourg, Switzerland, Austria, Spain and Australia.[16]

During 1990–1991, the FATF extended the membership further by inviting the remaining members of the Organisation for Economic Co-operation and Development (OECD) to join. This group included Denmark, Finland, Greece, Ireland, New Zealand, Norway, Portugal, Turkey. In addition, the FATF II invited Hong Kong, Singapore and the Gulf Co-operation Council (GCC) to participate. The latter three invitees were chosen on basis of their importance as offshore financial centres or as representative of offshore financial centres.[17] The GCC was invited to participate in order to reach a number of its members that are particularly important financial centres.[18] The membership of the GCC includes Saudi Arabia, Bahrain, the United Arab Emirates (UAE), Oman, Qatar and Kuwait.

The decision to invite the GCC rather than its member countries reflects the measured approach that the FATF adopts towards the question of its membership. Including the GCC allows the FATF to reach important financial centres in the region such as Bahrain and the UAE while limiting their influence in the decision-making process within the TASK Force. This is also reflected in the procedure followed for admission. In order to qualify for membership countries were required to endorse the Forty Recommendations. An entire meeting of the TASK Force on the 17th of December 1990 was dedicated to briefing them in order to help them assess the burden that they would incur by endorsing the Recommendations.[19]

In addressing the question of membership by the FATF in 1991–1992, the Task Force resolved not to accept any new members at that point. It justified its decision on the basis that its existing membership of 28 members is nearly the maximum possible if the body is to maintain its ability to achieve consensus and to operate informally.[20] The FATF reviewed the question of membership repeatedly in subsequent terms of operation. While deciding to keep the question under review, the decision not to extend the membership any further was maintained. The basis for the decision was always the desire not to jeopardise the 'flexibility and efficiency'[21] of the Task Force.

[15] FATF, *Report 1990* (Feb. 7, 1990), at 2.
[16] *Id.*
[17] FATF, *Report 1990–1991* (May 13, 1991), at 16.
[18] *Id.*
[19] *Id.*
[20] FATF, *Annual Report 1991–1992* (June 25, 1992), at para. 96.
[21] FATF, *Annual Report 1993–1994* (June 16, 1994), at para. 23.

During the comprehensive review of its future mission and programme that was carried out in 1997–1998, the FATF set its policy regarding future membership. It decided that as part of its efforts to spread the message of money laundering control worldwide, the FATF will consider expanding its membership to strategic countries. The criteria membership were set to include: (1) Having certain key anti-money laundering measures in place such as criminalisation, customer identification and suspicious or unusual transaction reporting. (2) Possessing the political determination to make a full commitment to implement the Forty Recommendations. (3) having the capacity to play a leading role in their regions in the process of combating money laundering.

The FATF launched its effort to expand its membership in 1998–1999. The criteria set out in 1997–1998 were further tuned. Potential members were now required to undergo two rounds of mutual evaluations and to be active members of the relevant FATF-style regional body or willing to take the lead on establishing such a body where no such body exists.[22] The FATF policy on expansion included taking into consideration the geographic balance of the Task Force and the need to re-enforce the FATF's representation in certain regions where it is under-represented. Accordingly, the FATF invited Argentina, Brazil and Mexico to become observers during the following term of the FATF. This status was only granted upon a written commitment from the target countries to endorse the Recommendations and to undergo mutual evaluations. The three Latin American countries became full members in 2000 following one round of mutual evaluation.[23] In its Report of 2000-2001, the FATF confirms its commitment to a policy of strategic expansion but it does not set out a specific plan.[24]

One of the features of the FATF is its multidisciplinary character. This is reflected in the representation of different members in the meetings of the Task Force. Countries are typically represented by experts from various ministries including finance, justice, interior and foreign affairs, financial regulatory authorities and law enforcement agencies. Annual meetings of the Task Force enjoy the participation of up to 150 experts. This multidisciplinary character is consistent with the nature of money laundering law and it is one of the strengths of the FATF.

In addition to its regular members, the FATF permits the participation of a number of observers from some of the main international organisations

22 FATF, *Annual Report 1998–1999* (July 2, 1999), at para. 150.

23 FATF, *Annual Report 1999–2000* (June 22, 2000).

24 FATF, *Annual Report 2000–2002*, (June 22, 2001), at para. 18. An interesting addition to this Report on the question of membership is that in footnote 5 the FATF indicates that the choice of strategic countries for the purposes of expansion will be regardless of their level of economic development. The lack of access to minutes of meetings prevents the researcher from understanding the origin and implications of such developments.

and regional bodies. The list currently consists of twenty organisations and bodies including the Asia /Pacific Group on Money Laundering (AGP), the Caribean Financial Action Task Force (CFATF), the Council of Europe PC-R-EV Committee, the African Development Bank, the Asia Development Bank, the World Bank and the International Monetary Fund.[25] The participation of international organisations in the FATF meetings is again subject to its discretion and strategic calculation.[26] In 1995–1996, the FATF decided to increase the participation of observer bodies and organisations in its plenary meetings as part of its strategy for spreading anti-money laundering efforts worldwide.[27]

In the same round (1995–1996), another important development has taken place. The FATF decided to cultivate co-operation with the financial services sector on on-going basis. For this purpose, it organised a Forum with representatives of the industry, which was held on 30 January 1996. The meeting brought together representatives from Member Countries and delegates from national banking and insurance associations as well as participants from the non-bank financial sector and organisations of the financial services industry. It was geared towards soliciting the advice and support of the financial sector. The practice of consultation with the financial sector continued in subsequent FATF rounds. This development is an illustration of the role of private parties in governance at all its levels.

IV. STRUCTURE OF GOVERNANCE

While the FATF is not an international organisation, which suggests that the use of the term 'governance' is probably inaccurate, the FATF is still an international body that expresses a form of collective will. Discussing the structure of the FATF in terms of governance is useful for the clarity of subsequent analysis and evaluation.

During the first four years of the life of the FATF (1990–1994) one could see an evolving structure of governance with some degree of formality, continuity and specialisation. In the first year of its operation (1989–1990) and for the purpose of developing its first report which introduced the now key Forty Recommendations on Money Laundering, the FATF worked through a series of plenary meetings and the work of three specialised *ad hoc* working groups. Working Group 1 worked on money laundering statistics and methods under the presidency of the United Kingdom; Working

[25] Consult the list of 'Observer Bodies and Organisations' on the FATF web site (www.oecd.org/fatf).

[26] 'Competent international organisations could be invited to participate as observers, at the discretion of the Presidency.' FATF, *Report 1990–1991* (May 13, 1991), at 25.

[27] FATF, *Annual Report 1995–1996* (June 28, 1996), at para.7.

Group 2 addressed the legal questions under the presidency of the United States and Working Group 3 focused on administrative and financial co-operation under the presidency of Italy. Each Group produced reports and documentation that formed the background material and basis of the First Report of the FATF and the Forty Recommendations. None of the background material compiled by the Groups, however, is published.

During the second round of the FATF in 1990–1991, the Task Force addressed explicitly its institutional structure.[28] One of three working groups created for the purposes of this round focused specifically on planning the future of the FATF.[29] Again none of the documents produced by this Working Group, nor the minutes of its deliberations is published or available for inspection. On the basis of the recommendations of this Working Group, the FATF resolved to continue on *ad hoc* and informal basis and to maintain its flexible structure.[30] The structure envisioned by the FATF at this stage involved a presidency, a steering group, a small secretariat and *ad hoc* working groups as necessary. The presidency was to be held by one of its members and to rotate amongst them on yearly basis. The presidency is allocated by the FATF, which could only mean the plenary, on basis of the geographical location and membership in international groupings. The Report does not elaborate on the exact meaning of these criteria.[31] The practice established in this Report has been followed in subsequent years. After the first two years of the French Presidency, the Presidency rotated for the first time in 1991–1992 and was passed to Switzerland.

The steering group envisioned in the FATF's 1990–1991 plan was to be constituted of representative of the Presidency for the last year and the next year plus the Chairmen of Working Groups if any such groups are formed.[32] There is limited reference to the Steering Group and its operations in subsequent reports. The practice of forming three Working Groups on the other hand continued in subsequent FATF rounds until 1994. In 1991–1992, signs of formalism in the structure were evident in two trends: (1) the Working Groups were formed with specific mandates; and (2) the mandates and the reports of the Working Groups were published as annexes to the FATF's Annual Report.[33] This pattern persisted in 1992–1993.[34]

The final limb in the FATF's institutional structure as established in 1990–1991 Report is the Secretariat. This is the only permanent organ in the structure of governance of the FATF. It is permanent in the sense that it remains in session throughout the year and continues for as long as the

[28] FATF, *Report 1990-1991* (May 13, 1991), at 25. [29] *Id.* at 4.
[30] *Id.* at 25. [31] *Id.* [32] *Id.*
[33] FATF, *Annual Report 1991–1992* (June 25, 1992), at para. 13 and the Annexes.
[34] FATF, *Annual Report 1992–1993* (June 29, 1993), at para. 14 and Annexes I, II and III.

FATF is in operation. While the UNIDCP had offered to act as the FATF's secretariat, the FATF chose instead to invite the OECD to provide the secretariat services for the Task Force. According to the FATF's Report, this choice was made on basis of the OECD's 'experience in areas related to those covered by the FATF, multidisciplinary nature, and compatibility with the aims of the FATF.'[35] The functions of the Secretariat include 'collating, co-ordinating and summarising responses from FATF members and supporting FATF presidency.'[36] The Secretariat could also conduct studies upon decisions by the FATF but it is explicitly excluded from getting involved in any enforcement activities.[37] The Report did not define what is meant by enforcement activities.

These various parts of the institutional structure of the FATF are managerial in nature. The decision-making power of the FATF resides entirely in the Plenary acting by consensus. Apart from the annual reports there is no information available on the procedures of the plenary meetings and such meetings are as a matter of rule not open to the public.

In addition to the various parts of the institutional structure of the FATF and its plenary meetings, the Task Force relies heavily on the endorsement of its decisions by the G7 Summits and by the Ministerial Meeting of the OECD.[38] It is a view repeatedly expressed in the FATF's reports that this endorsement is important to give the FATF's action the necessary political force.[39] It has been a regular practice for the G7 and the OECD to endorse the actions and decisions of the Task Force in their annual meetings.[40]

During the first review of the FATF's work and future mission and programme in 1993–1994, a major shift in the institutional arrangements has taken place. The FATF decided to discontinue the structure of three working groups and to strengthen the functions of the plenary.[41] *Ad hoc* working groups could be created to carry out specific functions. The Annual Report of that year marked the shift by not including in its Annex the reports of the three Working Groups, which were constituted for that round. The FATF also confirmed that it will continue to function as a 'free-standing ad hoc group'.[42] It is the view of the author that this decision by the FATF marks a shift towards stronger informality and had the effect of reducing an already meagre degree of transparency.

35 FATF, *Annual Report 1990–1991* (May 13, 1991) at 25.

36 *Id.*

37 *Id.*

38 The FATF reports regularly to the G7 Summit and to the OECD Ministerial Meeting.

39 *See e.g.* conclusion to that effect in the FATF's first report in 1990. FATF, *Report 1990* (Feb. 7, 1990), at 28.

40 *See e.g.*, FATF, *Annual Report 1997–1998* (June 1998), at paras. 22–25.

41 FATF, *Annual Report 1993–1994* (June 16, 1994), at para. 25.

42 *Id.* at para. 24.

V. FUNCTIONS

Since the third year of its operations, the FATF continued to organise its work into three priority areas: monitoring the implementation of the recommendations, review of the money laundering techniques and countermeasures and external relations. This Section translates the work of the FATF in these areas into specific functions. The analysis of the work of the FATF reveals that it exercises in the area of money laundering law the following six functions: research and analysis, rulemaking, enforcement, lobbying, technical assistance and co-ordination. Research and analysis is one of the primary functions of the FATF and one that was stipulated in its original mandate. It is also a function that is closely linked to its rulemaking function. The Recommendations advocated by the FATF are under constant review on basis of its findings regarding developments in money laundering typologies. [43] Each of these functions is analysed below in terms of its scope and the FATF's method of implementation.

Co-ordination, lobbying and technical assistance are all parts of what the FATF describes as its external relations priority area. This area, as indicated above, has become its priority area since 1997–1998. The FATF performs the function of co-ordinating the efforts of the ever-growing number of international organisations and bodies that are involved in combating money laundering.[44] It does so through inviting such organisations as observers in its meetings and attending, to the extent possible, any meetings organised by them. It also avoids duplication of efforts wherever possible. One of the most sophisticated aspects of the FATF's external relations efforts is its lobbying function. The FATF uses various mechanisms to promote its recommendations in the area of money laundering including setting up satellite secretariat in different regions in the world and encouraging the creation of FATF-style regional bodies and participating in their operations in some capacity. The technical assistance function is also part of this lobbying effort. The FATF is not an international organisation, which means that it does not possess independent resources to provide technical assistance. Its efforts in this regard consist of pooling the resources of its Member States and co-ordinating their allocation.

Detailed discussion of the research and analysis, co-ordination, lobbying

[43] Until 1997, the FATF has been publishing the findings of its research on money laundering typologies as part of the body of its annual report. The account of findings has therefore been in summary form. Since 1998, the FATF has been publishing the full report on money laundering typologies as an annex to the main report.

[44] For a summary table of the various international instruments in this area, current until 1999, *see* Simmons, B., 'International Efforts against Money Laundering', in Shelton, D. (ed.) *Commitment and Compliance: The Role of Non-Binding Norms in the International Legal System* 244 (2000), Table 6.1.

and technical assistance is beyond the scope of this study. The next two subsections will focus on the rulemaking function and the enforcement function. It is through these two functions that the FATF's supranational role is exercised.

A. Rulemaking

The Forty Recommendations of the FATF constitute the most important and most comprehensive international instrument on money laundering. The Forty Recommendations cover all aspects of combating money laundering. The substantive details of the recommendations have been discusses in Section (3) of Chapter Four above. This Section, therefore, focuses on the features of the Recommendations that illustrate the nature of the rulemaking power of the FATF.

The main feature of the Forty Recommendations is described in the first version of the Recommendations as published in the FATF's first Report in 1990. The Report states that the recommended action steps 'could constitute a *minimal standard* in the fight against money laundering for the countries participating in this Task Force, as well as for other countries.'[45] [emphasis added] Countries, therefore, are encouraged to go beyond the recommendations of the FATF wherever necessary.

The FATF's Recommendations are under continuous review in view of developments in the money laundering trends and typologies. This review is one of the priority areas of the FATF. Actual changes in the core text of the Recommendations are kept to a minimum. Responding to the changes is normally implemented through minor changes, annexes to the Recommendations and interpretative notes. The decision to recommend a certain course of action is adopted in a plenary meeting where the consensus rule applies. As a result of the secrecy and informality that surrounds the operation of the FATF, little is knows about the actual procedure that governs these decisions. The first Report of the FATF in 1990 however has explicitly provided that 'some of these recommendations reflect the view of a majority of delegates, rather than unanimity, so that they are not limited to the weakest existing solution in the participating countries on each topic.'[46]

The FATF's Forty Recommendations are now under comprehensive review, the results of which have not yet been published. In addition to the Forty Recommendations, following the events of September 11, the FATF has expanded its mandate to terrorist financing. On 31 October 2001, the FATF in an extraordinary meeting adopted eight 'Special Recommendations

[45] FATF, *Report 1990* (Feb. 7, 1990).
[46] FATF, *Report 1990* (Feb. 7, 1990), at 16.

on Terrorist Financing.'[47] This new set of recommendations is now subject to the same enforcement and review procedures as the original Forty Recommendations on money laundering.

The Recommendations are drafted in a non-binding language such as 'countries should consider the feasibility[. . .,]' 'Countries should further encourage[. . .,]' 'the appropriate national authorities should consider [. . .,]' 'wherever possible [. . .]' The forms of the recommendations is also indicative of the non-binding nature in that they do not prescribe detailed strict rules. Instead, the rules are drafted with sufficient flexibility to allow for variations in national legal systems. For example, Recommendation 4 provides that countries should criminalise money laundering of the proceeds of drug trafficking as stipulated in the Vienna Convention 1988. It, however, encourages countries to extend the scope of the predicate offence to include serious offences more generally and grants them the discretion to decide which serious offences to be included in the scope of money laundering offence.

This expression of the will of the Members of the FATF, as reflected in the language of the Recommendations, suggests that 'rulemaking' is an inaccurate description of the function of the FATF in this regard. The description is more consistent with the formalistic analysis of the instrument is probably standard-setting. This is also the reference most commonly used. It is the view of the author however that the elaborate and stringent character of the enforcement system that supports the recommendations renders this non-biding characterisation illusory. Arguing this point however is not possible until a description of the enforcement function and system of the FATF is provided. It is this description that the next Section provides.

B. *Enforcement*

Enforcement in this context means the measures taken by the FATF to pressure a member or non-member country to comply with the FATF's Recommendations either on money laundering or terrorist financing. The purpose of this discussion is to elaborate on the degree of coercion in the FATF's compliance system and to understand the procedural principles and safeguards that are followed in the process. The discussion will focus on the process of enforcing the Forty Recommendations as opposed to that of enforcing the Special Recommendations on Terrorist Financing. This is because of the mature stage that the former has reached as opposed to the latter. The discussion of this function is organised in two parts: (1) enforcement against Member Countries; and (2) enforcement against non-member countries.

[47] FATF, *Special Recommendations on Terrorist Financing* (Oct. 31, 2001).

1. Enforcement Against Member Countries

In order to secure compliance by its Members with the FATF's Recommendations, the FATF adopts two types of evaluation mechanisms that were agreed in 1991. The first monitoring mechanism is based on self-assessment and is carried out on annual basis. Countries are required to complete a standard questionnaire that is designed to measure the level of their compliance. The Secretariat uses this questionnaire to compile reports on the level of compliance with the Recommendations and also on the specific successes and failures in the reporting country's system.

The second mechanism of monitoring is one of mutual evaluation. The FATF has conducted two rounds of comprehensive mutual evaluation of the Forty Recommendations. The second round was completed in June 1999.[48] The process of mutual evaluation is governed by four core principles: participation,[49] efficiency, equality, objectivity and clarity.[50] Equality was specifically and repeatedly emphasised in the FATF's documents.[51] Consent is another principle that could be added to this list. In its 1991–1992 Annual Report, the FATF emphasised 'the consensual nature of all the different stages of the evaluation process'.[52]

The FATF has set a number of procedures in order to guarantee consistency and equality in the evaluation process. Primary responsibility lies on the Secretariat through its co-ordinating role.[53] Further, common mutual evaluation questionnaires were prepared[54] as well as a common outline and set form for all the reports.[55] In February 1997, a standard checklist of all the issues to be covered was prepared and given to the examiners as part of the same effort to guarantee equality and consistency.[56]

The evaluation process is conducted by three or four examiners through inspection of documents provided by the examined country and on-site visits. Each examination team is a multidisciplinary one consisting of legal, financial and enforcement experts. The examiners are selected from individuals voluntarily nominated by the Member Countries or directly solicited by the FATF Secretariat. The final decision on the selection is made by the President in co-operation with the Secretariat. In order to guarantee the principles of objectivity, the team consists of examiners from different countries and their background is taken into consideration.[57] In fulfillment

[48] FATF, *Review of FATF Anti-Money Laundering Systems and Mutual Evaluation Procedures 1992–1999* (February 16, 2001), para. 4.

[49] *Id.* at 144.

[50] *Id.*at para. 130.

[51] *See e.g. id.*, paras. 4, 131 & 133.

[52] FATF, *Annual Report 1991–1992* (June 25, 1992), at para. 57.

[53] FATF, *Review of FATF Anti-Money Laundering Systems and Mutual Evaluation Procedures 1992-1999* (February 16, 2001), para. 131.

[54] *Id.* at para. 132.

[55] *Id.* at para. 134.

[56] *Id.* at 133.

[57] *Id.* at 140.

of the principle of participation, all members are encouraged to provide at least one examiner. The majority of examiners, however, were provided by the United States in both rounds of evaluation. During the second round the principle of participation was satisfied, at least in token, when each member provided at least on examiner.[58]

The process of preparing and adopting the evaluation report is an elaborate one. The examiners' comments are provided to the Secretariat, which prepares the draft report according to a pre-set outline. The draft report is then sent to the examiners who provide their comments on the draft. Upon implementing the examiners' comments on the draft, the report is sent to the examined country for its comment. The country concerned communicates its comments to both the examiners and the Secretariat. The Secretariat prepares the final draft according to the examiners' advice and sends it to the delegates. Similar procedure is followed for the summary of the Evaluation Report, which is to be included in the FATF's Annual Report.

During the plenary the examiners and the country concerned with the involvement of the Secretariat resolve any disagreement on the wording through negotiation. The report is then discussed in the plenary following a brief presentation by the examiners and an opening statement by the country. This is followed by the comments of two intervener countries designated by the President and then the other delegates are invited to present five questions to the country concerned or the examiners. The report is then adopted verbally by the Plenary along with all the agreed amendments. The final report and summary is submitted to the following plenary for final adoption.[59]

In 1994, the FATF agreed a formal five-step non-compliance policy.[60] The purpose of this policy was to secure that the FATF's members achieve a satisfactory degree of compliance with the procedures. The FATF perceives that failure by its own members to comply with its policies hinders it international mission of spreading anti-money laundering measures. It was also agreed that the process should be 'a transparent one, based on a graduated approach, equality of treatment, and oversight by the Plenary of the various steps in the process.'[61]

Countries whose systems suffer serious failures to comply with the Forty Recommendations will be required to rectify the failures. Failure to do so would result in taking the following graduated steps as described by the FATF in its report:[62]

(1) Requiring the members to provide regular reports on their progress in implementing the Recommendations within a fixed timeframe;

[58] *Id.* at para. 144. [59] *Id.* at paras. 163–64. [60] *Id.* at para. 167.
[61] *Id.* at para. 168. [62] *Id.* at 168.

(2) Sending a letter from the FATF President to the relevant minister(s) in the member jurisdiction drawing their attention to non compliance with the FATF Recommendations;
(3) Arranging a high-level mission to the member jurisdiction in question to reinforce this message;
(4) In the context of the application of Recommendation 21 by its members, issuing a formal FATF statement to the effect that a member jurisdiction is insufficiently in compliance with the FATF Recommendations; and
(5) Suspending the jurisdiction's membership of the FATF until the Recommendations have been implemented.

This process since its inception was applied to twelve countries. In most cases the matter did not go beyond the submission of progress reports. In the case of Austria however, which was pressured with regard to its anonymous bank accounts system, the conflict reached a threat of suspension. Upon which and following two years of defiance, Austria took the initial steps to bring its law in conformity with the Recommendations.[63]

In conclusion, the FATF follows a strict but clearly procedural process of enforcement *vis-à-vis* its members. The core elements of the process are a procedure of mutual evaluation and a policy for non-compliance. The process of enforcement is governed by principles of transparency, equality, objectivity, clarity, efficiency and graduation. The procedures that govern the process are geared towards guaranteeing these principles. The process could be characterised as supranational to an extent. Although the basis of the process is consensual, once a country has joined the group, it is necessarily subject to accepting the enforcement mechanisms and the processes of mutual review. In that sense the process could be described as supranational. This is particularly so in view of the scope of mutual evaluation and the ways in which it affects the legislative autonomy of the States concerned.

2. *Enforcement Against Non-member Countries*

This is the aspect in which the FATF acts truly as a supranational agency. The enforcement of the FATF's Recommendations against non-member countries has always been part of the thinking within the FATF since its inception. The system of anti-money laundering measures as designed by the FATF is based on an assumption that 'any discrepancy between national measures to fight money laundering can be used potentially by traffickers, who would move their laundering channels to the countries and financial

[63] FATF, *Annual Report 1999–2000* (June 22, 2000), at paras. 89 *et seq.*

systems where no or weak regulations exist on these matters'.[64] Concern for regulatory discrepancy in non-member countries have resulted in Recommendation 21, which proposes two special measures in dealing with countries that do not sufficiently apply the Forty Recommendations. The first measure is special due diligence to be exercised by financial institutions in their dealing with individuals and entities from such countries, and the second measure is special record-keeping and reporting requirements regarding suspicious or unusual transactions emanating from these countries.

As early as 1990–1991, the FATF considered the imposition of collective measures against non-member countries, which do not comply with the Forty Recommendations.[65] The proposition was that Recommendation 21 should be applied collectively *vis-à-vis* a number of jurisdictions identified and publicly blacklisted. The FATF on specific advice of law enforcement experts deemed this exercise to be premature at that stage. Members, however, were left free to implement Recommendation 21 individually against jurisdictions they domestically deem as posing particular risk.[66]

It was not until 1998–1999 that the FATF started considering proposals on measures to be taken against countries that do not provide effective international co-operation in the fight against money laundering.[67] An *ad hoc* working group was formed to implement what was later on to be referred to as an initiative against Non-Co-operative Countries and Territories (NCCT). This initiative is comprised of a number of steps:[68]

(1) identifying the rules and practices that are detrimental to the effective implementation of anti-money laundering measures and to effective international co-operation;

- on basis of the previous exercise, determining criteria for defining the non co-operative countries and territories;
- identifying the jurisdictions which meet the pre-set criteria;
- agreeing on international action to encourage compliance; and
- agreeing on protective countermeasures designed to protect the economies of Members against money laundering.

In February 2000, a Report on Non-Cooperative Countries and Territories

[64] FATF, *Report 1990* (Feb. 7, 1990), at 16.

[65] FATF, *Report 1990–1991* (May 13, 1991), at 13.

[66] *Id.*

[67] FATF, *Annual Report 1998–1999* (July 2, 1999), at paras. 153 *et seq.* This initiative took place in the context of other similar developments in the OECD and some of its member countries. During the same period initiatives within the OECD geared towards coercing offshore financial centres to align their policies with the OECD countries' desire to enhance the effectiveness of their tax laws were also taking place. *See* Hay, R., 'Offshore Centre under Attack', 6 *Private Client Business* 345 (1999).

[68] FATF, *Annual Report 1998–1999* (July 2, 1999), at para. 155.

was published identifying twenty-five criteria for non-cooperation. Countries were to be measured against these criteria in order to determine the sufficiency of their anti-money laundering measures. The criteria were based on the Forty Recommendations and were drafted in very broad terms. Each criterion is an indicator of a broader failure in the jurisdiction's anti-money laundering measure that renders it ineffective in meeting the requirements of international co-operation. The indicators or criteria include absence of authorisation or registration requirements for financial entities,[69] the existence of anonymous accounts,[70] lack of adequate record-keeping requirements,[71] secrecy provisions that cannot be lifted by administrative or judicial authorities,[72] and failure to criminalise laundering of the proceeds from serious crimes.[73]

The next step in the initiative was the identification of non-cooperative countries and territories on basis of the pre-set criteria. This involved first selecting specific jurisdictions for review and then reviewing their laws and regulations in terms of the twenty-five criteria in order to determine their level of compliance. The choice of countries for review was based on two general tests: (1) the financial activities of the jurisdictions should be of such size and character that shortcomings in their legal systems would undermine the effectiveness of the anti-money laundering regime[74] and (2) the use of the jurisdiction for money laundering schemes on basis of the data gathered on law enforcement and money laundering typologies.[75] The selection of a particular jurisdiction was ultimately based on a complaint of an FATF members against 'jurisdictions, where in the recent past, there have been difficulties'[76] in soliciting co-operation. Members are required to explain the nature of these difficulties.[77]

In the period between 14 February and 22 June 2000, the FATF conducted a review of twenty-six jurisdictions.[78] The review was conducted by four regional review groups: Americas, Asia/Pacific, Europe and Africa and the Middle East.[79] The exact composition of each group is not revealed in the FATF's reports. The review groups were required to work with the

[69] *Criteria Defining Non-Cooperative Countries or Territories,* Criterion Non. 2, in FATF, *Report on Non-Cooperative Countries and Territories*, Annex (Feb. 14, 2000), at 10.

[70] *Id.* at Criterion No. 4.

[71] *Id.* at Criterion No. 6.

[72] *Id.* at Criteria Nos. 8 & 9.

[73] *Id.* at Criterion No. 19.

[74] FATF, *Report on Non-Cooperative Countries and Territories* (Feb. 14, 2000), at para. 38.

[75] *Id.* at para. 39.

[76] *Id.* at para. 39.

[77] *Id.*

[78] Antigua and Barbuda, Bahamas, Belize, Bermuda, British Virgin Islands, Cayman Islands, Cook Islands, Cyprus, Dominica, Gibraltar, Gurensey, the Isle of Man and Jersey, Israel, Lebanon, Liechtenstein, Malta, Marshall Islands, Mauritius, Monaco, Mauru, Niue, Panama, Philippines, Russia, Samoa, Kitts and Nevis, St. Lucia, Vincent and the Grenadines. FATF, *Review to Identify Non-Cooperative Countries or Territories: Increasing the Worldwide Effectiveness of Anti-Money Laundering Measures* (June 22, 2000), at paras. 10 *et seq.*

[79] FATF, *Review to Identify Non-Cooperative Countries or Territories: Increasing the Worldwide Effectiveness of Anti-Money laundering Measures* (June 22, 2000), at para. 8.

Secretariat of the FATF and allowed to work with the Secretariats of relevant regional groups.[80] The process of the review involved gathering information on laws and regulations in the jurisdiction concerned, contacting the jurisdiction for further information, drafting the report and submitting it to the jurisdiction with an opportunity for comment. The reports and the comments were discussed in face-to-face meetings between the Review Group and the relevant jurisdiction. The Review Group drafted a report indicating its assessment of the jurisdiction against the twenty-five criteria. The Review Reports were then endorsed by the Plenary.[81]

The first review of non-member countries resulted in black-listing fifteen jurisdictions as 'non-cooperative countries and territories' (NCCT's).[82] Subsequently, the jurisdictions were urged to address the deficiencies identified. FATF expressed willingness to provide technical assistance to the identified jurisdiction in the design of their relevant systems. As a response to the FATF's action, the black-listed countries reacted by a surge of rapid legislative activity. For example, in the period from 22 June to 29 December 2000, the Bahamas enacted *ten* new legislative acts covering areas of prudential regulations, commercial and corporate law, international co-operation and criminal law.[83]

The counter-measures envisioned by the FATF for failure to comply include, in addition to Recommendation 21, blanket requirements to report transactions with such jurisdictions to the competent authorities in Member countries; restrictions on the establishment of subsidiaries, branches or representative offices of NCCT countries in FATF member countries, warning non-financial sector businesses against transaction with entities and individuals within NCCTs in view of the risk of money laundering. The FATF first NCCT Report also suggested that FATF members might consider using measures to prevent financial institutions located in NCCTs from using facilities located in FATF member countries, such as information technology facilities.[84]

As originally envisioned, the FATF initiative indicated that the identified NCCTs will be kept under continuous review but it did not design a procedure

[80] FATF, *Report on Non-Cooperative Countries and Territories* (Feb. 14, 2000), at para. 39.

[81] FATF, *Review to Identify Non-Cooperative Countries or Territories: Increasing the Worldwide Effectiveness of Anti-Money Laundering Measures* (June 22, 2000), at para. 9.

[82] Bahamas, Cayman Islands, Dominica, Israel, Lebanon, Liechtenstein, Marshall Islands, Nauru, Niue, Panama, Philippines, Russia, St. Kitts and Nevis, St. Vincent and the Grenadines. FATF, *Review to Identify Non-Cooperative Countries or Territories: Increasing the Worldwide Effectiveness of Anti-Money Laundering Measures* (June 22, 2000), at para. 64.

[83] FATF, *Review to Identify Non-Cooperative Countries or Territories: Increasing the Worldwide Effectiveness of Anti-Money Laundering Measures* (June 22, 2001), at para. 20.

[84] FATF, *Report on Non-Cooperative Countries and Territories* (Feb. 14, 2000), at paras. 49 *et seq.*

for de-listing. This was established in June 2001.[85] According to June 2001 Report, the test applied in order to remove a jurisdiction off the list of NCCTs is whether the jurisdiction 'has taken sufficient steps to ensure continued effective implementation of the reforms.'[86] This test presumes that the relevant jurisdiction has enacted the necessary laws and regulations to meet the concerns raised by the FATF. It further requires evidence of sustainable effective implementation. The assessment of the latter requisite will depend on submissions by the concerned jurisdiction to the FATF of implementation plans and specific targets.[87] The assessment of the jurisdiction's eligibility for de-listing will be decided by the competent Review Group.[88] The decision to de-list will be taken by the Plenary on basis of the recommendation of the relevant Review Group.[89] The FATF's procedure requires continued monitoring of the de-listed jurisdiction as well as public announcement of any remaining concerns.[90] According to the FATF's policy, such continuous monitoring will be measured against the 'implementation plan, specific issues raised in 2001 progress reports and the experience of FATF members.'[91]

In June 2001, four previously listed jurisdictions were removed off the list of NCCTs on the basis of extensive and rapid legislative actions.[92] Thirteen countries were reviewed in the second round of reviews of non-members.[93] Six of the reviewed jurisdictions were listed as NCCTs.[94] In December 2001, the FATF decided to impose counter-measures on Nauru for its failure to address the concerns raised by the FATF in June 2000.[95] These counter-measures were determined to continue in the Plenary of February 2002.[96] While the countermeasures adopted by the FATF might seem mild and essentially preventive, their effect on increasing the transaction cost for countries operating within a target jurisdiction could be substantial. That in addition to the fact that liability risk could lead finan-

[85] FATF, *Review to Identify Non-Cooperative Countries or Territories: Increasing the Worldwide Effectiveness of Anti-Money Laundering Measures* (June 22, 2001), at paras. 13 *et seq.*

[86] *FATF Policy Concerning Implementation and De-listing in Relation to NCCTs*, in FATF, *id.*, Appendix 2, at para. 5.

[87] *Id.* at para. 2.

[88] *Id.* at para. 3.

[89] *Id.* at para. 5.

[90] *Id.* at para. 7.

[91] *Id.* at para. 30.

[92] Bahamas, Cayman Islands, Liechtenstein and Panama. FATF, *Review to Identify Non-Cooperative Countries and Territories: Increasing the Worldwide Effectiveness of Anti-Money Laundering Measures* (June 22, 2001), at paras. 18 *et seq.*

[93] Czech Republic, Egypt, Guatemala, Hungary, Indonesia, Myanmar, Nigeria, Poland, Seychelles, Slovak Republic, Turks and Caicos, Uruguay, and Vanuatu. *Id.* at paras. 57 *et seq.*

[94] Egypt, Guatemala, Hungry, Indonesia, Myanmar, Nigeria. *Id.* Para. 88.

[95] *FATF Decides to Impose Countermeasures on Nauru*, Press Release (Paris, 5 December 2001).

[96] *FATF Acts against Terrorist Financing, Money Laundering and Non-cooperative Jurisdictions*, Press Release (Hong Kong, 1 Feb. 2002).

cial institutions in FATF member countries to decline to deal with institutions from NCCT jurisdictions. Considering the reliance that offshore financial centres have on operating and conducting their business in onshore jurisdictions, such consequences could have extreme detrimental effects on the small economies of the offshore centres not just on the financial institutions operating there.

VI. FATF SUPRANATIONALISM: ANALYSIS AND CRITIQUE

In juridical terms the FATF recommendations are soft law instruments that are not, according to the prevailing view, legally binding.[97] The *de facto* nature of these instruments, however, is far from optional. The FATF has developed a sophisticated enforcement regime that sanctions failure to comply with its non-binding norms. This enforcement apparatus, as explained above, applies both to member countries and to non-member countries sometimes even more strictly to the latter. To the extent that the FATF sets norms that are *de facto* binding upon non-members and takes measures to sanction these rules, the FATF is a *supranational* agency. Its practices constitute a significant departure from the principle of consent in international law and are highly exceptional to State sovereignty.

In exercising these self-proclaimed powers, the FATF relies on substantive legitimacy.[98] This type of legitimacy depends on the desirability of the outcome, in this case money laundering control, and the capacity of the measures taken to achieve this outcome. This argument is based on the assumption that there is such a thing as a self-evident global public interest. This assumption is expressed repeatedly in the FATF reports. Recent developments do suggest the emergence of some common interests that might qualify as global public interests, such as the interest in controlling 'global warming.' The global legal order, however, still lacks legitimately constituted agencies vested with the task of determining the content of a global public interest. Absent notions such as natural law or divine laws, substantive legitimacy is not a substitute for procedural legitimacy.

The FATF is procedurally illegitimate on all scores. In rulemaking agencies, representation of relevant interests is a procedural requisite for legitimacy. The FATF is an elitist organisation with highly restrictive

[97] On this question *see* Aust, A., 'The Theory and Practice of Informal International Instruments', 35 I.C.L.Q. 787 (1986); Gruchalla-Wesierski, T., 'A Framework for Understanding 'Soft Law", 30 *McGill Law Journal* 37 (1984); Baxter, R., 'International Law in 'Her Infinite Variety", 29 I.C.L.Q (1980); Chinkin, C., 'Normative Development in the Internatioanl Legal System', in Shelden, D. (ed.), *supra* note , 2.

[98] FATF, *Annual Report 1991–1992* (June 25, 1992), at para. 99. The FATF 'substantive legitimacy stems from the political and moral obligations to implement the forty recommendations drawn in 1990.'

membership policies. Its core soft law instrument, the Forty Recommendations, reflects the views of the carefully selected fifteen countries, which were the total of the FATF membership in 1990. The care with which the FATF protects its culture to the exclusion of others to whom its instruments would eventually apply was reflected in its decision to decline the UN offer of secretariat facilities in favour of an OECD Secretariat. The Secretariat is the only permanent organ. It is an influential organ in terms of shaping the culture of an institution despite its seemingly administrative nature.[99] Allowing the Secretariat to be hosted by the United Nations was likely to create for the FATF a stronger perception of legitimacy even if it did not actually create an imprint on its culture.[100]

The FATF is an amorphous and faceless body. The affairs of the FATF are conducted in secrecy and all public reports of FATF meetings and operations are carefully edited. It is the declared policy of the FATF that its meetings are not open to the public. It is not an international organisation and it does not possess a charter or a constitution. Its operations are not subject to any specific set of principles apart from the principle of efficiency. During the early years of the FATF there were signs of an emerging formal structure and some reference to fairness and objectivity as principles governing the FATF operations.[101] This trend, however, was reversed in 1994–1995 in favour of a flexible and informal structure. Any reference to fairness was omitted. Limited references to principles such as equality appear in the context of the mutual evaluation process. The main cost of this shift to informality is lack of transparency.[102] Generally, the FATF does not operate under any code of conduct.

The legitimacy deficit is most striking in the context of the NCCT initiative. In this context the FATF exercises a quasi-judicial function reviewing the laws and regulations of the non-member countries against so-called international standards, which are principally the FATF Recommendations. The process was not governed by any principles. The procedural requirements are meagre. They are however worth listing in this context:

[99] On the role and structure of the international secretariat *see* Royal Institute of International Affairs (ed.), *The International Secretariat of the Future: Lessons from Experience by a Group of Former Officials of the League of Nations* (1944); Ranshofen-Wertheimer, E., *The International Secretariat: A Great Experiment in International Administration* (1945).

[100] On the significance of the location *see* Royal Institute of International Affairs (ed.), *id.*, at 47–49.

[101] FATF, *Annual Report 1991–1992* (June 25, 1992), at para. 99.

[102] Zaring, D., 'International Law by Other Means: The Twilight Existence of International Financial Regulatory Organizations', 33 Tex. Int'l L. J. 281–330 (1998). Discussing different examples of similar informal institutions such as Basel Committee and their tradition of secrecy.

- The Review Groups are required to involve the Secretariat in the process as a safeguard of the consistency between the various review reports;[103]
- The Review Groups are required to contact the jurisdiction under review for further information in order to secure the objectivity of their findings;
- The draft report should be sent to the relevant jurisdiction for comments;

The Review Group should hold face-to-face discussion of the findings with the competent authorities in the relevant jurisdiction.

In considering the de-listing of NCCTs, the chairmen of the Review Groups should meet , *if necessary*, to secure consistency in their responses to the NCCTs.[104]

The procedural failures are several:

- Some of the criteria of assessment are very broad, especially those pertaining to the effectiveness of the regulatory system and of international co-operation, which gives ample opportunity for abuse;
- The timeframe allocated for the review was short casting substantial doubt on the seriousness and reality of the process;
- According to an interview with a member of the Secretariat in August 2001, it was confirmed that there is no procedure to exclude the Member Country of the FATF whose complaints have triggered the review of a jurisdiction from acting as the reviewer of that jurisdiction. This a clear departure from the principle of the neutrality of the arbiter as a requirement of legitimacy;
- By contrast to the detailed procedures for the nomination and constitution of the examination team in the context of mutual evaluation amongst FATF Members, there is no reference whatsoever in the FATF documents to the constitution of the examination team in the context of an NCCT review;
- As explained above, the rights of the examined Member, in the context of a mutual evaluation process, to defend its position before the plenary and to influence the wording of the report are sufficiently protected by a lengthy negotiation process and detailed procedure for the adoption of the report. By contrast the reviewed country in the context of NCCT process does not possess any right of presentation before the Plenary.

The pressure of the FATF sanctions and the speed with which it requires compliance has resulted in a spree of legislative activity within the listed jurisdictions. This pressure undermines the democratic processes within the affected jurisdictions. This is yet another illustration of the conflict between

[103] FATF, *Report on Non-Cooperative Countries and Territories* (Feb. 14, 2000), at para. 39.

[104] FATF Policy Concerning Implementation and De-listing in Relation to NCCTs, in FATF, Review to Identify Non-Cooperative Countries and Territories: Increasing the Worldwide Effectiveness of Anti-Money Laundering Measures (June 22, 2001), Appendix 2, at para. 3.

different policies in the global sphere. While in other contexts, developed countries and international financial institutions are leading campaigns for democratisation in developing countries often supported by sanctions, the pressures of the money laundering control regime are undermining these nascent democratic values.

Finally, the FATF is an unaccountable institution. The sanctions applied by the FATF can be serious for the survival of a small economy. Any country that sustains damage by an FATF action will not have any venue for redress. These concerns are particularly alarming in view of the suggestion entertained by the FATF that it could ban NCCTs from using facilities, such as information technology services, that are located in FATF countries. Considering the concentration of clearing systems such as SWIFT in FATF Member countries and the indispensability of access to such facilities for the operation of any financial system, this proposition is serious. Leaving the decision on access to such facilities to the whims of a group of countries through an unregulated process is a clear symptom of the deficiency of global governance.

VII. CONCLUSION

Money laundering law provided a strong case of supranational rulemaking. Since the creation of the Financial Action Task Force in 1989, it has assumed a primary role in developing anti-money laundering legal and regulatory measures. Since the beginning, this fluid and informal body has intended to exercise an aggressive enforcement function for the sake of spreading its model worldwide. In 1998-1999, this intention was translated into reality through an initiative that aimed at assessing the compliance of non-members with the standards set by the FATF. The sanctions for failure were serious and this seriousness was reflected in the rushed legislative response by the countries that were subjected to the process.

While the Financial Action Task Force operated globally as a supranational organ with substantial sanctioning power that stems from the dominance of its members in global financial markets, it continued to operate internally on basis of strict commitment to unanimity. This dual nature of FATF is becoming a typical example of the emerging structures of global governance.

Innovations in international law are essential to fill gaps in governance that are created by new realities. These innovations, however, should continue to be subject scrutiny and responsive to criticism. The fact of the matter is that interests are still nationally determined and international governance still lacks the necessary structures to aggregate interests fairly and representatively.

CHAPTER NINETEEN

International Financial Stability—The Need for a Multilateral Response

*by George A. Walker**

CHAPTER OUTLINE

I. Financial Instability
II. Financial Crises
III. Policy Response
IV. International Financial Stability
V. The Financial Stability Forum
VI. Membership Structure And Operation
VII. Mandate
VIII. Working Groups And Task Forces
  A. Highly Leveraged Institutions (HLI)
  B. Capital Flows (CF)
  C. Offshore Financial Centres (OFC)
  D. Implementation Task Force
  E. Deposit Insurance Study Group
IX. General Activities
  A. Disclosure
  B. Standards
  C. Training
X. Financial Stability Standards
  A. Transparency
  B. Banking
  C. Securities
  D. Insurance
  E. Governance
  F. Payment And Settlement
XI. Closing Comment—Policy and Operational Integration and The Construction of a New Global Control Framework

* PhD, DPhil. Reader in Banking Law, Centre for Commercial Law Studies, University of London. Consultant to IMF (the views expressed herein are solely the personal views of the author). This chapter is derived in part from Chapter Five from the author's recent treatise, INTERNATIONAL BANKING REGULATION—LAW, POLICY AND PRACTICE (Kluwer 2001).

The debate between the relative advantages and disadvantages of unilateral[1] as opposed to multilateral[2] responses applies equally in the financial area. While the issue remains of continuing importance, and indeed difficulty, on various particular issues (such as with regard to currency alignments and re-valuations), the more general recent tendency has been towards the adoption of more cooperative and collective response programmes especially since the Asian and related financial crises during the 1990s.

Financial markets have been subject to significant recent turmoil and a number of attempts have been made to try to develop a series of new more integrated and effective responses.[3] These efforts have been variously referred to as the creating a new 'international financial architecture' or 'international financial stability' framework.[4]

The specific difficulty that arises in this area is that the structure and

[1] For the purposes of this chapter, unilateralism is understood to refer to the reliance by one state territory on its own capacity and resources to pursue its foreign policy and international relations. The 'Westphalia' arrangements adopted under the Munster and Osnabruck Treaties in 1648 can be considered to have been essentially unilateralist. Unilateralist policies include 'isolationism', 'neutralism' and 'non-alignment.' Unilateralism remains of importance especially where one territory is attempting to defend its perceived national interests against external intervention.

[2] Multilateralism refers to the establishment of a formal or informal system of relations between three or more states on the basis of an agreed set of rules or principles. Examples of multilateral responses in the financial and economic area include the operation of the'gold standard', the post-war Bretton Woods system and 'economic liberalism' more generally. Economic liberalism is based on the work of the Scottish Enlightenment writer, Adam Smith, and associated free market theories. *See* ADAM SMITH, THE WEALTH OF NATIONS (1776). Economic liberalism directs that government intervention should be kept to an absolute minimum and that free and open markets should prevail insofar as possible. In terms of inter-state relations, free trade should be promoted with government involvement being restricted to issues concerning state security. Early free trade ideas have since been replaced by more modern 'complex interdependence' ideas. Complex interdependence was developed by Keohane and Nye in 1971 as part of their attack on realism. Keohane and Nye questioned the coherence and dominance of state action and the effectiveness and precedence of force as a policy instrument. Societies can operate through a number of contact channels while no clear issue hierarchy exists with the use of force being significantly downgraded. *See* R. O. KEOHANE & J. S. NYE, TRANSNATIONAL RELATIONS AND WORLD POLITICS (Cambridge MA, Harvard University Press 1971). *See* C. BROWN, UNDERSTANDING INTERNATIONAL RELATIONS (Palgrave 2001), Ch 2.

[3] *See, e.g.*, IMF, *International Capital Markets: Developments, Prospects and Key Policy Issues*, World Economic and Financial Surveys (1995), Parts II and III; IMF, *International Capital Markets: Developments, Prospects and Key Policy Issues* (1996), Parts I and II; IMF, *International Capital Markets: Developments, Prospects and Key Policy Issues* (1997), Parts II, IV and VII; IMF, *International Capital Markets: Developments, Prospects and Key Policy Issues* (1998), Parts II and III; and IMF, *International Capital Markets: Developments, Prospects and Key Policy Issues* (1999), Parts II and IV. *See also* IMF, *World Economic Outlook: Interim Assessment*, World Economic and Financial Surveys (December 1997), Chapters II. and III; IMF, *World Economic Outlook* (October 1998), Chapters I-IV; IMF, *World Economic Outlook* (October 1999), Chapters I and II; and IMF, *Annual Report* (1999), Part I and Chapter 4.

[4] *See generally* G.A. WALKER, INTERNATIONAL BANKING REGULATION—LAW, POLICY AND PRACTICE (Kluwer, 2001), Ch. 5 and authorities cited.

operation of financial markets are particularly complex and affected by many national, regional and international factors. Recent trends in the markets have also been dominated by increased internationalisation, deregulation and integration which have all necessarily contributed to undermining the effectiveness of more traditional national jurisdiction-based regulatory responses. The result of these developments has been the creation of an essentially linked and inter-dependent global financial marketplace that allows twenty-four hour trading of almost all major stocks, bonds, derivatives, currencies and other financial instruments or claims, although one without any central or even co-ordinated oversight, control, support or crisis management arrangements.

Various attempts have been made to construct appropriate responses at the national level to the new risks and challenges that arise; although the core problem or conflict that remains is that the essentially interconnected nature of the new international financial marketplace of itself requires, and indeed necessitates, cooperative and collective rather than unilateral or even bilateral responses. The very existence and inherent structure and operation of modern global markets of themselves prevent any continued reliance on the possible use of more traditional essentially national, individual or separate, isolated or protectionist measures.

The emergence of multilateral as opposed to unilateral efforts has also been evident with the work of the various large international economic organisations that now exist. While some multilateral efforts date from last century (such as with regard to the early international commodity agreements), the dominant characteristic, especially of the post-war period, has been the growth and expansion of the role and function of multilateral organisations, in particular, in the economic area.[5] The emergence and significant contribution of such international economic organisations (IEOs) as the International Monetary Fund, the World Bank, the Bank for International Settlements and other more specific bodies further confirms the need for a multilateral response.[6]

Many of the recent 'schools' or 'debates' that have arisen in international law[7] and international relations[8] more generally also support the view that

[5] SERGEI A. VOITOVICH, INTERNATIONAL ECONOMIC ORGANISATIONS IN THE INTERNATIONAL PROCESS 108 (Martinus Nijhoff, Dordrecht 1995).

[6] *See infra* note 11. *See also* P. Verloren van Themaat, *The Changing Structure of International Economic Law* (Martinus Nijhoff Publishers, 1981).

[7] A number of more general 'schools' of international law can be identified. These include 'natural' and 'positive' law with more recent disciplines or doctrines although an important recent trend within international law has been the emergence of multilateralism this century. *See generally* Shaw, *International Law* (OUP 2001), ch. 2. For specific comment on the shift from bilateralism to multilateralism in International Economic Law, *see* VOITOVICH, *supra* note 5, at 108–109.

[8] A number of separate schools can be identified within international relations. Early

global exchanges and relationships have become much more complex and can no longer be understood on an individual state-centric basis. The adoption of more recent functionalist approaches, such as within the European Union and other regional systems, further confirms the need for more inclusive rather than exclusive policies and perspectives to be constructed.[9]

All of these types of analysis and approach are of use in attempting to understand the complex nature of modern international relations and politics more generally. The purpose of this chapter is nevertheless to focus on the nature of the emerging international response that is currently being constructed in response to the significant recent crises that have arisen.

The structure of this Chapter is as follows. The main recent events and major financial crises that have occurred are reviewed. The background to the establishment of the Financial Stability Forum (FSF) in particular is considered and its structure and operation assessed. This represents a significant example and successful model for the adoption of collective rather than more isolated responses in this area. The work of the FSF is then examined in further detail and conclusions drawn with regard to its contribution and importance. The emerging shape of the new international financial response is noted and its possible longer term validity and value referred to.

approaches were based on idealist or utopian ideas. Idealism or utopianism (or rationalism) is close to liberalism and stresses international development, the rule of law and the use of moral value systems in examining international relations. Idealism was quickly replaced by the conflicting approaches developed under 'realism' and 'behaviouralism'. Realism or 'power politics' focuses on the identity of the nation-state and its need for security and self-preservation. Behaviouralism borrowed social science techniques to question the earlier assumptions and state-centric based approach of the realists. This conflict is now understood in terms of 'neorealism' and 'neoliberalism' (with neorealism generally based on K. N. Waltz's THEORY OF INTERNATIONAL POLITICS (Addison Wesley, Reading MA 1979)). Neoliberalism or neoliberal institutionalism questions the state-centric and war and peace dominated analysis of the realists and neorealists in favour of 'institution building' alternative wealth and welfare driven policies and mixed actors models including international and transnational organisations and other non-state players including non-governmental bodies and multinational companies. For discussion, *see* Joseph Grieco, *Anarchy and the Limits of Co-operation: A Realist Critique of the Newest Liberal Institutionalism*, 42 International Organization 485–508 (1988). Although neorealism and neoliberalism represent the two dominant opposing schools, a number of other sub-disciplines or systems have since emerged including 'constructivists' and the 'English School', 'critical theory' and 'post-structuralists', 'world systems theory', and 'post-modernism'. *See generally*, BROWN, *supra* note 2, at 49–50. *See also* G. EVANS and J. NEWNHAM, DICTIONARY OF INTERNATIONAL RELATIONS 361–62 (Penguin 1998).

[9] Functionalism is generally concerned with the promotion of co-operation through specific economic activity. Subsequent more revisionist doctrines nevertheless include 'neo-functionalism,' 'neo-realism' (or 'liberal inter-governmentalism'), 'neo-federalism' and 'new institutionalism' or 'multi-level governance analysis.' For discussion, *see* Paul Craig, *The Nature of the Community in* THE EVOLUTION OF EU LAW ch 1, sec. 1; (P. Craig and G. de Burca, eds., 1999); K. Armstrong, *The New Institutionalism, in* LAW MAKING IN THE EUROPEAN UNION (P. Craig and C. Harlow, eds., 1998). These reflect the parallel debates that have taken place in international relations more generally. *See supra* note 8.

I. FINANCIAL INSTABILITY

With the recent crises which have been experienced in international financial markets, a number of significant concerns have arisen with regard to the value and effectiveness of the various control systems which are presently in place. The difficulties which have arisen and continuing problems being experienced in many parts of the world clearly demonstrate that the stability of the new global market place which has been created over the last two to three decades is far from secure and that a number of significant issues arise in connection with its continued efficient and sound operation. This has, in particular, resulted in a number of calls for the creation of a new supervisory and regulatory control framework,[10] and for the promotion of financial stability more generally, at the international level.

A number of international institutions, committees or other bodies are currently responsible for the supervision or management of various aspects of the new global system including monetary stability and currency support, regional or national development programmes, financial sector or cross-sector regulatory and supervisory policy and the construction of common standards in other important related areas of practice.[11] Each of these bodies, however, operates in accordance with their own separate sets of internal processes and procedures and historical mandates. A fundamental control gap or vacuum accordingly exists in international financial markets.[12]

[10] On the definition of the terms supervision and regulation, *see* Introduction n. 1. These definitions are generally consistent with the use of the terms by the principal organisations and in the main papers discussed to in this Chapter. *See infra.*

[11] These include the International Monetary Fund [IMF], the World Bank, the Bank for International Settlements [BIS], and the Organisation for Economic Co-operation and Development [OECD] as well as the Basel Committee on Banking Supervision, the International Organisation of Securities Commissions [IOSCO], the International Association of Insurance Supervisors [IAIS], the Committee on Payment and Settlement Systems [CPSS] and the Committee on the Global Financial System [CGFS], formerly the Eurocurrency Standing Committee. In connection with the roles and functions of each of these bodies, *see infra* note 21. For a review of the current work of each of these bodies, *see infra* Section 6. On the establishment, structure and operations of the Basel Committee, *see* Chapter 1. On the background, original functions and development of all IMF, World Bank, OECD and the BIS, *see generally* R. FRASER & C. LONG, THE WORLD FINANCIAL SYSTEM (1992). For the other committees and all relevant documentation, *see* http://www.imf.org; http://www. worldbank.org; http://www.oecd.org; http://www.bis.org; http://www.iosco.org; and http://www.iais.org. Information on and documentation produced by Basel Committee, the CPSS and the CGFS is provided through the BIS site at http://www. bis.org.

[12] This control gap is a concomitant part of the basic global market and local control conflict already identified. *See* Introduction and Chapter 4, Section 2.I. Both arise from the traditional doctrine of the sovereign autonomy of the nation state which creates exclusive jurisdictional areas within which, in connection with financial market, control the supervisory or regulatory authorities from other countries cannot operate without the consent of the host territory. *See* G. A. Walker, *Conglomerate Law and International Financial Market Supervision* 17 ANN. REV. BANKING L. 287 (1998). *See also* G. A. Walker, *A New Beginning*, FT FRR (June 1999), p. 1.

With this control gap, there has also been no co-ordination of the activities of any of these bodies until recently, nor any attempt made to try to construct any more complete and coherent programme of measures in this area. Serious deficiencies have accordingly been identified with regard to the ability of the institutional structures and substantive programmes currently in place to protect the stability and continued efficient operation of the international financial system.[13]

Following the 1990 crises, in Mexico in particular,[14] and then in Asia, Latin America and Russia,[15] three particularly important developments can be identified. There has, in the first place, been the emergence of a new degree of enhanced political involvement and direct concern especially at the G7[16] level in connection with international financial market stability and its early reform. While this has traditionally been an area which has been left to the various technical committees or other fora in place to consider under the oversight of the national central banks or supervisory authorities, the heads of government and finance ministries in the main industrialised and emerging market countries have recently become much more concerned with the success of the work currently being undertaken in this regard.[17]

This increased level of direct political intervention has then resulted in the emergence in a new climate or pressure for reform in the area of international market stability and, in particular, for the creation of a new inter-

[13] *See, e.g.*, Michel Camdessus (former IMF Managing Director), From the Asian Crisis Toward a New Global Architecture, Address to the Parliamentary Assembly of the Council of Europe, Strasbourg (June 23,1998). *See infra* Section 3.

[14] *See, e.g.*, IMF, *International Capital Markets: Developments, Prospects and Key Policy Issues* (1995), *supra* note 1. *See infra* Section 2.

[15] *See* M. Goldstein and P. Turner, *Banking Crises in Emerging Economies: Origins and Policy Options*, BIS ECONOMIC PAPER NO. 46 (Oct. 1996); P. Honohan, *Banking System Failures in Developing and Transition Economies: Diagnosis and Predictions*, BIS ECONOMIC PAPER NO. 39 (Jan. 1997) and IMF, *World Economic Outlook supra* note 3, ch. 1. *See also* M. GOLDSTEIN, THE ASIAN FINANCIAL CRISIS: CAUSES, CURES AND SYSTEMIC IMPLICATIONS (Inst. For Int'l Econ. 1998). *See infra* Section 2.

[16] The G7 was set up in Tokyo in May 1986 to strengthen co-ordination of international economic policy. It consists of Canada, France, Germany, Italy, Japan, the United Kingdom and the United States. *See* Introduction, n. 18.

[17] Following the G7 Halifax Summit in June 1995, the Heads of State and Government of the G7 confirmed their commitment to work together and with their other partners throughout the world, in particular to meet the challenges of the 21st century and to strengthening the global economy. *See* Introduction, n. 19. Closer international co-operation in the regulation and supervision of financial institutions and markets was stated to be essential to safeguard the financial system and prevent an erosion of prudential standards. *See* Heads of State and Government of the G7 and the President of the European Commission, Halifax, Nova Scotia Summit (June 15-17, 1995), Communiqué, Preamble at para 1. This concern with international financial market stability and the construction of a new architecture has been taken forward at all of the subsequent G7 Summits. *See* Communiqués issued following the subsequent G7 Lyons, Denver, Birmingham and Cologne Summits in 1996, 1997, 1998 and 1999. *See also infra* note 9 and Section 2.I.

national financial architecture. While the exact meaning of the term architecture is still far from clear,[18] this enhanced degree of political attention and direction has to be greatly welcomed, to the extent that it has provided a new impetus or momentum for change which has, in turn, facilitated the not inconsiderable amount of progress subsequently achieved in this area to date.

The second major development which has occurred has been growth of a new realisation or recognition that few, if any, of the problems which have arisen in international financial markets can be considered or treated separately and certainly not resolved on an individual basis. There has then, for the first time, been the emergence of new consensus that all of the different aspects of potential financial difficulty, inefficiency, risk or exposure which arise must be examined together or, at least, considered and treated in parallel manner. This then extends to all areas of market control including monetary stability and foreign exchange risk management, technical financial sector supervision or regulation, associated auditing and accountancy standards, linked payment and settlement problems as well as such larger issues as corporate governance and the prevention of financial crime and corruption. The primary objective is now then to construct a new integrated rather than essentially fragmented response as before, to all of these potential sources of instability and crisis.

A number of papers on the possible nature and content of the new control structure to be developed have since been published by various bodies including the G7,[19] the G10,[20] the G22[21] the International Monetary Fund [IMF][22] and the World Bank as well as by the Basel

18 For comment, *see* sub-section VII (3) *infra*.

19 *See* Report by Finance Ministers of the G7, Final Report to the G7 Heads of State and Government on Promoting Financial Stability (June 21, 1997); Report by Finance Ministers of the G7, Financial Stability—Supervision of Global Financial Institutions (May 1988). *See infra* Section 2.I.

20 *See also* G10, Report on the Implementation of the Concerted Strategy for Strengthening Financial Systems in Emerging Market Countries (November 1997). *See infra* Section 2.II.

21 Three papers were produced by the working groups set up, at the initiative of the United States, by the G7 and a number of other countries (the Group of 22 or 'Willard Group'), following a meeting of Finance Ministers and central bank Governors in Washington, D.C. in April 1998, to examine the stability of the international financial system and the effective functioning of global capital markets. *See* G22, Summary of Reports on International Financial Architecture (October 1998); Report of the Working Group on Transparency and Accountability (October 1998); Report of the Working Group on Strengthening Financial Systems (October 1998); Report of the Working Group on International Financial Crises (October 1998). The G22 was subsequently extended to include 26 and then 33 countries (following complaints about exclusion) and was then replaced by a new G20 in September 1999. *See supra* note 20 and *infra* Section 2.II.

22 *See* IMF, *Toward a Framework for Financial Stability* (January 1998). *See also* Michel Camdessus, *supra* note 13; The Role of the IMF: Past, Present and Future, Remarks by Michel Camdessus at Annual General Meeting of the Bretton Woods Committee, Washington, D.C. (Feb. 13, 1998). *See infra* Section 2.VI.

Committee and IOSCO.[23] Further papers have also been produced by the Organisation for Economic Co-operation and Development [OECD],[24] the G30[25] and a number of observations and recommendations for reform made by other political or private commentators.[26] With all of this, there has been a fundamentally new and enlightened examination of all the each of the core issues which arise and the range of possible responses or options which may be developed.

Concern with the creation of a new architecture has also resulted in the subsequent establishment of two new international bodies with the G20[27] and the Financial Stability Forum as well as the long overdue reform of the Interim Committee of the IMF which has now become the International Monetary and Financial Committee [IMFC].[28] The establishment of the G20 and IMFC represent important structural initiatives which will hopefully allow significant political and monetary issues to be considered at the international level and further necessary reforms adopted.

[23] *See* Basel Committee and IOSCO, Response of the Basle Committee and of the International Organisation of Securities Commissions to the Request of the G-7 Heads of Government at the June 1995 Halifax Summit (May 1996) [hereinafter 1996 Joint Statement].

[24] *See* OECD, *The OECD Report on Regulatory Reform* (1997).

[25] *See* G30, *Global Institutions, National Supervision and Systemic Risk* (1997); and G30, *The Future of Global Financial Regulation* (1998).

[26] *See*, *e.g.*, Robert Rubin, The Asian Financial Situation, Georgetown University (January 21, 1998); and Rubin, Strengthening the Global Financial System, Brookings Institute (April 14, 1998). *See also* President Bill Clinton, Speech on the Global Finance Crisis, Council of Foreign Relations (September 14, 1998); and Clinton, Remarks to World Economic Forum, Davos, Switzerland (January 29, 2000). *See infra* Section 2.V.

[27] The purpose of the G20 was primarily intended to be to generate discussion on proposals for international financial reform and to build legitimacy for the process among developing countries. It had been agreed at the G7 Cologne Summit that the G7 would establish an informal mechanism for dialogue between systemically important countries. Twenty countries, including the G7 and other systematically important developing countries, were expected to be invited to participate. The IMF and World Bank would also participate in the work of the new body. *See, e.g.*, *G Force*, FIN. TIMES (Sept. 13), at 27; *G7 prepares to give birth to its GX baby* FIN. TIMES (Sept. 20, 1999), at 4. *See supra* note 13. *See also* G. A. Walker, *Not Another Country Club*, FRR (April 2000), at 1. The role of the G20 is to extend the range of immediate countries involved in the current efforts to construct a new international financial market control framework, and in so doing lend a degree of authority and legitimacy to the larger processes concerned and essential work currently being undertaken. *Id.*

[28] The Interim Committee was the informal advisory ministerial body within the IMF structure. The Articles of Agreement of the IMF had been amended following the collapse of the Bretton Woods system of managed exchange rates in the early 1970s to allow a ministerial level council to be set up to supervise the management and adaptation of the international monetary system. The Interim Committee had then been set up as a temporary measure until a more formal agency could be created. One of the general functions of the Interim Committee was to act as a joint co-ordinating body between the IMF and World Bank. The Interim Committee was renamed the International Monetary and Financial Committee [IMFC] in September 1999. Despite this, the IMFC still has no formal decision making role in connection with major international issues or developments. For comment, *see* Michel Camdessus, Global Financial Reform: The Evolving Agenda, Council of Foreign Relations, New York (June 4, 1999); Michel Camdessus, The IMF We Need, Georgetown (February 2, 2000). *See also* Michel Camdessus, The Role of the IMF: Past, Present and Future, *supra.* note 22.

In the area of international banking and financial market control, the most important single event which has occurred has probably been the creation of the FSF as a new mixed or composite political, central bank with supervisory functions as well as related control over policy discussions and development mechanisms. The objective of the FSF is essentially to attempt to take forward a number of aspects of the supervisory and regulatory work required in this area in a much more balanced and integrated manner. In connection with this goal, a number of new initiatives have been undertaken, especially with regard to the membership composition, working group structures and operational mandate of the FSF to attempt to facilitate this process. Whether the FSF will be able to correct all of the continuing or residual deficiencies, however, in the existing system of international financial market control, remains to be seen.[29]

The purpose of this Chapter is to note briefly the nature of the financial crises which took place during the late 1990s and lead to the recent core initiatives identified. The policy response adopted by all of the various bodies concerned will be explained. The circumstances surrounding the establishment of the FSF, its structure and method operation, and its supervisory and regulatory policy programme will then be examined in further detail. The work of the FSF undertaken to date will be noted especially in the areas of disclosure, training and standards, and its contribution assessed. The content and value of the new Compendium of Standards currently being developed by the FSF will also be considered in further detail. Conclusions will, in particular, be drawn with regard to the contribution of the FSF in attempting to improve international financial market stability and to the construction of a new international architecture. Observations will also be made with regard to its possible future development.

II. FINANCIAL CRISES

The historical development of financial markets has always been accompanied by crisis and collapse. Financial crises are as old as the markets themselves.[30] Indeed, the development of bank and financial market control in most countries generally has often simply been one of attempting to respond to specific incidences of financial difficulty as they arise rather than

[29] For comment, *see* Walker, *A New Beginning*, *supra* note 12; G.A. Walker, *Working Groups and Global Standards*, FRR (Oct. 1999), at 1; G. A. Walker, *The New Global Rule Book*, FRR, (Nov. 1999), at 1; G. A. Walker, *Financial Stability Standards*, FRR (Nov. 1999), at 3. *See also* G. A. Walker, *New Dawn (New Risk)*, FRR (Jan, 2000), at 1.

[30] *See*, *e.g.*, C. KINDLEBERGER, MANIAS, PANICS AND CRASHES: A HISTORY OF FINANCIAL CRISES (Wiley & Sons 1989).

by attempting to construct any more complete and coherent programme of measures in advance. The nature and content of the new provisional international response which was beginning to develop during the 1980s and early 1990s has almost wholly been built up by attempting to correct specific deficiencies which have arisen following some particular closure or collapse such as Bankhaus Herstatt, Banco Ambrosiano, BCCI and Barings.[31]

Between 1980 and 1996, almost two-thirds of all IMF member countries had experienced significant banking sector problems much worse than during the 1950s or 1960s.[32] The frequency of banking crises had then significantly increased at the same time as their severity had become proportionately more serious. The potential impact of the instability created was also aggravated by the increasingly close linkages and mutual dependencies which had developed between the emerging economies, and between these and developed countries.[33] This meant that any financial problems which arose would no longer be localised within a particular country or region but would have significant knock-on effects in many other parts of the world.

While the crises which occurred during the 1990s had shared certain characteristics with those experienced elsewhere or before, certain new factors were present which meant that they were to some extent less predictable but certainly not wholly unpredictable. Of much more impor-

31 The establishment and evolution of the Basel Committee itself can be described as simply being one initially of responding to a particular problem in international banking on an essentially *ad hoc* basis and then of attempting to subsequently build up a more coherent supervisory and then regulatory response. *See* Chapters 1 and 2.

32 The costs of damage and recovery between developed and emerging market economies can be compared with regard to the much higher level of relative resolution costs involved: Spain (1997–85), 17 percent of GDP; Finland (1991–93), 8 percent of GDP; Sweden (1991), 6 percent of GDP; Norway (1987–89), 4 percent of GDP; and the United States (1984–91), 3 percent of GDP. In emerging markets, the equivalent figures are: Hungary 10 percent of GDP; the Czech Republic 12 percent of GDP; Bulgaria 14 percent of GDP; Tanzania 14.5 percent of GDP; Mexico 12–15 percent of GDP; Venezuela 8 percent of GDP; Argentina, Chile and Cote d'Ivorie over 25 percent of GDP. Since 1980, the resolution costs of banking crisis in all developing and transitional economies was almost a quarter of a trillion dollars. Goldstein and Turner, *supra* note 15 at introduction.

33 Although the spectacular growth experienced in Asia had benefited the region generally and other emerging economies as well as the rest of the world, the cost of collapse became correspondingly severe due to the increasingly close linkages which had developed between these countries and between these countries and the rest of the world. By the early 1990s, the industrialised world could no longer ignore problems in any particular emerging economy due to the increasing importance which they had on the world economy and international markets generally. One quarter of all industrial countries' exports had been purchased by developing countries. Between 1991 and 1994, they had received 40 percent of global inflows of foreign direct investment (£46 billion more than liabilities). By the end of 1985, the BIS reporting area banks had over $717 billion worth of outstanding claims against emerging countries; between 1990 and 1995, developing countries had issue $4,143 billions of bonds in international financial markets. Since the late 1970s, all IMF drawings had been made by developing countries.

tance, however, was the potential damage created for international financial stability more generally, especially as a result of the new levels of connection and interdependency which had been created between the emerging and developed markets.

The first major financial crisis of the 1990s was in Mexico in December 1994.[34] After massive outflows of foreign capital following the assassination of presidential candidate Colosio in March 1994, the Mexican government was forced unilaterally to devalue the peso by 15 percent on 20 December and then to let the currency float from 22 December.[35] By the end of 1994, the Mexican government had issued $28 billion worth of tesobonos or short-term government obligations indexed to foreign currencies. As it only had $6 billion of international reserves left, it had to use US and IMF funding to close out the tesobonos at full value on maturity.[36] Within six months, the immediate dangers had been avoided. This had, however, only possible with the support of external official credits made available.[37]

Many of the larger Latin American and other emerging market countries were then effected by a widespread process of portfolio rebalancing in many parts of the world as the risks involved in investing in these high return but essentially unpredictable economies were reassessed by international

[34] *See* United States General Accounting Office, *GAO Report—Mexico's Financial Crisis: Origins, Assistance, and Initial Efforts to Recover*, GAO/GGD-959-56 (Feb. 1996). *See also*, IMF, *Evolution of the Mexican Peso Crisis, in International Capital Markets: Developments, Prospects, and Policy Issues* (August 1995), at 53–64; D. Arner, *The Mexican Peso Crisis: Implications for the Regulation of Financial Markets*, 2 NAFTA REV. (Fall 1996); T. Slover, *Tequila Sunrise: Mexico Emerges from the Darkness of Financial Crisis,* 15 STUDIES IN INTERNATIONAL FINANCIAL AND ECONOMIC LAW (1998) and authorities cited.

[35] Large amounts of capital had flowed into Mexico following its accession to the North American Free Trade Agreement (NAFTA) and admission to the OECD. Subsequent political instability, however, undermined investor confidence which was further shaken by the threat of an imminent devaluation of the peso. When this occurred, President Ernesto Zedillo's government was not able to service its short-term debt obligations in dollar-denominated tesebonos. Following withdrawal of an immediate United States $40 billion loan guarantee support facility in January 1995, a $48.8 billion multilateral financial assistance package was made available. This was made up of a $20 billion facility collateralised against Mexican oil export revenues, $17.8 billion in IMF loans, and £10 billion in foreign government loans advanced through the BIS and certain other commercial bank resources. For comment, *see* J. J. Norton, *The Mexican Peso Crisis and the Future of Financial Integration in the Americas in* THE CHANGING NATURE OF INTERNATIONAL LAW IN THE TWENTY-FIRST CENTURY (J.J. Norton, M. Andenas and M. Footer , eds., 1998) at ch. 12. *See also* Arner, *supra* note 34 at 28; William A. Lovett, *Lessons from the Recent Peso Crisis in Mexico*, 4 TUL.J.INT'L & COMP L.143 (1996); Edwin M. Truman, *The Mexican Peso Crisis: Implications for International Finance*, 82 FED.RES.BULL. 199 (Mar. 1996).

[36] The peso would eventually fall to a low of 7.45 against the dollar in March 1995 with the Banco de Mexico having to raise interest rates to almost percent.

[37] *See* BARRY EICHENGREEN & C. FRED BERGSTEN, TOWARD A NEW INTERNATIONAL FINANCIAL ARCHITECTURE—A PRACTICAL POST-ASIA AGENDA, (Inst. for Int'l Econ., 1999).

institutional investors.[38] Despite this immediate 'Tequila Effect,' many of the core lessons to be learnt from the Mexican crisis were soon forgotten, or simply ignored, especially in many of the new 'Tiger' economies of East Asia.

Before the financial crises in Asia during 1997 and 1998, most of the major Asian economies had experienced strong and sustainable growth for almost 30 years. Some of the fastest growth in the world had been recorded in these countries as they transformed themselves from essentially peasant structured agrarian societies to modern industrial and trade based economies.[39] The main miracle countries concerned included the Republic of Korea, Singapore, Taiwan, Hong Kong, Japan and the three newly industrialised countries of Indonesia, Malaysia and Thailand. Average growth between 1992 and 1995 had reached 9% with an average of over 5% GNP between 1965 and 1990, twice the comparable rates in the United States and Europe. This growth was considered attributable to a number of indigenous factors common to these countries.[40]

Underlying this economic performance, however, a number of potential sources of instability had already arisen. These included high relative levels of bank credit[41] and short-term debt,[42] poor loan practices[43] and funda-

[38] *See* J. J. Norton, *Asian Contagion and Latin America*, *in* REFORM OF LATIN AMERICAN BANKING SYSTEMS (E. Aguirre and J. J. Norton, eds., Kluwer, 2000), at 291–92.

[39] *See* World Bank, *The East Asian Miracle: Economic Growth and Public Policy* (1993). Some 370 million people were lifted out of poverty between 1975 and 1985. This meant that the proportion of East Asians living below the absolute poverty level of $1 a day had fallen from 60 percent to 20 percent.

[40] These include: (a) policies of low inflation and macro-economic stability; (b) strong liberalisation policies followed in many areas across the region; (c) high investment and private savings rates; (d) high levels of human capital formation especially through training and educational programmes; and (e) consequent high profit levels and returns on investments. Mutual funds, pension funds and insurance companies as well as all other types of investors had been placing exceptionally large amounts of money in all of these emerging economies.

[41] One initial problem which arose was with regard to the high relative levels of bank credit which existed in almost of the emerging economies and the even higher more recent levels of demand which were experienced. This created an inherent risk of potential instability and exposure within the financial system which had become completely bank dependent for credit and funds. In terms of the ratio of bank credit to GDP, loan growth in Indonesia rose from 8.1 percent to 49.1 of GDP between 1980 and 1995, Malaysia from 33.1 percent to 46.9 percent and Thailand from 27.5 percent to 88.7 percent. During the same period, US loan growth only increased from 62.1 percent to 63.3 percent (a 1.2 percent difference).

[42] The major exposures had then been of a short-term nature to banks and other private sector counterparties. Less than twenty percent of the total funds made available were in the form of syndicated credits which meant that it was very easy to withdraw funds at short notice with no continuity or rescheduling issues. Derivative and other off balance sheet claims had increased prior to the crisis but the relevant exposure was still small. Over $1 billion had been invested in short-term investments such as equities, bonds and other money market instruments.

[43] Poor lending policies had been experienced during the third world debt crisis during the early 1980s. In this case, the poor lending was not by international banks to sovereign borrowers but by national banks to local or domestic borrowers. This was then aggravated by the high

mentally weak systems of bank supervision.[44] In such conditions, any subsequent currency instability could easily trigger massive funds withdrawal. This would then, in turn, undermine the already inherently weak and unstable underlying financial markets and systems.

The crisis in Asia then began with the devaluation of the Thai baht on 2 July 1997.[45] The Bank of Thailand had been forced to abandon its peg with the dollar.[46] The expectation of a depreciation after the float lead the heavily indebted corporate sector to purchase foreign exchange in the spot market to hedge exposure which forced baht down further. Despite a 14 percent fall in the value of the baht on onshore markets and 19 percent offshore, the reaction to the float was initially favourable and the stock market rose 8 percent on July 3. However, market opinion then quickly changed due to concern with the impact of the revaluation on the financial sector, continued uncertainty about the volatility of the baht and continuing high interest rates.[47]

Following the collapse in the value of the Thai baht, there was an almost

ratio of bank credit. *See supra* note 35. These poor lending policies resulted partly from weak bank supervision but also from the implicit government guarantee provided. This resulted in larger exposures lower spreads than would have been warranted by normal credit standards. *See infra* sub-section.

[44] In India, for example, the non-performing loans of the twenty-seven public sector banks totally 19.5 percent of GDP in 1995. In Eastern Europe, non-performing loans were 38 percent of GDP in the Czech Republic by 1994–95. In Sweden, 18 percent of loans had been lost between 1990 and 1993 and non-performing loans in Japan equalled 8 percent of GDP. Although 1,142 savings and loan associations and 1,395 banks had been closed in the United States between 1980 and 1992, this only cost 3 percent of GDP. In China, the largest four banks had $157 billion worth of bad or doubtful debts at the end of 1995 which represented 30 percent of the total loan portfolio.

[45] *See* T. Traissorat, *Thailand's Financial Crisis*, *in* YEARBOOK OF INTERNATIONAL FINANCIAL AND ECONOMIC LAW (J. J. Norton, ed., 1998). *See also* Goldstein and Turner, *supra* note 15; Honohan, *supra* note 15; Goldstein, *supra* note 15; and IMF, *International Capital Markets: Developments, Prospects and Key Policy Issues* (1996), *supra* note 3 at ch. 1.

[46] The IMF had advised that the Thai financial sector was vulnerable to high interest rates traditionally used to defend the exchange rate. Earlier pressure on baht in May had lead to controls on capital transactions to shield the domestic sector and make speculation expensive. These included prohibiting local banks from advancing credit to offshore companies, baht for dollar foreign exchange swaps and the sell of bahts for dollars in the spot market. These controls were maintained following float so that capital and exchange measures split onshore and offshore markets with huge rate differentials between them. The separation was, however, imperfect, and attempts to avoid lead further capital controls increasingly to difficult to enforce. All of these controls then became increasingly ineffective as both sets of exchange and interest rates converged. *See* Traissorat, *supra* note 45.

[47] The cause of the crisis in Thailand can principally be ascribed to unsound macroeconomic policy and fundamentally weak banking practices and supervision as well as economic and export growth slowdown, external factors including a speculative attack on the currency, and inherent political instability until the replacement of the Chevalit government. Further aggravating factors also included an underlying system of political patronage with an inherent tendency towards privilege and corruption, supported by the existence of an economy dominated by a number of powerful Sino-Thai family controlled business elites. For discussion, *see* Traissorat, *supra* note 45.

immediate knock-on effect in other countries such as Malaysia, Indonesia and the Philippines. During the third quarter of 1997, the value of all of these currencies depreciated by between 25% and 33%. The Taiwan dollar was then devalued in October. This, in turn, lead to a speculative attack on the Hong Kong dollar, with the contagion then spreading into South Korea.[48] Despite aid packages to Thailand, Indonesia and South Korea,[49] Japan subsequently announced worse-than-expected economic figures during the second quarter of 1998 and then Russia defaulted on its debt in August.[50]

The general loss of confidence in emerging market debt which had arisen had also spread as far as Latin America by late 1997 and early 1998 where Brazil had to raise interest rates and to implement a strong adjustment programme to protect the value of the real.[51]

A number of attempts have been made to explain the Asian and related crises.[52] The difficulty which arises, however, is that various traditional factors as well as certain new variables are both present. The complex chronology of events which took place also makes it almost impossible to consider the crisis as a single occurrence or incident but rather as a series of crises or events within a crisis. Two basic economic models can be distinguished based either on sound or unsound underlying fundamentals, to which a third can be added that combines elements of the other two.[53]

The nature and content of the emerging response developed to date is considered in the following section. The possible contribution of the FSF to

[48] *See* EICHENGREEN & BERGSTEN, *supra* note 37 at 149–50.

[49] Total amounts of US$17 billion were made available to Thailand, US$40 for Indonesia and US$57 for South Korea. *See* Traissorat, *supra* note 45. *See also*, J. Shim, *South Korea's Financial Crisis*; and D. Arner, *An Analysis of International Support Packages in the Mexican and Asian Financial Crises* both *in* Norton, *supra* note 38.

[50] *See* IMF, *International Capital Markets: Developments, Prospects and Key Policy Issues* (1996), *supra* note 3, pp. 2–16. *See also* IMF, 'Background Papers on Turbulence in Emerging Markets' *ibid*, p 33 *et seq*.

[51] *See* Norton, *supra* note 38, at 292 and authorities cited. *See also supra* note 3.

[52] *See, e.g.*, G. Corsetti, P. Presenti and N. Roubini, *What caused the Asian currency and financial crisis?* (March 1998) *available at* http://stern.nyu.edu/~nroubini/asia/AsianCrisis.pdf; EICHENGREEN & BERGSTEN, *supra* note 4, at ch. 1 and Appendix 2.

[53] In the first case, although the economic condition of a country may be essentially sound, this could be undermined by a financial panic resulting from a sudden shift in market expectation or confidence. *See, e.g.*, S. Radelet and J. Sachs, *The Onset of the East Asian Financial Crisis* (1998) *available at* http://www.hiid.harvard.edu. In the second case, the crisis can be explained in terms of an unsustainable deterioration in economic fundamentals and poor polices in the countries affected. *See, e.g.*, Paul Krugman, *What Happened to Asia?* (1998) available at http://web.mit. edu/krugman/ www. A third can also be developed which combines elements of the first two. This is based on the idea of 'self-fulfilling crises' in terms of which the crisis is facilitated by underlying fundamental weaknesses and errors but then triggered by market overreaction and response. *See, e.g.*, C. Wyplosz, Globalised Financial Markets and Financial Crises, conference paper at Amsterdam Forum on Debt and Development, (March 1987), *available at* http://heiwww.unige.ch/~wyplosz/ fondad.pdf. *See* Corsetti, et al., *supra* note 52.

the construction of some larger new supervisory and regulatory based market control framework is examined subsequently.

III. POLICY RESPONSE

Following the crisis experienced during the late 1990s in Asia and elsewhere, a number of immediate and then more substantial responses developed. While these were initially only concerned with the immediate strengthening of the financial systems in merging market countries affected by the crisis, they have subsequently developed into a more general attempt to protect the stability of international markets and the construction of a new international financial architecture.

As the severity and full range of the countries began to emerge, this discussion moved from being concerned with attempting to deal with specific problems, which had arisen in the immediate countries affected, to trying to construct a more complete and substantial framework of control for all international financial markets and their supporting clearance and settlement systems. While transparency and market supervisory and regulatory factors were clearly included, other related control issues, such as corporate governance, accountancy and audit standards and insolvency procedures, were added as this larger re-examination of the issues involved was expanded further.

Although this work has always been G7 or G10 led, much of it has involved co-ordinating the efforts of all of the existing separate sector bodies involved and other international financial institutions concerned. Various other separate proposals for reform have also been issued by other research institutions or private parties. Considerable differences have emerged in the recommendations made by all of these separate initiatives, although each has contributed to the development of a larger understanding of the issues involved and options for change available.

The most important single statement for some time was possibly the G7 Cologne Financial Ministers Report in June 1999.[54] The specific structure and content of this official control framework is still evolving.[55]

A number of other national or private proposals have been issued by various national government representatives or private individuals. The United Kingdom government recommended the creation of a new permanent Standing Committee for Global Financial Regulation which would bring together the IMF, the World Bank, the Basel Committee and other

[54] *See* G7, *Report by Finance Ministers of the G7* (June 1999).

[55] *See* WALKER, *supra* note 4, at ch. 5.

regulatory groups.[56] The principal function of the Committee would be to establish and implement international standards for financial regulation and supervision. Separate codes of conduct for fiscal policy, monetary policy, corporate governance and social policy would also be given effect by national governments through a policy of mandatory adherence. It was this new permanent standing committee that effectively became the FSF.[57]

The French government had also proposed transforming the Interim Committee of the IMF[58] while the Canadian government recommended a six point plan in response to global crises.[59] Various other private initiatives have included the creation of an international regulator and rating agency,[60] a new global central bank,[61] an international lender of last resort[62] and a new international bankruptcy or arbitration court which would be able to impose standstills in the event of financial crisis and impose settlement terms on creditors and debtor nations.[63] The creation of a new credit insurance agency has also been recommended.[64]

Other proposals include revising the IMF to offer limited discount window facilities at penal rates on strict conditions[65] or replacing the IMF with a new Global Information Agency, a Contingent Global Financial Facility and a Global Restructuring Agency.[66] Controls may also be placed

[56] *See* Gordon Brown, *Impose New Codes of Conduct*, WALL STREET JOURNAL, Oct. 6, 1998, at A22.

[57] *See infra* Section III.

[58] *See* Ministry for the Economy, Finances, and Industry, Facing International Instability: Twelve Proposals for European Initiative (Sept. 1998) (France).

[59] This includes enhanced vigilance on the part of the G7 central banks, pursuit of strong policies by emerging market economies, attention to the needs of the poorest countries, steps to strengthen national financial systems and international oversight, development of a specific strategy for prudent liberalisation of capital accounts, and adoption of mechanisms to involve private investors in the resolution of crises, especially through the negotiation of standing credit lines and modification of international bond contracts. *See* Press Release, Department of Finance, Finance Minister Announces Six Point Canadian Plan to Deal with Global Financial Turmoil, Release No. 98/094 (Sept. 29, 1998) (Canada).

[60] *See* Henry Kaufman, *Preventing the Next Global Financial Crisis*, WASHINGTON POST, January 28, 1998, at A17. *See also* H. Kaufman, Proposals for Improving the Structure of Financial Supervision and Regulation, Outline of remarks before the Brookings Institution Symposium on Limiting Model Hazard in Financial Rescues, Washington (June 4, 1998).

[61] *See* Jeffery Garten, *In This Economic Chaos, a Global Bank Can Help*, INTERNATIONAL HERALD TRIBUNE, Sept. 28, 1998), at 8.

[62] *See* Asian problems and the IMF (Feb 24, 1998) (testimony by Alan Meltzer prepared for the U.S. Cong.Joint Econ. Comm.).

[63] *See* Kunibert Raffer, *Applying Chapter 9 Insolvency to International Debts: An Economically Efficient Solution with a Human Face*, 18 WORLD DEVELOPMENT 301–11 (1990).

[64] George Soros, *Avoiding a Breakdown: Asia's Crisis Demands a Rethink of International Regulation*, FINANCIAL TIMES, Dec. 31, 1997, at 12. *See also* G. SOROS, THE CRISIS OF GLOBAL CAPITALISM: OPEN SOCIETY ENDANGERED: (PublicAffairs, 1998).

[65] *See* Charles W. Calomiris, *Blueprints for a New Global Financial Architecture* (Oct. 7, 1998), *available at* http://www.imfsite.org/reform/calomiris.html.

[66] Information will be provided in a timely and uncensored manner through the Global

on interbank credits such as through reduction in relevant interest rates or deductions in the event of early withdrawal or failure to rollover.[67] Other proposals have focused on creating enhanced currency stability, for example, through the use of target zones.[68]

A variety of possible reforms of the international financial system have accordingly been offered. It has to be stressed that none of these were developed in specific response to the Asian crisis. Many of these are obviously only of limited effect to the extent that they are concerned with taking action in connection with some particular sphere of activity. Even the institutional recommendations tend to relate only to setting come body to carry out some particular function. The only proposal which provides for both substantive policy construction across broad area of activity and associated institutional reform was that offered by Gordon Brown in October 1998.

In light of the complex and interconnected nature of the difficulties which have arisen in international financial markets and the need for some larger integrated reform package, it was only on the basis of such a combined broad issue and integrated support that any meaningful progress might be possible. Mr Hans Tietmeyer, the President of the Bundesbank, was accordingly asked to consider this idea further in his report on the strengthening of the international financial system which was published in February 1999.[69]

IV. INTERNATIONAL FINANCIAL STABILITY

The Finance Ministers and Central Bank Governors of the G7 countries commissioned Hans Tietmeyer to consider what new structures may be required for enhancing co-operation between the national and international

Information Agency. Contingent credit lines would be made available through the Global Financial Facility where countries experience liquidity problems provided that they otherwise followed fundamentally sound policies. Cooling-off periods or other stays of payment would be possible through the Global Restructuring Agency provided that countries were attempting to renegotiate debt in a realistic and good faith manner. *See* Sebastian Edwards, *Abolish the IMF*, FINANCIAL TIMES, Nov. 13, 1998, at A1. *See also* S. Edwards, *Capital Controls Are Not the Reason for Chile's Success*, WALL STREET JOURNAL, April 3, 1998), at A19.

[67] Countries would be required to adopt legislative provisions which give effect to these creditor laws—sharing recommendations failing which they would become ineligible for IMF assistance. *See* Robert Litan, et al., 'Statement of the Shadow Financial Regulatory Committee on International Monetary Fund Assistance and International Crises', Shadow Financial Regulatory Committee, Statement No. 145 (4 May 1998).

[68] *See*, Fred Bergsten, 'How to Target Exchange Rates', *Financial Times* (20 November 1998). *See also* Bergsten, 'Missed Opportunity', *The International Economy* [1998, 12] no. 6 (November 1998) pp. 26-27; and Bergsten and Randall Henning, *Global Economic Leadership and the Group of Seven* (1996) Institute for International Economics.

[69] *See* Hans Tietmeyer, *International Co-operation and Co-ordination in the Area of Financial Market Supervision and Surveillance* (11 February 1999).

supervisory bodies and international financial institutions which currently existed to promote stability in the international financial system and to make recommendations in this regard. A final Report was produced on 11 February 1999 which was presented to the G7 at their meeting in Bonn on 20 February 1999 and duly endorsed on that date.

The specific mandate of the G7 was to consult with all appropriate bodies and to consider the arrangements for co-operation and co-ordination between the various international financial regulatory and supervisory bodies and international financial institutions interested in such matters.[70] This original mandate was then restated and extended later the same month.[71] The G7 recognised that better processes were needed for the monitoring and promoting of financial stability in the international financial system which, in particular, depended upon both initial proper policy construction and its effective implementation.[72] A number of meetings were subsequently held with G7 representatives, the international financial institutions and international bodies concerned with a view to identifying key areas within the international financial system where improvements were necessary to safeguard the proper functioning of the markets.

The Report describes the current arrangements for the supervision and surveillance of the international financial system. Responsibility for the supervision and surveillance of the international financial system is shared by a number of international organisations. These include the international financial institutions comprising the IMF, the World Bank, the BIS, and the OECD, as well as such sector specific international groupings of regulators and supervisors as the Basel Committee, IOSCO, the IAIS and other central bank expert groupings including the Committee on Payment and Settlement Systems (CPSS) and the Committee on the Global Financial System (CGFS).[73]

[70] *See* G7 Communiqué, Oct. 3, 1998.

[71] *See* G7 Declaration, Oct. 30, 1998.

[72] The G7 stated that, '[W]e agree that better processes are needed for monitoring and promoting stability in the international financial system and for the International Financial Institutions, working closely with their international supervisory and regulatory bodies, to conduct surveillance of national financial sectors and their regulatory and supervisory regimes with all relevant information accessible to them'. The G7 would accordingly: '(i) support the establishment of a process for strengthened financial sector surveillance using national and international regulatory and supervisory expertise, including through a process of peer review and the IMF's regulatory surveillance of its member countries under Article IV; [and] (ii) to this end bring together the key international institutions and key national authorities involved in financial sector stability better to co-operate and to co-ordinate their activities in the management and development of policies to foster stability and reduce systemic risk in the international financial system and to exchange information more systematically on risks in the international financial system.' *Id.*

[73] The IMF is responsible for the surveillance of all member countries and the monitoring of developments in the global economy and financial markets. The World Bank assists countries in the design and implementation of reforms to strengthen financial systems including

The contribution of each of these bodies was recognised although the need for the development of a more integrated approach was stressed. The establishment of the Joint Forum on Financial Conglomerates, representing an initial response to the 'dichotomy of fragmented supervisory structures and increasingly integrated markets,' was noted.[74]

Areas in which improvements were required in the present control system were also considered. These included action to identify incipient vulnerabilities in financial markets with concerted efforts being required to be taken to mitigate systemic risk, develop and implement appropriate standards and codes of conduct and improve cross-sector financial supervision.

With regard to systemic risk, the Report notes that recent events had stressed the importance of assessing domestic vulnerabilities in light of evolving global conditions (and vice versa), and of the need to relay such assessments to all relevant parties to prevent delays in the correction of inadequate structures or destabilising trends.[75]

A systematic approach had also to be adopted to ensure that any remaining gaps in international standards or codes of conduct were properly identified

banking, capital markets and market infrastructure. The BIS provides analytical, statistical and secretarial support for various official groupings working to strengthen the global financial system. The OECD participates in the process of macro-economic and financial surveillance and formulated guidelines for evaluating and improving the framework for corporate governance. The OECD participates in the process of macro-economic and financial surveillance and formulated guidelines for evaluating and improving the framework for corporate governance. The CGFS (formerly the Euro-Currency Standing Committee) analyses global financial system conditions and made recommendations for improving market functioning.

[74] Such a more integrated approach had to be developed further and, in particular, applied in a more comprehensive manner. This included (a) overcoming the separate treatment of macro-prudential and micro-prudential issues, (b) bringing together the major international institutions and key national authorities involved in financial sector stability, and (c) integrating emerging markets more closely in this process.

This process of strengthening co-operation would in turn make a significant contribution to a better functioning of the financial markets especially by making possible a full utilisation of the considerable benefits which free market movements provided to all participants in the global financial system.

[75] While important work was undertaken by the international financial institutions in gathering and assessing data on segments of the whole financial system, none had the breadth of information or capacity to formulate a complete assessment of evolving risk. Better procedures were accordingly required for the systematic pulling and efficient use of such information.

The need to mitigate system risk had also been demonstrated by the range of potential risks which may arise and the threat of chain reactions within the financial sector. De-stabilising events included macro-economic weaknesses, the collapse of major individual institutions (such as hedge funds), and weaknesses in the underlying infrastructure which connected all of the separate financial systems concerned. The threat of systemic collapse required transparency, close monitoring and coherent and appropriate action to prevent risk acceleration where necessary.

The traditional micro-prudential approach adopted by the various regulatory groupings had to be extended to take into account larger marketing practices or aggregation effects, while instability created as a result of unsupervised financial or non-financial components within larger groups had also to be monitored.

and corrected through co-operation and co-ordination between all relevant bodies including emerging market participation. Effective implementation of, in particular, the various core standards which had already been developed had to be secured at the national level in co-operation with the international financial institutions. All relevant risk had to be properly managed and priced.

In connection with cross-sector supervision, existing efforts to improve supervisory co-operation through the issuance of minimum standards and risk-managing guidance had to be continued, although further work also had to be undertaken to deal with the additional problems created by the integration of financial markets, including the development of consistent rules for the treatment of relevant risk, arrangements for information pulling and closer co-operation between different sets of supervisory authorities. The need to ensure that all significant players were included within the scope of national regulatory control also had to be ensured.

Having considered the nature of the various issues which had to be dealt with, The Report concluded that specific action was required in the following areas:

(a) improving arrangements for the surveillance of global vulnerabilities (including the pooling of information available to the international financial institutions and the international regulatory groupings, the development and assessment of macro-early-warning indicators and the creation of procedures to ensure that information reaches all relevant parties);
(b) creating procedures for co-ordinating the work of national and international regulatory groupings and for the exchange and pooling of relevant information;
(c) assessing the need for the regulation of non-regulated entities; and strengthening and, where appropriate, encouraging the development and implementation of international best practices and standards (including improving in-house risk management at the individual institution level and promoting appropriate transparency and disclosure rules for all market participants).

In considering appropriate proposals for improved co-operation in terms of international financial market surveillance and supervision, it was accepted that fundamental institutional changes were not required. A new financial stability forum was, however, necessary which would meet regularly to assess issues and vulnerabilities affecting the global financial system and to identify and oversee actions needed to address the problems identified. This forum should report directly to the G7 Ministers and Central Bank Governors and replace the series of *ad hoc* groups which had been convened by the G7 in recent years.

A number of further directions were set out in the Tietmeyer Report concerning the composition and operation of the new forum.[76] The forum should also work through its members (taking into account their comparative advantages) in developing objectives, priorities and programmes for action. The chairperson would act in a personal capacity and be appointed for a period generally of not less than three years.[77] Andrew Crockett, General Manager of the BIS, was recommended for appointment as the first Chairman. Working groups should also be set up to develop a general response or consider specific *ad hoc* issues with a separate co-ordinating Chairman's Group.[78] The forum should meet as often as required to secure its objectives. It is significant that only two meetings per year were initially envisaged.

The Tietmeyer Report was significant in that it identified the specific deficiencies in the current international framework which the new body was designed to correct, as well as provided a number of detailed directions with regard to composition, structure and operation of the forum. The analysis of current gaps was significant in highlighting both the need for proper policy construction and its effective implementation in practice. In addition to this, however, all significant market risk would be identified and specific gaps within the scope of regulatory cover corrected. The degree of detail provided concerning the structure and operation of the new forum indicates that all of these operational issues were discussed and agreed in advance with relevant G7 and other institutional representatives. The forum itself could then be best considered to have arisen as the result of the consultations undertaken and general level of agreement secured between the relevant interested parties on the action required rather than of the final Report as such. This, however, in no way undermines the importance and value of the Report itself.

[76] The forum had, in particular, to be limited to a size which permitted an effective exchange of views and the achievement of action-oriented results within a reasonable time frame. Each G7 country would have three members. The international financial institutions and other international organizations would also have members. Participation would be extended over time to include representatives from a small number of additional non-G7 national authorities. These would either be invited to contribute substantively or to attend as guests.

The members of the forum would be representatives of the national and international authorities responsible for issues of international financial stability with the country members including the ministries of finance, central banks and senior supervisory authorities. Representation had to be at a high level including Deputy Ministers and Deputy Governors, Deputy Heads of the international financial institutions, Chairs and appointed members of the international groupings.

[77] This was recommended to ensure continuity of the work of the forum.

[78] This group would be composed of representatives of the international financial institutions and international regulatory groupings and national supervisors where necessary. This would meet around or between the forum's meetings to co-ordinate follow-up activities.

V. THE FINANCIAL STABILITY FORUM

The FSF was created by the G7 Ministers and Governors at their meeting in Bonn on 22 February 1999. While the many of the key aspects of the FSF's composition, mandate and working structure were set out in the Tietmeyer Report, other more specific operational issues were left to be dealt with at its first and second meetings.

The first meeting was held in Washington on 14th April at the offices of the IMF to discuss a range of organisational and other more preparatory or ancillary issues, including the establishment of the first three working groups in the areas of highly leveraged institutions, capital flows and offshore financial centres.[79]

The second meeting was held in Paris on 15 September 1999, which considered the interim reports prepared by the working groups (but not made publicly available), as well as progress in each of the more general areas of disclosure, standards and training.[80]

The next meeting was to be held in Singapore in April 2000 at which time all of the working and other groups which had subsequently been set up would report on their initial findings.

VI. MEMBERSHIP STRUCTURE AND OPERATION

The Financial Stability Forum is made up of thirty five representatives including three from each of the G7 countries. These generally consist of senior officials from the Treasury or Finance Ministry, the Central Bank and main supervisory authority. The Basel Committee, IOSCO and the IAIS have two representatives each with the IMF, the World Bank, the OECD, the BIS Committee on Payment and Settlement Systems and the BIS Committee on the Global Financial System (formerly the Euro-Currency Standing Committee) having one each.

Although direct membership was to be limited to the G7 efforts have been made from an early stage to extend the range of countries involved with its work. Senior representatives from Hong Kong, Australia and the Netherlands were accordingly invited to attend the second meetings in Paris while other countries will be involved through its working group structures.[81]

[79] *See* Press Release, FSF, First Meeting of the Financial Stability Forum (Apr. 6, 1999) [hereinafter FSF First Meeting]. Copies of all Press Releases are on the FSF web site, *available at* http://www.fsforum.org. For comment, *see* Walker, *A New Beginning*, *supra* note 12, at 1.

[80] *See* Press Release, FSF, Second Meeting of the FSF (Sept. 15, 1999). For Comment, *see* Walker, *Working Groups and Global Standards*, *supra* note 29, at 1.

[81] *See* Press Release, FSF, Broadening Representation in the Financial Stability Forum (June 21, 1999).

While the secretariat would be provided for by the BIS, other operational matters such as issue identification, information collection and analysis, decision taking and record and reporting procedures were left to the FSF to develop itself over time.

It is significant that no other resources were initially committed to assist the work of the FSF. The apparent intent, and certainly effect, of this was that the bulk of the FSF's work would have to be conducted through specially convened working groups made up of personnel from each of the underlying member bodies concerned. While the FSF would assume an important but essentially limited original policy analysis and paper production function in addition to acting as a general discussion vehicle, it is significant that it was only initially to act as a form of central processing or co-ordinating unit to the extent that it activities were still dependent on the secretarial and organisation support of all of the other bodies which made up its membership.

It was, however, significant that by the end of the first year of operation the assigned staff of the FSF had risen to four on secondment from the other member bodies in addition to its Chairman. Whether this will expand further will depend upon how its role and functions mature over time. Hopefully this can be achieved as the FSF assumes an increasingly clear, specific and central function in this area.

VII. MANDATE

The mandate of the FSF was to strengthen the surveillance and supervision of the international financial system. In connection with this, the FSF was to assess issues and vulnerabilities affecting the global financial system and to identify and oversee actions needed to address the problems identified.[82]

The particular nature and content of this role, however, was not expanded further and to some extent remained unclear for some time.[83] The most significant operational aspect which had to be determined was accordingly the actual role or function of the new body. To some extent, this still remains unclear.[84]

The core objective of the G7 in establishing the FSF was to create a new contact vehicle through which all of the separate bodies represented could meet and exchange views on systemically important issues. To assist these discussions, preparatory or reporting work would be carried out through the FSF's working and other internal groups. More formal decisions could

[82] *See supra* section 1.

[83] For comment, *see* Walker, *A New Beginning*, *supra* note 12, at 1.

[84] *See*, *e.g.*, Walker, *Working Groups and Global Standards*, *supra* note 29, at 1; Walker, *The New Global Rule Book*, *supra* note 29, at 1.

then be taken by the FSF following more detailed working groups analysis and report. The FSF could in this way both promote contact and understanding between all of the bodies involved as well as facilitate policy construction in any of the important areas identified and considered. The FSF would then act as both a discussion and policy originating device. This will clearly be of considerable value especially in the areas where all of the bodies concerned have not been able to work co-operatively before.

In terms of the underlying incentive to create the FSF, it could be argued that it was simply set up to allow the finance ministers to be able to follow and exercise more substantial control over developments in the financial market area. A number of difficulties had already arisen in various countries with regard to the degree to which they were fully informed and consulted. The FSF would then be seen as tool through which the finance ministers attempted to be more completely informed in this area against the wishes of national central bank and supervisory staff. The involvement of the finance ministries is not, however, resented in practice and everyone appears to recognise the need for a more complete and cross-interest as well as cross-sector response to be developed.

With regard to its future role, however, some difficulties still remain. the FSF could either simply produce further reports in such key areas of interest as those assigned to its first three working groups on hedge funds, off-shore centres and short-term capital movements or it could actually try to correct some of the key deficiencies which arise with regard to the current system (or non-system) of international financial market control.[85]

If the FSF was to assume a further originating or research and reporting role, it must be accepted that it could produce some valuable further insights and recommendations into the causes of instability or crises in national and international financial markets. It is, however, highly likely that these would then simply be added to all of the other papers already prepared by various agencies or bodies on international financial stability or a new financial architecture or other more specific related issues. Rather than simply produce more paper, it might be of more use if the FSF tried to do something with all of the often valuable material which has already been issued to date.

VIII. WORKING GROUPS AND TASK FORCES

Three working groups had been set up at the first meeting of the FSF to consider highly leveraged institutions, capital flows and off-shore financial centres.[86] Each of the groups met three times during 1999 to consider the

[85] *See* Walker, *A New Beginning*, *supra* note 12.
[86] *See* FSF First Meeting, *supra* note 79.

work already prepared in their area by various public and private sector bodies as well as conduct their own discussions with supervisory authorities and market participants.

The working groups reported on progress the degree of progress achieved to date at the Paris meeting in September 1999. Despite broad agreement on the need for better regulation in particular areas such as hedge funds, tax havens and capital flows, however, agreement could not be secured on the concrete measures necessary to achieve this with only slow progress being possible on new rules aimed at improving global financial stability. Participants would nevertheless keep up the pressure to adopt necessary changes in light of concerns that any sense of urgency might be lost as the recent financial crises fade.

Although the initial results were disappointing, it must be accepted that the FSF is dealing with complex and sensitive issues. More substantial progress was expected before the next meeting in Singapore in April 2000 at which the working groups were expected to submit their final recommendations.

The FSF also established, following its September 1999 Paris meeting, two further *ad hoc* study groups or task forces to consider standards implementation and deposit protection. The groups are made up of officials from developed and developing countries and were intended to draw on work completed or under way in various public and private sector fora.[87]

These are not referred to as working groups at this stage, as they are only intended to review existing work, or undertake some other more preparatory or separate research to be reported back to the FSF. If the FSF considers that some more substantial progress may be possible in either area, the matter can be considered at full forum level or a full working group appointed. It is also significant that the task force set up in November 1999 is not chaired by a full FSF member, as with the other working and study groups, but by only one of the other invited participation countries, although that is not the reason for its separate designation.

The assigned tasks and work carried out to date of each of the working and other groups is as follows:

A. Highly Leveraged Institutions (HLI)

The Highly Leveraged Institutions (HLI) working group had been set up under Howard Davies, Chairman of the UK Financial Services Authority, to consider whether hedge funds could be subject to some form of direct regulation. By the Paris meeting, it had not been possible to secure agreement between all of its members on the relevance and value of direct regulation

[87] *See* Press Release, FSF, FSF Establishes Working Groups, (Nov. 19, 1999).

and so other intermediate forms of control would be considered, such as imposing additional capital and disclosure requirements on market counterparties who provided investment funds.

This remains a difficult area.[88] Although the seriousness of the threats posed by hedge fund collapse have been recognised especially since Long Term Capital Management, it is unfortunate that some more substantial response has not been possible. Certain countries (including the United States) are reluctant to subject such institutions to direct control.[89] Indirect approaches can be used although they are possibly of considerably less value. The Basel Committee had recommended in January 1999 that a number of indirect measures be adopted including, in particular, improving the ability of bank counterparties to assess their risk exposures to HLIs and enhanced market transparency. Some direct regulation was considered although this was thought to have been problematic for definitional and jurisdictional reasons. Licensing requirements, fit and proper tests, and minimum standards in respect of capital and risk management may be introduced, but only if the other indirect measures and enhanced transparency fail. Such studies will be considered by the FSF working group and hopefully a final set of more substantial recommendations may be produced in due course.

B. Capital Flows (CF)

The Capital Flows (CF) working group was established under Mario Draghi, Director General of the Italian Treasury, to consider measures to reduce the volatility of capital flows and improve the assessment and management of the risks of excessive short-term external indebtedness in any financial system. The working group had, in particular, considered how the related risks should be managed on a country-wide basis (including public sector debt and liquidity management) and on an individual institu-

88 *See* Walker, *Working Groups and Global Standards*, *supra* note 29. *See also* G. A. Walker, *Hedge Fund Control*, FRR, (May 1999), at 1.

89 The first hedge fund was set up by Alfred Winslow Jones in 1949. They are established under an exemption within the Investment Companies Act 1940 that allows the SEC to regulate mutual funds. Section 3(c)(a) exempts, 'any issuer whose outstanding securities (other than short-term paper) are beneficially owned by not more than one hundred persons and which is not making and does not presently propose to make a public offering of its securities'. There are approximately 3,000 mutual funds which benefit from this exception. This means that they don't have to comply with onerous disclosure requirements and can hold both long and short positions in securities. Hedge funds are a small sub-group of these companies which specialise in developing highly geared speculative positions. This allows such funds as Quantum, Tiger and Steinhard to make annual returns in excess of thirty percent. Before its collapse, Long Term Capital Management was able to generate in excess of forty percent returns. In connection with the international response to these funds, *see* Basel Committee, Banks' Interactions with Highly Leveraged Institutions (Jan. 1999). For comment *see* Michael Taylor, *Hedgefund Regulation*, B.J.I.B.S.L, May, 1999, at 183–87.

tion basis. Information needs were considered and possible causes of capital distortions and high levels of volatility examined. Most significantly the possible use of controls on capital flows as a preventative risk management tool was discussed.

This is possibly an even more difficult area than HLIs. The dominant philosophy remains what is referred to as the Washington approach, which links maximum liberalisation and deregulation to the promotion of global growth. As has been seen repeatedly, however, the uncontrolled movement of funds can have devastating effects on the stability of national and international markets. It remains to be seen what controls on capital are considered desirable by the working group and how they may be given effect in practice.

C. *Offshore Financial Centres (OFC)*

The regulatory arbitrage problems which arise with certain countries have been considered by the Offshore Financial Centres (OFC) working group under John Palmer, the Canadian Superintendent of Financial Institutions. The activities of various offshore centres have been examined. The two key issues identified relate to relevant standards and implementation and compliance. The group was concerned to identify the most effective international standards which could secure proper financial supervision, cross-border co-operation and transparency. A number of core principles or standards have already been issued by the Basel Committee, IOSCO and the IAIS,[90] with work also being carried out by other bodies such as the Offshore Banking Group and the Caribbean Group of Banking Supervisors.

The even more difficult task of securing full implementation and compliance is being considered separately.[91]

D. *Implementation Task Force*

A special task force chaired by Mr. Andrew Sheng, Chairman of the Hong Kong Securities and Future Commission, was set up to examine ways of promoting the implementation of international standards relevant to the strengthening of financial systems. The task force was expected to consider official and market incentives to encourage implementation, explore strategies for assisting countries in the practical implementation of standards, and evaluate options when generating information on implementation progress.[92]

[90] *See infra* Section 5.
[91] *See* FSF, FSF Establishes Working Groups, *supra* note 87.
[92] The terms of reference of the Task Force on Implementation were as follows: (a) explore

Although no guidance is yet available, it would appear that the work of the task force will focus on encouragement and assistance rather than formal sanction.[93] The emphasis is then on the construction of a spirit of enlightened self-interest rather then threat of punishment. This is an intelligent way in which to proceed and hopefully a highly credible and effective policy can be produced.

In the event that pressure may be required in certain cases, the threat of some more formal response may still be thought appropriate.[94] The working group may, for example, then consider some system of enhanced peer group pressure supplemented by the co-ordinated exercise of unilateral rights of host territories to deny access to foreign institutions from suspect territories as well as the right of home authorities to impose restrictions on the overseas activities of locally incorporated or authorised institutions. While separate trade or other political sanctions may also have to be considered in certain almost exceptional circumstances, the co-ordinated exercise of all of the powers already available to national may be more than sufficient in almost all cases.

As a result of the fundamental importance of this problem, the production of the report by Andrew Sheng may be one of the most anticipated aspects of the FSF Singapore meeting. To the extent that this is only a task force, it can only be assumed that the FSF expects further work to be undertaken in this area. Hopefully a final set of balanced but effective recommendations on implementation policy can be produced in due course.

issues related to promoting the implementation of international standards relevant to strengthening financial systems; (b) consider a strategy for implementation of standards that may include countries announcing their commitment to implement standards and participate in credible assessments of compliance, technical assistance in support of implementation efforts being prioritised, relevant information on progress toward compliance being made available and compliance with sound practices being rewarded by market participants and others with a view to reinforcing efforts at implementation; (c) identify the set of international standards most relevant to strengthening financial systems and ways of disseminating these standards, explore strategies for assisting countries in the practical implementation of standards, explore official and market incentives that could encourage the process of implementation, outline options for generating credible self-assessments and independent assessments, consider how, what kind of and to whom information on progress toward compliance with standards could be made available and consider how the resources required to support implementation and assessment could best be mobilised; (d) consider how the various elements of the implementation strategy could best reinforce each other and what the roles and responsibilities of various bodies implementing it should be; and (e) in all of this, draw upon the work already done by the IMF, the World Bank, standards-setting bodies and others with respect to encouraging implementation of sound practices. *See* Press Release, FSF, Terms of Reference: FSF Study Group on Implementation of Standards, (Nov. 19, 1999) [hereinafter FSF Terms of Reference].

[93] The terms of the initial report were considered by the FSF at its third meeting in Singapore in March 2000 although not publicly released at that stage. *See* Press Release, FSF, Fifth Meeting, (Mar. 23, 2000).

[94] *See* Chapter 2, Section 2.X.

E. Deposit Insurance Study Group

A separate study group chaired by Jean Pierr Sabourin, President of the Canadian Deposit Insurance Co-operation, was invited to review recent experiences with deposit protection schemes and to consider developing international best practices for such arrangements.[95] This would include examining the issues involved in moving from implicit schemes to limited coverage schemes and the implications for deposit insurance design of different institutional settings.

The availability of some form of deposit protection remains a difficult issue from many perspectives. The value of providing some basic minimum type of deposit protection for less well off members of society is recognised in many countries. For this reason a number of different types of limited or partial cover schemes operate in various countries often financed through a bank levy or charging system. Against this obvious benefit, the actual costs of many more extensive forms of protection must be taken into account as well as the much more serious problem of moral hazard. To the extent that the depositor considers that he can not lose his deposit irrespective of how badly a particular bank is run, there will be no incentive to exercise any degree of supervision or control over management activities. The ultimate sanction is obviously withdrawal of the deposit. It is for this reason that many countries will only provide partial cover.

This is, however, also closely connected with the more general issue of financial support and lender of last operations. Further problems also arise with regard to funding full cover facilities as well as in regional systems, such as within the European Union where separate difficulties arose, including whether schemes should operate on a home or host country basis and what, if any, top up provision should be allowed.[96]

A number of difficult issues accordingly remain to be resolved in this area and it is to be particularly welcomed that this is the type of highly sensitive subject matter which the FSF is prepared to consider. It can only be hoped that the Study Group will make a serious attempt to examine and

[95] The terms of reference of the study group were (a) to study recent experiences with deposit insurance schemes by examining systems that worked well and those that did not with a view to synthesising the key lessons to be learned; (b) sketch the policy trade-offs presented by different types of schemes taking into account their distinct institutional settings; (c) examine the issues involved in transition from implicit or explicit blanket guarantees to limited coverage schemes; (d) assess the desirability and feasibility of setting out international guidance on deposit insurance, recognising that different country circumstances may imply distinct policy prescriptions; and (e) evaluate what form such guidance could take (including formulation of general principles for such schemes and setting out pitfalls to be avoided in their design and operation), and identify who would be best able to take this work forward. *See* FSF Terms of Reference, *supra* note 92.

[96] *See, e.g.*, Richard S. Dale, *Deposit Insurance: Policy Clash Over EC and US Reforms*, *in* THE EMERGING FRAMEWORK OF FINANCIAL REGULATION (Charles Goodhart, ed., 1998).

understand all of the related issues concerned and not just undertake some essentially limited descriptive examination of possible current deposit protection models.

IX. GENERAL ACTIVITIES

Since its establishment, the Forum has been concerned with extending its range of activities despite its limited size and resources. To some extent these are best regarded as being of value in co-ordinating the activities of others, although of no less importance for that reason.

In addition to noting its other important reporting activities, the FSF has produced a series of guidelines concerning its selection of issues for consideration.[97] Presumably the criteria were issued to allow the FSF to prioritise its work as it considers appropriate, although the qualification, in particular with respect to implementation (where appropriate), may be somewhat disappointing. Hopefully the criteria will not be used to constrain but only direct activity over time.

These are principally concerned with disclosure, training and standards. The general nature of the FSF's work in each of these areas is considered in turn. Its specific contribution to the construction of a new single rule financial market rule book is considered in the following section.

A. Disclosure

The Financial Stability FSF has also supported the activities of the separate Multidisciplinary Working Group on Enhanced Disclosure with the Basel Committee, IOSCO and the IAIS. This was set up at the initiative of the Committee on the Global Financial System (CGFS) earlier in the year. The Group has been assessing the value and feasibility of securing enhanced public disclosures by financial institutions through the use of a draft disclosure template which will be tested in a pilot study. Full disclosure is without doubt a very valuable control device. It facilitates greater understanding of market operations and conditions and consequent market discipline. This initiative has accordingly to be supported. The only problem is that even if large amounts of information are already available, as was the case before the Asian crisis, this may simply be ignored by many institutions.

[97] The selection criteria to be adopted are (a) to give impetus to work on issues that cut across the mandates and expertise of its members, (b) to co-ordinate work among members drawing on their comparative advantages, (c) to evaluate the completeness and fill in gaps in the body of work among members, (d) to endorse work by members that would benefit from such endorsement and (e) to monitor, where appropriate, implementation and any follow-up in areas where policy recommendations have been issued.

Disclosure, transparency and information provision may then never be sufficient instruments of market control in themselves.

B. Standards

More significantly, the FSF has being working on the compilation of a new Compendium of Standards. This has been designed to provide a common reference tool for economic and financial 'guidelines, principles and codes of good practice' which are internationally accepted as relevant to the 'sound, stable and well-functioning' of financial systems. The areas to be covered include transparency of fiscal, monetary and financial policies; dissemination of economic and financial data; the regulation and supervision of banking, securities and insurance firms; the disclosure, transparency and risk management practices of financial institutions; corporate governance; accounting, auditing and bankruptcy; and payment and settlement.

C. Training

A separate draft Financial Supervision Training Directory has also been prepared under the direction of the FSF, the World Bank, the IMF and the BIS. This currently provides information on training opportunities for bank supervisors and regulators and will be extended to include equivalent entries for securities and insurance personnel. The objective is to improve the technical capacity and quality of the line supervisors in national authorities. Although a considerably more modest area of activity, securing effective supervision of financial institutions at the national level in every country is essential to the effectiveness of the overall system of global control currently being constructed.

X. FINANCIAL STABILITY STANDARDS

The FSF's Compendium of Standards has still not been formally published but is available on its own website.[98] While this is clearly not complete, it does represent a significant development in the construction of a complete, coherent and effective single set of rules for all aspects of financial market supervision and control.[99]

Although the FSF has undertaken a significant amount of work in the areas of disclosure, standards and training,[100] most attention has focused

[98] http://www.fsforum.org. For comment, *see* G.A. Walker, *A Compendium of Financial Stability Standards*, FT-FRR (Nov. 1999), at 2.

[99] *See FT-FRR*, April, June and October 1999.

[100] *See supra* sub-section IV.(c).

on the second of these and, in particular, on the structure and content of its proposed new Compendium.[101]

The confirmed listing or structure of the Compendium's relevant measures is now public sector, banking, securities, insurance, corporate governance and payment and settlement.

A. Transparency

Under the FSF's new regime, policy transparency is to be secured through the IMF's 1998 *Code of Good Practices on Fiscal Transparency*[102] and its 1999 *Code of Good Practices on Transparency in Monetary and Financial Policies*.[103]

While the Fiscal Code sets out a series of transparency requirements to provide assurances to the public and capital markets that a sufficiently complete picture of the structure and finances of government is available to allow its fiscal policy to be properly assessed, a series of further desirable transparency practices are set out in the Monetary and Finance Code for central banks in relation to the conduct of monetary policy, and for central banks and other agencies with respect to their financial policies.

Two sets of Good Transparency Practices are set out under the July 1999 Code, which include provisions relating to the clarity of roles, responsibilities and objectives of central banks or financial agencies, open processes for formulating and reporting policies or policy decisions, public availability of information on relevant policies, and accountability and assurances of integrity.

The 1999 Code does acknowledge that full transparency may not be appropriate in all circumstances and that limitations may have to be included where, for example, the effectiveness of specific policies could be damaged or market stability or the legitimate interests of supervised and other entities could be affected. The key objective, however, remains transparency, although good policies are also promoted, for example, in the area of financial policy.

These are important measures which have begun the process of establishing new global standards of openness and accountability in these three key policy areas. Of possibly more value than their substantive content has been their contribution to the development a new culture of disclosure and open discussion in connection with such matters.

The release of more specific data in the public sector is also to be promoted through the IMF's 1996 paper on *Special Data Dissemination*

[101] *See* Walker, *supra* note 98, Tables 1–6.

[102] *See* IMF, *Code of Good Practices on Fiscal Transparency* (Apr. 1998).

[103] *See* IMF, *Code of Good Practices on Transparency in Monetary and Financial Policies* (July 1999).

Standards (SDDS)[104] and its 1997 paper on *General Data Dissemination System* (GDDS).[105] While the SDDS was designed to provide guidance for countries which might seek access to international capital markets in the dissemination of relevant economic and financial data, the GDDS assists in the provision of general economic, financial and socio-demographic data to the public in a comprehensive, timely, accessible and reliable manner.

By August 1999, there were 47 subscribers to the SDDS made up of industrial market countries, emerging market economies and transition economies. The GDDS was largely developed for countries which were not able to satisfy all of the requirements set out in the SDDS. The GDDS is then aimed at promoting or supporting improvements over time rather than acting as an assessment mechanism as such.

These are again important papers in the promotion of full, timeous and accurate disclosure of relevant market data. With the transparency papers, most countries should now be able to adopt clearer specific policies as well as a more general operating culture of openness, responsibility and accountability in public affairs within which modern capital market based finance structures can develop.

B. Banking

With regard to banking, the main document is, of course, the Basel Committee's *Core Principles for Effective Banking Supervision*.[106] This attempts for the first time to integrate all of the main aspects of supervisory and regulatory practice within a single paper and in so doing to provide a comprehensive model for national financial market control.

In addition to the twenty five core rules established, a number of 'precepts' for effective banking supervision are developed with regard to such matters as (a) key objectives (the maintenance of stability and confidence in the financial system), (b) the importance of market discipline and good corporate governance, (c) need for operational independence, (d) the ability of supervisors to understand bank activity and risk management as well as (e) the value of bank risk profile assessments, (f) adequate supervisory resources and (g) close co-operation between authorities.

The Core Principles also set out five further preconditions for effective banking supervision which comprise (a) a sound and sustainable macroeconomic policy, (b) a well-developed public infrastructure, (c) effective market discipline, (d) procedures for the efficient resolution of problems in

[104] IMF, *Special Data Dissemination Standards* (Mar. 1996).

[105] IMF, *General Data Dissemination System* (Dec. 1997).

[106] Basel Committee, *Core Principles for Effective Banking Supervision* (Sept. 1997). *See* Chapter 2, Section 1.V.

banks and (e) mechanisms for providing an appropriate level of systemic protection.

A number of principles are then set out dealing with all aspects of bank supervision and control. The most substantial of these is possibly Principle 1, which contains a number of preconditions for effective banking supervision. This then comprises eight separate conditions including (a) clear responsibilities and objectives for each supervisory agency, (b) operational independence and adequate resources, (c) a suitable legal framework which, in particular, secures (i) initial authorisation (or licensing) as well as effective on-going supervision of all relevant institutions, (ii) adequate powers to secure compliance with laws and safety and soundness concerns as well as (iii) legal protection for supervisors, (d) arrangements for sharing information between supervisors (where necessary) and (e) proper protections for the confidentiality of all information exchanged.

A number of further specific requirements are then set out with regard to licensing and structure (Core Principles 2–5), prudential regulation and requirements (Core Principles 6–15), methods of on-going banking supervision (Core Principles 16–20), information requirements (Core Principle 21), formal powers of supervisors (Core Principle 22) and cross-border banking (Core Principles 23–25).

The Core Principles have been criticised for their generality in many areas. The decision had, however, been taken at the beginning only to construct a general reference framework which could be used by all countries and not to try to create a detailed set of rules which may only be appropriate in a small number of jurisdictions. It would have been very difficult to balance these two competing considerations otherwise.

Most recently, the Committee has also issued a *Core Principles Methodology* which is designed to assist in the conduct of compliance assessments in particular countries with regard to the implementation of the Core Principles.[107] This restates the objectives of the Core Principles and sets out certain considerations in conducting assessments. It then contains a large amount of detailed guidance on the assessment of compliance with each of the principles issued by the Committee. This is a very useful document, especially for expert teams either preparing for or conducting on-site visits to determine material compliance with the Core Principles in any particular case. It accordingly adds further substance to the core rules and has to be strongly welcomed for that reason.

With regard to the supervision of international banks, the Committee's Compendium[108] contains the 1983 Revised Concordat[109] (which replaced

[107] Basel Committee, *Core Principles Methodology* (Oct. 1999). *See* Chapter 2, Section 1.V.
[108] *See* Basel Committee, *Compendium of Documents* (Apr. 1997).
[109] Basel Committee, *Principles for the Supervision of Banks' Foreign Establishments* (May

the Committee's original 1975 Concordat),[110]the 1992 Minimum Standards,[111] and the October 1996 twenty-nine recommendations for the supervision of cross-border banking.[112] The 1983 Revised Concordat was partly issued in the response to the collapse of Banco Ambrosiano (a replacement paper to the 1975 Concordat was already being considered to deal with such matters as consolidated supervision) while the Minimum Standards were issued following the collapse of BCCI. Although there are nominally only four Minimum Standards, the supporting text extends this considerably. The October 1996 paper was originally prepared as an implementation report on the Minimum Standards which was conducted by a joint working group set up by the Basel Committee and the Offshore Banking Supervisory Group.

These papers contain the core supervisory framework for internationally active banks although strangely the 1990 Information Supplement[113] is not included (this represented the results of an earlier 1986 implementation report[114] into the operation of the 1983 Revised Concordat), nor are the later Core Principles (23, 24 and 25) referred to separately which specifically deal with cross-border supervisory co-operation (although these may be considered only to reflect the rules set out in the other supervisory papers referred to).

Capital adequacy in respect of banks is to remain to be governed by the

1983); Basel Committee, *Compendium of Documents* (Apr. 1997), Vol. 3, at 7–13. *See* Chapter 2, Section 1.II.(a).

[110] Basel Committee, *Report to the Governors on the supervision of banks' foreign establishments* (Sept. 1975). This also gave effect to the Committee's recommendations in relation to consolidated supervision. *See* Basel Committee, *Consolidated Supervision of Bank's International Activities* (Mar. 1979). This followed an earlier 1978 paper by the Committee. *See* Basel Committee, *Consolidation of banks' balance sheets: aggregation of risk-bearing assets as a method of supervisory bank solvency* (Oct. 1978). *See also* Basel Committee, *Compendium of Documents* (Apr. 1997), Vol. 1, at 83–84. *See* Chapter 2, Section 1.I.(a).

[111] Basel Committee, *Minimum Standards for the supervision of international banking groups and their cross-border establishments* (July 1992). *See also* Basel Committee *Report on International Developments in Banking Supervision*, Report No. 8 (Sept. 1992), Ch III; Basel Committee, *Compendium of Documents* (Apr. 1997), Vol. 3, at 23–27. *See* Chapter 2, Section 1.IV.(b).

[112] Basel Committee, *The supervision of cross-border banking* (Oct. 1996). *See also* Basel Committee, *Report on International Developments in Banking Supervision*, Report No. 10 (June 1996), Ch IV; and Basel Committee, *Compendium of Documents* (Apr. 1997), Vol. 3, at 28–53. *See* Chapter 2, Section 1.IV.(c).

[113] Basel Committee, *Information flows between banking supervisory authorities* (Apr. 1990). This had earlier been reproduced in Basel Committee, *Report on International Developments in Banking Supervision*, Report No. 7 (Sept. 1990), Ch VI, at 31–42. *See also* Basel Committee, *Compendium of Documents* (Apr. 1997), Vol. 3, at 14–22. *See* Chapter 2, Section 1.IV (d).

[114] Basel Committee, *The Implementation of the Concordat*, reproduced in Basel Committee, *Report on International Developments in Banking Supervision*, Report No 5 (Sept. 1986), Ch VII at 50. *See* Chapter 2, Section 1.IV.(d).

Committee's July 1998 Capital Accord,[115] pending its future revision,[116] as well as the January 1996 Market Risk Amendment.[117] As the separate January 1996 paper on Back Testing is also to apply, the separate inclusion of the Market Risk Overview document is surprising, although this does incorporate the April 1998 amendments.

Transparency and disclosure in the banking area are to be secured under the Committee's September 1998 paper on Enhancing Bank Transparency and its July 1999 paper on Sound Practices for Loan Accounting, Credit Risk Disclosure and Related Matters.[118] The first of these is directed at securing improved supervisory and public disclosure as a device to promote enhanced market discipline while the second assists banks and banking supervisors make better provision for loan losses and connected matters.

The subsequent reference to the Committee's September 1998 paper on Internal Control Systems[119] is somewhat confusing. This should follow Capital Adequacy and not Transparency and Disclosure although this may be a minor matter. In considering financial market control, the core objective should be full and proper risk identification and control which begins with the internal risk management process of the individual bank. Transparency and disclosure and associated market discipline should be considered as supplements and not correctives to this.

The only unfortunate aspect of the Committee's work in this area has been the fact that it took it until September 1998 to issue or even outline guidance with respect to internal control systems (apart from in the area of financial derivatives where a considerable amount of progress had been possible with IOSCO). The supposed reason for the failure of international authorities generally to attempt to deal with the specific problem of operational risk control and the quality of internal systems before was supposedly that it was too complex and firm dependent.

Proper internal risk management must remain the fundamental function of every financial institution in any market. Consequently, firms must be

[115] Basel Committee, *International convergence of capital measurement and capital standards* (July 1988). *See* Chapter 2, Section 2.VI.

[116] For comment, *see* G.A. Walker, *So Close But So Far*, FT-FRR (May 1999); G.A. Walker, *Accord at Last*, FT-FRR (June 1999); G.A. Walker, *A New Capital Adequacy Framework*, FT-FRR (Aug./Sept. 1999).

[117] Basel Committee, *Market Risk Amendment* (Jan. 1996). *See also*, Basel Committee, *Overview of the Amendment to the Capital Accord to Incorporate Market Risks* (Jan. 1996); and Basel Committee, *Supervisory Framework for the Use of 'Backtesting' in Conjunction with the Internal Models Approach to Market Risk Capital Requirements* (Jan. 1996). *See* Chapter 2, Section 2.VI.

[118] Basel Committee, *Enhancing Bank Transparency* (Sept. 1998); Basel Committee, *Sound Practices for Loan Accounting, Credit Risk Disclosure and Related Matters* (July 1999). *See* Chapter 2, Section 2.VI.

[119] Basel Committee, *Framework for Internal Control Systems in Banking Organisations* (Sept. 1998). *See* Chapter 2, Section 2.VII.

able correctly to identify and control the full range and volume of risk which their activities generate. Their ability, or inability, to do so should then be the primary focus of supervisory attention.

All of the debate over the last two decades which has focused on credit and market risk capital adequacy has, to a large extent, simply distracted attention from this core function of effective financial market supervision.

Supervisory authorities must examine the quality of the internal risk management and control systems of every financial institution. Only if something goes wrong at that level does capital even become relevant. Capital is designed to absorb loss which subsequently arises while the immediate focus of financial market activity and supervision should be on loss prevention.

C. Securities

Securities firms are to be governed by IOSCO's 1998 core *Objectives and Principles of Securities Regulation.*[120] This establishes the three fundamental objectives for securities regulation of (a) protecting investors, (b) ensuring that markets are fair, efficient and transparent and (c) reducing systemic risk.

IOSCO then develops 30 core principles dealing with the regulatory authorities (Principles 1–5), self-regulation (Principles 6–7), enforcement (Principles 8–10), co-operation (Principles 11–16), collective investment schemes (Principles 17–20), market intermediaries (Principles 21–24) and secondary markets (Principles 25–30).

These Core Objectives and Principles are then supplemented by IOSCO's other more specific papers on Internet Trading,[121] Information Sharing,[122] Financial Derivatives[123] and Collective Investment Schemes.[124] All of these are valuable measures which attempt to develop further certain key aspects of best standard and practice in each of the main sub-areas of activity within securities markets. The only obvious omissions appear to be in connection with investment advice and brokerage although they are included within the core Objectives and Principles. The full range of papers

[120] IOSCO, *Objectives and Principles of Securities Regulation* (Sept. 1998).

[121] IOSCO, *Securities Activity on the Internet* (Sept. 1998).

[122] IOSCO, *Guidance on Information Sharing* (Nov. 1998).

[123] IOSCO, *Co-ordination between Cash and Derivative Markets: Contract Design of Derivative Products on Stock Indices and Measures to Minimise Market Disruption* (Oct. 1992); IOSCO, *The Application of the Tokyo Communiqué to Exchange-Traded Financial Derivatives Contracts* (Sept. 1998).

[124] IOSCO, *Principles for the Supervision of the Operators of Collective Investment Schemes* (Sept. 1997); IOSCO, *Report on Investment Management Principles for the Regulation of Collective Investment Schemes and Explanatory Memorandum* (Oct. 1994).

produced by all of the IOSCO's working groups will also have to be reviewed again to ensure that all relevant core standards are included.

Of slightly more surprise is the inclusion of the papers on Default Procedures,[125] MoUs[126] and mutual co-operation[127] within IOSCO's general section. These may have been more appropriately, and consistently, included in a separate co-operation sub-heading although IOSCO appears to have adopted a completely different approach to Basel on this. The specific paper on stock index futures may also have been better placed in a separate product sub-category or heading which could then be developed further over time.

Transparency and disclosure in the securities area are to be achieved under IOSCO's September 1998 paper on International Disclosure Standards[128] while risk management and internal controls are to be secured under its four papers on capital models,[129] OTC derivatives,[130] more general control guidance[131] and client asset protection.[132] These are all valuable contributions to the development of more stable national and international securities markets although again the selection and ordering are somewhat questionable. Risk management is arguably of more importance than transparency and disclosure while the May 1998 control guidance paper is the most important key paper in respect of risk management. The omission of a separate capital sub-heading is also somewhat strange although IOSCO is possibly still sensitive to its inability to agree any common standards with Basel in the area of market risk. The absence of any reference to the joint IOSCO and Basel papers on financial derivatives is also strange. Further discussions are presumably continuing in this regard.

The inconsistencies which arise between the basic structure of the Basel and IOSCO sub-area headings confirm that initial paper selection and structuring was left to the separate sector authorities and not determined by the FSF (see Editorial). While each of the two major sector bodies will obvi-

[125] IOSCO, *Report on Co-operation Between Market Authorities and Default Procedures* (Mar. 1996).

[126] IOSCO, *Principles of Memoranda of Understanding* (Sept. 1991).

[127] IOSCO, *Resolution: Principles for Record Keeping, Collection of Information, Enforcement Powers, and Mutual Co-operation to Improve the Enforcement of Securities and Futures Laws*.

[128] IOSCO, *International Disclosure Standards for Cross-Border Offerings and Initial Listings by Foreign Issues* (Sept. 1998).

[129] IOSCO, *Methodologies for Determining Minimum Capital Standards for Internationally Active Securities Firms which Permit the Use of Models under Prescribed Conditions* (May 1998).

[130] IOSCO, *Operational and Financial Risk Management Control Mechanisms for Over-the-Counter Derivatives Activities of Regulated Securities Firms* (July 1984).

[131] IOSCO, *Risk Management and Control Guidance for Securities Firms and their Supervisors* (May 1998).

[132] *See* IOSCO, *Client Asset Protection* (Aug. 1996).

ously adopt different approaches with regard to the discharge of their separate responsibilities and the development of appropriate rules and procedures for relevant risk control in their particular markets, it is unfortunate that more consistency has not been possible in this regard.

The ultimate objective of the FSF must, or, at least, should be the creation of a wholly integrated set of rules governing all aspects of market practice. To achieve this, each of the main papers selected should at some stage be reviewed to ensure their operational consistency. Before that can even be considered, however, each of the main sector committees involved must begin to try to develop some common approach to the identification of the type and function of the main policy papers required.

D. Insurance

Insurance undertakings are to be governed by the IAIS's September 1997 paper on *Insurance Supervisory Principles*[133](IAIS's Core Principles) as well as supporting papers on cross-border supervision[134] (the Insurance Concordat) and the supervisory standards on licensing,[135] on-site inspections[136] and derivatives.[137] Despite its much more recent creation, the IAIS has been able to make a significant contribution to the development of parallel standards in the insurance area.

The lack of consistent treatment between the banking and insurance subsite is, however even more surprising as the IAIS has generally always adopted a very Basel Committee-type approach to market control. The IAIS and the Basel Committee have always tended to work closely together in relation to all key issues. The IAIS is, of course, also based at the BIS in Basel.

If a common three sector approach is to be constructed, it would have been of assistance if Basel and the IAIS, at least, could have provisionally agreed on some common format between themselves which they could then have discussed with IOSCO. The absence of any initial consideration of the need for some basic degree of consistency between the banking and insurance and banking, securities and insurance sub-sites is highly regrettable. As has already been stressed, the overall objective must be to create an integrated compendium of relevant rules. This has to begin with some common understanding of agreed definitions and standard's structure.

The absence of any separate sub-area in respect of conglomerates is also

133 IAIS, *Insurance Supervisory Principles* (Sept. 1997).

134 IAIS, *Principles Applicable to the Supervision of International Insurers and Insurance Groups and their Cross-Border Establishments* (Sept. 1997).

135 IAIS, *Supervisory Standards on Licensing* (Sept. 1998).

136 IAIS, *Supervisory Standards on On-Site Inspections* (Oct. 1998).

137 IAIS, *Supervisory Standards on Derivatives* (Oct. 1998).

surprising. Presumably this may be added at a later stage. The inability for the three core sector fora to adopt a common approach with regard to the selection, identification and presentment of core documents make this even more unfortunate. As the FSF freely admits (as had Hans Tietmeyer before it), it is essential that an integrated cross-sector approach is adopted. More consideration should accordingly be given to securing consistency (although not necessarily uniformity) and coherence across the specific sector rules developed.

E. Governance

Corporate governance is initially to be secured solely under the OECD's May 1999 paper on *Principles of Corporate Governance*.[138] Unfortunately no papers have yet been issued in the areas of accounting and auditing and bankruptcy.

The OECD's May 1999 paper attempts to improve the legal, institutional and regulatory framework for corporate governance in both OECD and non-OECD countries. A number of principles are developed under the headings of the rights of shareholders, the equitable treatment of shareholders, the role of stakeholders, disclosure and transparency and the responsibility of the board of directors.

Although some of the principles are still drafted in fairly general language, this is an important document insofar as it attempts to establish a minimum level of common standards in this area at the international level.

The absence of any papers in connection with accounting and auditing and bankruptcy is unfortunate although work has been proceeding in each of these areas for a considerable period of time. Some recent progress has been possible, for example, in connection with international audit standards although this work must continue.

While all discussion at the international level attempts to resolve differences between relevant national systems, the additional difficulty which arises in these areas is that various private law as well as other related company and insolvency law issues have also to be dealt with. This makes negotiations more complex as differences in national laws have to be resolved first (if at all) before more specific supervisory or regulatory issues can even be considered. It is always more difficult to secure agreement where such issues of substantive law as opposed to pure supervisory or regulatory practice are involved. It can only be hoped that more substantial progress may be possible in these areas in due course.

138 OECD, *Principles of Corporate Governance* (May 1999).

F. Payment And Settlement

The payment and settlement section has been divided into a general and securities sub-heading. The titling is again somewhat strange as the first sub-area is clearly concerned with payment and settlement in banking and financial markets and the second with clearance and settlement in securities markets. The first is accordingly concerned with the completion of transfers of funds while the other with transfer and confirmation of title to security interests.

The main Committee on Payment and Settlement Systems (CPSS) has included its draft *Core Principles for the Design and Operation of Payment Systems*,[139] its 1996 paper on Foreign Exchange Settlement Risk,[140] 1977 paper on Real Time Gross Settlement Systems (RTGSS)[141] and the 1990 Lamfalussy Report.[142] Insofar as the Lamfalussy Report provided the background to much of the subsequent work in this area, it may have been better to include this as the introductory paper and then the outline Core Principles and RTGSS paper.

The CPSS's separate March 1996 paper on settlement risk and foreign exchange transactions is also included. It may have been better to have dealt with foreign exchange under a separate sub-heading within payment and settlement (which would then comprise banking, foreign exchange and securities). This may be reconsidered later.

With regard to securities, only the CPSS papers on Delivery Versus Payment (DVP),[143] OTC derivatives[144] and exchange-traded derivatives[145] papers are included. This suggests that there have been no attempts to integrate funds and securities transfers to date within a single section. This is unfortunate. Although distinct, the two core functions in both banking and securities markets are linked. One solution may have been to have a separate heading on *Payment and Clearance*. Alternatively, a separate clearance and settlement sub-heading could be included within securities. The failure to include any more specific securities papers within the existing *Payment and Settlement* area suggests that this sub-site was solely prepared by the CPSS without any wider initial discussion although hopefully again this can be corrected over time.

[139] CPSS, *Core Principles for the Design and Operation of Payment Systems* (Nov. 1999).

[140] CPSS, *Settlement Risk in Foreign Exchange Transactions* (Mar. 1997).

[141] CPSS, *Real Time Gross Settlement* (Mar. 1997).

[142] CPSS, *Report of the Committee on Interbank Netting Schemes of the Central Banks of the Group of Ten Countries* (Nov. 1990).

[143] CPSS, *Delivery Versus Payment in Securities Settlement Systems* (Sept. 1992).

[144] CPSS, *OTC Derivatives: Settlement Procedures and Counterparty Risk Management* (Sept. 1998).

[145] CPSS, *Clearing Arrangements for Exchange-Traded Derivatives* (Mar. 1997).

XI. CLOSING COMMENT—POLICY AND OPERATIONAL INTEGRATION AND THE CONSTRUCTION OF A NEW GLOBAL CONTROL FRAMEWORK

The objectives of the FSF remain highly ambitious. The FSF has already been able to create a new highly successful cross-interest and cross-sector discussion vehicle. It has also begun to make an important contribution in the area of international financial market policy construction. Much will, however, depend upon the quality of the final reports produced by the working and other groups appointed at the Singapore meeting.

The two most substantial achievements of the FSF would be the production of a final global rule book for all aspects of financial market supervision and control as well as a parallel set of effective implementation compliance, reporting and review practices and procedures.

The two major omissions which remain are concerned with the lack of any real attempt to integrate the separate sets of papers produced into any more coherent and unified whole and the equally fundamental problem of national implementation review and enforcement. It can only be hoped that the issue of sector specific rule book integration can be considered further at some time and that some more effective means of implementation review developed. The development of either a single integrated rule book or credible and effective implementation policy would be remarkable achievements, the production of both exceptional.

With the other structural initiatives which have been undertaken especially with the new G20 and the at least partially, if not wholly, reconstituted Interim Committee of the IMF, the shape of the new architecture is becoming more clear. None of these, however, represent fundamental changes in themselves. We are not then on the verge of a new international financial architecture but rather at a point of refinement of the old one.

The real success of the work undertaken in this area will also not be dependent on relatively minor structural changes as such, but on the substantive content of the work produced by all of the individual bodies involved. Our main objective should possibly then be to clarify the roles and functions of each of the main institutions currently in place and improve their operational relationship rather than waste time with the construction of new bodies as such.

The final value of the FSF may then not lie in the success of its co-ordination function or the quality or depth of its original reporting work (although this may still be quite substantial) but in the degree to which it brings together of all the separate political, central bank and national and international supervisory interests involved.

We may be closer to the creation of a new complete, coherent and effective international financial market control framework than we think.

Ultimately—as always—however, this will be dependent upon the commitment, support and enlightened self-interest of all parties concerned. Let us hope that we can find and secure that before the next major crisis. The structure and operation as well as significant recent successes of the FSF nevertheless continue to confirm the need for a collective or multilateral rather than unilateral or even bilateral response in the financial area.